MW01256325

A COMMENTARY

ON THE

GREEK TEXT OF THE EPISTLE OF PAUL

TO

THE GALATIANS

A COMMENTARY

ON THE

GREEK TEXT OF THE EPISTLE OF PAUL

TO

THE GALATIANS

JOHN EADIE, D.D., LL.D.

SOLID GROUND CHRISTIAN BOOKS
BIRMINGHAM, ALABAMA USA

Solid Ground Christian Books
2090 Columbiana Rd, Suite 2000
Birmingham, AL 35216
205-443-0311
sgcb@charter.net
http://solid-ground-books.com

A Commentary on the Greek Text of Galatians

John Eadie (1810-1876)

First published in 1869 by Richard Griffin and Co., London and Glasgow

Solid Ground Classic Reprints

First printing of new edition July 2005

Cover work by Borgo Design, Tuscaloosa, AL
Contact them at nelbrown@comcast.net

Cover image is taken from Rembrandt's 'The Apostle Paul.'

ISBN: 1-59925-003-9

PREFACE

THE object of this Commentary is the same as that stated in the prefaces to my previous volumes on Ephesians, Colossians, and Philippians. Nor do its form and style greatly vary from those earlier Works. Only it is humbly hoped, that longer and closer familiarity with the apostle's modes of thought and utterance may have conferred growing qualification to expound him. The one aim has been to ascertain the meaning through a careful analysis of the words. Grammatical and lexical investigation have in no way been spared, and neither labour nor time has been grudged in the momentous and responsible work of illustrating an epistle which contains so vivid an outline of evangelical truth. To find the sense has been my first step, and the next has been to unfold it with some degree of lucid and harmonious fulness. How far my purpose has been realized, the reader must judge; but, like every one who undertakes such a task, I am sadly conscious of falling far short of my own ideal. While I am not sensible of being warped by any theological system, as little am I aware of any deviation from recognised evangelical truth. One may differ in the interpretation of special words and phrases, and still hold the great articles of the Christian creed. I have gone over every clause with careful and conscientious effort to arrive at its sense, and without the smallest desire to find a meaning for it that may not jar with my theology. For "Theology," as Luther said, "is nothing else than a grammar and lexicon applied to the words of the Holy Spirit." I am well aware that scholastic theology has done no small damage to biblical interpretation, as may be seen in so many of the proof-texts attached to Confessions of Faith. The divine words of Scripture are "spirit and life," and have an inherent vitality, while the truth wedged into a system has often become as a mummy swathed up in numerous folds of polemical dialectics.

Several features of this epistle render its exposition somewhat difficult. In some sections, as in the address to Peter, the apostle's theology is but the expression of his own experience; brief digressions and interjected thoughts are often occurring; longer deviations are also met with before he works round more or less gradually to the main theme. The epistle is not like a dissertation, in which the personality of the author is merged; it is not his, but himself—his words welling up freshly from his heart as it was filled by varying emotions of surprise, disappointment, anger, sorrow, and hope. So, what he thought and felt was immediately written down before its freshness had faded; vindication suddenly passes into dogma, and dogma is humanized by intermingled appeals and warnings, —the rapid interchange of I, We, Thou, Ye, They, so lighting up the illustration that it glistens like the changing hues of a dove's neck. The entire letter, too, is pervaded by more than wonted fervour; the crisis being very perilous, his whole nature was moved to meet it, so as to deliver his beloved converts from its snares. One result is, that in his anxiety and haste, thought occasionally jostles thought; another idea presses upon him before the one under hand is brought to a formal conclusion; his faculty of mental association being so suggestive and fertile, that it pressed all around it into his service. These peculiarities show that the letter is an intensely human composition—the words of an earnest man writing in the fulness of his soul to other men, and naturally throwing himself on their affection; while there lies behind, in conscious combination, that divine authority which conferred upon him the apostleship in connection with the appearance and voice of the Saviour, and that divine training which opened up to him those sudden and perfect intuitions which he terms Revelation. The contents and circumstances of the epistle endeared it to Luther, for it fitted in wondrously to his similar experiences and trials, and he was wont to call it, as if in conjugal fondness, his Katherine von Bora. One may also cordially indorse the eulogy of Bunyan: "I prefer this book of Martin Luther's (except the Bible) before all the books that I have ever seen, as most fit for a wounded conscience." For the epistle unveils the relation of a sinner to the law which condemns him, and from which, therefore, he cannot hope for acceptance, and it opens up the great doctrine of justification by faith, which modern spiritualism either ignores or explains away. Its explicit theology is, that through faith one enjoys pardon and has the Spirit conferred upon him, so that he is free from legal yoke; while his life is characterized by a sanctified activity and self-denial, for grace is not in conflict with such obedience, but is rather the spring of it—death to the law being life to God. It is also a forewarning to all time of the danger of modifying the freeness and fulness of the gospel, and of allowing works or any element of mere ritual to be mixed up with the atoning death of the Son of God, as if to give it adaptation or perfection.

Any one writing on Galatians must acknowledge his obligation to the German exegets, Meyer, De Wette, Wieseler, and the others who are referred to in the last chapter of the Introduction. Nor can he forget to thank, among others at home, Bishop Ellicott, Dean Alford, and Prof. Lightfoot, for their learned and excellent labours. Each of these English commentaries has its distinctive merits; and my hope is, that this volume, while it has much in common with them, will be found to possess also an individual character and value, the result of unwearied and independent investigation. Ellicott is distinguished by close and uniform adherence to grammatical canon, without much expansion into exegesis; Alford, from the fact that his exposition extends to the whole New Testament, is of necessity brief and somewhat selective in his remarks; while Lightfoot himself says, that "in his explanatory notes such interpretations only are discussed as seemed at all events possibly right, or are generally received, or possess some historical interest;" and his collateral discussions occupy longer space than the proper exposition. I have endeavoured, on the other hand, to unite grammatical accuracy with some fulness of exegesis, giving, where it seemed necessary, a synopsis of discordant views, and showing their insufficiency, one-sidedness, ungrammatical basis, or want of harmony with the context; treating a doctrine historically, or throwing it into such a form as may remove objection; noticing now and then the views and arguments of Prof. Jowett; and, as a new feature in this volume, interspersing several separate Essays on important topics. Authorities have not been unduly heaped together; in the majority of cases, only the more prominent or representative names have been introduced. The text is for the most part, but not always, the seventh edition of Tischendorf, to whom we are indebted for the Codex Sinaiticus א, and for his recent and exact edition of the Vatican Codex of the New Testament.

My thanks are due to Mr. John Cross, student of Balliol College, Oxford, for looking over the sheets as they passed through the press.

And now, as an earnest and honest attempt to discover the mind of the Spirit in His own blessed word, I humbly dedicate this volume to the Church of Christ.

JOHN EADIE

6 Thornville Terrace, Hillhead,
Glasgow, 1*st January* 1869

CONTENTS

Some of the longer illustrations and separate discussions referred to in the Preface are noted in the following brief Table of Contents:—

GREEK WORDS AND PHRASES

INTRODUCTION

I—THE PROVINCE OF GALATIA

THE Galatia or Gallogræcia of the "Acts," the region to which this epistle was sent, was a central district in Asia Minor, bounded on the north by Bithynia and Paphlagonia, on the south by Cappadocia and Phrygia, on the east by Pontus and Cappadocia, and on the west by Phrygia and Bithynia. The Roman province of Galatia was considerably larger than this territory, and comprised Lycaonia, Isauria, Phrygia, and Pisidia—the kingdom as ruled by the last sovereign Amyntas.[1] Some critics therefore hold that this epistle was sent especially to believers in Lystra and Derbe; Mynster, Niemeyer, Paulus, Ulrich, Böttger, and Thiersch arguing that in the reign of Nero, Galatia included Derbe and Lystra along with Pisidia, and that therefore in Acts xiii. and xiv. there are full details of the apostle's missionary labours in the province. But Galatia is not used in the New Testament in this wide Roman sense; it has always a narrower signification. For by its side occur the similar names of Mysia, Pisidia, and Phrygia. Nay, Lycaonia, Pisidia, Phrygia—all included in the Roman province—are uniformly mentioned as countries distinct from Galatia; the obvious inference being that the terms denote various localities, without reference to political divisions. Thus the author of

[1] *Galatia quoque sub hoc provincia facta est, cum antea regnum fuisset primusque eam M. Lollius pro prætore administravit.* Eutropius, vii. 8.—Τοῦ δ' Ἀμύντου τελευτήσαντος οὐ τοῖς παισὶν αὐτοῦ τὴν ἀρχὴν ἐπέτρεψεν, ἀλλ' ἐς τὴν ὑπήκοον ἐσήγαγε, καὶ οὕτω καὶ ἡ Γαλατία μετὰ τῆς Λυκαονίας Ῥωμαῖον ἄρχοντα ἔσχε. Dion Cassius, liii. 3, vol. ii. p. 48, ed. Bekker. See also Strabo, xii. 5, 1. Pliny puts the *Lystreni* in the catalogue of the tribes occupying the Roman province: *Hist. Nat.* vii. 42.

the Acts describes the apostle and his party as going "throughout Phrygia and the region of Galatia" (Acts xvi. 6); and these are again distinguished from Lycaonia and Pisidia, Acts xiii. 14, xiv. 6, 24. Nay, the phrase first quoted—*τὴν Φρυγίαν καὶ τὴν Γαλατικὴν χώραν*, "the Phrygian and Galatian country"—implies that while Phrygia and Galatia were different, they were closely connected geographically; for the Galatian district was bounded south and west by Phrygia, nay, it had originally been Phrygian territory before it was conquered and possessed by the Gauls.[1] The towns of Lystra and Derbe, "cities of Lycaonia," with Iconium and Antioch, are never regarded as belonging to the apostolic Galatia, though the Roman Galatian province apparently included them. At the same time, in the enumeration of places in 1 Pet. i. 1, an enumeration running from east to west, Galatia may be the Roman province mentioned with the others there saluted.

The compound name *Γαλλογραικία*—Gallogrecia—Greek Gaul, is connected with the eastward migration of a fragment of the great old Keltic race which peopled western Europe. Indeed, Keltai, Galli, Galatæ, are varying forms of the same name. The first of these terms, *Κελτοί, Κέλται*, is probably the earliest, being found in Hecatæus[2] and Herodotus;[3] while the other form, *Γαλάτια*, is more recent (*ὀψέ*), as is affirmed by Pausanias,[4] though it came to be generally adopted by Greek writers as the name as well of the eastern tribes in Asia Minor, as of the great body of the people to the west of the Rhine. It occurs on the Augustan monument in the town of Ancyra; and being applied alike to the Asiatic and European Gauls, there needed occasionally some geographical notation to be added, such as that found in Ælian[5]—*Γαλάτας Εὔδοξος τοὺς τῆς Ἑῴας λέγει δρᾶν τοιαῦτα*; and it has been found on an inscription dug out from Hadrian's Wall in the north of England. Diefenbach[6] shows that this name had an

[1] Strabo writes: ἐν δὲ τῇ μεσογαίᾳ τήν τε Φρυγίαν, ἧς ἐστὶ μέρος ἥ τε τῶν Γαλλογραικῶν λεγομένη Γαλατία: *Geog.* ii. 5, 31.

[2] *Fragment.* 19, 20, 21, ed. Müller.

[3] *Hist.* ii. 33, iv. 49. Polybius, ii. 13; Diodorus Sic. v. 22. See Suidas, *sub voce* Γάλλοι, and the *Etymologicum Magnum*, *sub voce* Γαλατία.

[4] *Descript. Græc.* i. 3, 5, vol. i. p. 18, ed. Schubart.

[5] *De Nat. Anim.* xvii. 19, vol. i. p. 382, ed. Jacobs.

[6] *Celtica*, ii. p. 6, etc., Stuttgart 1839-40.

extensive range of application. Ammianus Marcellinus[1] says, *Galatas—ita enim Gallos Sermo Græcus adpellat;* and Appian[2] explains, *ἐς τὴν Κελτικὴν τὴν νῦν λεγομένην Γαλατίαν.* Galli —*Γάλλοι*, Gauls—was the current Roman name, though the other terms, Kelt and Galatian, are also used by Latin writers —the last being confined to the people who had settled themselves in Phrygia. Julius Cæsar's[3] words are, *tertiam qui ipsorum lingua, Celtæ, nostra Galli appellantur.* Livy,[4] in narrating the eastern wars in Galatia, calls the people Galli. *Γαλλία* is also employed by late Greek writers, and at a more recent period it almost superseded that of Galatia.[5] Theodore of Mopsuestia has *τὰς νῦν καλουμένης Γαλλίας—ad* 2 Tim. iv. 10, *Fragm.* p. 156, ed. Fritzsche. Diefenbach[6] quotes from Galen, *De Antidot.* i. 2, a clause identifying the three names: *καλοῦσι γὰρ αὐτοὺς ἔνιοι μὲν Γαλάτας, ἔνιοι δὲ Γάλλους, συνηθέστερον δὲ τῶν Κέλτων ὄνομα.* Strabo[7] reports some difference of language among the western Galatæ—a statement which may be at once believed, for, not to speak of Welsh and Erse, such variations are found in places so contiguous as the counties of Inverness and Argyle. Appian,[8] speaking of the Pyrenees, says, "that to the east are the Kelts, now named Galatians and Gauls, and to the west Iberians and Keltiberians." But the names are sometimes used vaguely, and sometimes also for the sake of inter-distinction, as in the definition of Hesychius, *Κελτοὶ ἔθνος ἕτερον Γαλατῶν*; in Diogenes Laertius,[9] *Κελτοῖς καὶ Γαλάταις*; and in fine, we have also the name *Κελτογαλατία.* These ethnological statements imply that the knowledge of ancient writers on the subject was not only vague and fluctuating, but often merely traditionary and conjectural, and that the various names—Greek and Roman, earlier and later, eastern and western—given to this primitive race, led to great confusion and misunderstanding. Perhaps it is not far from the truth to say that Kelt was the original name, the name em-

[1] xv. 9. [2] *Hann.* iv. p. 115, vol. i. ed. Bekker. [3] *Bell. Gall.* i.

[4] *Hist.* xxxviii. 12, 27. For these various names, see also Contzen, *die Wanderungen der Kelten*, p. 3, Leipzig 1861; Glück, *die bei C. J. Cæsar vorkommende Keltischen Namen*, München 1857.

[5] Wright's *Celt, Roman, and Saxon*, p. 325. [6] *Celtica*, ii. 7.

[7] *Geog.* iv. 1, 1. [8] *Hisp.* i. p. 48, vol. i. ed. Bekker.

[9] P. 1, vol. i. ed. Huebner.

ployed by the people themselves; and that the Greeks, on getting the name or some peculiar variation of it, represented it by Galatæ; while the Romans, by another initial change far from being uncommon, pronounced it Galli—the *t* or *at* in Kelt or Galat being a species of Keltic suffix.[1] Not only is the initial letter of Kelti and Galli interchangeable, but there is a form *Καλατία*, *Κάλατον*, allied, according to some, to Cael-don—the Gauls of the hills—Celadon, Caledonii. The northern form of the word is Gadhael, Gaidheal, or Gaoidheal, of which the Scottish term Gael is a contraction. Hence Argyle is *ar-Gadhael*, the coast of the Gael, and Argyle has become Argyll, just as Gael became Gall, Galli. The conflicting mythical derivations of the name need not be referred to; it seems to be allied to the Irish Gal, "a battle," Gala, "arms," and will therefore mean "armed"—*pugnaces, armati*.[2] This derivation is abundantly verified in their history, for they were, as Strabo says, "warlike, passionate, and ever prepared to fight."[3] The essential syllable in the earlier name is found in Celtiber, *Κελτίβηρ*; and the other form, Gall, makes the distinctive part of Gallicia, a province in the Spanish peninsula, of Galway and of Galloway, connected with the idea of foreign or hostile; hence the old Scottish proverb about "the fremd Scots of Galloway." The same syllable formed portion of the grand chieftain's name latinized by Tacitus into Galgacus, into whose mouth, in his oration before the decisive battle, the son-in-law of the Roman general puts those phrases which in their point and terseness have passed into proverbs: *omne ignotum pro magnifico; solitudinem faciunt, pacem appellant*.[4]

The Celtic races were among the earliest migrations from the East, and occupied western Europe; they were as far west, according to Herodotus, as to be "beyond the Pillars of Hercules"—"they are near the Kynetæ, which are the most western population of Europe."[5] They were also found in northern Italy, France, and the British Isles. Many Latin

[1] *T—derivans in nominibus Gallicis vel Britannicis vetustis. Singularis accedens ad radicem*—as Critognatus from *gnâ*. Zeuss, *Grammatica Celtica*, vol. ii. pp. 757, 758, Lipsiæ 1853.

[2] *Do.* vol. i. p. 993.

[3] *Geog.* iv. 4, 2.

[4] *Agricolæ Vita*, xxx. p. 287, *Op.* vol. iv. ed. Ruperti.

[5] ii. 33, iv. 49. Plutarch, *Vitæ*, *Marius*, p. 284, vol. ii. ed. Bekker.

terms connected with war are of Keltic origin.[1] But the ocean prevented any farther westward progress, and in their restlessness the Kelts retraced their steps, and commenced a series of movements towards the East. After some minor expeditions, and in the year 390 B.C., a portion of them, under Brennus or Bran, crossed the Apennines, captured Rome, and spread themselves over the south of Italy. According to Livy and Diodorus, these invaders came from the vicinity of Sens, and were therefore Kelts according to Cæsar's account of the races of Gaul. Others suppose them to have belonged to the Kymric branch of the Gauls: *Κίμβροι—Κιμμερίοι.*[2] About 279 B.C. another body of Gauls, under a leader of the same name, rushed eastward into Greece, overran Thrace and Macedonia, found immense wealth, and enriched themselves for another and more violent expedition,—their forces being said to consist of 150,000 infantry and 61,000 cavalry. These hardy hordes—*ὀψίγονοι Τιτῆνες*, late-born Titans—swarmed thick as snow-flakes—*νιφάδεσσιν ἐοικότες*, as the poet describes them.[3] On pushing their way to Thermopylæ so famed in olden story, they met 20,000 Greeks assembled to defend the pass, the shore being guarded also by an Athenian fleet. The Gauls, in spite of their numbers, were beaten back; and one party of them, crossing the mountains into Ætolia, ravaged the country with incredible barbarity. The leader then marched in haste on Delphi, gloating over the rich prize that should fall into his hands—the sacred treasures and statues and chariots dedicated to the sun-god; profanely joking, according to Justin,[4] that the gods were so rich that they could afford to be givers as well as receivers. But the Delphian Greeks, mustering only 4000, proved more than a match for Brennus and his impatient troops. The defenders had an advantageous situation on the hill, and, aided by a stern and intense wintry cold, they bravely repulsed the barbarians. Their general, wounded and carried off

[1] Prichard's *Eastern Origin of the Celtic Nations*, p. 124, Latham's ed.

[2] Appian, *Celtic.* vol. i. pp. 34, 42, ed. Bekker; Diodor. Sic. v. 32; Arnold's *History of Rome*, vol. i. p. 524, etc., 3d ed.

[3] Callimachus, *ad Delum.* 175, p. 33, ed. Blomfield.

[4] Justin, xxiv. 6. Contzen, *Wanderungen der Kelten*, p. 193, etc.; Wernsdorf, *De Repub. Galat.* vii.; Pausanias, *Descript. Græc.* x. 19.

the field, was unable to bear his mortification, and committed suicide; and the impetuous invaders, on being beaten, fled in panic—a national characteristic, and a few of them escaping the slaughter that accompanied their disorderly retreat through an unknown and mountainous territory, reached their brethren left behind at Thermopylæ. According to Greek legend, Apollo's help[1] led to the discomfiture of the invaders. Justin says that a portion of these marauders, the tribe called Tectosages, returned with their booty to Tolosa—Toulouse; but the story is uncertain, and the fluctuations of these Celtic tribes, ever in quest of new territories and plunder, cannot be distinctly traced—the hazy reports of their movements hither and thither cannot be clearly followed. The expedition to Delphi had bred fierce dissension among the leaders of the force, who, like all Keltic chiefs, were too self-willed and independent to maintain harmonious action for any length of time. Two leaders, named in a tongue foreign to their own, Leonnorius and Lutarius, had escaped the great disaster by refusing to join in the march; they and their followers fought their way through the Thracian Chersonese to the Hellespont, and after some quarrels and vicissitudes were carried across into Asia Minor. Nicomedes I., king of Bithynia, being at war at the time with his brother Zyboetes, gladly took these foreign mercenaries into his service, and by their help gained the victory, but at a terrible expense of misery to his country. In the campaign they had acted as it pleased them, and divided the prey among themselves. According to one statement, Nicomedes gave them a portion of the conquered country which was on that account called Gallogrecia. According to other accounts, the Gauls, disdaining all such trammels as usually bind allies or hired legionaries, set out to conquer for themselves, threw themselves over the country west and north of the Taurus, and either forced it to tribute or parcelled it out as a settlement. The Syrian princes were terrified into submission for a season; but their spirit at length revived, and one of them, Antiochus, got his surname of Soter from a victory over these truculent adventurers, or rather over one of their three tribes—the Tectosages. Such, however, was the importance attached to them, that the princes of various countries subsi-

[1] Diodorus, *Biblioth. Hist.* vol. iii. p. 52, *Excerpta Vaticana.*

dized them, and they are found in Egyptian as well as in Syrian battles. But they were dangerous friends; for after helping to gain a battle for Antiochus Hierax, they turned and compelled him to ransom himself and form a bond with them. Their spreading over the country like a swarm—*velut examen*, and the *terror Gallici nominis et armorum invicta felicitas*, are referred to by Justin.[1] In this way they became the terror of all states, an ungovernable army, whose two-edged sword was ever ready to be drawn to glut their own lust of booty, and which, when paid for, often cut on either side of the quarrel for which they had been bought, and was seldom sheathed. They knew their power, and acted according to their wild and rapacious instincts.

But their unquenchable turbulence became intolerable. Attalus, prince of Pergamus and father of Eumenes, gained a great victory over them, or rather over the two tribes, the Trocmi and Tolistoboii; he refused to pay them tribute, and hemmed them into the province proper of Galatia, about B.C. 230.[2] Yet we find Attalus employing another horde of the same hirelings in one of his wars, who, as their wont had been, broke loose from all restraint, and plundered the countries and towns along the Hellespont, till their defeat by Prusias, about B.C. 216.[3] But Rome was about to avenge its earlier capture. Some Gallic or Galatian troops had fought on the side of Antiochus at the battle of Magnesia; and the consul Manlius, against the advice of the *decem legati* who were with him, at once invaded their country, while the native Phrygian hierarchy, trodden down by the Gauls, encouraged the invaders. The Gauls, on being summoned to submit, refused—*stolida ferocia;* but they were soon defeated, in two campaigns and in a series of battles, with prodigious slaughter. Certain conditions were imposed on them, but their country was not wrested from them. They may by this time have lost their earlier hardihood, and, as Niebuhr remarks, have become quite effeminate and unwarlike, as the Goths whom Belisarius found in Italy. Fifty-two Gallic chiefs walked before the triumphal car of Manlius at Rome, B.C. 189. In subsequent years they were often employed as indispensable auxiliaries; they served both with Mithridates and with Pompey who showed them some favour, and some of them were at Actium on the side of Antony. Roman patronage, however,

[1] *Hist. Philip.* xxv. 2. [2] Livy, lib. xxxviii. 16. [3] Polybius, v. 11.

soon crushed them. Deiotarus, first tetrarch, and then made king by Pompey, was beaten at Pharsalia, but he was defended at Rome by Cicero; the second king of the same name was succeeded by Amyntas, on whose death Augustus reduced the country to the rank of a Roman province, B.C. 25, the first governor of which was the propraetor, M. Lollius. The difference between the limits of Galatia and the Roman province so named has been already referred to.

The Gauls who had so intruded themselves into Asia Minor, and formed what Juvenal[1] calls *altera Gallia*, were divided into three tribes: the names of course have been formed with Greek terminations from the native terms which may not be very accurately represented. These three tribes were the *Τολιστόβογιοι*, to the west of the province, with Pessinus for their capital; the *Τεκτοσάγες* in the centre, with Ancyra for their chief city which was also the metropolis of the country; and the *Τρόκμοι*, to the east of the territory, their principal town being Tavium.[2] Each tribe was divided into four tetrarchies, having each its tetrarch, with a judge and a general under him; and there was for the twelve tetrarchies a federal council of 300, who met at Drynaemetum, or oak-shrine—the first syllable of the word being the Keltic *derw*, oak (Derwydd, Druid), and *nemed* in the same tongue meaning a temple.[3] That, says Strabo, was the old constitution—*πάλαι μὲν οὖν ἦν τοιαύτη τις ἡ διάταξις.*[4]

The previous statements, however, have been questioned, and it has been denied that those fierce marauders were Gauls. There are, it is true, contradictions and uncertainties among the old writers about them,—statements that can neither be fully understood nor satisfactorily adjusted. The outline is

[1] *Sat.* vii. 16.

[2] Memnon in *Photii Bibliotheca*, pp. 227-8, ed. Bekker. The spelling of the names varies, and under the Emperor Augustus the epithet Σεβαστηνοί was prefixed to them. Who would not have thanked Tacitus, if in his *Life of Agricola*, instead of his stately Latin terminations, he had spelled the proper names as nearly as possible according to the pronunciation of the natives of Pictland or Caledonia? But the Romans looked with contempt on such an effort. Pliny sneers at a *barbara appellatio* (*Hist. Nat.* iii. 4), and a professed geographer says, *Cantabrorum aliquot populi amnesque sunt, sed quorum nomina nostro ore concipi nequeant.* P. Mela, *De Situ Orbis*, iii. 1.

[3] Diefenbach, *Celtica*, i. 160.

[4] xii. 5.

often dark, and the story is sometimes left incomplete, or filled in with vague reports, legends, or conjectures. But the wild wanderers referred to were generally believed to be Gauls proper from the west, and probably of the great division of Kymri or Welsh Kelts. Latham, in his edition of Prichard's *Eastern Origin of the Celtic Nations*, p. 104, etc., throws out the conjecture that the Galatians were from Austrian Gallicia, and therefore of Sclavonic origin; but his arguments are neither strong nor strongly put. Others maintain that those Gauls or Galatians were of a German stock. There are obscurities in the distinctions made by Greek and Latin authors between the German and Gothic races, of which Suidas under *Κελτοί* is an example; for he says the Kelts are called Germans, adding, that they invaded Albion, and are also called Senones —a Gothic race beyond all dispute. Dion Cassius falls into similar blunders. "Some of the Kelts," he says, "whom we call Germans, holding the whole of Keltike toward the Rhine, have made it to be called Germany."[1] He places the Kelts on both banks of the Rhine, or rather with this odd distinction, ἐν ἀριστερᾷ μὲν τήν τε Γαλατίαν . . . ἐν δεξιᾷ δὲ τοὺς Κελτούς. He also identifies Kelts and Germans, calling the latter *Κελτοί*, and the Belgians *Κελτικοί*; nay, vaguely regarding *Κελτική* as a Celtic territory bordering on Aquitania, he sometimes gives it the special meaning of Gallia, and at other times uses it in the broader sense of Western Europe containing Kelts and Germans.[2] Other old writers were apparently quite as bewildered on the subject, and as various in their references. A knowledge of the geography and the history of outlying regions could not be easily obtained in those days, and much of it must have been the result of oral communication, so liable to mistake, exaggeration, and distortion. But a distinction was usually made, though it was not consistently adhered to; and the hypothesis that these Gauls were of a Teutonic origin is quite contrary to the current traditions and the ordinary beliefs of the earlier times. There are extreme views on both sides; such as the theory of Mone,[3] that Germany as

[1] liii. 12, xxxix. 49.

[2] xxxix. 46, 49. See Brandes, *das Ethnographische Verhaltniss der Kelten und Germanen*, p. 203, Leipzig 1857.

[3] *Celtische Forschungen*, Freiburg 1857.

well as Gaul was peopled with Celts, and that of Holtzmann,[1] that the two peoples named Celts and Germans were both alike a Teutonic race. Something like national vanity has been mingled with this dispute, which is not unlike a fierce and famous quarrel nearer home as to the origin and blood of the Picts. Thus Hofmann, in his *Disputatio de Galat. Antiq.* 1726, cries: *En igitur coloniam Germanorum in Græcia—en virtutem majorum nostrorum quæ sua arma ad remotissima loca protulit.* Selneccer (Wernsdorf, *De Repub. Galat.*) is jubilant on this account: *cum ad Galatas scripsisse Paulum legimus, ad nostros majores Germanos eum scripsisse sciamus. Germani ergo epistolam hanc sibi vindicent, ut hæredes et posteri.*[2] Luther also says, "Some imagine that we Germans are descendants of the Galatians. Nor perhaps is this derivation untrue, for we Germans are not very unlike them in temper." "The Epistle to the Galatians is addressed to Germans," Olshausen writes; "and it was the German Luther who in this apostolical epistle again recognised and brought to light the substance of the gospel. It can scarcely be doubted that the Galatians are the first German people to whom the word of the cross was preached." Tournefort warms into enthusiasm when his travels carry him among Keltic affinities. Gleams of the same spirit are found in Thierry; and Texier says more distinctly, *Pour nous, nous ne devons pas nous rappeler, sans un sentiment d'orgueil national, que les Gaulois ont pénétré jusqu'à centre de l'Asie mineure, s'y sont établis, et ont laissé dans ce pays des souvenirs impérissables.*[3]

Now, first, the names of these Galatian tribes appear to be Keltic names. The Tolisto-boii, or perhaps Tolisto-boioi, are Keltic in both parts of their appellation. For Tolosa is yet preserved in France and Spain;[4] and the second portion of the word is Keltic also, the Boii being a well-known Gallic tribe—a turbulent and warlike race who left Transalpine Gaul, crossed into northern Italy by the pass of the Great St. Bernard, fought against the Roman power at intervals with

[1] *Kelten und Germanen*, Stuttgart 1855. See Prof. Lightfoot's Essay, in his *Commentary on Galatians*, p. 229.

[2] Wernsdorf, *De Repub. Galat.* 94.

[3] *Revue des Deux Mondes*, 1841, p. 575.

[4] Diefenbach, *Celtica*, ii. p. 339.

varying fortunes, but on being at length driven out of the country, settled on a territory named from them Boien-heim —home of the Boii—Bohemia.[1] The Tectosages bear also a Keltic designation. A Gallic tribe of the name is mentioned by Cæsar as being also a migratory one, like so many of its sisters: *Germaniæ loca circum Hercyniam silvam Volcæ Tectosages occupaverunt atque ibi consederunt;*[2] and Tolosa Tectosagum occurs in Pom. Mela, ii. 5, as among the cities of Gallia Narbonensis. The Tectosages are supposed indeed by Meyer and others to have been a German tribe, called by Cæsar Volcæ Tectosages; but Volcæ has no connection with the Teutonic *Folk* or *Volk*, for they were a Keltic race who had conquered a settlement in Germany and adopted German manners (Cæsar says these things not from his own knowledge), while the great body of the tribe occupied the basin of the Garonne, with Tolosa (Toulouse) for its capital. The name of the Trocmi is more obscure. Some, as Strabo, followed by Texier, derive it from a chief; Bochart took it from Togarmah;[3] others connect it with *Θρηϊκες*—Thraces; while others identify them with the Taurisci—mountain-dwellers.[4]—Secondly, the persons engaged in the expedition into Greece, and the chiefs noted among them afterwards, have Keltic names like the Gallic ones in Cæsar; ending in *rix* (chief), like Dumnorix; Albiorix, Ateporix occur after the lapse of two centuries; or in *marus* (*mar*, great), as Virdumarus, and in *tarus* or *torus*, as Deiotarus, *tar* being equivalent to the Latin *trans*. The leader Brennus (king) was called Prausus — terrible (Gaelic, *bras;* Cornish, *braw*). Brennus had a colleague or *Συνάρχων*; Pausanias calls him *Ακίχωριος*,[5] and Diodorus Siculus *Κιχώριος*. In the Kymric tongue the name would be Kikhouïaour, or Akikhouïaour, which without the augment *a* would be Cyçwiawr.[6]—Thirdly, names of places often end in the Keltic *briga* (hill) and *iacum*.[7]—Fourthly, Pausanias refers to a plant which the Greeks called *κόκκος*, the kermes berry, but which the Galatians *φωνῇ τῇ ἐπιχωρίῳ* call *ὗς*, or according to a better reading *ὕσγη*, the dye being called *ὑσγινόν*.[8] Now, the Kymric has *hesgen*, a sedge, and the Cornish has *heschen*.

[1] Tacitus, *De Germania*, c. 28.
[2] *De Bell. Gall.* vi. 24.
[3] *Phaleg*. iii. 11.
[4] Diefenbach, *Celtica*, ii. 256.
[5] x. 19.
[6] Thierry, *Hist. des Gaulois*, i. 129.
[7] Zeuss, *Celt. Gram.* 772.
[8] x. 36. Suidas, *sub voce*.

Pausanias[1] tells also that one mode of military arrangement among the invading Gauls was called *τριμαρκισία*, from their native name for a horse, *μάρκας*; *tri* or *trî* being Celtic for three, and *march* or *marc* the name of a steed. In Irish and Gaelic and Welsh, *trimarchwys* signifies "men driving three horses."—Fifthly, the long lance, the distinctive weapon of the infantry, was the *γαῖσον*; hence the epithet *γαισάται Γαλάται*.[2] It is in Irish *gad*, a lance, *gaide*, *gaisthe*, *s solitaria* often falling out.[3] It is often incorporated into proper names, as Radagaisus, Gaisatorix, not unlike Breakspear, Shakespear. It is allied to the Saxon *goad*, and the old Scottish *gad*, the name of a spear and a fishing-rod. The account of the word and epithet given by Polybius is wholly wrong. *Γαῖσος* occurs in the Sept., Josh. viii. 18, and in the Apocrypha, Judith ix. 9.—Sixthly, Jerome is a witness whose testimony may be trusted, for it is that of an ear-witness. He had sojourned both among the Treviri for some time when a young man—*adolescentulus*, and he had journeyed to Galatia, and seen its capital Ancyra. In a letter to Ruffinus he refers to a pilgrimage—*totum Galatiæ et Cappadociæ iter*.[4] In the preface to the second book of his *Commentary* he says, *Scit mecum qui videt Ancyram metropolim Galatiæ civitatem*.[5] Not only does he mention his being in Gaul, but he writes more definitely to Ruffinus, in the letter already quoted—*quum post Romana studia ad Rheni semibarbaras ripas eodem cibo, pari frueremur hospitio*. In his second book against Jovinian he tells a story about the cannibalism and ferocity of the *natio Scotorum* whom he saw in Gaul;[6] and more precisely still, he informs Florentius of a literary work, *librum Sancti Hilarii quem apud Treviros manu mea ipse descripseram*.[7] Now, Jerome's distinct words are:

[1] x. 19.

[2] Polybius, ii. 23. *Gæsum* occurs *Bell. Gall.* iii. 4. Athenæus, lib. vi. p. 548, *Op.* vol. ii. ed. Schweighäuser.

[3] Zeuss, *Celt. Gramm.* p. 64. [4] *Op.* vol. i. p. 10. [5] *Op.* vii. p. 430.

[6] Vol. ii. p. 335. The tribes called Scots in those days were Irish; and Irish wanderers came gradually over to Argyleshire, and founded the old kingdom of Dalriada. St. Columba is called *utriusque Scotiæ patronus*, there being a Scotia and a Dalriada in Ireland as well as in Britain. Probably the name Scot itself is allied to Scyth, the vague title assigned to a wild and distant race.

[7] *Op.* vol. i. p. 15, ed. Vallars. Venetiis 1766.

"It is true that Gaul produces orators, but Aquitania boasts a Greek origin"—*et Galatæ non de illa parte terrarum, sed de ferocioribus Gallis sint profecti. . . . Unum est quod inferimus, Galatas excepto sermone Græco quo omnis Oriens loquitur, propriam linguam eandem pene habere quam Treviros.*[1] So that six hundred years after their first settlement in Asia Minor their old language was spoken by them.

But, according to Meyer, Winer, Jablonski, Niebuhr, Hug, Hermes, Olshausen, Baumgarten-Crusius, Holtzman,[2] German was the language spoken then, as now, in and around Treves. This statement, however, though partially true, does not prove the point contended for. For there had been an intrusive change of population toward the end of the third century. A colony of Franks had settled in the territory of the Treviri, and naturally brought their language with them—*Γερμανοὺς οἱ νῦν Φράγγοι καλοῦνται.*[3] Yet the older tongue survived, and might survive for a long period afterwards, like the Welsh tongue of the present day, centuries after the annexation of the principality to England. Wieseler argues from the testimony of early writers as to the Germanic descent and blood of the Treviri. Tacitus says indeed that the Treviri and the Nervii affected a German origin,—a confession that they were not pure Germans, and he proceeds to distinguish them from peoples which were German *haud dubie.*[4] Strabo indeed seems to admit that the Nervii were a German race.[5] But the Treviri are called Belgæ and Gauls again and again, as by Tacitus in his *Annal.* i. 42, 43, iii. 44. In his *Hist.* iv. 71, 72, 73, Cerealis addresses them, *Terram vestram ceterorumque Gallorum. . . .* Cæsar says, *Treviros quorum civitas propter Germaniæ vicinitatem . . . .; hæc civitas longe plurimum totius Galliæ equitatu valet . . .; Gallus inter Gallos,*[6]—in which places they are distinguished from Germans; and Pom. Mela writes, *Clarissimi Belgarum Treveri.*[7] Their leaders' names are Keltic, such as Cingetorix. Some doubt is thrown on this by the way in which Pliny speaks of them,[8] and there may have been, as Thierry allows, some German

[1] *Op.* vol. vii. pp. 428–430.
[2] *Kelten und Germanen*, p. 88.
[3] Procopius, *Bell. Vandal.* i. 3.
[4] *De Germania* 28.
[5] *Geog.* iv. 24.
[6] *Bell. Gall.* viii. 25, v. 3, v. 45, vi. 2, vii. 8.
[7] iii. 2.
[8] *Hist. Nat.* iv. 31.

tribes mixed up with them, as was the case among the Keltic Belgians.[1] Cæsar's statement, *De Bell. Gall.* ii. 4, may be accounted for in the same way, and the apparently Teutonic names of some of the leaders in the invasion, such as Lutarius (Luther) and Leonnorius, may be thus explained. Great stress is laid on the names of these two leaders, and on the name of a tribe called Teutobodiaci, and a town oddly styled Germanopolis. Thierry supposes that the Tolistoboii were Teutonic, because of the name of Lutarius their leader. But the Teutonic origin of even these names has been disputed. With regard to the first word, there is a Keltic chieftain in Cæsar named Lucterius,[2] and Leonorius is the name of a Cymric saint.[3] The second syllable of the tribal name is found in the name of the warrior queen Boadicea, in the name Bodotria, and the *o* being resolvable into *ua*, the word assumes the form of *buáid*, *victoria*.[4] Zeuss also adduces such forms as Tribodii, Catbud, Budic, etc. Germanopolis, as Prof. Lightfoot remarks, is an exceptional word, and probably denotes some fragment of an exceptional population; or the name may have been one of later introduction, as the Greek termination may indicate. The name does not appear till more recent times, it being conjectured that a foreign colony had been planted there.[5] Still more, the dissyllable *German* itself, not being the native Teutonic name of the people, may have a Keltic origin,—according to Grimm, from *garm*, *clamor*, or according to Zeuss, from *ger* or *gair*, *vicinus*.[6]

Lastly, Ammianus Marcellinus, writing in former times, speaks of the tall stature, fair and ruddy complexion of the Gauls, and the blue eyes of their women;[7] and Diodorus[8] describes the white skins and yellow hair of the Ἑλληνογαλάται. If any faith can be placed in national resemblance of form and feature in

[1] *Hist. des Gaulois*, i. p. 225. [2] *Bell. Gall.* vii. 7.

[3] Diefenbach, *Celtica*, ii. 254. [4] Zeuss, *Gram. Celt.* vol. i. p. 27.

[5] Wernsdorf, *De Republica Galat.* p. 219.

[6] *G. C.* vol. ii. p. 375. Some deny that the Belgæ were Kelts. Cæsar distinguished them from the Celtæ and Aquitani; but it is admitted that among them were German colonies who had expelled the aborigines and settled near the Rhine, so that many Germans were mixed up with them. But the people itself was Keltic, and to them Cæsar gave the generalized name of Belgæ—the name being allied to Belg, Fir-bolg in Irish.

[7] xv. 12. [8] v. 28, 32.

two periods so remote, Texier may be listened to : *Sans chercher à se faire illusion, on reconnaît quelquefois, surtout parmi les pasteurs, des types qui se rapportent merveilleusement à certaines races de nos provinces de France. On voit plus de cheveux blonds en Galatie qu'en aucun autre royaume de l'Asie mineure, les têtes carrées et les yeux bleux rappellent le caractère des populations de l'ouest de la France. Cette race de pasteurs est répandue dans les villages et les yaëla (camps nomades) des environs de la métropole.*[1]

All these points enumerated are conclusively in favour of the old and common belief of the Keltic origin of the Galatians.

The original population of the province indeed was Phrygian, though in the current name no account is taken of that people, but of the Greeks who were settled in it, as in all the East since the period of Alexander's conquests, so that Strabo calls it *Γαλατία Ἑλλήνων.*[2] The partial amalgamation of these races must have occupied a long time. The Phrygian superstition may have taken hold of the Kelts from some points of resemblance to their ancestral faith and worship; and they learned to use the Grecian language, which was a kind of common tongue among all the tribes round about them, while neither the Phrygian nor the Gallic vernacular was wholly superseded. The Gauls had coins with Greek inscriptions prior to the Christian era. The consul Manlius, addressing his troops, says of the Galatians : *Hi jam degeneres sunt mixti, et Gallogræci vere quod appellantur . . . Phrygas Gallicis oneratos armis.*[3] The Galatian lady who is praised by Plutarch and others for killing her deforcer, spoke to her attendants in a tongue which the soldiers knew not. The Jewish dispersion had also been spreading itself everywhere, and was found in Galatia. The population was therefore a mixed one, but it was profoundly pervaded by a Keltic element which gave it character. The manifestations of that temperament occasioned this epistle, and are also referred to in it. The *Γαλατικά* of Eratosthenes has been lost, and we can scarcely pardon Jerome for giving us no extracts from Varro and other writers on Galatia, forsooth on this weak pretence,—*quia nobis propositum est, incircumcisos homines non introducere in Templum Dei.*

[1] *Revue des Deux Mondes*, 1841, p. 598.
[2] *Geog.* i. 4.
[3] Livy, xxxviii. 17.

II.—INTRODUCTION OF THE GOSPEL INTO GALATIA

It was during the apostle's second great missionary circuit that he first preached the gospel in Galatia, probably about A.D. 51 or 52. A mere passing hint is given, a mere allusion to evangelistic travel, as it brought the apostle nearer to the sea-board and his voyage to Europe. The simple statement is, "Now when they had gone throughout Phrygia and the region of Galatia, and were forbidden of the Holy Ghost to preach the gospel in Asia."[1] The apostle had proposed to visit Asia or Ephesus, but the set time had not come; and on arriving in Mysia, he and his party prepared to go north-east into Bithynia, but "the Spirit of Jesus did not suffer them"—such is the better reading. Thus checked and checked again, passing by Mysia, they were guided to Troas, the point of embarkation for Greece. They could not therefore purpose to preach in Bithynia after such a prohibition, and probably the prohibition to preach in Asia suggested the opposite continent of Europe. If the apostle had any idea of crossing to Europe at this time, the effort to advance into Bithynia may have been to reach Byzantium, and get to the West by the ordinary voyage and highway.[2] These brief words with regard to Galatia are thus a mere filling up of the apostle's tour, during which he was guided into a way that he knew not, and led by a path that he had not known. When it is said that he went through the Galatian territory, it is implied that he journeyed for the purpose of preaching, as is also shown by the contrast that he was forbidden "to preach" in Asia—preaching being the one aim and end of all his movements. In the cities of Galatia, then, the apostle preached at this time, and naturally formed associations of believers into churches. But nothing is told of success or opposition, of inquirers, converts, or antagonists.

The apostle's own reference to this visit is as brief, incidental, and obscure as the passage in Acts. "Ye know how, through infirmity of the flesh, I preached the gospel unto you at the first:" Gal. iv. 13. The plain meaning of this declaration is, that he was detained in the province by sickness, and that on this account, and not because of any previous plans and

[1] Acts xvi. 6, 7. [2] Wieseler, *Chronol.* p. 32.

arrangements, he preached the gospel at his first visit to Galatia. The phrase δι' ἀσθένειαν admits grammatically of no other meaning, and πρότερον refers to the earlier of two visits. See the commentary under the verse. But he reminds them of his cordial welcome among them as "an angel of God, even as Christ Jesus;" asserts, too, that in their intense and demonstrative sympathy they "would have plucked out their eyes, and given them to him," and that they overlooked that infirmity which tended from its nature to create loathing of his person and aversion to his message. See commentary on iv. 14. Their impulsive and excitable nature flashed out in enthusiastic reception of him; and their congratulations of one another on the message and the messenger were lavished with characteristic ardour,—all in sad contrast with their subsequent defection. But we learn, too, from some allusions in his appeals, that in Galatia as everywhere else, he preached Christ and His cross, —pictured Him clearly, fully, as the one atoning Saviour,—and announced as on a placard to them the Crucified One. That preaching was followed by the descent of the Spirit; miracles had been wrought among them, and their spiritual progress had been eager and marked—"Ye were running well." But the bright morning was soon and sadly overcast.

Some indeed suppose that an earlier visit than the one now referred to is implied in Acts xiv. 6, which says that Paul and Barnabas, on being informed of a persecution ripening against them in Iconium, "fled unto Derbe and Lystra, cities of Lycaonia, and unto the region that lieth round about." But these geographical notations plainly exclude Galatia, as we have seen in the previous chapter; and ἡ περίχωρος, the country surrounding Lystra and Derbe—cities toward the south of Lycaonia, cannot include Galatia which was situated so far to the north, Phrygia lying between. Such references as Macknight gives in proof to Pliny and Strabo have been already disposed of. Koppe maintains that the mention of Barnabas in Gal. ii. 13 presupposes a personal knowledge of him on the part of the Galatians, which could only be acquired through an earlier visit. But Acts xiv. 6 will not, as we have just seen, warrant any belief in such a visit; nor does the statement of the strength of that current of Judaistic influence which at Antioch carried even Barnabas away, really imply any more than that his name, as the apostle's recognised fellow-labourer, must have been in course of years quite familiar to them. It is a mistake on the part of Koppe and Keil to affirm that the visit on the second missionary circuit was one of confirmation only, which must therefore imply previous evangelical labour. It is true that Paul and Barnabas resolved on such a journey, and that, from a difference of opinion as to the fitness of Mark to accompany them, Paul and his new colleague Silas carried out the intention. "They went through Syria and Cilicia confirming the churches," xv. 41; then proceeded to Derbe and Lystra where Timothy joined them; and the result of the tour is formally announced thus: "So were the churches established in the faith, and increased in number daily." But this daily increase implies that the confirmation of believers was not the only service in which the apostle engaged; he also preached the gospel so as to gain numerous converts. The description of this journey ends at xvi. 5, and the next verse begins a new and different section—the account of a further journey with a somewhat different end in view, preaching being the principal aim and work.

During his third missionary circuit, a second visit was paid by the apostle to the Galatian churches, probably about three years after the first, or about A.D. 54. As little is said of this visit in Acts as of the first. It is briefly told in xviii. 23, that "he went over the Galatian country and Phrygia in order, strengthening all the disciples." The apostle passed through Phrygia in order to reach Galatia, and therefore Phrygia precedes in the first account; but at the next visit he passed through Galatia in order to reach Phrygia, and Galatia naturally stands first in the second account. The results are not stated, but we know that the effects of this "strengthening" were soon exhausted. It may be safely surmised that the allusions in the epistle to his personal presence among them, which have in them an element of indignation or sorrow, refer to his second visit—all being so fair and promising at his first residence. During the interval between the first and second visit, incipient symptoms of defection seem to have shown themselves; the Judaistic teachers had been sowing their errors with some success. The constitutional fickleness of the people had begun to develop itself when novelty had worn off. He did not need to warn them about "another gospel" at his first visit; but at the second visit he had felt the necessity of uttering such a warning, and that with no bated breath: He, the preacher of such a gospel, angel or man, let him be accursed. The solemn censure in v. 21 might be given at any of his visits, for it fitted such a people at any time; though perhaps, after a season of suppression at their conversion, these sins might reappear in the churches during the reaction which followed the first excitement. At the second visit, the earlier love had not only cooled and its effervescence subsided, but estrangement and misunderstanding were springing up. Such a change is implied in the sudden interrogation introducing an exposure of the motives of those who were paying them such court, and superseding him in their affections: "Am I become your enemy because I tell you the truth?" See commentary under iv. 15, 16, 17. The apostle had the fervent and abiding interest of a founder in the Galatian churches: in the crisis of their spiritual peril, he travailed in birth for them—suffered the throes of a first travail at their conversion, and those of a second now, that "Christ might be fully formed in their hearts."

It is probable that the apostle followed in Galatia his common practice, and preached "to the Jews first, and also to the Greeks." The historian is silent indeed on this subject, and it is wholly baseless in Baur, Schneckenburger, and Hilgenfeld to allege that the reason of the silence is because Paul did not follow his usual method, there being in fact no Jews to preach to. Hofmann inclines to the same view, though not for the same reasons. But the view of Baur assumes a primarily improbable hypothesis, that Luke constructed his narrative for the purpose of showing how the gospel was transferred from the rejecting Jews to the accepting Gentiles. In reply, besides, it may be stated, that on that ground the accounts of his labours at Lystra and at Athens must be taken as exceptions, which certainly show the improbability of the hypothesis. The reason alleged by Olshausen for the historian's brevity, viz. that he wished to bring the apostle over as speedily as possible to Rome, is nearer the truth; only Olshausen's argument can scarcely be sustained, that Luke thereby consulted the wishes and circumstances of his first readers. Nor is it less likely that the apostle at his first visit, and so far as his feeble health permitted, would labour in the great centres of population—in Ancyra, Pessinus, Tavium, and Gordium.[1] But we have several indirect arguments that many Jews had settled in the province and neighbourhood. We find in Josephus a despatch of king Antiochus, in which he says that he had thought proper to remove two thousand Jewish families from Mesopotamia and Babylon into Lydia and Phrygia.[2] Wherever there was an opening for gain, wherever traffic could be carried on, wherever shekels could be won in barter or commercial exchange, there the Jews were found, earnest, busy, acute, and usually successful,—the Diaspora surged into all markets; yet in the midst of its bargains, buying, selling, and getting gain, it forgot not to build its synagogues. Josephus quotes an edict of Augustus addressed to the Jews at Ancyra, protecting them in their special religious usages and in the enjoyment of the Sabbath; and he ordains that the *ψήφισμα* formally granted by them be preserved (*ἀνατεθῆναι*), along with his decree, in the temple dedicated by the community of Asia in Ancyra.[3] Names and symbols found in the inscriptions lead to the same conclusion. So that there was to be found in the territory a large Jewish population, to whom the apostle would prove that Jesus was the promised Messiah. How many of them received the gospel, it is impossible to say.

The churches, therefore, were not made up wholly of Gentiles, as Baur, Schneckenburger, and Hilgenfeld contend. That there was a body of Jews in them is probable also from the clauses in which the apostle identifies himself with them: "we Jews by nature," ii. 15; "redeemed us from the curse of the law," iii. 13; "we were kept under the law," iii. 23; "we are no longer under a schoolmaster," iii. 25; "we were in bondage under the elements of the world," iv. 3. Heathen believers are specially appealed to in many places, iv. 8–12; and to preach to them was his special function, i. 16, ii. 9: they are assured that to get themselves circumcised is of no avail, v. 2; and the party who would force cir-

[1] Strabo writes: *Πεσσινοῦς δ' ἐστὶν ἐμπορεῖον τῶν ταύτῃ μέγιστον*, *Geog.* xii. 5, 3; and Gordium is described by Livy—*id haud magnum quidem oppidum est, sed plus quam Mediterraneum, celebre et frequens emporium, tria maria pari ferme distantia intervallo habet:* xxxviii. 18.

[2] *Antiq.* xii. 3, 4.

[3] *Ibid.* xvi. 6, 2.

cumcision upon them are stigmatized as cowardly time-servers, vi. 12, 13. These Gentiles are regarded by Storr, Mynster, Credner, Davidson, and Jowett as proselytes of the gate; but the assertion has no sure foundation. Some may have been in that condition of anxious inquirers, but in iv. 8 they are accused of having been idolaters; and the phrase "weak and beggarly elements," to which again—*πάλιν*—they desired to be in bondage, may characterize heathenism in several of its aspects as well as Judaism. See commentary on iv. 8. But it is no proof of the existence or number of Jewish Christians to allege that Peter, i. 1, wrote to elect strangers in Galatia; for *διασπορά* may be there used in a spiritual sense, and it is certain that many words in that epistle must have been addressed to Gentiles: ii. 11, 12, iv. 3. Besides, the apostle makes a free and conclusive use of the Old Testament in his arguments—a mode of proof ordinarily unintelligible to a Gentile. Again and again does he adduce a quotation as portion of a syllogistic argument, conscious that his proof was taken from what was common ground to them both—from a source familiar to them and acknowledged to be possessed of ultimate authority. It is true that the Old Testament contained a divine revelation preparatory to the new economy, and that the apostle might use it in argument anywhere; but there is in this epistle a direct versatility in handling the Hebrew Scriptures, as well as an uncommon and esoteric application of them, which presupposes more familiarity with them and their interpretation than Gentiles by birth could be easily supposed to possess.

The amazing success of the apostle's first labours in the midst of numerous drawbacks, might be assisted by various secondary causes, such as the novelty of the message, and the unique phenomenon of its proclamation by one who was suffering from epileptic paralysis. The Celtic temperament, so easily attracted by novelty, might at once embrace the new religion, though, on the other hand, nothing could be more remote than the Phrygian *cultus* from the purity and simplicity of the gospel. Yet that gospel, presented in the enthusiastic eloquence of a man so wildly earnest as to appear "beside himself," and yet so feeble, so stricken, and so visibly carrying in himself the sentence of death, arrested and conquered them with ominous celerity. It is impossible to say what about the gospel specially captivated them, though there is no doubt that the cross was exhibited in its peculiar prominence. The appeal in iii. 1 would seem to imply, that as the public and placarded presentation of the Crucified One is brought forward to prove the prodigious folly of their apostasy, it may be inferred that this was the doctrine by which they had been fascinated, and which spoke home, as Prof. Lightfoot surmises, to their traditionary faith in the atoning efficacy of human blood.[1] That the blood of bullocks and of goats could not take away sin, was a profound and universal conviction in old Gaul, if Cæsar may be credited; and man for man appeared a juster and more meritorious substitution. Might not, then, the preaching of the man Jesus put to death as a sacrificial victim throw a wondrous awe over them, as they saw in it the realization of traditionary beliefs and hopes?

Still Christianity had nothing in common with the Phrygian religion, which was a demonstrative nature-worship, both sensuous and startling. The *cultus* was orgiastic, with wild music and dances led by the Corybantes—not without the usual accompaniment of impurities and other abominations, though it might have mystic initiations and secret teachings. Rhea or Cybele (and Rhea might be only another form of ἔρα, the earth), the mother of the gods, was the chief object of adoration, and derived a surname from the places where her service was established. The great Mother appears on the coins of all the cities, and many coins found in the ruins of the Wall of Hadrian have her effigy. At Pessinus her image was supposed to have fallen from heaven, and there she was called Agdistes. Though the statue was taken to Rome during the war with Hannibal, the city retained a sacred pre-eminence. Strabo says that her priests were a sort of sovereigns endowed with large revenues, and that the Attalian kings built for her a magnificent temple.[2] The Keltic invaders are supposed to have been accustomed to somewhat similar religious ordinances in their national so-called Druidism. But the Druidical system,

[1] *Quod, pro vita hominis nisi hominis vita reddatur, non posse aliter deorum immortalium numen placari arbitrantur, publiceque ejusdem generis habent instituta sacrificia.—Bell. Gall.* vi. 16. Strabo adds that some of their human victims were crucifièd, *Geog.* iv. 4, 5.

[2] *Ibid.* xii. 5, 3.

long supposed to be so specially characteristic of the Keltic races, has been greatly exaggerated in its character and results. The well-known description in Cæsar was based on reports which he harmonized and compacted; and the value of those reports may be tested by others which follow in the same Book as to the existence of a unicorn in the Hercynian Forest, and as to another animal found there like a goat, which had no knee-joints, and which was caught by sawing through the tree on which it leaned when asleep, for it could not rise when it had been thrown down.[1] The statement of Cæsar, based on mere unsifted rumour, was amplified by succeeding writers; and Pliny,[2] Strabo,[3] Ammianus Marcellinus,[4] and Pomponius Mela[5] have only altered and recast it, while Lucan[6] and Tacitus[7] added some new touches. If the Druids held the high and mysterious rank assigned to them in popular imagination,—if they dispensed laws, taught youth, offered sacrifices, possessed esoteric science, and held great conventions,—how comes it that they never appear in actual history, but are only seen dimly in the picturesque descriptions of these Greek and Roman authors, not one of whom ever saw a Druid? In all the previous intercourse of Gaul with Rome, no living Druids ever appear on the scene, and no one notices their presence or influence in any business—in any consultations or national transactions. Cæsar never alludes to them save in the abstract,—never, in his marches, battles, or negotiations in Gaul and Britain, comes into contact with one of them, or even hints at their existence. Tacitus relates that when the Capitol was burned during the struggle between Otho and Vitellius, the Druids predicted (*Druidæ canebant*) from that occurrence the fall of the empire.[8] The same author records, indeed, how at the invasion of Mona (Anglesea) they were seen in terrible commotion, the Druidesses like weird women or furies screaming and brandishing torches. His picture, however, is coloured for effect, since no genuine information is imparted by his description.[9] Ausonius describes the Druids as an ancient race, or rather caste, but he has no allusion to their sacerdotal character. Descent from them is in

[1] *Bell. Gall.* vi. 12–18, 25.
[2] *Hist. Nat.* xvi. 95.
[3] *Geog.* iv. 4, 4.
[4] xv. 9.
[5] *De Situ Orbis*, iv. 2.
[6] *Pharsalia*, p. 14, Glasguæ 1785.
[7] *Annal.* xiv. 3.
[8] *Hist.* iv. 54.
[9] *Annal.* xiv. 30.

his view a special honour, like that from any of the mythical deities: *stirpe Druidarum satus, si fama non fallit fidem; stirpe satus Druidum.*[1] Lucan also vaguely alludes to them in the first book of his *Pharsalia,* and they help to fill up his elaborate picture.[2] Again, if the Druids had possessed the authority claimed for them, how is it that we never find them in flesh and blood confronting the first Christian missionaries? The early church makes no mention of them; though there was a continuous battle with heathenism from the second century to the age of Charlemagne. It is remarkable that in no classic author occurs the term Druid as a masculine noun and in the singular number. The forms *Druides* and *Druidæ* do not always distinctly determine the sex; but the feminine term undoubtedly occurs so often as to induce a suspicion that the order consisted chiefly of females. It is somewhat remarkable that in the Keltic church of the Culdees in Ireland, the person holding the office of Co-arb was sometimes a female, and that office was one of very considerable territorial influence. The only living members of the Druidical caste that we meet with are women. Ælius Lampridius puts among the omens preceding the assassination of the Emperor Alexander Severus, that a Druidess accosted him with warning—*mulier Dryas eunti exclamavit Gallico sermone.*[3] Vopiscus[4] tells of Aurelian consulting Gallic Druidesses—*Gallicanas Dryadas*—on the question whether the empire should continue in his posterity; and he further relates that Diocletian, when among the Tungrians in Gaul, had transactions with a Druidess as to futurity: *cum in quadam caupona moraretur, et cum Dryade quadam muliere rationem convictus cotodiani faceret.* These Druidesses appear in a character quite on a level with that of a Scottish spaewife. Divitiacus the Æduan, a personal friend of Cicero, is said by him not to be a Druid indeed, but to belong to the Druids, and he is described as being famous for fortune-telling and guessing as to events to come.[5] The Druids were probably a sacerdotal caste of both sexes that dealt chiefly in divination. Suetonius says that Druidism, condemned by Augustus, was put down

[1] Pp. 86, 92, ed. Bipont. [2] P. 14, Glasguæ 1785.

[3] *Scriptores Historiæ Augustæ,* vol. i. p. 271, ed. Peter, Lipsiæ 1865.

[4] *Scriptores Historiæ Augustæ,* vol. ii. pp. 167, 223, do. do.

[5] *De Divinatione,* i. 40.

by Claudius.[1] An extirpation so easily accomplished argues great feebleness of power and numbers on the part of the Druids, and no one else records it. Yet Tacitus afterwards describes the seizure of Mona and the cutting down of the grove. The anecdotes given by Vopiscus—one of which he had heard from his grandfather (*avus meus mihi retulit*)—exhibit them as late as the third century. The nearest approach to the apparition of a living pagan Druid fighting for his faith is that of a Magus named Broichan at the Scottish court of Brud king of the Cruithne or Picts, who dwelt by the banks of the Ness. The magic of St. Columba proved more powerful than his; and the Magus, if he were a Druid, was not a whit exalted above the mischievous Scottish witches. In a Gaelic manuscript quoted by Dr. M'Lauchlan, and which he ascribes to the 12th or 13th century, this Magus is called a Druid.[2] Dr. M'Lauchlan is inclined to hold that the old Scottish heathenism had magi, and that these were of the order of the Druids; but he does not point out a single element of resemblance between the Scottish *Geintlighecht* and the description of the Druids in the sixth book of the *Gallic War*, or between it and the Zoroastrian system to which he likens it. The oriental aspect of the Scottish paganism is faint, save in superstitious regard for the sun in some form of nature-worship. The naming of the four quarters of the heavens after a position assumed towards the east, the west being behind or after, the north being the left hand, and the south the right hand, may spring not from the adoration of the elements, but from universal instinct, as it is common alike to Hebrew and Gaelic.[3] The connection of cromlechs, upright pillars and circles of stones, with the Druids is certainly not beyond dispute. The Roman

[1] *Vita Claudii*, xxv. But the spelling *Druidarum* in the clause is challenged; and as the interdiction by Augustus referred *tantum civibus*, the extirpation may have been also confined to Rome, and may be likened to the expulsion of Jews from the capital. Indeed the two events are told in the same breath.

[2] *Early Scottish Church*, p. 35, Edin. 1865.

[3] Druid is connected with *dru*, an oak. The supreme object of Druidical worship is called by Lucan, Teutatis: *Pharsalia*, i. 445. Maximus Tyrius says that the Kelts worshipped Dis, and that his image was an high oak. The name Teutatis is said to signify *strong*, and the oak was the symbol of strength. Max. Tyr. *Dissert.* p. 400, ed. Cantab. 1703.

Pantheon was not very scrupulous as to the gods admitted into it; and if the Druids were extirpated, it must have been for other reasons than their religion. What kind of theology they taught, it is impossible to say; the careless way in which Cæsar speaks of the population of Gaul as being divided into *equites* and *plebs* as in Roman fashion, and in which he gives Roman names to their objects of worship, takes all true historical value from his account. Not more trustworthy is Pliny's statement about the amulet used by the Druids which himself had seen,—a large egg, to the making of which serpents beyond number contributed;[1] and on his sole authority rests the tradition of the white robe of the arch-Druid, the misletoe, and the golden sickle. The Druids, if a sacerdotal caste, were apparently devoted to astrology or some other kinds of soothsaying, and they are socially ranked by Cæsar with the *equites*. According to Strabo[2] and Cæsar,[3] they affirmed that souls were immortal like the world—that matter and spirit had existed from eternity. Some liken Druidism to Brahmanism, and Valerius Maximus[4] pronounces it a species of Pythagoreanism. But so little is really known of the songs of the Bards, the ritual of the Ovates, or the teaching of the Druids—*φιλόσοφοι καὶ θεολόγοι*,[5] that all attempts to form a system rest on a very precarious foundation —"*y chercher davantage c'est tomber dans l'hypothèse pure.*"[6] They served in some idolatrous worship, and they taught immortality in the shape of transmigration, though they seem to have had also a Flaith-innis or Isle of the Blessed. Their

[1] *Hist. Nat.* xxix. 12: *Angues innumeri æstate convoluti salivis faucium corporumque spumis artifici complexu glomerantur . . . vidi equidem id ovum mali orbiculati modici magnitudine.* For an interesting dissertation on the Druids, see Burton, *History of Scotland*, vol. i. chap. vi., and an article by the same author in the *Edinburgh Review* for July 1863. On the other side, compare *The Celtic Druids, or an attempt to show that the Druids were the priests of Oriental colonies, . . . who introduced letters, built Carnac and Stonehenge*, etc., by Godfrey Higgins, London 1829.

[2] *Geog.* iv. 4, 4.

[3] *Bell. Gall.* vi. 14.

[4] *Memorab.* ii. 6, 9.

[5] Diodorus Sic. v. 31.

[6] Pressense, *Histoire des trois Premiers Siècles de l'Eglise Chrétienne*, deuxieme série, tome premier, p. 54, in which section a good account of Druidism is given, with a review of the theories of Henri Martin in his *Histoire de France*, vol. i. p. 48, and those of M. Reynaud in his article on Druidism in the *Encyclopédie nouvelle.*

system might find some parallel in the Phrygian worship, and be absorbed into it. But in a word, there is no foundation whatever for what has been apparently surmised sometimes, that so-called Druidical teaching might have disposed the Galatians to that immediate reception of the truth which is described in this epistle. The attempt to prove from a symbolic tree called Esus figured on an old altar found under Notre-Dame in Paris, that the Druids worshipped a personal god not unlike the Jehovah of the Old Testament, is only a romantic absurdity.

The Phrygian system of religion was one of terror,—Paul's was one of confidence and love; dark, dismal, and bloody had been the rites of their fathers,—the new economy was light, joy, and hope. Perhaps the friendless, solitary stranger, unhelped by any outer insignia, nervous and shattered, yet unearthly in his zeal and transported beyond himself in floods of tenderness and bursts of yearning eloquence on topics which had never greeted their ears or entered their imagination, might suggest one of the olden sages who spoke by authority of the gods, and before whose prophesying their fathers trembled and bowed. But apart from all these auxiliary influences, there was the grace of God giving power to the word in numerous instances; for though with so many—perhaps with the majority—the early impressions were so soon effaced, because profound and lasting convictions had not been wrought within them, yet in the hearts of not a few the gospel triumphed, and the fruit of the Spirit was manifest in their lives. The Christianity planted in Galatia held its place, in spite of numerous out-croppings of the national character, and in spite of the cruelties of Diocletian and the bribes and tortures of Julian. In the subsequent persecutions not a few were found faithful unto death.

III.—OCCASION AND CONTENTS OF THE EPISTLE

The Judaists had apparently come into the Galatian churches before the apostle's second visit (Credner, Schott, Reuss, Meyer), though at that period the mischief had not culminated. But the course of defection was swiftly run, and after no long time the apostle felt the necessity of decided interference. Neander and De Wette, however, date the intrusion of the false teachers after the second visit. Who these Judaists were, whether Jews by birth or proselytes, has been disputed. They might belong to either party,—might have journeyed from Palestine, like those who came down to Antioch, and said, "Except ye be circumcised after the manner of Moses, ye cannot be saved;" or some of them might be proselytes, contending for the obligation of that law to which they had conformed prior to the introduction of the gospel. Most likely what had happened in the Galatian province was only a repetition of what had taken place at Antioch, as the apostle himself describes it in the second chapter. There were myriads of Jews who believed, and who were all zealous of the law;[1] and an extreme faction holding such opinions were the inveterate enemies of the apostle of the Gentiles. It was so far innocent in Judæa to uphold the Mosaic law and its obligation on Jewish believers, but it was a dangerous innovation to enforce its observance on Gentile converts as essential to salvation. For the Mosaic law was not meant for them; the rite of circumcision was adapted only to born Jews as a token of Abrahamic descent, and of their inclusion in the Abrahamic covenant. The Gentile had nothing to do with this or with any element of the ceremonial law, for he was not born under it; to force it on him was to subject him to foreign servitude—to an intolerable yoke. Apart from the relation of circumcision to a Jew, the persistent attempt to enforce it as in any way essential to salvation was derogatory to the perfection of Christ's work, and the complete deliverance provided by it. Legal Pharisaism was, however, brought into Galatia, circumcision was insisted on, and special seasons were observed. To upset the teaching of the apostle, the errorists undermined his authority, plainly maintaining that as he was not one of the primary twelve, he could on that account be invested only with a secondary and subordinate rank and authority; so that his teaching of a free gospel, unconditioned by any Mosaic conformity, might be set aside. The apostle's doctrine on these points had nothing in the least doubtful about it. The trumpet had given no uncertain sound.

[1] Acts xxi. 20.

But while the false teachers were undermining his apostolic prerogative, they seem to have tried also to damage him by representing him as inconsistent in his career, as if he had in some way or at some time preached circumcision. He had circumcised Timothy, and had been, as his subsequent life showed, an observer of the "customs," and it was insinuated that he accommodated his message to the prejudices of his converts. Since to the Jews he became as a Jew, there might be found in his history not a few compliances which could be easily magnified into elements of inconsistency with his present preaching. In some way, perhaps darker and more malignant, they laboured to turn the affections of the Galatian people from him, and to a great extent they succeeded. We learn from the apostle's self-vindication what were the chief errors propagated by the Judaists, and what were the principal calumnies directed against himself.

These open errors and vile insinuations did immediate injury. The noxious seed fell into a congenial soil among the Galatians. Their jubilant welcome to the apostle cooled into indifference, hardened into antagonism. Their extreme readiness to accept the gospel indicated rather facility of impression than depth of conviction. The temperament which is so immediately charmed by one novelty, can from its nature, and after a brief period, be as easily charmed away by a second attraction. Their Celtic nature had sincerity without depth, ardour without endurance, an earnestness which flashed up in a moment like the crackling of thorns, and as soon subsided,—a mobility which was easily bewitched—witched at one time by the itinerant preacher, and at another time witched away from him by these innovators and alarmists. What surprised the apostle was the soonness of the defection, as well as the extent of its doctrinal aberrations and its numerical triumph. It had broken out like an infectious pestilence. The error involved was vital, as it supplanted his gospel by another "which is not another," neutralized the freeness of justification, rendered superfluous the atoning death of the Son of God, set aside the example of Abraham the prototype of all believers in faith and blessing, was a relapse to the weak and beggarly elements, and brought an obligation on all its adherents to do the whole law.

Besides, there was apparently in the Galatian nature a

strange hereditary fondness for ritualistic practices; the worship of Cybele was grossly characterized by corporeal maimings. What was materialistic with its appeal to the senses, what bordered on asceticism and had an air of superstitious mystery about it, had special fascinations for them—such as the circumcision of Hebrew ordinance in its innocent resemblance to Phrygian mutilation, or the observance of sacred periods with expectation of immediate benefit from ritualistic charms. As the errorists brought a doctrine that seemed to near some of their former practices, and might remind them of their national institute, they were the more easily induced to accept it. Having begun in the Spirit, they soon thought of being made perfect by the flesh. They were taught to rest on outer observances more or less symbolic in nature, to supplement faith with something done by or upon themselves, and to place their hopes of salvation, not on the grace of Christ alone, but on it associated with acts of their own, which not only could not be combined with it but even frustrated it. In no other church do we find so resolute a re-enactment of Judaistic ceremonial. The apostle bids the Philippians beware of the concision,—of the mere mutilators, implying that Judaizing influence had been at work, but not with such energy and success in Europe as in Asia Minor. Addressing the Colossians, he tells them that they had been "circumcised with the circumcision made without hands, in putting off the body of the sins of the flesh by the circumcision of Christ"—a statement of privilege perhaps suggested by some attempt to enforce a physical circumcision, while other elements of mystical theosophy had been propagated among them. The Judaism in Galatia is more Pharisaic, and that of Colossæ more Essenic in type. Separation from social intercourse with heathen believers, and the observance of Mosaic regulations as to diet, also characterized the Judaists; and perhaps they were on this point more readily listened to, as the people in Pessinus abstained from swine's flesh. Pausanias gives a mythological reason for the abstinence.[1]

The peril being so imminent, the alarmed and grieved apostle wrote to them in indignant surprise. He felt that their defection was all but incomprehensible, as it was in such con-

[1] vii. 15, 7.

trast to their early and hearty reception of the gospel and himself. He was filled with holy anxiety for them, though he has nothing but angry censure for their seducers who had no true respect for the law which they were trying to bind on them, for they did not themselves keep the whole of it, but were only by a wretched diplomacy endeavouring to escape from persecution, that is, by representing to the bigoted Jews that they made heathen believers Jewish proselytes as a first and indispensable step in their change to Christianity.[1]

And first, and formally, the apostle vindicates his full apostolic authority: affirming, that his office was primal like that of the original twelve; that his gospel was in no sense of human origin or conveyance, but came to him directly by the revelation of Jesus Christ; that his change from Judaism to Christianity was notorious; that his views as the apostle of the Gentiles had all along been decided; that when false brethren stealthily crept in to thwart him, he had opened out his teaching fully to James, Peter, and John, who acquiesced in it; that he would not circumcise Titus, his fellow-labourer; that the apostles of the circumcision acknowledged his mission and gave him the right hand of fellowship; and that so averse to any compromise on the point of a free gospel was he, that at Antioch he publicly rebuked Peter for his tergiversation. While his opponents were men-pleasers, his whole conduct showed that another and opposite motive was ever ruling him, for men-pleasing and Christ's service were incompatible; that the insinuation of his preaching circumcision was met and refuted by the fact that he was still persecuted; and that, finally, he desires to be no further troubled, for his connection with the Saviour had left its visible traces upon him, as he bears in his body the marks of Jesus.

Secondly, as to the doctrine of the Judaists, he utterly reprobates it; calls it a subversion of the gospel of Christ; asserts that justification is not of works, but only of faith in Christ; identifies this doctrine with his own spiritual experience; adduces the example of Abraham whose faith was counted for righteousness; proves that law and curse are associated, and that from this curse Christ has redeemed us; argues the superiority of the promise to the law in a variety of particulars;

[1] See Commentary under vi. 12, 13.

shows the use of the law as a pædagogue, while during pædagogy, and prior to the fulness of the time, the heir was a minor, differing nothing from a bond-slave; repeats his sense of their danger; fortifies his argument by an allegory based on the history of Abraham, the lesson of which is the spiritual freedom of the children of the promise, and in which they are exhorted to stand fast; utters a solemn warning, that if a man gets himself circumcised, Christ profits him nothing, and that all who seek justification by the law are fallen from grace; affirms that circumcision and uncircumcision are nothing in themselves, and that he who troubled the Galatians, whoever he might be, shall bear his judgment, exclaiming in a moment of angry contempt, "I would they were even cut off that trouble you." Toward the end of the epistle the apostle recurs to the same errors; accuses their patrons of being simply desirous of making a fair show in the flesh, and of wishing to avoid persecution; and he concludes by avowing his glorying in the cross, and his belief that what is outer is nothing, and what is inner is everything.

There are in the epistle some elements of Galatian character referred to or implied. The Galatians are warned against making their liberty an occasion for the flesh; against biting and devouring one another; against fulfilling the lusts of the flesh and doing its works which are specified; against vainglory, and mutual provocation, and envy. Exhortations are also tendered to them against selfishness and conceit; against sowing to the flesh, for the harvest is certainly of the same nature as the seed; against exhaustion or despondency in well-doing; and they are encouraged, at the same time, as they have opportunity, to do good.

It may be safely surmised that these advices were not tendered at random, but that they were meant to meet and check certain national propensities detected by the apostle in the Galatian people. Whatever modifying effect their long residence in Asia Minor might have had, however much certain earlier characteristics may have been toned down, they were not wholly obliterated. Their fickleness (Gal. i. 4) has been noticed by several observers. Cæsar pictures this feature of their western ancestors: *Partim qui mobilitate et levitate animi novis imperiis studebant.*"[1] Again he says, *Et infirmitatem*

[1] *Bell. Gall.* ii. 1.

Gallorum veritus, quod sunt in consiliis capiendis mobiles et novis plerumque rebus student;[1] and he adds some touches about their anxiety for news, and their sudden counsels on getting them.[2] In another place, where he repeats the sentiment, he asserts, *Ad bella suscipienda Gallorum alacer ac promptus est animus, sic mollis ac minime resistens ad calamitates perferendas mens eorum est.*[3] Livy observed the same feature: *Primaque eorum prœlia plus quam virorum, postrema minus quam feminarum esse.*[4] Tacitus speaks of one tribe as *levissimus quisque Gallorum et inopia audax.*[5] Polybius says, διὰ τὸ μὴ τὸ πλεῖον, ἀλλὰ συλλήβδην ἅπαν τὸ γιγνόμενον ὑπὸ τῶν Γαλατῶν, θυμῷ μᾶλλον ἢ λογισμῷ βραβεύεσθαι.[6] Their modern historian also thus characterizes them: *Les traits saillans de la famille Gauloise, ceux qui la distinguent le plus, à mon avis, des autres familles humaines peuvent se résumer ainsi, une bravoure personnelle que rien n'égale chez les peuples anciens, un esprit franc, impétueux, ouvert à toutes les impressions, éminemment intelligent; mais a côté de cela une mobilité extrême, point de constance, une répugnance marquée aux idées de discipline et d'ordre si puissantes chez les races Germaniques, beaucoup d'ostentation, enfin une désunion perpétuelle, fruit de l'excessive vanité.*[7]

The passion of their ancestors for a sensuous religion has been also marked: *Natio est omnium Gallorum admodum dedita religionibus.*[8] Diodorus Siculus relates the same characteristic.[9] Cicero tells of Deiotarus, that he did nothing without augury, and that he had heard from his own lips that the flight of an eagle would induce him to come back, after he had gone a considerable portion of a journey.[10] That the old nation was impetuous and quarrelsome has been told by several writers, and there is earnest exhortation in the epistle against a similar propensity in the Galatian churches. Ammianus brands them as extremely quarrelsome, and of great pride and insolence—"their voices are formidable and threatening, whether in anger

[1] *Bell. Gall.* iv. 5.
[2] *Ibid.* v. 5.
[3] *Ibid.* iii. 19. See Commentary under iii. 1.
[4] x. 28.
[5] *De German.* xxix. p. 136, *Op.* vol. iv. ed. Ruperti.
[6] ii. 35; *Opera*, vol. i. p. 204, ed. Schweighäuser.
[7] Thierry, *Histoire des Gaulois*, Introd. xii.
[8] Cæsar, *Bell. Gall.* vi. 16.
[9] v. 27.
[10] *De Divinatione*, i. 15, ii. 36, 37.

or in good humour."[1] Diodorus affirms their love of strife and single combats among themselves after their feasts; their disregard of life arising from their belief in the Pythagorean doctrine of transmigration: *Κάτοινοι δὲ ὄντες καθ' ὑπερβολὴν . . . μεθυσθέντες εἰς ὕπνον ἢ μανιώδεις.*[2] "The nation," says Ammianus Marcellinus, "is fond of wine, and of certain liquors resembling it; many of the lower class, their senses being weakened by continual intoxication, run about at random."[3]

The warring against the works of the flesh might also allude to certain national propensities. Their ancestors were marked by intemperance and quarrelsomeness—they are forbidden to bite and devour one another.

What effect was produced by the epistle we know not. The Judaistic influence may have been neutralized for a time, but it might not be uprooted. Some of the fathers witness that the errors rebuked still continued, with more or less modification. Jerome says without hesitation, that the traces of their virtues and their errors remained to his day.[4] They followed the Jewish reckoning of the paschal feast. One sect is described as *insanientes potibus et bacchantes.* Galatia was the region of later ecclesiastical strifes and heresies. Jerome gives a catalogue of them in his second preface to his commentary on the epistle.[5]

The epistle consists of two parts—the first doctrinal, and the second practical; or it may be taken as consisting of three sections: the first containing personal vindication, and in the form of narrative—the first two chapters; the second, doctrinal argument—the third and fourth chapters; and the third, practical exhortation—the fifth and sixth chapters. The autobiographical portion is linked on to the dogmatic section by the language addressed to Peter at Antioch; and the conclusion at which he arrives, at the end of the fourth chapter—the freedom of believers—suggests the admonition to stand fast in that freedom, and then not to abuse it, but to walk in love and in the spirit—the works of the flesh being so opposite. Other counsels follow, connected by some link of mental association.

[1] xv. 12.
[2] v. 26, 30.
[3] xv. 12. Compare Suidas, *sub voce* Ἄδην.
[4] Vol. vii. 417.
[5] See Milman's *History of Christianity*, vol. ii. 162, London 1867.

IV.—GENUINENESS OF THE EPISTLE

The earlier fathers have no direct citations from the epistle, but their allusions betoken unconscious familiarity with its language. Thus Clement writes: "Christ our Lord gave His blood for us by the will of God"[1]—not unlike Gal. i. 4; "His sufferings were before your eyes"[2]—a faint reminiscence of Gal. iii. 1. Ignatius says: "He obtained the ministry not of himself, nor by men,"[3] like Gal. i. 1; "If we still live according to Jewish law, we confess that we have not received grace,"[4] borrowed from Gal. v. 3, 4. Though these Ignatian epistles may not be genuine, they are early productions, and give us the echoes of a sub-apostolic writer. In the Syriac recension, Ignatius, *ad Polycarp.* enjoins: "Bear all men as the Lord beareth thee; bear the infirmities of all men, as thou saidst;" which may be compared with Gal. vi. 2. Polycarp is more distinct: "Knowing then this, that God is not mocked,"[5] Gal. vi. 7; "Built up into the faith delivered to us, which is the mother of us all,"[6] Gal. iv. 26; "The Father, who raised Him from the dead,"[7] Gal. i. 1. The allusions taken from Barnabas xix. and Hermas, *Simil.* ix. 13, may scarcely be quoted as proof. In the *Oratio ad Græcos*, ascribed to Justin Martyr, occurs the quotation from Gal. iv. 12, γίνεσθε ὡς ἐγὼ ὅτι κἀγὼ ἤμην ὡς ὑμεῖς; and the sins named in Gal. v. 20 are quoted with the apostle's addition: καὶ τὰ ὅμοια τούτοις. In his *Dial. c. Tryph.* cap. 90, 96, he adduces two quotations from the Old Testament like those in Gal. iii. 10, 13, and in the apostle's version too, which agrees neither with the Hebrew nor the Septuagint. The first quotation is introduced by the apostle's marked words, ὑπὸ κατάραν. In his *Apology*, i. 53, Justin quotes Isa. liv. 1, and works upon it, as does the apostle in Gal. iv. 27.

[1] Τὸ αἷμα αὐτοῦ ἔδωκεν ἐν θελήματι Θεοῦ.—*Ad Corinth.* i.

[2] Τὰ παθήματα αὐτοῦ ἦν πρὸ ὀφθαλμῶν ὑμῶν.—*Do.* ii.

[3] Οὐκ ἀφ' ἑαυτοῦ οὐδὲ δι' ἀνθρώπων.—*Ad Philadelph.* i.

[4] Εἰ κατὰ νόμον Ἰουδαϊκὸν ζῶμεν, ὁμολογοῦμεν χάριν μὴ εἰληφέναι.—*Ad Magnes.* 8. See *Cohortatio ad Græcos*, 40.

[5] Εἰδότες οὖν ὅτι ὁ Θεὸς οὐ μυκτηρίζεται.—*Ad Philip.* v.

[6] Πίστιν, ἥτις ἐστὶ μήτηρ πάντων ἡμῶν.—*Do.* 3.

[7] *Qui resuscitavit eum a mortuis.*—*Do.* 12.

Irenæus quotes the epistle by name: *Sed in ea quæ est ad Galatas sic ait, quod ergo lex factorum, posita est usque quo veniat semen cui promissum est.*[1] Allusions are also found in iii. 6, 5, to Gal. iv. 8, 9,—in iii. 16, 3, to Gal. iv. 4, 5, which is avowedly quoted from the apostle's letter to the Galatians—*in epistola quæ est ad Galatas;* and in v. 21, 1 are quoted Gal. iii. 15, 19, and iv. 4. The Alexandrian Clement quotes expressly Gal. iv. 19, under the formula *Παῦλος Γαλάταις ἐπιστέλλων.*[2] Tertullian is as explicit in referring to Gal. v. 20: *Paulus scribens ad Galatas.* The Epistle to Diognetus contains the expression: *παρατήρησιν τῶν μηνῶν καὶ τῶν ἡμερῶν ποιεῖσθαι.*[3] Melito repeats in spirit Gal. iv. 8, 9.[4] Athenagoras cites the phrase, "the weak and beggarly elements."[5] This epistle is found in all the canonical catalogues, in the Muratorian Fragment, and it is included also in the old Syriac and Latin versions. Marcion recognised it, and placed it in pre-eminence—*principalem adversus Judaismum.*[6] According to Hippolytus, the Ophites made considerable use of it, and their writings contain many quotations:[7] *ἡ ἄνω Ἱερουσαλήμ,* Gal. iv. 26, in *Hæres.* v. 7; and in *do.* v. 8, Gal. iv. 27 is quoted. The Valentinians were also well acquainted with the epistle, as Irenæus testifies in i. 3, 5. Celsus asserts that the Christians, whatever their wranglings and shameful contests, agreed in saying continually, "The world is crucified to me, and I to the world;" Origen quietly adding, *τοῦτο γὰρ μόνον ἀπὸ τοῦ Παύλου ἔοικε μεμνημονευκέναι ὁ Κέλσος.*[8] See commentary under ii. 11, and the attitude of the Clementine Homilies in relation to the passage.

The one exception against all critics is Bruno Bauer,[9] who regards the epistle as made up of portions of Romans and 1st and 2d Corinthians, and condemns the compilation as stupid, aimless, and contradictory. To review his assertions would be vain; they are so weak that the merit of perverse

1 *Hæres.* vii. 7, 2.
2 *Strom.* iii.
3 Just. Mart. *Opera*, vol. ii. 474, ed. Otto.
4 *Orat. ad Anton. Cæs.* Cureton's *Spicileg. Syr.* pp. 41–49.
5 Πρεσβεία, 16.
6 Tertullian, *Adv. Marc.* v. 2.
7 Pp. 106–114, ed. Miller.
8 Origen, *c. Celsum*, p. 273, ed. Spencer.
9 *Kritik der Paulinischen Briefe*, Erste Abtheil, Berlin 1850.

or learned ingenuity cannot be assigned to them. The process is a simple one, to find similar turns of thought and expression in the same man's letters on similar or collateral themes, and then, if he write three letters in such circumstances within a brief space of time, to argue that one of them must be spurious from its accidental or natural resemblances to the other two. The shortest, like the Epistle to the Galatians, may be selected as the one to be so branded. And yet such similarities of thought and diction as are adduced by Bruno Bauer are the standing proofs of identity of authorship, for every writer may be detected by the unconscious use of them. Some of the similarities which he arrays throughout his seventy-four pages are close like those taken by him from Romans where the apostle is illustrating the same truths as he has been discussing in this epistle; but many other instances have no real resemblance—are only the accidental employment of like terms in a totally different connection. Baur himself says of this epistle, that to Rome, and the two epistles to Corinth, *gegen diese vier Briefe ist nicht nur nie auch nur der geringste Verdacht der Unächtheit erhoben werden, sondern sie tragen auch den Character paulinischer Originalität so unwidersprechlich an sich, dass sich gar nicht denken lässt, welches Recht je der kritische Zweifel gegen sie gelten machen könnte.*[1]

The genuineness of the epistle has thus been unanimously acknowledged—the slight exception of Bruno Bauer not sufficing to break the universal harmony. The apostle's mental characteristics are indelibly impressed on the letter. In a doctrinal discussion or a practical dissertation, in a familiar correspondence on common things, or in any composition which does not stir up feeling or invoke personal vindication, one may write without betraying much individualism; but when the soul is perturbed, and emotions of surprise, anger, and sorrow are felt singly or in complex unity, the writer portrays himself in his letter, for he writes as for the moment he feels, what comes into his mind is committed to paper freshly and at once without being toned down or weakened by his hovering over a choice of words. The Epistle to the Galatians is of this nature. It is the apostle self-portrayed; and who can mistake the resemblance? The workings of his soul are quite visible in their strength and suc-

[1] Paulus, p. 248.

cession; each idea is seen as it is originated by what goes before it, and as it suggests what come after it in the throbbings of his wounded soul; the argument and the expostulation are linked together in abrupt rapidity, anger is tempered by love, and sorrow by hope; and the whole is lighted up by an earnestness which the crisis had deepened into a holy jealousy, and the interests at stake had intensified into the agony of a second spiritual birth. The error which involved such peril, and carried with it such fascination, was one natural in the circumstances, and glimpses of its origin, spread, and power are given us in the Acts of the Apostles. Who that knows how Paul, with his profound convictions, must have stood toward such false doctrine, will for a moment hesitate to recognise him as he writes in alarmed sympathy to his Galatian converts, who had for a season promised so well, but had been seduced by plausible reactionists—the enemies of his apostolic prerogative, and the subverters of that free and full gospel, in proclaiming and defending which he spent his life?

V.—PLACE AND TIME OF COMPOSITION

The place and time of composition have been, and still are disputed, and the two inquiries are bound up together. If the letter was written at Ephesus, the period was relatively early; but if at Rome, it was late in the apostle's life.

Those who hold that the gospel was preached in Galatia at an earlier epoch than that referred to in Acts xvi. 6, assign a correspondent date to the epistle. Others hold that it was written before the apostolic convention in Jerusalem, as Baumgarten, Michaelis, Schmidt. Koppe, Keil, Borger, Paulus, Böttger, Niemeyer, Ulrich, though not for the same reasons, generally maintain this view. Marcion seems to have believed, like these critics, that it was the earliest of Paul's epistles. According to Tertullian and Epiphanius, he set this epistle first in his catalogue; but as he places the Epistles to the Thessalonians after the Epistle to the Romans, no great credit can be reposed in his chronology, for which, however, Wieseler contends. Tertullian's words are, *principalem adversus Judaismum epistolam nos quoque confitemur quæ Galatas docet*, and there follows a running comment on the epistle. The epithet *principalis* has apparently an ethical meaning, placed first as being the most decided against Judaism. Epiphanius says of Marcion's canon, αἱ ἐπιστολαὶ αἱ παρ' αὐτῷ λεγόμεναί εἰσι πρώτη μὲν πρὸς Γαλάτας, δευτέρα δὲ πρὸς Κορινθίους.[1] Again: Αὕτη γὰρ παρ' αὐτῷ πρώτη κεῖται. Ἡμεῖς δὲ τὴν ἀναλογὴν τότε ἐποιησάμεθα οὐχ ὡς παρ' αὐτῷ, ἀλλ' ὡς ἔχει τὸ ἀποστολικὸν ῥητὸν, τὴν πρὸς Ῥωμαίους τάξαντες πρώτην.[2] But the chronology is wrong which dates the apostle's first visit to Galatia before Acts xvi. 6, and the relative οὕτως ταχέως in i. 6 is rather an indefinite term on which to found a distinct date.

But the epistle is by some supposed to be the last of Paul's epistles, and to have been written at Rome. The epigraph ἐγράφη ἀπὸ Ῥώμης is found in several MSS., as B², K, L, the two Syriac and Coptic versions. The same conjecture is found, among the fathers, in Eusebius of Emesa, Jerome, Theodoret, Euthalius, and Œcumenius; and their opinion has been followed in more recent times by Flacius, Baronius, Bullinger, Hunnius, Calovius, Lightfoot, Hammond, Schrader, Köhler, and Riccaltoun. Theodoret dates the epistle as the first of the Roman imprisonment; and Köhler dates it the last, in A.D. 69, two years before Nero's death. The notion that the apostle was in prison when he wrote the letter has partly given rise to the hypothesis. But the language of the apostle in iv. 20, "I desire to be present with you," does not prove that he was in bonds—does not bear out all Jerome's paraphrase, *vellem nunc præsens esse si confessionis me vincula non arctarent.* Jerome repeats the same idea under vi. 11 (*prohibebatur quidem vinculis*). Theodoret merely gives his opinion in his general preface, and Œcumenius in his brief prefatory note to this epistle. On iv. 20, the commentator named Eusebius in the *Catena* says, ἐπειδὴ ἐτύγχανε δεδεμένος καὶ κατεχόμενος.[3] Riccaltoun says on vi. 17, that "the clause, 'from henceforth let no man trouble me,' would go near to persuade one that this epistle was written near about the time when he finished

[1] *Panar.* lib. i. tom. iii.; *Hæres.* xlii. ps. 566, vol. i. ed. Œhler.

[2] *Panar.* lib. i. tom. iii. 68, p. 638, vol. i. ed. Œhler.

[3] *Catena*, p. 67, ed. Cramer. So also Carey.

his course, and much later than that which is commonly fixed on; and the note of being written from Rome, which is allowed not to be authentic, seems much nearer the true date than any other which has been pitched upon before he went thither." The clauses so referred to are otherwise better and more naturally explained. See the commentary under them. The conjecture that the epistle was sent from Rome has therefore no authority—no warrant from any expression in the letter itself, is plainly contradicted by the chronology of the Acts, and the *οὕτω ταχέως* would certainly be inapplicable to a period so very late.

Other opinions may be noticed in passing. Beza assigns Antioch as the place of composition, before the apostle went up to Jerusalem; Macknight fixes on the same place, but dates the epistle after the council; Michaelis supposes it to have been written from Thessalonica, and Mill from Troas; while Lardner, Benson, and Wordsworth hold that the apostle only once had visited Galatia, and that the epistle was written at Corinth during his first visit to that city, Acts xviii. 11. These opinions may be at once set aside. Wordsworth's argument based on the omission of any direction about a collection for the poor is exceedingly precarious, especially when viewed in connection with 1 Cor. xvi. 1.

It has been held by perhaps the majority that the epistle was written at Ephesus. The apostle, on leaving Galatia, after his second visit of confirmation, having "passed through the upper coasts," arrived at Ephesus, and there he remained three years, from A.D. 54 to 57. In this city he could easily and frequently receive intelligence of the Galatian churches; and if the news of their danger reached him, he would at once despatch a remonstrant epistle. The *οὕτως ταχέως* fits into this period, and to any year of it—his surprise that they were changing so soon after his second visit to them, or so soon after their conversion or after the intrusion of the false teachers. The elastic *οὕτω ταχέως* will suit any of these termini, but it would not so naturally suit an epoch very much later, though perhaps a year or so might make no great difference. In such a conclusion one might be content to rest, the sojourn at Ephesus being alike probable in chronology and in circumstances as the place and period of composition. The first Epistle to Corinth was written at this time and from Ephesus, and in that epistle there is a reference to the Galatian churches: "Now concerning the collection for the saints, as I have given order to the churches of Galatia, even so do ye," xvi. 1. These words may not mean that the apostle sent a written order to the Galatians, for they may refer to some command given by him during his second and recent visit.

But there are other letters written nearly at the same period which have a generic resemblance to the one before us. Between it and the first Epistle to the Corinthians there are no such striking points of similarity as would imply an all but simultaneous origin. The case is different with the second Epistle to the Corinthians and that to the Romans; and it has been suggested that the resemblances are so close and so numerous, as to furnish an argument for supposing the three epistles to have been written about the same period. The reasoning is quite legitimate. The state of mind under which one writes in any crisis does not soon subside, especially if similar topics are presenting themselves for illustration and similar perils are prolonging the excitement when another epistle is to be composed. The previous thoughts, if they are to be repeated, clothe themselves instinctively in the previous words; the old allusions recur; and though there may be much that is new,—though there may be fuller statement and varying appeal,—still there is a ground-tone of similarity, like the vibration of a chord which had been already struck a brief period before. What we refer to is not repetition or mechanical identity, nor the jejune iteration of characteristic idioms and turns of expression, nor the formal recalling and employment of the earlier diction; but the spirit has been so moved by a recent train of ideas and emotions as unconsciously to combine them with newer thoughts and fresher arguments.

In the second Epistle to the Corinthians there are themes akin to those more briefly handled in Galatians, but with marked difference of circumstance. The apostle's vindication of his office as compared with that of the original twelve, while it is as undaunted in spirit as in Galatians, is not so incisive—not so autobiographical in character, and is wrapt up with other elements of his career. The challenge to his enemies and to the false apostles is laden with touching allusions and crowded with vehement appeals, wrought out with a self-depreciation which yet could assert itself in ringing accents, if its divine prerogatives were impugned or thrust in any way into a lower place; for he was "not a whit behind the very chiefest apostles." But his conversion and his life prior to that change which involved his call to the apostleship are not alluded to in the letter to the Corinthians. The hostility to himself rested on a different ground—still Jewish, but not of that fanatical pharisaical type which it assumed in Galatia; and therefore the self-vindication takes another form—not the assertion of a divine call, but of work done, and especially suffering endured and pressing anxieties. 2 Cor. xi. 23–33, xii. 10, 11. The allusions in Galatians to bodily suffering and to the *στίγματα* of the Lord Jesus are brief, but in second Corinthians (xi. 21–33) the argument bursts out in a torrent of overwhelming force and grandeur. In the two first chapters, and toward the end, the descriptive appeals are so copious, that they would fill up the half of the Epistle to the Galatians. In Galatians his enemies are not directly flagellated, save in their subversion of the gospel, though their hostility is taken for granted; but in Corinthians his antagonists are openly pictured in various attitudes and assailed—"some who think of us as if we walked after the flesh;" there are allusions to his meanness of presence; there are "false apostles, deceitful workers, transforming themselves into the apostles of Christ," acting like the serpent that beguiled Eve through his subtlety: xi. 14, 15. In both epistles there is extreme anxiety about his converts, lest they should be seduced into error and estranged from himself. In both epistles, also, he is quite conscious of the power of the adverse influence used against himself, of the hollow court paid to his converts to wean them from him; in both there is a suspicion that his authority has been shaken, and that the seeds of evil and alienation have been sown. But in Galatians the sphere of enmity is more limited; the error threatening to come in a flood is palpable and simple, though multifarious in result; the people were passionate and demonstrative, and are appealed to in terms fitted to awe and impress them. In Corinthians, on the other hand, the sources of opposition are apparently numerous and complicated; there were rivalries and factions, so that there was a party taking for its motto, "I am of Christ;" there had been false philosophies at work denying the resurrection, along with propensities to idolatry, and the sexual impurities connected with it. Spiritual gifts, such as that of tongues, had been abused, and had led to scenes of disorder. The apostle is anxious to impress upon them his unabated love in the midst of his stern rebukes, and his disinterestedness in all his labours, which some had apparently called in question, and his care not to build on another man's foundation, which some had been mean enough to do. Little of this field of discussion is found in Galatians. In a word, both epistles are loving letters, not cold and impersonal treatises; and they let out more of the writer's heart—of his joys, his loves, his griefs, his anxieties, his fears, his hopes, his physical weakness and trials—than any other parts of his writings. They are a true cardiphonia, and in them you learn more of him as a creature of flesh and blood—of like passions with those about him; beneath the mantle of inspiration you find a man intensely human and sensitive—no one more alive to affront and disparagement, or more keenly desirous to stand well with those whose spiritual benefit he was spending himself to promote.

Now all these general points of similarity are certainly a token of identity of authorship, but they scarcely amount to a proof that both epistles were written at the same period. The diversity is as great as the resemblance; the crisis was somewhat alike in both cases; and though some time elapsed between the dates of the two letters, such resemblance would be easily accounted for. But there are other points of coincidence. The points first adduced by Prof. Lightfoot are not very striking, and little stress can be laid on them. "Christ redeemed us from the curse of the law, being made a curse for us,"[1] is quite different, save in general doctrinal import, from "He hath made Him to be sin for us who knew no sin."[2] The image, "Whatsoever a man soweth, that shall he also reap,"[3] is not "reproduced in almost the same words," "He that soweth sparingly, shall reap also sparingly;"[4] for in the first case it is the certain identity of the harvest with the seed, and in the second case it is its amount apart from its character, which is asserted; in Galatians it is like quality, but in Corinthians like quantity.

[1] Gal. iii. 13. [2] 2 Cor. v. 21. [3] Gal. vi. 7. [4] 2 Cor. ix. 6.

There are other and more striking similarities which Prof. Lightfoot has adduced, though he professes not to lay any great stress upon them:

Gal. i. 6, "another gospel," and in 2 Cor. xi. 4.
Gal. i. 9, v. 21, "tell you before," and in 2 Cor. xiii. 2.
Gal. i. 10, "persuade men," and in 2 Cor. v. 11, but in a different sense.
Gal. iv. 17, "zealously affect you," and in 2 Cor. xi. 2, "zealous over you."
Gal. vi. 15, "a new creature," and in 2 Cor. v. 17.

These are more than fortuitous cases; they indicate the use of favourite phraseology. Some words are peculiar to the two epistles. The figure *κατεσθίειν* occurs Gal. v. 15 and 2 Cor. xi. 20, *ἀπορoῦμαι*, Gal. iv. 20, 2 Cor. iv. 8; *φοβοῦμαι μήπως*, Gal. iv. 11, 2 Cor. xi. 3, xii. 20, and nowhere else; *τοὐναντίον*, Gal. ii. 7, 2 Cor. ii. 7, and nowhere else in Paul's epistles; *κυρόω* in Gal. iii. 15, 2 Cor. ii. 8, and nowhere else in the New Testament; and *κανών* is found in Gal. vi. 16, and in 2 Cor. x. 13. These words are not so distinctive or so numerous as to form a substantial proof, but they have some weight when taken along with other coincidences.

Prof. Lightfoot adduces one peculiar connection between the two epistles—the counsel to restore a fallen brother. In Galatians it certainly comes in abruptly, and seems to have been suggested by something without, not by anything in the immediate course of thought. It is surmised that what had happened at Corinth gave rise to the admonition. A member of that church had fallen into sin, and the apostle had bidden the church subject him to discipline. But the church had in severity gone beyond what was necessary, and the apostle pleads for his forgiveness and restoration. Such an event so happening at the time might suggest the injunction, "Restore such a one in the spirit of meekness," guarding against excessive severity.

The similarity of the Epistle to the Galatians in many points to that to the Romans has often been remarked. Jerome, in the preface to his *Commentary*, says: *ut sciatis eandem esse materiam et Epistolæ Pauli ad Galatas et quæ ad Romanos scripta est, sed hoc differre inter utramque, quod in illa, altiori sensu et profundioribus usus est argumentis.* Similar themes are surrounded with similar illustrations. There is very much more material in Romans, both at the beginning and end of the epistle, but the Epistle to the Galatians is imbedded in it. The one is like an outline, which is filled up in the other, but with less of a personal element. The Epistle to the Romans is more massive, more expansive, and has about it as much the form of a discussion or a didactic treatise as of a letter. The presumption then is, that as the likeness between the two epistles is so close, they were written much about the same time. Nobody doubts the likeness, though many deny the inference, for the plain reason that this similarity will not prove immediate connection of time, since the inculcation of analogous truths may, after even a considerable interval, lead to the use of similar diction. No one can safely or accurately measure the interval from the nature or number of such similarities. It is certain, however, that no long time could have elapsed between the composition of the Epistle to the Galatians and that to the Romans, and their juxtaposition in point of time may not exceed the relative limit implied in *οὕτως ταχέως*.

The points of similarity between Galatians and Romans are, generally, as follows in this table:—

Gal. ii. 16. Knowing that a man is not justified by the works of the law, but by the faith of Jesus Christ, even we have believed in Jesus Christ, that we might be justified by the faith of Christ, and not by the works of the law: for by the works of the law shall no flesh be justified.	Rom. iii. 20. Therefore by the deeds of the law there shall no flesh be justified in his sight: for by the law is the knowledge of sin.
Gal. ii. 19. For I through the law am dead to the law, that I might live unto God.	Rom. vii. 4. Wherefore, my brethren, ye also are become dead to the law by the body of Christ; that ye should be married to another, even to him who is raised from the dead, that we should bring forth fruit unto God.
Gal. ii. 20. I am crucified with Christ: nevertheless I live; yet not I, but Christ liveth in me: and the life which I now live in the flesh I live by the faith of the Son of God, who loved me, and gave himself for me.	Rom. vi. 6. Knowing this, that our old man is crucified with him, that the body of sin might be destroyed, that henceforth we should not serve sin.

Gal. iii. 5, 6. He therefore that ministereth to you the Spirit, and worketh miracles among you, doeth he it by the works of the law, or by the hearing of faith? Even as Abraham believed God, and it was accounted to him for righteousness.	Rom. iv. 3. For what saith the scripture? Abraham believed God, and it was counted unto him for righteousness.
Gal. iii. 7. Know ye therefore that they which are of faith, the same are the children of Abraham.	Rom. iv. 10, 11. How was it then reckoned? when he was in circumcision, or in uncircumcision? Not in circumcision, but in uncircumcision. And he received the sign of circumcision, a seal of the righteousness of the faith which he had yet being uncircumcised: that he might be the father of all them that believe, though they be not circumcised; that righteousness might be imputed unto them also.
Gal. iii. 8. And the scripture, foreseeing that God would justify the heathen through faith, preached before the gospel unto Abraham, saying, In thee shall all nations be blessed.	Rom. iv. 17. (As it is written, I have made thee a father of many nations,) before him whom he believed, even God, who quickeneth the dead, and calleth those things which be not as though they were.
Gal. iii. 9. So then they which be of faith are blessed with faithful Abraham.	Rom. iv. 23, 24. Now, it was not written for his sake alone, that it was imputed to him; but for us also, to whom it shall be imputed, if we believe on him that raised up Jesus our Lord from the dead.
Gal. iii. 10. For as many as are of the works of the law are under the curse: for it is written, Cursed is every one that continueth not in all things which are written in the book of the law to do them.	Rom. iv. 15. Because the law worketh wrath: for where no law is, there is no transgression.
Gal. iii. 11. But that no man is justified by the law in the sight of God, it is evident: for, The just shall live by faith.	Rom. i. 17. For therein is the righteousness of God revealed from faith to faith: as it is written, The just shall live by faith.
Gal. iii. 12. And the law is not of faith: but, The man that doeth them shall live in them.	Rom. x. 5. For Moses describeth the righteousness which is of the law, That the man which doeth those things shall live by them.
Gal. iii. 15–18. Brethren, I speak after the manner of men: Though it be but a man's covenant, yet if it	Rom. iv. 13–16. For the promise, that he should be the heir of the world, was not to Abraham, or to

be confirmed, no man disannulleth, or addeth thereto. Now to Abraham and his seed were the promises made. He saith not, And to seeds, as of many; but as of one, And to thy seed, which is Christ. And this I say, that the covenant, that was confirmed before of God in Christ, the law, which was four hundred and thirty years after, cannot disannul, that it should make the promise of none effect. For if the inheritance be of the law, it is no more of promise: but God gave it to Abraham by promise.

his seed, through the law, but through the righteousness of faith. For if they which are of the law be heirs, faith is made void, and the promise made of none effect. Because the law worketh wrath: for where no law is, there is no transgression. Therefore it is of faith, that it might be by grace; to the end the promise might be sure to all the seed: not to that only which is of the law, but to that also which is of the faith of Abraham, who is the father of us all.

Gal. iii. 22. But the scripture hath concluded all under sin, that the promise by faith of Jesus Christ might be given to them that believe.

Rom. xi. 32. For God hath concluded them all in unbelief, that he might have mercy upon all.

Gal. iii. 27. For as many of you as have been baptized into Christ have put on Christ.

Rom. vi. 3, xiii. 14. Know ye not, that so many of us as were baptized into Jesus Christ were baptized into his death?—But put ye on the Lord Jesus Christ, and make not provision for the flesh, to fulfil the lusts thereof.

Gal. iv. 5–7. To redeem them that were under the law, that we might receive the adoption of sons. And because ye are sons, God hath sent forth the Spirit of his Son into your hearts, crying, Abba, Father. Wherefore thou art no more a servant, but a son; and if a son, then an heir of God through Christ.

Rom. viii. 14–17. For as many as are led by the Spirit of God, they are the sons of God. For ye have not received the spirit of bondage again to fear; but ye have received the Spirit of adoption, whereby we cry, Abba, Father. The Spirit itself beareth witness with our spirit, that we are the children of God: And if children, then heirs; heirs of God, and joint-heirs with Christ; if so be that we suffer with him, that we may be also glorified together.

Gal. iv. 23, 28. But he who was of the bond woman was born after the flesh; but he of the free woman was by promise. . . . Now we, brethren, as Isaac was, are the children of promise.

Rom. ix. 7, 8. Neither, because they are the seed of Abraham, are they all children: but, In Isaac shall thy seed be called: That is, They which are the children of the flesh, these are not the children of God: but the children of the promise are counted for the seed.

Gal. v. 14. For all the law is fulfilled in one word, even in this, Thou shalt love thy neighbour as thyself.

Rom. xiii. 8–10. Owe no man anything, but to love one another: for he that loveth another hath fulfilled the law. . . . If there be any other commandment, it is briefly comprehended in this saying, namely, Thou shalt love thy neighbour as thyself. Love worketh no ill to his neighbour: therefore love is the fulfilling of the law.

Gal. v. 16. This I say then, Walk in the Spirit, and ye shall not fulfil the lust of the flesh.	Rom. viii. 4. That the righteousness of the law might be fulfilled in us, who walk not after the flesh, but after the Spirit.
Gal. v. 17. For the flesh lusteth against the Spirit, and the Spirit against the flesh: and these are contrary the one to the other; so that ye cannot do the things that ye would.	Rom. vii. 23, 25. But I see another law in my members warring against the law of my mind, and bringing me into captivity to the law of sin which is in my members. . . . So then with the mind I myself serve the law of God, but with the flesh the law of sin.
Gal. vi. 2. Bear ye one another's burdens, and so fulfil the law of Christ.	Rom. xv. 1. We then that are strong ought to bear the infirmities of the weak, and not to please ourselves.

These resemblances are very striking, and would seem to indicate nearness of period in the composition. But Dean Alford interposes thus: "It may be that the elementary truths brought out amidst deep emotion, sketched, so to speak, in rough lines in the fervent Epistle to the Galatians, dwelt long on St. Paul's mind, even though other objects of interest regarding other churches intervened, and at length worked themselves out under the teaching and leading of the Spirit into that grand theological argument which he afterwards addressed, without any special moving occasion, but as his master-exposition of Christian doctrine, to the church of the metropolis of the world." The statement is true, but it does not on this point bring out the whole truth. For the resemblances are closer, more definite, and in every way more characteristic than the objection allows. Not only is the Galatian outline preserved in Romans, but its minutiæ, its sudden turns, its rapid logic beating down opposition, its peculiarities of quotation and proof are rewritten; the smaller touches are reproduced as well as the more prominent courses of argument; forms of thought and imagery suggested and sharpened by personal relations and direct collision in the shorter letter, are reimpressed on the longer and more impersonal production, without any immediate necessity. The parallel is about as close in many sections as between Ephesians and Colossians. See our Introductions to these epistles. There are also words peculiar to the two epistles, such as *κῶμοι*, *μακαρισμός*, *μέθη*, *δουλεία*, *βαστάζειν*, *ἐλευθερόω*, *ἴδε*, *κατάρα*, *καταρᾶσθαι*, *ὀφειλέτης*, *παραβάτης*; and phrases also, as *τί ἔτι; παρ' ὅ, οἱ τὰ τοιαῦτα πράσσοντες, τί λέγει ἡ γράφη;* So that Prof. Lightfoot's argument becomes very plausible, and, to use his own words, "The reasons given certainly do not amount to a demonstration, but every historical question must be decided by striking a balance between conflicting probabilities; and it seems to me that the arguments here adduced, however imperfect, will hold their ground against those which are alleged in favour of the earlier date." He ingeniously concludes that the epistle may have been written between the second Epistle to the Corinthians and the Epistle to the Romans, and on the journey between Macedonia and Achaia. This view is adopted by Bleek,[1] and virtually by Conybeare and Howson, who date the epistle from Corinth, while Grotius and De Wette do not definitely commit themselves to it.

Looking, in a word, at both sides of the question, we feel it still to be impossible to arrive at absolute certainty on this point, and critics will probably oscillate between Ephesus and Greece. The opinion that Greece was the place where the epistle was written has certainly very much to recommend it, though we may not be able to reach a definite and indisputable conclusion.

VI.—COMMENTARIES ON THE EPISTLE

There are the well-known commentaries of Chrysostom, Theodoret, Œcumenius, and Theophylact, with some extracts from Eusebius Emesenus, Severianus, and Theodore of Mop-

[1] *Einleitung in das Neue Testament*, p. 418, Berlin 1862. Storr has a good essay with this heading, *Prolusio de consensu Epistolarum Pauli ad Hebræos et Galatas* (*Comment. Theol.* ed. Velthusen, Kuinœl, et Ruperti, vol. ii. p. 394), Lipsiæ 1795.

suestia in Cramer's *Catena*. Extracts from Gennadius and Photius are found in Œcumenius. Among the Latin fathers may be named Marius Victorinus (Abbe Migne's *Pat. Lat.* viii.), the pseudo-Ambrose or Hilary, Jerome, Augustine, Pelagius, Primasius, and others of less note. Mediæval writers may be passed over. Luther follows, with Calvin, Beza, Erasmus, Musculus, Bullinger, Calovius, Zanchius, Crocius, Cocceius, Piscator, Hunnius, Tarnovius, Aretius, Wolf, etc.; and the Catholic commentators, Estius and a-Lapide. Wetstein, Grotius, and the writers in the *Critici Sacri* and *Fratres Poloni* are well known, and so are the collectors of annotations, as Elsner, Kypke, Krebs, Knatchbull, Lœsner, Alberti, Küttner, Palairet, Heinsius, Bos, Keuchenius, Doughtæus, and Hombergk. There are also the older English expositors, Ferguson, Dickson, Hammond, Chandler, Whitby, Locke, Doddridge, etc. etc. We have also the general commentaries of Koppe, Flatt, Morus, Rosenmüller, Jaspis, Hyperius, Cameron, and Reiche 1859.

The following more special commentaries may be noted: Luther, 1519; Pareus, 1621; Wesselius, 1756; Semler, 1779; Schulze, 1784; Mayer, 1788; Krause, 1788; Carpzov, 1794; Borger, 1807; Paulus, 1831; Rückert, 1833; Matthies, 1833; Usteri, 1833; Schott, 1833; Zschokke, 1834; Sardinoux, 1837; Olshausen, 1841; Windischmann, 1843; Baumgarten-Crusius, 1845; Peile, 1849; Conybeare and Howson, 1850; Jatho, 1851; Hilgenfeld, 1852; Brown, 1853; Jowett, 1855; Bagge, 1856; Trana, 1857; Ewald, 1857; Bisping, 1857; Winer, 4th ed., 1859; Wieseler, 1859; Wordsworth's *New Test.* P. iii., 1859; Webster and Wilkinson, *do.* vol. ii., 1861; Meyer, 1862; Schmoller, *Lange's Bibelwerk*, viii., 1862; Kamphausen, *Bunsen's Bibelwerk*, viii. Halb-band, 1863; Hofmann, 1863; Gwynne, 1863; Ellicott, 3d ed., 1863; Alford, *New Test.* vol. iii., 4th ed., 1865; Matthias, 1865; Lightfoot, 1865; Vömel, 1865; Carey, 1867; Larsen (Kjobenhavn), 1867. Reference may be made also to Bonitz, *Exam. Gal.* iii. 20, 1800; Hauk, *Exeget. Versuch über Gal.* iii. 15, 22, *Stud. u. Kritik.* 1862; Hermann, *de P. Epist. ad Galat. tribus primis capitibus*, 1832; Elwert, *Annot. in Gal.* ii. 1–10, 1852; Keerl *in Gal.* vi. 1–10, 1834; Holsten, *Inhalt, etc., des Briefes an die Galaten*, 1859, enlarged and reprinted, 1868; Fritzsche, *de nonnullis ad Galat. Epistolæ locis, Opuscula,* p. 158, etc., 1838.

Of a popular and practical nature are—Perkins, 1609; Riccaltoun, 1772; Barnes, 1840; Haldane, 1848; Anacker, Leipzig 1856; Twele, Hannover 1858; Kelly, 1865; Bayley, 1869. Exegetical remarks on portions of the epistle may also be found of a rationalistic nature in Holsten's *Zum Evangelium des Paulus und des Petrus,* Rostock 1868; and of an opposite character in Œrtel's *Paulus in der Apostel-geschichte,* Halle 1868.

When Buttmann, Matthiæ, Kühner, Winer, Scheuerlein, Bernhardy, Madvig, Schmalfeld, Krüger, Schirlitz, Green, A. Buttmann, and Jelf are simply named, the reference is to their respective Grammars; and when Suidas, Hesychius, Rost und Palm, Wahl, Wilke, Bretschneider, Robinson, Cremer, Liddell and Scott are simply named, the reference is to their respective Lexicons. The references to Hartung are to his *Lehre von den Partikeln der griechischen Sprache,* Erlangen 1832.

COMMENTARY ON GALATIANS

CHAPTER I

THE apostle's standing had been challenged by a faction in the Galatian churches, in order that his distinctive teaching might be disparaged or set aside. To undermine his doctrine, they denied or explained away his apostleship. It seems to have been alleged against him, that as he had not been a personal disciple of Jesus, he could not claim the inspiration enjoyed by those on whom He breathed, as He said, "Receive ye the Holy Ghost;" that his gospel had been communicated to him through a human medium, and therefore was not primary and authoritative truth; and that his position in the church was only of secondary or intermediate appointment, and on that account quite subordinate in rank and prerogative. Or there may have been an impression that the first number could not be augmented; and as it bore a relation to the twelve tribes of Israel, no one could be regarded as equal in office and honour to the *δώδεκα, οὓς καὶ ἀποστόλους ὠνόμασεν* (Luke vi. 13). The number was hallowed as a sacred one (Rev. xxi. 14). Justin also speaks significantly of the twelve: *ἄνδρες δεκαδύο τὸν ἀριθμόν* (*Apol.* i. 39, *Opera*, vol. i. p. 216, ed. Otto). If the Clementines be taken as embodying to some extent the traditionary opinions and prejudices of the Jewish Christians, then Paul's official standing would be disallowed, as being unattested by credentials from the twelve; his doctrine denied, as unsanctioned by James, called "the Lord's brother," and the head of the church in Jerusalem; and his apostleship ignored, because he had not "companied" with Jesus and the twelve in the days of His flesh (*Homiliæ*, xi. 35, xvii. 19, pp. 253, 351, ed. Dressel. 1853). In the *Recognitiones* it is more distinctly stated: *neque propheta neque apostolus in hoc tempore speratus a vobis aliquis alius præter nos. . . . Ipse enim est annus Dei acceptus nos apostolos habens duodecim menses* (iv. 35). Besides, Paul's official affinity with the Gentiles, and his characteristic assertion of their freedom—their non-obligation to submit to the Mosaic law, excited suspicion and hostility against him on the part of all—*ζηλωταὶ τοῦ νόμου*—who held that it was to be rigidly enforced on heathen converts, who were to be permitted only through the gate of virtual proselytism to enter into full communion with the church. Perhaps this depreciation arose also from some false view of his connection with Barnabas, and of their relation to the prophets of the church at Antioch, by the laying on of whose hands both had been separated and designated to missionary work. The apostle therefore enters at once on self-vindication—*non superbe sed necessarie* (Jerome)—not because of the mere slander, *διαβολήν* (Theodoret), or because they held him cheap, *ἐξηυτέλιζον* (Œcumenius); but because the slight cast upon him was not only a denial of Christ's authority to rule in His own church, and to choose and endow any one to serve in it, but was also a preliminary step to the promulgation and advocacy of a mass of errors, which detracted from the fulness of His atoning work by suspending Gentile salvation on the observance of Gentile Jewish ritual. True, indeed, he was not one of the original twelve, but he claims a parity of rank, as his call was as real as theirs though posterior to it: *ὡσπερεὶ τῷ ἐκτρώματι ὤφθη κἀμοί* (1 Cor. xv. 8). The same Jesus who summoned the twelve by the Lake of Galilee, did, after being taken up into heaven, appear in glory "above the brightness of the sun," and make him "a minister and a witness," and send him to the Gentiles. He saw "that Just One, and heard the voice of His mouth," and therefore had a commission as divine, distinct, and independent as any one of those whom he calls *οἱ πρὸ ἐμοῦ ἀπόστολοι*. So that he opens by a sharp and resolute assertion of his full apostolic prerogative; and the first verse contains, not exactly what Jowett calls "the text of the whole epistle," but an assertion of official dignity, which underlies the grand question discussed in it.

Ver. 1. *Παῦλος, ἀπόστολος οὐκ ἀπ' ἀνθρώπων οὐδὲ δι' ἀνθρώπου*—"Paul, an apostle, not from men nor by man." There needs no participle to be inserted after ἀπόστολος, as Borger, Bloomfield, and others suppose, its relations being sufficiently marked and guarded by the following prepositions. In most of the other epistles the same assertion is made, though in quieter and more general terms. For its different forms, see on Phil. i. 1; and for the meaning of "apostle," see on Eph. iv. 11, and this epistle, i. 19, in the essay at the end of this chapter. But now, the reality of his apostleship being impugned, and that for a selfish purpose, he at once asserts its divinity with bold and unmistakeable emphasis. Sometimes, when the opposition to him was not so fierce, he uses other arguments: "the seal of mine apostleship are ye in the Lord;" "truly the signs of an apostle were wrought among you;" "I am not a whit behind the chiefest of the apostles;" but the antagonism to him in Galatia demanded a more incisive vindication. The statement is made by a change of prepositions and a change of number. The use of two prepositions in successive clauses is indeed quite characteristic of the apostle's style; and ἀπό and διά are not to be confounded, as if the whole meaning were, that in no sense did Paul receive his apostleship from a human source. On purpose he puts the fact very distinctly: he was an apostle, not from men, ἀπό, referring to remote or primary source; nor by man, διά referring to medium or nearer instrumental cause. Winer, § 47; Bernhardy, p. 222. Some expositors, as Koppe, Borger, Usteri, and Gwynne, neglecting the change of preposition, lay the stress on the change of number. Gwynne denies the distinction between ἀπό and διά, but without foundation in any of the instances alleged by him. Nor does he see, in the case of ἀπό, how the literal so naturally and necessarily passes into the ethical meaning of a particle, or how "remotion from" comes to signify origination. The οὐδὲ implies a difference of relation in the second clause from the first. Διά may not always denote instrument in the strict sense, for means may be blended in conception with source, especially when God is spoken of, as in Rom. xi. 36: "for of Him (ἐξ αὐτοῦ) and by Him (δι' αὐτοῦ) are all things," being His alike in origin and agency, Himself the worker of His own will or purpose—one or both aspects of relationship being equally applicable to Him (compare Heb. ii. 10; 1 Cor. i. 9, viii. 6). It is true that διά is used with both nouns in the following clause; but here, as in contrast with ἀπό, it has its distinctive meaning, and is the first step in the argument. Bengel's distinction, therefore, is baseless, that his call (*vocatio*) is referred to in ἀπό, and instruction (*institutio immediata*) in διά. But it is wrong in Hofmann to say that any distinction of meaning between the two prepositions serves no purpose. Borger errs far in supposing that ἀπό and διά are both used for ὑπό which points to an active and more immediate cause. In the decaying stage of a language, the precise distinction of similar particles, with the more delicate shades of relation indicated by them, ceases to be felt; and thus, as Winer remarks, ἀπό is frequently used for ὑπό after passive verbs in Byzantine Greek, and the two prepositions are often exchanged both in classical and New Testament codices (§ 47, *b*). On the difference of meaning, see also Poppo, *Thucydides*, vol. i. p. iii. p. 158; Stallbaum, *Plato*, vol. iii. p. 137. The apostle's office flowed from no body of men, nor was it given him through an individual man, either by himself or as representing any body of men and acting in their name. He was no delegate of the original twelve, and was in no way dependent on them; nor even did he stand in any official subordination to James, Cephas, or John—*οἱ δοκοῦντες στύλοι εἶναι*. Or if ἀνθρώπου be taken as the abstract, the clause may mean that his was no dependent charge delegated to him from any party of men, nor was it an independent charge conveyed to him through mere humanity. It may, however, be doubted whether it be the abstract, or whether any direct personal allusion is intended; for the change to the singular forms a designed antithesis to the following clause, while it denies the intervention of human agency in any form and to any extent. It does not seem likely that, in this vindication of his independent standing, the apostle alludes to the false teachers as having no divine commission (Jerome, De Wette, and Lightfoot); for to have brought himself into any comparison with them would have been a lowering of his plea. Rather, as we have said, these Judaizers, the more thoroughly to controvert his doctrine and undermine his influence, denied his true apostleship. He might, in their opinion, be a δοῦλος, διάκονος, εὐαγγελιστής, but not an apostle; for they seem to have maintained that there was the taint of a human element in his commission, and they assigned him a far lower platform than the original twelve.

But Christ had called him immediately, *οὐρανόθεν ἐκάλεσεν οὐκ ἀνθρώπῳ χρησάμενος ὑπουργῷ* (Theophylact); and he was not therefore like Silas or Timothy in his relation to Christ and the ruling powers in the churches. What the apostle asserts of his office, he afterwards as distinctly asserts of his doctrine (vers. 11, 12, etc.). Negatively, his apostleship was not from men as its *causa principalis,* nor by man as its *causa medians;* but positively,

'Αλλὰ διὰ 'Ιησοῦ Χριστοῦ καὶ Θεοῦ πατρὸς τοῦ ἐγείραντος αὐτὸν ἐκ νεκρῶν—"but by Jesus Christ, and God the Father who raised Him from the dead." Had the apostle consulted mere rhetorical fulness, he might have repeated *ἀπό* before *Θεοῦ πατρός*. But both nouns are governed by the same preposition *διά,* and are included under the same relation. For, to his mind, so much were Christ and God one in purpose and act, that the *διά* not only implies the *ἀπό,* but absorbs it, primary source in God being identified with mediate agency in the appearance and call of the Lord Jesus. The phrase is therefore placed first, as being nearest his thought at the moment, and as it was the relation expressed by *διά* which formed the question in dispute. The apostleship might be admitted as being from God, and yet not by Him as its immediate agent; *ἀπό* does not of itself prove *διά,* but *διά* certainly implies *ἀπό*. *Διά* is not used therefore for the sake of shortness, as Olshausen says, and as Ellicott partly allows; but it points to the direct agency of God, manifested in raising His Son from the dead. By Jesus Christ was the apostle selected and directly called, and by God the Father acting in and through Him whom He had raised from the dead; for it was the risen and glorified Saviour who bestowed the apostolate on him. See above on the prepositions, and Fritzsche on Rom. i. 5. In ver. 3, again, the usage is reversed, and *ἀπό* is employed with both names. Both nouns here want the article, and *Θεὸς πατήρ* has all the force of a proper name (Gal. i. 3; Eph. vi. 23; Phil. ii. 11; 1 Pet. i. 2). The genitive *νεκρῶν* wants the article, too, as usually when preceded by *ἐκ* (Winer, § 19), the quotation in Eph. v. 14 being an exception, and there being in Col. ii. 12 various readings with authorities almost balanced. God is called *πατήρ,* not generally as Father of all (De Wette, Alford), nor specially as our Father (Usteri and Wieseler), nor directly as

Christ's Father, as is the opinion of Meyer, Ellicott, and the rendering of the Syriac; but the name is probably inclusive of all those relations. Because He sustains such a relation to Christ and Christ's, because of His foremost place in the gracious economy, and His fatherly manifestations in it and through it, may He not receive the characteristic and almost absolute name of Father? The relation of Christ and believers to the Father is often indicated by a following genitive (i. 4; Eph. i. 2, 3; Col. i. 2, 3; 1 Thess. i. 3, iii. 11, etc.).

The predicate is, *τοῦ ἐγείραντος αὐτὸν ἐκ νεκρῶν*. Why this addition, for it must have some connection with the apostle's self-vindication? The addition is not a vague one, as if the act asserted had become an attribute of God (Jowett); nor is it the mere token of almighty power (Olshausen), nor an affirmation of His resurrection against Jews (Chrysostom), nor chiefly a refutation of the objection that he had not seen Christ (Semler, Morus), nor a passing historical notice that he had been called by the risen Saviour, nor a recognition of the Father as the *Urheber*, originator of Christ's redeeming work (De Wette, Usteri), nor only the historical confirmation of the *καὶ Θεοῦ πατρός* (Meyer); nor is it principally to exhibit the resurrection as awaking faith in the Risen One and in God as our reconciled Father in Him (Wieseler); but it is the proof that Jesus who died could call him, though He had not called him at the period when the twelve were commissioned in the days of His flesh, and that the apostleship was one of the gifts which specially belonged to Him as the ascended Lord. Eph. iv. 11. It may be said generally, the Father raised Him from the dead, so that all His apostles could proclaim the truth of which His resurrection was the primal evidence and a distinctive tenet (Rom. i. 4, iv. 24; Eph. i. 20; Phil. ii. 9); and specially, God the Father entrusted Paul with the apostleship, and did it through Jesus, whom He had raised from the dead: so that the risen Saviour invested with supreme authority, added, by a direct and personal act, one to the number of the twelve, with every element of qualification and prerogative which had been conferred upon them. There is no need to say, with Luther, that the clause condemns *justitiam operum*. It would be at the same time laying too great stress on the words, to suppose, with Augustine, Erasmus, Beza, and Calvin, that the apostle is claiming a superiority over the other apostles, inasmuch as he alone had been called by the risen Saviour, but they by Him *adhuc mortali.* But the clause plainly implies that he possessed all the qualifications of an apostle; that he had been commissioned immediately by Jesus Himself, having not only heard Him but seen Him, and could be a witness of His resurrection equally with any of the twelve; and that he possessed the gift of the Holy Ghost in such fulness and adaptation as fitted him for all spheres of his work (1 Cor. ix. 1, 2). It is a strange lection which is ascribed by Jerome to Marcion, which omitted the words *Θεοῦ πατρός*, and seems to have read *I. X. τοῦ ἐγείραντος ἑαυτὸν ἐκ νεκρῶν*, for it is opposed to the uniform teaching of the Pauline theology. The Greek fathers lay no little stress on the fact that *I. X.* and *Θεὸς πατήρ* have a common bond of connection in *διά*. Chrysostom speaks of it as "fitted to stop the mouths of the heretics who deny Christ's divinity, and to teach us not to prescribe laws to the ineffable nature, nor to define the degrees of Godhead which belong to the Father and the Son." Theodoret presses the inference to prove *οὐδεμίαν φύσεως διαφοράν* between Father and Son. But such a theological pressure upon the passing phrase cannot be sustained in all its weight, though the words do imply economic unity of will and operation, and show that to the mind of the apostle Christ and the Father were one in authority and prerogative. Nay more, *I. X.* is placed in direct opposition to *ἀνθρώπου*, as if, in Augustine's phrase, He were *totus jam Deus.*[1] The reason why Crellius and Le Clerc and others insist on inserting *ἀπό* before *Θεοῦ* is, that they may impugn the equality which the common *vinculum* of *διά* implies. Brown inclines very needlessly to their exegesis, though certainly not for their doctrinal grounds. In a word, this self-assertion of the apostle is in no way opposed to what he says elsewhere in self-depreciation, as when he calls himself "the least of the apostles," "not meet to be called an apostle," 1 Cor. xv. 8, 9, for these are the utterances of conscious personal unworthiness. Nor is the statement before us in conflict with the record in Acts xiii. 1–3. Paul was an apostle, as himself felt and believed, prior to this scene in the church

[1] This phrase is guarded and explained in his *Retractationes*, *Opera*, vol. i. p. 74, ed. Paris, 1836.

of Antioch. Acts xx. 24, xxii. 14, 15, xxvi. 16–20. Was not the formal apostolic commission given in the hour of his conversion—*ἐθνῶν, εἰς οὓς ἐγώ σε ἀποστέλλω*? See also Gal. i. 12, 15, 16, 22, 23; 1 Tim. i. 12, 13. The fasting, prayer, and imposition of hands were not, as Hammond, Wake, Wordsworth, and the Catholic commentators Bisping and Windischmann,[1] argue, a consecration to the apostleship, but a solemn designation of Saul and Barnabas to a special missionary work, which on their return is said to have been "fulfilled." Even Calvin speaks of the call of the apostle as being followed by the *sollennis ritus ordinationis;* see under Eph. i. 1. But if ecclesiastical ordination was essential to full apostleship, what becomes of the *οὐδὲ δι' ἀνθρώπου*?

After this decided assertion of his apostleship—an assertion necessary in the circumstances, at once for his own vindication, and the confirmation of the gospel which he preached, as also to give their due weight to the censure, counsels, warnings, and teachings which were to form the contents of the epistle—he passes on to say—

Ver. 2. *Καὶ οἱ σὺν ἐμοὶ πάντες ἀδελφοί*—"and all the brethren who are with me." This phrase, designating a number of persons beyond such names as Timothy, Sosthenes, and Silvanus, found in some of the other epistles, cannot refer exclusively, as Brown after Beza supposes, to official colleagues, nor generally, as Schott, Victorinus, Jatho, Schmoller, Jowett, take it, to the brethren or community in the place from which the epistle was written. It denotes an inner circle of friends, in special companionship with the apostle—at one with him in opinion at the present moment; *πάντες* emphatic—referring not so much to number, though it must include several, as to unanimity,—no exception among them, all of them in the crisis sympathizing with the Galatian churches, and sharing his anxiety to deliver them from imminent jeopardy. In fact, in Phil. iv. 21, 22, the apostle distinguishes "the brethren with him" from "all the saints." The question as to who might be included in the *πάντες* is answered in various ways, according to the opinion adopted about the place where the epistle was written—in Ephesus or Corinth. Wherever they were, they joined in the salutation; but their position and unanimity added no authority

[1] Estius is an exception.

to the epistle (Chrysostom, Luther, Calvin, Olshausen, Meyer, and De Wette, hold the opposite view), though probably they might strengthen its appeals, as showing how wide and warm an interest was felt in the Galatian defection. Tit. iii. 15. The authority of the epistle rests exclusively on the official prerogative of Paul himself, singly and apart from the *ἀδελφοί*. For the association of other names with the apostle's own in his salutations, see under Phil. i. 1.

The epistle is not sent to one community in a town, but

Ταῖς ἐκκλησίαις τῆς Γαλατίας—"to the churches of Galatia" —the letter being therefore a circular. Acts xvi. 6, xviii. 23; 1 Cor. xvi. 1; 1 Pet. i. 1. It has been often remarked, that *ἐκκλησίαις* occurs without any qualifying element or additional clause; and it has been explained since the time of Chrysostom, that, on account of their defection, the apostle could not give them any title of honour or endearment. Usteri denies this, and appeals to both epistles to Thessalonica; but there the words *ἐν Θεῷ πατρὶ* are added. In both epistles to Corinth, *τοῦ Θεοῦ* is annexed to *ἐκκλησία*, passages strangely referred to also by Hofmann and Sardinoux, as if proving that Paul had felt, in writing to these churches, as he did in writing to those of Galatia. It is quite baseless on the part of Theophylact, to find in the plural a reference to divisions—*ἐπεὶ δὲ καὶ διεστασίαζον*. For the places where those churches were probably situated, see Introduction.

Ver. 3. *Χάρις ὑμῖν καὶ εἰρήνη ἀπὸ Θεοῦ πατρὸς καὶ Κυρίου ἡμῶν Ἰησοῦ Χριστοῦ*—"Grace be to you and peace from God the Father and our Lord Jesus Christ." The pronoun *ἡμῶν* is placed after *Κυρίου* on good authority, though A and ℵ, with some of the Latin fathers, insert it after *πατρός*, as in other salutations. Rom. i. 7; 1 Cor. i. 3; 2 Cor. i. 2; Eph. i. 2, etc. As *διά* in the first verse, so *ἀπό* in this verse governs both the genitives, as both are sources of divine blessing, according to the aspect in which each is viewed, primarily indeed from God and proximately from Jesus Christ. This contiguous use of two prepositions, each of them in application both to the Father and to Christ, shows that to the apostle God and Christ were so much one in will and operation ("God in Christ"), that no sharp dogmatic distinction of origin and medium needed to be drawn between them in such a prayer offered for the churches. See under ver. 1.

For the meaning of the benediction, see under Eph. i. 2, and also the note of Wieseler. As the West embodied its wishes in χάρις, and the East in שָׁלוֹם—εἰρήνη,—so the apostle, in catholic fulness, uses both terms in their profoundest Christian significance: no ordinary greeting, or "as the world giveth," but a prayer for all combined and fitting spiritual blessings.

In connection with Christ, and as an unusual addition to his salutations, he now describes His distinctive work in its blessed purpose and in its harmony with the divine plan; for the passing statement presents a truth in direct conflict with the errors prevailing in the Galatian churches. Thus the first and fourth verses contain in brief the two themes of the epistle,—a vindication of his apostleship and of the free and full salvation by faith without works of law, which he rejoiced to proclaim.

Ver. 4. *Τοῦ δόντος ἑαυτὸν περὶ τῶν ἁμαρτιῶν ἡμῶν*—"who gave Himself for our sins." The ὑπέρ of the received text is found in B and א[3], and some of the Greek fathers, but περί has the authority of A, D, F, K, א, several minuscules, and is apparently the preferable reading. The correction to ὑπέρ might appear to be more in the apostle's manner (Meyer). The two prepositions, so similar in meaning, are often exchanged in New Testament MSS. Meyer holds that they are not different in meaning.

The act here ascribed to Christ Himself is often ascribed to God, as in Rom. viii. 32; sometimes it assumes the form of a simple statement, as in Rom. iv. 25, v. 8; but here, as also in other places, especially in the pastoral epistles, it is regarded as the spontaneous act of the Self-offerer, as in John x. 18, 1 Tim. ii. 6, Tit. ii. 14, Eph. v. 2 where a compound verb is used. (Rom. v. 6, 8, etc.; 1 Macc. vi. 44.) Wetstein quotes in illustration from Xiphilinus, the abbreviator of Dio Cassius (in *Othone*, p. 193), the following clause: ὅστις οὐκ ὑμᾶς ὑπὲρ ἑαυτοῦ, ἀλλ' ἑαυτὸν ὑπὲρ ὑμῶν δέδωκε. Meyer says, and so far correctly, that the idea of satisfaction lies not in the meaning of the preposition, but in the whole *Sachverhältniss;* quoting also *Iliad*, i. 444:

Φοίβῳ θ' ἱερὴν ἑκατόμβην
ῥέξαι ὑπὲρ Δαναῶν ὄφρ' ἱλασόμεσθα ἄνακτα.

Wesselius cites the *versiculus notissimus* of Cato:

"Ipse nocens cum sis, moritur cur victima pro te?"

Περί, as might be expected from the meaning of the words in such a connection, is often used with the thing, and ὑπέρ with the persons: περὶ ἁμαρτιῶν, ὑπὲρ ἀδίκων (1 Pet. iii. 18; Sirach xxix. 15). But the usage is not uniform, as Heb. v. 3, περὶ τοῦ λαοῦ, . . . περὶ ἑαυτοῦ, . . . ὑπὲρ ἁμαρτιῶν; and in the first verse also of the same chapter, ὑπὲρ ἁμαρτιῶν. In 1 Cor. xv. 3, ὑπέρ is used with ἁμαρτιῶν, but ἡμῶν is a personal qualification. In Matt. xxvi. 28 we have περὶ πολλῶν, but the personal design is introduced, εἰς ἄφεσιν ἁμαρτιῶν; and in the parallel passages, Mark xiv. 24, Luke xxii. 19, ὑπέρ occurs, and the personal explanatory clause is wanting. In 1 Thess. v. 10 the various reading is περί—ὑπέρ, and a personal purpose follows. The preposition ὑπέρ denotes a closer relation—"over," or "for the benefit of," "on behalf of," personal interest in, that interest being often an element of conscious recognition (Gal. ii. 20; 1 Cor. v. 20; Rom. xiv. 15), and has a meaning verging very close on that of ἀντί, "in room of," as the context occasionally indicates (chap. iii. 13; Eph. v. 2; Philem. 13). See Fritzsche on Rom. v. 7, 8; Poppo on the phrase ὑπὲρ ἑαυτοῦ, which he renders *suo loco, ὑπὲρ pro ἀντί, Thucydides*, part iii. vol. i. p. 704; Euripides, *Alcestis*, 690; Polybius, i. 67, 7; Matthiae, § 582; Rost und Palm, *sub voce*. *Περί* is more general in meaning, and may denote "on account of," "in connection with," bringing out the object or motive of the act: Jesus Christ gave Himself for our sins—on account of them, or in such a connection with them—that He might deliver us. See under Eph. vi. 19. The distinction between the two prepositions is often very faint, though frequently περί expresses only *mentis circumspectionem, ὑπέρ simul animi propensionem* (Weber, *Demosth.* p. 130). See also Schaefer's full note on the phrase of Demosthenes, οὐ περὶ δόξης οὐδ' ὑπὲρ μέρους, *Annot.* vol. i. p. 189; and the remarks of Bremi, *Demosthenes, Orat.* p. 188. The two prepositions may, as commonly employed, characterize the atonement or self-oblation of Christ; the first in its object generally, the second specially in its recipients, and the benefits conferred upon them. Christ gave Himself for us, on account of our sins, that expiation might be made, or on behalf of sinners, that by such expiation they might obtain forgiveness and life. See more fully under Eph. v. 2, 25. 'Αντί is more precise, and, signifying "in room of," points out the substitutionary nature of Christ's death. Matt.

v. 38; Luke xi. 11; 1 Cor. xi. 15; Jas. iv. 15; Matt. xvii. 27, etc.

The meaning is, that He gave Himself to death (not *volenti diabolo*, Ambrosiast.), or, as in other places, gave His life. Matt. xx. 28; Mark x. 45. Sometimes a predicate is added, as ἀντίλυτρον, 1 Tim. ii. 6; προσφορὰν, Eph. v. 2. Such a predicate is here implied in the clause defined by περί, and in the purpose indicated by ὅπως. The freeness of the self-gift is prominent, as well as its infinite value—HIMSELF. We pause not over theological distinctions as to the two natures of the Mediatorial person in this act: He gave Himself—a gift impossible without incarnation—a gift valueless without a mysterious union with divinity, as is at least indicated by the common *vinculum* of διά in the first verse, and of ἀπό in the second verse. The ἡμῶν refers primarily to the apostle, the brethren with him and the persons addressed by him in Galatia, but does not by its use define in any way the extent of the atonement, either as limiting it to "us" believers, as some have argued, or extending it to "us" "mankind sinners," as others contend. The doctrine taught is, that Jesus Christ did spontaneously offer Himself as the one propitiation, so that He is the source of grace and peace; and the inference is, because He gave Himself, the oblation is perfect as also the deliverance secured by it, so that obedience to the Mosaic law as a means of salvation is quite incompatible with faith in Him.

The self-oblation of Jesus is surely no mere Jewish image, as Jowett represents it, something now in relation to us like a husk out of which the kernel had fallen. True, as he says, "the image must have had a vividness in the days when sacrifices were offered that it may not have now;" but the truth imaged has not therefore faded out. Take away all that is Jewish in the presentation of that truth, yet you alter not its essence and purpose; for through the death of Christ, and its relation to or influence on the divine government, God is just while He is justifying the ungodly. The teaching of Scripture is something more than that "Christ took upon Him human flesh, that He was put to death by sinful men, and raised men out of the state of sin—in this sense taking their sins upon Him:" that is, in no true sense bearing our guilt. For not only expiation or propitiation, but reconciliation, justification, acceptance, redemption from the curse, are ascribed to His death. Men are raised out of a state of sin when their guilt is forgiven, and the power of sin is destroyed within them; and both blessings are traced to the Self-sacrifice of the Son of God. The sinfulness of the men that put Him to death is not incompatible with the voluntariness and atoning merit of His death; for it was more than a tragedy or a martyrdom, though it is not without these aspects. The figures, as Jowett says, are varied; but such variation does not prove them to be "figures only," and the truth underlying them has varying and connected phases of relation and result. "The believer is identified with the various stages of the life of Christ;" true, but his life springs from Christ's death, and is a life in union with the risen Lord. Gal. ii. 20. The definite doctrine of Scripture is, that in dying, Christ bore a representative or a substitutionary relation to sin and sinners, as is expressed by ἀντί, and implied in περί and ὑπέρ. This teaching of Scripture in the age of the apostles is the truth still to us, even though its imagery may be dimmed. Moulded for one age, and given primarily to it, it is adapted to all time as a permanent and universal gospel. The palpable terms fashioned in Jewry ray light through the world. The apostolic theology, though bodied forth by Hebrew genius, and glowing with illustrations from Hebrew history and ritual, is all the more on that account adapted to us, for it speaks in no dull monotone, and it is no exhibition of such abstract and colourless formulas as would satisfy the scanty creed of modern spiritualism. The purpose of the self-sacrifice is

Ὅπως ἐξέληται ἡμᾶς ἐκ τοῦ αἰῶνος τοῦ ἐνεστῶτος πονηροῦ—"that He might deliver us out of the present world—an evil one:" *nequam*, Vulg.; *malo*, Clarom.; *maligno*, Aug. Perhaps this is the better reading, and it is supported by A, B, א[1]. The received text places ἐνεστῶτος before αἰῶνος, omitting the article, and is also well supported by a large number of MSS., some versions and fathers. The verb, from its position, is emphatic, and πονηροῦ is virtually a tertiary predicate. Ἵνα is the apostle's favourite term, and the relative particle ὅπως—"in such manner that"—is rarely used by him. In the New Testament it is construed with the subjunctive, sometimes with ἄν, but it is found with other moods in classical writers (Krüger, § 54, 8, etc.; Klotz-Devarius, vol. ii. pp. 629, etc., 681, etc., in which sections *ἵνα* and *ὅπως* are distinguished in meaning and use). The verb *ἐξαιρεῖσθαι* (*eriperet*, Vulgate) occurs only here in Paul's epistles. In other passages of the New Testament it has the sense of rescue from peril by an act of power, as of Joseph (Acts vii. 10); of the Hebrews out of slavery (Acts vii. 34); of Peter from the hand of Herod (Acts xii. 11); of Paul from the mob in Jerusalem (Acts xxiii. 27); and it is the word used by the Divine Master to the apostle in reference to his frequent deliverances from danger (Acts xxvi. 17). Compare Gen. xxxii. 11, Isa. xlii. 22, Ps. cxl. 1. The noun *αἰών* connected with *ἀεί*, Latin *ævum*, and the Saxon *aye* ("God shall endure for aye"), means "duration;" its adjunct determining whether that duration reach indefinitely backwards or forwards, as in *ἀπ'* or *ἐκ αἰῶνος* in the one case, and *εἰς τὸν αἰῶνα* in the other. The latter is a common meaning both in the classics and in the New Testament: Ast, *Lexicon Platon. sub voce.* With a more restricted duration, it often means in the New Testament, the age or present course of time, with the underlying idea of corruption and sinfulness, though, as having a temporal sense in more or less prominence, it is not to be identified with *κόσμος*. Luke xvi. 8; Rom. xii. 2; Eph. i. 21, ii. 2. In rabbinical usage, there was the עוֹלָם הַזֶּה, the present or pre-Messianic age, and עוֹלָם הַבָּא, the coming age, or period after Messiah's advent. Allusions to such use would almost seem to be in Matt. xxiv. 3, Heb. vi. 5, ix. 26. The *αἰῶν μέλλων*, however, of the New Testament is not so restricted as the corresponding rabbinical phrase, Matt. xii. 32, Mark x. 30, Luke xviii. 30, Eph. i. 21. The noun, in Christian use, and in both references, acquires a deeper significance. The *ὁ νῦν αἰῶν* of the pastoral epistles, 1 Tim. vi. 17, 2 Tim. iv. 10, Tit. ii. 12—*ὁ αἰῶν οὗτος*, Rom. xii. 2—has a pervading element of evil in it, in contrast to the *ὁ αἰῶν μέλλων*, *ὁ αἰῶν ὁ ἐρχόμενος*, which is characterized by purity and happiness (Mark x. 30; Luke xviii. 30). The *αἰῶν* is this passing age—this world as it now is—fallen, guilty, and corrupt, in bondage to a "god" (2 Cor. iv. 4), and to *ἄρχοντες* who are opposed to God (1 Cor. ii. 6; Eph. vi. 12). We often use the word "world" very similarly, as signifying a power opposed to Christ in its maxims, fashions, modes of thought, and objects of pursuit, and as continually tempting and often subduing His people; the scene of trial and sorrow, where sense ever struggling for the mastery over faith, embarrasses and overpowers the children of God. See Cremer, *Biblisch-theolog. Wörterb. sub voce*, Gotha 1866.

The participle *ἐνεστώς* has two meanings, either time present actually, or present immediately—time now, or time impending. The first meaning is apparent in Rom. viii. 38, *οὔτε ἐνεστῶτα οὔτε μέλλοντα*, "nor things present, nor things to come"—present and future in contrast. Similarly 1 Cor. iii. 22, vii. 26; Heb. ix. 9. Instances abound in the classics and Septuagint, Esdras v. 47, ix. 6, *τὸν ἐνεστῶτα χειμῶνα*; 3 Macc. i. 16; frequently in Polybius, i. 60, 75, xviii. 38; Xen. *Hellen.* 2, 1, 6; Joseph. *Antiq.* xvi. 6, 2; Philo, *de Plantat. Noe*, *Opera*, vol. iii. p. 136, Erlangæ 1820. Phavorinus defines it by *πάροντα*, and Hesychius gives it as *ὁ τῆς ζωῆς χρόνος*. The Syriac renders it "this age," and the Vulgate *præsenti sæculo*. Sextus Empir. divides times into *τὸν παρῳχημένον καὶ τὸν ἐνεστῶτα καὶ τὸν μέλλοντα*, *Advers. Phys.* ii. 192, p. 516, ed. Bekker. It is also the term used by grammarians for "the present tense;" thus *ἐνεστῶσα μετοχή*—the present participle. Theodore of Mopsuestia, *in loc.*, defines the term by *παρών*, and explains it as the period stretching on to the second advent, ed. Fritzsche, p. 121. Compare Clement. *Hom.* ii. 40, Ignat. *ad Eph.* xi., Corpus Ignatianum, ed. Cureton, p. 29. While there may be a few passages in which it will bear the sense of impending (Polybius, i. 71–4), or ideally present, as good as come or seen as certainly coming, it is questioned whether it has such a meaning in the New Testament, even in 2 Thess. ii. 2, compared with 2 Tim. iii. 1. See Schoettgen's *Horæ* on this place. But this view is taken by Meyer, Bisping, and Trana, the phrase denoting, according to them, impending time,—the evil time predicted as coming and preceding the second advent. 2 Pet. iii. 3; 1 John ii. 18; Jude 18; 2 Tim. iii. 1. Matthias, a recent annotator (Cassel 1865), holds the same view, and would punctuate *αἰῶνος, πονηροῦ κατά*—that is, the evil is allowed by God to culminate just before the second advent, that it may be effectually and for ever put down. The first interpretation is preferable. It accords with the simple meaning of the passage, which states, without any occult or prophetic allusion, the immediate purpose of Christ's death; and such is, in general, the theme of the epistle. Nor does there seem to be anything in the context to suggest to the apostle's mind the idea of the last apostasy, or to deliverance from it as the design of tho atonement. His thoughts, so soon to find utterance, concern present blessing through Christ, and Him alone; the reception of such blessing being prevented by looking away from Him, and putting partial or complete trust in legal observances.

The phrase "this present evil world" cannot therefore mean merely the Mosaical constitution (Locke, Krause), or the entire system of things defective and unsatisfactory connected with it (Carpzov, Gwynne),—an exegesis too technical and narrow, and which comes far short of the meaning of the apostle's pregnant words. The meaning of the verse is, that the purpose of Christ's self-sacrifice was to rescue believers out of (ἐκ) a condition fraught with infinite peril to them—the kingdom of darkness—and bring them into a condition safe and blessed—"the kingdom of His dear Son." This change is not, in the first instance, one of character, as so many assert, but one of state or relation having reference rather to justification than to sanctification, though change of relation most certainly implies or entails change of character (De Wette, Meyer, Hofmann). Believers are rescued out of "this present age," with all its evils of curse, corruption, sense, and selfishness, not by being removed from earth, but being translated into another "age"—accepted, blessed, adopted, regenerated. John xvii. 15, 16. Not that redemption is confined in any sense to the present age, for its recipients are at length received up into that glory which lasts εἰς τοὺς αἰῶνας τῶν αἰῶνων. Chrysostom and Jerome are anxious to guard against the Manichæan heresy, that the age or world is essentially and in itself evil, for it is only made so by evil προαιρέσεις; the latter dwelling on the *deliramenta* of the Valentinians, and the mystical meanings which they attached to the Hebrew עולם, as written with or without the ו, and as meaning eternity in the first case, and the space reaching to the year of jubilee in the other.

Κατὰ τὸ θέλημα τοῦ Θεοῦ καὶ πατρὸς ἡμῶν—"according to the will of God and our Father." Theophylact distinguishes *θέλημα* from *ἐπιταγή*, and identifies it with *εὐδοκία*. (See under Eph. i. 11.) Is *ἡμῶν* connected only with *πατρός*, or is the proper rendering "our God and Father?" It is rather difficult to answer. The article is omitted before *πατρός*, according to usage. Middleton, p. 57; Winer, § 19, 4. The *καί* seems to have its ordinary connecting force. The phrase *Θεὸς καὶ πατὴρ* occurs with a genitive following in several places, Rom. xv. 6, 2 Cor. i. 3, Eph. i. 3, Col. i. 3, 1 Pet. i. 3; and in these places the dependent genitive is *τοῦ Κυρίου ἡμῶν Ι. Χ.* See under Eph. i. 3. A simple *ἡμῶν* follows the phrase, Phil. iv. 20, 1 Thess. iii. 11, 2 Thess. ii. 16; and it stands alone in 1 Cor. xv. 24, Eph. v. 20, Jas. i. 27. That *ἡμῶν* is connected only with *πατρός* is probable, because not only, as Ellicott says, is the idea in *Θεός* absolute, and that in *πατήρ* relative—the relation being indicated by the pronoun—but also because *πατήρ* has often, in the apostle's usage, a genitive after it when it follows *Θεός*: Rom. i. 7, 1 Cor. i. 3, 2 Cor. i. 2—"God our Father." The places last quoted, however, have not the conjunction. Nor will the article before *Θεοῦ* indicate that both clauses are connected with *ἡμῶν*, for it is usually inserted in such a connection of two predicates. Winer, § 19, 3, footnote 2. The rendering, then, is, "According to the will of God who is also our Father"—He who is God is also our Father—the article not repeated before the second noun, as both are predicates of the same person. In fine, this statement underlies the whole verse, and is not in mere connection with *τοῦ δόντος* (Chrysostom, Wieseler), nor with the clause before it—*ὅπως* (Meyer, Schott); nor is *θέλημα* the elective will of God in the rescue of certain individuals (Usteri). But Christ's Self-sacrifice, with its gracious and effective purpose, was no human plan, and is in no sense dependent on man's legal obedience. Its one source is the supreme and sovereign will of God, and that God is in relation to us a father who wins back his lost child. Luke xv. 11. The process of salvation stands out in divine and fatherly pre-eminence, and is not to be overlaid by man's devices which would either complicate or enfeeble it. In harmony with the eternal purpose, the Son of God incarnate gave Himself for us, and for our rescue. This redemptive work was no incident suddenly devised, nor was it an experiment made on the law and government of God. Alike in provision and result, it was in harmony with the highest will, and therefore perfect and permanent in nature—an argument against the Judaists.

Ver. 5. *Ὧ ἡ δόξα εἰς τοὺς αἰῶνας τῶν αἰώνων· ἀμήν*—"To whom be the glory for ever. Amen." Most probably the verb *εἴη* is understood (1 Pet. i. 2; 2 Pet. i. 2; Jude 2), not *ἐστί*, which some editions and versions present (the Vulgate having *cui est gloria*), and which is preferred by Lightfoot and Hofmann; nor *ἔστω*, though it be found in 2 Chron. ix. 8. It is more natural to regard the verse as a wish than as an affirmation, it being the devout aspiration suggested by the blessed and wonderful assertion of the previous verse, and quite in the apostle's style. Rom. ix. 5, xi. 36; 2 Cor. ix. 15; Eph. iii. 20. In such doxologies *δόξα* usually has the article, when, as here, it stands alone. Rom. xi. 36, xvi. 27, Eph. iii. 21, Phil. iv. 20, 2 Tim. iv. 18; but Luke ii. 14, xix. 38, are exceptions. Occasionally it wants the article when other substantives are added to it (Rom. ii. 10, which, however, is not a doxology; 1 Tim. i. 17; Jude 25); but it has the article in 1 Pet. iv. 11, Rev. i. 6, vii. 12. *Δόξα*, translated "praise" in the older English versions, does not here take the article, not as being an abstract noun (Matthies; Middleton, v. 1); but the meaning is, the glory which is His, or which characterizes Him and is especially His due. The doxology is based on the previous statement: To Him, for His gracious will that wrought out our deliverance through His Son's self-sacrifice, be the glory "to the ages of the ages." This last expression is not a pure Hebraism. Winer, § 36, 2. See under Eph. iii. 21. These ages of ages—still beginning, never ending—are as if in contrast to "this present age, an evil one," out of which believers are rescued. And this blessed change is not of law or of works in any sense, but solely from His will as its source, and by the self-oblation of Christ as its intermediate and effective means —means which have this rescue for their direct object—*voluntas Filii Patris voluntatem implet* (Jerome).

The Hebrew אָמֵן, "truly," is sometimes transferred in the Septuagint—*ἀμήν*, sometimes rendered by *γένοιτο* in praise and response, while Aquila translated it by *πεπιστωμένως*. "So ought it to be, so let it be, so shall it be" (Brown).

Ver. 6. *Θαυμάζω, ὅτι οὕτω ταχέως μετατίθεσθε ἀπὸ τοῦ καλέσαντος ὑμᾶς ἐν χάριτι Χριστοῦ*—"I marvel that you are so soon turning away (are removing yourselves) from Him who called you in the grace of Christ." The apostle now rushes, as one may say, on the main subject of the epistle, disclosing in a moment the feeling of disappointment which he could not repress or modify. By a sharp and sudden *θαυμάζω* he shows his surprise, not unmingled with anger and sorrow. The result had not been as he had fondly anticipated; nay, it was so contrary to previous manifestations on which he seems to have trusted, that his censure and chagrin are expressed by his amazement. Rebuke lurks under his surprise. The verb often from the context gathers into itself the ethical notion of what is culpable—surprise excited by what is object of censure. Mark vi. 6. Sometimes it is followed by *εἰ*, when what is thought of is matter of doubt, and by *ὅτι*, as here, when it is matter of fact. 1 John iii. 13. Sturz, *Lex. Xen. sub voce.*

Μετατίθεσθε, the present middle—not the aorist—will not bear the rendering, "ye are removed," nor, as Dr. Brown gives it, "ye have removed yourselves;" but, "ye are removing yourselves." Gal. iv. 9, 11, v. 10. The falling off was in process, not completed, as Chrysostom says: *οὐκ εἶπε μετεθέσθε, ἀλλὰ, μετατίθεσθε; οὐδέπω πιστεύω οὐδὲ ἡγοῦμαι ἀπηρτισμένην εἶναι τὴν ἀπάτην.* The verb cannot be aoristic in sense, for it is not a historical present (Matthies). Bernhardy, p. 372. Nor is it passive, as Beza, Erasmus, and others take it—*ut culpam in pseudapostolos derivet.* The Vulgate gives also *transferimini.* The verb signifies to transfer or put in another place locally, as Heb. xi. 5, Sept. Gen. v. 24; and then tropically, to put to another use, or to change place ideally. Jude 4. In the middle voice it signifies to change what belongs to one—*τὰ εἰρημένα*, Xen. *Mem.* iv. 2, 18, or *τὴν γνώμην*, Joseph. *Vita*, § 33, Herodotus, vii. 18; then to fall away from one party—*ἐκ* or *ἀπό*, 2 Macc. vii. 24—to another, *εἰς* or *πρός*, Polybius, iii. 118, 8, and often in the Sept. 1 Kings xxi. 25. Dionysius of Heraclea, who became an Epicurean from being a Stoic, rejoiced to be called *Μεταθέμενος*—*transpositus sive translatus* (Jerome). Athenæus, vii. p. 25, vol. iii. ed. Schweighaüser; Rost und Palm, *sub voce.*

There was special surprise that this changing of sides was going on *οὕτω ταχέως*, "so quickly." These words have been taken either in a positive or a relative sense. In the first sense, or as referring to manner, they have been supposed to signify *οὕτω εὐκόλως* (Koppe), *parum considerate* (Schott, Chrysostom), "*gewiss zu rasch*" (Rückert), or "so readily," "so rashly" (Lightfoot, Gwynne, and Hofmann). But relatively they have been taken as signifying "so soon" after—

1. The last visit of the apostle to them, as Bengel, Hilgenfeld, and Wieseler. No chronological inference can indeed be based on this exegesis, for it is untenable. The idea of his own visit is not in his mind, so far as his language implies, for *καλέσαντος* does not refer to him;—

2. Or "so soon" after their conversion, as Usteri, Olshausen, Meyer, Alford, Trana, Bisping, Jatho. This is no doubt true; but such a terminus does not seem directly in the apostle's eye. The points before his mind are: the one from which they are changing away—"Him who called them;" and that into which they were sinking—"another gospel." His mind turns at once to the false teachers, and their seductive influence; and therefore the meaning may be,

3. "So soon" after the intrusion of the false teachers among them. Chrysostom describes it as *ἐκ πρώτης προσβολῆς* (De Wette, and Ellicott). The apostle refers at once to these men, and to their disturbing and dangerous power. The Galatians had not the courage or constancy to resist the fascination of these unscrupulous Judaizers. But if the false teachers came among them after the apostle's recent visit (Acts xviii. 23), these two last opinions may so far coalesce. Their conversion, however, was a point further back, and connected with an earlier visit. But though, if one adopt the relative sense, the last opinion be preferable, yet probably the apostle had no precise point of time in his reference. The unexpectedness of the apostasy—involving, it is true, some latent temporal reference—appears to be his prominent element of rebuke. Taking in the whole crisis, so sudden and speedy,—so contrary to earlier auspicious tokens,—he might well say, without any distinct allusion to a precise date, *οὕτω ταχέως*. While the remark of Jerome, *Galatia translationem in nostra lingua sonat*, is without basis, this fickleness was quite in keeping with the Gallic character. See Introduction.

'Απὸ τοῦ καλέσαντος ὑμᾶς ἐν χάριτι Χριστοῦ—"from Him that called you in the grace of Christ." The words are not to be construed thus, *ἀπὸ τοῦ καλέσαντος—Χριστοῦ* ("from Him that called you—Christ"), as the Syriac, Jerome, Calvin,

Bengel, a-Lapide, and Brown. As Meyer remarks, however, against Schott and Matthies, the absence of the article would be no objection to this exegesis. Rom. ix. 5; 1 Pet. i. 15. The calling of believers is uniformly represented as the work of the Father in the Pauline theology, Rom. viii. 30, ix. 24, 1 Cor. i. 9, Gal. i. 15, 1 Thess. v. 24; and therefore τοῦ καλ. cannot be understood of the apostle, as Piscator, Balduin, Paulus, Bagge, Olearius, Gwynne, and even Doddridge. Their defection was all the more sinful, as the calling was from God. He alone effectually summons the soul to forgiveness and life, for He has access to it, and as His love yearns over it, His power is able to work the blessed change. God called them, and there is emphasis in the omission of Θεοῦ; as they needed not to be told who the Caller was, their defection was no sin of ignorance. It would be very strange if the apostle should in this place arrogate to himself what everywhere else he ascribes to God. Reuss, *Theol. Chret.* ii. 144. His own special work is thus characterized by him—εὐηγγελισάμεθα.

Ἐν χάριτι Χ.—"in the grace of Christ." Χριστοῦ is wanting in F, G, and in some of the Latin fathers, and is wrongly rejected by Griesbach. The phrase ἐν χάριτι is neither to be identified with διὰ χάριτος, nor εἰς χάριτα; Vulgate, *in gratiam*, that is, "to a participation of that grace," as Borger and Rückert explain it. The preposition ἐν denotes the element—that element here viewed as possessing instrumental power. Eph. ii. 13, vi. 14. It may thus be the instrumental adjunct (Wunder, *Sophocles*, *Philoct.* 60; Donaldson, § 47, 6), but the instrumentality is here regarded as immanent. Jelf, § 622. In some other passages with καλέω the preposition has its usual force. 1 Cor. vii. 18; 1 Thess. iv. 7. It is only or chiefly after verbs of motion that ἐν as result combines the sense of εἰς (Winer, 50, § 5), though originally they were the same word, related to each other; as μείς, μέν—δείς, δέν. Donaldson, *New Cratylus*, p. 318. They were called "in the grace of Christ;" for the call of God works only in that grace, never apart from it. Rom. v. 15. That call, sphering itself in Christ, and thus evincing its power, is on this account opposed to the νόμος, to the entire substance and spirit of the Judaizing doctrine. This grace of Christ, so rich and free, crowned in His atoning death and seen in all the blessings springing out of it, seems to be suggested by, or connected in the apostle's mind with, the phrase just used—"gave Himself for our sins." But they are falling off—

Εἰς ἕτερον εὐαγγέλιον—"to a different gospel"—the ruling element of which was not the grace of Christ, nor was its leading doctrine that "He gave Himself for our sins." No moral feature is expressed by the adjective, though it may be implied—not *corruptum et adulterinum*, as Calvin has it. The adjective *ἕτερον* marks distinction, *ἄλλος* indicates addition. 2 Cor. xi. 4. This signification of difference is seen in such compounds as ἑτερόγλωσσος, Ps. cxiii. 1; ἑτερογενής, Deut. xxii. 11; ἑτερόζυγος, Lev. xix. 19. It represents the Hebrew חָדָשׁ, "new," in Ex. i. 8, and זָר, *alienus*, in Ex. xxx. 9, "strange incense." It is found with an ethical sense also, Ex. xxi. 2, Num. xiv. 24; often as applied to false divinities, Dan. vii. 5, 6, 8. The adjective thus generally denotes distinction of kind. Even in Matt. xi. 3, adduced by Ellicott to show that *ἕτερος* does not always keep its distinctive meaning, it may signify not simply another individual, but one different in position and function. But *ἄλλος* is used in the parallel passage, Luke vii. 20. Tittmann, *De Synon.* p. 155. The Judaizing gospel, for it might be named gospel by its preachers and receivers too, was of a totally different genus from that proclaimed by the apostle, differing from it as widely as *νόμος* and *χάρις*, *ἔργα* and *πίστις*, bondage and liberty, flesh and spirit. But the apostle at once checks himself, lest the phrase *ἕτερον εὐαγγ.* should be misinterpreted, on the plea that by its use he had admitted the possibility of another and different gospel. Therefore he abruptly adds,

Ver. 7. *Ὃ οὐκ ἔστιν ἄλλο, εἰ μή*—"which is not another, save that:" it is no new or additional gospel—*οὐκ*, the negative being emphatic,—there is only one gospel. The *εὐαγγέλιον* expressed after *ἕτερον* stands vaguely and imperfectly, as the Judaizers might so name their system, but the *εὐαγγ.* implied after *ἄλλο* is used in its strict and proper sense. The connection with the following clause is variously understood.

1. Schott, preceded by a-Lapide, connects *εἰ μή* with *θαυμάζω*, making the previous clause a parenthesis: "*Miror vos tam cito deficere ad aliam doctrinam salutarem* (*quanquam hæc alia salutaris nulla est*) *nisi nonnulli sint.*" But such an utterance requires *ἐθαύμαζον ἄν*: "I should have wondered" that you fell away so soon, unless there had been some troubling

you. The sentence also becomes disjointed, and would make the apostle give only a hypothetical statement of the cause of his surprise.

2. Some make the whole previous sentence the antecedent to ὅ, such as Calvin, Grotius, Winer, Rückert, Olshausen: Your defection to another gospel is nothing else but this, or has no other source but this, that some are troubling you. But why should the apostle, after the censure implied in the last verse, really lift it by throwing the entire blame on the Judaizers? It would be to blame them in one breath, and make an apology for them in the next; and to refer *καλέσαντος* to Paul himself, as Gwynne does, does not remove the difficulty.

3. Others, again—and this has been the prevailing opinion—take *εὐαγγέλιον* as the antecedent: "which is no other gospel, because indeed there can be no other." So the Greek fathers, with Luther, Beza, Koppe, Borger, Usteri, De Wette, Hilgenfeld; the Peschito, ܐܝܢܐ ܕܠܐ ܐܝܬܘܗܝ, "which does not exist;" and the Genevan, "seeing there is no other."[1] But it seems plain that ἕτερος and ἄλλος, occurring together, must be used with some distinctiveness, for the one sentence suddenly guards against a false interpretation of the other.

4. The antecedent is, as Meyer, Hofmann, Wieseler, and others suppose, *ἕτερον εὐαγ.*: which different kind of gospel is no additional or co-ordinate gospel. The apostle does not say, it is not gospel; but it is not a second or other gospel, which may take a parallel or even subordinate rank with his. And he adds,

Εἰ μή—"save that." By this phrase, not equivalent to *ἀλλά*, as Dr. Brown argues in support of his exegesis, an exception is indicated to a negative declaration preceding, and it signifies *nisi*, "unless," "except," even in Matt. xii. 4, 1 Cor. vii. 17. Klotz-Devar. ii. p. 524; Herodotus, iv. 94, *ἄλλον Θεὸν, εἰ μή*; Xen. *Cyrop.* ii. 2, 11, *τί δ' ἄλλο, εἰ μή*; Aristoph. *Eq.* 615, *τί δ' ἄλλο; εἰ μή*; Poppo, *Thucyd.* vol. iii. P. 1, 216; Gayler, *Partic. Neg.* p. 97. The Vulgate has, *quod non est aliud nisi.* The meaning is, this gospel is another, only in so far as

[1] The Gothic of Ulfilas reads, "which is not another." Vömel translates, *Welches anderartige Evangelium in nichts anderem besteht als*, Frankfurt 1865.

Τινές εἰσιν οἱ ταράσσοντες ὑμᾶς—"there are some who are troubling you." In this participial phrase, as Winer says, the substantivized participle is a definite predicate to an indefinite subject. A. Buttmann, p. 254. The apostle says of the *τινές*, that it was their function or their characteristic to be disturbing the Galatian converts. Luke xviii. 9; Col. ii. 8. Bernhardy, p. 318. *Τινές* neither marks insignificance, *ἀνώνυμοι* (Semler), nor *infelices* (Bengel), nor yet paucity, *pauci duntaxat sunt* (Winer). Though not named, they were well known, but the apostle would not further characterize them. An extraordinary interpretation of *τινές* is given by Wordsworth, who takes it as the predicate: "unless they who are troubling you are somebody," persons of some importance. The exegesis is not sustained by any of the examples which he has adduced, for *τινές* in them is marked by its position as a predicate, and the use of *τι* is not to the point. Nor would the clause so misunderstood bring out any self-consistent meaning. The verb *ταράσσω*, used physically (John v. 7), signifies to put in fear or alarm (Matt. ii. 3), then to disquiet (John xii. 27), to perplex (Acts xv. 24). The apostle adds of those disturbers, what their desire or purpose was:

Καὶ θέλοντες μεταστρέψαι τὸ εὐαγγέλιον τοῦ Χριστοῦ—"and desiring to subvert the gospel of Christ." The verb *μεταστρέφω* is to change, to change into the opposite (Acts ii. 20; Jas. iv. 9), or to change to the worse. Aristot. *Rhet.* i. 15, p. 60, ed. Bekker; Sept. 1 Sam. x. 8; Sirach xi. 31. The genitive *τοῦ Χριστοῦ* may either mean the gospel which is Christ's as proclaimed by Him, or that which has Him for its object. One might say that the former is preferable, as then the different gospel preached by the Judaizers would stand in contrast to that proclaimed by Christ Himself. Still there would in the latter exegesis be this contrast, that as the gospel preached by them was conformity to the Mosaic ritual, it was in antagonism to that gospel which has Christ for its theme, for by its perversion it would render "Christ of none effect." Whatever would derogate from the sufficiency of Christ's gospel, or hamper its freeness, is a subversion of it, no matter what guise it may assume, or how insignificant the addition or subtraction may seem. Bengel's oft-quoted remark, *Re ipsa non poterant, volebant tamen obnixe*, is true in result. Yet they in their preaching revolutionized the gospel, and such is the apostle's charge against them.

Ver. 8. Ἀλλὰ καὶ ἐὰν ἡμεῖς ἢ ἄγγελος ἐξ οὐρανοῦ εὐαγγελίζηται ὑμῖν παρ' ὃ εὐηγγελισάμεθα ὑμῖν, ἀνάθεμα ἔστω—"But if we, or an angel from heaven, should preach to you any other gospel different from what we have preached to you, let him be accursed." There is some difference of reading. K, Theodoret, Œcumenius, have εὐαγγελίζεται; while A, ℵ, and others, have εὐαγγελίσηται. There are also variations with regard to ὑμῖν: F and ℵ omit it; B, H, place it before the verb; the majority of MSS. place it after the verb; while D[1] has ὑμᾶς. "But" be the τινές who they may who seek to subvert the gospel, they incur an awful peril. The καί belongs to ἐάν, "even if." The case put so strongly is one which may never have occurred; but its possibility is assumed, though it may be very improbable. Hermann, *Opuscula,* iv. p. 95; Hermann, *Vigerus,* vol. ii. 664, London 1824; Jelf, § 861. On the difference of εἰ καί and καὶ εἰ, see under Phil. ii. 17; Kühner, § 824; Hartung, vol. i. pp. 139, etc. The ἡμεῖς—not himself alone, the pronoun being expressed and emphatic—may take in, though not necessarily, ἀδελφοὶ σὺν ἐμοὶ of ver. 2, or perhaps Silvanus and Timothy, fellow-preachers (Hofmann).[1] He was speaking by divine commission when he preached, and he had no right to alter the message. If it should ever by any possibility happen that he did so, on him should fall the anathema. "We or an angel from heaven"—no fallen spirit who might rejoice in falsehood, but one ἐξ οὐρανοῦ; the phrase being joined to ἄγγελος, and not to the verb (2 Cor. xi. 14), which agrees with ἄγγελος. An angel from heaven is highest created authority, but it cannot exalt itself against a divine commission. An angel preaching a Judaizing gospel would be opposing that God who had "called them in the grace of Christ." Chrysostom supposes allusion to other apostles. The verb εὐαγγελίζηται is here followed by the dative of person: iv. 13; Luke iv. 18; Rom. i. 15; 1 Cor. xv. 1; 1 Pet. iv. 6. The variety of construction which it has in the New Testament—it being found sometimes absolutely, sometimes with accusative or dative, often with accusative of thing and dative of person—may have

[1] Against the view of Hofmann, see Laurent, *Neutestam. Studien*, p. 120, Gotha 1866.

originated the variations connected with ὑμῖν, though Lightfoot, from these variations, regards the word as doubtful. The spurious preaching is characterized as

Παρ' ὃ εὐαγγελισάμεθα ὑμῖν—"contrary to that which we preached to you" (Ellicott), or "beyond" it (Alford). The *παρά* can bear either meaning. Bernhardy, p. 259. The Vulgate has *præterquam*, and some of the Greek fathers give the same sense, so Beza also; while "against," *contra*, is the interpretation of Theodoret, Winer, Rückert, Matthies, De Wette, Jatho, Turner, Estius, Windischmann. Thus Rom. i. 26, *παρὰ φύσιν*; Acts xviii. 13, *παρὰ νόμον*; Xen. *Mem.* i. 1, 18. Examples may be found in Donaldson, § 485. What is specifically different from it, must in effect be contrary to it. Rom. xi. 24, xvi. 17. Usually Catholic interpreters take the sense of "contrary to" (Estius, Bisping); and Lutherans adopt that of "beyond," or "in addition to," as if in condemnation (*aus blinder Polemik*, Bisping) of the traditions on which the Romish Church lays such stress. But the apostle refers to oral teaching only, and the preposition *παρά* glancing back to *ἕτερος*, naturally signifies "beside," that is, in addition to, or different from, the gospel,—or what is really another gospel. But the gospel is one, and can have no rival.

Ἀνάθεμα ἔστω—"let him be accursed" (v. 10). *Ἀνάθεμα*: the earlier classical form was *ἀνάθημα*, *Ἀττικῶς* (Moeris). Lobeck, *Phrynichus*, p. 249. Thus *ἐπίθεμα*, *ἐπίθημα*; *εὕρεμα*, *εὕρημα*.[1] The general sense is, "laid up," set apart to God: *τῷ Θεῷ ἀνατιθέμενον* (Suidas). The meaning of the word in the New Testament is derived through the Septuagint, where it represents the Hebrew חֵרֶם, something so set apart to God as to be destroyed or consecrated to divine vengeance. The other form, *ἀνάθημα*, retained its original meaning, comprehending all gifts to the gods. Xen. *Anab.* v. 3, 5. Such gifts were often ornamental, and Hesychius defines it by *κόσμημα*; but the other form, *ἀνάθεμα*, he identifies with *ἐπικατάρατος*. The distinction begins to appear in the Septuagint, though differences of reading prevent it being fully traced and recognised. In Lev. xxvii. 28, 29, the living thing devoted to God is to be surely put to death: *Πᾶν ἀνάθεμα ἅγιον ἁγίων ἔσται*

[1] *Πάντες πεζολόγοι ἐπίθημα καὶ ἀνάθημα λέγουσιν.* Cramer, *Anecd. Græca*, vol. i. 165, Oxon. 1835.

τῷ Κυρίῳ . . . θανάτῳ θανατωθήσεται: the city of Jericho, and all in it, was declared ἀνάθεμα Κυρίῳ Σαβαώθ. Josh. vi. 16, 17. This consecration of Jericho to utter ruin was in obedience to the command, Deut. xiii. 14–16, ἀναθέματι ἀναθεματιεῖτε αὐτήν, and was a reproduction of an older scene (Num. xxi. 1-3), where a city was devoted, and then truly named חָרְמָה, ἀνάθεμα. Comp. Josh. vii. 11. In the case of Jericho, portion of the spoil was set apart for the sacred treasury, and part was to be utterly destroyed—two modes of consecration to God, for divine blessing and for divine curse—God glorified in it, or glorified on it. Trench, *Syn.* p. 17, 1st ser. In Ezek. xliv. 29, the offering of a dedicated thing given to the priests (the same Hebrew term) is rendered ἀφόρισμα in the Septuagint, but ἀνάθημα by Aquila, Symmachus, and Theodotion. Orig. *Hex.* tom. ii. p. 321, ed. Montfaucon. In the Apocrypha the distinction appears to be preserved: 2 Macc. ix. 16, καλλίστοις ἀναθήμασι κοσμήσειν; 3 Macc. iii. 14; Judith xvi. 19; also in Joseph. *Antiq.* xv. 11, 3, *Bell. Jud.* ii. 17, 3. So in the New Testament, Luke xxi. 5, the temple adorned with goodly stones, καὶ ἀναθήμασι, "and gifts." But the other form, ἀνάθεμα, occurs six times, and in all of them it has the meaning of accursed. Acts xxiii. 14; Rom. ix. 3; 1 Cor. xii. 3, xvi. 22; and Gal. i. 8, 9. Theodoret, on Rom. ix. 3, recognises this διπλῆν διάνοιαν, which he gives to ἀνάθημα; also on Isa. xiii., and on Zeph. i. See also Suidas, *sub voce;* Chrysostom on Rom. ix. 3; and Suicer, *sub voce.* Among the ecclesiastical writers, ἀνάθεμα came to signify excommunication, the cursing and separation of one put out of communion. Bingham, *Antiquities, Works,* vol. v. p. 471, London 1844. Such a use of the word was natural. Council of Laodicea, *Canon* xxix. But to justify this use by any appeal to the New Testament is vain. Nowhere has it this meaning, but a darker and a more awful one. Nor does חֵרֶם in the Old Testament ever signify ecclesiastical separation; it is synonymous with ἀπωλεία, Isa. liv. 5; ἐξολόθρευμα, 1 Sam. xv. 21; ἀφάνισμα, Deut. vii. 2. On the various forms of the Jewish curse, see Selden, *De Syned.* viii.; *Opera,* vol. i. p. 883, etc. The idea of excommunication cannot be adopted here (Grotius, Semler, Flatt, Baumgarten-Crusius, Hammond, and Waterland); for it is contrary to the usage of the New Testament, and could not be applicable to an "angel from heaven." Excommunication is described in very different terms, as in John ix. 22, xii. 42, xvi. 2, or Luke vi. 22, 1 Cor. v. 2, 13. Winer, *sub voce.* How tame Grotius, *cum eo nihil vobis sit commercii;* or Rosenmüller, *excludatur e cœtu vestro.* The preacher of another gospel exposes himself to the divine indignation, and the awful penalty incurred by him is not inflicted by man: he falls "into the hands of the living God." See Wieseler's long note.

Ver. 9. Ὡς προειρήκαμεν—"as we have said before." The reference implied in προ. is doubtful. By a great number—including Chrysostom, Bengel, Winer, Neander—the reference is supposed to be simply to the previous verse: "As we have just said, so I repeat it." 2 Cor. vii. 3; 2 Macc. iii. 7; and Winer, § 40. Others, as the Peschito, Borger, Usteri, Hilgenfeld, Meyer, Wieseler, suppose the allusion to be to a previous visit of the apostle. The use of the perfect, though not decisive, and the antithesis of ἄρτι in the following clause, favour this view. The language would have been different had the apostle wished to say nothing more. See v. 21; 2 Cor. xiii. 2; 1 Thess. iv. 6. This opinion is confirmed by the sameness of tense of the two verbs, as if they referred to the same event. The re-asseveration in v. 2, 3 is no case in point to be adduced as an objection; for it has no verb compounded with προ, and the statement in ver. 3 is far from being a repetition of the second verse. *Εὐαγγελισάμεθα, προειρήκαμεν—καὶ ἄρτι* mark a more distinct lapse of time than a recurrence to what had just been written, and the change from εὐαγγελίσαμεθα to παρελάβετε points to the same conclusion: As he had said when among them by way of affirmation and warning.

Καὶ ἄρτι πάλιν λέγω—"and now again I say." The change from the plural προειρήκαμεν to the present λέγω is significant. The previous warning was uttered by the apostle and his fellow-labourers, but the following sentence is based on his sole apostolical authority. This is not, as Rückert makes it, part of the *protasis* or preceding sentence: "As I said before, I now say again." The meaning is: As we said before, so now I say again,—πάλιν referring to repetition of the same sentiment, and ἄρτι in contrast with προ. in composition with the verb. The first of these opinions preserves, as Ellicott says, the classical meaning of ἄρτι, for it refers to a time just passed away. Matt. ix. 18. *Tempus quodque proximum, ἄρτι et ἀρτίως significant,*" Lobeck, *Phryn.* pp. 18–20. But later writers use it as it is employed in this clause, "now," or in this next sentence. Matt. iii. 15; John ix. 19, 25, xiii. 7; 1 Cor. xiii. 12. The statement is:

Εἴ τις ὑμᾶς εὐαγγελίζεται παρ' ὃ παρελάβετε—"If any man is preaching to you a gospel different from what ye received, let him be accursed." The Rheims version tries to preserve the original in both verses: "evangelize to you beside that which we have evangelized to you." The statement is now made merely conditional, or the fact is assumed by *εἰ* with the indicative. The case is put as one that may be found real. Donaldson, § 502. See also Tischendorf, *Præf.* p. lvii. 7 ed.; Klotz-Devarius, vol. ii. 455; Luke xiii. 9; Acts v. 38, 39. The verb *εὐαγγ.* is here followed by the accusative of person, *ὑμᾶς*, emphatic from its position. No other example occurs in the writings of the apostle. But we have the same construction in Luke iii. 18, Acts viii. 25, 40, xiii. 32, xiv. 15, 21, xvi. 10, 1 Pet. i. 12. *Phrynichus*, ed. Lobeck, 266, etc.; Winer, § 32. For *παρ' ὅ*, see on previous verse. The verb *παραλαμβάνω*, followed either by *ἀπό* or by *παρά*, pointing to the source, is to receive, to take into the mind, what is given by instruction, and corresponds to the *ὑμῖν* of the preceding verse. In this verse the evangel, which is the theme of the verb, goes out on them as its direct objects—*ὑμᾶς*; in the other it is given to them, or for their benefit—*ὑμῖν*—and they received it. The change may have been intentionally suggestive. For *ἀνάθεμα ἔστω*, see previous verse.

Ver. 10. *Ἄρτι γὰρ ἀνθρώπους πείθω, ἢ τὸν Θεόν;*—"For do I now conciliate men or God?" or, "Now, is it men I am conciliating, or God?" The emphatic *ἄρτι* of this verse must have the same sense as that of the preceding verse—"now," at the present moment, or as I am writing. It cannot contrast vaguely the apostle's present with his previous unconverted Jewish state, as is held by Winer, Rückert, Matthies, Bisping, Olshausen, Neander, and Turner. For, grammatically, we cannot well sever the second *ἄρτι* in meaning and reference from the first; and historically, the favour of men was not a ruling motive with the apostle in his pharisaic state. Phil. iii. The connection is somewhat more difficult, as expressed by *γάρ*. It might mean, "Well, now, am I pleasing men?" Klotz-

Devarius, ii. 245. But it rather states an argument. It is no apology, as Dr. Brown takes it, for the preceding language; nor, as Alford similarly asserts, "softening the seeming harshness of the saying." It states the reason idiomatically why he pronounces anathema on the Judaizers,—that he did it from divine sanction, or in accordance with the divine will. His fidelity was so stern, that it might be unpalatable to his enemies; but he was securing through it the friendship of God. There is some probability that he is rebutting a calumny of his opponents (Usteri, Lightfoot), based on a misconstruction of some previous portion of his career, such as the circumcision of Timothy. The verb πείθω, to persuade, signifies, by a natural transition, to conciliate by persuasion or to make friends of. Acts xii. 20, xiv. 19. Josephus, πεῖσαι τὸν Θεὸν, *Ant.* iv. 6, 5; Ζηνὸς ἦτορ ἔπεισε, Pindar, *Ol.* ii. 80, ed. Dissen; δῶρα Θεοὺς πείθει, a portion of a line ascribed by Suidas to Hesiod; Plato, *De Repub.* iii. 344, 390 E, do. *Opera*, vol. iii. pp. 146, 231, ed. Stallbaum; similarly Euripides, *Medea*, 960. There is no occasion to attach to the verb the idea of *conatus* as distinct from *effectus:* "For am I, at the moment of uttering such an anathema against perverters of the gospel, making friends of men or of God?" What but faithfulness to my divine commission can prompt me to it? It was no human passion, no personal animosity, no envious or jealous emotion at being superseded in the affections of the Galatian churches: it was simply duty done in compliance with the ruling motive of his soul, and to enjoy and secure the divine complacency. The noun ἀνθρώπους, wanting the article, is "men generally," while Θεόν has it, as if to specialize it by the contrast. The connection of πείθω with τὸν Θεόν is no formal zeugma, though the sense is necessarily changed with such a change of object. What fully applies to men can only in a vaguer reference apply to God; but it has suggested several improbable forms of exegesis. Calvin goes the length of interposing a κατά before the two nouns, owing to what he calls the ambiguity of the Greek construction; and nothing, he adds, is more common with the Greeks than to leave κατά understood: "Do I persuade according to men or God?" Webster and Wilkinson apparently follow Estius, *non apud homines judices, sed apud tribunal Dei causam hanc ago*, but without any warrant or adduced example. Piscator renders, "Do I persuade you to believe men or God?" *Utrum vobis suadeo ut hominibus credatis an ut Deo?* Luther, Erasmus, Vatablus, and others give, *Num res humanas suadeo an divinas?* But πείθω governing a person is distinct in meaning from πείθω governing a thing or object; πείθειν τινα being, as Meyer remarks, quite distinct from πείθειν τι. The meaning is more fully explained in the following clause, where the apostle adds more broadly:

Ἢ ζητῶ ἀνθρώποις ἀρέσκειν;—"or am I seeking to please men?" the stress being on ἀνθρώποις. To please men was not his endeavour or pervading aim: it was no motive of his; for he adds:

Εἰ ἔτι ἀνθρώποις ἤρεσκον, Χριστοῦ δοῦλος οὐκ ἂν ἤμην—"If still men I were pleasing, Christ's servant I should not be." The leading nouns, ἀνθρώποις and Χριστοῦ, are in emphatic contrast. The received text reads εἰ γὰρ ἔτι, after the slender authority, D[2, 3], E, K, L, the Syriac and Greek fathers; whereas A, B, D[1], F, G, ℵ, the Vulgate, and many Latin fathers want it. The asyndeton, however, is the more powerful. Tischendorf, indeed, says, *a correctore alienissimum est;* but the γάρ seems really to be a natural emendation, as if giving point to the argument by it as a connecting particle. There is no *conatus* in the imperfect, as Usteri, Schott, Bagge, and others hold. He says, not, "if I were studying to please;" but, "if," the study being successful, "I were pleasing men." The result implies the previous effort. The particle ἔτι, "still," gives intensity to the declaration, and looks back to ἄρτι. Bäumlein, *Griech. Part.* p. 118. If, after all that has happened me, my devoted service to Christ, and the deadly hostility I have encountered, I were yet pleasing men,—if yet such a motive ruled me, Christ's servant I should not be. The form of the imperfect ἤμην is peculiar, being used Ἑλληνικῶς, according to Moeris. It occurs in the later writers, and is used by Xenophon, *Cyro.* vi. 1, 9, and Lysias, *Areopag.* p. 304, ed. Dobson. Its use is not confined to its occurrence with ἄν. Lobeck, *Phrynichus*, p. 152. It is quite common in the New Testament: Matt. xxv. 35, John xi. 15, Acts x. 30, xi. 5, 17, 1 Cor. xiii. 11,—all without ἄν. After εἰ with a past indicative in the protasis, ἂν in the apodosis points out an impossible condition. Donaldson, § 502. The apostle calls himself δοῦλος in various places. Compare John xiii. 16, xv.

15, 20; Rom. i. 1; Tit. i. 1; Phil. i. 1; Col. iv. 12; 2 Tim. ii. 24. Here he may refer to the inner nature of all Christian service, which admits of no compromise between the Master and the world, and especially to such service embodied and wrought out in the varied spheres and amidst the numerous temptations of his apostleship. See under Phil. i. 1. The Greek fathers, followed by Koppe, Paulus, Rückert, take the words in a historical sense: If my object had been to please men, I should not have become a servant of Christ. But, as has been remarked, *οὐκ ἂν ἐγενόμην* would have been more fitting words to express such an idea. Besides, such a contrast does not seem to be before the apostle's mind, nor could such a reference be in harmony with the supernatural and resistless mode in which he had become a servant of Christ. It is better to take the words in an ethical sense: "I should not be Christ's servant:" man-pleasing and His service are in direct conflict. No one can serve Him who makes it his study to be popular with men. For to His servant His will is the one law, His work the one service, His example the one pattern, His approval the continuous aim, and His final acceptance the one great hope. 1 Cor. iv. 2–4; 2 Cor. xi. 23. This declaration of the apostle as to his ruling motive is not opposed to what he says of himself in 1 Cor. ix. 20, x. 33: "To the Jews I became as a Jew;" "all things to all men;" "to please all men in all things." There he is referring to his versatility of accommodation to national and individual humours and failings in cases where no principle was involved. Though he claimed entire liberty, he would not, by acting it out, wound unnecessarily the feelings of a "weak brother." To please himself, he would not stir up prejudices in fellow-believers. To conciliate them he "made himself the servant of all," by continuous self-denial in things indifferent. He might, but he did not; he could, but he would not. He had a claim of support from the churches, but he preferred at Corinth to labour with his own hands for his maintenance. He believed that an idol was "nothing in the world," and that one could without sin sit down to a repast in a Gentile's house; but if his liberty were challenged by a scrupulous conscience, he should at once abstain. Without a grudge he yielded his freedom, though he felt the objection to be frivolous, for he sought "the profit of the many." But while there was such wise and tender forbearance in minor matters which were naturally left open questions among believers, many of whom could not rise to the realization of "the perfect law of liberty," his adherence to principle was uniform and unyielding towards all classes, and on all occasions. These two modes of action are quite coalescent in a mind so upright, and yet so considerate,—so stern, and yet so unselfish,—so elevated, and yet so very practical, as was that of the apostle of the Gentiles.

The apostle in the first verse had asserted the reality and divine origin of his apostleship,—that it came from the one highest source, Jesus Christ; and then, in vers. 8, 9, he had maintained, in distinct and unmistakeable phrase, that the gospel preached by him was the one true gospel. He now takes up the apologetic part of the epistle, and proceeds to explain and defend his second position, for both were livingly connected. The gospel preached by him was in no sense human, as his apostleship rested in no sense on a human basis. He had not been one of the original twelve, and he had not companied with Christ; and this posteriority had been apparently laid hold of to his disadvantage, as if his gospel were but secondary, and he had been indebted for it and his office to human teaching and authority. But the truth proclaimed by him and the office held by him, not only sprang from a primary relationship to Christ, but had even no human medium of conveyance. The apostle therefore argues this point, that his gospel had Christ for its immediate source, and revelation for its medium of disclosure to him; that he was not indebted to the other apostles for it; that he had held no consultation with them as his tutors or advisers, for his apostleship rested on a basis of its own but identical with theirs; and that, in fine, they recognised it not as a derived and dependent office, or as in any way holding of them, but as a distinct, collateral, and original commission. Therefore he says:

Ver. 11. *Γνωρίζω δὲ ὑμῖν, ἀδελφοί*—"Now I declare unto you, brethren." Instead of δέ, which is found in A, $D^{2,3}$, K, L, ℵ, Chrysostom and Theodoret, and in the Coptic and Syriac versions, γάρ is read in B, D^{1}, F, $ℵ^{1}$, and by Jerome, the Vulgate, and Augustine. Tischendorf has γάρ in his second edition, but δέ in his seventh; and the reading is adopted by

Scholz, Griesbach, Lachmann, and the Textus Receptus. Authorities are thus nearly balanced. Possibly the apologetic nature of the section might suggest to a copyist to begin it with *γάρ*, argumentative; whereas *δέ* is only transitional to another topic, or to some additional illustration of it. It may, however, be replied, that the insertion of *δέ* by copyists was influenced by its occurrence with this verb in 1 Cor. xv. 1, 2 Cor. viii. 1. The topic has been twice referred to, in 1 and 9; so that this verse does not spring by direct logical connection out of the last verses, but rather gathers up the pervading thought of the previous paragraph. *Γνωρίζω* is a term of emphatic solemnity with the apostle (1 Cor. xii. 3, xv. 1; 2 Cor. viii. 1), as if he were obliging himself to repeat, formally and fully, what had before been so explicitly made known. They are called *ἀδελφοί*—still dear to him, in spite of their begun aberration, as in iii. 15, iv. 12, v. 13, vi. 1. What the apostle certified them of was:

Τὸ εὐαγγέλιον τὸ εὐαγγελισθὲν ὑπ' ἐμοῦ ὅτι οὐκ ἔστι κατὰ ἄνθρωπον—"As to the gospel preached by me, that is not after man." This clause may characterize his gospel wherever preached, *ὃ κηρύσσω ἐν τοῖς ἔθνεσι* (ii. 2); but the pointed language of vers. 6–9 specializes it as the gospel preached by him in Galatia. The attraction here is a common one, especially after verbs of knowing and declaring, the principal clause attracting from the dependent one, as if by anticipation. 1 Cor. iii. 20, 2 Cor. xii. 3; Winer, § 66, 5; Krüger, § 61, 1. The noun and participle give a fulness and impressiveness to the statement, as if referring back to vers. 8 and 9 (compare i. 16, ii. 2). The gospel preached by me is not *κατὰ ἄνθρωπον*—"after man." The phrase does not express origin, as Augustine, a-Lapide, and Estius assert, though it implies it. The Syriac renders ܡܢ, "from," as it does *ἀπό* in ver. 1, and *παρά* in ver. 12. It means "after man's style." Winer, § 49. Xen. *Mem.* iv. 4, *κατ' ἄνθρωπον νομοθέτου*; Sophocles, *Ajax*, 747, *μὴ κατ' ἄνθρωπον φρονεῖ*; *Œdip. Col.* 598, *ἢ κατ' ἄνθρωπον νοσεῖς*. For in form, quality, and contents, it was not human or manlike; it was Godlike in its truths, and in their connection and symmetry. It was God's style of purpose and thought—in no sense man's, and all about it, in disclosure and result, in adaptation and destiny, proves it to be "after" Him whose "ways are not our ways." Turner presses too much upon the phrase, when he gives as its meaning, "in character with human weakness and infirmity."

Ver. 12. *Οὐδὲ γὰρ ἐγὼ παρὰ ἀνθρώπου παρέλαβον αὐτὸ*— "For neither did I receive it from man." *Γάρ* assigns the ground: The gospel I preach is not according to man, for man did not teach it to me. Through no human medium did I get it, not even from James, John, or Cephas, who are reckoned "pillars." I got it from the same source as they—from the one Divine Teacher. I was no more man-taught than they were, for I had apocalyptic intercourse with the Lord as really as they had personal communications; and I received what they received. This side-glance at the other apostles is plainly implied in the emphatic position or relation of the first three words, *οὐδὲ γὰρ ἐγώ*. *Οὐδὲ γάρ* is different from the absolute *οὐ γάρ*, and also from *οὐδὲ ἐγὼ γάρ*, which might give a different turn to the thought. The pronoun expresses emphatic individuality, and *γάρ* occupies its usual place. It is not *οὐδέ* for *οὐ* (Schirlitz, § 59); nor is the meaning *nam ne ego quidem* (Winer), "not even I, who might have been expected to be man-taught." *Οὐδέ*, as Hartung remarks, is in negative sentences parallel to *καὶ γάρ* in positive sentences (vol. i. p. 211); Herodot. i. 3; Æschylus, *Agam.* 1501. This implied reference in *οὐδέ* is common: *ut aliquid extrinsecus adsumendum sit, cui id, quod per οὐδέ particulam infertur, opponatur.* Klotz-Devar. ii. 707; Kühner, *Xen. Mem.* p. 94; and Borneman, *Xen. Conv.* p. 200, says truly that *οὐδὲ γάρ* and *οὐ γάρ* differ as *neque enim* and *non enim.* Lightfoot objects that this interpretation is not reflected in the context; but surely the following paragraph plainly implies anxiety on the apostle's part to free himself from a charge of human tuition, and thus place himself in this matter on an equality with the twelve. Matt. xxi. 27; Luke xx. 8; John v. 22, viii. 11, 42; Rom. viii. 7. The reference cannot be, as Rückert and Schott make it, to those taught by himself, *quibus ipse tradiderit evangelium;* for that is in no sense the question involved.

The source denied is, *παρὰ ἀνθρώπου*, "from man," with the notion of conveyance, *παρά* denoting a nearer source than *ἀπό*.

It might have been *ἀπὸ X.*, and yet *παρὰ ἀνθρώπου*—ultimately from Jesus, yet mediately to him from a human source. But man was not the nearer source of it, as some had apparently insinuated; it was to him no *παράδοσις*. The distinctive meanings of *παρά* and *ἀπό*—for this verb may be used with either—seem in some cases almost to blend. The apostle in a matter of revelation which excludes all human medium, may drop the less distinction of near or remote. He adds:

Οὔτε ἐδιδάχθην—"nor was I taught it." The reading *οὐδὲ* is found in A, D[1], F, ℵ, and is but ill supported, being probably an unconscious assimilation to the previous particle commencing the verse. The adverb *οὔτε* often occurs similarly, and, as Winer says, divides the negation (§ 55–6). The *οὐδέ* belongs only to the previous clause, and its connection with the foregoing verse. The *οὔτε* is not co-ordinate with *οὐδέ*, but subordinate. Hartung, vol. i. 201; A. Buttman, 315; Klotz-Devarius, ii. 709. The difference between the verbs in this denial is, that the first may refer to truth presented in an objective or historical form (1 Cor. xi. 23), while the other may refer to his subjective mastery of it in a doctrinal or systematic connection, the first verb being, as Bengel says, to learn *sine labore*, and the second to learn *cum labore.* The verbs do not differ, as Brown following Beza maintains, as if the first denoted reception of authority to preach, *apostolatus onus Paulo impositum*, and the other referred to instruction; for *αὐτό* goes back distinctly to *εὐαγγέλιον*. See Mark vii. 4; 1 Cor. xv. 1–3; Phil. iv. 9.

Ἀλλὰ δι' ἀποκαλύψεως Ἰησοῦ Χριστοῦ—"but through revelation of Jesus Christ." *Ἀλλά* is strongly adversative. The one medium was revelation, and that revelation came from Christ; the genitive being that of author as in formal contrast to *παρὰ ἀνθρώπου*, denoting origin. But one may say, that a revelation from Jesus Christ is also a revelation of Jesus Christ, Himself being theme as well as source; and thus the phrase, though not grammatically, yet really and exegetically, includes a contrast also with *κατὰ ἄνθρωπον*, and virtually asserts of his teaching what he had declared of his apostleship, that it was *οὐκ ἀπ' ἀνθρώπων οὐδὲ δι' ἀνθρώπου* (i. 1). See under ver. 16.

The apostle now proceeds to give an autobiographical proof

of his position: that his gospel came from direct communication with Christ; that it was as original and trustworthy as those of the others who were apostles before him; that for a long period after his conversion he had no communication with any of them; that three years elapsed before he saw one of the twelve, and then he saw Peter only for a fortnight; and that fourteen years additional passed away ere he had any interview with the pillars of the church. His gospel was therefore in no sense dependent on them, nor had his first spheres of labour been either assigned or superintended by them. He had felt no dependence on them, and was conscious of no responsibility to them. Separate and supreme apostolical authority, therefore, belonged to him; and it sealed and sanctioned the message which it was the work of his life to publish.

Ver. 13. Ἠκούσατε γὰρ τὴν ἐμὴν ἀναστροφήν ποτε ἐν τῷ Ἰουδαϊσμῷ—"For ye heard of my manner of life in Judaism." *Γάρ* formally commences the historical proof, and the verb ἠκούσατε beginning the sentence has the stress upon it: Ye heard, not have heard, referring to an indefinite past time. It was matter of rumour and public notoriety. His mode of life or his conduct he calls ἀναστροφή,—literally and in Latin, *conversatio*, "conversation" in old English. He uses in Acts xxvi. 4, in reference to the same period of his life, τὴν βίωσίν μου. Comp. Eph. iv. 22, 1 Tim. iv. 12, Heb. xiii. 7, Jas. iii. 13, 2 Macc. ii. 21, viii. 1. The word in its ethical sense belongs to the later Greek. Polybius, iv. 82, 1. The position of ποτέ is peculiar, no article as τήν is attached to it, and it occurs after the noun. It is used with the verb in Eph. ii. 3, and in Eph. iv. 22 the phrase occurs, κατὰ τὴν προτέραν ἀναστροφήν. In the same way, words are sometimes separated which usually come in between the article and the substantive (Winer, § 20). The apostle places ποτέ as he would if he had used the verb. Such is one explanation. Similarly Plato, *De Leg.* 685 D, ἡ τῆς Τροίας ἅλωσις τὸ δεύτερον, where Stallbaum says that τὸ δεύτερον is placed *per synesin ob nomen verbale* ἅλωσις. *Opera*, vol. x. p. 290; Ellendt, *Lex. Sophoc. sub voce.* The entire phrase contains one complete idea, as the absence of the article seems to imply. Winer, § 20, 2*b*. As the verb is followed by ἐν, denotive of element, in 2 Cor. i. 12, Eph. ii. 3, so the noun is here closely connected with a similar ἐν; and, according to Donaldson, the position of ποτε is caused by the verb included in the noun. The element of his mode of life was—

Ἐν τῷ Ἰουδαϊσμῷ—"in Judaism," not Mosaism, not exactly the old and primitive Hebrew faith and worship, nor the modern or current theology, but rather ritualism and the mass of beliefs and traditions held by Pharisaism. The abstract noun is specialized by the article, and it occurs in 2 Macc. ii. 21, xiv. 38, 4 Macc. iv. 26, and the correspondent verb meets us in Gal. ii. 14. Similarly he says, Acts xxvi. 5, τῆς ἡμετέρας θρησκείας, this last noun being more special and referring to worship or ceremonial. Judaism is here the religious life of the Jews or Pharisees, in its varied spheres of nutriment and service. See under Phil. iii. The apostle now honestly adduces one characteristic of his previous life in Judaism—

Ὅτι καθ' ὑπερβολὴν ἐδίωκον τὴν ἐκκλησίαν τοῦ Θεοῦ, καὶ ἐπόρθουν αὐτήν—"how that beyond measure I was persecuting the church of God, and was destroying it." The conjunctive ὅτι, frequently used after ἀκούω without any intervening sentence (Madvig, § 159), introduces the first special point in the apostle's previous life in Judaism which he wishes to specify. The imperfects ἐδίωκον and ἐπόρθουν are to be taken in the strict sense (Schmalfeld, § 55). The second verb has been often rendered, "was endeavouring to destroy." So Chrysostom, Theodoret, Theophylact, give it this sense—σβέσαι ἐπεχείρει. The imperfects represent an action carried on during his state of Judaism, but left unfinished owing to his sudden conversion. He was in the very act of it when Jesus called him on the road to Damascus, and that mission to lay waste was not carried out. Nor is the meaning of the verb to be diluted, as is done by Beza, Winer, Schott, and Usteri, the last of whom says that Winer is right in denying that it means *evertere*, but only *vastare*. But Passow, Wahl, and Bretschneider give it the meaning which these expositors would soften. Examples are numerous. It occurs often in the strongest sense (Homer, *Il.* iv. 308), is applied to men as well as cities (Lobeck, *Soph. Ajax*, p. 378, 3d ed.), and is sometimes associated with καίειν (Xen. *Hellen.* v. 5, 27). Compare Wetstein, *in loc.* What the apostle says of himself is abundantly confirmed. Saul,—"he made havoc of the church," etc., Acts viii. 3; "yet breathing out threatenings and slaughter against the disciples of the Lord," ix. 1; his mission to Damascus was, "that if he found any of this way, whether they were men or women, he might bring them bound to Jerusalem," ix. 2; "is not this he that destroyed them which called on this name in Jerusalem?" ix. 21; "I persecuted this way unto the death," xxii. 4; "I imprisoned and beat in every synagogue them that believed on Thee," xxii. 19; "when they were put to death, I gave my voice against them, being exceeding mad against them," xxvi. 10, 11. No wonder, then, that he uses those two verbs, and prefixes to the first *καθ' ὑπερβολήν*, one of his favourite phrases. Rom. vii. 13; 1 Cor. xii. 31; 2 Cor. i. 8, iv. 17. It was no partial or spasmodic effort, either feeble in itself, or limited and intermittent in operation. It was the outgrowth of a zeal which never slept, and of an energy which could do nothing by halves, which was as eager as it was resolute, and was noted for its perseverance no less than for its ardour. And he distinctly sets before his readers the heinousness of his procedure, for he declares the object of his persecution and fierce devastation to have been

Τὴν ἐκκλησίαν τοῦ Θεοῦ—"the church of God." 1 Cor. xv. 9. The possessive genitive *τοῦ Θεοῦ* points out strongly the sinfulness and audacity of his career. It may be added that the Vulgate reads *expugnabam;* and F has *ἐπολέμουν*. This Greek was probably fashioned from the Latin. The Vulgate has, Acts ix. 21, *expugnabat* for *ὁ πορθήσας*, without any various reading in Greek codices. The object of this statement is to show that the apostle, during his furious persecution of the church, could not be in the way of learning its theology from any human source; its bloody and malignant enemy could not be consorting with the apostles as a pupil or colleague.

Ver. 14. *Καὶ προέκοπτον ἐν τῷ Ἰουδαϊσμῷ ὑπὲρ πολλοὺς συνηλικιώτας ἐν τῷ γένει μου*—"and was making progress in Judaism beyond many my equals in my own nation." The tropical sense of the verb is, "to push forward," and intransitively "to make advancement," followed by *ἐν*, and sometimes with a different reference by *ἐπί* or a simple dative, as in Luke ii. 52. His progress in Judaism was

Ὑπὲρ πολλοὺς συνηλικιώτας—"beyond many contemporaries." Such compound terms as *συνηλικ.*, which the apostle uses only here, belong to the later age; the simple noun sufficing at an earlier and fresher stage. Diodor. Sic. i. 53, in which place, however, several codices have the simple term. So, too, Dionysius Halicar. x. 49. The persons referred to are those of similar age and standing,—fellow-pupils, it may be, at the feet of Gamaliel. And they were his countrymen—

Ἐν τῷ γένει μου. Compare Acts xviii. 2, 2 Cor. xi. 26, Phil. iii. 5. Numerous contemporaries of pure Jewish blood, and not simply Jews from Tarsus, were excelled by him. His zeal pervaded every sphere of his life and labour. He could not be lukewarm, either in persecution or in study. His whole soul was ever given to the matter in hand; for he thus assigns the reason of his forwardness and success in the following clause:

Περισσοτέρως ζηλωτὴς ὑπάρχων τῶν πατρικῶν μου παραδόσεων—"being more exceedingly a zealot for the traditions of my fathers." This participial clause may be modal, as Meyer and Ellicott take it (*ὑπάρχων*, "as being"), but it may be causal: He excelled his contemporaries, inasmuch as he was more exceedingly zealous than they were. In *περισσοτέρως* the comparison is not surely, as Usteri explains, *mehr als gewohnlich*, but more than those contemporaries to whom he has just referred. Strange and unfounded is the notion of Gwynne, that the comparison in *περισσοτέρως* is not between Paul and his contemporaries, but between "the precepts and ordinances of the law of Moses of which his appreciation was not so high, nor his zeal for them so fervid as for his ancestral traditions." Such a comparison comes not into view at all. The noun *ζηλωτής* signifies one filled with zeal for what is contained in the following genitive—*τοῦ Θεοῦ*, Acts xxii. 3; *τοῦ νόμου*, Acts xxi. 20; *πνεύματων*, 1 Cor. xiv. 12; *καλῶν ἔργων*, Tit. ii. 14: the genitive of person being sometimes preceded by *ὑπέρ*; 2 Cor. vii. 7, Col. iv. 13. The noun is not here used in the fanatical sense attaching to the modern term zealot, though it came also to denote a fanatical party in the last days of the Jewish commonwealth. The object of his intense attachment was—

Τῶν πατρικῶν μου παραδόσεων—"for the traditions of my

fathers," the genitive being that of object, as in the places already quoted. The noun παράδοσις, *traditio*, "giving over," is literally employed as with πόλεως (Thucydides, iii. 53; Josephus, *De Bello Jud.* i. 8, 6; Sept. Jer. xxxii. 4; Esdras vii. 26); then it signifies handing over or down an inheritance (Thucydides, i. 9), and by a natural trope it is used of narration. Josephus, *contra Apion.* i. 6. So it came to denote instructions delivered orally, as Hesychius defines it by ἀγράφους διδασκαλίας. It is used of apostolical mandate, 1 Cor. xi. 2, 2 Thess. ii. 15, iii. 6; and especially of the Jewish tradition, Matt. xv. 2, 3, 6, τὴν παράδοσιν τῶν πρεσβυτέρων, τὴν παράδοσιν ὑμῶν, in opposition to the written divine law. Mark vii. 3, 9, 13; Col. ii. 8. So in Josephus, *Antiq.* xiii. 10, 6, and 16, 2. Thus the term seems to denote not the Mosaic law itself, but the accretions which in course of ages had grown around it, and of which the Mishna is an example. Luther and Calvin think that the term denotes the Mosaic law—*ipsam Dei legem*, as the latter says; and many suppose that the law is included, as Estius, Winer, Usteri, Schott, Hilgenfeld, Olshausen, and Brown. The law may be included, in the sense that a commentary includes the text, or that a legal exposition implies a statute. But the terms, from their nature, cannot primarily refer to it or formally comprehend it, for the law written with such care, and the sacred parchment kept with such scrupulosity, could not well be called traditions. In Acts xxii. 3 the phrase is τοῦ πατρῴου νόμου—"the law of my fathers"—and refers to traditionary pharisaic interpretation; but the traditions are here called πατρικαί μου. The adjectives πάτριος, πατρικός, πατρῷος, generically the same in meaning, are supposed to have been used with specific difference, though what the precise difference was has been disputed. Ellendt, *Lex. Soph. sub voce;* Kühner, *Xen. Anab.* iii. 2, 17; also Schoemann, *Isaeus*, p. 201; and Hermann, *Opuscula*, vol. iii. 195. The apostle, however, uses in these two places the two adjectives πατρικός and πατρῷος with much the same reference. We cannot agree with Meyer, followed by Alford, Ellicott, and others, in saying that the adjective and pronoun limit these traditions to the sect of the Pharisees, Paul being φαρισαῖος, υἱὸς φαρισαίου, "a Pharisee, the son of a Pharisee." We rather think, with Wieseler, that the reference must be as wide as in the phrase ἐν τῷ γένει; that the traditions described as handed down from his fathers are viewed as national and not as sectarian; and that though in effect they were pharisaic, still, as the Pharisees were the mass of the nation, they are regarded as having characterized the people to whom Paul belonged. It cannot therefore be supposed that the apostle would be learning Christianity during the period when his progress in Judaism was so marked, when his zeal for patristic traditions so far outran that of his contemporaries,—a zeal in utter and burning antagonism to the new religion. He had kept from all contact with it, save the contact of ferocity with the victim which it immolates. Luther touchingly applies this verse to his own previous history.

Ver. 15. Ὅτε δὲ εὐδόκησεν ὁ Θεὸς, ὁ ἀφορίσας με ἐκ κοιλίας μητρός μου—"But when God was pleased, who set me apart from my mother's womb." The ὁ Θεός of the received text has for it, D, K, L, א; but B, F, G, omit it. The Greek fathers are doubtful, but the Vulgate and Jerome have it not. The words are left out by Tischendorf and Alford; but if they are a gloss, they are an old one. Ellicott refers to Θ. preceded and followed by Ὁ, as the probable source of omission. One may say, on the other hand, that the supposed demands of syntax might seem to warrant the insertion of the words; yet the phraseology of the following clauses is so precise, God's destination and call of the apostle, the revelation of His Son in him with his commission to preach to the Gentiles, that though in the hurry and glow of thought the nominative was omitted, nobody could doubt what it was. "I persecuted the church of God, yet HE was pleased to select me,"—all the more solemn from the omission of the name. Comp. i. 6, ii. 8; Rom. viii. 11; Phil. i. 6. He, provoked as He might have been, εὐδόκησεν—"was pleased" of His own sovereign grace. The verb is, as usual with Paul, followed by an infinitive, though it is found in other constructions with a simple accusative. Heb. x. 6. It occurs with an accusative and εἰς in 2 Pet. i. 17; and with ἐν and a dative in Matt. iii. 17, and probably in 2 Thess. ii. 12.

The verb ἀφορίσας is not used here in a mere physical sense (Aquinas, Cajetan, Paulus), as if ἐκ were local, but is ethically "to set apart," and is followed by εἰς, pointing to the end, as in Acts xiii. 2, Rom. i. 1. Instead, however, of being followed here by εἰς, the construction leads on to an infinitive of purpose, but connected with the previous verb. The ἐκ points out the time from which his destination is to be reckoned (Winer), and the phrase is an imitation of open Hebrew speech. Judg. xvi. 17; Ps. xxii. 11, lxx. 6; Isa. xliv. 2, xlix. 1, 5; Matt. xix. 12; Acts iii. 2, xiv. 8. It is equivalent in sense to ἐκ γενετῆς, John ix. 1, and does not glance in any way at pharisaic separatism (Wessel). The apostle means to say that God destined him from his birth to his vocation, no matter how wayward and unlikely had been the career of his youth. The words do not mean from eternity (Beza), though, indeed, every act of God is but the realization of an eternal purpose; nor do they mean, before he was born. To support this sense, advocated by Jerome, Grotius, Semler, Rückert, Wieseler, and Hofmann, reference is made to Jer. i. 5; but there the language is different, πρὸ τοῦ με πλάσαι σε ἐν κοιλίᾳ. It is therefore only an inference, but not the sense, to say, If he was chosen from the womb, he was chosen in it. His being set apart from his birth was of God's sovereign good pleasure. The phrase may imply also, in an undertone, that his education had been, under God, adapted to his high function. Not only from his birth was he a designated apostle; but he adds:

Καὶ καλέσας διὰ τῆς χάριτος αὐτοῦ—"and called me by His grace." Designation was not enough: he brings out another essential link—that of vocation—as a second step in his progress. The participles are closely connected, no article being before the second one—the designation showed itself in the κλῆσις. The διά is instrumental—by means of His grace (1 Cor. xv. 10); and the call came to him near Damascus. This is the plain historical sense and allusion. The apostle refers to the period of his conversion, and to its medium, as not of merit but of grace. Now he proceeds to show how his call to the apostolate was connected with qualification for it.

Ver. 16. *'Αποκαλύψαι τὸν Υἱὸν αὐτοῦ ἐν ἐμοὶ*—"to reveal His Son in me." The infinitive is not connected with one or both of the participles, but with εὐδόκησεν, and its aorist form denotes the past and completed act. The phrase ἐν ἐμοί is "in me,"—in my soul, in my inner self. It cannot mean "to me;" nor is it to be taken for the simple dative (Calvin,

Rosenmüller, Koppe, and Flatt), for what then should be the force of the preposition? In Matt. xi. 27, 1 Cor. ii. 10, Eph. iii. 5, Phil. iii. 16, the simple dative following the verb has a different meaning. Winer, § 31, 8, § 48*a*; Bernhardy, p. 213. As little can the phrase mean "through me," as Jerome, Pelagius, Grotius, Estius, Lightfoot, and Bagge. Nor can it mean *coram me* (Peile), or "on me" (P. Lombard, Seb. Schmidt), as if it were a manifest token of divine power.[1] Œcumenius says, *ἐν ἐμοὶ δὲ εἶπε δεῖξαι θέλων οὐ λόγῳ μόνον μαθόντα αὐτὸν ἀλλὰ καὶ νῷ καὶ καρδίᾳ.* Lightfoot's objection to the natural meaning is only a hasty anticipation of the following clause, which tells the purpose of the revelation.

The object of this divine revelation was "His Son;" not the truth about Him, or His work, or His death, or His glory, but Himself—Himself including all. His person is the sum of the gospel. See, for some remarks on "Son," under Eph. i. 3, 17. This revelation may have been in some sense subsequent to the direct call, or it may refer also to the appearance of the Redeemer near Damascus qualifying him for the apostleship. 1 Cor. ix. 1. It gave him full and glowing views of the Redeemer's person, including His various relations to God and to man,—such views as fixed the apostle's faith upon Him, centred his love in Him, and enabled him to hold Him out in his preaching as the one living and glorified Saviour. It was by no process of reasoning that he came to such conclusions, by no elaborate and sustained series of demonstrations that he wrought out his Christology. God revealed His Son in him, divine light was flashed in upon him, so that he saw what he had not seen before, fully, suddenly, and by a higher than intuitive suggestion. He had not been taught, and he did not need to be taught, by any of the apostles. The purpose of this revelation is then stated:

Ἵνα εὐαγγελίζωμαι αὐτὸν ἐν τοῖς ἔθνεσιν—"in order that I should preach Him among the Gentiles." The Son of God was the living theme of his preaching, and the good news about Him was what is stated in the fourth verse—that "He gave Himself for our sins"—the theme which the apostle elsewhere characterizes thus, "We preach Christ crucified." The enlightenment of the apostle was not for his own individual

[1] Even Blomfield says, *ἐν ἡμῖν pro εἰς ἡμᾶς vel ἡμῖν.—Agamemnon*, 1425.

luxury; it was to fit him to make known what had been so conveyed to him. Acts xxii. 15, 21, xxvi. 17–19. The ἵνα points out the purpose, and the present tense of the verb describes the work of evangelization as no passing or isolated act, but an enduring function. And the sphere of his labours is distinctly avowed—"among the heathen." Rom. i. 5, 13, xi. 13, xv. 16; Eph. iii. 8; 1 Tim. ii. 7. The verb εὐαγγελίζω has already been used with the simple dative, ver. 8, and with the accusative, ver. 9; here it is followed by ἐν—among the heathen peoples or all other races beyond the chosen seed. He forgot not his own people—they were ever dear to him; but his characteristic work—to which he had been set apart, called, qualified—was to be the apostle of the Gentiles; and this, so specially his own office, he magnified.

Revelation is opposed to knowledge gained by prolonged and patient thought. It is unlike the common process by which an intellectual conclusion is reached, the inference of one syllogism forming but the premiss of another, till by a series of connected links, primary or abstract truth is reached. For it is sudden and perfect illumination, lifting the receptive power into intensest susceptibility, and so lighting up the whole theme disclosed, that it is immediately and fully apprehended in its evidence and reality. We know not, indeed, what the process is, what the waking up of the higher intuition is, or what the ecstasy which throws into momentary abeyance all the lower faculties. It may resemble that new sphere of vision in which genius enjoys gleams of unutterable beauty, or that "demonstration of the Spirit" which gives the truth new aspects of richness and grandeur to the sanctified soul in some mood of rapt meditation. But still it is different and higher far both in matter and purpose. It was God's revelation of His Son,—not glimpses of the truth about Him, but Himself; not merely summoning his attention to His paramount claims, so as to elicit an acknowledgment of them,—not simply presenting Him to his intellectual perception to be studied and comprehended,—nor even shrining an image of Him in his heart to be loved and cherished,—but His Son unveiled in living reality; and in him—in his inner self, not in any distinct and separate realm of his being,—with the conscious possession of all this infallible and communicable knowledge which was given perhaps first in clear and vivid outline—παρέλαβον—and then filled in surely and gradually—ἐδιδάχθην.

Εὐθέως οὐ προσανεθέμην σαρκὶ καὶ αἵματι—"immediately I conferred not with flesh and blood;" "I communed not of the matter with flesh and blood" (Tyndale). It would almost seem that the apostle meant to write εὐθέως . . . ἀπῆλθον εἰς Ἀραβίαν—I went at once into Arabia; but other explanations of a negative kind struggle first for utterance (Jowett). Still εὐθέως, standing emphatically, may qualify the whole paragraph, as Chrysostom hints. What he describes happened immediately after his conversion,—non-conference, non-visitation of Jerusalem, departure for Arabia,—all told in the same breath. The construction is close; for the intermediate negative statement, "neither did I go off to Jerusalem," is connected by οὐδέ as a denied alternative with the first clause, and then by the directly adversative ἀλλά with the last clause, εὐθέως underlying all of them but specially pointing to, "I went off to Arabia." Rückert, after Jerome, against all MSS., would join εὐθέως to the previous clause, and so Credner, *Einleit.* p. 303. The adverb might stand at the end of the clause. See some examples not wholly analogous in Stallbaum's note, *Phaedrus*, p. 256 E, or vol. iv. p. 134. The phrase σάρξ καὶ αἷμα, בָּשָׂר וָדָם, here denotes human nature, or man generally, not specially in contrast with higher powers, as in Eph. vi. 12; nor in his more earthly nature, as in 1 Cor. xv. 50; but man as in contrast with divine agency, the contrast suggesting, however, the idea of inferiority, Matt. xvi. 17. The verb προσανεθέμην is classically "to add a burden to," or "on one's own self;" and then, as here, "to make address to," or "hold communion with." The *non acquievi* of the Vulgate is not the correct rendering, though it may be so far according to the sense. In the double compound, the first preposition indicates "direction towards" (Meyer), and not addition, *præterea* (Beza, Bengel). "I did not address myself to," or "did not take counsel with,"—two successive phases of the one idea, "I did not consult." Diodorus Sic. xvii. 116; Ὦ Ζεῦ . . . ἐμοὶ προσανάθου, Lucian, *Jup. Tragœd.* i. *Opera*, vol. vi. p. 223, ed. Bipont.; Suidas, *sub voce.* The phrase "flesh and blood" does not refer to the other apostles (Chrysostom), nor is it a contemptuous allusion to them, as Porphyry insinuated; nor does the apostle mean himself (Koppe, Gwynne), for the verb would not be in harmony; nor does it include the apostle and the others, with whom conference is denied (Schott, Winer, Matthies). The reference, as is held by the majority of expositors, is simply to others, as the spirit of the context also shows, his object being to prove that he was in no sense *ἀνθρωποδίδακτος*. The apostle is not alluding to any self-denial or any victory over his own desires and preferences, but is only stating the fact that, after his conversion, he had studiously shunned all human conference. The *non acquievi* has been unduly pressed. Tertullian speaks of some who held that flesh and blood meant Judaism, and that the apostle is to be thus understood: "Statim non retulerit ad carnem et sanguinem, id est, ad circumcisionem, id est ad Judaismum, sicut ad Galatas scribit." *De Resurr. Carnis*, cap. i. p. 534; *Opera*, vol. ii. ed. Oehler. Primasius writes, "*Continuo non acquievi*, continuo non fui incredulus cœlesti visioni quia non carnis et sanguinis voces audivi."

Ver. 17. *Οὐδὲ ἀπῆλθον εἰς Ἱεροσόλυμα πρὸς τοὺς πρὸ ἐμοῦ ἀποστόλους*—"Neither did I go away to Jerusalem to them who were apostles before me." The *ἀνῆλθον* of the received text is very well supported, having in its favour A, K, L, א, Chrysostom, and the Latin, both Vulg. and Clarom.; while *ἀπῆλθον* is found in B, D, F, the Syriac, and in Basil. The form *ἀνῆλθον* is the one usually employed,—going up to Jerusalem, not only as the capital city, but as one built on high land, —and may be fairly supposed to be a correction of the more general *ἀπῆλθον*. It may be indeed replied, as by Tischendorf, that it is improbable that Paul should have written *ἀπῆλθον* twice consecutively; but we find *ἐλάβετε . . . ἐλάβετε* in Rom. viii. 15; Heb. ii. 16. There was no temptation to change *ἀν.* into *ἀπ.*, but to change *ἀπ.* into *ἀν.*, so as to harmonize it with general usage. Acts ii. 15, xxi. 15, xxv. 1. In the *οὐδέ* there is reference to the previous negation, while another more definite is added, so that there is something more than the *fortuitus concursus* given by Klotz-Devar. ii. 707, and acquiesced in by Ellicott. Generally he held conference with nobody, with no members of the church in Damascus; and specially, as the contrary might have been expected or insinuated, he did not go off to Jerusalem, and consult the elder apostles. Rom. xvi. 7. He did not rehearse his experience to them, or receive either authority or instruction from them. In fact, he carefully kept aloof from them; and so far from journeying to Jerusalem, and to the leaders in the mother church, he went away in quite a different direction—

'Αλλ' ἀπῆλθον εἰς 'Αραβίαν—"but I went away into Arabia." The *ἀλλά* is found in its full form in A, B, D, F, L, and א; and as introducing an affirmative after a negative statement, it has its strong adversative force. Arabia may mean Arabia Deserta, a portion of which comes so near Damascus.[1] Not to speak of wider geographical descriptions of the name, as in Herod. ii. 12, Xen. *Anab.* i. 5, Plin. *Hist. Nat.* vi. 32, Justin Martyr says, *Δαμασκὸς τῆς 'Αραβικῆς γῆς ἦν καὶ ἔστιν. Dial. c. Tryph. Op.* vol. ii. p. 268, ed. Otto, 1843; and Tertullian repeats the account, *Adv. Marcion.* iii. 13, *Adv. Jud.* 9. Or if Arabia be used more strictly, as in iv. 25, then, as some have fancied, he may have visited, like Elijah, the grand scene of the old legislation. But probably, had he done so, there would be some allusion to such a pilgrimage of honour in a letter in which he unfolds the relations of a law which he was accused of rashly undervaluing and setting aside.[2] The point cannot be determined; and in the brief narrative of the Acts the journey is omitted. Nor can the definite motive of the apostle be ascertained. It does not seem to have been to preach the gospel (Meyer, Wieseler, Ewald), though he would not decline such work if opportunity offered, but rather to prepare himself for his coming labour. Jerome thus allegorizes the matter: "The *Itus ac reditus* mean nothing in themselves; but Arabia, the country of the bond slave, is the Old Testament, and there he found Christ; *reperto illo*, he returned to Damascus, *ad sanguinem et passionem Christi*,"—a play upon the Hebrew meaning of the first syllable; and "so strengthened, he went up to Jerusalem, *locum visionis et pacis*,"—an allusion again to the signification of the name. At all events, the journey to Arabia is here adduced, not as an illustration of his early preaching of Christ among the heathen, but as a proof that he had

[1] Conybeare and Howson, vol. i. 104.

[2] There was at that time a large and flourishing kingdom of Jews in Arabia Felix. Milman, *History of the Jews*, vol. iii. p. 85, 4th ed. 1866.

held no consultation with flesh and blood; so that probably he retired to enjoy solitary thought and preparation, sounding the depth of his convictions, forecasting possibilities, receiving revelations and lessons,—truth presented inviting him to earnest study,—divine communications viewed on all sides and in all lights, till they were mastered in sum and detail, and became a portion of himself; a lifetime in awfulness and intensity of thought and feeling crowded into a few months. He in this way followed the Master, who, after enjoying the divine manifestation at His baptism, was led of the Spirit into the wilderness. It is not likely that Paul's object was to find safety from Jewish persecution under king Aretas in some part of Arabia (Thiersch).

Καὶ πάλιν ὑπέστρεψα εἰς Δαμασκόν—"and again returned to Damascus." The phrase implies through *πάλιν* that he had been in Damascus before he went into Arabia. His work on his return to Damascus, was "proving that this is very Christ;" and he "confounded" the Jews by his arguments, anticipating every objection, removing every scruple; remembering how himself had felt and reasoned, and diffusing that new light which had been poured into his soul. A conspiracy was formed against him, but he escaped by night and by a peculiar stratagem, as himself tells, 2 Cor. xi. 33. Thus early did he begin to realize what was said to Ananias, "I will show him how great things he must suffer for my name's sake."

Ver. 18. *Ἔπειτα μετὰ ἔτη τρία ἀνῆλθον εἰς Ἱεροσόλυμα*—"Then after three years I went up to Jerusalem." What must have been his emotions as he passed the scene of his conversion, or if he entered the holy city by the gate through which he had left it? The adverb *ἔπειτα*, "then"—after his return to Damascus—is a connecting link in his narrative. The point from which the three years are to be computed is fixed by some at the return from Arabia (Borger, Rückert, Jatho). The majority, however, date them from his conversion. That event had just been referred to by him, in its origin, nature, and design. God had set him apart, called him and qualified him, and this event of events to him stood out so prominently in its solitary grace and grandeur, that he reckons from it without any formal reference. The *ὁ Θεὸς εὐδόκησεν* dominates the whole paragraph. How much of this time was spent in Arabia, and how much in the two sojourns at Damascus, is a question for the solution of which we have no proper data. The first stay seems to be indicated by the words *ἡμέραι τινές*, and the second by *ὡς δὲ ἐπληροῦντο ἡμέραι ἱκαναί*, in Acts ix. 19, 23. This last phrase is indefinite, but coupled with the verb seems to denote a considerable space. Eichhorn, Howson, Anger, suppose the three years to have been wholly spent in Arabia. The *μετὰ ἔτη τρία* are in contrast with the *εὐθέως* of ver. 16, and *ἀνῆλθον* refers back to the previous *ἀπῆλθον*. The object of the visit to Jerusalem was

Ἱστορῆσαι Κηφᾶν—"to make the acquaintance of Cephas." The reading *Πέτρον* of the received text is well sustained, having in its favour D, F, K, L, ℵ[3], the Vulgate, and many of the fathers; while *Κηφᾶν* has A, B, ℵ[1], three MSS., Syriac, Coptic, and Æthiopic. The rarer name is to be preferred. The verb *ἱστορῆσαι*, occurring only here, has sometimes in earlier Greek the sense of knowing through inquiry, or of asking; Hesychius defines it by *ἐρωτᾶν*. In later Greek it denotes "to visit" as applied to places or things, and to persons in the sense of making the acquaintance of—*coram cognoscere*. It differs from *ἰδεῖν* in that it implies that what is to be seen is worthy of a visit of inspection. See Kypke, *in loc.*, and so Chrysostom illustrates it. Thus *ἱστορῆσαι Ἐλεάσαρον*, Josephus, *Antiq.* viii. 25; similarly, *Bell. Jud.* vi. 1, 8, he says of Julian the Bithynian centurion, *ὃν ἐγὼ ἱστόρησα*; and often in the Clementines, as adduced by Hilgenfeld: *Homiliæ*, i. 14, ix. 22, ix. 6, etc. But these instances, as usual, refer to things, not persons.

Paul did not go to consult Cephas, or get any information essential to the validity of his office and work, but to visit him as a noted apostle,—one whom it would be gratifying to know through private and confidential intercourse.

But even this first visit to Jerusalem, three years after his conversion, was a very brief one:

Καὶ ἐπέμεινα πρὸς αὐτὸν ἡμέρας δεκαπέντε—"and I abode with him fifteen days." *Πρός* so used does not differ in meaning from *παρά* with a dative. Matt. xxvi. 55; John i. 1; 1 Cor. xvi. 6, 7–10. A similar construction is often quoted from Æschyl. *Prom.* 351; Eurip. *Ion*, 916. Fritzsche on Mark vi. 3 warns, however, that there are many cases in which, though somewhat similar, πρός cannot have this meaning—*quæ aliquam motus significationem habeant*,—cases which even Wahl has not distinguished *satis feliciter*. Luke xvi. 20, xxii. 56; Acts v. 10, xiii. 31.

It is needless to lay special stress on the ἐπί in ἐπέμεινα, for it seems to be neither distinctly local nor intensive. It may denote rest (Ellicott), and thus give a fuller meaning to the compound verb than the simple one would have borne. The verb is followed in the New Testament by ἐπί, Acts xxviii. 14; by ἐν, Phil. i. 24; by πρός, 1 Cor. xvi. 7; and by a simple dative, Rom. vi. 1, xi. 22, 23, Col. i. 23, 1 Tim. iv. 16. In the latter case there is a difference of meaning, *qui in aliqua re manet et perseverat*. Winer, *De verborum cum præp. compos.* ii. 11. The form δεκαπέντε is for the more classical and the fuller πεντεκαίδεκα. Kühner, § 353. The later form occurs often at an earlier period, as in the *Tabulæ Heracleenses* (Lightfoot). Jerome, finding a hidden meaning in the number fifteen, supposes it to mean here *plena scientia*. Why the visit was so brief is told in Acts ix. 29. The Hellenists with whom he had been disputing "went about to slay him," and the brethren, on becoming aware of the conspiracy, "brought him down to Cæsarea, and sent him forth to Tarsus." A simultaneous reason is assigned by himself. He was praying in the temple, and fell into a trance,—identified on slight grounds by Schrader and Wieseler as the rapture described in 2 Cor. xii. 2, —and the Master appeared and said to him, "Make haste, and get thee quickly out of Jerusalem, for they will not receive thy testimony concerning me." He pleads now for Jerusalem as a field of labour, because his history was so well known to the Hellenists whose prejudices he understood from experience. The excuse is not listened to: not Hellenism but heathenism was again formally assigned to him as his field of labour. "Begone," was the reply, "I will send thee far hence unto the Gentiles." Acts xxii. 17–21.

Ver. 19. Ἕτερον δὲ τῶν ἀποστόλων οὐκ εἶδον, εἰ μὴ Ἰάκωβον τὸν ἀδελφὸν τοῦ Κυρίου—"And another of the apostles I did not see, except James the Lord's brother;" or, "None other of the apostles did I see, save James the Lord's brother."

The adjective ἕτερον is simply numerical, not qualitative. Two different meanings have been assigned to the verse.

Victorinus, Grotius, Fritzsche (on Matt. xiii. 55), Bleek, and Winer supply simply *εἶδον* after *εἰ μὴ*—"none other of the apostles did I see, except that, or but, I saw James the Lord's brother;"—the inference being, that this James was not an apostle. In this case *εἰ μὴ* still retains its exceptive force, which is, however, confined to the verb. Thus in Matt. xii. 4 it is rendered "but only;" Luke iv. 26, 27, "save," "saving;" Rev. xxi. 27, "but." Others more naturally supply *τὸν ἀπόστολον*—"none other of the apostles did I see, except the Apostle James, the Lord's brother;" or, "none other of the apostles saw I, save James the Lord's brother;"—the inference plainly being, that the Lord's brother was an apostle. Thus 1 Cor. i. 14, *οὐδένα ὑμῶν ἐβάπτισα, εἰ μὴ Κρίσπον καὶ Γάϊον*—"none of you I baptized, save Crispus and Gaius:" I baptized them, and they were *ὑμῶν*—"of you." The *εἰ μὴ* being suggested by *ἕτερον*, thus refers to the whole clause. See under i. 7, ii. 16.[1]

Ver. 20. *Ἃ δὲ γράφω ὑμῖν*—"but as to the things which I am writing to you,"—the reference being to the assertions just made—his visit to Jerusalem, and his brief residence with Peter, and that during that fortnight he saw only him and the Lord's brother. Some, as Calvin, Winer, Matthies, refer the declaration to the whole paragraph from ver. 12, or from ver. 15 (Estius and Hofmann), some of the elements of which were not, however, matter of dispute. The apostle becomes fervent in his affirmation, and calls God to witness:

Ἰδοὺ ἐνώπιον τοῦ Θεοῦ ὅτι οὐ ψεύδομαι—"behold before God that I lie not." The construction is broken. Schott denies it, *γράφω* being supplied—*quæ vobis scribo, ecce coram Deo scribo, siquidem non mentior.* So generally Jerome and Ambrose. The ellipse is striking, and *ἰδοὺ ἐνώπιον τ. Θ.* is a virtual oath. *Ἰδού*, as Lightfoot remarks, is never used as a verb, so that here it cannot govern *ὅτι*. The word to be supplied to resolve the ellipse has been variously taken: *γράφω* by Meyer; *λέγω* by De Wette, Olshausen, and Bisping; *ὄμνυμι* by Usteri; *μαρτυρῶ* by Hilgenfeld; and *ἐστί* by Rückert and Bengel—*i.e.* it is before God that I lie not. In 2 Cor. xi. 31 we have *ὁ Θεὸς . . . οἶδεν . . . ὅτι οὐ ψεύδομαι*. In 1 Tim. v. 21, *διαμαρτύρομαι* occurs with *ἐνώπιον τ. Θ.*; *διαμαρτυρόμενος* with

[1] See note at end of chapter.

ἐνώπιον τοῦ Κυρίου in 2 Tim. ii. 14; similarly 2 Tim. iv. 2. This verb might therefore be the most natural supplement, if any supplement be really necessary. But the ellipse, abrupt, terse, and idiomatic, needs not to be so diluted, and probably no supplementary term was in the apostle's mind at all as it suddenly threw out this solemn adjuration. Besides, a similar construction occurs in the Sept.: *ἴδε ὅτι τὰς ἐντολάς σου ἠγάπησα*, Ps. cxix. 159; *ἴδε Κύριε ὅτι θλίβομαι*, Lam. i. 20. "Behold before God" is equivalent to saying, I call God to witness that, *ὅτι* (Lightfoot). There might be no human proof, but there was divine attestation. Augustine, *in loc.*, enters into the question of the lawfulness of swearing. One can scarcely suppose that the apostle would have used this solemn adjuration, unless the statement had been liable to be questioned, or a different account of his early Christian history had been in circulation. It would seem that a totally different account of his visits to Jerusalem after his conversion, and of the relation he sustained to the elder apostles, had been in use among the Judaists, to undermine his independent authority and neutralize his teaching. And because what he now tells would contradict received opinion as to his earlier actings and journeys, he confirms what he says by a virtual oath, though the phrase as in Hebrew, לִפְנֵי־יְהוָֹה, is not formally always used of oaths.

Ver. 21. *Ἔπειτα ἦλθον εἰς τὰ κλίματα τῆς Συρίας καὶ τῆς Κιλικίας*—"afterwards I came into the regions of Syria and Cilicia." The noun *κλίματα*, found also in Rom. xv. 23, 2 Cor. xi. 10, originally means inclination or declivity, such as that of a hill; then a space of the sky, so named from the inclination of the heaven to the poles—*κλῖμα μεσημβρινόν*, Dion. H. *Ant.* i. 9; *βόρειον*, Aristot. *De Mund. Opera*, vol. iii. p. 133, ed. Bekker, Oxford 1837; *γῆς μέρος ἢ κλῖμα οὐρανοῦ*, Herodian, ii. 11, 8;—then a tract of earth, so called in reference to its inclination towards the pole—*τοῖς πρὸς μεσημβρίαν κλίμασι*, Polyb. v. 44; *τοῦτο τὸ κλῖμα . . . τῆς Ἰταλίας*, *ib.* x. 1;—and then, as in Joseph. *De Bell. Jud.* iii. 7, 12, approaching the modern sense of climate. Thus Athenæus, *εὐδαιμονίαν τοῦ σύμπαντος τούτου κλίματος*, referring to Siris in the south of Italy, lib. xii. p. 445, vol. iv. p. 444, ed. Schweighaüser. Lobeck (*Paralip.* 418) shows that the true accentuation is *κλῖμα*, a properispomenon like *κρῖμα* which is long in Æschylus, *Supp.* 397; Lipsius,

Gramm. Untersuch. über die Bibl. Græcität, pp. 40, 41, Leipzig 1863. Codices A, L, have *κλήματα*. Syria is naturally Syria proper, which he reached from Cæsarea,—not Cæsarea Philippi (Eichhorn, Olshausen), and not the country formerly called Phœnicia (Usteri, Schott): the supposition of such a near vicinity is not in harmony with the apostle's argument. Cilicia was his native province; and Barnabas soon after found him in Tarsus, and brought him to Antioch. According to the narrative in Acts, he seems to have sailed from Cæsarea to Tarsus. Cilicia was more allied to Syria than Asia Minor, and both countries are collocated vaguely by the *τὰ κλίματα*. The apostle is not stating his tour with geographical precision, but is merely showing how far he travelled away from all Judæan influence. and recognition.

Ver. 22. *Ἤμην δὲ ἀγνοούμενος τῷ προσώπῳ ταῖς ἐκκλησίαις τῆς Ἰουδαίας ταῖς ἐν Χριστῷ*—"and I was unknown by face to the churches of Judæa which are in Christ." The first words are a strong form of the imperfect, equivalent to "I remained unknown." Jelf, § 375, 4. The *τῷ προσώπῳ* is the dative of reference, carrying in it that of limitation or the defining or qualifying element which characterizes this case. Winer, § 31, 6; Bernhardy, p. 82; Donaldson, § 459. The apostle was known to these churches in many aspects, but he was unknown in this one thing—in person or face. The churches in Judæa did not know him personally, and they are thus distinguished from the churches in Jerusalem, many of whom had a knowledge of his person, and could recognise him if they saw him, for he had been "going in and out" among them, "speaking boldly and disputing," having sojourned fifteen days with Peter. Acts ix. 28. The object of Hilgenfeld, following Baur and others of the same school, in maintaining that the church in Jerusalem is here included, is to bring the statement into conflict with the Acts, so as to ruin the credibility of the narrative. But compare John ii. 23 with John iii. 22, Acts i. 8, x. 39, xxvi. 20; and for an analogous foreign example, Acts xv. 23. The churches in Judæa are characterized as *ταῖς ἐν Χριστῷ*, "that are in Christ,"—in Him as united to Him, the Source of life and power, and having fellowship with Him,—so included in Him as the members are organically united to the head. It is not certain that this definition is added because unconverted Jewish communities might be called churches of God (Lightfoot). Is there any example in the New Testament? The apostle was hurried away to Cæsarea, where he took shipping for Tarsus, and thus had no opportunity of becoming acquainted with the Judæan churches; nor had they, for the same reason, any opportunity of gaining a personal knowledge of him. He is not showing that he could not learn the gospel from Judæan Christians, as Œcumenius and Olshausen suppose, nor, as Chrysostom thinks, that he had not taught circumcision in Judæa. For these are not topics in dispute. The apostle means to affirm, that so little intercourse had he with the apostles, that the church in Judæa, having constant correspondence with those apostles, did not know him, so wholly was he away from their home sphere of labour. The notion of Michaelis is out of the question, that the church of Jerusalem is included among those that did not know him personally, because, though known to a few individuals of them, he was not known to them as a body, since his labours were principally among his unconverted brethren.

Ver. 23. *Μόνον δὲ ἀκούοντες ἦσαν*—not *audierant* (Estius), nor "they had heard" (Luther, Brown),—"only they were hearing," they continued hearing: fresh and pregnant reports were brought from time to time. The *δέ* contrasts this clause with the previous *ἤμην ἀγνοούμενος*. *'Ακούοντες*, not the *ἐκκλησίαι* formally, but the members of them. Such constructions *κατὰ σύνεσιν* are not uncommon. Winer, § 21, § 58, § 67; A. Buttmann, p. 113. The "resolved imperfect" conveys the idea of duration more fully than the simple tense. The usage is found in classic writers (Kühner, § 416, 4; Winer, § 45, 5), but with a closer connection with the subject than in the freer style of the New Testament, which may in this case be influenced by Aramaic usage. In the Sept. it is chiefly employed in clauses which in Hebrew have a special significance, *ubi etiam in Hebraico non sine vi sua adhibita erat*, as Gen. iv. 17, Ex. iii. 1, where the Hebrew has the same construction of substantive verb and participle, or where there is only a participle, Gen. xviii. 22. The periphrasis occurs often with the future. Thiersch, *de Pent. Vers.* p. 163. What they were hearing was startling to them:

"Οτι ὁ διώκων ἡμᾶς ποτέ—"that he who once persecuted

us," that is, our former persecutor,—the participle with the article losing its temporal significance and becoming a substantive. Schmalfeld, § 222; Winer, § 45, 7; Schirlitz, § 47. The participle *διώκων* is not for *διώξας* (Grotius, Rückert), nor is *ὅτι* superfluous (Koppe). The *ποτέ* is out of its usual place. According to Schott, Matthies, Hilgenfeld, and Trana, the *ὅτι* is recitative; and it might be so if the following clause be regarded as a quotation. They might say one to another, "that our former persecutor is now become a preacher." This use of *ὅτι* is limited in Paul to quotations from the Old Testament: iii. 8, Rom. iv. 17, viii. 36, ix. 17; somewhat differently, 2 Thess. iii. 10. The address here passes in *ἡμᾶς* from the oblique introduced by *ὅτι*, to the direct form in the pronoun, as in Acts xiv. 22, xxiii. 22, 1 Cor. xiv. 23, 25. Krüger, § 65, 11, Anm. 8, gives examples from classical writers, so that the diction here is neither so lax nor inaccurate as Gwynne supposes it. It seems a mere refinement on the part of Meyer to deny the passing of the indirect to the direct form, by alleging that Paul might now as a Christian include himself among the *ἡμᾶς*, and call himself "our former persecutor." He—

Νῦν εὐαγγελίζεται τὴν πίστιν ἥν ποτὲ ἐπόρθει—"is now preaching the faith which he once was destroying." Some MSS., the It., and Vulg., with many of the Latin fathers, have *ἐπολέμει*. The present and the imperfect are to be taken in their full and proper meaning.

Πίστις has an objective reference, but not in the later ecclesiastical sense. It was the distinctive pervading element of the new evangel, and soon gave its name to it. Its facts and truths claim faith; its blessings are suspended on faith; its graces are wrought by faith; its Lord and Saviour is the object of faith; and its disciples are called faith-ful—believers. In the New Testament, the word seems always to carry in it reference to the inner principle, the governing power in the soul, for "we walk by faith." On *ἐπόρθει*, see ver. 13.

The result of their knowledge of this momentous and notorious change was—

Ver. 24. *Καὶ ἐδόξαζον ἐν ἐμοὶ τὸν Θεόν*—"And they glorified God in me." The *ἐν ἐμοί* is not *δι' ἐμέ* (Photius), "on account of me" (Brown), as if it were בִּי for עָלַי (Beza), or *de me, vel propter me* (Estius). The preposition marks the sphere in which the action takes place. Winer, § 48, 2, *a*; Bernhardy, 210; Ex. xiv. 4, ἐνδοξασθήσομαι ἐν Φαραῷ; Isa. xlix. 3, καὶ ἐν σοὶ δοξασθήσομαι. To glorify God is a favourite Pauline phrase: Acts xi. 18, xxi. 20; Rom. i. 21, xv. 9; 1 Cor. vi. 20; 2 Cor. ix. 13. "In him"—and the change wrought within him, with its marvellous and enduring effects—they glorified God. Not only did his conversion give them occasion to glorify God, but they glorified God working in him, and in him changing their malignant and resolute persecutor into a bold enthusiastic preacher. They were thankful not simply because persecution had ceased, but they rejoiced that he who did the havoc was openly building up the cause which he had laboured to overthrow. On hearing of a change in so prominent and terrible an adversary—a change not leading merely to a momentary check or a longer neutral pause, but passing into unwearied activity, self-denial, and apostolical pre-eminence—they glorified God in him, for in him God's gracious power had wrought with unexpected and unexampled might and result. They did not exalt the man, though they could not but have a special interest in him; but they knew that by the grace of God he was what he was. If the churches even in Judea were so grateful to God for His work in Paul, were they not a rebuke to the Judaizers, who now questioned his apostleship and impugned his teaching? Eph. iii. 7, 8; 1 Tim. i. 16. Chrysostom adds, he does not say ὅτι ἐθαύμαζόν με, ἐπῄνουν με, ἐξεπλήττοντο, ἀλλὰ τὸ πᾶν τῆς χάριτος ἔδειξεν ὄν. . . .

NOTE ON CHAP. I. 19

Ἰάκωβον τὸν ἀδελφὸν τοῦ Κυρίου—"James the Lord's brother."

What, then, is meant by the phrase, "the Lord's brother?" If, as here implied, he was one of the apostles, was he one of the twelve—James, son of Alphæus? or if he did not belong to the twelve, why is he ranked among the apostles?

First of all, who are these ἀδελφοί, brothers of our Lord, to whom this James belonged? One may surely discuss this theme without incurring the censure of Calvin: *Certe nemo unquam hac de re questionem movebit nisi curiosus, nemo vero pertinaciter insistet nisi contentiosus rixator.*—On Matt. i. 25. For, after all, it is simply an attempted answer to the question, Are there two only or are there three Jameses mentioned in the New Testament? What, then, from the simple narrative may be gleaned about the ἀδελφοί? They are referred to nine times in the four Gospels, once in the Acts, and once in the first Epistle to the Corinthians. From these incidental notices we learn the following:—1. The "brothers" are a party distinct from the apostles. Thus, John ii. 12: "After this He went down to Capernaum, He, and His mother, and His brethren, and His disciples;" Matt. xii. 46, 47: "While He yet talked to the people, behold, His mother and His brothers stood without, desiring to speak with Him. Then one said, Behold, thy mother and thy brothers stand without, desiring to speak with thee." Mark iii. 31; Luke viii. 19. Again, the men of "His own country" cried, "Is not this the carpenter's son? is not his mother called Mary? and his brothers, James, and Joses, and Simon, and Judas? and his sisters, are they not all with us?" Matt. xiii. 55. "Is not this the carpenter, the son of Mary, and brother of James and Joses, and of Judas and Simon? and are not his sisters here with us?" Mark vi. 3. "His brothers said to Him, Depart hence, and go into Judæa, that thy disciples also may see the works that thou doest. For neither did His brothers believe on Him. But when His brothers were gone up, then went He also up unto the feast." John vii. 3, 5, 10. Four times do this party, so nearly related to Him, pass before us in the gospel history: immediately after His first miracle; as wishing an interview with Him; as sneeringly referred to by His fellow-townsmen; and as not yet believing on Him. The same distinction is still marked after the ascension: "These all (the apostles) continued with one accord in prayer and supplication, with the women, and Mary the mother of Jesus, and with His brothers."[1] Acts i. 14. The plea of the Apostle Paul is: "Have we not power to lead about a sister, a wife, as well as other apostles, and as the brothers of the Lord, and Cephas?" 1 Cor. ix. 5. 2. The

[1] Strange is the view of Guericke—"with His brethren," *i.e.* with His other three brothers, besides James that had just been named. *Einl.* p. 156.

brothers appear always in connection with Mary, save in John vii.—the scene and expression of their unbelief, and she could not be entangled in that unbelief; and she is always found in company with them, save in Luke ii. 42, Joseph being then alive, and in John xix. 25, where she was commended to John and not to one of them. Four times is she—a widow probably by this time—connected with them as their parental head. 3. As a family they are once named as consisting of four brothers—"James, and Joses, and Judas, and Simon"—and of at least *two* sisters, as the word "all" (πᾶσαι ἀδελφαί) would seem to imply. 4. We have in the verse before us "James the Lord's brother," not to distinguish him from the son of Zebedee, as Hug supposes, for then his patronymic Alphæi would have been quite sufficient. He was therefore one of these ἀδελφοί.

Now, had there been no theological intervention,—no peculiar views as to the perpetual virginity of Mary, or at least no impression that the womb chosen for the divine infant was so sacred—so set apart in solitary honour and dedication, that it could have no other or subsequent tenant,—the natural or usual domestic meaning would have been the only one given to the previous quotations, and Jesus, His brothers, and His sisters would have been regarded as forming one household having the common relationship of children to Mary their mother. The employment of the anomalous double plural "brethren,"[1] instead of "brothers," in all these places of the Authorized Version, lessens or diverts the impression on the English reader; for "brethren" now never denotes sons of the same parents, but is official, national, functional, or congregational in its use. But the simple and natural meaning of ἀδελφοί has not been usually adopted, and two rival explanatory theories have had a wide and lasting prominence.

The theory so commonly held among ourselves is, that the brothers of our Lord were His cousins—either children of the Virgin's sister, wife of Clopas, or children of Clopas, Joseph's brother.[2] The first hypothesis is real cousinhood; the second

[1] Bruder, Brüder (Brither, Breether, *Scottice*),—"*-en*" belonging to another plural form, as in ox, oxen. Latham calls these last forms "collectives," rather than true plurals. *English Language*, p. 503.

[2] Clopas, not Cleophas, is the proper reading of John xix. 25, and is so given in the margin. Cleopas is the name in Luke xxiv. 18.

is only legal and unreal in reference to Him who was not Joseph's son.

Jerome, who is identified with the theory of cousinhood, as being the first who gave it an elaborated form, refers (under Gal. i. 19) to his *Adversus Helvidium de perpetua Virginitate Beatæ Mariæ*, written about 382,—an essay which he wrote, as he says, *dum Romæ essem, impulsu fratrum.* Now, to hold, according to the title of this tract, the perpetual virginity of Mary, forecloses the discussion as to the question of full and natural brotherhood; and Jerome's avowed and primary object was to show that no theory about the *ἀδελφοί* was permissible which brought the perpetual virginity under suspicion or denial. But the dogma has no scriptural support, so that it cannot demand acceptance as an article of faith. For,

I. What does *πρωτότοκος* imply? We read, Matt. i. 25, *καὶ οὐκ ἐγίνωσκεν αὐτὴν ἕως οὗ ἔτεκε τὸν υἱὸν αὐτῆς τὸν πρωτότοκον*—"and knew her not till she brought forth her first-born son." Lachmann, Tischendorf, and Tregelles exclude *πρωτότοκον*, but only on the authority of B, Z, and א, and on the suspicion that the phrase was taken from Luke ii. 7. It may be replied, however, that this intense belief in the perpetual virginity formed a strong temptation to leave out the epithet; for from it, as Jerome bitterly asserts, some men *perversissime* suspected that Mary had other and subsequent children. The epithet, however, occurs in Luke ii. 7, where there is no difference of reading. Now, in ordinary language, "first-born" implies that others are born afterward; and Jesus could have been as easily called her *only* as her first-born son. The force of this argument is somewhat neutralized by the opinion, that the word "first-born" may have had a technical sense, since in the Mosaic law it might be applied to the first child, though none were born after it,—"the firstling of man and beast being devoted to God." Ex. xiii. 2; Luke ii. 23. Thus Lightfoot says: "The word is to be understood here according to the propriety and phrase of the law," and he instances 1 Chron. ii. 50, where "Hur is called the first-born of Ephrath, and yet no mention made of any child that she had after."[1] But "first-born" occurs generally in these genealogical lists in its relative sense; and as sons are usually

[1] *Works*, vol. iv. 194, ed. Pitman.

registered only, might not Ephrath have had daughters? The Hebrew law, as originally ordained, was a present enactment with a prospective reference as regards the first child or son, whether an only child or not, and the statute was easily interpreted. The same principle is applicable to the term "first-born" as belonging to the Egyptian families that suffered under the divine judgment, and to Jerome's objection that the law of redemption applying to the first-born would, if the word be taken in its relative sense, be held in suspense till the birth of a second child. But Jerome's definition is true only in a legal sense: *Primogenitus est non tantum post quem alii, sed ante quem nullus.*[1] For the diction of law and history are different. The law ordained the dedication of that child by the birth of which a woman became a mother, and called it the firstling or first-born irrespective of any subsequent children, and at its birth the redemption must be made. But in writing the history of an individual many years after his time, it would be strange to call him a first-born son, or to say of his mother that she brought forth her first-born son, if there were in that family no subsequent births. A biographer would in that case most naturally call him an only son. Epiphanius must have been greatly at a loss for an argument to prove "first-born" to be the same as "only," when he bases it on the position of *αὐτῆς* in Matt. i. 25: *τὸν υἱὸν αὐτῆς . . . καὶ οὐκ εἶπε τὸν πρωτότοκον αὐτῆς . . . ἀλλὰ πρωτότοκον μόνον,*[2] as if *αὐτῆς* did not belong to both words.

Besides, the epithet "first-born" is used by an evangelist who in subsequent chapters speaks of brothers and sisters of Jesus; and what could he suppose would be the natural inference of his readers when they brought *πρωτότοκος υἱός* and *ἡ μήτηρ καὶ οἱ ἀδελφοὶ αὐτοῦ* together, there being no hint or explanation that the relations indicated are other than the ordinary and natural one of blood? The epithet, too, does not seem to have an absolute sense as used in the New Testament: *πρωτότοκον ἐν πολλοῖς ἀδελφοῖς*, Rom. viii. 29. Compare Col. i. 15, 18; Heb. xi. 28; Rev. i. 5. The inference of Eunomius is a natural one: *εἰ πρωτότοκος οὐκέτι μονογενής.* Helvidius, who, as is well known, holds the natural kinship,

[1] *Opera*, vol. ii. p. 214, ed. Vallars.

[2] *Panaria*, vol. ii. pp. 431–2, ed. Œhler, Berlin 1861.

and against whom Jerome fulminated in the tract already referred to, argues, as might be supposed, in the same way; and Lucian says: *εἰ μὲν πρῶτος, οὐ μόνος, εἰ δὲ μόνος οὐ πρῶτος.*[1]

II. No definite argument can be based on the particle ἕως in the same verse, for it does not always mean that what is asserted or denied up to a certain point of time is reversed after it. In 2 Sam. vi. 23, where it is said "she (Michal) had no child till the day of her death," the meaning cannot be mistaken. But the sense must be determined by the context, whether what is asserted as far as ἕως ceased or continued after it.[2] See Fritzsche on Matt. xxviii. 20; Meyer on Matt. i. 25.

This verse undoubtedly affirms the virginity of Mary up to the birth of Jesus, and this prior virginity is the principal fact; but it as plainly implies, that after that event Mary lived with Joseph as his wife. Even prior to the birth she is called "Mary thy wife," and her virginity is stated as if it had been a parenthesis in her wifehood. Basil himself, while asserting that her virginity before the birth was necessary, and that the lovers of Christ cannot bear to hear that she, *ἡ θεοτόκος*, ever ceased to be a virgin, admits that the phrase *ἕως οὗ ἔτεκεν* creates a suspicion, *ὑπόνοιαν*, that afterwards this prenuptial condition ceased: *τὰ νενομισμένα τοῦ γάμου ἔργα μὴ ἀπαρνησαμένης τῆς Μαρίας.*[3] The theory of Jerome, on the other hand, was intended, in fact, to conserve the perpetual virginity both of Joseph and Mary. It is beside the point, and a mere assumption, to say, with Olshausen on Matt. i. 25, Joseph might justly think that his marriage with Mary had another purpose than that of begetting children. "It seems," he adds, "in the order of nature, that the last female descendant of

[1] *Demonax*, 29; *Opera*, vol. v. p. 245, ed. Bipont.

[2] Isidore the Pelusiot, repeated by Suidas, says: *τὸ ἕως πολλάκις καὶ ἐπὶ τοῦ διηνεκῶς ἐν τῇ θείᾳ γραφῇ εὑρίσκομεν κείμενον.* Theophylact, on Matt. i. 25, gives as the result, *οὐδέ ποτε αὐτὴν ἔγνω.* Strauss quotes from Diogenes Laertius, iii. 1, 2 (p. 195, vol. i. ed. Huebner), the case of Plato's father, of whom it is said, in consequence of a vision of Apollo, *ὅθεν καθαρὰν γάμον φυλάξαι ἕως τῆς ἀποκυήσεως*, and Plato had brothers. But when Strauss says of Mary, that she had children younger than Jesus—*jüngere und vielleich auch ältere*, "younger, and perhaps older also"—the audacious assertion makes the *πρωτότοκον* a falsehood. *Das Leben Jesu*, vol. i. p. 246.

[3] *Opera*, vol. ii. p. 854, ed. Gaume, Paris 1835.

David, in the family of which the Messiah was born, closed her family with this last and eternal scion." This is only sentiment without any proof, though I confess that one naturally clings to such a belief. The perpetual virginity cannot, however, be conclusively proved out of Scripture; but an inference decidedly against it may be maintained from both the terms πρωτότοκος and ἕως in Matt. i. 25.

If the ἀδελφοί were only cousins, the perpetual virginity becomes at least possible. Jerome's first argument on behalf of cousinhood is, that in Gal. i. 19, James is recognised as an apostle, and must therefore be James son of Alphæus, one of the twelve. If not, he reasons that there must have been three Jameses,—the son of Zebedee, the son of Alphæus or James the Less, and this third one; but the epithet τοῦ μικροῦ given to the one James implies that there were only two; so that the imagined third James is identical with the son of Alphæus. Mark xv. 40. But in reply, *first*, James the Lord's brother was not, in our view, one of the twelve, so that such an argument forms no objection; and, *secondly*, the comparative *minor*, "the Less," is not the proper rendering of the positive ὁ μικρός; and though it were the true rendering, it might still be given to James the Lord's brother, to distinguish him from James the son of Alphæus. Probably the epithet is absolute, and alludes to stature and not to age;[1] at all events, the other James is never called James the Great. Gregory of Nyssa, indeed, gives him that title because he was among the apostles; the Lord's brother, on the other hand, being called "Little" as not being among them,—a conjecture on a par with that of Lange, that James was named "the Less" from his later entrance into the apostolic college in comparison with the other James. It is highly probable, too, that "the Little" was not the epithet he bore at the period of the resurrection, but was his individualizing epithet when the Gospel was written.

[1] Aristophanes, *Ranæ* 709, names the bathkeeper Kleigenes, ὁ μικρός, having just styled him πίθηκος, an ape; μικκός γα μᾶκος οὗτος are used similarly, *Acharn.* 909. In Xenophon, *Mem.* i. 4, 2, we have the phrase πρὸς Ἀριστόδημον τὸν Μικρὸν ἐπικαλούμενον; and the meaning is apparent, for the diminutive atheist is called σμικρός in Plato, *Symp.* 173 B, vol. i. p. 8, ed. Stallbaum.

2. The other steps of Jerome's argument are: Alphæus father of James, was married to Mary sister of the Virgin; so that James was the Lord's cousin, and might be called His brother according to Jewish usage. That is, Mary the mother of James the Little is asserted to be wife of Alphæus his father,—it being assumed, *first*, that James the Little is the same with the son of Alphæus; *secondly*, that this Mary is the wife of Clopas and the Virgin's sister; and *thirdly*, that Alphæus and Clopas are the same person. Yet Jerome says in his very tract against Helvidius that he does not contend earnestly for the identity of Mary of Clopas with Mary mother of James and Joses, though one should say that it was the key to his whole argument. Nay, in his epistle to Hedibia he writes: *Quatuor autem fuisse Marias, in Evangeliis legimus, unam matrem Domini Salvatoris, alteram materteram ejus quæ appellata est Maria Cleophæ, tertiam Mariam matrem Jacobi et Jose, quartam Mariam Magdalenam. Licet alii matrem Jacobi et Jose materteram ejus fuisse contendunt.*[1]

But Clopas and Alphæus cannot be identified with certainty. The names are not so like as some contend. In Matt. x. 3, Mark iii. 18, Luke vi. 15, Acts i. 13, we have James the son of Alphæus, and in Mark ii. 14 we have Levi the son of Alphæus; but whether these two Alphæuses are the same or different, it is impossible to decide.[2] Then we have Κλῶπας (Clopas) in John xix. 23, and Κλέοπας (Cleopas) in Luke xxiv. 18, the proper spelling of the two names in the Greek text. The original Syro-Chaldaic form, as given in the Syriac version, is ܚܠܦܝ, Chalphai,[3] and is found in the five places where Ἀλφαῖος occurs, but it gives ܩܠܝܘܦܐ for the two names Clopas and Cleopas in John and Luke. The names are

[1] Ep. cxx., *Opera*, vol. i. p. 826.

[2] The Greek Church has a feast for St. James the Just, October 23d; and another on the 9th of the same month for St. James son of Alphæus, "and brother of Matthew the publican and evangelist." The Syrian and Coptic Churches observe the same festivals. Chrysostom also makes Matthew and James brothers: on Matt. x. 3.

[3] The name Χαλφί occurs in 1 Macc. xi. 70, and represents, perhaps, such a Hebrew form, חַלְפַּי.

thus evidently regarded as quite different by the author or authors of this oldest version. Clopas therefore is not, as is often affirmed, the Aramaic form of Alphæus; and to assert that Alphæus and Clopas are varying names is opposed to philological analogy. The Syriac *Cheth* may pass into the Greek *'A* with the *spiritus lenis*, as in *'Αλφαῖος*, for the Hebrew ח is so treated by the Seventy, חַוָּה becoming *Εὔα*, though often it is represented by the Greek *X* or *K*. But would *'A* have any alliance with the consonantal *Kuph* in Clopas or Klopas? At least the Hebrew *Koph* seems never to be represented by a vowel in the Septuagint, but by *K*, *X*, or *Γ*. Frankel, *Vorstudien*, etc., p. 112. In fine, it cannot be safely held that by James the Little must be meant the son of Alphæus, for, as Hegesippus says, "there were many Jameses."

Nor can any solid assistance for this theory of cousinhood be got from John xix. 25, for it cannot be proved that the words "His mother's sister" are in apposition with "Mary the wife of Clopas." The punctuation of the verse is, probably, not *τοῦ 'Ιησοῦ ἡ μήτηρ αὐτοῦ, καὶ ἡ ἀδελφὴ τῆς μητρὸς αὐτοῦ Μαρία ἡ τοῦ Κλωπᾶ*—"Mary His mother, and His mother's sister Mary wife of Clopas;" but there should be a comma after *μητρὸς αὐτοῦ*, so that Mary of Clopas becomes a third and different person, the "sister's" name not being given: "His mother and His mother's sister, Mary wife of Clopas and Mary Magdalene." The Peschito inserts "and" before *Μαρία* —ܘܡܪܝܡ; and in the Greek the four clauses are arranged in couplets, as in Matt. x. 2–4. This punctuation is preferable, for it is not very likely that two sisters in one family should have the same name, and there is no parallel case in Scripture; for the name of Herod, an example adduced by Mill, comes not, as being a royal name repeated in the family, into comparison. But again, there is no certainty that *ἡ τοῦ Κλωπᾶ* is "wife of Clopas;" for it may be either wife, mother, or daughter of Clopas, as the context may determine. Thus a Mary is called mother of James and Joses in Matt. xxvii. 56, *Μαρία ἡ τοῦ 'Ιακώβου καὶ 'Ιωσῆ μήτηρ*; but in Mark (xv. 47) she is named simply *Μαρία 'Ιωσῆ*, and in Luke (xxiv. 10), *Μαρία 'Ιακώβου*. Why may not these two last places guide us to interpret *Μαρία ἡ τοῦ Κλῶπα* as "Mary mother of

Clopas?" It cannot, then, be demonstrated, either that Alphæus and Clopas are the same person, or that Mary of Clopas is necessarily his wife, and to be identified with Mary mother of James and Joses. But it has been triumphantly asked, If a Mary, not the Virgin, is called for distinction's sake "mother of James," what James can be meant but the most famous of the name—James of Alphæus called the Lord's brother, and in the early church James the Little, and therefore the cousin of our Lord? But be James the Little who he may, his position does not seem of sufficient prominence to distinguish his mother, for the name of another son, Joses, is added, as if for such a purpose, in Mark xv. 40. The combination of both names was apparently required to point out the mother, so that it is natural to infer that this James, like his brother Joses, was of small note in the church, and could not therefore be the son of Alphæus. And to show what confusion reigns on this point, it may be added that not a few identify Mary mother of James with Mary mother of our Lord. This is virtually done in the apocryphal gospel *Historia Josephi*, cap. iv., by Gregory of Nyssa, by Chrysostom, by Theophylact, by Helvidius, by Fritzsche, and by Cave who makes Alphæus another name of Joseph. The James and Joses who had this Mary as their mother could not, therefore, be the brethren of our Lord, as the four would most likely have been mentioned together; and it is not possible either that "mother" should have a vague significance, or that her maternal relation should be ignored, and two other sons or step-sons placed in the room of her First-born.

Again, if the brothers were merely cousins, sons of Alphæus, how could they be called again and again ἀδελφοί? Jerome replies, *Quatuor modis fratres dici, natura, gente, cognatione affectu; natura, Esau, Jacob; gente qua omnes Judæi inter se fratres vocant; . . . cognatione qui sunt de una familia, id est patria, Abraham, Lot,—Laban, Jacob; affectu . . . Christiani fratres*, etc. Then he asks, Were these cousins *fratres juxta naturam? non; juxta gentem? absurdum; juxta affectum? verum si sic, qui magis fratres quam apostoli? . . . Restat igitur fratres eos intelligas appellatos cognatione.*[1] But in these examples re-

[1] Theophylact also says, εἴωκεν ἡ γραφὴ τοὺς συγγενεῖς ἀδελφοὺς ὀνομάζειν. Monod's reference to Matt. i. 11, in defence of the same opinion, cannot be sustained.

ferred to, the context prevents any confusion of sense. Lot is called a brother of Abraham, and Jacob of Laban, they being only nephews, and specially beloved for the original fraternal relation. These indefinite terms of relation are found in the oldest book of Scripture; but there is no instance of this laxity in the New Testament found with *ἀδελφός* in reference to kinship, nor with *ἀδελφή* unless it is used tropically, Rom. xvi. 1. The New Testament has special terms, as *συγγενεῖς*, *ἀνεψιός*: Mark vi. 4; Luke i. 36, ii. 44; Col. iv. 10. Even in the old books of the Old Testament, when relation is to be marked, there is perfect definiteness in the use of אָח, as in Gen. xxxvii. 10, l. 8, Lev. xxi. 2, Num. vi. 7, Josh. ii. 13. When it is employed along with father, mother, or sister, it evidently bears its own proper meaning. In the same way, in those clauses of the New Testament already referred to, *ἀδελφός* is used along with *μήτηρ αὐτοῦ*; and it would be strange if in such a connection, where the maternal relation is indicated, the fraternal should not correspond,—if along with "mother" in its true meaning, "brother" should be found in a vague and unusual sense. Do not the phrases, "His mother and His brothers," "thy mother and thy brothers," suggest that Mary stood in a common maternal relation to Him and to them? And if these brothers were only first cousins, sons of Mary's sister and Alphæus, why are they always in the evangelical history associated with the mother of Jesus, but never with their own mother, while they are uniformly called His brothers?

It is also held by many, though not by Jerome, that along with James Alphæi there were among the twelve two other brothers, a *Ἰούδας Ἰακώβου*, "Jude brother of James," and a Simon called the Zealot; the proof being that in the lists of Luke and Acts, James is placed between these two, as if he had belonged to the same family. See Matt. xiii. 55, Luke vi. 16, and Jude 1. That is, His "brothers" are James, Joses, Simon, and Judas; and these being cousins, three of them are found among the primary apostles. But if in the same list *Ἰάκωβος Ἀλφαίου* be James *son* of Alphæus, why should *Ἰούδας Ἰακώβου* not mean Jude *son* and not brother of James, especially as brotherhood is marked by *ἀδελφός* in a previous part of the catalogue in Luke vi. 16? Son is the more natural supplement, as in the Peschito, and the opinion is adopted by Luther, Herder, Jessien, Dahl, and Wieseler. As Lightfoot has remarked, "Had brotherhood been intended, the clause would have run as in other cases, such as that of the sons of Zebedee,—'James the son of Alphæus, and Jude his brother,' or 'James and Jude, sons of Alphæus.'" Simon Zelotes is never called brother of James; and Jude is termed Lebbæus whose surname was Thaddæus in Matt. x. 3, in Mark iii. 18 simply Thaddæus, and Judas not Iscariot in John xiv. 22. It is likewise passing strange, that if three out of the four brothers were apostles, not one of them should be ever designated by that honourable appellation. Nor is there any probability at all that Jude and Simon are two of the four; nor is the case different with James and Joses, for if Joses be not one of the so-called brethren, neither was his brother James. One of the Lord's brothers is called by the Nazarenes, in Matt. xiii. 55, *'Ιωσήφ* (Joseph), according to the best reading; but the son of a Mary is called *'Ιωσῆς* (Joses), making a genitive *'Ιωσῆτος*, in Matt. xxvii. 56, according to the highest authorities. These Greek words may represent different Syro-Chaldaic forms, and the Syriac has for Joses ܝܘܣܐ, the other form being ܝܘܣܣ. But no great stress can be laid on such variations, unless we had faith in the minute exactness of copyists. Schneckenburger's identification of Joses with Joseph Barsabas surnamed Justus in Acts i. 23, is for many reasons quite a gratuitous conjecture. Levi (Matthew) is called "of Alphæus," Mark ii. 14: was he another son of Alphæus, or is the father of Matthew a different person of the same name?

But further, after this disposal of the names individually, we may ask, If three out of the four of Christ's "brothers" were among His called and consecrated, how could they come with His mother desiring to speak with Him; how could they as a party be always named as distinct from the apostles; and especially, how could it be said of them at a period so far advanced in our Lord's ministry, that they did not believe on Him? For it is declared of them: *οὐδὲ γὰρ οἱ ἀδελφοὶ αὐτοῦ ἐπίστευον εἰς αὐτόν,*—"for neither were His brothers believing on Him." John vii. 5. They certainly could not be His apostles and yet be unbelievers in Himself or in His divine mission. Jerome indeed holds that James was a believer, and his theory allowed him to single out James; but the brethren are plainly spoken of as a body. Nor would this alleged faith of James serve Jerome's purpose, or warrant James' enrolment among the twelve; for the brethren, even after they did believe, are described as a party quite distinct from the apostles, Acts i. 14, 1 Cor. ix. 5. It is remarkable, too, that our Lord's reply to His brothers is the same as that to His mother, John ii. 4, "My time is not yet come,"—as if He had detected in them a similar spirit to hers at the marriage, when, the wine being done, she ventured to suggest His immediate interposition. The force of this argument from the unbelief of the brothers has been sometimes set aside, as by Ellicott after Grotius, Lardner, and Hug, who assert that the verb ἐπίστευον may be used in an emphatic sense, as if it meant, did not fully believe on Him. The context is against such a view; for whatever their impressions and anticipations about Him and His miracles, they wanted faith in Him, and spoke either in selfish or satirical rebuke: "Depart hence, and go to Judæa, that thy disciples also may see the works that thou doest." Ellicott refers, in vindication of his statement, to John vi. 64, "There are some of you—μαθηταί—that believe not;" but there the assertion is an absolute one,—and in proof we are told in the 66th verse, that "many of them went back, and walked no more with Him." The 67th verse, by the question, "Will ye also go away?" does not, as Ellicott alleges, imply any doubt, for it was only a testing challenge proposed to draw out the noble response of Peter for himself and his colleagues. See Meyer, Lücke, *in loc.* Further, to say, in opposition to what has been advanced, that two at least of the ἀδελφοί were among the apostles, assumes the correctness of the theory that they were cousins, but the phrase οἱ ἀδελφοὶ αὐτοῦ seems to include the domestic party as a whole; and there was no need, as Pott and Monod imagine, for inserting πάντες in order to get this sense. The exegesis of Lange on this passage is quite untenable, and is no better, as Alford calls it, than "finessing."[1] He says that the unbelief of the Lord's brother is parallel to (*auf eine linie mit*) the unbelief of Peter, Matt. xvi. 23, and of Thomas, John xx. 25. "The evangelist does not," he adds, "speak of unbelief in the ordinary sense, which rejected the

[1] Article *Jacobus* in Herzog's *Encyclopædie.*

Messiahship of Jesus; but of that want of trust, compliance, and obedience, which made it difficult for His disciples, apostles, and even also His mother, to find themselves reconciled to His life of suffering and to His concealment of Himself." Now the phrase introducing the statement is *οὐδὲ γάρ*, "for neither did His brethren believe on Him,"—the relative *οὐδέ* bringing a previous party into view, that is, the Jews, who sought to slay Him,—the worst form of unbelief; or if *οὐδέ* be taken absolutely, "not even," it still brings out a very strong assertion of unbelief. The unbelief ascribed to Peter and Thomas, on the occasions to which Lange refers, was a momentary stagger,—the first at the idea of the Master enduring the sufferings which Himself had predicted, and the other was a refusal to admit without proof the identity of the apparition which the ten had seen with Him who had been crucified. The phrase *πιστεύειν εἰς αὐτόν* has but one meaning in the narrative portion of John, as in ii. 11, 23, iv. 39, vii. 31, 39, ix. 36, x. 42, etc.; and that simple and natural meaning does not bear out the ingenious exegesis by which Ellicott and Lange would exculpate the Lord's brethren. Nay more, the evangelist records the saying in vi. 69, "We believe and are sure that Thou art that Christ, the Son of the living God,"—and this is said of the apostles as a body; but when he says a few verses farther on, vii. 5, "Neither did His brothers believe on Him," the contrast is surely one of full significance. In fine, the *ἀδελφοί* distinctly, and one would almost say tauntingly, exclude themselves from the wider party when they name them *οἱ μαθηταί σου*. They went up to the feast separately from Jesus and the apostles. Other shifts have been resorted to in order to take its natural significance of fraternal unbelief from the passage. While Chrysostom (on John vii. 5) distinctly places James among the brethren—the James of Gal. i. 19; Grotius and Paulus imagine that the same persons are not always represented by the *ἀδελφοί*, some of whom believed, and some did not. Pott and Gabler conjecture more wildly that the *ἀδελφοί* were brothers of James who was only a cousin, and not comprehended therefore in this position of unbelief. But why should James the "Lord's brother" be put into a different category from the Lord's brothers, one of whom is called James? It may be added in a word, that the unbelief of the Lord's brothers so incidentally stated, becomes a proof of the veracity of the evangelists. They hesitate not to say that His nearest kindred opposed Him, and they did not deem the unlikely fact to be derogatory to His character. Their unbelief proves, at the same time, that there was no inner compact, no domestic league, to help forward His claims. He did not first win over His family, so as to enjoy their interested assistance as agitators and heralds. The result then is, that the theory which holds that these brothers of our Lord were His first cousins seems very untenable, as is shown by this array of objections viewed singly and in their reciprocal connection.

The tractate of Jerome, who first argued out at length the hypothesis of cousinhood, and of the identity of James the Lord's brother with James son of Alphæus, was an earnest vindication against Helvidius of the *ἀει-παρθενία* of the blessed Virgin as a dogma not to be questioned without presumption or impugned without "blasphemy." So much is his soul stirred by the daring outrage, that he begins with invoking the assistance of the Holy Spirit; and of the Son that His mother may be defended *ab omni concubitus suspicione;* and of the Father, too, that the mother of His Son may be shown to be *virgo post partum quæ fuit mater antequam nupta.* What he defended was to him a momentous article, the virginity of Mary after the Lord's birth being as surely held and revered as her virginity prior to it. He professes to be guided solely by Scripture: *Non campum rhetorici desideramus eloquii, non dialecticorum tendiculas, nec Aristotelis spineta conquirimus.* He shows no little ingenuity in his interpretation of various phrases; is especially exultant on the meaning of *donec* or *usque* in the clause *donec peperit filium,* and of *primogenitus* in connection with the Hebrew priesthood[1] and the destruction of the first-born in Egypt; cries out on Helvidius, who thought that Mary the mother of Jesus is she who is called mother of James and Joses among the women at the cross;[2] then develops his theory of cousins-brothers, and thinks that he has obtained

[1] He pictures a Hebrew as saying to himself, *Nihil debeo sacerdoti nisi et ille fuerit procreatus per quem is qui ante natus est, incipiat esse primogenitus.* Advers. Helvid. p. 215, vol. ii. ed. Vallars.

[2] Yet, as we have said, Gregory of Nyssa, Chrysostom, Fritzsche, and Cave, hold the same view.

a decided victory by a *cornuta interrogatio*, when he winds up a paragraph by affirming that in the same way as Joseph was called His father, they were called His brothers.[1] He next passes into a eulogy on virginity, not forgetting, however, that the saints in the Old Testament had wives, nay, that some had a plurality of them; but proceeds to a very spirited picture of the woes of married life,—the wife painting before the mirror, and busied in dusting, knitting, and dressing, infants screaming, children kissed, cooks here and dressmakers there, accounts to be made up, correction of servants, scenes of revelry,—*Responde quæso inter ista ubi sit Dei cogitatio?* Any house otherwise ordered, must, he adds in his celibate wit, be *rara avis.* At length he ventures to go so deeply into the privacies of the matter that we forbear to follow him. His tone towards his opponent is one of utter contempt and savage humour: he brands him as *hominem rusticanum* and *vix primis quoque imbutum literis*,—cries on one occasion, *doleamne an rideam, nescio;* upbraids his style,—*vitia sermonis, quibus omnis liber tuus scatet;* salutes him as *imperitissime hominum;* accuses him of a love of notoriety madder and incomparably more flagitious in result than his who set fire to Diana's temple at Ephesus, for he had done a similar outrage to the temple of the Lord, and had desecrated the sanctuary of the Spirit; compares his eloquence to a camel's dance,—*risimus in te proverbium, camelum vidimus saltitantem;* and ends by assuring him that his censure would be his (Jerome's) highest glory, since he would in that case suffer the same *canina facundia* as did the mother of the Lord. This sternness of rebuke and outpouring of scorn and indignation on the subject, are an index to that general state of feeling which Helvidius was so luckless and daring as to offend, *solus in universo mundo;* and yet he was all the while so obscure an individual that his respondent, living in the same city with him, knows nothing of him, and cannot tell whether he be fair or dark of visage,—*albus aterve sis, nescio—quis te, oro, ante hanc blasphemiam noverat, quis dupondii supputabat?* It is at the same time to be borne in mind, that Jerome, in the midst of this fury, claims no support from the ecclesi-

[1] Chrysostom, on Matt. i. 25, gives the same opinion. He asks, How are James and the others called His brothers? and his reply is, *ὥσπερ καὶ αὐτὸς ἐνομίζετο ἀνὴρ τῆς Μαρίας ὁ Ἰωσήφ*

astical writers before him, quotes no one in his favour, appeals to no father of an earlier century, even while he admits that Tertullian held his opponent's views, and curtly dismisses him as not belonging to the church.

The general purpose of his treatise was to prove the perpetual virginity, and to root up and scatter to the winds the argument against it, that Mary had other sons besides her "First-born." Ignatius, Polycarp, Irenæus, Justin Martyr, and "many other apostolic and eloquent men," are appealed to by him as holding the general opinion, *hæc eadem sentientes;* but he does not aver that they held his special hypothesis that the brothers were cousins, though certainly he does not intimate that he and they differed on the point. Jerome refers to this treatise ten years afterwards in an epistle to Pammachius, and vindicates the doctrine of *virgo perpetua mater et virgo*, by bringing such strange analogies in proof as—Christ's sepulchre "wherein was never man yet laid;" His entrance into the chamber, "the doors being shut;" and the prophetic utterance about the gate, "No man shall enter in by it, because the Lord the God of Israel hath entered in by it; therefore it shall be shut."[1] Ezek. xliv. 2.

Now, Jerome's object being to prove Mary virgin *post* as well as *ante partum*, it was quite enough for his purpose to show that the brethren of Joseph were not her true and proper sons. Ambrose, ten years afterwards, contents himself with this simpler declaration: *Potuerunt autem fratres esse ex Joseph non ex Maria. Quod quidem si quis diligentius prosequatur inveniet. Nos ea persequenda non putavimus, quoniam fraternum nomen liquet pluribus esse commune.*[2] Jerome, however, in his zeal, and from the impulses of an ardent and impetuous temperament, deliberately preferred a theory in conflict with the well-known tradition on the subject, which he scouted as being taken from the *deliramenta Apocryphorum.* He was thus well aware of the alternative; for in his note on Matt. xii. 49, he says: *quidam fratres Domini de alia uxore Joseph filios suspicantur;*—again, in *De Viris Illustribus: Jacobus qui appellatur frater Domini, ut nonulli existimant, Joseph ex alia uxore, ut autem mihi videtur, Mariæ sororis*

[1] Ep. xlviii. vol. i. p. 234.

[2] *De Institut. Virg.* vi. *Opera*, vol. ii. p. 317, ed. Migne.

matris Domini cujus Joannes in libro suo meminit, filius.[1] So Pelagius and Isidore Hispalensis, who says, *Jacobus Alphæi sororis matris Domini filius.*—Tom. v. p. 153, ed. Migne. The view of Jerome, which was a comparative novelty among the Western churches, was not at first adopted by his great contemporary Augustine. In his note on Gal. i. 19, he says: *Jacobus Domini frater vel ex filiis Joseph de alia uxore vel ex cognatione Mariæ matris ejus debet intelligi.* These words indicate no fixed opinion; but otherwise he appears to maintain a view not unlike that of Jerome. Thus, in a spiritualistic interpretation of the second verse of Ps. cxxvii., he describes the brethren as *cognati consanguinitate.*[2] Again, *Non mirum est dictos esse fratres Domini ex materno genere quoscumque cognatos, cum etiam ex cognatione Joseph dici potuerint fratres ejus ab illis qui illum patrem Domini esse arbitrantur.*[3] Further: *Unde fratres Domini? Num enim Maria iterum peperit? Absit. Inde cœpit dignitas virginum. Cognati Mariæ fratres Domini, de quolibet gradu cognati.*[4] He does not in these places call them cousins, though he repeats in some of them the stock argument about the brotherhood of Abraham and Lot, Laban and Jacob. He is content with the more general terms, *consanguinei et cognati,*—their *cognatio,* however, being derived through Mary, not through Joseph. The same opinion had, however, some few advocates in the Eastern church. Chrysostom, on Gal. i. 19, calls James son of Clopas ὅπερ καὶ ὁ εὐαγγελιστὴς ἔλεγεν, thus identifying Clopas with Alphæus and regarding James as an apostle. But Chrysostom is far from being consistent with himself; since, as he identifies Μαρία Ἰακώβου (on Matt. xxvii. 25) with the Lord's mother, he must have held either that James was full brother, or at least step-brother. In other places he does not place James among the twelve at all, as on 1 Cor. xv. 7, but calls him an unbeliever with the rest of the Lord's brethren, and says that they bore this name as Joseph was the reputed husband of Mary (on Matt. i. 25). Theodoret says explicitly that James was brother,—not, however, οὔτε μὴν ὥς τινες ὑπειλήφασι τοῦ Ἰωσὴφ υἱὸς ἐτύγχανεν, ὢν ἐκ προτέρων γάμων γενόμενος, ἀλλὰ

1 Tom. ii. p. 829.

2 *Opera*, vol. iv. p. 2058, Paris 1835.

3 On Matt. xii. 55, *Opera*, vol. iii. p. 1669.

4 *Ib.* i. pp. 1793, 1998; *Opera*, vol. viii. 594, and v. 934.

τοῦ Κλωπᾶ μὲν ἦν υἱὸς, τοῦ δὲ Κυρίου ἀνεψιός (on Gal. i. 19). But this view did not obtain wide currency in the East.

The theory of mere cousinhood thus won its way into the Western churches, and became the common one among ourselves. Professor Lightfoot has said that Jerome "did not hold his theory staunchly and consistently," and that in his comment on this verse he speaks like "one who has committed himself to a theory of which he has misgivings." Certainly Jerome did not hold his view at a future period so tenaciously, or with so keen and impatient an opposition to others, as he did at its first promulgation. Thus in the Epistle to Hedibia he says: "There are four Maries: the mother of our Lord; another her aunt, Mary of Clopas; a third, the mother of James and Joses; and a fourth, Mary Magdalene; though others contend that Mary mother of James and Joses was the Virgin's aunt." (See Latin on p. 64.) Again, on this verse, he refers to his treatise written when he was a young man, and then, curtly dismissing it, advances a new argument, that James was called the Lord's brother *propter egregios mores et incomparabilem fidem sapientiamque non mediam*, and that for the same reason the other apostles also were called *fratres Domini*. But where do they get this distinctive appellation? The first of these quotations is virtually an abandonment of his whole theory, at least of its principal proof, and the second is the occupation of entirely new ground; but there is no preference indicated for the other hypothesis, that of step-brothers, as Professor Lightfoot would infer. Lastly, in his commentary on Isa. xvii. 6, Jerome formally admits fourteen apostles: *duodecim qui electi sunt et tertium decimum Jacobum qui appellatur frater Domini et Paulum. . . .*[1]

This theory of Jerome, whose adherence to it did not grow with his years, does not however appear to be the absolute novelty which some would assert it to be. The opinion of Clement is somewhat doubtful, and we can only guess at it from extracts, some of which may not be genuine. Cassiodorus quotes from his *Hypotyposeis* thus: "Jude, who wrote the catholic epistle, being one of the sons of Joseph and the Lord's brother, a man of deep piety, though he knew his relationship to the Lord, yet did not say he was His brother; for this is true, he *was* His

[1] Vol. iv. p. 194.

brother, being Joseph's son." It is hard to say whether the last explanatory words are those of Clement, or are inserted by the Ostrogothic statesman Cassiodorus, his Latin translator, who may not have held the theory of Jerome.

But Eusebius, speaking of the Lord's brother, gives other extracts from Clement of quite a different character: "Peter, James, and John, after the ascension of the Saviour, were not ambitious of honour; . . . but chose James the Just Bishop of Jerusalem."[1] James the Just was therefore a different person from the three apostolical electors; and if the first James is the son of Zebedee, the last is James son of Alphæus. For the historian adds another illustrative quotation: "The Lord after the resurrection imparted the *gnosis* to James the Just, and John, and Peter. These delivered it to the rest of the apostles, and the rest of the apostles to the seventy, of whom Barnabas was one. Now there were two Jameses—one the Just, who was thrown from a battlement of the temple, and the other who was beheaded."[2] These extracts from Clement favour the theory of Jerome; for James the Just, as seen in this statement, which admits two persons only of the name of James, cannot be a son of Joseph, but must be the son of Alphæus, and not a half-brother, though he may be a cousin. There is no room to doubt the genuineness of the epithet *τῷ Δικαίῳ* in the beginning of the second excerpt, in order to make the triad the same in the first and second quotations; for it is in connection with James the Just that the second quotation is made, and it is introduced by the words *ἔτι καὶ ταῦτα περὶ αὐτοῦ φησίν*.

Nor, on the other hand, was the opinion of Helvidius so great a novelty as Jerome represents it. Victorinus of Petavium is said to have taken the word "brethren" in its natural sense, but Jerome denies it. Tertullian, who was claimed by Helvidius, is rudely thrown out of court by Jerome because he did not

[1] Πέτρον γάρ φησι καὶ Ἰάκωβον καὶ Ἰωάννην μετὰ τὴν ἀνάληψιν τοῦ Σωτῆρος . . . Ἰάκωβον τὸν Δίκαιον ἐπίσκοπον Ἱεροσολύμων ἑλέσθαι.

[2] Ἰακώβῳ τῷ Δικαίῳ καὶ Ἰωάννῃ καὶ Πέτρῳ μετὰ τὴν ἀνάστασιν παρέδωκε τὴν γνῶσιν ὁ Κύριος . . . Δύο δὲ γεγόνασιν Ἰάκωβοι, εἷς ὁ Δίκαιος ὁ κατὰ τοῦ πτερυγίου βληθεὶς . . . ἕτερος δὲ καρατομηθείς. These extracts from the sixth and eighth books of Clement's *Hypotyposeis* are found in Euseb. *Hist. Eccles.* lib. ii. 1, vol. i. pp. 93, 94, ed. Heinichen.

belong to the catholic church. In discussing the reality of the incarnation, Tertullian seems to employ *mater et fratres* in their ordinary sense, evidently regarding that sense as essential to his argument: *Et Christum quidam virgo enixa est, semel nuptura post partum, ut uterque titulus sanctitatis in Christi censu dispungeretur, per matrem et virginem et univiram.*[1] Again, in his treatise against Marcion, and on the assertion, *inquiunt, ipse (Christus) contestatur se non esse natum, dicendo quæ mihi mater et qui mihi fratres?* among other elements of reply, he asks: *Dic mihi, omnibus natis mater adivit? omnibus natis adgenerantur et fratres? non licet patres magis et sorores habere vel et neminem? . . . et vere mater et fratres ejus foris stabant,—si ergo matrem et fratres eos fecit qui non erant, quomodo negavit eos qui erant?*[2] Tertullian thus took *mater* and *fratres* in their natural sense, and the opinion is strengthened by Jerome's treatment of him. Helvidius had quoted Tertullian as being in his favour, and Jerome does not deny it, but tartly says: *nihil amplius dico quam ecclesiæ hominem non fuisse.* Now Tertullian does not regard his view as an uncommon one, and the likelihood is that it was widely held; for if so pronounced an ascetic as he was did espouse it, it must have been by the compulsion of undeniable evidence. Still we do not find any express testimonies on the subject in other quarters; nor do we know any sufficient grounds for Neander's assertion, that many teachers of the church had in the preceding period maintained, that by the brothers of Jesus mentioned in the New Testament were to be understood the later-born sons of Mary—*später geborne Söhne der Maria.* Vol. iii. p. 458, Engl. Trans.

The other theory which Jerome scouted, maintains equally with his that the ἀδελφοί were not relations in near blood or uterine brothers, but were children of Joseph by a former marriage. This hypothesis seems to have been, if not originated, yet perpetuated by the grammatical necessity of giving ἀδελφός its natural meaning on the one hand, and the theological necessity, on the other hand, of maintaining the postnuptial virginity of Mary. Cousinhood would suffice for the dogma, but not for the philology. "Brothers," in the position which they repeatedly occupy in the Gospels, could not well be

[1] *De Monogam.* viii. *Opera*, vol. i. p. 772, ed. Œhler.

[2] *Advers. Marcion.* xix. *Opera*, vol. ii. pp. 206–7.

relatives so distant as cousins; but they might be earlier children of Joseph, yet related in no degree of blood to Jesus as the son of Mary. Indeed, had they been the children of Mary herself, they were only through her related to Jesus, who in fatherhood was separated by an infinite distance from them. This view is presented by Theophylact in a peculiar form —to wit, that they were the children of Joseph by a levirate marriage with the widow of his brother Clopas who had died childless.[1] But was Joseph husband of the widow of Clopas and of Mary mother of Jesus at one and the same time? and if this widow were the Mary wife of Clopas supposed by so many to be the sister of the Virgin, what then would be the nature of such a marital connection? Or was Mary widow of Clopas dead before he espoused the Virgin Mary? Or are the two women, unrelated in blood, called sisters because married to two brothers? There is no proof that such a connection would warrant a designation of sisterhood.

Now, first for the theory of step-brotherhood, there is no explicit evidence in Scripture—no hint or allusion as to Joseph's age or previous history. Nor are the *ἀδελφοί* ever called the sons of Joseph, as if to identify them more particularly with him; nor are they ever associated with him, save remotely in the exclamation of the Nazarenes. Nor, indeed, are they called the children of Mary,—through her they are always associated with Jesus. Dr. Mill, however, says that the theory "imparts a meaning to the Nazarenes' wondering enumeration of those (now elder) brethren, which on the other supposition is senseless." This is mere hypothesis. No question of comparative age has anything to do with the sceptical amazement at Nazareth. The ground of wonder was, how one member of a family still among themselves, and with whom they were or had been so familiar, could start into such sudden pre-eminence,—displaying such wisdom and putting forth such unearthly power. As for the

[1] His words are: *ἀδελφοὺς καὶ ἀδελφὰς εἶχεν ὁ Κύριος τοὺς τοῦ Ἰωσὴφ παῖδας οὓς ἔτεκεν ἐκ τῆς τοῦ ἀδελφοῦ αὐτοῦ Κλωπᾶ γυναικός. Τοῦ γὰρ Κλωπᾶ ἄπαιδος τελευτήσαντος ὁ Ἰωσὴφ ἔλαβε κατὰ τὸν νόμον τὴν γυναῖκα αὐτοῦ*,—the sequel being, that he begat by her six children—four sons and two daughters, one of whom was Mary called daughter of Clopas according to the law, and the other Salome.—On Gal. i. 19.

"tone of authority" ascribed by Dr. Mill to the ἀδελφοί, we find it not; the phrases, "desiring to speak with Him," and in a spirit of unbelief urging Him to go up to the feast, are certainly no proof either of it or of superior age on which they might presume. For any appeal on this point to Mark iii. 21 cannot be sustained: *καὶ ἀκούσαντες οἱ παρ' αὐτοῦ ἐξῆλθον κρατῆσαι αὐτόν· ἔλεγον γὰρ, Ὅτι ἐξέστη.* Now the persons called here *οἱ παρ' αὐτοῦ, οἱ οἰκεῖοι* (different, certainly, from *οἱ περὶ αὐτόν* (Mark iv. 10)), who wished to seize Him under the impression that He was "beside Himself," could not be exclusively the ἀδελφοί who are formally mentioned in a subsequent part of the same chapter, Mark iii. 31. Meyer, indeed, and many others identify them. Nor can the phrase mean, "those sent by Him," or the apostles; nor can it denote the Pharisees;—a most absurd conjecture. Nor does it characterize a wider circle of disciples (Lichtenstein, *Lebens-geschich. d. Herrn.* p. 216). Least of all were they guest-friends who were with Him in some house of entertainment (Strauss). Nor is it necessary, with Lange, to include among them the apostles. The persons called *οἱ παρ' αὐτοῦ* were relations of Jesus, either of near or remote kinship. Bernhardy, p. 256; Susann. v. 33; Fritzsche, *in loc.* The phrase *οἱ παρ' αὐτοῦ* is plainly the nominative to ἔλεγον, and ὄχλος cannot be the nominative to ἐξέστη, as if they had told Him that the multitude was mad against Him. The argument of Hilary and Epiphanius, that if the brothers had been sons of Mary herself, her dying son would have commended her to one of them rather than to John, is just as strong against the supposition that the brothers, though not her own children, were Joseph's. Lange's theory, that Joseph had undertaken the charge of his brother Clopas' children after their father's death, so that the "brothers" were only foster-brethren, is no less a hypothesis unsupported in Scripture than the opposite one of Schneckenburger, that Joseph dying at an early period, Mary became domiciled in the house of her sister, wife of Clopas or Alphæus, so that his children, brought up under the same roof with Jesus, might be called His brothers. Quite as baseless is the statement of Greswell, that while the brothers were full brothers, the sisters of our Lord were probably only His cousins, because they are said to be living in Nazareth, while the brothers are supposed to have their abode in Capernaum. But the notices in the Gospels are too indistinct to warrant the opinion of such a separation of abode; and as the brothers were married (1 Cor. ix. 5), why might not the sisters be married and settled in Nazareth?

If, then, the ordinary meaning of the term *ἀδελφοί* is not to be retained, or rather, if it is allowed to *μήτηρ* but inconsistently refused to *ἀδελφοί* in the same connection—an inconsistency which would be tolerated in the biography of no other person; if mere cousinhood cannot be satisfactorily vindicated,—if it is opposed to the natural sense, and rests on a series of unproven and contradictory hypotheses; and if the other theory of mere affinity, unsupported by any statements or allusions in the evangelical narrative, was yet the current opinion among the fathers,—we may now inquire as well into their statement and defence of it, as into the source whence they got it. If they had it from tradition, was that tradition at all trustworthy? If Scripture is silent on some historical points, these points may be found in some old tradition which details minuter or more private circumstances of which inspiration has taken no cognisance. But if the general character of that tradition be utterly fabulous and fantastic; if its staple be absurd exaggeration and puerile legend; if its documents are forgeries composed in furtherance of error, pious frauds or fictions ascribed in authorship to apostles or evangelists; and if some fragments are coarse and prurient as well as mendacious,—then, as we cannot separate the true from the false, the reality from the caricature, we must reject the entire mass of it as unworthy of credit, unless when any portion may be confirmed by collateral evidence. No one can deny, indeed, that there must have been a real tradition as to many of those points in the first century and in Palestine. The first two chapters of Luke, with the exception of the exordium, are so Hebraistic in tone and style, so minute in domestic matters and so full and so characteristic in individual utterances, that they must have been furnished from traditions or from documents sacredly preserved in the holy family. The relationship of the *ἀδελφοί* must also have been known to the churches in Galilee and Judæa; and had it been handed down to us on assured authority, we should have accepted it without hesitation. But we have no such reliable record, nay, none earlier than the second century. One class of documents very minute and circumstantial in detail as to the family of Nazareth is utterly unworthy of credit, and many of them were composed in defence of serious error. The Clementine *Homilies* and *Recognitions*—dating somewhere in the second century—support a peculiar form of Ebionitism; the "Gospel according to Peter"[1] was Doketic in its doctrines and aims,—so much so, that Serapion was obliged to denounce it; the *Protevangelium* of James is a semi-Gnostic travesty of many parts of the sacred narrative, and might be almost pressed into the service of the immaculate conception of Mary; the "Gospel of St. Thomas" was Doketic also in its tendencies, —filled with silly prodigies done by the boy Jesus from His very cradle; the "Gospel according to the Hebrews," or "the Twelve Apostles," was translated into Greek and Latin by Jerome: some fragments, however, which have been preserved show that it has little connection with our canonical Matthew, but was the work of early Jewish converts, manufactured from some older narrative—perhaps from one of the products of the many, πολλοί, who, according to Luke, had "taken in hand to set forth in order a declaration of the things most surely believed." If the tradition be uniform on any point, it deserves attention, though one must still inquire whether any impressions or opinions might help to create and sustain such a belief, and what is its real value and authority; for its authors, instead of being independent witnesses, may be all of them only repeating and copying without investigation what a predecessor had originated and diffused. Besides, if we find the "brothers" called simply sons of Joseph, it is open for us to question who their mother was. Might not the phrase, *sons of Joseph*, mean children by her who is so familiarly known as his wife in the sacred narrative? We should maintain this inference in any other case, if no other mother be distinctly stated; and the canonical Gospels are silent as to any earlier conjugal relation of Joseph.

We may observe in passing, that it is remarkable that in the genuine Gospels Joseph is not mentioned *by name* as father

[1] *Evangelia Apocrypha*, ed. Tischendorf, 1853. See also the *Testimonia et Censuræ* prefixed to each of the books by Fabricius in his *Codex Apocryphus Novi Test.* 1763

of Jesus, though it must have been the current belief on the part of all who were ignorant of the supernatural conception, or did not credit it. Mary indeed says, "Thy father and I;" but how else could she have alluded to the relation? The contemptuous exclamation was, "Is not this the carpenter's son?" or, "Is not this the carpenter?" and then His mother Mary is named in the same connection. Probably Joseph was dead by that time, though his age cannot be certainly inferred from any period assigned to his death. The sinister purpose of Strauss is apparent in his explanation: "Joseph had either died early, or had nothing to do with the subsequent ministry of his son. But it is not improbable that, on dogmatic grounds, the person who was not to be supposed to be the real father of Jesus was removed from the traditions about him." Yet we cannot but be struck with the fact, that while the inspired Gospels have so little about Joseph, many of the apocryphal Gospels are full of him, and give him a primary place, in the same way as they abound with romance about the unrecorded infancy and early years of Jesus. Such legends must be discarded; and though they are so closely interwoven, it is hard to discover in them any thread or basis of genuine tradition. To proceed:

Origen is quite explicit in his belief that the brethren were children of Joseph by a former wife. In his note on Matt. xiii. 55, he states this opinion, says it was held by some though not by all, and adopts it as his own.[1] "And I think it reasonable, that as Jesus was the first-fruit of purity and chastity among men, so Mary was among women; for it is not seemly to ascribe the first-fruit of virginity to any other woman than her." Again, on John ii. 12, "They were," he says, "Joseph's children ἐκ προτεθνηκυίας γυναικός, by a predeceased wife." In the first quotation he ascribes this opinion to some only, φασί τινες,—a minority perhaps is naturally designated by the term. But what opinion was in that case held by the majority? Was it not very probably that of uterine brotherhood rather than that of cousinhood? for the last upheld

[1] Καὶ οἶμαι λόγον ἔχειν ἀνδρῶν μὲν καθαρότητος τῆς ἐν ἁγνείᾳ ἀπαρχὴν γεγονέναι τὸν Ἰησοῦν, γυναικῶν δὲ τὴν Μαρίαμ. . . . See *Commentarii*, vol. i. p. 223, ed. Huet. No small amount of this kind of traditional lore may be found in Hofmann's *Das Leben Jesu nach den Apocryphen*, etc., Leipzig 1851.

the perpetual virginity equally with the view which Origen espoused. If he took the same side, chiefly or solely, as he says the persons referred to did, "to preserve the honour of Mary in virginity throughout," and because of his own belief in the same dogma, is it rash to infer that the other opinion, because it denied it or set it aside, was rejected by him? Origen traces the opinion held by the "some," and advocated by himself, only to the "Gospel of Peter, as it is called," or "the book of James,"[1] and does not claim for it a clear uninterrupted tradition. He could have no great respect for those uncanonical books, and he does not allude to any remoter relationship. Nor does he hold his opinion consistently or firmly, for in one place he assigns a wholly different reason, and in another place he affirms that James was called the Lord's brother not so much "*διὰ τὸ πρὸς αἵματος συγγενές*," as "*διὰ τὸ ἦθος καὶ τὸν λόγον*"—"not so much on account of blood-relationship as on account of his character and discourse." *Contra Celsum*, i. 35, ed. Spencer. Origen had plainly made no investigation into the matter, perhaps shrunk from it on account of his belief in the perpetual virginity, and was ready to adopt any opinion of the origin of the name that did not come into conflict with this belief.

Epiphanius wrote a treatise on the subject against the Antidikomarianites, who, as their name implies, refused certain honours to the blessed Virgin,—a sect, he says, "who from hatred to the Virgin or desire to obscure her glory, or from being blinded with envy or ignorance, and wishing to defile the minds of others, dared to say that the holy Virgin, after the birth of Christ, cohabited with her husband Joseph." At one point of the treatise he incorporates an address which he had formerly written against the sect, and dedicated *ὁμοπίστοις ὀρθοδόξοις*. The pastoral abounds in wailings, censures, and expressions of astonishment at the audacity, profanity, and ignorance of these heretics. "Who ever," he exclaims, "used the name of the holy Mary, and, when asked, did not immediately add, the virgin?" But we still use the same epithet, though with reference specially to the miraculous conception. James, he adds, is called the Lord's brother, *οὐχὶ κατὰ φύσιν ἀλλὰ κατὰ χάριν*,—and Mary only appeared as the wife of Joseph, *μὴ ἔχουσα πρὸς αὐτὸν σωμάτων συνάφειαν*. Joseph,

[1] Τοῦ ἐπιγεγραμμένου κατὰ Πέτρον εὐαγγελίου καὶ τῆς βίβλου Ἰακώβου.

he goes on to say, was fourscore or upwards when the Virgin was espoused to him, his son James being then about fifty; and his other sons were Simon, Joses, and Jude, and his daughters, Mary and Salome,—these two names, he strangely avers, being warranted by Scripture—ἡ γραφή. In the *Historia Josephi* they are called Asia and Lydia. His conclusion is: *οὐ γὰρ συνήφθη ἔτι παρθένος, μὴ γένοιτο.* He then resorts to another style of argument taken from *φυσιολογιῶν σχέσεις*; one of them being, that as the queenly lioness, after a gestation of six-and-twenty months, produces a perfect animal which by its birth makes physically impossible that of any second cub, so the mother of the Lion of Judah could be a mother only once. Joseph was old—*πρεσβύτου καὶ ὑπερβάντος τοῦ χρόνου*[1]—at the birth of Jesus with all its prodigies; and though he had been younger, he would not have dared to approach his wife afterwards—*ἐνυβρίζειν σῶμα ἅγιον ἐν ᾧ κατῳκίσθη Θεός.*[2] His argument in a word is virtually this, that the cohabitation of Joseph with Mary was on his part a physical and ethical impossibility. Besides, he maintains that as Jesus was *πρωτότοκος* of the Father in the highest sense, *ἄνω πρὸ πάσης κτίσεως*, and really alone in this relation—*μονογενής*; so it was and must have been also on earth between Him and His mother. And not to dwell upon it, the good father thought that he was holding an even balance when he proceeds in his next section to oppose the Collyridians,—a sect which offered to the Virgin divine honours and such kind of meat-offering as was often presented to Ceres. The theory of Epiphanius is quite clear in its premises, but he finds difficulty in defending it out of the simple evangelical narrative, and is obliged to guard it by proofs taken from apocryphal legend and ascetic theology. Nay, he has doubts of the Virgin's death;[3] such is his extravagant opinion of her glorification.

Hilary of Poitiers holds a similar view;[4] and so does Hilary

[1] *Panaria*, vol. ii. p. 428, etc.

[2] *Εἰ γὰρ καὶ προσεδοκᾶτο ἡ παρθένος τῷ Ἰωσὴφ εἰς συνάφειαν ὡς οὐδὲ ἐπεδέχετο διὰ τὸ γηραλέον. . .* Again, *πῶς ἄρα ἐτόλμα συναφθῆναι τῇ τοσαύτῃ καὶ τοιαύτῃ ἁγίᾳ παρθένῳ Μαρίᾳ. . .—Ib.*

[3] *Οὐ λέγω ὅτι ἀθάνατος ἔμεινεν, ἀλλ' οὔτε διαβεβαιοῦμαι εἰ τέθνηκεν.—Ib.*

[4] *Verum homines pravissimi hinc presumunt opinionis suæ auctoritatem quod plures Dominum nostrum fratres habuisse sit traditum,*—and argues that

the deacon or Ambrosiaster, on Gal. i. 19, one of his arguments being, that if these were His true brothers, Joseph was His true father—*si enim hi viri fratres ejus, et Joseph erit verus pater;* while those who hold the opposite view, that is, of their being *veri fratres,* are branded with insanity and impiety. Gregory of Nyssa, brother of Basil the Great, also maintained that Mary is called the mother of James and Joses as being only their step-mother.

Now, as all these fathers held the perpetual virginity, they were therefore shut up to deny the obvious sense of *ἀδελφοί.*[1] The theory of Joseph's previous marriage suited their views, and they adopted it. It was already in existence, and they cannot be accused of originating it to serve their purpose. The theory of cousinhood was equally valid to their argument, but they make no reference to it. Either they did not know it, or they rejected it as not fitting in to the sacred narrative, or as not coming up to what they felt must be the sense of the term *ἀδελφός.*

The apocryphal sources of these beliefs are well known. The *Protevangelium* of James[2] enters fully into the matter: recounts the prodigies attending the Virgin's birth, she being the predicted daughter of Joachim and Anna; describes the wonders of her infancy, she being brought up in the temple and fed by an angel; tells how, when she was twelve years of age, all the widowers among the people were called together by the advice of an angel, each to bring a rod in his hand,—that Joseph, throwing his hatchet down as soon as he heard the proclamation, snatched up his rod,—that the rods were

they are children of Joseph *ex priore conjugio*, because Jesus on the cross commended His mother to John and not to one of them. On Matt. i.—*Opera*, vol. i. p. 922, ed. Migne.

[1] Origen says explicitly: *οἱ δὲ ταῦτα λέγοντες τὸ ἀξίωμα τῆς Μαρίας ἐν παρθενίᾳ τηρεῖν μέχρι τέλους βούλονται.* *Comment.* vol. i. p. 223, ed. Huet. See Basil. *Opera*, vol. ii. p. 854, Paris 1839.

[2] An old Syriac version of several of these documents may now be thankfully read in the excellent edition of Dr. Wright, London 1865; and see also, for another recension of some of them, in the *Journal of Sacred Literature*, 1865. Ewald, in reviewing Dr. Wright's work, characterizes the tract called *Transitus Mariæ*, or Assumption of the Virgin, as the source—*der feste Grund für alle die unselige Marienverehrung und hundert abergläubische Dinge. . . . Der ganze Mariencultus der Päpstlicher Kirche beruhet*

received by the high priest, who, having gone into the temple and prayed over them, returned them to their owners,—that on the reception of his rod by Joseph a dove flew out of it and alighted on his head, and that by this gracious omen he was pointed out as the husband of Mary. But Joseph refused, "saying, I am an old man with children;" and he was also ashamed from so great disparity of years to have Mary registered as his wife.[1] The other incidents need not be recounted. The pseudo-Matthew's Gospel is very similar, mentioning in chap. xxiii. Joseph's four sons and his two daughters. In Codex B, Tischendorf's edition, p. 104, Anna, mother of the Virgin, is said on Joseph's death to have married Cleophas, by whom she had a second daughter, named also Mary, who became the wife of Alphæus, and was mother of James and Philip, and who on the decease of Cleophas married a third time, her husband being Salome, by whom she had a third daughter, named also Mary, who was espoused to Zebedee, and became mother of James and John. It is needless to refer to the other legends, unequalled in absurdity and puerility.

The *Apostolical Constitutions* do not give a decided testimony; but they uniformly assert that the brother of our Lord was not James the apostle, and reckon, with the addition of Paul, fourteen apostles. James is severed alike from apostles, deacons, and the seventy disciples. They speak in one place of the mother of our Lord and His sisters (iii. 6);—James more than once calls himself *κἀγὼ Ἰάκωβος ἀδελφὸς μὲν κατὰ σάρκα τοῦ Χριστοῦ*. viii. 35, etc. *Constitut. Apostolicæ*, pp. 65, 79, 228, ed. Ueltzen. As the perpetual virginity is not insisted on in these writings, perhaps these extracts favour the

auf diesem Buche. . . . Götting. gelehrte Anzeigen, 1865. This statement is true, though Pope Gelasius would not admit the document among the canonical writings; but the further truth is, that the appearance of this tract, probably during the second half of the fourth century, shows that the worship of Mary already existed. It did not originate the *Marien-cultus*, but it is an index of that state of feeling out of which it had grown, and by means of which it attained a rapid development,—the worship *τῆς παναγίας ἐνδόξου θεοτόκου καὶ ἀειπαρθένου Μαρίας*. A Greek edition of the same tract, Κοίμησις τῆς Θεοτόκου, is now also printed in Tischendorf's *Apocalypses Apocryphæ*, p. 95, Lipsiæ 1866.

[1] An excellent edition of several of these Gospels may be found in Hilgenfeld's *Novum Testamentum extra Canonem receptum*, Lipsiæ 1866.

idea that sisters and brothers are taken in their natural and obvious meaning. The Clementine *Homilies* and *Recognitions* give James the chief place among the apostles, as ὁ λεχθεὶς ἀδελφὸς τοῦ Κυρίου (*Hom.* xi. 35); which may either mean, one who ordinarily went by that appellation, or one so called without any natural right to the name,—called a brother as he *was* one, or *called* a brother though not really one. As James, however, was universally known by the title, the clause may be thought to express real brotherhood. *Recognit.* i. 66, etc.

The testimony of Hegesippus has been variously understood. One excerpt preserved by Eusebius runs thus: "There were yet living of the family of our Lord the grandchildren of Jude called the brother of the Lord according to the flesh."[1] Eusebius calls this same Jude "the brother of our Saviour according to the flesh, as being of the family of David." The participle λεγόμενος is doubtful in meaning; it may refer to a reputed brotherhood, or it may mean simply that such was the common and real designation. Whatever be the meaning of ἀδελφός—real or reputed brother—it cannot mean cousin. Hegesippus supplies no hint that he did not believe the brotherhood to be a full and not simply a step-brotherhood. Again, Eusebius (*Hist. Eccles.* ii. 23) inserts a long extract from Hegesippus which gives a graphic account of James' death, and in which he says "the church was committed, along with the apostles, to James the brother of the Lord, who, as there were many of the name, was surnamed the Just by all from the Lord's time to our own."[2] In a subsequent excerpt from Josephus, the same appellation is given to James, "the brother of him who is called Christ." The meaning of another extract

1 Ἔτι δὲ περιῆσαν οἱ ἀπὸ γένους τοῦ Κυρίου υἱωνοὶ Ἰούδα τοῦ κατὰ σάρκα λεγομένου αὐτοῦ ἀδελφοῦ.—*Hist. Eccles.* iii. 19, 20.

2 Διαδέχεται δὲ τὴν ἐκκλησίαν μετὰ τῶν ἀποστόλων, ὁ ἀδελφὸς τοῦ Κυρίου Ἰάκωβος ὁ ὀνομασθεὶς ὑπὸ πάντων Δίκαιος ἀπὸ τῶν τοῦ Κυρίου χρόνων μέχρι καὶ ἡμῶν. Jerome's translation of μετά by *post*, in the phrase μετὰ τῶν ἀποστόλων, is wrong; but Stier adopts it, as he holds that James Alphæi is referred to in Gal. ii. 9–12, and that he was the first head of the church in Jerusalem, James the Lord's brother being his successor. Lange's interpretation of μετὰ τῶν ἀποστόλων (in his article in Herzog) is quite fallacious. The phrase plainly implies that James was not a primary apostle; but Lange argues that he was an apostle, and that only in holding episcopal office was he distinct from the other apostles. The state-

from Hegesippus has been keenly disputed. He says: "After James the Just had been martyred, as also the Lord was on the same charge (or for the same doctrine), his uncle's son, Symeon son of Clopas, is next appointed bishop, whom all put forward as second, being a cousin of the Lord."[1] The meaning is, not that Symeon was another son of his uncle, or another cousin in addition to James, as Mill and others contend, but that the second bishop was Symeon, son of Christ's or James' paternal uncle Clopas; that is, James is brother, but Symeon is only cousin of the Lord. Hegesippus in another place calls him *ὁ ἐκ θείου τοῦ Κυρίου ὁ προειρημένος Συμεὼν υἱὸς Κλωπᾶ*. Euseb. *Hist. Eccl.* iii. 32. Hug, Schneckenburger, and Lange suppose him to be the Apostle Simon the Canaanite, who in the two lists of Luke is mentioned immediately after James Alphæi. See Bleek, *Einleit.* p. 544. Hegesippus thus calls Symeon second bishop and cousin of the Lord, and he carefully distinguishes between the relationship of Symeon and James; for though Symeon was a cousin, he never calls him the Lord's brother. Eusebius himself does not speak distinctly on the subject when he says, "James called the Lord's brother, because also He (*οὗτος*) was called the son of Joseph, Joseph being thus regarded as the father of Christ."[2] He does not seem to mean that James was called the son of Joseph, but that Jesus was so called. There is, however, another reading, and the words do not clearly assert what James' natural connection with Christ was. If he was Christ's brother as Joseph was His father, then there was no relationship in blood, and he might only be a cousin; or if *οὗτος* refer to James, then James was a real as

ment that the superintendence of the church was committed to him along with the apostles, excludes him from the number; but Lange draws an opposite inference, quoting in support of his exegesis, *ὁ Πέτρος καὶ ἀπόστολοι*, Acts v. 29, which is a very different form of phrase. See Alford's *Prolegomena to the Epistle of James.*

[1] Μετὰ τὸ μαρτυρῆσαι Ἰάκωβον τὸν Δίκαιον, ὡς καὶ ὁ Κύριος ἐπὶ τῷ αὐτῷ λόγῳ, πάλιν ὁ ἐκ τοῦ θείου αὐτοῦ Συμεὼν ὁ τοῦ Κλωπᾶ καθίσταται ἐπίσκοπος, ὃν πρόεθεντο πάντες ὄντα ἀνεψιὸν τοῦ Κυρίου δεύτερον.—*Hist. Eccles.* iv. 22, p. 382, vol. i.

[2] Τότε δῆτα καὶ Ἰάκωβον τὸν τοῦ Κυρίου λεγόμενον ἀδελφὸν, ὅτι δὴ καὶ οὗτος τοῦ Ἰωσὴφ ὠνόμαστο παῖς, τοῦ δὲ Χριστοῦ πατὴρ ὁ Ἰωσήφ.—*Hist. Eccl.* ii. 1.

Jesus was a reputed son of Joseph; and if a real son of Joseph, why not by Mary? Eusebius (*Comment. on Isaiah,* xvii. 6), in a mystical interpretation of the "gleaning of grapes" and "shaking of the olive-tree," "two, three berries left on the top of the uppermost bough, four, five on the outmost branches," makes out from the addition of those numbers that James was a supplementary apostle as Paul was, counting fourteen apostles in all.[1] But the apocryphal theory of step-brotherhood was current in that age, and Eusebius may be supposed to have held it, as he does not formally disavow it. Cyril of Jerusalem distinguishes James from the apostles, calls him *τῷ ἑαυτοῦ ἀδελφῷ*, and the first bishop *τῆς παροικίας ταύτης*—"of this diocese." *Catechesis,* xiv. 11, p. 199; *Opera,* ed. Milles, Oxon. 1703. Hippolytus may be passed over; and the Papias who is sometimes referred to, is, as Prof. Lightfoot has shown, not the bishop of Hierapolis. The extract sometimes taken from this Papias of the eleventh century may be found in Routh's *Reliq. Sac.* vol. i. p. 16.

If, then, the theory of step-brethren or cousins be surrounded with difficulties, and rest on many unproved hypotheses; if the one theory can be made the means of impugning the other; if the first has its origin in apocryphal books filled with silly legend and fable, and the second has no true basis in the evangelical narrative; if both have been held from the earliest times avowedly to conserve the ecclesiastical dogma of the perpetual virginity; and if there be nothing in Scripture or sound theology to upset the belief that gives our Lord's "brothers" the natural relationship which the epithet implies,—what should hinder us from taking *ἀδελφοί* in the same sense as *μήτηρ*?

There are indeed objections, but none of them are of any serious moment. One objection that weighs with many is thus stated by Jeremy Taylor: "Jesus came into the world without doing violence to the virginal and pure body of His mother; He did also leave her virginity entire, to be as a seal that none might open the gate of that sanctuary." *Life of Christ,* § 3. Bishop Bull also asserts, "It cannot with decency be imagined that the most holy vessel which was thus once consecrated to

[1] Similarly also Jerome, as before quoted. Compare also what he says, *Opera,* vol. iv. p. 280.

be a receptacle of the Deity, should afterwards be desecrated and profaned by human use." Bishop Pearson adds, "Though whatever should have followed after could have no reflective tendency upon the first-fruit of her womb, yet the peculiar eminency and unparalleled privilege of that mother . . . have persuaded the church of God to believe that she still continued in the same virginity." Spanheim holds it as *admodum probabile sanctum hoc organum ad tam eximium conceptum et partum a Deo selectum non fuisse temeratum ab homine. Dubia Evang.* i. p. 225. Mill himself admits, "They hold themselves free to include this doctrine as a matter of pious persuasion, but by no means of the same gravity or indispensable necessity as the belief of the immaculate conception." *Mythical Interpretation of the Gospels*, p. 269. So also some Lutheran confessions, *Artic. Smalcald.* p. i. art. 4, and in the *Formula Concordiæ*. Numerous persons of opposite views on many other points, as Zwingli and Olshausen, Lardner and Addison Alexander of Princeton, agree on this theme. Both Taylor and Pearson quote Ezek. xliv. 2, the first as an argument, and the second as an illustration of the dogma under review. The words of the prophet are: "Then said the Lord unto me, This gate shall be shut, it shall not be opened, and no man shall enter in by it; because the Lord, the God of Israel, hath entered in by it, therefore it shall be shut." But these utterances have no connection with the subject in any way. Still I suppose that every one feels somewhat the force of the sentiments contained in the previous extracts. They may be superstitions, but they are natural even to those who by force of evidence are not able to make the perpetual virginity an article of faith. It is not, however, a belief basing itself on Scripture even by one remote inference. That Jesus should be born of a virgin, fulfilled prophecy; still, whether virginity was essential to immaculate conception is open to question, for the mere suspension of male instrumentality would not remove the sinfulness of the mother. But divine agency wrought out its purpose in its own way, and the child of the Virgin was a "holy thing." The supernatural origin of the babe did not depend for its *reality* on her virginity, but very much for its visible proof and manifestation. A second-born child might, for anything we know, be born by immediate divine power, but the absence of human intervention would not so palpably present itself. Jesus, virgin-born, was thus set apart in unique and awful solemnity from all mankind,—as born pure, not purified,—divine, not deified,—"the second Adam, the Lord from heaven."

That the Virgin had no other children is the impression of many who do not believe in the perpetual virginity. Thus Lange says: "We must not forget that Mary was the wife of Joseph. She was according to a ratified engagement dependent upon her husband's will. . . . As a wife, Mary was subject to wifely obligations; but as a mother, she had fulfilled her destiny with the birth of Christ. . . . And even for the very sake of nature's refinement, we cannot but imagine that this organism which had born the Prince of the new Æon would be too proudly or too sacredly disposed to lend itself, after bringing forth the life of Christ, to the production of mere common births for the sphere of the old Æon." *Life of Christ*, vol. i. 425, English Trans. But the theory of natural brotherhood throws no shadow over the glories of Mary, ever blessed and pre-eminent in honour. It does not in any way lessen the dignity of her who was so "highly favoured of the Lord" and "blessed among women." For though one may shrink from calling her *θεοτόκος*—*Deipara*,[1]—an unwarranted epithet that draws after it veneration and worship,—yet her glories, which are without parallel and beyond imagination, and which are hers and hers alone, are never to be veiled. For she was the elected mother of a child whose Father was God,—her son "the only-begotten of the Father;" through her parthenic maternity the mystery of mysteries realized—"God manifest in flesh;" her offspring the normal Man, and the Redeemer of a fallen race by His atoning blood,—the Man of Sorrows and the Lord of all worlds,—crowned with thorns, and now wearing on His brow the diadem of universal dominion,—the object of praise to saints, to angels, and to the universe; for of that universe He is the Head, in that very nature of which, through and in Mary the mother-maid, He became a partaker.

It is therefore unfair on the part of Mill to allege against the natural and obvious interpretation of the term *ἀδελφοί*, that it "aims at no less than the error of the grosser section of

[1] James has also been called ὁ ἀδελφόθεος.

the Ebionites, who held that Jesus was in the same manner her son as all the rest are supposed to have been." The two beliefs have no natural alliance. Equally futile is it in the same author to tell us that Helvidius was the disciple of an Arian Auxentius, and that Bonosus is said to have impugned the Divine Sonship. *Mythical Interpretation of the Gospels*, pp. 221, 274. For whatever errors may have been held along with the theory of natural relationship, and whatever the character of such as may have espoused it, it stands out from all such adventitious elements of connection. One may hold it and hold at the same time the supreme divinity of the Lord Jesus Christ with most perfect consistency. It does not concern the cardinal doctrine of His divinity, nor the equally precious doctrine of His true and sinless humanity. It impugns not His immaculate conception, or His supernatural birth, He being in a sense peculiar to Himself the seed of the woman, the child of a virgin—Immanuel, "God with us." It refers only to possibilities after the incarnation which do not in any way affect its divineness and reality. It leaves her first-born in the solitary glory of the God-man. Jesus indeed passed among the Jews as the ordinary son of Joseph and Mary, yet this belief was very erroneous; but the ground of the error does not apply to this theory. The first chapter of Matthew tells the mystery of the incarnation, and the event is at once taken out of the category of all ordinary births; but if Mary had other children, no such wonder surrounded them, and no mistake could be made about them. The Jewish misconception as to the parentage of Jesus could not be made regarding subsequent members of His family, whose birth neither enhances nor lessens the honour and the mystery of His primogeniture. It was a human nature which He assumed; they were persons born into the world. Neither, then, in theology nor in piety, in creed nor in worship, can this obvious theory of natural relationship be charged with pernicious consequences. It is vain to ask, Why, if there were births subsequent to that of Jesus, are they not recorded? The inspired narrative keeps steadily to its one primary object and theme—the life of the blessed Saviour, first-born son of Mary and the Son of God.

Another objection against the natural interpretation of ἀδελφός is the repetition of names in the family of Mary and in the company of the apostles;—James, Joses, Simon, and Judas, brothers,—and two Jameses, two Simons, two Judes, among the apostles. Or, identifying Clopas and Alphæus, there would be James and Joses as cousins; and if the Ἰούδας Ἰακώβου, Luke vi. 16, Acts i. 13, be rendered "Jude brother of James," there would be two sets of four brothers having the same names. It is not necessary, however, to render the Greek phrase by "brother of James," and the sons of Alphæus are only James and Joses. But surely the same names are found among cousins every day, and would be more frequent in a country where a few favourite names are continually repeated. There are in the New Testament nine Simons, four Judes, four or five Josephs; and in "Josephus there are twenty-one Simons, seventeen named Joses, and sixteen Judes." Smith's *Dict. Bible Antiq.*, art. "Brother."

A crowning objection against the view we favour is, that Jesus upon the cross commended His mother to the care of the beloved disciple. This objection, says Lightfoot, "has been hurled at the Helvidian view with great force, and, as it seems to me, with fatal effect;" and Mill has also put it in a very strong form. Hilary adopts the same argument, as also Ambrose, Epiphanius, Chrysostom, and Jerome. That is to say, if Mary had children or sons of her own, her first-born would not have handed her over to a stranger. The objection has never appeared to us to be of very great force; for we know nothing of the circumstances of the brothers, and there may have been personal and domestic reasons why they could not receive the beloved charge. They might not, for a variety of reasons, be able to give Mary such a home as John could provide for her. As we cannot tell, it is useless to argue. We are wholly ignorant also of their peculiar temperament, and their want or their possession of those elements of character which would fit them to tend their aged and widowed parent. Especially do we know, however, that up to a recent period they were unbelievers in her divine first-born; and though He who did not forget His mother in His dying moments foreknew all that was to happen, still their unbelief might disqualify them for giving her the comfort and spiritual nursing which she required, to heal the wounds inflicted by that "sword" which was piercing her heart as she contemplated the shame and agony of the adored Sufferer on the cross. Every attention was needed for His mother at that very moment, and He seized that very moment to commend her to John, who had been to Him more than a brother, and would on that account be to her more than a son. John was "standing by," and so was His mother; so that perhaps his ministrations to her had already commenced. The close vicinity of the two persons whom He most loved on earth suggested the words, "Woman, behold thy son," who will supply, as far as possible, my place; "Son, behold thy mother:" be what I have been to her. "And from that hour that disciple took her to his own home." The brothers might not be there, or might be unfitted, as poor and unbelieving Galileans, for doing what John did,—for immediate obedience to such a command. Nay, if the commendation of His mother to John in the words, "Behold thy mother," be a proof that Jesus had no brothers, might it not prove, on the other hand, that John had no mother? Besides, if James were either a cousin or half-brother, and therefore a blood-relation, why in that case pass over him? So that the objection would tell against the theory of cousinhood, though not so strongly as against that of brotherhood. Wieseler,[1] indeed, contends that Salome was a sister of Mary, so that the sons of Zebedee were cousins of our Lord, and that as Salome was present at the crucifixion, John might designate her as the "sister of Mary," just as he calls himself "the disciple whom Jesus loved." No conclusive argument can thus be drawn from this last scene of Christ's life as to the relation of the ἀδελφοί to Himself. Far from us, at the same time, be the thought of Strauss, that the esoteric tendency of the fourth Gospel sets aside the real brothers of Jesus as unbelieving, "in order to enable the writer to transfer under the very cross the place of the true son of Mary, the spiritual brother of Jesus, to the favourite disciple."[2]

Nor has Renan's opinion anything in its favour. He imagines that the Virgin's sister, named Mary also, was wife of Alphæus; that her children, cousins-german of Jesus, espoused

[1] *Die Söhne Zebedäi Vettern des Herrn. Studien und Kritiken*, 1840, p. 648.

[2] *Neu Leben Jesu*, § 31.

His cause, while His own brothers opposed Him; and that the evangelist, hearing the four sons of Clopas called brethren of the Lord, has placed their names by mistake in Matt. xiii. 55, Mark vi. 3, instead of the names of the real brothers who have always remained obscure. *Vie de Jésus*, p. 25, 11th ed. The statement is only a piece of gratuitous wildness, devoid even of critical ingenuity. It has no basis,—is but a malignant dream.

But apart from these theories as to relationship, it seems plain, for many reasons, that James the Lord's brother was not one of the twelve, though he is virtually called an apostle according to our exegesis of the verse. The name *apostle* was given by Jesus specially to the twelve, Luke vi. 13; but it is not confined to them. In 2 Cor. viii. 23 certain persons are called ἀπόστολοι ἐκκλησιῶν, and in Phil. ii. 25 Epaphroditus is called ὑμῶν ἀπόστολον. In these instances the word is used in its original or common signification, and is not implicated in the present discussion. But the title (see under i. 1) is given to Barnabas, though Acts xiii. 2, 3 is not an account of his consecration to the office, but of his solemn designation to certain missionary work. In Acts xiv. 4, 14, he is called an apostle, in the first instance more generally: σὺν τοῖς ἀποστόλοις, that is, Paul and Barnabas; and in the second, the words are οἱ ἀπόστολοι Βαρνάβας καὶ Παῦλος. Compare 1 Cor. iv. 9, ix. 5; Gal. ii. 9. Besides, why should it be said in 1 Cor. xv. 5, 7 that Jesus appeared "to the twelve," and then "to all the apostles," if the two are quite identical in number? Paul also vindicates himself and his fellow-labourers, "though we might have been burdensome to you ὡς Χριστοῦ ἀπόστολοι," 1 Thess. ii. 6—Silas being in all probability the person so referred to by the honourable appellation (Acts xvii. 4). In none of these cases, however, is any person like Barnabas or Silas called an apostle directly and by himself, but only in connection with one or other of the avowed apostles. Again, in Rom. xvi. 7 Andronicus and Junia are thus characterized: οἵτινές εἰσιν ἐπίσημοι ἐν τοῖς ἀποστόλοις,—rendered in our version, "who are of note among the apostles." The meaning may either be, "highly esteemed in the apostolic circle" (Reiche, Meyer, Fritzsche, De Wette), or, "highly esteemed among the apostles," reckoned in some way as belonging to them. Such is the more natural view, and it is taken by the Greek fathers, by Calvin, Tholuck, Olshausen, Alford. On the stricter meaning of the term ἀπόστολος, see under Eph. iv. 11. We cannot, however, agree with Chrysostom, that the phrase "all the apostles," in 1 Cor. xv. 5–7, included such persons as the seventy disciples; nor with Calvin, that it comprehends *discipulos etiam quibus evangelii prædicandi munus injunxerat;* since some distinction is apparently preserved between ordinary preachers and those who in a secondary sense only are named apostles. For, as it is pointed out by Professor Lightfoot, Timothy and Apollos are excluded from the rank of apostles, and the others not of the twelve so named may have seen the risen Saviour. Eusebius speaks of very many apostles—πλείστων.[1] The Lord's brother, then, was not of the primary twelve. He is placed, 1 Cor. xv. 7, by himself as having seen Christ; or rather, Cephas is mentioned, and then "the twelve," of which Cephas was one; James is mentioned, and then "all the apostles," of which James was one. One cannot omit the beautiful legend founded apparently on this appearance: "The Lord after His resurrection went to James and appeared to him, for James had sworn that he would not eat bread from that hour in which he had drunk the cup of the Lord until he had seen Him risen from the dead. Then He said, Bring hither a table and bread. Then He took bread, and blessed it, and brake it, and gave it to James the Just, and said to him, My brother, eat thy bread, for the Son of man has risen from the dead." This scene is taken by Jerome from the Gospel according to the Hebrews, which he translated into Greek and Latin. *De Viris Illustr.* ii. Some for *biberat calicem Domini* read *Dominus,* and render "before the *Lord* drank the cup," or suffered. The Greek has πεπώκει τὸ ποτήριον ὁ Κύριος, which is also the more difficult reading. The other reading, *Domini,* would imply that the Lord's brother had been present at the Lord's Supper. The writer of the legend did not, however, regard him as one of the twelve.

James appears as the head of the church in Jerusalem, and is called simply James in Acts xii. 17 and in Acts xv. 13. Such was his influence, that his opinion was adopted and em-

[1] *Hist. Eccles.* i. 12, p. 77, ed. Heinichen.

bodied in the circular sent to "the churches in Antioch, and Syria, and Cilicia." Acts xv. 13. Paul, on going up to the capital to visit Peter, saw James also, as we are told in Gal. i. 19; and on his arrival at Jerusalem many years afterwards, he at once "went in with us unto James"—πρὸς Ἰάκωβον,—a formal interview. Acts xxi. 18. In Gal. ii. 9, too, we read, "James, and Cephas, and John, who were reputed to be pillars,"—most naturally the same James, the Lord's brother, referred to in the first chapter; and again in the same chapter reference is thus made—"certain came from James." James was thus an apostle, though not one of the twelve.

The original apostles were, according to their commission, under the necessity of itinerating; but the continuous residence of James in the metropolis must have helped to advance him to his high position. Lange, indeed, objects, that "on such a supposition the real apostles vanish from the field," and quite correctly so far as the book of Acts is concerned. For the assertion is true of the majority, or of eight of them; and a new apostle like James—he of Tarsus—fills the scene. Another of Lange's objections is, "the utter untenableness of an apocryphal apostolate by the side of that instituted by Christ."[1] But his further inference, that the elevation of James to a quasi-apostolate lifts Jude and Simon, too, to a similar position, is without foundation as to the last. The apostleship of Paul, however, is so far of the same class; only he became through his formal call equal to the twelve in rank,—his grand argument in that paragraph of the epistle out of one statement of which the previous pages have sprung. Jude and James were not regarded as primary apostles, and could not claim such a standing, though they received the general name. True, the book of Acts is silent about James Alphæi, and introduces without any explanation another James. But if this James had been the son of Alphæus, he would probably have been so designated, as, indeed, he is everywhere else. One may reply, indeed, that the paternal epithet is omitted because by this time James son of Zebedee had been slain, and there remained but one of the name. Still, it would be strange that he is not formally called an apostle, when there is nothing said

[1] *Die völlige Unhaltbarkeit eines apokryphischen Apostelstandes neben dem von Christus gestifteten Apostolat.*

to identify him. A James unidentified is naturally taken to be a different person from one who is always marked by a patronymic. And to how few of the apostles is there any reference made at all in the Acts! Luke's habit is not to identify formally or distinguish persons in the course of his narrative. It is therefore worse than useless on the part of De Wette to insinuate that Luke has exchanged the two Jameses in the course of his history, or forgotten to distinguish them. The apostles at the period of Paul's visit were probably absent from Jerusalem on missionary work. Peter and John happened to be there; but James was the recognised or stationary head. The difficulty, too, is lessened, if, with Stier,[1] Wieseler,[2] and Davidson,[3] we take the James whose opinion prevailed in the council, and who is mentioned in Gal. ii. 9, to be the apostle, son of Alphæus; but the view does not harmonize with the uniform patristic tradition.

The relation which James bore to Christ must also have invested him with peculiar honour in the eyes of the Jewish church. Nor was his character less awful and impressive; he was surnamed "the Just." According to Hegesippus, he was holy from his mother's womb, and lived the life of a Nazarite,—neither shaved, nor bathed, nor anointed himself; wore linen garments; was permitted once a year to enter the holy of holies; and was so given to prayer, that his knees had become callous like a camel's. Euseb. *Hist. Eccl.* ii. 23. Much of this, of course, is mere legend. Yet, though he was a believer, he was zealous of the law,—a representative of Jewish piety, and of that peculiar type of it which naturally prevailed in the mother church in Jerusalem, still the scene of the temple service, and the centre of all sacred Jewish associations. In his epistle the same elements of character are exhibited. The new dispensation is to him *νόμος*, but *νόμος τῆς ἐλευθερίας*. He was a stranger to all the practical difficulties which had met Paul and Peter who had to go and form churches among the uncircumcised; for his circle was either of Jews or circumcised proselytes. He was the natural head of the "many thousands of Jews who believed, and who were all zealous of

[1] *Andeutungen*, i. 412.

[2] *Ueber die Brüder des Herrn. Studien und Kritiken*, 1st Heft, 1842.

[3] *Introduction to New Testament*, vol. iii. p. 310.

the law" (Acts xxi. 20); and he was able to guide the extreme party, for they had confidence in his own fervent observance of "the customs."[1]

Such was his great influence even in distant places, that when "certain came" from him to Antioch, Peter dissembled, and even Barnabas succumbed. His shadow overawed them into a momentary relapse and inconsistency. His martyrdom, recorded by Hegesippus, and by Josephus in a paragraph the genuineness of which has been questioned, was supposed by many[2] to have brought on the siege of Vespasian as a judgment on the city. St. James is glorified in the *Clementines* as "lord, and bishop of bishops."[3] In the *Chronicon Paschale* he is called apostle and patriarch of Jerusalem, and is said to have been enthroned by Peter on his departure for Rome (vol. i. 460, ed. Dindorf). So strangely do opinions grow into extremes, that Victorinus the Rhetorician, a man mentioned cautiously by Jerome,[4] but extolled by Augustine,[5] denies James to be an apostle, affirms him to be *in hæresi,* and reckons him the author of those Judaistic errors which had crept into the Galatian churches. His interpretation is: "I saw James the Lord's brother (*habitus secundum carnem*); as if Paul meant thereby to affirm, 'You cannot now say, "Thou deniest James, and therefore rejectest the doctrine we follow, because thou hast not seen him." But I did see him, the first promulgator of your opinions—*ita nihil apud me valuit.*'" "The Symmachians make James," he adds, "a supernumerary apostle, *quasi duodecimum,* and all who add the observance of Judaism to the doctrine of our Lord Jesus Christ follow him as master."[6]

On a question so difficult, critics, as may be supposed, are much divided. Against the theory put forward in the previous pages are Baronius, Semler, Pott, Schneckenburger,

[1] What the name 'Ωβλίας, given him by Hegesippus, means, it is impossible to say, for no solution is satisfactory. See Heinichen's note, Routh's *Reliquiæ Sacræ,* vol. i. p. 233, 2d ed.; Fuller's *Miscellanea Sacra,* lib. iii. cap. i.; Suicer, *sub voce;* Schaff, *Kircheng.* § 35.

[2] As Hegesippus, in Euseb. *Hist. Eccl.* ii. 23.

[3] Τῷ κυρίῳ καὶ ἐπισκόπων ἐπισκόπῳ, διέποντι δὲ τὴν 'Ιερουσαλὴμ ἁγίαν 'Εβραίων ἐκκλησίαν.—*Homiliæ,* p. 10, ed. Dressel.

[4] *De Viris Illust.* cap. 101.

[5] *Confessionum,* lib. viii. cap. 2, vol. i. p. 252, Paris 1836.

[6] Mai, *Script. Vet. Nova Collectio,* vol. iii.

Guericke, Steiger, Olshausen, Lange, Hug, Friedlieb, Lichtenstein, and Arnaud; on the other side are De Wette, Rothe, Herder, Neander, Stier, Niedner, Winer, Meyer, Ewald, Gresswell, Wieseler in a paper *Ueber die Brüder des Herrn, Stud. und Kritik.* 1 Heft, 1842; Blom, *Disputatio de τοῖς ἀδελφοῖς καὶ ταῖς ἀδελφαῖς τοῦ Κυρίου*, Lugduni Batav. 1839; Schaff, *das Verhältniss des Jacobus Bruders des Herrns zu Jacobus Alphæi auf Neue exegetisch und historisch untersucht*, Berlin 1843. In a later work (*Church History*, § 95, 1854), Dr. Schaff has modified his view of some of the proofs adduced by him, saying that he had made rather too little of the dogmatic argument against the supposition that Mary had other children, and of the old theory that the brothers were sons of Joseph by a former marriage (vol. ii. p. 35, English transl.). See also an essay of Laurent, *Die Brüder Jesu*, in his *Neutestamentliche Studien*, Gotha 1866.

CHAPTER II. 1–10

AFTER his conversion, the apostle had held no consultation as to his course or the themes of his preaching with the other apostles; and in proof he still continues his narrative. He had been in Jerusalem once, and had seen Peter and James, but he had stayed only for a brief period. The apostles whom he met did not question his standing, neither did they sanction his commission nor add to his authority. He now in his historical argument refers to another visit to Jerusalem, when he saw the chief of the apostles; but met them as an equal, on the same platform of official status, and took counsel with them as one of the same rank and prerogative. Nay more, at a subsequent period he confronted the eldest, boldest, and most highly honoured of them, when he was in error; did not privately warn him or humbly remonstrate with him as an inferior with a superior, but solemnly and publicly, as one invested with the same authority, rebuked Cephas, the apostle of the circumcision.

Ver. 1. *Ἔπειτα διὰ δεκατεσσάρων ἐτῶν πάλιν ἀνέβην εἰς Ἱεροσόλυμα μετὰ Βαρνάβα, συμπαραλαβὼν καὶ Τίτον*—"Then after fourteen years I went up again to Jerusalem with Barnabas, having taken along with me also Titus." *Ἔπειτα* marks another step in the historical argument, as in vers. 18 and 21 of the previous chapter,—another epoch in his travels and life. The period is specified by *διὰ δεκατεσσάρων ἐτῶν*—"after fourteen years." It is vain to disturb the reading, as if it might be read *τεσσάρων* (*διὰ ιδ' ἐτῶν* changed into *διὰ δ' ἐτῶν*), as is maintained by Semler, Capell, Guericke, Rinck, Winer, Reiche, and Ulrich in *Stud. u. Kritik.* 1836. The *Chronicon Paschale*, sometimes adduced, is no authority, nay, very probably it also read fourteen years, as it computes them from the ascension—*ἀπὸ τῆς ἀναλήψεως*. Vol. i. p. 436, ed. Dindorf. See Anger,

Wieseler, and the reply of Fritzsche, *Fritzschiorum Opuscula*, p. 160, etc.

The phrase διὰ δεκατεσσάρων ἐτῶν is rightly rendered "after fourteen years," διά denoting through the whole period, and thus emphatically beyond it or at the end of it; *post* in the Vulgate, Acts xxiv. 17, Mark ii. 1, 4 Macc. xiii. 21, Deut. ix. 11; Xen. i. 4, 28; Winer, § 47; Bernhardy, p. 235. Thus διὰ χρόνου, "after a time," Sophocles, *Philoct.* 285, wrongly rendered by Ellendt "slowly,"—nor is the translation of Wunder and Ast more satisfactory; διὰ χρόνου, Xen. *Mem.* ii. 8, 1, and Kühner's note; δι' ἔτους, in contrast with ἐμμήνους, Lucian, *Paras.* 15, vol. vii. p. 118, ed. Bipont. Hermann, *ad Viger.* 377, remarks, διὰ χρόνου *est interjecto tempore.* Schaefer, Bos, *Ellips.* p. 249, ed. London 1825. In Deut. ix. 11, the unmistakeable Hebrew phrase מִקֵּץ, "at the end of" forty days, etc., is rendered by the Sept. διὰ τεσσαράκοντα ἡμερῶν. Others give διά a different sense, the sense of *intra:* at some point within the fourteen years, in which I have been a Christian. Œder, Rambach, Theile, Schott, and Paulus take this view. The preposition apparently may bear such a sense, though Meyer denies it, Acts v. 19, xvi. 9. But with such a meaning, we should have expected the article or the demonstrative pronoun. Nor would the expression with such a sense have any definite meaning, as it would afford no distinct date to give strength and proof to the apostle's statement of self-dependence. But the main question is, From what point does the apostle reckon the fourteen years?

1. Many date it from the journey mentioned in i. 18, as Jerome, Usher, Bengel, Winer, Meyer, Usteri, Rückert, Trana, Reiche, Jatho, Bisping, Hofmann, Prof. Lightfoot, Kamphausen in Bunsen's *Bibelwerk*, and Burton, *Works*, vol. iv. p. 45.

2. Some date it from his conversion, as Estius, Olshausen, Fritzsche, Hilgenfeld, Windischmann, Wieseler, Meyer, Ebrard; also in former times, Baronius, Spanheim, Pearson, and Lightfoot.

3. Others date it from the ascension, as the *Chronicle* referred to, Peter Lombard, and Paulus. This last opinion may be discarded, and the difficulty lies between the previous two.

It does seem at first sight in favour of the first view, that the apostle has just spoken of a previous journey; and now when he writes ἔπειτα . . . πάλιν, you may naturally infer that he counts from it. And then, as it is part of his argument for his independent apostolate to show how long a time he acted by himself and in no concert with the other apostles, the dating of the time from his first journey adds so much more weight to his declaration, so much longer an interval having elapsed; and he also places διὰ δεκατεσσάρων in the position of emphasis.

Yet the second opinion is the more probable. The grand moment of his life was his conversion, and it became the point from which dates were unconsciously measured,—all before it fading away as old and legal, all after it standing out in new and spiritual prominence. His conversion divided his life, and supplied a point of chronological reference. As he looked back, it faced him as a terminus from which he naturally counted. Not only so, but in the commencement of this vindication he recurs to his conversion and its results, for it severed his former from his present self, and it was not till three years after it that he went up to Jerusalem. He lays stress on the lapse of so long a time, wishing it to be noted that he speaks of years, and so he writes μετὰ ἔτη τρία, the emphasis on ἔτη; but now, the idea of years having been so emphatically expressed, when he refers again to them, their number becomes prominent, and he writes, as if still reckoning from his conversion, διὰ δεκατεσσάρων ἐτῶν. Had this verse occurred immediately after i. 18, we might have said that the fourteen years dated from the first visit to Jerusalem; but a paragraph intervenes which obscures the reference, and describes some time spent and some journeys made in various places. It is natural, therefore, to suppose, that after a digressive insertion, the apostle recurs to the original point of calculation—his conversion. The second ἔπειτα of this verse thus refers to the same *terminus a quo* as the first in i. 18, and he now uses διά, not a second μετά, as if to prevent mistake.

Πάλιν ἀνέβην—"I again went up." On the question, with which of the visits of the apostle to Jerusalem recorded in the Acts of the Apostles this visit is to be identified, see remarks at the end of this section, after ver. 10. The πάλιν does not qualify μετὰ Βαρνάβα, as if, according to Lange, a previous journey with Barnabas had been alluded to. Paul on this journey was the principal person, Barnabas being in a subordinate, and Titus in a still inferior relation. Acts xv. 2. There had, indeed, been an intermediate visit (Acts xi. 29, 30); but the apostle makes no allusion to it, either because he was sent up on a special errand of beneficence, or because, as under the Herodian persecution the apostles might be absent, he did not see any of them (Spanheim). The record of this visit was not, on that account, essential to his present argument, and the mere use of *πάλιν* will not prove that this second visit is the one intended. Compare John xxi. 1, 14.

Συμπαραλαβὼν καὶ Τίτον—"having taken with me also Titus:" "also," as he is going to speak of him immediately, and he is thus singled out from the *τινας ἄλλους* of Acts xv. 2. Compare Job i. 4. The precise circumstances attending this visit are minutely dwelt on, as corroborating his statement that he was an accredited apostle, working and travelling under a parallel commission with the others for a lengthened period. Therefore he adds—

Ver. 2. *'Ανέβην δὲ κατὰ ἀποκάλυψιν*—"But I went up by revelation." Jerusalem stood on a high plateau; but to "go up" refers, as with us, to it as the capital. 1 Kings xii. 28; Matt. xx. 17, 18; Mark iii. 22; Acts xv. 2, etc. See C. B. Michaelis, *Dissertatio Chorographica notiones superi et inferi evolvens*, etc., § 37, in vol. v. of *Essays* edited by Velthusen, Kuinoel, and Ruperti. Lest the visit should be misunderstood, the *ἀνέβην* is repeated and put in emphasis, while the iterative and explanatory *δέ* at once carries on the argument, and has a sub-adversative force: I went up, as I have said, "but I went up according to revelation." Klotz-Devarius, ii. 361; Hartung, i. 168. The nature of that divine revelation we know not. The apostle was no stranger to such divine promptings. He had received the gospel by revelation, and in the same way had often enjoyed those divine suggestions and counsels which shaped his missionary tours. Acts xvi. 6, 7, 9. The apostles did not summon him to account, asking why he had assumed the name and professed to do the work which so specially belonged to them. Granville Penn renders *κατὰ ἀποκάλυψιν* "openly," *palam*, as if opposed to *κατ' ἰδίαν*, privately,—a useless departure from usage.[1] Schrader, Schulz, and Hermann render the same phrase in the words of the latter: *explicationis*

[1] Morehead proposes to put a comma after *ἀποκάλυψιν*: "I went up

causa, ut patefieret inter ipsos, quæ vera esset Jesu doctrina. The preposition itself may bear such a meaning (Winer, § 49), but this phrase cannot; for it would be contrary to the New Testament use of the noun, and would be in the face of the apostle's very argument for his independent position. Nor is *κατά τινα ἀποκ.* required for the common interpretation. See Eph. iii. 3; also, Gal. i. 12, 16. The apostle does not specify the individual revelation, but affirms absolutely that it was under revelation that he went up, and not under human suggestion or control. He went up "by revelation," not by a particular revelation. Yet the turn given to the words by Whitby is inadmissible: "according to the tenor of my revelation, which made me an apostle of the Gentiles." What happened in Jerusalem is next told:

Καὶ ἀνεθέμην αὐτοῖς τὸ εὐαγγέλιον ὃ κηρύσσω ἐν τοῖς ἔθνεσι—"And I communicated to them the gospel which I preach among the Gentiles."

'Ανεθέμην is rendered in the Vulgate *contuli cum eis.* Compare Acts xxv. 14; 2 Macc. iii. 9; and Wetstein *in loc.* It does not exactly mean, "to leave in the hands of" (Green, *Gr. Gram.* p. 82), but to tell with a view to confer about it. Jerome adds: *inter conferentes æqualitas est.* The noun implied in *αὐτοῖς* is to be found in the term *'Ιεροσόλυμα*—no uncommon form of antecedent. Matt. iv. 23, ix. 35, xi. 1, xii. 9; Luke v. 14; Acts viii. 5; Winer, § 22, 3, *a*; Bernhardy, p. 288. The *αὐτοῖς* are the Christians in Jerusalem, not the elders, as is held by Winer hesitatingly, and by Matthies decidedly—*auf die Vorsteher und Aeltesten in der Gemeinde;* nor yet the apostles (Calvin, Schott, and Olshausen),—a view which would not only make a distinction among the apostles, but also a difference in the mode and extent of the communication, as if he had told as much as he chose to the apostolic college, but opened himself more fully and unreservedly to a select committee of them. The gospel propounded by him was—

"Ο κηρύσσω ἐν τοῖς ἔθνεσιν—the present indicating its continuous identity and his enduring work; that conference made no change upon it. The gospel so characterized was, indeed, the great scheme of mercy, but especially in the free

and communicated according to revelation," or, according to his own full light, his gospel to them.—*Explanation of Passages*, etc., Edin. 1843.

form in which he presented it,—unhampered by legal or Mosaic restrictions, unconditioned by any distinctions of race or blood —*τὸ χωρὶς περιτομῆς*, as Chrysostom describes it—its characteristic tenet being justification without works of law. Though he was speaking in the heart of Judaism, and among Jewish believers who were zealous of the law, he did not modify his vocation in describing it, or present it as his exceptional work. Where it was most suspected and opposed, where it was sure to provoke antipathy, he gloried in it. But, as if correcting himself, he suddenly adds—

Κατ' ἰδίαν δὲ τοῖς δοκοῦσιν—"but privately to them of reputation." These words seem to qualify the *αὐτοῖς* and to confine them to a very particular class, though to state the persons communicated with, first so broadly and then with pointed restriction, seems peculiar. Some therefore suppose that there were two conferences—a first and more public one, and a second and more select one. Such is the view of De Wette, Meyer, Windischmann, Ellicott, Bisping, and many others. But why should the apostle first to all appearance proclaim his gospel publicly, and then afterward privately—first to the mass, and then to a coterie? The doctrine of reserve propounded by the Catholic Estius is not to be admitted. We prefer the view of Chrysostom who admits only one conference; and he is followed by Calovius, by Alford apparently, and Webster and Wilkinson. There is no occasion, however, to mark the clause with brackets, as is done by Knapp. Going up under revelation, the apostle made known his gospel "to those in Jerusalem, privately, however, to them who were of reputation." The reason, as given by Theodoret, is, that so many were zealous for the law—*ὑπὲρ τοῦ νόμου ζῆλον ἔχοντες*. That there was a public meeting and discussion is true, as recorded in Acts xv.; but the apostle does not allude to it here in definite terms. He seems to state the general result first, and then, as if referring to the revelation under which he acted, he suddenly checks himself, and says he communicated with them of reputation. Thus he may have distinguished his general mission, which is perhaps alluded to in Acts xv. 4, from the special course of conduct which his revelation suggested. The church at Antioch deputed the apostle in consequence of the Judaizers; the Judaizers in Jerusalem thought their cause betrayed by the favourable reception given to Paul, and their agitation in the metropolis seems to have necessitated the public conference. But "the revelation" may have referred more to the matters which were treated of in confidence with the noted brethren.

The phrase κατ' ἰδίαν is "privately." Matt. xvii. 19, xx. 17, xxiv. 3; Mark iv. 34. It does not mean "*especially*" (Baur), or "preferably," as Olshausen and Usteri give it. The margin of the common version has "severally," and the Genevan reads "particularly;" but the Syriac correctly, ܒܝܢܝ ܘܠܗܘܢ, "between me and them." It corresponds to ἰδίᾳ in the classics as opposed to κοινῇ or δημοσίᾳ. The peculiar phrase τοῖς δοκοῦσι is rightly rendered, "to them which are of reputation"—ἐπισήμοις (Theodoret), or, as Hesychius defines it, οἱ ἔνδοξοι. There needs no supplied insertion of τι after the participle, as Bagge supposes. Thus Ælian says of Aristotle, σοφὸς ἀνὴρ καὶ ὢν καὶ εἶναι δοκῶν, *Hist. Var.* xiv.; ἀδοξούντων is in contrast with δοκούντων, in reference to the weight of their word or opinions. Euripides, *Hecuba*, 294, 295. Pflugk in his note refers to Pindar, *Nem.* vii. 30, ἀδόκητον ἐν καὶ δοκέοντα; to Eurip. *Troad.* 608, and *Heracl.* 795. See Pindar, *Ol.* xiii. 56, and Dissen's note. Borger quotes from Porphyry a clause in which τὰ πλήθη is in contrast to οἱ δοκοῦντες. Similarly the Hebrew חָשׁוּב. See Fürst, *Lex. sub voce.* Wycliffe's version is wrong in rendering "to those that semeden to be summewhat." And there is no ground for the supposition of Cameron, Rückert, Schott, and Olshausen, that the phrase was chosen as one often in the mouths of the party who preferred them as leaders. Nor is there any irony in it, for the apostle is making a simple historical reference—τοῖς κορυφαίοις (Œcumenius)—to his intercourse with them and its results,—all as confirmatory of his own separate and independent commission.

Μή πως εἰς κενὸν τρέχω ἢ ἔδραμον—"lest I might be running or have run in vain." The figure of the two verbs is a common one. Phil. ii. 16; 2 Tim. iv. 7; Gal. v. 7; and also 1 Cor. ix. 24, Heb. xii. 1. The meaning of εἰς κενόν, "in vain," may be seen, 2 Cor. vi. 1, Phil. ii. 16, 1 Thess. iii. 5, Sept. Isa. lxv. 23; Kypke, *in loc.* It is surely prosaic in Jowett to refer ἔδραμον to the journey to Jerusalem, which he had already accomplished. Homberg, Gabler, Paulus, and Matthies connect this clause with τοῖς δοκοῦσιν—*qui putabant num forte in vanum currerem.* Wieseler says that he mentions this connection simply as a *philologische Antiquität.*

Allied to this view is one originally held by Fritzsche (*Conjectanea*), by Green, and similarly by Wieseler, that μή πως may mean *num forte.* In such a case the verb is in the present indicative. Green renders it thus: "I laid my gospel before them, that they might judge whether I was running or had run in vain" (*Gr. Gram.* pp. 80–83). But μή πως is *ne forte,* and is dependent on ἀνεθέμην. Hofmann also regards the clause as a direct question to which a negative answer is anticipated; but the question in such a case would, as Meyer says, be made by εἴ πως. Œcumenius proposes also to take it κατ' ἐρώτησιν, but as containing a confirmatory result, that he had not run in vain. Gwynne, finding that all his predecessors have mistaken the real meaning, thus puts it: "I submitted the gospel which I preach among the Gentiles, so that I run not now, nor was then running in vain;" but it is simply ungrammatical to make μή πως signify *adeo non,* and his doctrinal arguments rest on a misconception. At the same time the inference of Augustine is too strong, that if Paul has not conferred with the apostles, *ecclesia illi omnino non crederet. Contra Faust.* lib. 28. The verb τρέχω is subjunctive, 1 Thess. iii. 5, and ἔδραμον indicative. Stallbaum, *Plato, Phæd.* p. 84, E, vol. i. 127–8. It does not require that the first should be indicative because the second is, for the use of the mode depends on the conception of the writer. Krüger, § 54, 8, 9. The first verb in the present subjunctive, where perhaps an optative might have been expected, describes Paul's activity as still lasting; and the past ἔδραμον is regarded by Fritzsche in a hypothetical sense—*proposui . . . ne forte frustra cucurrissem,*—that is to say, which might perchance have been the case if I had not held this conference at Jerusalem. Or the change of mood, causing also change of tense, may mark that the event apprehended had taken place. Winer, § 56, 2, and examples in Gayler, *Partic. Negat.* p. 327; A. Buttmann, p. 303. There was fear in the apostle's mind of something disastrous, and that generally is expressed: "whether I be running or had run in vain,"—the idea of apprehension being wrapt up in the idiom.

Matt. xxv. 9; Rom. xi. 21. But to what does or can the apostle refer?

1. The *εἰς κενόν* cannot refer to his commission, the validity of which depended not on human suffrage, and of which he never could have any doubt, nay, which he was employed at that moment in justifying.

2. Nor can the phrase refer to the matter of his preaching. He had received it by revelation, and its truth was independent altogether of the results of any conference or the decisions of any body of men. Chrysostom asks, "Who would be so senseless as to preach for so many years without being sure that his preaching was true?" Some Catholic expositors hold, however, that his preaching needed the sanction of the other apostles or of the church. See Corn. a-Lapide, *in loc.*, who stoutly contends against all *Novantes* or Reformers who do not act like Paul, and consult mother church.

3. Nor can the words mean that he doubted the efficacy or success of his labours. So many sermons preached, so many sinners converted, so many saints blessed and revived, so many churches founded, so many baptisms administered by himself or in connection with his apostleship and followed so often by the visible or palpable descent of the Divine Spirit, were surely manifold and unmistakeable tokens that he had not run in vain. And these realities were unaffected by the opinions of any parties in Jerusalem. Tertullian is bold enough in hitting Marcion to barb his weapon by the supposition, that the apostle was in doubt as to his system, that he wished *auctoritas antecessorum et fidei et prædicationi suæ*. *Adver. Marcion.* iv. 2, vol. ii. p. 163, *Opera*, ed. Œhler.

4. Nor probably can we regard the whole matter as merely subjective, with Chrysostom, Beza, Borger, Winer, Rückert, Meyer, and Ellicott,—that is, lest in the opinion of others I be running or had run in vain; or as Theodoret plainly puts it, *οὐ περὶ ἑαυτοῦ τέθεικεν ἀλλὰ περὶ τῶν ἄλλων*. This, we apprehend, is only the truth partially, not wholly. It was not the mere opinion others might form of the gospel which he preached among the Gentiles, but more the mistaken action to which it might lead. He was now under a commission to ask advice on a certain point, the point which characterized his gospel among the Gentiles. This private conference enabled him

to state what his views were on this very question; and his apprehension was, that if it should be misunderstood, all his labour would be lost, if his free and unhampered mode of offering Christ to poor heathens were disallowed. Should the church, in defiance of his arguments, experience, and appeals, insist on compliance with circumcision as essential to admission to the church, then on this point which signalized his preaching as the apostle of the Gentiles, his labour would be so far in vain, and the Gentile churches would be in danger of losing their precious freedom. No man who had laboured so long and so hard to maintain a gospel unrestricted by any ceremonial conditions would wish his labour to be in vain, or so in vain as to be authoritatively interfered with, and frustrated as far as possible by being disowned. And the question involved so much, that to enjoin it was to introduce another gospel. No wonder that in connection with so momentous a matter fraught with such interest to all the Gentile churches, the apostle of the Gentiles went up by revelation. But he gained his point, and that point was the non-circumcision of Gentile converts, as the next verse shows. We do not suppose, with Thiersch, that the reality of his apostleship was the matter laid before the private conference after the public settlement of the controversy, so that thus the "faithful at large were spared the trial of a question for which they were not prepared, the recognition of Paul's apostleship being much more difficult than the rights of the Gentiles." *History of the Christian Church*, p. 121, Eng. trans. But it was his gospel, not his office, which he set before them. Winer's view is as remote from the point: *Ut ne, si his videretur paribus castigandus, publica expostulatione ipsius auctoritas infringeretur.* He had not run in vain—

Ver. 3. *'Αλλ' οὐδὲ Τίτος ὁ σὺν ἐμοί, Ἕλλην ὤν, ἠναγκάσθη περιτμηθῆναι*—"Howbeit not even Titus, who was with me, though he was a Greek, was forced to be circumcised." The reference is not to what had happened at Antioch prior to the visit (Hofmann, Reiche), but to what took place at Jerusalem during the visit. The *ἀλλά* is strongly adversative. So far from my having run in vain; in the very headquarters of Jewish influence or Judaistic leaning, my Greek companion Titus, heathen though he was, had not circumcision forced upon him. The apostle's position was tested in the case of Titus, and was not overthrown. Ἀλλ' οὐδέ is a climactic phrase—*at ne quidem;* "neuerthelesse nother" (Coverdale). Luke xxiii. 15; Acts xix. 2. Titus is the emphatic word: his was a ruling case,—"a strong and pertinent instance," as Locke calls it. For various reasons that might have been deemed expedient at the moment and in the place, his circumcision might have been demanded, and yet the tenor of the apostle's preaching among the Gentiles not disallowed. But *not even* Titus—

Ἕλλην ὤν—"Greek though" or "as he was,"—καίτοι, Theodoret,—the participle declaring the reason by stating the fact. Donaldson, § 493. Titus was a Greek, or of Greek extraction, and circumcision might on that account have been exacted from him as also my companion; but on the very same account it was resisted. "Greek" is equivalent to being of heathen extraction. Mark vii. 26.

The verb ἠναγκάσθη, the opposite of πείθειν, is a strong expression, denoting to compel even by torture, to force by threats, more mildly by authority (Acts xxvi. 11); then to constrain by argument: Matt. xiv. 22; Mark vi. 45. See under ver. 14.

Two wrong and extreme inferences have been drawn from the word:

1. The Greek fathers, Winer, De Wette, Usteri, Matthies, and Schott go to one extreme, and give this meaning, that the circumcision of Titus, as a Greek and Paul's companion, was not insisted on, so much did Paul find himself at one with the leading authorities in the mother church. But this hypothesis does not harmonize with the strong expression ἠναγκάσθη, nor with the well-known state of opinion and feeling in the church at Jerusalem. Such a statement at this point, too, would be a forestalling of the argument as based on the results of the conference. The apostle is showing that he had not laboured in vain,—that the very point which characterized his gospel was gained, that point being the free admission of uncircumcised Gentiles into the church; for even in Jerusalem the circumcision of Titus was successfully resisted,—the enemy was worsted even in his citadel. Titus was "with me," and my authority in the matter was equipollent with that of the other apostles.

2. Some have gone to another extreme, and have drawn this inference from the language, that Titus was not forced to

circumcision,—that is, he was circumcised voluntarily, and not of constraint. Such is the idea of Pelagius, Primasius, Wieseler, Baur, Trana, and others. The verse may bear the inference, but the context disallows it. The circumcision of Timothy is no case in point; and such an interpretation is in direct conflict with the course of argument. For the circumcision of Titus would have been a concession of the very point for which the agitators were disturbing these churches, first in Antioch, and afterwards in Galatia. The "false brethren" for whose sakes, or to whose prejudices, the apostle is supposed to have yielded, are the very persons with whom he could have no accommodation. How could he say that he "yielded not," if at the very time and on a vital doctrine he had succumbed? "The apostle might be accused of preaching uncircumcision; but had he allowed Titus to be circumcised, a far more pointed charge might have been brought against him" (Jowett). And how could such a compromise in such a crisis, a compromise which the council virtually condemned, secure the truth of the gospel coming to or remaining with the Galatian churches (ver. 5)? If Paul yielded in Jerusalem, why not in the provinces? His conduct would have been quoted against himself; the Judaizing teachers would have had warrant for their fettered and subverted gospel, and "the truth of the gospel" among the Galatians would have been seriously endangered. Would not the Judaists there have pleaded Paul's example, proposed Titus as a noted precedent, and ingeniously pictured out similarity of circumstance and obligation? Holding the *οἷς οὐδέ* to be genuine, we regard him as affirming that very strenuous efforts were made, by whom he says not, to have Titus circumcised,—efforts so keen and persistent as to amount almost to compulsion, but which the apostle strenuously and effectively resisted. Such a view is in harmony with the course of the historical argument. Though there is no sure ground for Lightfoot's assertion, that "probably the apostles recommended Paul to yield the point," yet they may have left him to contend alone on this point with the alarmists; for the subsequent *ἰδόντες . . . γνόντες* certainly imply, that if they did not alter their views, they came at all events to clearer convictions. The apostle proceeds to give the reason, or rather the explanation, of the statement just made:

Ver. 4. *Διὰ δὲ τοὺς παρεισάκτους ψευδαδέλφους*—"now it was because of the false brethren stealthily introduced." The difficulty of this connection lies in the δέ, and the Greek fathers, expounding their own language, were puzzled with it: ὁ δὲ σύνδεσμος περιττός (Theodoret). The statement is repeated by Theodore of Mopsuestia, and Theophylact transforms it into οὐδέ. Jerome says, *Sciendum vero quod* autem *superflua sit, et si legatur non habeat quod ei respondeat.* But δέ gives an explanation which virtually contains a reason. Klotz-Devarius, ii. 362. Rom. iii. 22 (Alford, *in loc.*), Phil. ii. 8, are similar, but somewhat different. The connection is not, Titus was not forced to be circumcised, which, if it had happened, would have happened on account of the false brethren; but rather, Titus was not forced to be circumcised, and the reason was, because of the false brethren,—either they pressed it, or would have made a handle of it, and divided the council on that point and others allied to it.[1] Nor is δέ adversative, and περιετμήθη to be supplied—"but he was circumcised on account of false brethren" (Pelagius, Rückert, Elwert, Schmoller),—nor is ἠναγκάσθη to be simply repeated. The construction is probably of a more general nature, and apparently refers to some unexpressed connection between the expected and the actual result of the conference with the apostles, the difference being caused by the efforts of the false brethren. The clause has also a sort of double connection,—one suggested by δέ with the verse before it, and one carried on by οἷς with the verse after it. The connection is thus peculiar. The suppositions of an anakolouthon—διὰ τ. ψευδ. . . . οἷς οὐδε, ver. 5—or of a blending of two constructions, the οἷς of ver. 5 being redundant or resumptive (Winer, Wieseler, Hilgenfeld, Windischmann, Rinck, and Hofmann), need not be detailed. The apostle's words, though loose in connection, may be otherwise unravelled, though not perhaps to one's complete satisfaction. There is, as Lightfoot says, some "shipwreck of grammar. He must maintain his own independence, and not compromise the position of the twelve. There is need of plain speaking, and there is need of reserve." Yet one may say with Luther, *Condonandum est Spiritui Sancto*

[1] Augustine says, *Nam et Titum circumcideret, cum hoc urgerent Judæi nisi subintroducti falso fratres idem vellent, etc. De Mendacio*, 8, p. 718, vol. vi.

in Pauló loquenti si peccet aliquando in grammaticam. Ipse magno ardore loquitur. Qui vero ardet, non potest exacte in dicendo observare regulas grammaticas et præcepta rhetorica.

It is an unnatural and far-fetched connection given by Storr, Borger, Rosenmüller, Stroth, Olshausen, Hermann, and Gwynne, to connect this verse with ἀνέβην, or with ἀνεθέμην (Turner). Nor was it necessary to write, "Titus was not allowed to be circumcised, *yea not;* on account of false brethren." The preposition διά assigns the reason—*propter.* Matt. xxiv. 22; Acts xvi. 3; Rom. viii. 20. The more abstruse meaning assigned by Wieseler is not in point, at least is not necessary. The διά gives the ground for the preceding statement as a whole, but specially for the non-circumcision of Titus.

Who the ψευδάδελφοι in Jerusalem, not Antioch (Fritzsche), precisely were—and the article gives them a known prominence—we know not. 2 Cor. xi. 26. The apostles certainly did not coincide with them; and they must have been Judaizers, though all Judaizers might not be called "false brethren," for many were no doubt sincere Christians, though zealous of the law. But this faction who clamoured for circumcision were Christians only by profession,—owning the Messiahship so far as to secure admission to the church, but still Jews in their slavish attachment to the old economy and its ritual, and in their belief of its permanent and universal obligation. Epiphanius affirms that they were Cerinthus and his party: *Hæres.* xxviii. 4. Their mode of introduction showed what they were —τοὺς παρεισάκτους. The word occurs only here; the verb is used in 2 Pet. ii. 1, and the term is also found in the prologue to the son of Sirach. It appears to be sometimes used simply for a stranger, and is rendered by Hesychius and Suidas ἀλλότριος, and it is found with the same meaning in Polybius more than once; but the additional sense of surreptitious (*subintroductitios,* Tertullian) was in course of time attached to it, as its verb here implies. Or may not the term mean that their falsehood lay in their surreptitious introduction to the company of the apostles, not their admission into the church,—that they were false in professing to be brethren, while yet they were only spies, not from curiosity, but from an earnest and insidious longing to enslave the Gentile converts? Further are they characterized:

Οἵτινες παρεισῆλθον—"who came in stealthily." *Οἵτινες*, "as being a class of men who." Jelf, § 816; Ellendt, *Lex. Soph. sub voce—significatio non tam causalis, quam explicativa*; Bornemann, *Scholia in Luc.* p. 135, comp. Jude 4. The verb is applied to Simon Magus in the *Clementine Homilies*, ii. 23. Their first object was—

Κατασκοπῆσαι τὴν ἐλευθερίαν ἡμῶν ἣν ἔχομεν ἐν Χριστῷ Ἰησοῦ—"to spy out our liberty which we have in Christ Jesus." Josh. ii. 2, 3; 2 Sam. x. 3, 1 Chron. xix. 3, where it stands for the Hebrew רַגֵּל; Xen. *Mem.* ii. 1, 22; Polybius, v. 20, 2; Eurip. *Hel.* 1607. Their work was that of spies—inspection for a sinister purpose. The aorist may refer to the act as done before they were detected; or they had no sooner done with spying out our liberty, than their design became apparent. The liberty referred to in the clause is not spiritual liberty in general, nor independence of human authority (Köhler), but freedom in the sphere where it was menaced and threatened to be curtailed. It was freedom from the Mosaic ritual, but not in and by itself; for that freedom contained in it at the same time justification by faith without deeds of law. This liberty is precious—

Ἣν ἔχομεν ἐν Χριστῷ Ἰησοῦ—"which we have in Christ Jesus." It is ours, *ἡμῶν*, for we are having it in Christ Jesus. It is our present, our asserted possession. See Eph. i. 7. Its element of being is "in Christ Jesus,"—not by Him (Fritzsche, Brown), though He did secure it, but in Him through living faith, and in Him by fellowship with Him. By Him it was secured to us, but in Him we possess it. Their purpose was—

Ἵνα ἡμᾶς καταδουλώσουσιν—"in order that they might bring us into utter bondage." The *ἡμᾶς* are not all Christians, or the apostle and the heathen Christians (Usteri, Meyer, Wieseler, Hofmann), but as in contrast with *ὑμᾶς* it is more distinctive, and is restricted at the moment to the apostle, Titus, and Barnabas, with perhaps the deputation from Antioch representing the freer party in the church. Still, what was true of the *ἡμεῖς* at that moment as a representative party holds true of all believers. F, G read *ἵνα μή*. The Textus Receptus has *καταδουλώσωνται*, vindicated by Reiche, with K and the Greek fathers who virtually use the middle; but the other reading has in its favour A, B[1], C, D, א, and it is received by Lachmann and Tischendorf. B², F, G have the subjunctive *καταδουλώσωσιν*. The future is the most probable as the rarest form of construction, for the future indicative is very uncommon after *ἵνα*, though found in John xvii. 2 (*Lect. Var.*), Rev. iii. 9, viii. 3, xxii. 14. Winer, § 41. The change to the subjunctive is thus easily accounted for. There is no reason whatever for Bloomfield's assertion, that the received reading was altered on account of ignorance of the proper force of the middle voice, for the middle voice would be inappropriate here, since the subjection is not to themselves, but to the law; or for Fritzsche's opinion, that the future is only the subjunctive aorist—*depravatum.* The term *ἵνα* points to the final cause, and the *κατά* in composition deepens the meaning of the verb. The connection with the future is rare, though *ὅπως* is so employed. Gayler, *Part. Neg.* p. 169, says that it is used *sensu improprio finem spectante.* Hom. *Il.* vii. 353, xxi. 314. In connection with *ὅπως μή*, see Schæfer, *Annot. in Demosth. Ol. III.* vol. i. p. 277. According to Winer, § 41, the future expresses duration, or a continued state; according to others, confident anticipations of the result; or, as Alford gives it, "certain sequence in the view of the agent;" or as Meyer puts it, they expected the result as certain and enduring—*als gewiss und fortdauernd.* Schmalfeld, § 142; Klotz-Devarius, p. 683. It probably indicates purpose realized in the view of the false teachers.

Ver. 5. *Οἷς οὐδὲ πρὸς ὥραν εἴξαμεν τῇ ὑποταγῇ*—"To whom not even for an hour did we yield in subjection." The reading *οἷς οὐδέ* has preponderant authority. The words are found in all Greek uncial codices except D at first hand, and in almost all the cursives, in a host of versions and originally in the Vulgate. Many of the Greek and Latin fathers so read also. Ambrosiaster refers to the reading, and so does Jerome: *quibus neque.* But some of the Latin fathers omitted the negative. Tertullian justifies the omission, reading *nec ad horam*, and accuses Marcion of *vitiatio Scripturæ*, for Paul did sometimes yield, *ad tempus.* The omission thus arose from the grammatical difficulty, and the desire to preserve the consistency of the apostle who had circumcised Timothy. The verb occurs only here, and by the aorist refers to the historic past. The dative *ὑποταγῇ* is that of manner, the article *τῇ* before the abstract noun specifying it as the obedience which was demanded or expected, not "the submission we were taunted with," in the circumcision of Titus (Lightfoot). The noun does not signify obedience to Christ—*Jesu obsequio* (Hermann), but refers to the οἷς, the false brethren in Jerusalem, on account of whom and whose conduct Titus was not compelled to be circumcised. The ὑποταγῇ claimed was a specimen of the καταδούλωσις designed against them. Its resolution by Winer and Usteri into εἰς τὴν ὑποταγήν, or by Bloomfield into πρὸς τ. ὑποτ., is not to be thought of; nor can it mean, as with the older interpreters, δι' ὑποταγῆς, *per subjectionem* (Calvin), nor is it in apposition with οἷς (Matthies). The subjection was not yielded for the briefest space, οὐδὲ πρὸς ὥραν—"not even for an hour." 2 Cor. vii. 8; Philem. 15. This natural interpretation of the clause goes directly against those who, thinking that Paul voluntarily circumcised Titus, are obliged to strain the meaning thus: *obsequium se præstitisse Paulus profitetur, sed non ita præstitisse ut illis se victum donet vel de jure suo aliquid cederet.* See Elwert. And the purpose was—

Ἵνα ἡ ἀλήθεια τοῦ εὐαγγελίου διαμείνῃ πρὸς ὑμᾶς—"that the truth of the gospel might continue with you." "The truth of the gospel" is not simply the true gospel, but truth as a distinctive element of the gospel,—opposed to the false views of its cardinal doctrine which the reactionary Judaists propounded. That truth was, in its negative aspect, the non-obligation of the Mosaic law on Gentile believers,—in its positive aspect, justification by faith. The long theological note of Matthies is foreign to the point and the context. The διά in the verb is intensive—"might endure," *ad finem usque.* Heb. i. 11; 2 Pet. iii. 4; Wilke, *sub voce.* The phrase πρὸς ὑμᾶς means, with you—you Galatians, the readers of the epistle. It is an instance, as Alford remarks, "in which we apply home to the particular, what, as matter of fact, it only shares as included in the general." The apostle's motive in resistance was pure and noble, and the Galatians should have highly appreciated it.

Ver. 6. Ἀπὸ δὲ τῶν δοκούντων εἶναί τι—"But from those high in reputation." The construction is plainly broken and involved. It is evident from this clause that the first intention was to end the sentence with οὐδὲν προσελαβόμην; or, judging from the words actually employed, it might or would have been ἐμοὶ οὐδὲν προσανετέθη—"but from those high in reputation nothing was added to me;" instead of which he writes: "From them who are high in reputation—to me those persons high in reputation added nothing." The construction begins with ἀπό, and passively, then two parenthetical clauses intervene, and the parenthesis is not formally terminated, but passes into the connected active clause, ἐμοὶ γάρ. Winer, § 63. The apostle is still asserting his apostolic independence. First, generally, he went into conference with the οἱ δοκοῦντες, and he got nothing from them—no additional element of information or authority. His commission did not receive any needed *imprimatur* from them. But, secondly, the apostle, on referring to the οἱ δοκοῦντες, and while such a result as we have just given is before his mind, is anxious that his relation to them should be distinctly apprehended—that he met them on a perfect equality; and so he interjects, "Whatsoever they were, it maketh no matter to me." Then, thirdly, to show that this declaration was no disparagement of them on any personal ground, he subjoins, as if in defence or explanation, "God accepteth no man's person." And, lastly, going back to his intended statement, but with an emphatic change of construction, he concludes, "To me, it is true, those who are high in reputation added nothing." The anakolouthon is the result of mental hurry, the main thought and subordinate ideas struggling for all but simultaneous utterance,—his anxiety to be distinctly understood in a matter of such high moment as the independency of his apostleship and teaching, leads him to commence with a statement, then to guard it, and then to explain the very guard. This throng of ideas throws him off from his construction which he does not formally resume, but ends with a different and decided declaration. Such, generally, is, we think, the structure of these clauses of terse outspokenness.

More particularly: ἀπὸ δὲ τῶν δοκούντων εἶναί τι—"But from them who were esteemed something,"—literally, "who were" or "are in high estimation;" *qui videbantur*, Vulgate; "which seme to be great," Tyndale. The δέ is resumptive of the thought first alluded to in ver. 2, but going off from the previous statement. The phrase is not to be taken subjectively, or as meaning "who thought themselves to be something." Examples of similar language are: ὑπὸ πολλῶν καὶ δοκούντων εἶναί τι, Plato, *Gorg.* p. 472, A; ἐὰν δοκῶσί τι εἶναι μηδὲν ὄντες, *Apolog.*

41, E. See also Wetstein, *in loc.* There is apparently a slight element of depreciation in these quotations, but not in the clause before us. If those in whose estimation they stood so high were the Judaizing faction, such an inference might be legitimate, and Bengel and Wieseler adopt it; but if the persons who held them in honour were the church—and such seems the case from ver. 9—then the words simply indicate the high position of the individuals referred to. See under ver. 2. The next clause is explanatory—

Ὁποῖοί ποτε ἦσαν, οὐδέν μοι διαφέρει—"whatsoever they were, it matters nothing to me;" *quales aliquando fuerint*, Vulgate. Some give *ποτέ* the sense of *olim*, and understand the reference to be to the apostles and their past connection with Christ during His public ministry (Luther, Beza, Hilgenfeld, Olshausen); while others refer it to the life of the apostles prior to their call by Christ—"Whatever they had been"—sinners (Estius after Augustine); or but unlearned and ignorant fishermen (Ambrosiaster, Thomas Aquinas, Anselm, Cajetan, and a-Lapide). Others suppose a reference to previous opinions subversive of the gospel held by them (Gwynne), or to the past time, when they were apostles, but himself was *alienus a fide Christi* (Calvin). Hofmann and Usteri make it "whether apostles or not." The first of these views is not without plausibility, for the prevailing sense of *ποτέ* in the New Testament is temporal; but it is too pointed to be contained in these simple words, and the reference is one not employed by the apostle usually when he maintains his equality. He says that he had what they had as in 1 Cor. ix. 1, xv. 10, but does not refer to their personal connection with Christ as giving them any official advantage over him, for he was not a "whit behind the very chiefest apostles" —*τῶν ὑπερλίαν ἀποστόλων.* 2 Cor. xi. 5. The apostle speaks simply of their position in the church when he conferred with them, or rather, of the honour they were held in at the period of his writing. The *ποτέ*, therefore, may be used in an intensive sense—*cunque*—as often in interrogations.

Οὐδέν μοι διαφέρει—"nothing to me it matters:" the stress on *οὐδέν*—utter indifference. The present *διαφέρει* does not express his present view of the case, but his view at the time, vividly recalled, or assuming the present. Phrynichus says, p. 394, *λέγε οὖν τί διαφέρει*, quoting Demosthenes against the use of the dative τίνι, as μοι here. Lobeck, however, quotes in correction from Aristotle, τίνι διαφέρει τὰ ἄῤῥενα, *De Part. Animal.* viii. 555; Xenophon, *Hier.* 1, 7, οὐκ οἶδ' εἴ τινι διαφέρει. Plato uses both dative and accusative, *Alcibiades*, i. 109 B; and Ælian also has ζεῦγος γὰρ ἤ τινι ἢ οὐδὲν διαφέρει, *Hist. Animal.* xiv. 26, vol. i. p. 327, ed. Jacobs. Chrysostom writes too strongly in saying that "he presses hard on the apostles for the sake of the weak." Theophylact, on the other hand, says, οὐκ ἐξουθενῶν τοὺς ἁγίους—"not vilipending those holy men." It matters nothing to me, and the reason is—

Πρόσωπον Θεὸς ἀνθρώπου οὐ λαμβάνει—"God accepteth no man's person." The asyndeton, or want of any connecting particle, gives point to the statement (Winer, § 60), and by the peculiar order of the words the emphatic Θεός is placed next the contrasted ἀνθρώπου. The phrase πρόσωπον λαμβάνει is a Hebraism, a translation of נָשָׂא פָּנִים, which means "to favour, to show favour,"—used first of all in a good sense—of God in Gen. xix. 21: Gen. xxxii. 20; 1 Sam. xxv. 35; 2 Kings iii. 14; Job xlii. 8;—then specially in a bad sense to show undue favour to, Lev. xix. 15; Deut. x. 17; Ps. lxxxii. 2; Prov. xviii. 5; Sirach iv. 27. But in the New Testament the phrase is invariably used in a bad sense: Matt. xxii. 16; Mark xii. 14; Luke xx. 21, etc.;—to favour one for mere face or appearance, Jas. ii. 1–7. Hence the nouns προσωποληψία, προσωπολήπτης, and the corresponding verb. God is impartial in the bestowment of His gifts and in the selection of His instruments. The apostle takes God for his model, and he judges and acts accordingly. "I acted," as if he had said, "in my estimate of these men, and in my conference with them, without regard to such external elements as often influence human judgments and occasionally warp them." He showed no undue leaning on them, though they justly stood so high in the esteem and confidence of the mother church in Jerusalem. Koppe's conjecture, that the apostle might be thinking of his mean bodily appearance, is really bathos. Chrysostom gives another turn to the thought: "Although they allow circumcision, they shall render an account to God; for God will not accept their persons because they are great in rank and station." But this future and judicial reference is not in the context, which is describing present feeling and events.

The resumed statement is :

'Εμοὶ γὰρ οἱ δοκοῦντες οὐδὲν προσανέθεντο—"to me in fact those in repute communicated nothing,"—*ἐμοί* emphatic. If *γάρ* assign a reason, it may be connected with *οὐδέν, μοι διαφέρει*—"it matters nothing to me, for they added nothing to me;" or it may be joined to the preceding clause, *πρόσωπον Θεὸς ἀνθρώπου οὐ λαμβάνει*—God is impartial, for He has put me on the same level (*auf so gleiche Linie*, Meyer) with the persons so high in reputation. Both connections appear unnatural, linking what is the main thought to a clause subordinate and virtually parenthetical. Nor will *ἐμοὶ γάρ* bear to be translated *mihi inquam* (Peile, Scholefield). But *γάρ* may be regarded rather as explicative. Donaldson, § 618, says *γάρ* is often placed first with an explanatory clause. Composed of *γε*, verily, combined with *ἄρα*, "therefore," it signifies "the fact is," "in fact, as the case stands." Klotz-Devarius, ii. 233; Kühner, § 324, 2.

The verb *προσανατίθημι* is to impart, to communicate; in the middle voice—"on their part." This is the real signification of the verb, though the idea of "additional" or new be found in it by Beza, Erasmus, Bengel, Winer, Usteri, Wieseler, Hilgenfeld, and others; but *προσ-* in composition will not signify *insuper*. Though, however, the signification of the verb be simply "they imparted," the sense or inference plainly is, they imparted nothing new,—as Meyer has it, *um mich zu belehren*. The men of note, *οἱ δοκοῦντες*, imparted nothing—nothing which was so unknown, that he felt himself instructed in his preaching or strengthened in his commission. The least that can be said is, they did not interfere with him, and they felt that they could not. Chrysostom is therefore too strong when he explains it, *τουτέστι, μαθόντες τὰ ἐμὰ οὐδὲν προσέθηκαν, οὐδὲν διώρθωσαν*. In a word, the apostle makes this statement in no spirit of vainglory, but simply narrates the naked facts.

Other forms of exegesis have been tried. 1. Some render the first clause, as Gomarus, Borger, Bagge, *quod attinet ad*—as regards the persons high in repute,—thus giving *ἀπό* the sense of *περί*, and rendering the next clause, as Theophylact, *οὐδεμία μοι φροντὶς*, or as Olshausen paraphrases, "I do not trouble myself about the distinguished apostles in the matter." 2. Homberg in his *Parerga*, p. 275, thus renders: *ab illis vero, qui videntur esse aliquid, non differo. Vult enim,* he adds, *se non esse minorem reliquis, quanticunque etiam fuerint.* This interpretation makes *ἀπό* superfluous, and also *μοι, consueto pleonasmo;* and Homberg quotes in justification several examples which are far from bearing him out—admitting, too, that the clause is the same in meaning with *οὐδὲν διαφέρω.* (Similarly Ewald.) 3. Elsner, throwing *ἀπό* aside, renders, *qui videbantur esse aliquid nihil ad me, nulla ab illis pervenit ad me utilitas.* 4. Heinsius, keeping *ἀπό*, renders, *de iis autem qui existimantur esse aliquid, qualescunque ii fuerint, nihil mihi accedit,*—a meaning which the verb will not bear. 5. Bengel's paraphrase is, *Nihil mea interest quales tandem fuerint illi ex insignioribus,* etc.: this would require in the last clause *ἀπὸ τῶν δοκούντων*, and the paraphrase is very loose and disjointed. 6. As remote from the context, and subversive of the order of thought, are the two methods proposed by Kypke, which need not be given at length; one of them, reckoned by him the preferable, being, "It matters not to me whether these false brethren were held in high esteem or not." 7. Rückert gives the sense as, *Was ihn anlangt, ist es mir ganz gleichgultig*—an exegesis not unlike that of Castalio, Calovius, Zachariæ. 8. Still worse is the exegesis of Zeltner, given by Wolf: "Of those who seemed to be somewhat—*τί*, what? What, in a word, of those in repute? What they were formerly, whether they held another opinion or not, I am not concerned;"—the view also of Schrader. 9. Hermann proposes an aposiopesis, *ἀπὸ τῶν δοκούντων εἶναί τι—quid metuerim?* But this is not the kind of style for such an oratorical pause. 10. Köhler joins the clause to the last clause of the previous verse: "That the truth of the gospel might remain with you, (as a gift) from those who were high in reputation." But this exegesis mars the unity of thought, and the persons high in reputation were not specially concerned with the preaching and permanence of a free gospel among the Gentiles. 11. Wordsworth, after Bengel, calls *ἀπό* paraphrastic, and takes it as indicating origin or quarter: "But it is no matter to me what sort of persons were from those who seemed to be somewhat." So also Gwynne, who finds the syntax to be remarkably simple, and its parsing a "schoolboy's" exercise. On the other hand, Laurent conjectures that the difficulty arises from the apostle's habit of adding marginal notes to his epistles after he had dictated them, and that ver. 6 is one of these notes: *Neutest. Studien*, p. 29, Gotha 1866. 12. Hofmann contrives to construe without any anakolouthon, making the parenthesis begin with *ὁποῖοι*, and ending it with *ἀλλὰ τοὐναντίον*, which words he dissevers from ver. 7 for this purpose,—a clever but quite unnatural mode of sequence. All these forms of exegesis, more or less ingenious, are out of harmony with the context and the plain significance of the terms employed, in such broken and hurried statements.

They not only gave me no instructions, as if my course had been disapproved by them, "but on the contrary"—*ἀλλὰ τοὐναντίον*—their conduct was the very opposite; neither jealousy, nor disparagement of me—far from it,—"but on the contrary, they gave me the right hand of fellowship."

Ver. 7. *Ἀλλὰ τοὐναντίον, ἰδόντες ὅτι πεπίστευμαι τὸ εὐαγγέλιον τῆς ἀκροβυστίας, καθὼς Πέτρος τῆς περιτομῆς*—"But on the contrary, seeing that I have been entrusted with the gospel of the uncircumcision, even as Peter was with that of the circumcision." The passive verb governs the accusative of the thing, the active combining a dative with it. Rom. iii. 2, 1 Cor. ix. 17, 1 Tim. i. 11; Winer, § 32, 5; Polybius, xxxi. 26, 7. Other examples may be found in Fischer, *ad Weller. Gram. Græc.* vol. iii. p. 437. The perfect passive, emphatic by position, denotes the duration of the trust, or that he still held it. The resolution of the more idiomatic *πεπίστευμαι τὸ εὐαγγ.* into *πεπίστευταί μοι τὸ εὐαγ.* is found in F, G.

The noun *ἀκροβυστίας*, "of the uncircumcision," is equivalent to *τῶν ἀκροβύστων*, Rom. ii. 26, iii. 30,—the gospel as addressed to them or belonging to them, the gospel as it was preached by him among the Gentiles. Of course, the gospel of the circumcision is that belonging to Jews, as specially preached to them by Peter—*καθώς*. It is plain that this agreement was the result of the apostle's frank disclosures. They had confidence in his statements, and seeing that his was a divine stewardship for a special sphere of labour, they could not, they durst not, oppose it. It might not be in all points to their perfect liking, it might not quite tally with their ideas of becomingness; but they could not set themselves against it. They now did more than allow Paul "to fight his own battle"

(Jowett): not only did they leave him undisturbed in the field, but the council, after a characteristic address by Peter, the apostle of the circumcision, and on the motion of James, sent out an edict which must have smoothed away some prejudices and confirmed the success of the apostle among the Gentiles. One should like so much to know what the beloved disciple said at the private conference, or what he who lay in the Master's bosom addressed to the public assembly.

The verse implies that Peter was a representative of the other apostles who laboured among the circumcision. Yet he had been the first to evangelize and baptize the heathen (Acts x. xi.); and on being challenged for his conduct, he had made a pointed and successful vindication. It is not implied by this language that there were two gospels, or even two distinct types of one gospel. But circumcision formed the point of difference. The Jew might practise it, for it was a national rite; but it was not to be enforced on the Gentile. The first Epistle of Peter shows the accordance of his theology with that of Paul. In Peter there are Jewish imagery and allusions, but no Judaistic spirit. The relation of the old economy to Gentile converts is not once glanced at. He does not refer to its overthrow, for to him the old Israel had passed into the spiritual Israel which had burst the national barriers. He does not write of Judaism and Christianity as rival faiths, or of the one supplanting the other; but to him Judaism had reached a predicted spirituality and fulness of blessing in the Messiah, by "the sprinkling of the blood of Him" who was the "Lamb without spot." So that, as Tertullian tersely puts it, this arrangement was only *distributio officii*, not *separatio evangelii, nec ut aliud alter sed ut aliis alter prædicarent. De Præscript. Hæret.* xxiii. vol. ii. p. 22, ed. Œhler.

Ver. 8. This parenthetical verse gives the ground of the preceding statement. The same God who wrought effectually for Peter wrought effectually for Paul too; therefore the mission of Paul, divine in its source and sustentation, could not but be recognised.

Ὁ γὰρ ἐνεργήσας Πέτρῳ εἰς ἀποστολὴν τῆς περιτομῆς, ἐνήργησε καὶ ἐμοὶ εἰς τὰ ἔθνη—"For He who wrought for Peter toward the apostleship of the circumcision, the same wrought for me also towards the Gentiles." This he adds,

Jerome says, *ne quis eum putaret detrahere Petro.* The datives Πέτρῳ and μοι, as Meyer observes, are not governed by ἐν in the verb which is not a pure compound, as ἐν could not stand independently. They are therefore *dativi commodi.* The purpose of the divine inworking is expressed fully in the first portion, εἰς ἀποστολήν—"with a view to the apostleship," for its successful discharge; at least such is the sense implied, 2 Cor. ii. 12, Col. i. 29. The last clause, fully expressed, as in the Syriac version, would have been εἰς ἀποστολὴν τῶν ἐθνῶν; but the curter form is used by the apostle (*comparatio compendiaria*). Winer, § 66, *f.* The inworker is God, and that inworking comprehends every element of commission and qualification—outpouring of the Spirit, working of miracles, and all the various endowments and adaptations which fitted both men so fully for their respective spheres. Acts xv. 12.

Ver. 9. *Καὶ γνόντες τὴν χάριν τὴν δοθεῖσάν μοι*—"And coming to the knowledge of the grace which was given to me, James and Cephas and John, who are reputed pillars, gave to me and Barnabas right hands of fellowship; that we should go or preach to the Gentiles, but they to the circumcision." First, ἰδόντες, perceiving,—that is, probably struck by Paul's representation of his work as the apostle of the Gentiles,—a phrase parallel to καὶ γνόντες, "and learning," from the details communicated to them. The χάρις here is not barely the apostolic office (Piscator, Estius), nor yet the success of his labours—*potissimum de successu* (Winer, Fritzsche),—but all that divine gift embodied as well in the apostolate as in all the freely bestowed qualifications for the successful discharge of its duties. See under Eph. iii. 8. They came to a knowledge of the divine gift enjoyed by Paul, implying that they had not distinctly understood it before. If they added nothing to Paul, he certainly added something to them. Rom. i. 5, xii. 3.

Ἰάκωβος καὶ Κηφᾶς καὶ Ἰωάννης—"James and Cephas and John." The order of the names differs. A omits καὶ Κηφᾶς; D, F, G, and the Itala read Πέτρος καὶ Ἰάκωβος, followed by few supporters; while the reading as we have given it is found in B, C, K, L, א, and versions and fathers. The placing of Κηφᾶς first is a natural correction from the mention of Peter in the previous verse; but James is first, from his immediate official status, and he must have had great influence at the consultation. So much did he become the central figure, that Irenæus characterizes the other apostles as *hi autem qui circa Jacobum apostoli. Advers. Hæres.* iii. 12, vol. i. p. 494, ed. Stieren. See Essay at the end of previous chapter. There is no good reason for supposing that the James of this verse is other than the Lord's brother, i. 19, who according to all tradition was head of the church in Jerusalem. Stier, Wieseler, and Davidson, however, take the James of this verse for the Apostle James, son of Alphæus. But is it not likely that some clause or epithet would have been given to the James of the second chapter, if he were different from the James of the first? or how were his readers to be guided to make the necessary distinction? See p. 98. The two participles have these proper names as substantives. Of them the apostle adds—

Οἱ δοκοῦντες στύλοι εἶναι—"who have the reputation of being pillars,"—not, as in Authorized Version, "who seemed to be," either in tense or signification. The Genevan has, "which are taken to be pyllers." There is no pleonasm in *δοκοῦντες*. Mark x. 42; Luke xxii. 24; Josephus, *Antiq.* xix. 6, 3; Winer, §§ 65-7. The figure in the term *στύλοι* is a common and natural one. It represents the Hebrew עַמּוּד in Ex. xiii. 21, 22, xiv. 24, referring to the pillar of fire, and it occurs often in a literal sense in the description of the tabernacle. Its tropical use may be seen in the New Testament, 1 Tim. iii. 15, Rev. iii. 12. It is employed often by rabbinical writers as an epithet of great teachers and saints. See Schoettgen, i. 728, 9; compare Prov. ix. 1. It occurs in a personal sense in the Epistle of the Church at Lyons—*στύλους ἑδραίους*, Euseb. *Hist. Eccl.* v. 1; in the first Epistle of Clement, i. 5, Peter and Paul are *οἱ μέγιστοι καὶ δικαιότατοι στύλοι εδιώχθησαν.* See *Hom. Clement.* xviii. 14, *ἑπτὰ στύλους κόσμῳ.* Many examples from the Greek and Latin fathers will be found in Suicer, *Thes. sub voce.* The figure is found also in the classics: *στῦλοι γὰρ οἴκων εἰσὶ παῖδες ἄρσενες*, Euripides, *Iph. Aul.* 57; *ὑψηλῆς στέγης στῦλον ποδήρη*, Æschylus, *Agam.* 897; also, *stantem columnam*, Horace, *Od.* i. 35. The accent of *στυλος* is doubtful, though probably evidence preponderates for *στῦλος*—perhaps the old Æolic form: Lipsius, p. 43, Leipzig 1863. Ellicott and Tischendorf print it *στῦλοι*, and the *υ* is invariably long in poetry, though it is short in the Latin *stylus*. *Rost und Palm, sub voce*. These three men were esteemed as "pillars," and deservedly so, as they supported and graced the Christian edifice—which is not necessarily imaged here as a temple,—zealous, gifted, mighty, and successful labourers, able to look beyond the narrow and national boundary within which some would confine the gospel, and qualified to guide the church in any crisis with enlightened and generous advice; for they solemnly and formally recognised Paul on this occasion.

Δεξιὰς ἔδωκαν ἐμοὶ καὶ Βαρνάβᾳ κοινωνίας—"gave to me and Barnabas right hands of fellowship." The first noun is far removed from the genitive which it governs. Such a separation when the genitive follows sometimes happens from the sudden intervention of some emphatic or explanatory phrase. John xii. 11; Rom. ix. 21; 1 Cor. viii. 7; Phil. ii. 10; 1 Thess. ii. 13; 1 Tim. iii. 6; Winer, 30, 3, note 2. One may say in this case that *δεξιὰς ἔδωκαν* stand first, referring to the visible hearty pledge of recognition; and that *ἐμοὶ καὶ Βαρνάβᾳ* follow, from their close relation to *ἔδωκαν* and *κοινωνίας*, which are put in immediate connection with the explanation. Both nouns are anarthrous. The first noun with this verb is often used without the article, the second wants it by correlation. Middleton, pp. 36, 49, ed. Rose; Apollonius, *de Synt.* p. 90; 1 Macc. xi. 50, 62, xiii. 50. Compare, however, Gersdorf's *Beiträge*, pp. 314–334. For *κοινωνία*, see under Phil. i. 5. The giving of the right hand was a common pledge of friendship or covenant then as now. While the Hebrew נָתַן יָד means "to surrender," as in 2 Chron. xxx. 8, Lam. v. 6, it denotes also to pledge, 2 Kings x. 15, Ezra x. 19. Compare Ezek. xvii. 18, Prov. xi. 21, Lev. vi. 2; Diodor. Sic. 16, 43; Xen. *Anab.* ii. 3, 11; Aristoph. *Nub.* 81; Euripides, *Medea*, 91, and Porson's note. This giving of right hands was the pledge of fellowship, the recognition of Paul and Barnabas as fellow-labourers. Chrysostom exclaims, Ὢ συνέσεως ὑπερβολὴ καὶ συμφωνίας ἀπόδειξις ἀναντίῤῥητος. "It was no such parting as when Luther in the castle of Marburg refused the hand of Zuingle, or when James Andreæ refused that of Theodore Beza at Montbeliard" (Thiersch). The purpose was—

Ἵνα ἡμεῖς εἰς τὰ ἔθνη—"in order that we unto the heathen." The particle *μέν* is found after *ἡμεῖς* in A, C, D, א, many cursives, and several of the fathers; but the simple pronoun is read in B, F, H, K, L, ℵ[1], Vulgate and Clarom. and Gothic version, in Origen, Theophylact, Œcumenius, and in most of the Latin fathers. Griesbach marks it as probable, Tischendorf omits it, Lachmann and Meyer accept it; but Wieseler, Ellicott, Alford, and Lightfoot rightly reject it. It seems to have been inserted to produce a correspondence with the following δέ. The clause wants a verb, and is all the more emphatic, as if no verb of sufficient fulness and distinction had presented itself readily or at the moment to his mind. The words "we to the Gentiles" say all that is needful. His readers could easily divine what the phrase implied. Compare Rom. iv. 16, 1 Cor. i. 31, 2 Cor. viii. 13,—ἵνα being similarly placed in all these quotations.

Αὐτοὶ δὲ εἰς τὴν περιτομήν—"and they unto the circumcision,"—the abstract used as in ver. 7 for the concrete. Are not the Jews so named here on purpose, as if the reference were not only to the covenant rite, but also to what had been the theme of dissension at Antioch and the subject of present consultation in Jerusalem? while ἔθνη is used in its broad sense, of all the nations beyond Palestine, as nations in want of a free and unclogged offer of the gospel. Some would supply εὐαγγελιζώμεθα—ωνται, as Winer and others; but εἰς with a personal reference is not used by Paul after this verb. Yet we have a very similar connection in 2 Cor. x. 16, and this preposition follows the corresponding noun, 1 Thess. ii. 9; see 1 Pet. i. 25. Meyer in his last edition drops his objection to εὐαγγελ. as the supplement, which he had stated in his third edition. Others propose πορευθῶμεν—θῶσιν, as Bengel and Fritzsche; but the apostle's idea implies both these verbs; Erasmus and Schott fill in by *apostolatu fungeremur*. Though this agreement referred generally to spheres of labours, it cannot strictly be called a geographical division; nor was it a minute mapping out of future travels. Thousands of Jews were in "the dispersion," among whom the three apostles might labour; and Paul, "as his custom was," went first to the Jews: Acts xvii. 2, 10, xviii. 5, xix. 8. He speaks in his imprisonment of some of his companions "who are of the circumcision," Col. iv. 11; and Peter and John travelled into heathen countries. Peter is found in Paul's way at Antioch; but Paul "would not build on another man's foundation"—"would not boast in another man's line of things made ready to our hand."

Ver. 10. *Μόνον τῶν πτωχῶν ἵνα μνημονεύωμεν, ὃ καὶ ἐσπούδασα αὐτὸ τοῦτο ποιῆσαι*—"Only they asked us that we should remember the poor, which very thing I also was forward to do." The adverb belongs to the previous clause beginning with *ἵνα*. There is no formal ellipse, and no verb like *αἰτοῦντες* or *προσκαλοῦντες* needs to be supplied (Borger, Winer, Rückert, Usteri): vi. 12; 2 Thess. ii. 7. The clause is scarcely a limitation of the compact, but is rather an understanding, so slight as not to contradict what the apostle has just said—"they communicated nothing to me." They gave us the right hand of fellowship, that we should go to the Gentiles; only we were to remember the poor of the circumcision. Rom. xv. 26, 27; 1 Cor. xvi. 3. The order of the words is peculiar, and *μόνον ἵνα τῶν πτωχῶν* in D, F, etc., is an evident emendation. The position of *τῶν πτωχῶν* is emphatic, John xiii. 29, 2 Thess. ii. 7; and this irregular position occurs in a different form in the previous verse. Winer, § 61, 3. For a similar position of *ἵνα*, see 1 Cor. vii. 29, 2 Cor. ii. 4. The emphasis is thus on "the poor,"—the understanding being that Paul and Barnabas were to remember them. The subjective verb *μνημονεύω* governs here the genitive, though occasionally it is followed by the accusative, indicating a different aspect of idea. Matthiae, § 347; Winer, § 30, 10, *c*. Many believers in Judæa were poor, and the victims of persecution. It would be wrong to limit the poor to the city of Jerusalem (Piscator and Estius). In the contract that they should go to the Gentiles to make them the special field of labour, they were, however, to take with them this understanding, that they were to remember the Jewish poor believers. To "remember the poor" is a quiet Christian way of expressing generous pecuniary benefaction,—not the idle and cheap well-wishing reprobated by the Apostle James. The apostle now adds this brief explanation for himself; for he and Barnabas soon after parted:

Ὃ καὶ ἐσπούδασα αὐτὸ τοῦτο ποιῆσαι—"which very thing I was also forward to do." The repetition of *αὐτὸ τοῦτο* after the relative is no direct imitation of a well-known Hebraism. Nordheimer, *Heb. Gram.* §§ 897, 898. In such cases *αὐτός* is the pronoun most commonly employed in the Septuagint.

Thiersch, *De Pentat. Alex.* p. 123, has noted some examples in the Seventy, as Gen. xxiv. 37, xxviii. 13, xlviii. 15; Ex. xxx. 6; Num. xiii. 20: and also in the New Testament, as Rev. vii. 2, xii. 14. Ellicott adds Mark i. 7, vii. 25. The idiom before us is thus no Hebraism (Rückert, Baumgarten-Crusius); nor are *αὐτὸ τοῦτο* redundant, as Piscator and many of the older interpreters affirm. The idiom is well known. Kühner, ii. p. 527; Winer, § 21, 3, 2, § 22, 4; Stallbaum, *Plato, Gorgias*, p. 285 (509 E.); Sophocles, *Philoctet.* 315, and there Hermann's note in reply to Porson's conjecture in his *Adversaria*, p. 199. See under Phil. i. 6. The emphasis is on the verb—the apostle was forward to do it, and needed not any such recommendation. The past tense of the verb needs not have either a perfect (Conybeare) or a pluperfect signification, as denoting time past with reference to the conference, that is, before it (Jatho, Webster and Wilkinson); but it signifies, that at that past period now referred to, he was forward to remember the poor—"also," *καί*—as forward to do it as they were to stipulate for it. Probably the Galatians did not need to be told this, for he informs the Corinthians, 1 Cor. xvi. 1, "Now concerning the collection for the saints, as I have given order to the churches of Galatia, even so do ye." Compare Rom. xv. 26, where Macedonia and Achaia are said to make a collection *εἰς τοὺς πτωχοὺς τῶν ἁγίων τῶν ἐν Ἱερουσαλήμ*, and the argument which follows in ver. 27. Such benevolence shows the unity of the church amidst this apparent diversity of procedure. The special spiritual obligations under which the Gentiles lay to the Jews, were partially and cheerfully fulfilled in those temporal charities which the Jews did not hesitate to receive from their Gentile brethren. But the sending of this money was no tribute, no token of their dependence on the mother church (Olshausen): Acts xxi. 17, xxiv. 17, and Acts xi. 29 at an earlier period; 2 Cor. viii. and ix. To take *ὅ* for *δι' ὅ*, a conjecture hazarded by Schott, is vague and inadmissible here, though it may occur in poetry. Allied to this is another meaning, *eben deshalb*, "for that very reason:" 2 Pet. i. 5; Xen. *Anab.* 1, 9, 21; Plato, *Protag.* 310 E; Winer, § 21, 3, 2; Matthiae, § 470. Such a mode of construction is here quite unnecessary. Nor can the reference be that which Usteri quotes from his friend Studer, "even this," that is, "nothing more did the apostles communicate;" nor can it be "which also, that same, trifling and inconsiderable as it was" (Gwynne). It simply refers to the fact that the very thing stipulated was the very thing the apostle was forward to do, and independently altogether of the stipulation. It is needless to ascribe the poverty of the believers in Jerusalem to any such remote cause as the free table established after Pentecost, and which was furnished by a kind of voluntary communism; for we know not how long the experiment lasted, or to what extent it was supported. Nor need we think of any abuse of the doctrine of the second advent as being near at hand (Jowett),—an error in the Thessalonian church which apparently unhinged its social relations. We have but to remember "the spoiling of your goods" in the Epistle to the Hebrews, and what the apostle says to the Thessalonians, 1 Thess. ii. 14, 15, "For ye, brethren, became followers of the churches of God which in Judæa are in Christ Jesus: for ye also have suffered like things of your own countrymen, even as they have of the Jews; who both killed the Lord Jesus and their own prophets, and have persecuted us; and they please not God, and are contrary to all men."

The three apostles here referred to, whatever their prepossessions, yield to the force of Paul's statements. Peter also at the council called the imposition of the law on Gentile converts an intolerable yoke, for the Gentile was saved by the same grace as the Jew. Peter appealed only to the great facts which had met him unexpectedly in his own experience; but James, in the old theocratic spirit, connected the outburst of Christianity with ancient prophecy as its fulfilment. In his thought, God takes out of the Gentiles a people for His name, and by an election as real as when He separated Israel of old from all the nations. The prophecy quoted by him describes the rebuilding of the tabernacle of David, not by restoring his throne in Jerusalem over Jews, and over heathen who as a test of their loyalty become proselytes, but by the reconstitution of the theocracy in a more spiritual form, and over myriads of new subjects—"all the Gentiles"—without a hint of their conformity to any element of the Mosaic ritual. This expansion of the old economy had been foreseen; it was no outgrowth unexpected or unprovided for. Believers were not to be surprised at it, or to grudge that their national supremacy should disappear amidst the Gentile crowds, who in doing homage to David's Son, their Messiah, should raise "the tabernacle of David" to a grandeur which it had never attained, and could never attain so long as it was confined to the territory of Judæa. The Jewish mind must have been impressed by this reasoning—this application of their own oracles to the present crisis. So far from being perplexed by it, they ought to have been prepared for it; so far from being repelled by it, they ought to have anticipated it, prayed for it, and welcomed its faintest foregleams, as in the preaching of Philip in Samaria, and of Peter to Cornelius. Paul and Barnabas, in addressing the multitude—"the church, the apostles and elders"—did not launch into a discussion of the general question, or attempt to demonstrate abstract principles. First, in passing through Phenice and Samaria, they "declared the conversion of the Gentiles;" and secondly, at the convention theirs was a simple tale which they allowed to work its own impression—they "declared what miracles and wonders God had wrought among the Gentiles by them." The logic of their facts was irresistible, for they could not be gainsaid. Let their audience account for it as they chose, and endeavour to square it with their own opinions and beliefs as best they might, God was working numerous and undeniable conversions among the Gentiles as visibly and gloriously as among themselves.

The haughty exclusiveness of the later Judaism made it impossible for the church to extend without some rupture and misunderstanding of this nature. That exclusiveness was nursed by many associations. For them and them alone was the temple built, the hierarchy consecrated, and the victim slain. Their history had enshrined the legislation of Moses, the priesthood of Aaron, the throne of David, and the glory of Solomon. The manna had been rained upon their fathers, and the bright Presence had led them. Waters had been divided and enemies subdued. Sinai had been lighted up, and had trembled under the majesty and voice of Jehovah. Their land was hallowed by the only church of God on earth, and each of them was a member of it by birth. His one temple was on Mount Moriah, and they gloried in the pride of being its sole possessors. The archives of their nation were at the same time the records of their faith. Nothing was so opposed to their daily prepossessions as the idea of a universal religion. Or if the boundaries of the covenanted territory were to be widened, Zion was still to be the centre. Foreign peoples were to have no separate and independent worship; all nations were to flow to the "mountain of the Lord's house, established in the top of the mountains, and exalted above the hills." It is impossible for us to realize the intensity of Jewish feeling on these points, as it was ever influencing Hebrew believers to relapse into their former creed, and leading others into the self-deceptive and pernicious middle course of Judaizers. In such circumstances, the work of the Apostle Paul naturally excited uneasiness and suspicion in the best of them, for it was so unlike their own sphere of service. But the elder apostles were at this period brought to acquiesce in it, and they virtually sanctioned it, though there might not be entire appreciation of it in all its extent and certain consequences.

There is no ground, therefore, for supposing that there was any hostility between Paul and these elder apostles, or any decided theological difference, as many strenuously contend for. They all held the same cardinal truths, as is manifest from the Gospel and Epistles of John, and from the Epistles of Peter. There are varying types of thought arising from mental peculiarity and spiritual temperament,—accidental differences showing more strongly the close inner unity. Nor is the Epistle of James in conflict with the Pauline theology. It was in all probability written before these Judaistic disputes arose; for, though addressed to Jews, it makes no mention of them. Its object among other things was to prove that a justifying faith must be in its nature a sanctifying faith; that a dead faith is no faith, and is without all power to save; and that from this point of view a man is justified by works—the products of faith being identified with itself, their one living source.

Nor can we say that there were, even after the convention, no misunderstandings between Paul and the other apostles. While they were at one with him in thought, they seem not to have had the same freedom to act out their convictions. There was no opposition on any points of vital doctrine; but though they held that his success justified him, they did not feel at liberty, or had not sufficient intrepidity, to follow his example.

Though their earlier exclusiveness was broken, their nationality still remained,—their conservatism had become an instinct—"they to the circumcision." This mere separation of sphere might not give rise to division, but these pharisaic Judaists, who were not so enlightened and considerate as their leaders, were the forefathers of that Ebionitism which grew and fought so soon after that period, having its extreme antagonism in Marcion and his adherents. How the other apostles who had left Jerusalem at the Herodian persecution, and may have been in different parts of the world, acted as to these debated matters, we know not. It is storied, indeed, that John, living amidst the Hellenic population of Ephesus, kept the paschal feast on the fourteenth day of the month, in accordance with the Jewish reckoning; and that he wore in his older years one special badge of a priest. Such is the report of Polycrates;[1] but no great credit is to be attached to it, for it may be only a literal misapplication to the "Divine" of the sacerdotal imagery of his own Apocalypse. But the stand made by Paul subjected him to no little obloquy and persecution from Jews and Judaists. His apostleship was depreciated as secondary, and his doctrine impugned as not according to truth. His perils were not sympathized with; nay, some during his imprisonment preached Christ "of envy and strife," intending thereby to "add affliction to his bonds." The mournful admission is wrung from him during his last hours, "All they which are in Asia be turned away from me." For his bold and continuous assertion of Gentile freedom he was frowned upon during his life, and no doubt censured as pragmatic, vehement, and unreasonable in the advocacy of his latitudinarian views; and after his death, he was for the same reason caricatured in the *Clementines* under the name of Simon Magus, the malignant and worsted antagonist of the apostle of the circumcision. And yet Paul was the truest Jew of them all,—true in spirit and in act to the Abrahamic promise which contained in it a blessing for "all families of the earth"—to the divine pledge, "I will give Thee the heathen for Thine inheritance"—and to the oracular utter-

[1] The words of Polycrates are, ὃς ἐγενήθη ἱερεὺς τὸ πέταλον πεφορηκώς. Euseb. *Hist. Eccles.* v. 24. The word πέταλον is rendered by Jerome (*De Viris Illus.* 4, 5), *aurea lamina*—the plate on the high priest's mitre. Epiphanius records the same thing also of James the Just, *Hæres.* 39, 2.

ance, "I will give Thee for a light to the Gentiles, that Thou mayest be my salvation unto the end of the earth." Truer by far was he to the old covenant, and those numerous fore-showings of a better and broader dispensation, than they "which were scattered abroad upon the persecution that rose about Stephen, and who travelled as far as Phenice, and Cyprus, and Antioch, preaching the word *to none, but unto the Jews only*," and than those who, by insisting on the circumcision of Gentile converts, were barring the way while they professed to open it, and clogging the gift in their mode of presenting it with conditions which robbed it of its value by hampering its freeness.

The power of early association, which grows with one's growth, is very difficult to subdue; for it may suddenly reassert its supremacy at some unguarded moment, and expose inherent weakness and indecision. He who, on being instructed by a vision, had preached to Cornelius and admitted him by baptism into the church, and who, when "they of the circumcision contended with him," had nobly vindicated his procedure, and rested his concluding argument on the remembered words of the Master,—who had spoken so boldly in the synod, and joined in the apostolic circular,—sunk at Antioch so far beneath himself and these former experiences, that Paul was obliged to withstand him to the face.

NOTE ON CHAP. II. 1

Ἀνέβην εἰς Ἱεροσόλυμα—"I went up again to Jerusalem."

Five visits of the apostle to Jerusalem are mentioned in the Acts, and the question is, which of them can be identified with the visit so referred to in the first verse of this chapter, or is that visit one not mentioned in the Acts at all?

These visits are: 1. That recorded in Acts ix. 26, and referred to already in Gal. i. 18. See p. 50.

2. The second visit is described in Acts xi. 27–30, and the return from it in Acts xii. 25. In consequence of a famine, "which came to pass in the days of Claudius Cæsar," Barnabas and Saul carried up from Antioch "relief to the brethren

which dwelt in Judæa;" and their mission being accomplished, they "returned from Jerusalem."

3. The third visit is told in Acts xv. In consequence of Judaistic agitation in the church at Antioch, it was resolved "that Paul and Barnabas, and certain other of them, should go up to Jerusalem to the apostles and elders about this question." The agitation was renewed in Jerusalem, and after the deputies had been "received of the church," a council was held, and a letter was written. Then Paul and Barnabas returned to Antioch, accompanied by Silas and Judas Barsabas, who carried the epistle, and had it also in charge to expound its contents—"to tell the same things by mouth."

4. The fourth visit is inferred from Acts xviii. 21, where the apostle says, "I must by all means keep this feast that cometh in Jerusalem,"—followed by the announcement, that "when he had landed at Cæsarea, and gone up and saluted the church, he went down to Antioch."

5. The fifth visit is given at length in Acts xxi. 1–17, etc. The apostle sailed from Philippi "after the days of unleavened bread;" and he would not spend any time in Asia, for "he hasted if it were possible for him to be at Jerusalem the day of Pentecost."

Now the first and last visits may be at once set aside. He sets aside the first himself by affirming that the one under discussion was a subsequent visit to it—*ἔπειτα*; and he did not return to Antioch after his last visit, but he went down to it after this visit, as is implied in ii. 11. Nor is it likely that his visit to Jerusalem as a delegate from Antioch on a theological controversy was the fourth visit, for its only asserted purpose was to keep a Jewish feast. Whiston, Van Til, Credner, and Rückert virtually, with Köhler, Hess, Huther (on 1 Pet. p. 8), and Lutterbeck, adopt this view, which has been strenuously contended for by Wieseler in his *Chronologie d. apostol. Zeitalters*, p. 179, and in a *Chronologischer Excurs* appended to his commentary on this epistle. Wieseler, struck by Paul's circumcision of Timothy after the visit referred to in this epistle, and by some objections adduced by Baur, tries to escape from the difficulty by adopting this hypothesis. But in this visit of the Galatian epistle, the apostle describes his interview with the apostles as a novelty; while the entire narrative implies that they met for the first time, and came to a mutual understanding as to their respective spheres of labour. Such a visit cannot therefore be the fourth, for at the third visit Paul had most certainly met with the apostles and elders, and there had been a public synod and debate. Besides, Barnabas was with Paul at the visit in question; but there is no mention of him in the account of the fourth visit, for the two apostles had separated before that period. If what Paul relates in this epistle, as to the results of his consultations with the older apostles, had happened at the fourth visit, it would have been surely mentioned in Acts; but Acts is wholly silent on the matter, and dismisses the visit by a single clause—"having saluted the church." Can those simple words cover, as Wieseler argues, business so momentous, prolonged, and varied as that described in the epistle before us? Besides, if this fourth visit, which appears to be limited to the exchange of cordial greetings, is the one here described by the apostle, then his historical argument for his independence breaks down, and he conceals that at a previous period he had been in company with the apostles, and had obtained from them a letter which was meant to suspend an agitation quite of the kind which was placing the Galatians in such serious peril. In arguing his own independence from the fact of his necessary distance during a long period from the primary apostles, could he have concealed such a visit as that which led to an address from Peter and a declaration from James on points of such importance, and so closely allied to those which he is about to discuss at length in the letter under his hand? Wieseler's arguments are futile. One of them is, that not till the time of the fourth visit could Paul have risen to such eminence as to be on a virtual equality with Peter, nor would Paul have ventured at an earlier period to have taken a Gentile like Titus with him to Jerusalem. This is only an assumption, for during those fourteen years the churches must have been learning to recognise Paul's independent mission, since he had so successfully laboured in Antioch, the capital of Syrian heathendom, had gone a long missionary circuit, and returned to the same city, where he "abode long time." There was therefore, before his third visit, an ample period of time and labour, sufficient to place him and Barnabas in the high position assigned to them. The record of the fourth visit in Acts is also silent about Titus;

but at such a crisis as that which necessitated the third visit, Titus, a person so deeply interested that in his person the question was virtually tested, is very naturally found along with the champion of Gentile freedom in the Jewish metropolis. Wieseler indeed attempts to find Titus in Acts xviii. 7, where the common reading *'Ιούστου* is found in some MSS. as *Τίτου 'Ιούστου* or *Τιτίου*—a reading rejected by Lachmann and Tischendorf, and probably a traditional emendation. He again argues that the clause, ii. 5, "that the truth of the gospel might remain with you," implies that Paul had been in Galatia before he could so write of any purpose of his at the convention. But the apostle merely identifies, as well he might, a more proximate with a more future purpose. See on the verse. Another of Wieseler's proofs that the visit must be the fourth one is, because it allows unrestricted freedom to the Gentile converts, whereas at the third visit the circular issued and carried down to Antioch laid them under certain restrictions. But in making this affirmation he travels beyond the record in Gal. ii. 1–10, which speaks only of the apostolic concordat, and says not a syllable about the general standing of the Gentile converts. There is thus a certainty that his fourth visit is not the one referred to by the apostle in the words, "Then fourteen years after I went up to Jerusalem."

Nor in all probability was it the second visit, when he went up with funds to relieve the poor. This opinion is given in the *Chronicon Paschale*,[1] and held by Calvin, Keil, Küchler, Gabler, Heinrichs, Kuinœl, Koppe, Bottger, Fritzsche, and by Browne, *Ordo Sæclorum*, p. 97. The prophecy of Agabus could not be the "revelation" by which he went up; and this visit could not have been so long as fourteen years after his conversion. On such a theory, too, he must have spent nearly all the intermediate and unrecorded time at Tarsus. But, according to Acts, no period of such duration can be assigned to his sojourn in his native city, for we find him very soon afterwards at Antioch. Prior to the visit of this chapter, Paul and Barnabas were noted as missionaries among the heathen; the elder apostles saw that Paul had been entrusted with the gospel of the uncircumcision, for he described to them the gospel which he was in the habit of

[1] *Καὶ ὅ εἶπε πάλιν, δηλονότι ἑτέρα ἐστὶν ἀναβάσις αὕτη.* Vol. i. p. 436, ed. Dindorf, Bonn 1832.

preaching among the Gentiles. These circumstances were impossible at the second visit, for at that period the conversion of the Gentiles had not been attempted on system and over a wide area. It may be indeed replied, that as the apostle refers to one visit, and then says, "After fourteen years I went up again," the natural inference is, that this second must in order of time be next to the first: *Primum proximum iter* (Fritzsche). But the inference has no sure basis. The apostle's object must be kept in view; and that is, to show that his mission and ministry had no originating connection with Jerusalem; because for a very long period he could hold no communication with the twelve, or any of them; for it was not till three years after his conversion that he saw Peter for a fortnight, and a much longer interval had elapsed ere he conferred with Peter, and James, and John. Any visit to Jerusalem during which he came into contact with none of the apostles, did not need to be mentioned; for it did not assist his argument, and was no proof of his lengthened course of independent action. But the second visit was one of this nature—the errand was special; the Herodian persecution, under which James son of Zebedee had fallen, and Peter had been delivered from martyrdom by a singular miracle, had driven the apostles out of Jerusalem, and the money sent by the church was, in absence of the apostles, given into the custody of "the elders." This view is more in accordance with the plain meaning of the narrative than that of Ebrard and Düsterdieck, Meyer, Bleek, and Neander, who conjecture that this visit to Jerusalem was made by Barnabas only, Paul having gone with him only a part of the way. So that the so-called third visit was therefore really the apostle's second. But this view charges inaccuracy on the Acts of the Apostles, and is only a little better than the assumption of Schleiermacher, that the historian has confounded his authorities, and made two visits out of one. Nor had Paul at the second visit risen to an eminence which by common consent placed him by the side of Peter. We dare not say with Wordsworth that he was not an apostle at the period of the second visit, for the apostleship was formally conferred on him at his conversion, but certainly he had not as yet made "full proof" of his ministry. In the section of the Acts which narrates the second visit he even appears as secondary—the money was sent "by the hands of Barnabas and Saul;" "Barnabas and Saul returned from Jerusalem." Acts xi. 30, xii. 25. If one object that the visit under review could not be the second visit, because Peter, on being released from prison, had left Jerusalem (Acts xii. 17), and could not therefore come into conference with Paul and Barnabas, Fritzsche replies, *perperam affirmes*, for Paul and Barnabas had finished their stewardship prior to the martyrdom of James and the arrest of Peter. But to sustain his view, he breaks up the natural coherence and sequence of the narrative.

The probabilities are therefore in favour of its being the third visit recorded in Acts xv., when Paul and Barnabas went up as deputies from the church at Antioch on the embarrassing question about the circumcision of Gentile converts. The large majority of critics adhere to this view; and among authors not usually referred to in this volume may be named, Baronius, Pearson, Hemsen, Lekebusch, Ussher, Schneckenburger, Thiersch, Lechler, Baumgarten, Ritschl, Lange, Schaff, Anger, *de Temporum in Actis ratione*, iv.; and Trip, in his *Paulus nach der Apostelgeschichte*, Leiden 1866. Baur, Schwegler, Zeller, and Hilgenfeld hold the same opinion, only for the sinister purpose of showing that the discrepancies between Acts and Galatians in reference to the same event are so great and insoluble, that Acts must be given up as wholly wanting historical basis and credit. But in Acts, Paul and Barnabas were commissioned, and "certain others;" in the epistle, Titus is mentioned as being with the two leaders. The question at Antioch was virtually the same as that discussed in the public conference at Jerusalem; and as a testing case, the circumcision of Titus was refused, after it had been apparently insisted on with a pressure that is called compulsion. At this visit Paul stood out in the specific character and functions of an apostle of the Gentiles; the other apostles acquiesced in his work, not as a novel sphere of labour, but one which he had been filling with signal success. True, he says, "I went up by revelation;" but the statement is not inconsistent with the record in Acts, that he was sent as a deputy. Commission and revelation are not necessarily in antagonism. The revelation might be made either to the church to select him, or to himself to accept the call. Or it might open up to him the true mode of doing the work, and of securing Gentile liberty. Or it might take up the more personal question of his own standing; and he chiefly refers to this point in the epistle, for it concerned the argument which he was conducting, and closely touched the more public theme of disputation. The first form of revelation is found in the history of the same church, Acts xiii., but the case is not analogous to the one before us. Quite a parallel case, however, is related by the historian, and told by Paul himself: the efforts of the brethren to save his life were coincident with a vision vouchsafed to himself. Acts ix. 30, 31, xxii. 17–21.[1] As the *πάλιν* of ver. 1 does not make it of necessity a second visit, so the history of the third visit in Acts xv. is not in opposition to the paragraph of the epistle before us. The historian, looking at the mission in its more public aspects, describes the assembly at Jerusalem to which Paul and Barnabas were deputed; but the apostle, looking at it from his own line of defence, selects what was personal to himself and germane to his argument—his intercourse with the three "pillars," and their recognition of his independent apostleship. It is vain for Baur and his school to insist on any notorious discrepancy; for private communication is not inconsistent with, but may be preparatory to a public convention, or may spring out of it. It is true that John is not mentioned in Acts as being present at the assembly, as he might have taken no prominent part in the consultation, though he is spoken of as being at the interview in Galatians. It is further argued, as by Wieseler, that the third visit to Jerusalem and its convocation cannot be the one referred to in this epistle, because in the epistle no notice is taken of the decrees of the council. This silence about these local and temporary decrees, which were simply "articles of peace," as Prof. Lightfoot calls them, is one of Baur's curious arguments for denying that such a document was ever issued at all. The abstinence enjoined in them was to produce conformity in three things to the Jewish ritual; and the moral veto refers probably not to incest or marriage within the Levitical degrees, but to the orgies so often con-

[1] Biley, however, without any good ground, places this vision at the second visit, during the Herodian persecution. Supplement to Paley's *Horæ Paulinæ*, p. 6.

nected with heathen worship, and to indulgence in which the heathen converts, from custom and a conscience long seared as to the virtue of chastity, and not yet fully awake to its necessity, might be most easily tempted.[1] But the apostle never refers to the decrees at any time, when he might have made naturally some allusion to them, as in 1 Cor. x. and in Rom. xiv. Nay, in the first of these places, he virtually sets aside one of the articles of the apostolic letter. It forbade the eating of "meats offered to idols;" but he represents it to the Corinthians as a matter of indifference or of liberty, the question of eating or of abstinence depending on the degree of enlightenment one may have, and on the respect he ought to show to a brother's scruples. In the Epistle to the Romans he takes similar ground, not that it is wrong in itself to eat certain meats—"I know, and am persuaded by the Lord Jesus, that there is nothing unclean of itself;" but the law laid down is, that no one in the exercise of his just liberty is to put a stumbling-block in his brother's way. The apostle probably did not regard the decrees as having any force beyond the churches for which they were originally enacted and designed—"the brethren which are of the Gentiles in Antioch, and Syria, and Cilicia." The apostolic circular, which was a species of compromise in a peculiar and vexing crisis, was not meant for the churches in Galatia which at the time had no existence. The circumstances, too, were different. The Gentile section of the church at Antioch wanted to guard itself against Judaistic tyranny, and there is no proof that any of its members had succumbed. But many in Galatia had become willing captives, and the enactment of the council had therefore no special adaptation to them. The churches in Antioch, Syria, and Cilicia were exhorted to conform on some points to Jewish observances, with the guarantee that no further exactions should be demanded; while many in the Galatian churches were willing to observe, as far as possible, the entire Hebrew ritual.

It is sometimes alleged, as by Keil, that Paul after the council became more lax in his treatment of Jews, for he circumcised Timothy; so that this controverted visit must be one

[1] See in Deyling specimens of an attempt to show that the "decrees" were meant to comprise the so-called Noachic precepts, vol. ii. p. 469.

earlier than the third, for at it he strenuously resisted the circumcision of Titus. But while there is no general proof of the assertion, the special case adduced in illustration is not in point. Titus was wholly a Gentile, and his circumcision was resisted. Timothy was a Jew by one side, and might receive, according to law and usage,[1] a Jewish ordinance which was a physical token of his descent from Abraham. Paul circumcised Timothy "because of the Jews in those quarters," to gain them by all means; but he would not have Titus circumcised to please the Judaists, for their demand was wrong in motive and character. To circumcise the son of a Jewish mother that he might have readier access to those of his own race as one of themselves, is one thing; but it is a very different thing to circumcise a Gentile on the stern plea that submission to the rite was essential to his salvation. Nor can the objection taken from Peter's conduct at Antioch, as recorded in the following verses, be sustained, viz. the strong improbability that one who had taken such a part in the apostolic council at Jerusalem should so soon after at Antioch act so unlike himself, and in opposition to the unanimous decree of the synod. Some, indeed, place the scene at Antioch before this council, as Augustine, Grotius, Vorstius, Hug, and Schneckenburger; but it seems most natural, according to the order of this chapter, to place it after the council. Wieseler and Neander date it after the fourth journey, with as little reason, though Wieseler, in accordance with his own theory, places it not long after the council. But granting for a moment that Peter did act in opposition to the decrees, his conduct at Antioch affords no proof that he had changed his opinion in any way. What he is accused of is not any sudden, violent, and unaccountable alteration of opinion, but he is formally charged with dissimulation,—not *Selbstwiderspruch*, self-contradiction (Hilgenfeld), but hypocrisy,—not the abjuring of his former views, but shrinking from them through timidity. His convictions were unchanged, but he weakly acted as if they had been changed. Such vacillation, as will be seen in our commentary, is quite in keeping with those glimpses into Peter's character which flash upon us in the Gospels. Besides, while occasional vacillation characterized Peter, his conduct at Antioch was not a formal

[1] See Wetstein on Acts xvi. 1–3.

transgression of the decrees. They did not distinctly touch the point on which he slipped; for while they enjoined certain compliances, they said not a word as to the general social relations of the Gentile to the Jewish brethren. This question was neither discussed nor settled at the council. So that Peter cannot be accused of violating rules in the enactment of which he had borne a principal share, and the objection based on his alleged and speedy disobedience falls to the ground. See under the 11th and 12th verses.

Some of the objections against the identity of the third visit with the one referred to in Galatians, disposed Paley to the notion that the Galatian visit is one not recorded in Acts at all. Some of these objections he certainly solves himself with his usual sagacity, particularly that based on the omission of all notice of the decrees in the epistle. He says that "it is not the apostle's manner to resort or defer much to the authority of the other apostles;" that the epistle "argues the point upon principle;" and Paul's silence about the decrees "is not more to be wondered at, than it would be that in a discourse designed to prove the moral and religious duty of keeping the Sabbath, the writer should not quote the thirteenth canon." *Works*, vol. ii. p. 350, ed. London 1830. Still, as he is inclined to think that the journey was a different one from the third, he puts it after Acts xiv. 28; and he is followed by his annotator, Canon Tate, in his *Continuous History of St. Paul*, pp. 141, etc., London 1840. Beza held a similar opinion; and Schrader would insert the journey after the 20th verse of Acts xix.,—that is, the visit was made during the apostle's long sojourn at Ephesus, and is thus placed between the fourth and fifth visits. *Der Apostel Paulus*, vol. ii. pp. 299, etc. But while there are difficulties in spite of all explanations, there seems great probability at least that the visit recorded in the epistle is the same as that told in Acts xv.—the third recorded visit of the apostle to Jerusalem. The remarks of Hofmann on the harmony between Acts and Galatians on the point before us may be read with advantage.

Approximate chronology reckoning, according to ordinary Jewish computation, a fragment of a year as a whole one, leads to the same result. His first journey to Jerusalem was probably in A.D. 41, his conversion having happened three years before; his second visit with funds for the poor may be placed in A.D. 44, for in that year Herod Agrippa died, Acts xi., after a reign of seven years; his third visit may be assigned to A.D. 51, or fourteen years after his conversion; his fourth visit may be dated A.D. 53; and his fifth and last A.D. 58. Then he was kept prisoner two years in Cæsarea; Festus succeeded Felix as procurator in A.D. 60, and probably the same year the apostle was sent under his appeal to Rome. See Schott's *Prolegomena; Rückert, in loc.;* Davidson, *Introduction*, vol. ii. p. 112; and Conybeare and Howson, vol. i. p. 244, etc.

CHAPTER II. 11-21

THE apostle pursues his vindication no further in the same strain. He has said that he received his commission and gospel immediately from the same source as did the other apostles; that he owed nothing to them; that he did not on his conversion rush up to Jerusalem and seek admission among them, or ask counsel or legitimation from them; that three years elapsed before he saw one of them, and him he saw only for a brief space; that fourteen years afterwards he went up again to the metropolis, when he met them, or rather three of the most famous of them, as their equal; that he did not and would not circumcise Titus; that the original apostles gave him no information and no new element of authority, nay, that they cordially recognised him, and that he and they came to an amicable understanding as to their respective departments of labour. Who then could challenge the validity of his apostleship, or impugn the gospel which he preached, after Peter, James, and John had acquiesced in them? Who would now venture to question their opinion? for they were satisfied,—even Peter, specially marked in contrast as having the gospel of the circumcision divinely committed to him. Nay more—and such is now the argument—he was not only officially recognised as a brother apostle by Peter, and as possessed of equal authority, but he had opposed and rebuked Peter on a solemn and public occasion, and in connection with one of the very points now in dispute. While Peter had resiled for a moment, he had never done so: his conduct in Jerusalem and in Antioch had been one and the same. He thus proves himself invested with the same high prerogative, measuring himself fully with Peter as his equal, nay, more than his equal.

Antioch, a large and magnificent city, had communication by the Orontes and its port of Seleucia with all the territories bordering on the Mediterranean, and it was connected by an overland route with Arabia and the countries on and beyond the Euphrates. Men of all nations easily found their way into it for business or pleasure; and into this capital named after his father, Seleucus had introduced a large colony of Jews who lived under their own ethnarch. From being the metropolis of Greek sovereigns, it became through the fortune of war the residence of Roman proconsuls. The gospel had been brought to it at an early period. Persons who had fled on the martyrdom of Stephen travelled as far as Antioch, "preaching the word to none but unto the Jews only," acting according to their light and their national prepossessions. But a section of these itinerating preachers, "men of Cyprus and Cyrene," had larger hearts and freer views, and they at Antioch "spake unto the Grecians, preaching the Lord Jesus." Great results followed these ministrations. Tidings of the immense success were carried to the church in Jerusalem, which at once, and probably from a combination of motives, sent Barnabas to visit the Syrian capital. The earnest and self-denying Cypriot at once undertook the work, and rejoiced in the spectacle which he witnessed; but he felt the labours so augmenting, that he went and fetched Saul to be his colleague. Their joint ministry among the mixed people that thronged the streets and colonnades of this Rome in miniature lasted a year; and such were its numerous converts, that the native population were, for the sake of distinction, obliged to coin a name for the new and rising party, and they called them Christians. Antioch thus became the metropolis of Gentile Christianity, and Jerusalem looked with jealousy on its northern rival. In it originated the first formal Christian mission, and Paul made it his headquarters, starting from it on his three great evangelistic journeys. The peace of this society, however, was soon disturbed by Jewish zealots from Jerusalem, and Paul and Barnabas went up to the mother church "about this question." Gal. ii. 1. A council was held, the decrees were issued and sent down, and the two deputies returned to Antioch and resumed their old work—"teaching and preaching the word of the Lord." At some period after this, Peter happened to come down to Antioch, and the scene here described took place. Just as from attachment to Jesus he followed "into the palace of the high priest,' and found himself in almost the only circle where he could be tempted to deny his Lord; so now he had travelled to almost the only city which presented that strange variety of circumstances by which, from his peculiar temperament, he could be snared into this momentary cowardice and dissimulation.

Ver. 11. *Ὅτε δὲ ἦλθεν Κηφᾶς εἰς Ἀντιόχειαν*—"But when Cephas came to Antioch." *Κηφᾶς* is found in A, B, C, H, א, in the Vulgate, Syriac, and Coptic versions; but *Πέτρος* has in its favour D, F, K, L, and the Greek fathers. The Hebrew name was more likely, however, to be altered than the usual Greek one. By *δέ* he passes to another and different argument. Paul and Barnabas went down after the council, and Peter seems to have followed them, though his visit is not recorded in Acts. Augustine, Hug, and Schneckenburger refer the visit to an earlier epoch, yet the apostle appears to follow the order of time; while Neander, Sardinoux, Baumgarten, Lange, and Wieseler of course, assign it to a later year. But Barnabas had separated from Paul before the time alluded to in Acts xviii. 22, and they were together in Jerusalem at the period of the council. There is no authority for saying either, with Schrader, that Peter had accompanied Paul and Barnabas from Jerusalem, or with Thiersch, that it was his first visit to the metropolis of Gentile Christianity.

Κατὰ πρόσωπον αὐτῷ ἀντέστην, ὅτι κατεγνωσμένος ἦν—"I withstood him to the face, because he had been condemned." The Syriac reads ܡܛܠ ܕܡܬܟܫܠܝܢ ܗܘܘ ܒܗ, "because they were stumbled by him." The last clause sets out the reason of the conflict, and then it is historically stated. The verb *καταγιγνώσκω*, generally followed by the genitive of the person and accusative of the thing, means to know or note something against one, next to lay this to his charge, and then naturally to condemn him—accusation followed by the passing of sentence. The perfect participle passive with *ἦν* has its natural meaning, "because he had been condemned,"—not simply accused, but condemned. Compare 1 Cor. xi. 5, Heb. v. 14, x. 22. The Vulgate reads doubly wrong, in sense and in syntax, *quia reprehensibilis erat;* and so Calvin, *reprehensione dignus.* And this rendering is followed by many, as Beza, a-Lapide, Küttner, Borger, Matthies, Brown, and the English Version. Others, as Winer, Schott, De Wette after Luther, and Jowett, take the milder meaning, which is, however, grammatically correct, *quia reprehensus erat*—"because he was blamed." But the phrase "I withstood to the face" necessitates the full signification of the participle. The instances commonly adduced in behalf of the adjectival meaning will not bear it out. It is true that in Hebrew, from its want of verbal adjectives, the passive participle may occasionally bear the sense of one ending in *bilis*, or a participle ending in *ndus*. Gesenius, *Lehrgeb.* § 213; Nordheimer, § 1034, 3, *b*. The idiom is based on the notion that what is praised is praisable, that what is loved is lovable or deserves to be loved. Thus one passes easily from the idea of incorrupt to that of incorruptible, from that of seen to that of visible, from that of touched to that of touchable or palpable. But it is difficult to say in regard to the Hebrew idiom when and how far the one notion is expanded into the other, and there is no reason why this usage should be transferred into Greek. The common proofs taken from the classics—τετελεσμένος, *Iliad*, i. 388, and Lucian, *de Saltatione*, p. 173 (vol. v. ed. Bipont.), where the same word occurs as in the passage before us—will not bear it out, and those quoted from the New Testament are also defective. For the aorist participle ἐκριζωθέντα in Jude 12 has its regular meaning, "rooted out;" the perfect participle ἐβδελυγμένοις in Rev. xxi. 8 is not "abominable," but "covered with pollutions," or abominated; and the present participle in Heb. xii. 18, ψηλαφωμένῳ, has its literal meaning of being touched. See Alford, Delitzsch, and Bleek, *in loc.*; Winer, § 45, 1. So that the strong term used by the apostle leads us to infer that the condemnation was not simply self-condemnation or conscious inconsistency (Bengel, Bagge, Windischmann, Hofmann), but condemnation pronounced in no measured terms by those who were aggrieved by Peter's hypocritical conduct. Tergiversation on the part of such a man could not but produce deep and wide sensation in such a church as Antioch; and the outraged feelings of the Gentile portion of it so suddenly shunned, and to all appearance so decidedly disparaged, must have condemned the apostle. They had but to compare himself, not with his former self, as he had championed them twice over in Jerusalem, but with his recent self on his arrival in their city. The hollowness of his withdrawal from them carried with it at the same time its own condemnation.

Peter therefore being signalized as a condemned man, Paul was obliged to interfere on behalf of honesty, consistency, and spiritual freedom—

Κατὰ πρόσωπον αὐτῷ ἀντέστην—"to the face I withstood him"—not simply *coram omnibus* (Erasmus, Beza, Matthias, and Conybeare), for the preposition retains its sub-local meaning, as may be inferred also from the attitude described in the verb *ἀντέστην*. Acts iii. 13, xxv. 16. Comp. 2 Cor. x. 1, 7; Sept. Deut. vii. 24, ix. 2; 2 Chron. xiii. 7, 8; *κατὰ πρόσωπον τάξας*, Polyb. iii. 65, 6; similarly xi. 14, 6. This meaning is not very distinctly brought out in Winer, § 49. The antagonistic sense of the verb may be seen in Eph. vi. 13, 2 Tim. iii. 8. These two words—*πρόσωπον, ἀντέστην*—have the emphatic position as an index to the fidelity of the argument. Private remonstrance, written correspondence, appeals against Peter or crimination of him in his absence, would not have proved Paul's conscious equality of status so truly as a face-to-face rebuke, and that publicly, of the apostle of the circumcision. The iniquitous gloss *κατὰ σχῆμα*—"in appearance only"—as if the whole scene had been got up between the apostles, is as little to be thought of as the assertion that this condemned Peter was not the well-known apostle, but another individual of the same name. See the history of that controversy at the end of this chapter.

Ver. 12. *Πρὸ τοῦ γὰρ ἐλθεῖν τινὰς ἀπὸ Ἰακώβου*—"for before that certain from James came." What is the connection of the word *ἐλθεῖν* with *τινὰς ἀπὸ Ἰακώβου*?

1. The preposition seems to be used in no vague sense, as if they only came from James' locality, or from Jerusalem, for they came from himself. Augustine, Beza, Olshausen, Schaff, Baumgarten-Crusius, and Brown incline to this view. But why name James, if locality only be alluded to? As easy, since *ἀπό* has so often a local meaning, would it have been to write at once, from Jerusalem—*ἀπὸ Ἱεροσολύμων*.

2. Usteri, Winer, and Zeller connect *τινὰς* with *ἀπὸ Ἰακώβου*—certain dependants or followers of James, as in the phrase

οἱ ἀπὸ Πλάτωνος. Bernhardy, p. 222. Winer's explanation of this conjecture is loose—*qui Jacobi auctoritate utrum jure an secus usi fuerint.* But this idiom is specially connected with names of places and abstract nouns (Ellicott), and James never appears as the head of a party. His name never seems to have been used as the watchword of any faction of Jacobites, like that of Paul, Cephas, and Apollos; and this probably because he was resident in Jerusalem where the church thought and felt so much at one with himself, whereas Peter must have constantly come into contact with persons of opposite sentiments, and preached to communities of divided opinion.

3. The inference seems to be well grounded that they were persons sent from James (De Wette, Meyer, Trana). Matt. xxvi. 47; Mark v. 35; Mark xiv. 43; *καὶ ἄρτι ἀπ' ἐκείνου ἔρχομαι,* Plato, *Protag.* 309B. It may, on the one hand, be too strong to affirm that they were formally sent by James on an express mission, though it may be fairly inferred that he knew of their coming, and that they appeared in Antioch with at least his sanction; but, on the other hand, it unduly softens the phrase to give it the meaning of persons who "gave out themselves as from James" (Winer, Ellicott). There is no warrant for Prof. Lightfoot's supposition, that they came "invested with some powers from James, *which they abused.*" For there is no hint that they were the same very extreme party described in Acts xv. 24, a party which Peter would rather have resisted than succumbed to. Who those men were, or what their mission was, we know not. The narrative of Acts says nothing of the occurrence. But from the result one may infer, that they were sent to see as to the obedience of the church to the decrees. These decrees respected the Gentiles, and indeed they originated in a reference regarding their position. No additional burden was to be placed on them; but the believing Jews were expected to keep "the customs," and not to mix freely with the Gentiles. Acts xv. 19. It may, therefore, have been suspected at Jerusalem that the Jewish believers, through intercourse with Gentile brethren, were relaxing, and were doing what Peter had begun to do at Antioch with increasing freedom; so that the business of this deputation may have been, to see that the circumcision did not presume on any licence in consequence of the opinion of the council. See

Alford. Other purposes have been imagined for these "certain from James," without any foundation. At all events, they could not be the false brethren already mentioned by Paul, nor those disowned by James in his address before the council, and in the apostolic circular. Nor could they be the bearers of the decrees, as Ritschl (*Altkath. Kirche*, p. 128) supposes, for these documents had been sent down at an earlier period. Before these certain came from James, we are told of Peter—

Μετὰ τῶν ἐθνῶν συνήσθιεν—"he was eating with the Gentiles." As he had done before (Acts x.), and had defended the act at Jerusalem so nobly and conclusively, as is told in the following chapter (Acts xi.). The charge at that time was *καὶ συνέφαγες αὐτοῖς*,—himself admitting to Cornelius that by Jewish ordinance such intercourse was *ἀθέμιτον*. Compare Luke xv. 1; 1 Cor. v. 11. Some, as Olshausen and Matthies, widen the meaning of the phrase too much, as if it signified general social intercourse; and others, as Thiersch and Hilgenfeld, emphasize it too much, and refer it not to ordinary diet, but also to communion in the love-feasts and eucharist. Peter then had been acting according to conviction, and as the vision had long ago instructed him. But on the question of eating with Gentiles the council had said nothing, it only forbade certain articles of food; and the circular did not settle the general relation of converted Gentiles to the law, for it only spoke out against the necessity of circumcising them. But this last enactment releasing them from circumcision virtually declared them no longer common or unclean; and for a time at Antioch Peter thus understood it, so that his tergiversation was a violation in spirit at least of the "decrees." There is no ground for Wieseler's assumption, which is based on the late date which he assigns to this meeting at Antioch, that Peter's conduct had reference simply to the articles of food forbidden by these "decrees" which in lapse of years had fallen into comparative desuetude, and that, in withdrawing from social intercourse with the Gentiles, he only obeyed them. The reproof of Paul on such a supposition would have been uncalled for and unjust; and for such a withdrawal, hypocrisy could not be laid to Peter's charge. The "certain from James" seem to have insisted that the decision of the council was to be limited entirely to the points specified in it, and that it did not warrant such free intercourse with believing Gentiles as Peter had been practising. The believing Gentiles were, on that view, to be an inferior caste in the church.

῞Οτε δὲ ἦλθον, ὑπέστελλεν καὶ ἀφώριζεν ἑαυτόν—"but when they came, he withdrew and separated himself." The reading *ἦλθεν* has B, D[1], F, ℵ, two other MSS., and the Itala in its favour; but the plural form has preponderant authority. The singular *ἦλθεν*, accepted by Lachmann, may have come from the following verse, from some reminiscence of the previous *ἐλθεῖν* in ver. 11, or from some odd meaning attached to *τινὲς ἀπὸ Ἰακώβου*; for Origen has *ἐλθόντος Ἰακώβου πρὸς αὐτόν*, as if James himself had followed his *τινές*. *Contra Celsum*, ii. 1, p. 56, ed. Spencer. The two connected verbs represent Peter first as withdrawing himself, and then, as the fear grew, ultimately and formally separating himself. The imperfects show that not one act only, but the course which he was following is depicted as if placed before one's eyes. Jelf, § 401, 3.

Φοβούμενος τοὺς ἐκ περιτομῆς—"fearing," or "inasmuch as he feared them of the circumcision"—that is, Jews in blood, but Christians in creed, called *Ἰουδαίων τῶν πεπιστευκότων* in Acts xxi. 20; Tit. i. 10, 11. The participle has a causal sense. Schmalfeld, § 207, 3. Before the *τινές* who had arrived at Antioch he quailed; and they certainly represented, though not by any formal commission, the creed and practice of the mother church (Wieseler). Peter might imagine that his position as the apostle of the circumcision was endangered. It would thus appear, that though he was the apostle of the circumcision, and might naturally be regarded as the head of that section of the church, there was an influence in it higher than his, and a power resident in Jerusalem of which he stood in awe. Chrysostom is anxious to show that his fear had no connection with himself, but was only anxiety about the disciples, his fear being parallel to that expressed by Paul in iv. 11; and Theophylact adds, that he was condemned wrongfully by men who did not know his motive. Somewhat similar opinions are held by Erasmus, Piscator, Grotius, and Dr. Brown, and most naturally by Baronius and Bellarmine.

Ver. 13. *Καὶ συνυπεκρίθησαν αὐτῷ καὶ οἱ λοιποὶ Ἰουδαῖοι*—"and the other Jews also dissembled with him." The compound verb—the aorist passive with a deponent sense (Polyb. iii. 31, 7)—means "to act a part along with," "to play the hypocrite in company with." The rest of the believing Jews in Antioch acted as Peter did—withdrew themselves, and shunned all social intercourse, of the kind at least referred to, with their fellow-believers of the Gentiles. Now this secession was hypocrisy, for Peter and these other Jewish converts transgressed against their better convictions. They concealed their real views, or acted as if they thought that it was really wrong to eat with Gentiles. Probably they felt as if they had gone beyond the understood compact, in enjoying such familiar intercourse with their Gentile brethren; and on account of the party which came from James, they suddenly and decisively asserted their rigid Judaism, and acted as if they had been convinced that their salvation depended on complete ritual conformity. This hypocrisy involved a denial of one of the primary truths of the gospel, for it had a tendency to lead the Gentiles to believe that they too must observe the law in order to justification and life. It is added, in fine, to show the marvellous strength of the current—

Ὥστε καὶ Βαρνάβας συναπήχθη αὐτῶν τῇ ὑποκρίσει—"so that even Barnabas was carried along with them by their dissimulation." The *καί* is ascensive—"even." Winer, § 53, 3, *e*. The verb is used only tropically in the New Testament, but not always *in malam partem:* Rom. xii. 16 with the dative of thing. The particle *ὥστε* is usually joined with the infinitive, that mood, according to grammarians, being used when the result is a matter of necessity; but the indicative, as here, is employed when the result is represented as a matter of fact. Klotz-Devarius, ii. 772; Kühner, ii. 563; Winer, § 41, 5, 1. The vacillation of Barnabas was the direct but not the necessary result of their dissimulation. The dative *ὑποκρίσει* may be that of instrument, or it may be governed by *συν* in composition, as our version gives it. 2 Pet. iii. 17; *ἡ Σπάρτη συναπήγετο τῇ κοινῇ τῆς Ἑλλάδος ἁλώσει*, Zosimus, *Hist.* v. 6, p. 409, ed. Reitemeier,—in which places also both forms of construction are possible. The first, said to be so harsh, is probably the true one. They were swept along with others by their hypocrisy, and of course swept into it, though the translation cannot be that of the Vulgate, *in illam simula-*

tionem. That, however, is the undoubted inference, as συν implies it. Fritzsche on Rom. xii. 16. The contagion of such an example infected Barnabas, "a good man, and full of the Holy Ghost, and of faith," who had shared in Paul's labours among the Gentiles, and must have possessed no little of his free and elevated spirit. Even the apostle's colleague was swept away from his side by the influence of Peter, and perhaps by a similar awe of the τινές. If Peter and Barnabas had changed their views, hypocrisy could not have been laid to their charge. But with their opinions unchanged, they acted as if they had been changed; therefore are they accused of dissimulation. It was "not indecision" of opinion, as Jowett affirms, but indecision certainly in acting up to their unaltered convictions. Nor was it error or inconsistency, induced by want of clear apprehension, that is laid to their charge (Hilgenfeld, Bisping); but downright hypocrisy, and that is the proper term to describe their conduct. What Peter could say in his genuine state may be read in his first Epistle, i. 22, 23. This dissimulation, so wide and powerful, was compromising the freedom of the gospel, for it was subverting the doctrine of justification by faith; and therefore the apostle, who could on fitting occasions "to the Jews become a Jew," was obliged to visit it with immediate and stern rebuke.

Ver. 14. Ἀλλ' ὅτε εἶδον ὅτι οὐκ ὀρθοποδοῦσι πρὸς τὴν ἀλήθειαν τοῦ εὐαγγελίου—"But," or "howbeit," "when I saw that they were not walking according to the truth of the gospel." The compound verb occurs only here, and is translated in the Vulgate, *recte ambularent;* in Tertullian, *non recte pede incedentes: Contra Marc.* iv. 3. Ὀρθόπους (Soph. *Antig.* 972) occurs also in later ecclesiastical writers, and the use of ὀρθός in other compounds leads to the correct apprehension of its meaning here, which is "to foot it straight," to walk straight, that is, in no crooked paths—to conduct one's self uprightly or honestly. The apostle often uses περιπατεῖν and στοιχεῖν. See under Eph. ii., etc. The present tense employed as in this clause denotes action beginning at a previous period and still continuing—"a state in its entire duration." Kühner, § 846; Winer, § 40, 2, *c.* Schmalfeld says that in such a case *das Subjekt in dem Processe der Ausführung seines That vergegenwärtigt wird,* p. 96. The πρός, pointing to the norm or rule, signifies "according to." Luke xii. 47; 2 Cor. v. 10; Winer, § 49, *h;* Bernhardy, p. 265. But Estius, Baumgarten-Crusius, Meyer, and Alford give it its more ordinary sense of "in the direction of," or marking aim, that aim being, according to Meyer, to uphold and further the truth of the gospel. The apostle generally uses *κατά,* as denoting rule or measure, after *περιπατεῖν.* Ellicott says, indeed, in reply, that "motion is much more obscurely expressed in ὀρθοποδεῖν than περιπατεῖν." Hofmann affirms that the verb means "to stand with equal feet," ὀρθόπους (*Antigone*, 972) meaning *ein gerad aufrecht stehender.* Usage seems to declare for the second meaning, and the idea of norm may be implied in the verb itself. The "truth of the gospel" is not the true gospel, but the truth which it contains or embodies—evidently the great doctrine of justification by faith, implying the non-obligation of the ceremonial law on Gentile converts, and the cessation of that exclusiveness which the chosen people had so long cherished. See ii. 5.

Εἶπον τῷ Κηφᾷ. The reading *Κηφᾷ* has the authority of A, B, C, ℵ, the Vulgate, Syriac, and many other versions, with several of the Greek fathers; but *Πέτρῳ* has only in its favour D, F, K, L. The apostle uses no strong term, does not say in any overbearing spirit, "I challenged him, or I rebuked him;" but simply, "I said to him." The expostulation, however, was in public (not *κατ' ἰδίαν* now), and he puts his own apostolic independence in direct conflict with that of Peter. He was in this publicity only following the injunction which he afterwards gave to Timothy, 1 Tim. v. 20. But while the words *ἔμπροσθεν πάντων,* "before them all," describe the publicity of the address, there is no warrant for saying expressly, as Thiersch does, that the phrase means "in a meeting of both sections of the congregation specially summoned for the purpose."

The scene is quite in keeping with the respective antecedents and character of the two apostles. See note at end of chapter.

The address is somewhat difficult and involved, from its brevity and compactness, and its passing away from the direct second person singular to the first person singular which rehearses in wondrous words the depth of Paul's own experience. Yet Gwynne, in opposition to all who have written on the subject, says, "Methinks a plainer, simpler, more intelligible line of argument is not to be found within the compass of the Bible."

The commencement is bold and somewhat abrupt—

Εἰ σὺ, Ἰουδαῖος ὑπάρχων, ἐθνικῶς καὶ οὐχ Ἰουδαϊκῶς ζῇς—"If thou, being a Jew, livest after the manner of Gentiles and not after the manner of the Jews." The place of the verb in our text has the authority of A, B, C, F, ℵ, MSS., and Latin fathers. Cod. Clar., Sang., with the text of Ambros. Sedulius, Agap., omit *καὶ οὐχ Ἰουδαϊκῶς*. The position of *ζῇς* in the received text after *ἐθνικῶς* has the authority of D, K, L, nearly all MSS., the majority of versions and of the Greek fathers, and is followed by Tischendorf. Instead of *οὐκ*, *οὐχ* is found in A, C, ℵ[1], etc., and is accepted by Tischendorf, B and D[1] having *οὐχι*. Winer, § 5. Paul brings the matter home at once to him. If a Jew as thou art—*ὑπάρχων,* stronger than *ὤν,* which is found in D[1]. The *εἰ* throws no doubt on the case, but puts it syllogistically, as in Rom. v. 10, xv. 27; 2 Cor. iii. 7, 9, 11; Eph. iii. 2. If thou, being a Jew—born and brought up a Jew as thou hast been—the stress lying on *Ἰουδαῖος*. By the present *ζῇς* is represented the usual life of the apostle—his normal conduct; for at that very moment he had receded from his ordinary practice, and was again living *Ἰουδαικῶς*. The present *ζῇς* is certainly not for the past *ἔζης,* either actually (Flatt) or in effect (De Wette), nor is *εἰ* for *ἐπειδή,* nor *ζῇς* for *ἔζησας* (Usteri). Like all Jews, he had felt it unlawful—*ἀθέμιτον*—*κολλᾶσθαι ἢ προσέρχεσθαι ἀλλοφύλῳ*—to associate with or come unto a foreigner. Acts x. 28; Joseph. *Cont. Ap.* ii. 28. Such association was limited and defined by *συνέφαγες* when Peter was challenged for his free social intercourse with Cornelius. Since that period of divine warning and illumination at Joppa, as to what was *κοινὸν ἢ ἀκαθάρτον,* Peter had so broken through Jewish custom that he freely ate and drank with Gentile converts. He had been doing so till the moment of his present withdrawal. To live *ἐθνικῶς* was to disregard the old distinction of meats, drinks, and races; and this Peter did, as is said in ver. 12. And he had not renounced his liberty; he had in no sense retracted his principles of life; he had not refused to eat with Gentiles from force of conviction that such association was wrong, but only from pressure of circumstances—undue deference to the prejudices of some he desired to stand well with. So that Paul justly and with emphasis says ζῇς—"thou art living"—the word by the present form rebuking his inconsistency, as if overlooking his momentary defection. Wholly out of question is the view of Usteri, that the adverbs ἐθνικῶς and Ἰουδαικῶς are to be taken ideally and not in their ordinary objective sense, the first meaning "wrongly," and the second "with spiritual rectitude," Rom. ii. 23; that is, Peter had acted ethnically or *sinfully*, in his dissimulation, since he was not "an Israelite in whom is no guile." But it is not to the morality, it is to the hollowness and inconsistency of the action that the apostle refers. The charge is, Thou art living after the manner of the Gentiles, and, though a Jew, not after the manner of the Jews. Now, this being admitted and undeniable, the challenge is—

Πῶς τὰ ἔθνη ἀναγκάζεις Ἰουδαΐζειν;—"how art thou compelling the Gentiles to live after the manner of the Jews?" Wycliffe has it more tersely idiomatic—If thou that art a Jewe lyuest hethenlich and not jewliche, how constreynest thou hethen men to bicome jewis? We read πῶς on the authority of A, B, C, D, F, א, the majority of versions and the Latin fathers. The other reading τί of the Received Text, has K, L, the majority of minuscules, and the Greek fathers in its favour, and it is retained by Tischendorf, in violation of his own critical principles. The verb ἀναγκάζειν, used here as often with an accusative followed by an infinitive, passes away from its strict original meaning into the kindred one of moral compulsion—by suasion, menaces, or authority. So often in Plato and in Xenophon. Ast defines it as *argumentis cogo aliquem ut concedat*, *Lex. Platon. sub voce;* Sturz, *Lex. Xen. sub voce*, gives it as *necessitas quam presens rerum conditio efficit.* Matt. xiv. 22; 2 Cor. xii. 11. See under ver. 3. Libanius has τί ἡμᾶς ἀναγκάζεις τοῖς ἤθεσιν Ἀθηναίων ἀκολουθεῖν, 455. Comp. *Hom. Clement.* xiv. 7, and *Recogn.* ix. 38. It has been supposed by De Wette, Wieseler, Lechler, and Ritschl, that the τινὲς ἀπὸ Ἰακώβου had insisted on the observance of the ceremonial law, and that Peter did not merely remain silent or passive, but openly and actively defended their view. But this verb and the context afford no sure ground for this extreme supposition. All we are warranted to say is, that Peter belied his own principles in his conduct; for there is no proof that either he had changed them, or had intimated that he had changed them. The Jewish party naturally followed Peter, even Barnabas among them; and such an example in the circumstances, and connected with the arrival of these men from the mother church, exerted a pressure amounting to a species of compulsion on the Gentile converts. What inference could they draw from the sudden change of Peter but an obligation to follow him and submit? The direct tendency of Peter's conduct was so to act upon them as to constrain them into Judaism,—a result which, by the concealment of his real principles, he was doing his best to bring about. The verb *Ἰουδαΐζειν* is apparently more pointed and full than *Ἰουδαϊκῶς ζῆν*—the one depicting the condition of, and the other implying the entrance into, the Jewish life, and properly used of a conforming Gentile. Joseph. *Bel. Jud.* ii. 18, 2; Sept. Esther viii. 17. Wieseler, according to his theory already referred to, takes "to Judaize" as equivalent to, "to keep the decrees of the council." *Ἰουδαΐζειν* is formed like *ἑλληνίζειν, φιλλιππίζειν, λακωνίζειν, μηδίζειν.* Buttmann, § 119–8, *d.* The *πῶς* represents the case as incomprehensible and surprising—*qui fit ut, quo jure* (Winer); Mark xii. 35; John iv. 9; Rom. iii. 6, vi. 2;—puts his conduct in such a light, that it needed immediate vindication.

How far the address of the apostle extends, has been disputed. Beza, Grotius, Semler, Koppe, Matthies, Hermann, Wieseler, and Hofmann hold that the address ends with ver. 14; Luther and Calvin that it ends with ver. 16; Cajetan, Neander, Turner, Gwynne, that it ends with ver. 17; and Flatt with ver. 18. On the other hand, the majority of commentators suppose that the address extends to the end of the chapter. For it would be strange if, in such a crisis, these two clauses alone, or these and ver. 15, formed the entire expostulation.

Wieseler argues, and he is joined in this portion of his argument by Hofmann, that if the two apostles were at one in principle, then, though Peter dissembled, how could Paul so earnestly prove to him the truth which he did not deny? But Peter was not alone concerned; the words were spoken "before them all," and the inconsistency between principle and practice needed to be fully exposed. The appeal in iii. 1, it is argued, is abrupt if the address to Peter be carried on to the end of the chapter. But the abruptness is not more than that expressed by θαυμάζω in i. 6; and the conclusion of Paul's expostulation so shapes itself as to accord with, and form an introduction to, the train of argument and appeal with which the epistle is to be filled. Wieseler objects again, that the direct σύ is not found after ver. 14, and that the tone of a personal address is wanting. But the σύ is taken up by the ἡμεῖς, and the apostle does not reproduce his exact words; he gives only the substance without the precise original form. Nay, the ἐγώ in the hypothetical case put in ver. 18 plainly arraigns the conduct of Peter, and is an indirect description of his inconsistency—"For if the things which I destroyed, these again I build up, I constitute myself a transgressor." In the 15th verse the words are ἡμεῖς φύσει Ἰουδαῖοι, which could not be said directly to the Galatian churches, the majority of whom were Gentiles. Nor are there any marks of transition, indicating where he passes from the address to Peter to the general style of the epistle, till we come to the sharp and startling words of iii. 1, ὦ ἀνόητοι Γαλάται. The verses, too, are all closely connected—the 15th and 16th verses by syntax; these to the 17th by the adversative inference in εἰ δέ; it to the 18th by the argumentative εἰ γάρ; and it to the 19th by γάρ, rendering a reason,—while the remaining clauses are logically linked together to the end of the chapter. Vers. 15, 16, 17 are in the first person plural ἡμεῖς, and the remainder in the first person singular,—not precisely the apostle's "musing or arguing with himself with an indirect reference to the Galatians" (Jowett), but the vindication of his consistency, which had its roots deep in his own personal history. The apostle is not "speaking to himself," nor can we regard the words as "the after comment of the narrator" (Lightfoot); but he brings out some elements of his own spiritual consciousness to vindicate the part which he had taken, and to show by this representative *I* that he, and those who had passed through his experience, of all of whom he was a prominent specimen, could not but regard Peter's tergiversation not only as unworthy of him and detrimental to the cause of the gospel, but as utterly in conflict with the inner life and trust of every believer. Nor does the apostle really "drift away from Peter at Antioch to the Judaizers in Galatia" (Lightfoot); rather, the apostle's reminiscence of his address to Peter naturally throws into relief the points which had reference to the letter which he was writing at the moment. That is to say, his immediate object was to show his perfect independence of the primary apostles, even of Peter; for he opposed him resolutely on a certain occasion, when by taking a retrograde step he was exercising an adverse Judaistic influence; but this theme of dispute was in itself intimately connected with the Judaizing reaction in Galatia, so that in his narrative of the interview and expostulation he brings out its bearing on the immediate object of the epistle, to which he passes at once without any formal transition. The apostle gives only an abridged report of what he said to Peter; and he introduces what he says of himself, first, because he was the object of suspicion and attack, and secondly, because at the same time it carried him into the line of thought which he was about to pursue in the parchment under his hand. He is not to be supposed as calling up his very words, but he writes the general purport in brief, at once vindicating his independence, or in a human sense his autonomy, and exposing in the process the very error which had seduced the Galatian converts.

Ver. 15. *Ἡμεῖς φύσει Ἰουδαῖοι, καὶ οὐκ ἐξ ἐθνῶν ἁμαρτωλοί* —"we by nature Jews, and not of the Gentiles sinners." Primasius, Elsner, Schmidt, Bagge, Grotius, and Brown connect *ἁμαρτωλοί* with *Ἰουδαῖοι*—*nos natura Judæi, licet non ex Gentibus, peccatores,*—we being by nature Jews, and not of the Gentiles, yet sinners; or, Jews, and though not Gentiles, still sinners. True, the apostle concludes all under sin; and Jews are not only no exception, but their sinfulness has special aggravations. Rom. ii. 3, 22, iii. 9, 23, 24. Yet he does not here say that the Jews are not sinners, but the heathen are characterized as "sinners" from the Jewish standpoint—sinners inasmuch as they are Gentiles, or in consequence of being Gentiles; and it would be as unfair to infer from this language, on the one hand, that those who were by birth Jews were therefore not sinners (Hofmann), as, on the other hand, that the Gentilism of the contrasted party excused their sin. The term is not taken in a strict spiritual sense, but with the signification it carried in Jewish parlance as a designation of all who were beyond the limits of the theocracy. The apostle thus speaks relatively: Men born Gentiles, being without the law, were by the privileged Jews reckoned "sinners." Rom. ii. 12; Eph. ii. 12; 1 Cor. ix. 21; Luke xviii. 32, xxiv. 7, compared with Matt. xxvi. 45, xviii. 17; 1 Sam. xv. 18; 1 Macc. ii. 44; Tobit xiii. 6; *Hom. Clement.* xi. 16, p. 241, ed. Dressel. It is perhaps better to supply *ἐσμέν* than *ὄντες*. We (himself and Peter) are Jews by nature, not of Gentile extraction, and therefore, from our national point of view, sinners. Wieseler, according to his view, takes the *ἡμεῖς* to be Paul and the other Jewish believers like-minded with him. The stress is on *ἡμεῖς*, and *καὶ οὐκ* normally follows an affirmative assertion. The dative *φύσει* (Winer, § 36, 6) affirms that they were Jews in blood and descent, not proselytes,—*ἐκ γένους καὶ οὐ προσήλυτοι*, Theodore Mopsuest. See under Eph. ii. 3. But the opposite phrase *ἐξ ἐθνῶν* has not the very same meaning, as it signifies, though not so distinctively, "out of or belonging to the Gentiles," as in Acts xv. 23. The *καί* may have a consecutive force: Gentiles, and being such, sinners. Phil. iv. 9; Matt. xxiii. 32. The particle *μέν* is not needed in such a connection, nor is there an ellipse, as Rückert, Schott, and others suppose. Fritzsche, Rom. x. 19, vol. ii. 423; Donaldson, § 563. The verse seems in a word to be a concessive statement to strengthen what follows: Though we are Jews by descent, and not Gentiles who as such are regarded by us from our elevation as sinners, yet our Judaism, with all its boasted superiority, could not bring us justification. Born and bred Jews as we are, we were obliged to renounce our trust in Judaism, for it was powerless to justify us. Why then go back to it, and be governed by it, as if we had not abandoned it at all?

Ver. 16. *Εἰδότες δὲ ὅτι οὐ δικαιοῦται ἄνθρωπος ἐξ ἔργων νόμου*—"but knowing as we do that a man is not justified by the works of the law." The *δέ* is not found in the Received Text, nor in A, D[3], K, some versions and Greek fathers; but it occurs in B, C, D[1], F, L, א. Some connect the verse with the preceding, regarding its *ἡμεῖς* as taken up by the following *καὶ ἡμεῖς*, the nominative to *ἐπιστεύσαμεν*: "We by nature Jews, knowing that a man is not justified by the works of the law, even we believed into Christ." This is the view of Winer, Matthies, B.-Crusius, De Wette, and Alford—the whole forming one sentence. But the previous verse may be taken as a complete statement: "We are Jews by nature; but, knowing as we do that a man is not justified by works of law, even we believed." Such is the view of Beza, Borger, Schott, Hilgenfeld, Ellicott, Lightfoot, Ewald, Hofmann, Meyer, and Turner. The construction is supported by the δέ, which was probably omitted in favour of the other view. Nor can δέ well mean "nevertheless," as Alford renders it, nor "and," as Bagge gives it; nor can *obgleich*, "although," be supplied to the previous verse, as is done by De Wette, or *quamquam*, as by Trana. None of these supplementary ekes are required.

The δέ then is "but," with its usual adversative meaning, pointing to a different course from that to which the previous verse might be supposed to lead, and indicating a transition from a trust in Judaism, so natural to a born Jew, to faith in Christ. The participle εἰδότες has a causal sense (Schmalfeld, § 207, 3); but the meaning is not that it was a logical conclusion from the premiss, "a man is not justified by the works of the law," which led to the conversion of Peter and Paul. The faith of Peter had showed itself in attachment to the person and life of the Master, and must have developed within him the conviction, that He to whom he had ascribed "the words of eternal life" could alone bestow the blessing. Paul, on the other hand, had been arrested in a moment by the sudden challenge of Jesus (Phil. iii. 12); and his first thought was, the identity of Him that spoke out of that "glory" with Him who had been put to death on the cross. This earliest belief, begotten in an instant, must have created the persuasion, that in Jesus and not in works of law a man is justified. But the apostle now speaks in the light of present knowledge, puts into a definite shape the result of those mingled impressions which led to their discipleship, or at least sustained it.

The phrase ἐξ ἔργων νόμου, the stress on ἔργων, may be rendered "by works of law," as virtually by Peile, Brown, and Gwynne; for if a man cannot be justified by the Mosaic law, he cannot be justified by any other. But,

I. Such a generalization, or the idea of obligation arising out of law, though it is the blessed truth, could scarcely be attributed to so early a period in the religious history of the apostle and that of the Jewish converts.

II. The law referred to is certainly the law in dispute, the Jewish law, the law which Peter was so inconsistent as to allow himself to observe through pressure of Jewish influence—his hypocrisy in the matter leading to the whole controversy. That a man cannot be justified by any law whatever on the score of duty done, is indeed the ultimate inference, but it was not the immediate point of discussion. That a man cannot be justified by the works of the Mosaic law, was the doctrine demanding immediate defence, the doctrine so far invalidated by Peter's dissimulation; nay, it was this conviction which led so many Jews in possession of that law to put their trust in Christ.

III. *Νόμος*, in the sense of the Mosaic law, does not require the article, as some suppose; for it was to the Jewish mind the only divine law, the only law revealed and sanctioned for them. In the Gospels it has the article indeed, except in Luke ii. 23, 24, in which places there is the qualifying genitive *κυρίου*. But it wants the article in Rom. ii. 12, 23, iv. 13, 14, 15, v. 13, 20, vii. 1, x. 4; 1 Cor. ix. 20; Gal. iii. 10, 11, 18; and as Winer remarks, "it always occurs as a genitive when the principal noun has no article," § xix. Middleton, *Gr. Art.* p. 48.

The preposition *ἐκ*, "out of," denoting source, passes often into a causal meaning, "resulting from," and is not in such use distinguishable, as Fritzsche remarks, from *διά*, as frequently in Herodotus, or even from *ὑπό* or *παρά*: *Epist. ad Rom.* i. pp. 332–3; Jelf, § 621, 3. Source or origination may be the relation here indicated: works are not the source out of which justification springs; or, with a slight change of relation, works are not the cause of justification. The genitive *νόμου* is taken as that of subject by Augustine,—by the Catholic interpreters, Aquinas, Bellarmine, and Salmero,—by Windischmann and Maier, as also by Usteri, Neander, Olshausen, Lepsius, Hofmann, and Gwynne who calls it a genitive of quality "with an adjectival force." Under that view the meaning is, "works capable of satisfying the requirements of God's law, *i.e.* meritorious works." But *ἔργα νόμου* are works which fulfil the law, in contrast, as Meyer remarks, to *ἁμαρτήματα νόμου*, Wisdom ii. 12, deeds which transgress the law. In this way it is regarded as the genitive of object by Beza, Rückert, De Wette, Wieseler. And the νόμος or law we regard as the whole Mosaic law, and not merely its ceremonial part, as is the opinion of Theodoret, Pelagius, Erasmus, Michaelis, Semler, Schott. And the ἔργα are not works external in character and proceeding from no inner principle of love or loyalty, ἔργα νεκρά, which Catholic commentators place in contrast to *spes, charitas, timor;* the plural ἔργα does not of itself convey this insinuation (Usteri). See under Eph. ii. 10. See Calvin, *in loc.;* Philippi on Rom. iii. 20, p. 89, etc., 3d ed.—his opinion being changed from that expressed in his first edition. Neither *meritum de congruo* nor *meritum de condigno* has any place in a sinner's justification. The so-called ceremonial part of the law may indeed have been specially in the apostle's mind, as suggested by Peter's withdrawal from eating with the Gentile converts, but the modern distinction of moral and ceremonial is nowhere formally made or recognised in Scripture; the law is regarded as one code. See under iii. 10–13.

Ἐὰν μὴ διὰ πίστεως Ἰησοῦ Χριστοῦ—"except by faith in Jesus Christ,"—the stress lying on πίστεως. This is the order of the proper names in C, D, F, K, L, and א, the majority of cursives, versions, and the Greek fathers, Chrysostom, Theodoret; also, Jerome and Ambrose. The inverse order, adopted by Tischendorf in his 7th ed., has in its favour only A, B, Victorinus, and Augustine. The phrase ἐὰν μή has the usual meaning of εἰ μή, and refers only to the οὐ δικαιοῦται—a man is not justified by the works of the law, or a man is not justified except by faith in Jesus Christ. See under i. 7, 19, pp. 33, 51; Matt. xii. 4; Luke iv. 26, 27; Rom. xiv. 14, and the remarks of Fritzsche on that place, vol. iii. 195. The verb δικαιοῦται is the ethical present—the expression of an enduring truth. The relation indicated by ἐκ in the former clause is indicated in this clause by διά,—the reference being to source or cause in the former, in the present to means or instrument; or, as Meyer says, it is causality in two forms—"*des Ausgehens und des Vermitteltseins.*" It is the apostle's manner to exhibit relations in various connected phases by a change of prepositions. Rom. iii. 30; 1 Cor. viii. 6, etc. The διά is changed again into ἐκ in the next clause, showing that they indicate the same relation with a slight difference of view,—πίστις being taken as cause or as instrument in connection with—that is, originating or bringing about—the same result. Besides ἐκ and διά, ἐπί with the dative occurs Phil. iii. 9, and the simple genitive is used Rom. iv. 11. Bengel's strange distinction is, that διά refers to Gentiles, and ἐκ to Jews. Like the preceding νόμου, the genitive *I. X.* is that of object. Rationalists, according to Wieseler, make it the genitive of subject. Thus Schultess, *der Glaube Christi, Glauben wie Christus an Gott den Vater hatte und bethätigte.* But others, not rationalists certainly, hold a similar view. Thus Gwynne, who takes the genitive subjectively or possessively, "Faith not only of Christ as author or giver, but of Christ as the author or possessor—Christ, in a word, believing within them." See also Stier, *Eph.* i. 447. Whatever theological truth may be in the statements, they do not lie naturally or apparently in the words before us. The faith which justifies is characterized by its object, for by its object it is distinguished from all other kinds of belief; the difference being, not how one believes, but what one believes.

These clauses seem sometimes to have been understood in the following fallacious way, chiefly by Catholic expositors: "A man is not justified by works or by the law, except through faith in Christ; that is, on condition of faith in Christ, works of law will justify a man, or works acquire justifying power through faith in Christ." *Non justificatur homo ex operibus legis nisi per fidem Jesu Christi, i.e. opera legis non justificant quatenus sint legis, sed quatenus ex fide fiunt, ita ut opera vim justificandi a fide accipiant* (a-Lapide, Holsten). But this opinion is plainly against the grammatical meaning and the entire logical bearing of the apostle's argument. See Paræus in reply.

The notion of Jatho is peculiar, as he takes ἔργα νόμου to mean, in some way or other, the works done in fulfilment of the law by Christ—the *obedientia activa, die Gesetzeserfüllung Christi,* on which faith lays hold. A man is not justified by Christ's fulfilment of the law, except through faith in Him who had so acted. The idea is far-fetched, and wholly foreign to the natural meaning of the terms, for it comes not within the scope of the apostle's statement.

No man can fulfil the law, and therefore no man can be justified by it; for as he breaks it, so he is exposed to the threatened penalty. Law detects and convicts transgressors; it has warrant to condemn, but it is powerless to acquit. It pronounces every man a violator of its precepts, and leaves him under the curse of death. But the law is holy; it does not create his guilt, save in the sense of showing many acts to be sinful which without its light and power might be regarded as indifferent, and of stirring up desire after forbidden things: it only declares his guilt; and "we abandon it," as Chrysostom says, "not as evil, but as weak." Faith is a principle wholly different from works. It does not merit justification; but as it has its root in Him who died for us, it brings us into union with Him, and into a participation of all the blessings which His obedience unto death has secured for us. It is not the ground (*propter*), but only the instrument (διὰ πίστεως, and never διὰ πίστιν or *propter fidem*, Lightfoot) by which Christ's merit is laid hold of—"the hand," as Hooker says, "that putteth on Christ to justification." See under chap. iii.

Καὶ ἡμεῖς εἰς Χριστὸν Ἰησοῦν ἐπιστεύσαμεν—"we also believed into Christ Jesus." There is some variation of reading as to the proper names. B, some versions, Theodoret, and Augustine place Ἰησοῦν first, so that it is precarious to lay stress on the change. The aorist is not "we have believed," but indefinite, or at a previous point of time "we believed." The καί may be taken in its ascensive force—"even we," born Jews as we were. Its ordinary meaning, however, is just as emphatic—"we also," as well as the Gentiles—"we too," born under the law, renounced all trust in the works of the law, and putting ourselves quite on a level with Gentile sinners who never had the law,—we as well as they believed into Christ Jesus. In ἡμεῖς there is the personal application of the precious doctrine—a man is not justified by the works of the law, but by the faith of Christ Jesus. In order to be so justified, "we too" believed on Christ, is the exhaustive statement; and Paul reminds Peter how they had both brought this truth home to themselves, and acted in harmony with it. The relation indicated by εἰς—not so frequent a usage in Paul as in John—is more than mere direction, and means "into" (Winer, § 30), in the same way as the other expression, εἰς Χριστὸν ἐβαπτίσθητε, in iii. 27. The faith enters into Christ through union with Him. But faith is not to be identified with this union or incorporation (Gwynne), for it is rather the means of creating and sustaining it—the Spirit being the agent, the Spirit in the Head giving organic union to all the members.

The verb *πιστεύω* is used with various prepositions. Thus, it sometimes governs the dative, expressing an act of simple credence, a usage common in the Septuagint. See Matt. xxi. 25, 28-32; Mark xi. 31; Luke xx. 5, in reference to the Baptist; John v. 38, 46; Acts xviii. 8; Gal. iii. 6. Sometimes, though rarely, it is followed by the dative with *ἐν*, expressing confidence in or in union with: Mark i. 15, Sept. Jer. xii. 6, Ps. lxxviii. 22, הֶאֱמִין בְּ;—sometimes, but very seldom, by the dative with *ἐπί*, implicit reliance on: Luke xxiv. 25, spoken of divine oracles, 1 Tim. i. 16, Matt. xxvii. 42;—sometimes with the simple accusative of the thing believed: John xi. 26;—occasionally with *εἰς*: 1 John v. 10;—sometimes with accusative of person and *εἰς*—faith going out toward and entering into,—often, as might be expected, in John, and also in Peter; and sometimes with an accusative and *ἐπί*—faith going out with a view of being reposed upon—*fidem alicui adjungere*,—only once in Sept. Wisdom xii. 2. The accusative with *εἰς* or *ἐπί* is more specially characteristic of believing in the New Testament—of that faith which implies union with its object, or consciously places calm confidence on it. Rom. iv. 5. The ecclesiastical uses of the verb and noun, the more correct and the laxer, will be found in Suicer's *Thes. sub voce.* See also Reuss, *Theol. Chret.* vol. ii. p. 129.

Ἵνα δικαιωθῶμεν ἐκ πίστεως Χριστοῦ—"in order that we might be justified by the faith of Christ." This reading is well supported, and is generally accepted. X. is omitted in F, Theodor., Tert.,—the omission made apparently on account of the previous repetition of the name. The *ἵνα* reveals the final purpose or object of their believing—the momentous end sought to be realized. The use of *ἐκ* shows that it does not essentially differ from *διά* in the previous part of the verse, and it was preferred probably as being directly opposed to the repeated *ἐξ ἔργων*. Justification springs out of faith in Christ, not as its ultimate source, but as its instrumental cause. Or may not *ἐκ* have been suggested by the previous *εἰς*—*πίστις εἰς X. . . . ἐκ πίστεως X.*—out of this faith so uniting us with Him into whom it enters as its object, comes justification? The apostle adds in contrast, *καὶ οὐκ ἐξ ἔργων νόμου*—"and not by the works of the law." See on the first and last clauses.

If the reading of the previous clauses as here given be adopted as correct, there are three ways in which the Saviour is mentioned—Jesus Christ, Christ Jesus, Christ. It is hard to say what suggested such variations to the apostle's mind in this verse or elsewhere. The nouns are all anarthrous, and, as may be expected, there are often various readings. In this epistle the names Jesus Christ and Christ Jesus occur about equally; but with *ἐν* it is always *X. I.*, as with *εἰς* in this verse. If the variations of name are designed to be significant, then they may be explained thus: In the first clause where the name occurs, it is Jesus Christ—"the faith of Jesus Christ"—faith which has for its object the living and loving man brought so close to us by His humanity indicated by His birth-name Jesus, and that Jesus the Messiah or Christ, the double name being connected with a proposition of universal application. Then in the next clause it is Christ Jesus—"we also believed into Christ Jesus"—into Him, the promised and anointed Deliverer, His mission and work giving our faith its warrant, and our union with Him its saving reality, this Messiah being He who was called Jesus,—a proposition made by the *καὶ ἡμεῖς* especially Jewish in its aspect, and therefore naturally giving the name Christ or Messiah the prominence in thought and order. Next it is simply "Christ"—"that we might be justified by the faith of Christ." The solitary Jewish name in its recurrence is all-inclusive to the *ἡμεῖς*—"we"—"you, Peter, and I:" we Jews believed on our Messiah, on whose mother and for Him rested the unction of the Holy One, and on whom at His baptism the Spirit visibly descended, in fulfilment of the oracles and promises of the Old Testament. In the Gospels these names are used with distinctive propriety; and it may be added, that *'Ιησοῦς*, the familiar name of the Man, occurs in the Gospels 620 times,—61 of these, however, being various readings; that *ὁ Χριστός*, the official designation, occurs 47 times, four of these being various readings; and *Χριστός* five times,—the form *Χριστὸς 'Ιησοῦς* not occurring once. But in the Epistles such precision is not preserved: the ascended Lord had become more than mere Jesus, and *'Ιησοῦς* occurs only 62 times, 10 of these being various readings; the promised Deliverer now stood out to view, and ὁ Χριστός occurs 108 times, 22 being various readings; and the simple Χριστός 148 times, 17 being various readings. The compound name is also naturally employed: Ἰησοῦς Χριστός being used 156 times (nine various readings); and Χριστὸς Ἰησοῦς, which is never used in the Gospels and only two or three times in the Acts, occurs in the Epistles 64 times (two various readings). These changes are natural, and are easily accounted for. Χριστός lost its official distinctiveness and passed into a proper name, though there are places where the names could not be interchanged. The name Ἰησοῦς (Joshua) is from יֵשׁוּעַ, Neh. viii. 17, the later form of יְהוֹשֻׁעַ, "*Jehovah—help*," Num. xiii. 16, Matt. i. 21. Compare Acts vii. 45, Heb. iv. 8. Some of the Greek fathers absurdly derived the word from Ἰάομαι, as Eusebius, Clement of Alexandria, and Cyril of Jerusalem who says "it means saviour among the Hebrews, but in the Greek tongue Ἰώμενος"—Healer. Χριστός, הַמָּשִׁיחַ, or the anointed one, is applied to such as had enjoyed the sacred unction. The priest is often called ὁ χριστός, Lev. iv. 3, 5, 16; the king was also called ὁ χριστός, 1 Sam. xii. 3, 5, as is also Cyrus, Isa. xlv. 1; and the prophets also get the same title—τῶν χριστῶν μου, Ps. cv. 15—my anointed ones, Abraham being specially referred to, Gen. xx. 7. The word is applied in pre-eminence to Jesus, and the reason is given in Luke i. 35; Matt. iii. 16, xii. 18; John iii. 34; Acts x. 38. In the Received Text the last clause of the verse reads—

Διότι (ὅτι) οὐ δικαιωθήσεται ἐξ ἔργων νόμου πᾶσα σάρξ —"because by the works of the law no flesh shall be justified." This order of the words is found only in K, L, in the Gothic version, and in some of the Greek fathers. But the order ὅτι ἐξ ἔργων νόμου οὐ δικαιωθήσεται is found in A, B, C, D, F, א, in the Itala, Vulgate, Syriac, and in many Latin fathers. The reading διότι is doubtful. It is found in C, D[3], K, L, many MSS., versions, and fathers, and is adopted by Tischendorf and Ellicott; whereas the shorter ὅτι has in its favour A, B, D[1], F, א, etc., and is received by Lachmann, Alford, Meyer, and Lightfoot. It may be said that διότι was taken from Rom. iii. 20; but it may be replied that ὅτι is a correction of the longer διότι: the latter, however, is not so likely. The clause is a free use of Old Testament language, and in Paul's manner it is naturally introduced by *ὅτι* which in meaning is not materially different from *διότι* in the later writers—"because that," "because." It is not a formal quotation introduced by a formula, but rather a reminiscence of Ps. cxliii. 2 in the Sept., *ὅτι οὐ δικαιωθήσεται ἐνώπιόν σου πᾶς ζῶν*. That the allusion is to that psalm, is indicated by the Hebraism *οὐ πᾶσα*. The apostle leaves out *ἐνώπιόν σου*, which implies an appeal to Jehovah; and to give the clause special adaptation to the case before him, he adds *ἐξ ἔργων νόμου*. The Hebrew reads, כִּי לֹא־יִצְדַּק לְפָנֶיךָ כָל־חָי. The negative לֹא belongs to the verb, as the Masoretic punctuation shows (Ewald), and forms a universal negative. Ex. xii. 43; Josh. xi. 12; Jer. xxxii. 16. So in the Greek: non-justification is predicated of all flesh. Compare Matt. xxiv. 22, Luke i. 37, Acts x. 14. The idiom is found chiefly in "sentential quotations," though it occurs often in the Septuagint. Ex. xii. 16, xx. 10; Deut. v. 14; 2 Sam. xv. 11. It is put by Leusden in the sixth section of his sixteenth class of Hebraisms: *Philologus Heb. Græc.* p. 118, ed. 1785, Lugd. Batav. See also Vorstius, *De Heb. N. T.* p. 91; *Pars Altera*, p. 91, ed. 1705, Lipsiæ. The Seventy now and then render by *οὐ—οὐδείς*, or simply *οὐδείς*. Compare Deut. viii. 9, Josh. x. 8, xxiii. 9. It is especially when the negative precedes the article that the Hebraism occurs. Winer, § 26, 1. The *πᾶσα σάρξ*, equivalent to כָל־חָי, is perhaps chosen in preference to the *ζῶν* of the Septuagint, as in the apostolic times, and so close on the life-giving work of Christ, *ζωή* with its associates was acquiring a new and higher meaning. *Πᾶσα σάρξ* is all humanity—the race without exception,—Luke iii. 6; John xvii. 2; Acts ii. 17; 1 Pet. i. 24,—representing in the Septuagint כָּל־בָּשָׂר, there being apparently in the phrase no accessory notion of frailty, or sin, or death (Beza, Schrader). It means, however, man as he is, though not insinuating his inability *in naturâ adfectibus et cupiditatibus sensuum obnoxia* (Schott); nor does it carry any allusion to the overweening estimate placed by the Jews on their fleshly descent from Abraham (Windischmann). The future *δικαιωθήσεται*, as the ethical future, affirms possibility under the aspect of futurity, and with the negative particle denotes "something that neither can or will happen." Webster, *Syntax of the New Testament*, p. 84. It thus expresses a general truth which shall ever continue in force—*quæ omnino non fiunt, et ne fieri quidem possunt.* Thiersch, *de Pentat.* p. 160. The future contains no allusion to a coming day of reckoning (Hofmann); nor is there any such allusion in the psalm, for the phrase "enter not into judgment with Thy servant" refers to present divine inquisition or trial. Peile, p. 238. The apostle in the clause bases his reasoning upon an assertion of the Old Testament familiar to Peter and to his Jewish auditors. The quotation is more than "an axiom in our theology" (Alford), and it is not a mere repetition of what is found in the first clause of the verse, but it is an authoritative confirmation of the major premiss of the argument. Usteri, *Lehr-begr.* p. 90; Messner, *Die Lehre der Apostel*, p. 219.

Ver. 17. *Εἰ δὲ ζητοῦντες δικαιωθῆναι ἐν Χριστῷ εὑρέθημεν ἁμαρτωλοί, ἆρα Χριστὸς ἁμαρτίας διάκονος; μὴ γένοιτο*—"But if, while seeking to be justified in Christ, we were found sinners, is Christ therefore a minister of sin? God forbid." Of this difficult verse various interpretations have been given.

The verse plainly takes up an assumption, and reduces it to an absurdity. Theodoret says at the conclusion of his remarks on the previous verse, *εἶτα συλλογίζεται τὰ εἰρημένα.* "But if, in accordance with these premises of thine, or assuming the truth of these thy retrogressive principles" (Ellicott). The apostle had said, "we believed into Christ," *ἵνα,* with this end in view—justification; and he now uses *ζητοῦντες*, describing the action in unison with it, or which had been prompted by it. It is to be noted, that with the active participle he uses the aorist infinitive, which, though it cannot be expressed in English, "gives a momentary character to the action." Jelf, § 405, 2. Not as if two justifications are spoken of—one enjoyed already, and another yet sought after" (Wieseler, Lipsius). The apostle throws himself back to an earlier period; and indeed some regard *ζητοῦντες* as an imperfect. He does not insinuate any doubts as to the reality of his justified state, but only represents the general attitude of an earnest soul—its uniform aspiration toward Christ and justification in Him; as it still feels its sins and shortcomings, still prays for a growing faith and an intenser consciousness of union with Him, and the possession of its blessed fruits. The phrase ἐν Χριστῷ has its usual meaning, "in Christ"—in union with Christ, and not "by Christ," as in our Authorized Version, which follows Cranmer, Tyndale, and the Genevan. Wycliffe and the Rheims have, however, "in Christ." The faith possessed by Peter and Paul, which had gone out of themselves and into Christ, εἰς, was the nexus of a living union—ἐν Χριστῷ. They were justified διὰ πίστεως, for it was the means, or ἐκ πίστεως, as it was the instrumental cause; but they were also justified ἐν Χ., as only in such a union has faith any power, or divine grace any saving efficacy. The soul out of union with Christ is faithless, unforgiven, and lifeless. So that the relation indicated by ἐν Χ. differs from that indicated by διὰ Χ. The phrase "by Christ" may cover the whole extent of His work as Mediator; but ἐν Χ. narrows the meaning to the more special point of union with Him—the inner and only source of life. Wieseler, followed by Schmoller, wrongly takes the phrase to mean, the "ground, or Christ as *causa meritoria*." But the ἐν and διά are used with distinctive significance, as in Eph. i. 7. See under it. The two prepositions cannot be so distinguished here, or in such an argument, as if the one pointed to a mere inquirer and the other to a professed member of Christ (Gwynne). In εὑρέθημεν lies a contrast to ζητοῦντες: "if while seeking," or, "if after all our seeking, we ourselves also were found to be sinners." The verb εὑρίσκω has been often regarded as a periphrasis of the subjunctive verb—*idem est ac* εἶναι. Kypke, *Observat.* i. p. 2. Even Gataker makes it a Hebraism—γενόμενος *et* εὑρεθεὶς *idem valent. Antonin. Med.* p. 329, ed. London 1697. By this dilution of meaning the point and force of the verb are taken away. Not only the Greek verb, but the נִמְצָא of the Hebrew idiom also, keeps its proper meaning (2 Chron. xxxvi. 8; Mal. ii. 6), and denotes not simply the existence of anything, but that existence recognised or discovered. Matt. i. 18; Luke xvii. 18; Rom. vii. 10. Soph. *Trach.* 411; *Ajax,* 1135; Winer, § 65, 8. The aorist refers to a point of time past; that is to say, "but if, while seeking justification in Christ, we too were found to be, or turned out to be" (perhaps with the idea of surprise, Lightfoot), or "after all," ἁμαρτωλοί. It is surely requisite that this word be taken in the sense which it has in ver. 15—"sinners" as the Gentiles were regarded from the Jewish point of view, because not living in subjection to the Jewish law.

The particle which begins the next clause may be accented *ἄρα* or *ἆρα*. *Ἄρα—ῥα* has in it, according to Donaldson, the idea of distance or progression in an argument, and may involve the idea that the existing state of things is at variance with our previous expectations—"so then," or "as it seems." *Cratylus*, pp. 364, 365. In Attic usage it indicates both direct and oblique allusions, the idea of surprise being sometimes implied; or, as Stallbaum defines it, *Eam habet vim ut aliquid præter opinionem accidere, significet; also, doch.* Plato, *Republ.* 375 D; *Apolog.* 34 E. It does not usually stand first in the sentence among classical writers, nay, sometimes is placed at the end. Herod. iii. 64; Xen. *Hell.* vii. 1, 32. Hermann says, *ἄρα συλλογιστικόν in initio poni non potest: Antig.* 628. But in the New Testament it stands first. Matt. xii. 28; 2 Cor. v. 15; Gal. ii. 21; 2 Thess. ii. 15; Klotz-Devarius, ii. 160, 1. Some take it here as the conclusive *ἄρα*. As Chrysostom says, *εἶδες εἰς ὅσην ἀνάγκην περιέστησεν ἀτοπίας τὸν λόγον.* More fully his argument is: "If faith in Him does not avail for our justification, but if it be necessary to embrace the law again; and if, having forsaken the law for Christ's sake, we are not justified, but condemned for this abandonment; then shall we find Him for whose sake we abandoned the law the Author of our condemnation." This opinion changes, however, the meaning of *ἁμαρτωλοί* into *κατακρινομένοι.* Theodoret gives the same view, but more distinctly: *εἰ δὲ ὅτι τὸν νόμον· καταλιπόντες τῷ Χριστῷ προσεληλύθαμεν διὰ τῆς ἐπ' αὐτὸν πίστεως ἀπολαύσασθαι προσδοκήσαντες, παράβασις τοῦτο νενόμισται, εἰς αὐτὸν ἡ αἰτία χωρήσει τὸν δεσπότην Χριστόν.* In this case the apostle is supposed either to take up the objection of a Judaizer thus put: "To forsake the law in order to be justified, is to commit sin; and to make this change or commit this sin under the authority of Christ, is to make Christ the minister of sin,—a supposition not to be entertained; therefore it is wrong to plead His sanction for renunciation of law." Or the statement may be the apostle's own argument: "It cannot be a sinful thing to abandon the law, for such abandonment is necessary to justification; and if it were a sinful thing to pass over from the law to faith, it would thus and therefore make Christ the minister of sin: but far from our thoughts be such a conclusion." So generally Koppe, Flatt, Winer, Borger, Schott, and many others.

2. But ἄρα is supposed by some to put a question; and it needs not with this meaning to be changed into ἆρα, because it introduces an unauthorized conclusion rebutted by μὴ γένοιτο (Hofmann, Wieseler). It is better, however, to take the particle as ἆρα. True, indeed, in the other places where it occurs, Luke xviii. 8, Acts viii. 30, it introduces a question to be followed by a negative answer; but here, from the nature of the case, an affirmative—that is, on the principle admitted—but virtually a negative, which μὴ γένοιτο thunders out. On the other hand, it may be said, that in Paul's epistles μὴ γένοιτο occurs only after a question, and denies an inference false in itself but drawn from premises taken for granted, as is pointed out by the indicative εὑρέθημεν. The ἆρα expresses a perplexity, so natural and striking in the circumstances. It hesitates in putting the question, and has a shade of irony in it. Are we then, pray, to conclude that Christ is the minister of sin? *Simplex ἆρα aliquid sive veræ sive fictæ dubitationis admiscet.* Stallb. *Plato, De Repub.* 566A. It does not necessarily stand for ἀρ' οὐ, *nonne* (Olshausen, Schott), which prepares for an affirmative reply. Jelf, § 873, 2; Hermann, *ad Viger.* 823. *Unde fit, ut ubi ἆρα pro ἆρ' οὐ dictum videatur orationi sæpe color quidam ironiæ admisceatur.* Kühner, *Xen. Mem.* ii. 6, 1, p. 244. The general meaning then is: But if we, seeking to be justified, are found to be sinners; if we, having renounced the law as the ground of justification, have placed ourselves on a level with the heathen who are sinners from our point of view; is it to be inferred, pray—*ἆρα, ergone*—that Christ is a minister of sin? Ellicott and Lightfoot find an irony in ἁμαρτωλοί: We look down upon the Gentiles as sinners, and yet, in order to be justified, we must put ourselves on a level with them. Our possession of the law as born Jews gives us no element of justification; we renounce it, and thus become as Gentile sinners who never had it. Is Christ in that case, in whom alone justification is to be sought without works of law, a minister of sin? The lesson given by Peter's dissimulation in reverting to legal observance was, that renunciation of legal observance had been wrong. But the renunciation had been made under the autho-

rity of Christ; so that you, and they who hold with you, must be prepared to affirm that Christ, necessitating such renunciation, is a minister of sin.

The expositors who attach a different sense to *ἁμαρτωλοί* in this verse from what it plainly bears in ver. 15, bring out forms of exegesis which do not harmonize with the apostle's reasoning, or with the special circumstances in which he was placed.

1. A common exegesis among the older interpreters generally, as Paræus, Wesseling, etc., and recently Twele, Webster and Wilkinson in their New Testament, has been this: If men seeking or professing to seek justification in Christ are yet found living in sin, is Christ to blame for such an abuse of His gospel? vi. 1. It is a monstrous inference to teach, that "to dispense with works of law in regard to justification is to allow men to continue in sin." But surely this exegesis does not follow out the apostle's train of thought. It is not the abuse of the doctrine of faith or *fides sola* at all, but the virtual denial of its sole efficacy, that the apostle is reprehending in this verse.

2. Others, as Calovius, Locke, Zschokke, Haldane, bring out this idea: If while seeking to be justified in Christ, we are yet found sinners or unjustified; if His work alone cannot justify, but must have legal observance added to it; then Christ after all leaves us sinners under condemnation. As Dr. Brown remarks, the inference in such a case would be, not, Christ is the servant of sin, but, Christ's expiation has been incomplete. This exegesis does not suit the context, nor is it fairly deducible from the words.

3. The same objection may be made to Calvin's notion: "If justification by faith puts Jews and Gentiles on a level, and if Jews, 'sanctified from the womb,' are guilty and polluted, shall we say that Christ makes sin powerful in His own people, and that He is therefore the Author of sin? He who discovers the sin which lay concealed is not therefore the minister of sin." Compare Piscator and Wordsworth. This, however, is not by any means the point in dispute to which the apostle is addressing himself.

4. Nor better is the supposition of Grotius, that the apostle has in his eye the flagitious lives of Judaizers, though he puts

it in the first person: The inference that Christ is the minister of sin, will be gathered from our conduct, unless it far excel the life both of Gentiles and Judaizers.

5. The opinion of Macknight needs scarcely be noticed: "If we practise the rites of the Mosaic law contrary to our conscience, will Christ promote such iniquity by justifying teachers who delude others in a matter of such importance?"

6. Olshausen's view of the last clause is as objectionable, for it overlooks the special moments of the verse: "If justification depends on the law, while Christ ordains the preaching of faith for that purpose, then He is the minister of sin, as He points out a false method of salvation."

7. The form in which Jowett puts the question changes the meaning of *ἁμαρτωλοί*: "If we too fall back under the law, is Christ the cause of this? Is He the author of that law which is the strength of sin, which reviving we die?" etc.[1] This paraphrase introduces a new idea from the Epistle to the Romans; and it is not so much to the inner working of the law, as to its powerlessness to justify, that the apostle is here referring. The point before him suggested by Peter's inconsistency is rather the bearing of the law on our relation to God than on our character, though both are inseparably connected.

The phrase *ἁμαρτίας διάκονος* is a pregnant one (2 Cor. xi. 2), the first word being emphatic,—not a furtherer of lawlessness, as Morus, who gives *ἁμαρτωλοί* the meaning of lawless, or without law—*gesetzlos*,—and Rosenmüller, who sums it up, *Christum esse doctorem paganismi!*

The apostle protests against the inference—

Μὴ γένοιτο—"God forbid"—let it not be; *absit*, Vulgate. The phrase is one of the several Septuagint translations of חָלִילָה, *ad profana*, sometimes joined to a pronoun of the first or second person, and sometimes to the name of God. The Seventy render it by *μηδαμῶς* or *μὴ εἴη*; *ἵλεώς σοι* occurs in Matt. xvi. 22; and the Syriac has ܚܣ = *propitius sit Deus*. The phrase is not confined to the sacred writers, but is found abundantly in Arrian's *Epictetus* and in the same sense, but

[1] "*Meint Ihr, dass Christus dann an uns Gefallen, grösseres Gefallen, als an den Heiden finden, und so uns in unsrer Sünde stärken und fördern werde? Das wird er nicht.*"—Rückert.

with a change of reference in Herodotus, v. 111; Xen. *Cyrop.* v. 5, 5. It is used only by Paul among the writers of the New Testament: Rom. iii. 4, 6, 31, vi. 2, 15, vii. 7, 13, ix. 14, xi. 1, 11; 1 Cor. vi. 15; Gal. iii. 21; and with a difference in Gal. vi. 14. It is spoken by the people in Luke xx. 16. It is usually and suddenly interjected against an opponent's inference. "God forbid" that any one, for any reason or to any extent, from any misconception or on any pretext, should either imagine or suspect Christ to be a minister of sin; or should be involved in any course of conduct, the vindication of which might imply such an inference; or be entangled in any premisses which could lead by any possibility to such an awful conclusion. Perish the thought! Let it be flung from us as an abominable thing!

Ver. 18. *Εἰ γὰρ ἃ κατέλυσα ταῦτα πάλιν οἰκοδομῶ, παραβάτην ἐμαυτὸν συνιστάνω*—"for if the things which I destroyed, these again I build up, I constitute myself a transgressor." The *συνίστημι* of the Received Text rests only on the slender authority of D[3], K, L.

This verse has a close connection with the preceding one. The *γάρ*, in spite of Wieseler's objection, is a confirmation of the *μὴ γένοιτο*, as in Rom. ix. 14, xi. 1. Why say I *μὴ γένοιτο* so sharply? the reason is, For if I set up again what I have pulled down, my rebuilding is a confession that the work of demolition was wrong. And if I claim the authority of Christ for both parts of the process, then I make possible an affirmative to the startling question, "Is He after all a minister of sin?" Nay, if I re-enact legal observances as indispensable to justification, after having maintained that justification is not of legal merit but of grace, my second work proves my sin in my first work. Or: Is Christ the minister of sin? God forbid; for in the renunciation of the law, and in the consequent finding of ourselves sinners in order to justification, there is no sin; but the sin lies in returning to the law again as the means or ground of acceptance, for such a return is an assertion of its perpetual authority. There is yet another and secondary contrast,—not so primary a contrast as Olshausen, Winer, Schott, and Wieseler would contend for, since *ἐμαυτόν* coming after *παραβάτην* has not the emphatic position: You, from your point of view toward us who have forsaken the law and only believe in Christ to justification, find us sinners—ἁμαρτωλοί, and would implicate Christ; but in rebuilding what I destroyed, it is not Christ who is to blame, but *myself* I show to be a transgressor. Or: You Judaists regard as ἁμαρτωλοί all non-observers of the law, yet this non-observance is sanctioned by Christ; but would you dare to impeach Him as the promoter of anything that may really be called ἁμαρτια? No, far from us be the thought! But a direct παράβασις must be charged on him who, like Peter, sets up in Galatia what at Cæsarea and at Antioch he had cast down so firmly, and that as the result of a supernatural vision and lesson. The structure of the verse, which prevents it from being well rendered into English, is emphatic: ἃ . . . ταῦτα. The change to the first person was probably *clementiæ causâ—mitigandi vituperii causâ* (Jaspis),—for it might well have been—σύ. The figure is a common one with the apostle, as in Rom. xv. 20; 1 Cor. viii. 1, x. 23; Eph. ii. 20. The tropical use of καταλύω, to loosen down, is common in the New Testament, as applied to νόμος, Matt. v. 17, and ἔργον, Acts v. 38, 39, Rom. xiv. 20. The apostle utters a general principle, though the intended application is to the Mosaic law. There is a distinct emphasis on ταῦτα: "these, and nothing else than these,"—a rebuilding of the identical materials I had cast down. The verb οἰκοδομέω in the present tense is suggested by the general form of a maxim which the verse assumes, while it also glances at Peter's actual conduct. The rarer form συνιστάνω, not different in meaning from the other form συνίστημι, signifies "I prove, or am proving," not *commendo* (Schott). Hesychius defines it by ἐπαινεῖν, φανεροῦν, βεβαιοῦν, παρατιθέναι. The true meaning comes—*e componendi significatione:* Rom. iii. 5, v. 8; 2 Cor. vi. 4; Sept. Susan. 61; Jos. *Antiq.* ii. 7, 1; and as here with a double accusative it occurs in Philo, συνίστησιν αὐτὸν φροφήτην, *Quis rer. div. Haer.* p. 114, vol. iv. ed. Pfeiffer; and in Diodor. Sic. xiii. 91, συνιστὰς αὐτοὺς οἰκείους, vol. i. pt. 2, p. 779, ed. Dindorf, Lipsiæ 1828. Bengel's notion of a mimêsis, and Schott's of irony, in the selection or use of the verb, are far-fetched and groundless. Παραβάτης is a transgressor, to wit, of the law,—a more specific form than ἁμαρτωλός, for it seems to imply violation of direct law: Rom. ii. 25, 27, iv. 15; Jas. ii. 9, 11.

But what law is referred to? It cannot be the law of

faith or of the gospel (Koppe, Matthies); but it is the Mosaic law itself. For Peter was guilty of notorious inconsistency in preaching the abrogation of legal observance, and then in re-enacting it in his conduct; and specially, that conduct was a confession that he had transgressed in overthrowing the law. So Borger, Usteri, Hilgenfeld, De Wette, and Ewald. Alford takes the phrase as the explanation of *ἁμαρτωλοὶ εὑρέθημεν*—"found sinners," that is, in setting aside the law. Various modifications of this view have been given. Pelagius places the *παράβασις* specially in this, that Peter was confessing himself *meæ sententiæ prævaricator;* Morus, in that by his inconsistency he was showing himself to be one, *qui non observat officium doctoris*. Hammond takes the noun to signify an apostate. Wieseler understands the verse in a general sense as enforcing the connection of justification and sanctification,—sin being an actual rebuilding of what in justification had been thrown down; an opinion which Schmoller is justified in calling *ein starkes Exempel dogmatisirender Exegese*. Hofmann, too, gives a peculiar view: The sinner, to be justified, must acknowledge himself guilty of a violation of law; and such a confession shows himself and not Christ the servant of sin—his very attempt to obtain righteousness in Christ is an acknowledgment of transgression. But these opinions are aside from the context. Bagge's view is too vague: "If a justified man seek justification by law, he again binds himself to the law, and thus declares himself a transgressor." So is that of Rollock: *Ego sum transgressor quoniam reædifico peccatum, quod per fidem in Christum, quoad reatum et maculam destruere desideravi*. Similarly Webster and Wilkinson. The apostle's general argument is, there was no sin in declaring against the validity of legal observance in order to faith in Christ, who is "the end of the law;" this emancipation was only obedience to Christ, and He cannot be the minister of sin. Men, Jews especially, renouncing the law as a ground of justification, will find themselves sinners from their previous point of view, and Christ is not to be blamed. But this renunciation of law must be sin to all who, now regarding themselves as having been in a false position, not only recoil from it, but go back to the old Judaic ordinances, and seek acceptance through subjection to them. Abrogation and re-enactment cannot both be right.

But there lies a deeper reason which the apostle now proceeds to develop. This deeper reason it might be difficult to trace in this verse by itself, but the *γάρ* of the next verse brings it out. It is also recognised by the Greek expositors; and it is this, that the law itself was leading on to faith in Christ. From its very form and aspects it taught its own typical and temporary character,—that it was an intermediate system, preparing for Christ and showing the way to Him; and in serving such a purpose it indicated its own supersession. But if, after Christ has come, you re-enact it, you not only confess that you were wrong in holding it to be abrogated, but you also prove yourself a transgressor of its inner principles and a contravener of its spirit and purpose; for the next words are, *ἐγὼ γὰρ διὰ νόμου νόμῳ ἀπέθανον*. Chrysostom gave as the meaning: "The law has taught me not to obey itself; and therefore if I do so, I shall be transgressing even its teaching." Theophylact explains, *ὁ νόμος με ὡδήγησε πρὸς τὴν πίστιν καὶ ἔπεισεν ἀφεῖναι αὐτόν.*

The objection of Alford to this view is, as Ellicott remarks, "of no real force." The Dean says, "The *ἐγώ* of the illustration has given up faith in Christ, and so cannot be regarded as acknowledging it as the end of the law." The Bishop truly replies, that "the *ἐγώ* had not given up faith in Christ, but had only added to it." Peter certainly had not renounced faith in Christ, but he had given occasion for others to suppose that he regarded legal observance to be either the essential complement of faith or an indispensable supplement to it. His view of the relation of the law to faith may not even have been obscured, for his inconsistency was dissimulation. How the law was transgressed, if re-enacted either to compete with faith or give it validity, the apostle proceeds to show:

Ver. 19. *Ἐγὼ γὰρ διὰ νόμου νόμῳ ἀπέθανον*—"for I through the law died to the law." *Διὰ νόμου* cannot mean "on account of the law." The *γάρ* has its full force: If I build up that law which I pulled down, I prove myself a transgressor of it, for by it I became dead to it; or as Lightfoot happily expresses it, "In abandoning the law, I did but follow the leading of the law itself." The position and expression of *ἐγώ* are alike emphatic—"I for my part;" it being the revelation of his own experience. The *ἐγώ* is not merely representative in its nature, as is held by Olshausen, Baumgarten-Crusius, Kamphausen, and

Wieseler who understands it *von Paulus und seinen judenchristlichen Gesinnungsgenossen.* This is true as an inference. But Paul's personal experience had been so profound and decided, and had so moulded the entire course of his life, that it may certainly isolate him from other believing Jews,—even from those who could trace in themselves a similar change,—even, in a word, from Peter, whose momentary reaction had challenged this discussion. So far as the result is concerned, the experience of believers generally is pictured out; but the apostle puts himself into prominence. The experience of others, while it might approximate his, could never reach a perfect identity with it in depth and suddenness. That both words, *νόμου νόμῳ*, should by necessity refer to the same law, has not been universally admitted. The genitive has been referred by very many to the law of the gospel,—such as Jerome, Ambrosiast., Erasmus, Luther, Calovius, Hunnius, Vatablus, Vorstius, Bengel, Koppe, Morus, and Borger. It is also an alternative explanation of the Greek fathers and Pelagius. Küttner quietly says, *Intellige πίστεως quod omisit ut elegantior et acutior fieret sententia.*

But this signification cannot be received as even plausible. It is true that *νόμος* is a term occasionally applied to the gospel, but some characterizing element is added,—as *πίστεως*, Rom. iii. 27; *τ. πνεύματος τ. ζωῆς*, Rom. viii. 2; *δικαιοσύνης*, Rom. ix. 31; Justin Mart. *Dial. cum Tryph.* p. 157, ed. Thirlby. The word can bear here no meaning but the law of Moses, the law of God embodied in the Jewish economy. The Mosaic law is the point of dispute, the only divine law known to the speaker and his audience. The article is not necessary. The want of the article in some clauses, even when the reference is to Mosaic system, may express to some extent the abstract idea of law, but it is ever divine law as exemplified or embodied in the Jewish economy. See pp. 163, 164.

How, then, did the law become the instrument of the apostle's dying to itself,—for *διὰ νόμου* has the stress upon it? How through the instrumentality of the law was he released from obligation to law; or, more briefly, How did the law free him from itself?

1. Some find this power in the outspeaking of the law as to its own helplessness to justify. Thus Winer: *Lex legem*

sustulit, ipsa lex cum non posset mihi salutem impertire mei me juris fecit atque a suo imperio liberavit. Similarly Olshausen, Matthies, Hilgenfeld, and Matthias. But this statement does not contain the whole truth.

2. Some ascribe to the law the peculiar function of a *παιδαγωγός*. Thus Beza: *Lex enim terroris conscientiam ad Christum adducit.* So Calvin, Schott, Bagge, Trana, and virtually Lightfoot. But surely this abandonment of the law forced upon sinners by its terrors does not amount to the profound change described in the very significant phrase *τῷ νόμῳ ἀπέθανον.*

3. Some refer this instrumental power to the Messianic deliverances of the law, as Gen. xv. 6, explained in Rom. iii. 21, or Deut. xviii. 18—*Διά τε τῶν Μωσαϊκῶν λόγων καὶ τῶν προφητικῶν*, Theophylact. Theodoret, Hammond, Estius, Wetstein, and Baumgarten-Crusius. It is also an alternative explanation of Œcumenius, Pelagius, Augustine, Crocius, and Grotius. But the written law would be *ὁ νόμος*, and it did not as such embrace the prophets by whom those utterances were most fully and vividly given. Besides, as Lightfoot remarks, "such an appeal" based on type and prophecy would be "an appeal rather to the reason and intellect than to the heart and conscience." The apostle's words are indeed an argument,—one not based however on written external coincidences or propaideutic and typical foreshowings, but drawn from the depths of his spiritual nature. Marian. Victor. puts it peculiarly: *Ego enim per legem, quæ nunc spiritualiter intelligitur legi mortuus sum, illi scilicet legi quæ carnaliter intelligebatur.*

But to aid inquiry into the meaning of *διὰ νόμου*, the meaning of *νόμῳ ἀπέθανον* must be first examined. The noun is a kind of *dativus commodi* as it is called. Such a dative is found with this verb Rom. vi. 2, 10, vii. 4, xiv. 7. To die to the law, is to die as the law demands—to bear its penalty, and therefore to be no longer under its curse and claim. In Rom. vii. 4 the apostle says, "The law has dominion over a man as long as he liveth;" but that dominion over him ceases at his death. This is a general principle; and for the sake of illustration he adds, that the *γυνὴ ὕπανδρος* dies to the law of marriage in her husband's death, and therefore may "marry another." So believers died to the law in the death of Christ

—*ἐθανατώθητε τῷ νόμῳ διὰ τοῦ σώματος τοῦ Χριστοῦ.* They were freed from the law (*κατηργήθημεν*, nullified), and so are discharged from it. The common reading *ἀποθανόντος* in Rom. vii. 6 is to be rejected—"that being dead in which we were held;" for the true reading is *ἀποθανόντες*—"we having died to that *ἐν ᾧ κατειχόμεθα*—in which we were held bound," and so we are freed from it. But how can a man die by the law to the law and be relieved from its curse? The apostle explains in the following verse—

Χριστῷ συνεσταύρωμαι—"I have been crucified with Christ." Wondrous words! I am so identified with Him, that His death is my death. When He was crucified, I was crucified with Him. I am so much one with Him under law and in suffering and death, that when He died to the law I died to the law. Through this union with Him I satisfied the law, yielded to it the obedience which it claimed, suffered its curse, died to it, and am therefore now released from it—from its accusations and its penalty, and from its claim on me to obey it as the means of winning eternal life. By means of law He died; it took Him and wrought its will on Him. As our Representative in whom we were chosen and in whom we suffered, He yielded Himself to the law, which seized Him and nailed Him to the cross. When that law seized Him, it seized at the same time all His in Him, and through the law they suffered and died to it. Thus it is that by the law taking action upon them as sinners they died to the law. This is the view generally of Meyer, Ellicott, Alford, and Gwynne. At the same time, the passage is not parallel to the latter portion of the seventh chapter of Romans; for there the apostle shows the powerlessness of the law to sanctify as well as to justify. Yet the law is not in itself to blame, for it is "holy, and just, and good;" and it has its own functions—to reveal sin in the conscience, to irritate it into activity, and to show its true nature as being "exceeding sinful." When sin revives, the sinner dies—not the death referred to in the passage before us, but spiritual death and misery. And now certainly, if the law, avenging itself on our guilt, has in this way wrought our release from itself—has set us for ever free from its yoke, and we have died to it and have done with it; then he who would re-enact legalism and bring men under it, proves himself its transgressor, nay, opposes its deepest principles and its most gracious design. See Usteri, *Paulin. Lehrb.* p. 171, 5th ed.

But release from law is not lawlessness. We die to sin as well as to the law which is "the strength of sin,"—and "Christ died unto sin once." But death to the law is followed by life to God as its grand purpose:

Ἵνα Θεῷ ζήσω—"that I might live to God," even as Christ "liveth unto God." Life in a high spiritual form succeeds that death to the law—life originated and fostered by the Spirit of God—the life of faith—the true life of the soul or Christ living in it. The dative *Θεῷ* is opposed to *νόμῳ*, and with the same meaning. The verb *ζήσω* is the subjunctive aorist (Winer, 41, p. 257), in keeping with the historical tense of the principal sentence. The phrase *ζῆν τινι*, *vivere alicui*, is common: *ἑαυτῷ ζῆν*, opposed to *τῷ κυριῷ ζῶμεν*, Rom. xiv. 7; *ἐμαυτῷ ζῆν*, Euripides, *Ion*, 646; *Φιλίππῳ ζῶντες*, Demosth. *Philip. Epist.* vol. i. p. 100, ed. Schaefer; *τῷ πατρὶ ζῶντες*, Dion. Halicar. iii. 17, vol. i. p. 235, ed. Kiessling, 1860; *τοῦτ' ἐστι τὸ ζῆν οὐχ ἑαυτῷ ζῆν μόνον*, Menander in *Philadelpho*, Stobæus, *Flor.* 121, 5, ed. Gaisford; *αἰσχρὸν γὰρ ζῆν μόνοις ἑαυτοῖς*, Plutarch, *Ag. et Cleom. Opera*, vol. iv. p. 128, ed. Bekker; *ζῶσιν τῷ Θεῷ*, 1 Macc. xvi. 25; *Θεῷ μόνῳ ζῆσαι*, Philo, *de Nom. Mut.* p. 412, *Op.* vol. iv. ed. Pfeiffer; *ζῆσαι Θεῷ μᾶλλον ἢ ἑαυτῷ*, *Quis rer. Div.* do. p. 50; *non sibi soli vivere*, Ter. *Eun.* iii. 2, 27; *mihi vivam*, Hor. *Ep.* xviii. 107; *vive tibi, vive tibi*, Ovid, *Tr.* iii. 4, 4. These current phrases were therefore well understood. To live to one's self is to make self the one study—to bend all thoughts, acts, and purposes on self as the sole end; so that the inquiry, how shall this or that tell upon self either immediately or more remotely, deepens into a species of unconscious instinct. To live to God is to be in Him—in union with Him, and to feel the assimilating influence of this divine fellowship—to give Him the first place in the soul, and to put all its powers at His sovereign disposal—to consult Him in everything, and to be ever guided by His counsel—to do His will, because it is His will, at all times—to regard every step in its bearing on His claims and service, and to further His glory as the one grand end of our lives. Such is the ideal in its holy and blessed fulness. Alas, how seldom can it be realized! Such a life must be preceded by this death to the law through the law, for the legal spirit is one of bondage, failure, and unhappiness,—works done in obedience to law to ward off its penalty, with the consciousness that all the while the perfect fulfilment of the law is impossible,—God being viewed as the lawgiver and judge in their sterner aspects, and not in His grace, so as to win our confidence and our unreserved consecration. The clause is connected with the one before it, and not with the following one.

Ver. 20. *Χριστῷ συνεσταύρωμαι*—"I have been crucified with Christ." The meaning of the words has been already considered—the wondrous identity of the saint with his Saviour. See under Phil. iii. 9, 10, 11. Compare Rom. vi. 4, 8; Rom. viii. 17; Eph. ii. 5; Col. ii. 12, 20; 2 Tim. ii. 11. Lightfoot errs in giving it a different meaning from *νόμῳ ἀπέθανον*, of which it is the explanation, as if the one were release from past obligation, and this were the annihilation of old sins. For the allusion here is not to the crucifixion of the old man as in v. 24 (Ambros., Grotius),—the image of spiritual change, self-denial, and "newness of life." The apostle is describing how death to the law and release from legal bondage were brought about. Some connect the clause *ἵνα Θεῷ ζήσω* with the one before it—"in order that I may live to God, I am crucified with Christ" (Chrysostom, Cajetan, Calvin). But the position of *ἵνα*, and the contrast of *ἀπέθανον* and *ζήσω*, show that the first clause is a portion of what is introduced by *γάρ*. The punctuation of the following clauses has been variously attempted. In one way the arrangement is—

Ζῶ δὲ οὐκέτι ἐγώ· ζῇ δὲ ἐν ἐμοὶ Χριστός—"but it is no longer I that live, but it is Christ that liveth in me;" or, "I live however no longer myself, Christ however liveth in me." It has been common, on the other hand, to put a point after the first *δέ*, as in our version—"nevertheless I live, yet not I, but Christ liveth in me;" and so Bagge, Gwynne, Scholz, Luther, Morus, etc. As Alford remarks, however, that punctuation would require *ἀλλά* before *οὐκέτι* in such a negative assertion. It is difficult, indeed, to translate the clauses; but that is rather in favour of the idiomatic structure which the newer punctuation brings out. Still, under the older punctuation there is something like the Pauline antithesis, *ἐκοπίασα· οὐκ ἐγὼ δέ*, 1 Cor. xv. 10; 2 Cor. vi. 8–10. But here the phrase "I am crucified with Christ" is a kind of parenthetical explanation suddenly inserted; and the ζῶ δέ, therefore, is not in contrast with it, as the older punctuation supposes, but goes back to the previous clause—Θεῷ ζήσω.

The ζῶ . . . ζῇ have the emphatic place—the idea of life after such death fills the apostle's thoughts: "living, however, no longer am I; living, however, in me is Christ." The first δέ has its proper force, referring to ἵνα Θεῷ ζήσω: "That I may live to God;" but "it is not I that live." I have said "I," but it is not *I*. It is something more than the *fortschreitendes* δέ (De Wette, Rückert). This ἐγώ is my old self—what lived in legalism prior to my being crucified with Christ; it lives no longer. The principle of the old life in legalism has passed away, and a new life is implanted within me. Or, When I speak of my living, "I do not mean myself or my natural being;" for a change as complete is spoken of as if it had sundered his identity. The explanation of the paradox is—this new life was not himself or his own, but it was Christ living in him. His life to God was no natural principle—no vital element self-originated or self-developed within him;—it sprang out of that previous death with His Lord in whom also he had risen again; nay, Christ had not only claimed him as His purchase and taken possession of him, but had also entered into him,—had not only kindled life within him, but was that Life Himself. When the old prophet wrought a miracle in restoring the dead child by stretching himself upon it so exactly that corresponding organs were brought into contact, the youth was resuscitated as if from the magnetic influences of the riper and stronger life, but the connection then terminated. Christ, on the other hand, not only gives the life, but He is the life—not as mere source, or as the communicator of vitalizing influence, but He lives Himself as the life of His people; for he adds—

Ζῇ δὲ ἐν ἐμοὶ Χριστός. There are idiomatic reasons for the insertion of this second δέ, for it marks the emphatic repetition of the same verb. The idiom is a common one.

ἥσθην δὲ βιαιὰ, πάνυ δὲ βιαιά.—Aristophanes, *Acharn.* v. 2.

καλῶ δὲ τάσδε δαίμονας καλῶ δ' Ἄρη.—Soph. *Œdip. Col.* 1391.

πολλὰ δὲ σῦκη πολὺ δ' ἔλαιον, Xen. *Cyrop.* ii. 22. Many other examples are given in Hartung, i. p. 168; Klotz-Devarius, ii. 359, who adds, *significatio non mutatur etiam tum, cum in ejusdam rei aut notionis repetitione ponitur;* Kühner, *Xen. Mem.* i. 1; Dindorf, *Steph. Thes.* ii. p. 928. That is to say, δέ is not wholly adversative; but it introduces a new, yet not quite a different thought—*similis notio quodam modo opponitur.* Living is the emphatic theme of both clauses; the contrast is between ἐγώ and Χριστός in relation to this life; the one clause does not contradict or subvert the other, but the last brings out a new aspect under which this life is contemplated.

The utterance is not, as might be expected, I live in Christ; but, "Christ liveth in me." Some, as Riccaltoun and Olshausen tell us, take this expression "for a mere metaphor" or "a mere oriental figure," or if not, "for cant and unintelligible jargon;" while others, as Olshausen also informs us, base a species of pantheism upon it—*ein Verschwimmen ins allgemeine Meer der Gottheit.* But Christ-life in us is a blessed fact, realized by profound consciousness; and the personality is not merged, it is rather elevated and more fully individualized by being seized and filled with a higher vitality, as the following clauses describe. What a sad interpretation of Semler, that "Christ" in this clause means *illa perfectior doctrina Christi!*

Ὃ δὲ νῦν ζῶ ἐν σαρκί—"but the life which I am now living in the flesh," the stress lying on *νῦν*. The δέ is used as in the first of the two previous clauses, and it rebuts an objection suggested by the words *νῦν—ἐν σαρκί*. The *νῦν*, glancing back to *οὐκέτι*, has been supposed to allude to the apostle's unconverted state: my present life dating from my conversion; as Alford, Meyer, Wieseler, Trana. Others take it to be in contrast to the future state, as Rückert, Usteri, Schott, Bisping: my present life, my life now in contrast with what it shall be, is a life of faith; Meyer adding, though he adopts the previous interpretation, that Paul expected at the second coming to be among the living who shall only be changed. The idea of Chrysostom, followed by Ellicott, comes nearer to our mind, that *νῦν* characterizes simply his life as a present one, life in the flesh—*hæc vita mea terrestris.* The words *ἐν σαρκί* would be all but superfluous if a contrast with his former unbelieving state were intended, for he lived ἐν σαρκί then as now. As for the construction, it is needless with Winer to fill it out as *quod vero ad id attinet*, or καθ' ὃ δὲ νῦν ζῶ, the alternative and preferred explanation in his *Gram.* § 24, 4, 3. Here ὅ is simply the accusative to the verb ζῶ (Bernhardy, p. 297); not precisely, as Ellicott resolves it, τὴν δὲ ζῶην ἣν νῦν ζῶ, for ὅ limits and qualifies the idea of life, as is more fully seen in Rom. vi. 10. See Fritzsche *in loc.* The implied repetition of the noun in connection with its own verb is common. Bernhardy, p. 106. The ἐν σαρκί, in this body of flesh, is not *carnaliter* or κατὰ σάρκα; there is no ethical implication in the term; it merely describes the external character of his present life. My present life—so true, so blessed, and so characterized by me—is a life in the flesh. Granted that it is still a life in the flesh, yet it is in its highest aspect a life of faith. This idea or objection suggested the δέ, which is simply explicative, and is more than *nämlich*, to wit (Meyer): "but what I now," "or so far as I now live in the flesh." "I live indeed in the flesh, but not through the flesh, or according to the flesh" (Luther), for the believer's life externally resembles that of the world around him. Thus Tertullian, in vindication against the charge of social uselessness: *Quo pacto homines vobiscum degentes, ejusdem victûs, habitûs, instinctûs, ejusdem ad vitam necessitatis? Neque enim Brachmanæ, aut Indorum gymnosophistæ sumus, sylvicolæ et exules vitæ. Meminimus gratiam nos debere Deo Domino creatori, nullum fructum operum ejus repudiamus, plane temperamus, ne ultra modum aut perperam utamur. Itaque non sine foro, non sine macello, non sine balneis, tabernis, officinis, stabulis, nundinis vestris cæterisque commerciis, cohabitamus in hoc seculo; navigamus et nos vobiscum et militamus, et rusticamur et mercatus proinde miscemus, artes, opera nostra publicamus usui vestro.*—*Apologet.* cap. 42, vol. i. p. 273, ed. Œhler. While his life was in this visible sense an earthly one, it was characterized at the same time by a higher principle—

'Εν πίστει ζῶ τῇ τοῦ υἱοῦ τοῦ Θεοῦ—"I live in the faith of the Son of God;" or, "in faith," to wit, "the faith of the Son of God." Codex A omits ζῶ; τῇ τοῦ Θεοῦ καὶ Χριστοῦ is read in B, D[1], F, and is accepted by Lachmann; but the usual text is supported by A, C, D[2,3], K, L, א, and by many of the versions and fathers. It is difficult, indeed, to see how the other reading could have originated; unless, as Meyer supposes, *υἱοῦ τοῦ* had been omitted, and some other copyist, to bring the clause into harmony with what follows, added *τοῦ Χριστοῦ*.

He lived *ἐν πίστει*, "in the faith," not by the faith, either as the simple dative, or as if it were *διὰ πίστεως*, though the Greek fathers, with Michaelis, Beza, Balduin, so render it; and our version has also "by the faith," the only place where the phrase is so translated. *'Εν*, indeed, with the dative has an instrumental sense; but here, while that is not wholly excluded, it falls into the background. Faith was the element in which he lived; his life was not only originated instrumentally by it, but it was also sustained in faith. A weak dilution of the phrase is given by Grotius, *Sub spe vitæ melioris*, and by Koppe, who explains the clause by *omne studium religionis Jesus*. How odd is the notion of Vatablus, *Propter fidem, i.e. ut fidem doceam!*

This faith is held up or is particularized as *τῇ τοῦ υἱοῦ τοῦ Θεοῦ*. The article, as inserted at this point, gives it special prominence or moment—"in faith, and that of the Son of God." The genitive is that of object—faith resting on Christ, as in ver. 16. And the name is chosen with fitting solemnity. It is as the Son of God that He has and gives life. John v. 25, 26. Divine personality and equality with the Father are implied in the Blessed Name. Both names are specified by the article. See under Eph. i. 3. That faith rested on no creature, but on God's own Son—so like Him as to be His "express image," and so loved by Him as to be in His bosom. And what He has done for the apostle is stated in glowing terms—

Τοῦ ἀγαπήσαντός με καὶ παραδόντος ἑαυτὸν ὑπὲρ ἐμοῦ—"who loved me, and gave Himself for me." See under i. 4, and under iii. 13. The *καί* is illustrative—*et quidem*, Winer, § 53, 3, c, though he warns correctly, that "this epexegetical force has been attributed to *καί* in too many passages." The participles, emphatic in position, are aorists, referring the facts to the indefinite past; and they show how well warranted that faith was, by the relation which the Son of God bore to him, for He loved him with a love which none but He can feel—a love like Himself, and by the gift which He gave for him, and which none but He could give—Himself, the fruit of His love. *Μέ*, though repeated,—for it is still the same *ἐγώ*,

—has not a position of special prominence. But it shows the depth and individualizing nature of his faith; he particularizes himself: No matter who else were loved, He loved me; no matter for whom other He gave Himself, He gave Himself for me. Is it any wonder, then, that my life even now is a life of faith in Him, and no longer one in legal bondage? Paul had been many years in Christ ere he used this language of assurance. That assurance was unchanging. If the Son of God loved him, and so loved him that He gave Himself to death for him, and if his faith had been resting on that love crowned in His sacrifice, how could he think of disowning this divine Redeemer, slighting His love and disparaging His self-gift, by relapsing into legal observances and rebuilding what He had been so strenuously throwing down? His confidence in the Son of God, and the near and tender relation of the Son of God to him, made such retrogression impossible; for these elements of life were weightier than all arguments—were the soul of his experience, and identified with himself. He must deny himself and forget all his previous history, before he could turn his back on that cross where the Son of God proved the intensity and self-denying nature of His love for him in that atonement which needs neither repetition nor supplement. "Wilt thou bring thy cowl, thy shaven crown, thy chastity, thy obedience, thy poverty, thy works, thy merits? What shall those do?" (Luther.) To be faithless is to be lifeless, without union with Him who has life and imparts it. Faith rests on His ability and will as a divine Redeemer—"the Son of God;" feels its warrant and welcome—"He loved me;" and revels in the adapted and numerous blessings provided—"He gave Himself for me." These blessings are all summed up in "life," as awaking it, fostering it, and crowning it, so that its receptive faculties are developed, and it pulsates healthfully and freshly in sympathetic unison with its blessed Source. Faith brings the soul into close and tender union with Him "who is our life," keeps it in this fellowship, and creates within it a growing likeness to Him in the hope that it shall be with Him for ever. Faith gives Him a continuous influence over the conscience, writes His law on "the fleshly tables of the heart," and enables the believer to realize His presence as his joy and power. In short, the new existence which springs from co-crucifixion with

Christ, "lives, and moves, and has its being" in this faith of the Son of God. It is a lamentably superficial view which is taken by Rosenmüller of these clauses—*ἐν πίστει, in religione Messiæ excolenda et propaganda.*

Prof. Jowett at this point makes an apparent assault on the common theology, because it does not follow the apostle's special order of thought in this place. "We begin," he says, "with figures of speech—sacrifice, ransom, Lamb of God—and go on with logical determinations—finite, infinite, satisfaction, necessity in the nature of things. St. Paul also begins with figures of speech—life, death, the flesh; but passes on to the inward experience of the life of faith, and the consciousness of Christ dwelling in us." But this use of the apostle's present form of argument is partial and one-sided. Prof. Jowett's accusation implies that "we" do not reason on these subjects in the apostle's order; and he institutes a needless comparison between theology and experience, between objective and subjective Christian truth. But it is surely quite possible to begin with such "figures" as those he refers to—"sacrifice, ransom, Lamb of God"—and move on naturally to the other figures which more delight him, as "death, and death with Christ." May not one—after referring to the fact that "Christ has given Himself for us an offering and a sacrifice to God," to the "price" with which men "are bought," and to "the Lamb of God taking away the sin of the world,"—and these are realities of Scripture,—pass without any incongruity to the necessity of faith as a means of appropriation, to the inability of the law to justify, and to the blessed fact that the same law has no power to condemn believers—they being dead to it—while their faith originates a new life within them, of which Christ is the true vital element? Nay, might not a man put all this as the record of his own experience? Might not he say, Christ my "passover has been sacrificed" for me; I "have redemption through His blood;" I have been "redeemed with the precious blood of Christ, as of a lamb without blemish and without spot?" And what then should hinder him either to drop altogether the scholastic terms "finite, infinite, satisfaction," or, making his own use of them as the inadequate symbols of momentous truth, to go on to vital union with the Life-giver, and that fellowship with Him in His death which emancipates from legal bondage and gives a community of life with the Son of God in whom faith ever rests. If it be common for divines to do as Prof. Jowett alleges, if it be their normal progress of argument, it is because they have some purpose in view which is different from that of the apostle in this report of his address to Peter. For, in referring to Christ's death in this paragraph, it was foreign to his purpose either to discuss or illustrate such aspects of it as the terms "finite, infinite, satisfaction, and necessity," point to. Neither these words, nor any words like them, are ever used indeed by the apostle, for they had their rise chiefly in mediæval times; but the ideas suggested by them, we will not say represented by them, are occasionally illustrated by him. His object, however, here is to connect the death of Christ subjectively with his own experience which shadows out that of all true believers, and he required not to consider its value, extent, or connection with the divine government. That is to say, the apostle does not himself follow a uniform order of thought on this central theme; and why should blame be insinuated against those who do not follow him in the special style of reasoning adopted here for a specific object and in personal vindication?

Finally, the apostle begins at a point more remote than that selected by Prof. Jowett, from which to start his depreciatory contrast. He commences with an objective declaration that justification is impossible by the works of the law, and that this blessing comes through faith as its instrument,—with an assertion that under this creed or conviction himself and Peter had renounced Judaism and had believed in Christ. But while Peter had recoiled and partially gone back to the law, he would not and could not go back to it, for he had died to the law. He did not need to fortify his position by argument; his own history was conscious and undeniable evidence. Unless, therefore, writers on theological science have a purpose identical with the apostle's before us, there is no reason why they should walk in his steps; nor, if they deviate, are they to be tacitly censured, for in such deviation they may be only following the apostle in some other section of his epistles. Let, then, these "logical determinations" be dismissed as not being scriptural terms, but only inferential conclusions, and not perhaps in all their metaphysical senses and uses warranted by Scripture; still, one may hold the scriptural ideas which by common understanding they are intended to symbolize, and may from them pass over, by closely connected steps and in the apostle's mode, to spiritual experience in its elevation and rapture. There is no occasion, then, to contrast the method which men may ordinarily adopt in the construction of creeds with the apostle's special and limited illustration in the present paragraph. The presentation of doctrine in its scientific aspects and relations is surely a warranted effort, and not incompatible with a living spiritual experience as the result of the truth accepted. A sound creed or Scripture teaching arranged and classified, and a true and earnest life acted on by faith and reacting on it, are not necessarily at opposite poles. Still it had been better if, in our treatises on divinity, it had been more deeply borne in mind—*Pectus est quod theologum facit.* The whole truth contained in an inspired utterance can never be fully expressed by any human dogma; but the divine and illimitable will always outstretch its precision and logic. Confessions of faith, however necessary and exact they may be, are only as cisterns; and no matter how skilfully and capaciously they are hewn out, the water from the living fountain will not be confined, but will always overflow them.

Ver. 21. *Οὐκ ἀθετῶ τὴν χάριν τοῦ Θεοῦ*—"I do not frustrate the grace of God." The verb, which is used first by Polybius, has various shades of meaning. As applied to persons, it means "to despise" or "reject." Mark vi. 26; Luke vii. 30, x. 16 four times; John xii. 48; 1 Thess. iv. 8; Sept. 1 Sam. ii. 17. So Theodoret here has *οὐκ ἀτιμάζω*; Grotius, *non vilipendo;* and the Vulgate, *non abjicio.* The definition of Œcumenius falls short of the full import: *τὸ ἀπιστεῖν, τὸ ἐξευτελίζειν, τὸ διαπαίζειν.* In a stronger sense it denotes "to cast off" or violate, such as *νόμον*, Heb. x. 28, or one's faith, 1 Tim. v. 12; then it means "to annul or make void." This last sense it has in the clause before us; as *τὴν ἐντολήν*, Mark vii. 9; *τὴν σύνεσιν*, 1 Cor. i. 19; Sept. 1 Macc. xv. 27; Ps. xxxiii. 10; Polyb. ii. 58, 5; Gal. iii. 15. The sweeping conclusion *δωρεὰν ἀπέθανεν* shows that this must be its meaning. The "grace of God" is not in a general sense the gospel, nor exactly the work of Christ (Gwynne), though that work was its proof and channel, as the last clause indicates; but His sovereign kindness manifested in the death of His Son, spontaneous on His part and wholly unmerited on ours. See Eph. ii. 4–9. The apostle's realization of identity with his Lord, dying with Him and rising with Him, his conscious possession of Christ as his life within him, and that life moving and being sustained in its element of faith in the Son of God,—all were proofs to him that he was not frustrating the grace of God. For he felt that the one source of justification was grace, and that the medium of it was grace embodied in the incarnate Son. In trusting in Christ, and in Him alone, he was magnifying the grace of God; while Peter, on the other hand, by his reactionary dissimulation, was in effect putting aside that grace. For if any one put faith in works, or revert to works, or in any way, either wholly or in part, give them place in justification, either as opposed to faith or as supplementing it,—if any one hope to merit what God so freely bestows, he frustrates the grace of God, regards it as void, or as an unneeded arrangement. For most surely—

Εἰ γὰρ διὰ νόμου δικαιοσύνη, ἄρα Χριστὸς δωρεὰν ἀπέθανεν—"for if through the law comes righteousness, then Christ died without cause." *Γάρ* introduces strong confirmatory proof. The phrase *διὰ νόμου*, emphatic in position, is in contrast with *Χριστός* in the same position. *Δικαιοσύνη* is supposed by some to be the result of justification (Alford); by others, righteousness imputed and inherent (Ellicott); by others, the possession of *δικαίωσις* (Wieseler). Righteousness is that by which a man becomes right before God—that on his possession of which he is rightened or accepted as righteous in God's sight. Such a basis of justification may come through law, and be personal righteousness, but that is impossible for fallen man. The law which he has broken can only arraign him, convict him, and work his death; works of law can therefore in no sense justify him. Another provision has been made by God, and a righteousness wrought out by the obedience unto death of His Son, becomes his through faith. See under Phil. iii. 9. It comes not *διὰ νόμου*, but *διὰ πίστεως*; and law and faith are antagonistic instrumentalities. But if righteousness did come by the law, then there was no necessity for Christ's death. If man by works of law can justify himself, what need was there that Christ should die to provide for him what he can win for himself?

Ἄρα—"then," "after all"—standing first in the apodosis after the previous conditional sentence—then as an undoubted inference. Matt. xii. 28; Luke xi. 20; 1 Cor. xv. 18; Klotz-Devarius, ii. p. 160.

Δωρεάν does not mean "in vain," *frustra* (Erasmus, Piscator), or *μάτην* (Theophylact), nor *gratis*, as often in classical use. Matt. x. 8; Rom. iii. 24. From this meaning, *nulla prægressa causa*, it comes to signify *sine justa causa*. Tittmann, *Synon.* i. 161, gives it as *nulla erat causa moriendi*. Sept. 1 Sam. xix. 5, *θανατῶσαι τὸν Δαυὶδ δωρεάν*—rendered in our version "without a cause;" Ps. xxxiv. 7, *δωρεὰν ἔκρυψαν*—"without cause they hid for me a net," rendered by Symmachus *ἀναιτίως*, but followed by *μάτην ὠνείδισαν*; חִנָּם being used in both clauses. So Sirach xx. 23, *καὶ ἐκτήσατο αὐτὸν ἐχθρὸν δωρεάν*—"and made him his enemy for nothing;" John xv. 25, *ἐμίσησάν με δωρεάν*—"they hated me without a cause,"—quoted from Ps. xxxiv. 19, *οἱ μισοῦντές με δωρεάν*. Gesenius and Fürst, *sub voce* חִנָּם. If there can be righteousness through the law, Christ's death was uncalled for—was gratuitous; *περιττὸς ὁ τ. Χ. θάνατος*, Chrysostom. The sense is not, if works are necessary, Christ's death is ineffectual or in vain; but, if works can secure righteousness, Christ's death was needless. But Christ's death could not be needless, therefore righteousness comes not of the law; it is the purpose and result of the great atoning sacrifice. His theme is, I do not constitute myself a transgressor; the reason is given, "I do not frustrate the grace of God;" and then the proof contained in the last clause is added. The former declaration was connected with *ἄρα* (ver. 17), and this similarly with the same particle—two conclusions alike absurd and impious, but to which the inconsistency of Peter assuredly led by necessary consequence.

What reply Peter made, or how his subsequent conduct at Antioch was shaped, we know not. Nor know we how the crisis ended—whether the believing Jews recovered their earlier freedom, or whether any compromise was brought about. Yet in spite of this misunderstanding and rebuke, evincing the superior consistency of one of the apostles, tradition, with the exception of the *Clementines*, has placed Peter and Paul on a similar level in many points. The *Apostolical Constitutions* (vii. 46) report Peter as saying, "Evadius was ordained bishop by me at Antioch, and Ignatius by Paul;" but whether simultaneously or in succession, cannot be ascertained.

The same authority adds, that Paul ordained Linus the first bishop of Rome, and Peter Clement as the second bishop. Irenæus says, again, that the church of Rome was founded *a gloriosissimis duobus apostolis Petro et Paulo*—a false assertion indeed, but showing what honour both apostles enjoyed. *Contra Hæres.* iii. 3, 2; *Opera*, vol. i. p. 428, ed. Stieren. Dionysius, bishop of Corinth, as quoted by Eusebius (ii. 25), says, "Peter and Paul planted us at Corinth, and likewise instructed us." And this is very much in the spirit of the Acts of the Apostles, where Peter is found vindicating free Pauline doctrine, and Paul goes into the temple to show that he "walked orderly," while miracles similar in character are ascribed to each. We may hold this opinion without going the length of asserting that the "Acts" was written for the apologetic purpose of defending the apostolate of Paul, or of placing him on the same official standing as Peter. Baur, Schwegler, and Lutterbeck admit that, if judged by the first Epistle of Peter, there is no essential difference between the Pauline and Petrine doctrine. The original apostles are, indeed, found in the temple again and again after the ascension; but after what was agreed to by them at the council, they cannot be justly accused of Ebionitism. The address of Peter at the council pointed indeed at the free and untrammelled admission of Gentiles, while the modifications are proposed by James; but even these restrictions gave up circumcision—the initial rite, the necessity for submission to which had been so fanatically contended for,—and proposed only certain compliances with the national ritual, along with obedience to the law of chastity, for the breach of which Syrian idolatries and the Antiochene grove of Daphne afforded so many facilities and temptations. Still, that conformity to the Jewish ritual should prevail especially in Palestine, is scarcely to be wondered at. Eusebius enumerates fifteen bishops, "all of the circumcision," who held office in Jerusalem prior to the last Jewish rebellion, the church being entirely made up of "believing Hebrews," *Histor. Eccles.* iv. 5. Sulpicius Severus records: *Namque tum Hierosolymæ non nisi ex circumcisione habebat ecclesia sacerdotem . . . pæne omnes Christum Deum sub legis observatione credebant.* *Chron.* ii. 31; *Opera*, vol. i. 36, ed. Halm, Vindobonæ 1866. Jerome describes the church at Alexandria founded by Mark, Peter's *interpres et disciplus*, as *adhuc judaizans*, that is, in the period of Philo, *De Viris Illust.* viii.[1] But the insurrection under Bar Cochba brought the vengeance of Hadrian upon the capital, and by him the Jews were forbidden to enter it under its new heathen title of Ælia Capitolina. Christians had on the other hand free permission to settle in this Roman colony; and then, the Jewish element being so thoroughly eliminated, the church elected Marcus as the first Gentile bishop or "presiding elder." Probably Jews who had fully renounced Judaism, who had denationalized themselves in embracing Christianity, might also be enfranchised. But the exiled Jews of the stricter party, who clung to their old Judaism like ivy to a ruined tower, and clung to it all the more keenly on account of this proscription, repaired to Pella, their refuge under the first siege, and the Ebionite community so originated survived till the fifth century. In course of time the Christian element had nearly faded out among them, and, as Origen informs us, there was little left to distinguish them from ordinary Jews. There were, however, various modifications both in the theology and practices of the party; and a section called Nazarenes, the original Jewish appellation of believers, were noted for their more orthodox creed and for their stern anti-pharisaic tendencies. See Neander; Lechler, *das Apostol. u. das nachapostol. Zeitalter*, p. 235.

NOTE ON CHAP. II. 11

Κατὰ πρόσωπον αὐτῷ ἀντέστην—"I withstood him to the face, because he had been condemned."

THIS scene at Antioch—Peter's dissimulation and Paul's rebuke—was soon laid hold of by infidel opponents to damage the truth of Christianity. Jerome in the preface to his *Commentary on Galatians* refers to Porphyry, who took such an advantage of the altercation,[2] and under ii. 11 he puts this

[1] Compare Schwegler, *Nachapost. Zeitalter*, i. p. 113.

[2] *Volens et illi maculam erroris inurere et huic procacitatis et in commune ficti dogmatis accusare mendacium, dum inter se ecclesiarum principes discrepent.*

alternative: *ad extremum, si propter Porphyrii blasphemiam, alius nobis fingendus est Cephas.* Opposing parties also in these early times made the most of the occurrence. The Ebionites through it attacked Paul, as in the *Clementines*, in which Peter assaults the apostle of the Gentiles under the name of Simon Magus. We need not say a word about the date of the *Clementines—Homilies* and *Recognitions.* Nor need we discuss the critical opinions of Schliemann, Hilgenfeld, Uhlhorn, and Ritschl as to their relations and origin; nor the elaborate efforts of Neander, Credner, Baur, and Schwegler to evolve their doctrinal system.[1] Suffice it for our present purpose to say, that in the letter of Peter prefixed to the *Homilies* he says, "Some of those among the Gentiles have rejected my lawful preaching—*νόμιμον κήρυγμα*, having embraced the lawless and foolish teaching of the enemy,"—"hostile man"—*τοῦ ἐχθροῦ ἀνθρώπου.* "Some have tried by diverse interpretations to shape my words into an abolition of the law—*εἰς τὴν τοῦ νόμου κατάλυσιν*, as if this were my sentiment, and I did not dare openly to preach it;"—with more to the same purpose, in evident allusion to the *ὑπόκρισις* charged upon him at Antioch. *Homiliæ*, pp. 4, 5, ed. Dressel. In Homily xvii. 19 (p. 351, *do.*) Peter then refers in sneering depreciation to the visions and revelations which Paul enjoyed, and places his own honours and privileges in very favourable comparison—the personal instructions of the Divine Teacher for a year being put into contrast with instructions for but an hour, adding: "For me, being a firm rock, the foundation of the church, as an adversary thou hast withstood; if thou hadst not been an enemy, thou wouldest not have reviled me and calumniated my preaching, that I might not be believed when I declared what I had heard from the Lord myself in His presence—as if I were condemned, and not to be approved; or if thou calledst me condemned, thou accusest God who revealed Christ to me."[2]

[1] Uhlhorn supposes an earlier work than either the *Homilies* or *Recognitions* to have existed among the Elxaites in eastern Syria, and argues that the *Recognitions* are a recasting of the *Homilies*, because the quotations from the New Testament in the former agree better with the canonical text. But this better harmony may have been the work of the Latin translator, though he certainly professes a strict adherence to his original.

[2] See the critical note of F. Wieseler in his appendix to Dressel's edition of the *Clementinorum Epitomæ duæ*, pp. 308, 309, Lipsiæ 1859.

The reference is plainly to this section of Galatians. The phrases ἐναντίος ἀνθέστηκάς μοι—ἐμοῦ καταγνωσθέντος—ἤ εἰ κατεγνωσμένον με λέγεις, are borrowed from it. That Simon represents the Apostle Paul is now generally agreed. Many proofs may be found in Schliemann's *Clementinen*, p. 96, and in Zeller, *Die Apostelgeschichte*, p. 158. This opinion is denied, but on insufficient grounds, by Ernest de Bunsen (*Hidden Wisdom*, vol. ii. pp. 12–14), who, however, regards these documents as genuine, and "as based on originals dating from apostolic times."

On the other hand, the conflict at Antioch afforded an opportune handle for Marcion to depreciate Peter, and to prove the direct opposition of the true gospel to Judaism. Irenæus thus meets the objection: "This dispute about the law did not argue a different origin to it from the gospel."[1] Tertullian, occupied with the same objection, rebukes his opponents thus: *credunt sine scripturis ut credant adversus scripturas;* and his explanation is, that Peter's fault lay not in his preaching, but in his life—*utique conversationis fuit vitium non prædicationis.*[2]

This Antiochene controversy was thus sadly misunderstood, and its meaning perverted for sceptical and polemical purposes. But it did not touch the truth of the gospel, nor militate against the inspiration of the apostles. For inspiration does not charge itself with the government of personal conduct, but is connected only with official labour done in Christ's name. Peter's momentary timidity, so like himself, and yet so unworthy of him, did not influence his preaching, since he acted against his own theory, and shrunk from his asserted freedom. Peter and Paul preached all the while the very same gospel,

[1] *Religiose agebant circa dispositionem legis, quæ est secundum Moysem ab uno et eodem significantes esse Deo.*—Vol. i. p. 494, ed. Stieren, Lipsiæ 1853.

[2] *De Præscript. Hæret.* xxiii.; *Opera*, vol. ii. p. 22, ed. Oehler. . . . . . *Tamen doceant ex eo quod allegant Petrum a Paulo reprehensum aliam evangelii formam a Paulo superductam citra eam quæ præmiserat Petrus et ceteri. . . . . Non enim ex hoc alius Deus quam creator et alius Christus quam ex Maria, et alia spes quam resurrectio.* See also i. 20, p. 69, *ib. Plane reprehendit, non ob aliud tamen quam ob inconstantiam victus, quem pro personarum qualitate variabat, non ob quam divinitatis perversitatem.*—*Advers. Marc.* v. 3, p. 280, *do.*

though at this startling crisis Peter did not act in harmony with it, but allowed earlier feelings to acquire for the time a second and cowardly predominance. To eat with one of another nation had been his first abhorrence; and though a vision helped him, nay, forced him, to surmount the antipathy, it had never wholly died out within him. Traditionary education and habit produce certain associations which may have a dormant co-existence with a better creed, but which in an unexpected hour and under strong temptation may reassert the mastery. To make a bold assertion, and then on a sudden to recoil from it, had been Peter's temperament. "Lord, bid me come to Thee on the water," was in a few moments followed by "Lord, help me!"—the avowal, "Though all men forsake Thee, yet will not I," "though I should die with Thee, yet will I not deny Thee," was only a prelude to the denial a few hours afterwards, "I know not the man;"—"Thou shalt never wash my feet," was said one instant, but the next brought out the changed desire, "Lord, not my feet only, but also my hands and my head." His answer to those who "contended with him," saying, "Thou wentest in to men uncircumcised, and didst eat with them," had been, "God hath showed me that I should not call any man common or unclean," and his intrepid conclusion had been, "What was I that I could withstand God?" Nay, to those who insisted on the Gentiles being circumcised and keeping the law of Moses, his reply had been noble and unfearing: "God made choice among us that the Gentiles by my mouth should hear the word of the gospel. Why tempt ye God, to put a yoke upon the neck of the disciples?" And yet, after all this undaunted and unreserved vindication, he turns his back on himself, abjures his own protest, and in a fit of weakness bows his own neck to that very unbearable yoke. Paul's record of the scene shows how free and open the founders of the church were—without any collusion which a misunderstanding might break up, or any compact the fraudulent basis of which a sudden alienation might expose. The worst that could be said of Peter was, that overawed by the presence of "certain from James" and the mother church, he fell into a momentary vacillation; and that his courage and constancy sank for a time under a conservative influence, before which even Barnabas, first the patron and then the colleague of Paul, and filled with no small portion of his spirit, quailed and fell.

In this debated matter of Gentile freedom, while others stumbled or advanced with unsteady step—for theirs were but "broken lights"—Paul moved onwards without hesitation or pause, and by his single courage and consistency secured to the churches a liberty which, though it might be grudged or suspected in many quarters, could not be withdrawn, but has descended as an invaluable legacy to modern times. As he knew Peter's character, it must have cost him a pang to confront him whose name stands first in all the catalogues of the apostles; but the claims of truth were paramount. The unhappy entanglement of Barnabas in the controversy, and this rebuke, in which he must have shared, perhaps helped to exacerbate the misunderstanding or "contention" which soon afterwards severed the two fellow-labourers, when they "departed asunder the one from the other." Who that knows anything of human nature will not sympathize with Peter in his sudden weakness, so characteristic of persons of his temperament, which, without a steady self-control and true all the while to the ultimate motive, so vibrates under proximate influences as to swerve for a season into devious courses? His dissimulation was an honest obedience to the impulse of the moment, and that impulse was the sudden awakening of early and deep impressions. What bitter regrets must have followed such aberrations! what prayers for a steadier walk and for an unbroken unity of will! what reluctance to forgive himself, even though he had the assurance of divine forgiveness! But it needed the greater nature of Paul to ward off the injuries which such tergiversation was so certain to produce. He was a stranger to that infirmity by which Peter had been overtaken. With an emotional nature as profound though not so variable as Peter's, his temperament was as decided as it was ardent, as lofty as it was inflexible. He saw truth on all sides of it, both in theory and result, in germ and in development; and obstacles unforeseen by others did not, as they started up, so surprise him as to make him question or re-examine his leading principles.

It is pitiable, therefore, to see what shifts have been resorted to in order to explain away a scene so life-like in the case of Peter, and so true to his character in that of Paul. And first it was hinted that this Cephas was not the Apostle Peter, but another bearing the name, and who was one of the seventy disciples. This opinion was started by the Alexandrian Clement. In the fifth book of his *Hypotyposeis*, as cited by Eusebius, when speaking of the Cephas whom Paul withstood to the face at Antioch, he says: *ἕνα γεγονέναι τῶν ἑβδομήκοντα μαθητῶν, ὁμώνυμον Πέτρῳ τυγχάνοντα τῷ ἀποστόλῳ. Hist. Eccles.* 1–12, pp. 75, 76, vol. i. ed. Heinichen. Eusebius simply reports the opinion without controverting it; but his neutrality is construed by Œcumenius into positive agreement, —with the addition, *καὶ πιθανὸς ὁ λόγος*, the argument being the great moral improbability of its being that apostle who had seen the vision and baptized Cornelius, and who had already stood out so boldly on the subject—*οὐ γὰρ ἦν ὁ εἰπὼν ταῦτα.* Jerome repeats the same conjecture, though he does not hold it; adding, that its advocates argue that Luke makes no mention of the dissension, or ever places Peter and Paul together at Antioch—*et locum dari Porphyrio blasphemanti; si autem Petrum errasse, aut Paulus procaciter apostolorum principem confutasse credatur.* Chrysostom, in his homily on the clause, "I withstood him to the face," refers to the same opinion, but asserts that it is refuted by the context—*καὶ ἐκ τῶν ἀνωτέρω καὶ ἐκ τῶν μετὰ ταῦτα. Opera*, vol. iii. p. 446, Gaume, Paris 1837. Gregory the Great mentions it too, but denies it.[1] Nay, this Cephas appears in the list of the seventy in the *Paschal Chronicle: Κηφᾶς ὁμώνυμος Πέτρου ᾧ καὶ ἐμαχήσατο Παῦλος κατὰ Ἰουδαϊσμοῦ*; and in the list ascribed to Dositheus, the martyred bishop of Tyre, the addition is made: *Κηφᾶς ὃν ὁ ἀπόστολος Παῦλος ἐν Ἀντιοχείᾳ ἤλεγξεν, ὅς καὶ ἐπίσκοπος Κονίας ἐγένετο. Chron. Pasch.* vol. i. p. 400, vol. ii. p. 126, ed. Dindorf, Bonn 1832. This wholly groundless

[1] *Patet ergo de quo Petro Paulus loquitur, quem et apostolum nominat et præfuisse evangelio circumcisionis narrat.* In the previous paragraph also, when telling that Paul rebuked Peter, and Peter called him afterwards *charissimus frater noster*, he adds: *quatenus qui primus erat in apostolatus culmine esset primus et in humilitate.—Homil. in Ezek.* lib. ii. Hom. vi.; *Opera*, vol. ii. pp. 1002–3, ed. Migne, Paris.

opinion has not wanted favourers in more modern times, as may be seen in Vallarsi's editorial note on Jerome, which has also guided us to some of the previous references. Hardouin the Jesuit revived it, and its refutation in Deyling's *Observ. Sac.* (cap. xlv. vol. ii. p. 520) degenerates ultimately into an antipapal polemic. See also Calmet, *Dissert.* tom. iii. p. 519, Paris 1720. This absurd opinion originated in a fear that the great apostle of the circumcision might be disparaged; but it is rightly and honestly repudiated by many exegets and controversialists who owe allegiance to the chair of St. Peter.

To gain a similar end, another method was adopted; and it was held that the dispute was only a feigned one, the apostles being quite agreed in opinion, and that the scene was got up in order that Peter might submit to a rebuke, as a lesson to the Judaizers who were censured and condemned in him. Jerome asserts that Origen first propounded this extraordinary notion.[1] Jerome himself adopted it, and it was advocated by Chrysostom,[2] first in his *Commentary on Galatians*, and also in a separate treatise referred to in the footnote.[3] The Latin father, who, according to Luther, "neither understood this place, nor the whole epistle besides," in various ways justifies this acting of a lie, *quasi in publico contradicens.* The apostles must have been at one, he argues; for Paul was just as much committed as Peter by "shaving his head in Cenchrea, for he had a vow," by his carrying offerings to Jerusalem, and by his circumcision of Timothy, so that, *ejusdem simulationis tenebitur reus.* Then he asks in triumph, "How, then, could Paul resist and rebuke with a good grace, when himself was guilty of similar inconsis-

[1] His words, in a letter to Augustine, are: *Hanc autem explanationem quam primus Origenes in decimo Stromateôn libro, ubi epistolam Pauli ad Galatas interpretatur, et ceteri deinceps interpretes sunt sequuti, illa vel maxime caussa subintroducunt, ut Porphyrio respondeant blasphemanti, qui Pauli arguit procacitatem,* etc.—*Epist.* 112; *Opera*, vol. i. ed. Vallarsi.

[2] *Quid dicam de Joanne qui dudum in Pontificali gradu, Constantinopolitanam rexit Ecclesiam; et proprie super hoc capitulo latissimum exaravit librum, in quo Origenis et veterum sententiam est sequutus.*—*Ep.* 112, *do.*

[3] The treatise of Chrysostom thus referred to by Jerome is in the third volume of his works, p. 431, Gaume, Paris, and is a homily preached at Antioch on the clause—Κατὰ πρόσωπον αὐτῷ ἀντέστην.

tencies?" This *tu quoque* reply is heartily and admiringly endorsed by Stap in his *Etudes,* an attempt to popularize the criticism of the Tübingen school for French readers.[1] But the proofs adduced do not come at all under the same category of personal inconsistency or hypocrisy. Jerome then refers for an instance of *utilis simulatio* to the treachery of Jehu, without which the priests of Baal could not have been assembled to be all massacred. "Call unto me all the prophets of Baal, all his servants, and all his priests: let none be wanting; for I have a great sacrifice to do to Baal," were also the words of Elijah. But the adduction of such a case is truly as melancholy as his next is ridiculous, which is David's feigning of madness for his personal safety at Gath. Another of his proofs is based on the publicity of the rebuke; for such publicity, if the censure were genuine, would, in his opinion, be a direct violation of the Master's precept, "Tell him his fault between thee and him alone." But the inconsistency of Peter was no private offence; it scandalized the entire Gentile portion of the church. His next reference to the practices of pleaders in the Roman forum is pithily put, but is still farther from the point, and needs not be replied to. Chrysostom, in the midst of his rhetoric, is as precise as Jerome. In his commentary his deliverance is, "Peter's conduct, as Paul well knew, was dictated by two secret motives: to avoid offending the Jews, and to give Paul a good opportunity for animadverting. . . . Now that the one refutes, and the other submits, the Jewish faction is seized with great fear."[2] His explanation of the clause *κατὰ πρόσωπον ἀντέστην* is *σχῆμα ἦν,* it was a feint, or merely in outer appearance; for if they had been in earnest, they would not in public have censured each other. Peter's inconsistency was only a sham—*ὡς ἁμαρτάνων*—that the Judaizers through him might be rebuked. The plot was this: "If Paul had reproved these Jews, they would have been indignant and contemptuous, for they held him in small honour; but when they saw their

[1] *Etudes historiques et Critiques sur les Origenes du Christianisme,* par A. Stap, 2d ed., Paris 1866.

[2] *Δύο ταῦτα οἰκονομῶν, καὶ τὸ μὴ σκανδαλίσαι τοὺς ἐξ Ἰουδαίων, καὶ τὸ παρασχεῖν τῷ Παύλῳ εὔλογον τῆς ἐπιτιμήσεως πρόφασιν. . . . Διὸ καὶ Παῦλος ἐπιπλήττει καὶ Πέτρος ἀνέχεται ἵνα ἐγκαλουμένου τοῦ διδασκάλου καὶ σιγῶντος εὐκολώτερον οἱ μαθηταὶ μεταθῶνται.*

teacher under rebuke and yet silent, they could not despise nor gainsay what was spoken."[1] Chrysostom is eloquent on the impossibility of one who had spoken and acted as Peter had, falling into the alleged inconsistency. In his homily on the subject his motive is apparent, for he espoused the theory on account of the bad use that was made of the incident—*παρὰ τῶν ἔξωθεν καὶ τῶν τῆς πίστεως ἀλλοτρίων*. "Would not one," he adds, "be struck with terror if he heard that the pillars of the church had come into collision? The great wisdom and benevolence of the two apostles would have prevented them from coming into actual strife. Could Peter be a coward—*δείλος καὶ ἄνανδρος*—he to whom the name of Rock had been given; who had himself been the first to confess the Messiahship and boldly to preach it; whose ardent impulses outstripped all his fellows, and who had protested before the rulers, 'We cannot but speak the things which we have seen and heard;'—could he who had been so bold at Jerusalem in the midst of enemies waver at Antioch—*ἐν τῇ Χριστιανικωτάτῃ πόλει*?" Time, place, and circumstances alike forbid the thought. Besides, Paul, who was "as weak to the weak," was too modest and loving, and must have had too much respect for Peter's prerogative, to have rebuked one, to make whose acquaintance he had not long before gone up to Jerusalem, and with whom he had sojourned fifteen days. This, and a vast deal more poured out in impassioned declamation and challenge, does not touch the matter. In the case of a man of Peter's temperament, it is dangerous to argue from only one side of his antecedents, leaving the other side in discreet abeyance, such as his boast and his subsequent denial of the Master. Similar things will be found in Œcumenius, and in Theophylact, who calls the dispute *σχηματισθεῖσα μάχη*. Theodoret's commentary is wanting at this part; but he elsewhere characterizes Peter's conduct as dissimulation—*καὶ τῷ Πέτρῳ σχηματισαμένῳ τοῦ νόμου φυλακήν*. *Op.* vol. ii. p. 536, ed. Sirmondi.

The interpretation of Jerome came at length into the hands

[1] Εἰ μὲν γὰρ τοῖς ἐξ Ἰουδαίων ὁ Παῦλος ἐπέπληξεν, ἠγανάκτησαν καὶ διέπτυσαν· οὐ γὰρ πολλὴν περὶ αὐτοῦ δόξαν εἶχον· νυνὶ δὲ τὸν διδάσκαλον ὁρῶντες ἐπιτιμώμενον καὶ σιγῶντα, οὔτε καταφρονῆσαι, οὔτε ἀντειπεῖν τοῖς λεγομένοις εἶχον; and in this the Greek father discovers πολλὴν σύνεσιν.

of Augustine,[1] and greatly shocked him,[2]—*non mediocriter doleo*. *Ep*. 28, probably A.D. 394 or 395. He wrote at once to Jerome as the reputed author—*quædam scripta quæ tua dicerentur;* but he was not perfectly sure—*si alius illa scripsit.* He puts the case very plainly, not as one of lying on the part of good men, but whether it behoved the writers of sacred scripture to lie. The same allegation, he adds, may be made regarding other passages, such as those regarding marriage, 1 Tim. iv. 3. The authority of Scripture is thus destroyed—*nusquam certa erit in sanctis literis castæ veritatis auctoritas.* Augustine writes firmly, but in all modesty—*nec me onerosum aut impudentem judices.* This first letter does not touch the context, nor its bearing on the subject; it deals only with ethics, and not with criticism. In another letter (*Ep*. 40) he refers to the same subject, and enters into it more fully in its various aspects, has a word on the value of Origen's authority, and urges Jerome to sing a palinode, "for the truth of Christendom is more incomparably beautiful than the Grecian Helen." Augustine is in profound earnest, and yet quite without arrogance. *Nequaquam vero mihi arrogaverim ut ingenium tuum divino dono aureum, meis obolis ditare contendam.* The first letter, which had been entrusted to Profuturus, had been lost in the conveyance, but its contents had got into general circulation. Jerome's temper was none of the best, and this supposed slight was enough to exasperate him. He could not bear to be attacked by a younger rival (*Ep*. 102). Through Sysinnius the deacon, he had got, he says, a copy of a letter purporting to be addressed to him—*epistolæ cujusdam quasi ad me scriptæ,*—in which Augustine urged him to recant and imitate Stesichorus.[3] If the letter be genuine, he

[1] The letters of Jerome are quoted as numbered in the first volume of his works edited by Vallarsi, Venetiis 1769; and those of Augustine, as in the second volume of his works published *apud Gaume fratres*, Paris 1836.

[2] *Opera*, vol. ii. p. 68, *ib*.

[3] The legend was, that Stesichorus, "the poet of Himera" in Sicily, wrote an attack on Helen, and was punished with blindness for the libel; but recovered his sight on composing a recantation—a palinode. Pausanias, iii. 19, 11, vol. i. pp. 541-2; *Opera*, ed. Schubart, Lipsiæ 1838. The unlucky allusion stuck fast in Jerome's memory, and again and again he makes reference to it, as in a sense "the unkindest cut of all."

bids him *aperte scribe, vel mitte exemplaria veriora.* Augustine explained afterwards that the person entrusted with the letter had neither delivered it nor returned it. Jerome was therefore suspicious and irritated, because he had seen only an anonymous copy of a document, which, though addressed to himself, he had never received, while the attack upon him found in it had come to be generally known in Rome and over the churches. Augustine solemnly denied on oath that he had circulated any book against Jerome. *Deum nostrum testor hoc me non fecisse* (*Ep.* 67.) It turned out, however, as Augustine admitted afterwards, that this denial was caused by the distinction which he made between *liber* and *epistola.* He had not written any *liber* against Jerome, nor had he sent that ill-fated *epistola* to the capital. But Jerome was not aware of this at the time, and consequently his indignation begins to glow at what he reckoned unhandsome treatment, and he warns his youthful tutor of the juvenile weakness of crowing over illustrious men, as if it were a way to fame. He reminds him that the writer (Jerome) had had his day; and lest Augustine should suppose that poetic allusion was specially his property, he hints in return for the reference to Stesichorus, that Entellus, aged though he was, might crush the younger Dares.[1] In another communication (*Ep.* 105) Jerome returns to the letter on the subject which had been circulated in Africa and in Italy; and he plainly suspects Augustine of using undue means for its publication, as it had never reached him, save in some anonymous form. Busy friends, too, had been at his elbow—*familiares mei et vasa Christi,* and they had insinuated doubts of Augustine's integrity of motive, and the hints officiously whispered in his ear lose nothing through his telling of them. The old and suspicious story of the letter, and Augustine's denial of its authorship, again turn up with the sharp innuendo: "Thou hast not written, and yet how are there brought to me reports of my being censured by you? If the book is not yours, deny its authorship; if yours, say so honestly, that I may write in my defence."[2] Augustine had quietly asked Jerome to cor-

[1] Virgil, *Æneid,* v. 362, etc.

[2] *Quod autem juras te adversum me librum nec scripsisse, neque Romam misisse quem non scripseris. Non scripisti librum et quomodo mihi reprehensionis a te meæ per alios scripta delata sunt? Cur habet Italia quod tu*

rect anything wrong in his works; but Jerome tartly retorts, "that he had not given special attention to them, and had seen indeed but few of them, but that there were opinions in his book on the Psalms not consonant to the views of the old Greek interpreters." The next letter of Augustine (*Ep.* 73) is a long and pointed one. It takes up the allusion to Entellus and to his own works—*fortasse dura sed certe salubria verba;* reciprocates his protestations of love; declares that he wrote about the Galatian *Comment.* when he was a young man, and that now, though he was an old man, he had got no reply. Probably ten years had elapsed, so slow was correspondence in those days. The letter is occupied not with recriminations certainly, but it shows that the writer had been touched by some of Jerome's hard words: "If we cannot correct what may be wrong in one another's writings without suspicion of envy, or breach of friendship, let us give it up—*quiescamus ab his et nostræ vitæ salutique parcamus;*" and he ends with sentences of noblest Christian charity. So boldly challenged, Jerome replied at length (*Ep.* 112), perhaps A.D. 404, to what he calls *tres epistolas imo libellos breves.* In the introduction and at the end he purposely omits all compliments, even those with which his opponents had tried to soften his censures. In defence of his *Commentary on Galatians*, he quotes a portion of the preface which enumerates the authorities which had been consulted by him—Origen, Didymus, the Laodicene (Apollinaris), Alexander (an ancient heretic), Eusebius of Emesa, and Theodore of Heraclea; and he challenges Augustine to produce one supporter of his view. The old arguments are then repeated: the various points of Peter's life; his sayings and doings which make the tergiversation ascribed to him so unlikely, for he was the first to advocate the freedom which he was now accused of having deserted; and then he sets upon Paul, to show him guilty of the very course for which he reprehended Peter.[1]

non scripsisti? Qua ratione poscis, ut rescribam ad ea quæ scripsisse te denegas? . . . Igitur aut tuum negato librum, aut si tuus est ingenue confitere; ut si in defensionem mei aliqua scripsero, in te culpa sit qui provocasti, non in me, qui respondere compulsus sum.

[1] *O beate Apostole Paule, qui in Petro reprehenderas simulationem, quare subtraxisset se a gentibus propter metum Judæorum qui ab Jacobo venerant, cur Timotheum filium hominis gentilis, utique et ipsum gentilem (neque enim*

The abuse which Porphyry had made of the scene is still the stumblingblock which Jerome could not surmount or thrust aside. Augustine had spoken in a previous letter of the comparative harmlessness of a Jew observing the Mosaic institutions of his country, that being a different thing from fixing their observance on the Gentiles; but with striking inconsistency, Jerome's blood boils at the thought, and he declares the opinion to be vilest error bordering on Ebionitism;[1] and this thought is elaborated in various ways, and with increasing vehemence. The letter then passes into some biblical questions, among which the proper Latin translation of Jonah's "gourd"[2] is a source of irritation; and it draws to a close with a request to be let alone, so as not to be provoked into further contest, and with an advice to Augustine—who, though young, was a bishop—to teach the people and enrich the Roman church with the fruits of his African genius; concluding with a sigh, perhaps of wounded pride—*mihi sufficit cum auditore et lectore pauperculo in angulo monasterii susurrare.* To this epistle Augustine sent a distinct and formal reply (*Ep.* 82), in which he carefully reviews all the points of the argument; lays stress on Paul's declaration, "When I saw that they walked not uprightly according to the truth of the Gospel,"—a handle to the falsifying Manichæans if it were not true; analyses the conduct and motives of Paul; shows that his becoming a Jew to the Jews was *non mentientis astu, sed compatientis affectu;* dwells on the relations of the law to believers; throws off all Jerome's authorities but three as being heretics; opposes to them the two fathers Ambrose and Cyprian; and asserts that if he had read much, he could easily have found a third (*ut tres tribus opponam*). In default, however, of a third, he will summon the apostle himself, and ask him if, when he accused Peter, he had spoken *dispensativa falsitate;* and his reply is, what he had stated in a previous verse, "Now the things which

Judæus erat qui non fuerat circumcisus) contra sententiam tuam circumcidi coegisti? Respondebis mihi; propter Judæos qui erant in illis locis. . . . Qua igitur fronte, qua audacia Paulus in altero reprehendit quod ipse commisit?

[1] *Ego e contrario loquar, et reclamante mundo, libera voce pronuntio: cæremonias Judæorum, et perniciosas esse et mortiferas Christianis; et quicumque eas observaverit sive ex Judæis, sive ex gentibus, eum in barathrum diaboli devolutum.*

[2] Whether it should be *hedera* or *cucurbita.*

I write unto you, behold, before God I lie not." The epistle concludes with warm expressions of attachment, and some undervaluing of Jerome's biblical labours. To this last letter Jerome does not seem to have replied. Augustine gives another and a very clear and succinct view of the subject in his *De Mendacio*.[1] The reasoning of Augustine must have told upon Jerome; but there is no answer extant to Augustine's last epistle. Jerome's pride was hurt: the beginning of the correspondence had been so awkward and unfortunate, that it had given him an adverse bias; the allusion to Stesichorus evidently rankled in his mind, as it is often alluded to in his letters; he expected his opponent to pay greater deference to his age and standing, and had some suspicions of his motives; and he was ruffled by his calm and dignified arguments and expostulations, to which he answered in a style of vaunting vehemence. In attempting to vindicate Peter from a charge of inconsistency, and Paul from that of procacity, he really finds both of them guilty of a darker sin by far when he describes them as conspiring to act what Augustine calls *officiosum mendacium*. But it would seem that afterwards and on reflection Jerome was at length convinced of his error, and he appears to have adopted the view which Augustine had so warmly and conclusively pressed upon him. In his treatise or dialogue *Contra Pelagianos*, written after this correspondence, he gives the honest and straightforward view, and at the end of it he refers to his former opponent as *vir sanctus et eloquens episcopus Augustinus*.[2] In his tract against Jovinian the same view is given as a passing reference;[3] similarly in the midst of a few sharp words at

[1] *Qui et Petrum coram omnibus in rectam viam revocavit, ne gentes per eum Judaizare cogerentur, et ipse suæ prædicationi attestatus est, qui cum putaretur hostis paternarum traditionum, eo quod nolebat eas imponere gentibus, non aspernatus eas more patrio celebrare, satis ostendit hoc in eis Christo adveniente remansisse, ut nec Judæis essent perniciosæ, nec gentibus necessariæ, nec jam cuiquam hominum salutares.*—Vol. vi. p. 718, *ib.*

[2] *Opera*, vol. ii. 804, *ib.* In the same treatise he says: *Si enim ipse apostolus dicit de Petro, quod non recto pede incesserit in evangelii veritate et in tantum reprehensibilis fuerit, quis indignabitur id sibi denegari quod princeps apostolorum non habuit* (*ib.* p. 718); and all this to show that when it is affirmed that a bishop ought to be *irreprehensibilis*, the epithet is not to be taken in a universal sense, because *aut nullus aut rarus* can claim the epithet.

[3] *Et certe castigaverat Galatas Petrumque reprehenderat quod se propter

the beginning of his tract against Ruffinus;[1] and again in his *Commentary on Philemon*, *Opera*, vol. vii. p. 755. In these places there is only a simple allusion to the scene at Antioch, but such an allusion as would honestly seem to imply his conviction of the reality of the dispute, involving the error of Peter and the necessity of the rebuke. Only, he makes these references without a syllable indicative of his own past or present opinion. But the dates are uncertain, and some of those treatises may have been written during the correspondence; if so, Jerome did not hold his view tenaciously, though he could not but accept the challenge of an opponent and junior rival who was in no way abashed before his age, fame, and position. It was not in him to make a formal acknowledgment of defeat in such circumstances. Yet no matter how Porphyry reviled Christianity through its two apostles, he could say nothing of them so severe as Origen and Jerome had said of them, in asserting that they had conspired to act a hollow drama. A traditionary halo was already gathering round Peter, and the veracity of Paul must be sacrificed to save Peter's consistency, as if infallibility of conduct and the utter elimination of every human element of character were a necessary result of a divine commission. It was, however, quite like Peter and his antecedents to shrink in a moment from a perilous and bold step, and quite as like Paul to rebuke without a moment's hesitation such cowardice. The straightforward meaning of his words in his own account of the occurrence, must therefore be maintained. Honest interpretation must be listened to, no matter what traditionary dogma it upsets, or what unwelcome inferences may be suggested by it. Augustine's opinion prevailed in the western churches, even though it exposed a constitutional weakness in their great primate's character. In a word, Augustine believed that Jerome had changed his opinion, yet he does not take any credit for producing the change.[2] But

observationes Judaicas a gentibus separaret.—Adversus Jovin. vol. ii. p. 264, *ib.*

[1] *Nonne idem Paulus in faciem Cephæ restitit quod non recto pede incederet in Evangelio?—Advers. Ruffin.* vol. ii. p. 532, *ib.*

[2] To Oceanus he writes (*Ep.* 180, vol. ii. p. 948): *Sed quid hinc diutius? cum de hac quæstione inter nos, ego et prædictus venerabilis frater Hieronymus satis litteris egerimus; et in hoc opere recentissimo, quod sub nomine Critobuli adversus Pelagium modo edidit, eamdem de ista re gesta*

there is uncertainty still about Jerome's real or ultimate view, for in his *Commentary* on Isa. liii. 12 (perhaps A.D. 410) he says, those who regard the controversy between Peter and Paul as real *ut blasphemanti Porphyrio satisfaciant, debent et auream in mille annis expectare Jerusalem.* Zöckler's *Hieronymus, sein Leben und Wirken*, p. 275, Gotha 1865.

Some remarks on this controversy may be found in Thomas Aquinas, *Summæ Theologicæ prima secundæ*, Quæst. 103, Art. 4, vol. ii. p. 849; *et secunda secundæ*, Quæst. 43, Art. vi. vol. iii. p. 349. The first volume of Moehler's *Gesammt. Schriften* contains a paper on this subject, giving a fair critical estimate of the controversy. He says that Jerome put himself into the position of many whose zeal for truth and goodness is greater than their insight into what is true and good, and Augustine's last letter (82) he characterizes as crushing Jerome's argument *mit der Gewalt eines überlegenen Geistes.*

dictisque apostolicis sententiam tenuit, quam beatissimi Cypriani etiam nos secuti sumus. Cyprian's opinion so referred to is found in one of his letters, in which he says of Peter when rebuked by Paul: *Nam nec Petrus quem primum Dominus elegit et super quem ædificavit ecclesiam suam, cum secum Paulus de circumcisione postmodum disceptaret, vindicavit sibi aliquid insolenter aut arroganter assumpsit, ut diceret se primatum tenere et obtemperari a novellis et posteris sibi potius oportere. Nec despexit Paulum quod ecclesiæ prius persecutor fuisset, sed consilum veritatis admisit.*—*Ep.* 71, *Opera*, ed. Fell, vol. ii. 194-5, Bremæ 1690. Similarly thought also Zosimus of Tharassa at the Council of Carthage, A.D. 256. Compare Tertullian, *De Præscrip.* 23; *Contra Marc.* iv. 3; Gregory the Great, Hom. vi. lib. ii. in Ezek. vol. ii. p. 1002, *Op.* ed. Migne; and Cyril. Alex. vol. ix. p. 999, ed. Migne.

CHAPTER III

THE apostle has now finished his self-vindication. He has maintained his apostleship to be divine in origin and in fulness of prerogative; and the discussion at Antioch proved his equality with Peter, nay, it evinced his superiority as compared with the momentary relapse and dissimulation of the apostle of the circumcision. His rebuke of Peter does not rest simply on logical argument, but it has its source and power in the living depths of his own spiritual experience. The address as here presented concludes the first portion of the discussion, and is so moulded in its parting words that it naturally introduces us into the second division of the epistle. The object of this second or theological part is to illustrate and defend the doctrine of a free justification through faith, without the works of the law. He concludes his address to Peter by affirming, "I do not set aside the grace of God;" but all who rest justification on legal merit put aside divine grace. I am not guilty of this error, nor can I, for the Son of God died for the great and blessed purpose of providing pardon and acceptance: you Galatians knew this—"for Christ was set forth in you, crucified." How foolish, then, to fall away from Him, to resile for justification to the works of the law, and so to nullify the grace of God, and bring on you the fearful but inevitable conclusion that the death of Christ was superfluous and unneeded, and might have been dispensed with!

Having therefore vindicated his apostolic prerogative, he now turns sharply round on his readers, and, as their sudden change seemed so inexplicable, he cries—

Ver. 1. *Ὦ ἀνόητοι Γαλάται*—"O foolish Galatians!" "O senseless Celts!" The epithet *ἀνόητος*, sometimes taken among the classics in a passive sense, but always having an active sense in the New Testament when applied to persons (Luke

xxiv. 25; Rom. i. 14; 1 Tim. vi. 9; Tit. iii. 3), means foolish—acting in a spirit which manifests the absence of wisdom. Tittmann, *De Syn.* p. 144. The apostle does not, as Jerome wrongly supposes, charge them with foolishness as a national characteristic—*regionis suæ proprietas*. Their temperament was rather different. It was not stupidity, but fickleness; not dulness, but susceptibility so quick as to be at variance with decision and permanence. Their folly showed itself in that facility of fascination by which they had been characterized. True, indeed, Callimachus says,

> *αἳ Γαλάτῃσι κακὴν ὁδὸν ἄφρονι φύλῳ*
> *στήσονται.*—*Hym. εἰς Δ.* 184, p. 33, ed. Blomfield.

On the other hand, Themistius calls the Galatians *ὀξεῖς καὶ ἀγχίνοι καὶ εὐμαθέστεροι τῶν ἄγαν Ἑλλήνων. Orat.* 23. See Wernsdorf, *de Republica Galatarum*, p. 268. Jerome informs us, too, that Hilary, *Gallus ipse et Pictavis genitus*, calls his own race, in one of his Hymns, *Gallos indociles*.[1] The *ἄνοια* had showed itself in the senseless change which they had made. See Introduction. Chrysostom is anxious to vindicate the apostle's use of such an epithet from being a violation of Christ's law, Matt. v. 22. The Syriac reads ܚܣܝܪܝ ܪܥܝܢܐ —"deficient in understanding."

Τίς ὑμᾶς ἐβάσκανεν;—in some of the Greek fathers, etc., *ἐβάσκηνεν* (Winer, § 15; A. Buttmann, p. 35)—"who bewitched you?" This expressive verb still indicates the apostle's surprise, as if he could not explain their change, or as if ordinary causes could not account for it. *Βασκαίνω* (not as the scholiast on Aristophanes puts it = *φάεσι καίνειν*—"to kill with the

[1] Jerome had spoken of the word Galatia as connected with the Hebrew גלה, to migrate, as if their name had indicated their fickleness—*Galatia translationem sonat in nostra lingua.* Weinrich, for the same purpose, connects the name with גלגל, *rota: Comment. in Ep. ad Galat.* p. 119; see Borger *in loc.* Luther brings the matter home thus: *Quinam putant nos Germanos oriundos esse ex Galatis. . . . In omnibus enim rebus sub initia prima valde calemus, ut ubi deflagravit is ardor primorum affectuum mox sumus remissiores.* Lactantius, in a work not extant, had, as Jerome tells us, connected the name with *γάλα*, milk, as if they had been so named *a candore corporis*—which some have improved upon, as if the apostle here meant to stigmatize them as sucklings. The name of Lac-tantius himself has been fancifully supposed to image the milk-like character of his style.

eyes," but) from *βάζω, βάσκω*—Latin, *fascino* (Benfey, ii. 104),—signifies to hurt by an evil tongue, to slander, then to talk over, or mislead by insidious speech. The word occurs only here in the New Testament. The eye is sometimes the organ of witchery as well as the tongue. *Βασκαίνων τῷ ὀφθαλμῷ*, Sirach xiv. 8; "*oculus obliquus*," Horace, *Ep*. i. 14, 37; also Virgil, *Eclog*. iii. 103. It is not in unison with the context to take the verb, with the Greek interpreters, as signifying to envy, for the word with that sense usually governs the dative (Lobeck, *Phryn*. 463), but sometimes the accusative also, with an ideal difference. Jelf, § 589, 3, obs. 2. Chrysostom renders it *τίς ἐφθόνησε*;—who has envied you? your previous privileges excited envy. Jerome adds that the evil eye was specially hurtful to the young, and therefore to the Galatians, as they were but recent converts—*in Christo fide nuper nati*. The stress is on *ἡμᾶς*, "you:" who has juggled you?—you, who possessed and so appreciated your high privileges,—he must have wielded very uncommon powers of fascination. In *τίς* there is no reference to the seducer's imagined piety or power, as Brown thinks; nor is there any apology, as Luther supposes, in the question, as if he "laid the fault on the false apostles." Prof. Lightfoot lays too much stress on the mere popular image employed by the apostle, and Hammond supposes that sorcery was practised. Winer, *Real-Wört.*, art. Zauberei.

The next clause of the Received Text, *τῇ ἀληθείᾳ μὴ πείθεσθαι*—"that you should not obey the truth"—is generally rejected as without authority, and as having been probably taken from v. 7. It is not found in A, B, D[1], F, ℵ, nor in many versions and fathers. There was also some doubt about the reading in Jerome's time—*in exemplaribus Adamantii non habetur*. The reason why the apostle, in his sorrow and surprise, puts the striking question is now given. Their privilege having been so great, it was passing strange that they should have been so quickly tempted to abandon it.

Οἷς κατ' ὀφθαλμοὺς Ἰησοῦς Χριστὸς προεγράφη ἐν ὑμῖν ἐσταυρωμένος—" before whose eyes Jesus Christ was evidently set forth in you—crucified."[1] The words *ἐν ὑμῖν* are not

[1] Macknight gives, "crucified for you," and innocently adds—"the common translation of this clause is not true: Christ was not crucified among the Galatians." Tirinus puts it alternately: "either in Judæa,

found in A, B, C, א, and were omitted, perhaps, because they were not understood, or were regarded as superfluous. But as they create a difficulty, it is almost impossible to regard them as an interpolation. Much depends on the meaning assigned to προ in προεγράφη—whether the local meaning of *palam*, "openly," or the temporal meaning of *antea*, "before." The phrase κατ' ὀφθαλμούς and the classical usage seem to favour the former, and it is espoused by Winer, Usteri, Rückert, Wieseler, Ewald, Schott, Lightfoot, and Hofmann; but the Pauline usage is as strong for the latter (Rom. xv. 4; Eph. iii. 3), which is adopted by Erasmus, Beza, a-Lapide, Trana, and Meyer. The simple verb sometimes signifies to paint or depict, but not so the compound, though Jowett translates, "as in a picture was set." The meaning then is, that Jesus Christ had been at a prior period, or when Paul preached to them, described to them κατ' ὀφθαλμούς, so that as the placard fronted them they could easily comprehend it. Comp. Sept. 2 Chron. xxxii. 23, Jer. lii. 10, Ezek. iv. 12, xxi. 6; Aristoph. *Ranae*, 626. Compare κατ' ὄμμα, Eurip. *Androm.* 1064; Soph. *Antig.* 760. There is no reference to the foreannouncements contained in the prophets (Jerome, Hermann). The ordinary reading of the Vulgate is *præscriptus est*, but some codices have *proscriptus;* and Augustine, Ambros., and Lyra take the words in a kind of legal sense—"*pro-scribed*"—Rheims Version. The Claromontane has *proscriptus est in vobis.* This sense it sometimes has. Comp. Aristoph. *Aves*, 450; Demosthenes, vol. ii. p. 228, ed. Schæfer; Dio Cass. ii. p. 46, ed. Bekker; Jude 4. The phrase ἐν ὑμῖν cannot be regarded as tautological nor as epexegetical of οἷς, nor does οἷς preceding and agreeing with it form a Hebrew construction, אֲשֶׁר בָּכֶם. Winer, § 22, 4. It is annexed to προεγράφη as a species of local qualification—in you. This division of the words is better than to assign ἐν ὑμῖν to the ἐσταυρωμένος, as if the sense were—crucified among you, the idea of Calvin, Borger, and Matthies; or, for, or on account of you (Koppe), or by you. Ἐν ὑμῖν, bearing the emphasis (compare ἐν ἐμοί, i. 1, and ii. 20), shows the nature of the description, or where it could be read. Compare 2 Cor. iii. 2.

near you, or by some of you who happened to be present in Jerusalem;" while the Jesuit Gretzer argues that the apostle's language implies the use of pictures and crucifixes.

Before their eyes had it been posted, and in them was it apprehended. What the apostle preached, they accepted. It was not unintelligible, or they might be pardoned. It was not a transient impression meant only for the senses; it had penetrated into them. They understood, appreciated, and believed. Had it not been openly made, and inwardly understood and realized, there would have been no wonder at the sudden revolution; for men cannot hold tenaciously anything of which they have no just perception or cordial appreciation. Had it been only *κατ' ὀφθαλμούς*, it might have faded away; but it was also *ἐν ὑμῖν*, and therefore the apostle was amazed that it should so very soon lose its hold. There is no need of taking *ἐν ὑμῖν* in any proleptic sense, "So that in you He becomes a crucified one," or dead, as Jatho, and his references to Bremi and Stallbaum are not to analogous instances. Nor is there any allusion to Jewish phylacteries or to heathen amulets: "Your frontlet of faith—Christ crucified" (Wordsworth).

And there is special moment on the last word *ἐσταυρωμένος*, not to be diluted by "as if" (Turner), but the One who has been crucified, who still in this character is preached, or who still maintains the relation of a crucified One. Winer, § 45, 1. The previous and patent presentation of Christ Jesus was of Him as the Crucified One (1 Cor. i. 23, ii. 2); and Theophylact adds, that with the eye of faith they saw the cross more distinctly than *τῶν τότε παρόντων καὶ θεωμένων*. The theme of preaching was Christ crucified, and it was the object of commemoration in the Lord's Supper. The death of Christ really involved the whole question in dispute, and the *ἐσταυρωμένος* of this verse repeats the fact of the previous verse, "He gave Himself," nay, is an echo of an earlier utterance—"I have been crucified with Christ." He had made atonement by His obedience and sufferings, and had thus provided a free and complete salvation received through faith in Him. This doctrine of salvation by His blood they had accepted; and what then could induce them to turn away so speedily, and seek by the law of Moses what they had believed to be attainable only by the cross? Luther's notion is strange and foreign to the point, and the image is unnatural here, that the Galatians had by their inconsistency crucified Christ afresh: Heb. vi. 6. So Ambros., Storr. Out of place also is Bengel's view, that the form of

His cross was so portrayed in their hearts that they might be crucified with Him (Windischmann, Ewald); and Cajetan's, that by their sufferings they had become partakers of Christ's sufferings; and that of Mar. Victor., that in persuading them to follow Judaism, their enemies crucified Christ in them. Hofmann, without any good reason, divides the clauses by a comma after *I. X.*—"*abrupt und gewaltsam*," as Moeller in De Wette calls it. The same remark may be made on the punctuation proposed by Matthias.

Ver. 2. *Τοῦτο μόνον θέλω μαθεῖν ἀφ' ὑμῶν*—"This only I would learn of you." This only—this one thing out of many; for this one point is sufficient for the purpose, and is in itself decisive of the controversy. There is no irony in the language (Luther); he wished information on this one point. Acts xxiii. 28; Sept. Ex. ii. 4, 2 Mac. vii. 2; Soph. *Œd. Col.* 504; Xen. *Hell.* ii. 1, 1. *'Αφ' ὑμῶν* is less direct or immediate than *παρ' ὑμῶν*. Winer, § 47, 2, note. The one thing so conclusive of their folly lies in the question—

'Εξ ἔργων νόμου τὸ Πνεῦμα ἐλάβετε, ἢ ἐξ ἀκοῆς πίστεως;—"Did ye from the works of the law receive the Spirit, or by the hearing of faith?" The meaning of *Πνεῦμα* is restricted erroneously, by Chrysostom, Jerome, and others, to miraculous gifts. It is no argument on the part of Schott and Meyer against this view, that the apostle writes to the entire churches, and that only a fraction could enjoy the *χαρίσματα,* because the gift of a few was really the gift of the church at large, as a church may be said to enjoy a revival though all its members without exception may not have partaken of the heavenly gift. That the *Πνεῦμα* included extraordinary gifts is evident from ver. 5; but that it included greatly more is evident from its contrast with *σάρξ* in the next verse, from the allusion of the 14th verse, and from the entire strain of the epistle, especially of the fifth chapter. The Holy Spirit was the characteristic possession of believers. To settle a previous dispute, Peter had said, "The Holy Ghost fell on them as upon us." Though the Spirit was bestowed under the law, it was with scantiness; but fulness of gift was a prominent element of the promise in Joel ii. 28. That fulness seemed to overflow at the first descent, and miracles, tongues, and healings were the result—as if the prismatic sparkling of the baptism of fire. The

Spirit, as the originator and sustainer of the new life, is the special endowment of believers, and was received openly and visibly by many of the converts to Christianity from Judaism.

What, then, was the source of that spiritual influence possessed by them? Was it *ἐξ ἔργων νόμου—ἐκ*, as in ii. 16, denoting origin or cause—the works of the law, which have the law for their object and are done to fulfil it?

The precise meaning of *ἀκοὴ πίστεως*—which, however, cannot mean "faithful hearing" (Gwynne)—has been disputed. The noun *ἀκοή* may be taken either in an active sense—the hearing of faith, that is, the hearing or reception of that gospel in which faith is the distinctive doctrine, in which it is presented as the rule of life; or in a passive sense—that which is heard of faith—that "report" or message which holds out faith as its prominent and characteristic element—"the preaching of the faith" (Tyndale). *Πίστις* is used generally in a subjective sense (see i. 23). The passive sense is the prevailing, if not the only one of *ἀκοή* in the New Testament. Matt. iv. 24; John xii. 38; Rom. x. 16, 17; 1 Thess. ii. 13; Heb. iv. 2. Herod. ii. 148; Plato, *Tim.* 23, A, D. It represents in the Sept. the Heb. שְׁמוּעָה, a passive participle. The contrast also justifies this meaning: on the one hand are works done, on the other hand a report or declaration is made—states of mind quite opposite. Works done in obedience to law is the one alternative, the presentation of a message about faith is the other. The contrast is not so defective as Jowett supposes. Schott and Sardinoux represent that the parallelism of the contrast demands, that as the first clause is subjective, the second must be subjective too. Granted that the first clause is subjective, the second is all the stronger a contrast that it is objective—works that ye do, placed in opposition to a report brought to you. Did they receive the Spirit in obeying the law, or in so trying to obey it as to merit eternal life by it? or was it when the message of faith was preached to them, and they embraced it? for it is to the period of the introduction of the gospel that the apostle refers. They could at once determine the matter—it was one of experience and history. The apostle does not give the answer, for he knew what it must be. It was under the hearing of faith that they first enjoyed the Spirit—that Spirit which enlightens, sanctifies, certifies of sonship, makes inter-cession for us as being in us, seals us, and is the earnest and first-fruits. Opposed to usage and correctness is the interpretation of Rollock, Matthies, and Wahl, that *ἀκοή* stands for *ὑπακοή*—obedience. It is needless to object, with Gwynne and Hofmann, that the hearing of the gospel does not in itself secure the gift of the Spirit, as the apostle is alluding in the contrast to open and usual instrumentality. Jerome starts and answers the question—*si fides non est nisi ex auditu quomodo qui surdi nati sunt possunt fieri Christiani?* It is needless to debate the question raised by De Wette and Wieseler, whether, as the first holds, the parties specially addressed were Jews or proselytes once under the law, or whether, as the second maintains, they were Gentiles who had never been under the law at all. The challenge, however, has a special point as spoken to Jews, to whom their law had been everything.

Ver. 3. *Οὕτως ἀνόητοί ἐστε;*—"Are ye so very foolish?"—*οὕτως* being used of degree or extent: i. 6; Mark vii. 18; John iii. 16; Heb. xii. 21; *οὐκ ἔστιν οὕτω μῶρος ὃς θανεῖν ἐρᾷ*, Soph. *Antig.* 220; Xen. *Cyr.* ii. 2, 16. The folly is again noticed, and the *οὕτως* refers to it.

Ἐναρξάμενοι πνεύματι, νῦν σαρκὶ ἐπιτελεῖσθε;—"having begun in the Spirit, are ye now being completed in the flesh?" The words *ἐναρξάμενοι* and *ἐπιτελεῖσθε* occur in Phil. i. 6. See also 2 Cor. viii. 6. The two datives are those of manner. Winer, § 31, 7; Bernhardy, p. 101. The two clauses are so arranged in contrast, that they make what grammarians call a Chiasma. Jelf, 904, 3. They had begun in or with the Spirit; that is, the beginning of their spiritual life might be so characterized. His influences, enjoyed through the hearing of faith, are the commencement—the one way in which life is to be enjoyed and sustained. The natural course would be, begun in the Spirit, and in the Spirit perfected—reaching perfection in Him as He is more copiously given and His influences work out their end more thoroughly, and with less resistance offered to them. But the apostle adds abruptly, "are ye now being carried to perfection in the flesh?" The verb *ἐπιτελεῖσθε* contains more than the idea of end as in contrast to that of commencement in *ἐναρξάμενοι*, the notion of perfection being in it, not simply and temporally—but a perfect end ethically. 1 Sam. ii. 12; Luke xiii. 32; Rom. xv. 28;

2 Cor. vii. 1, viii. 6; Rost und Palm, *sub voce.* The verb may be either middle or passive. In the former it often occurs in the classics, but usually with an accusative of object. Windischmann, De Wette, Hilgenfeld, Ewald, Bisping, Hofmann, Wieseler, and Winer so take it here. Some in this way render, "Are ye now for finishing—do ye think that you can finish or be perfect, or do ye seek to be perfected, or do ye bring yourselves to perfection?" But the passive form only is found in the Septuagint and the New Testament, and thus Chrysostom and others regard it; the Vulgate has *consummamini.* The use of the present (not the Attic future, Usteri) implies that they were at the moment cherishing this mistaken perfection. The language, perhaps, is not irony, but springs from a deeper source. It depicts their own experience and their folly. Is it possible that you can suppose that a beginning in the Spirit can be brought to maturity in the flesh? Are ye so senseless as to imagine it? Are you living under such a delusion? As the *ἀνόητοι* is repeated in his fervour from the first verse, it being there the warning epithet; so *πνεύματι* comes from the second verse, it being there the testing word. By *πνεῦμα* is meant here again the Holy Spirit—the Life and Power of the gospel which fills the spirit of believers, and not vaguely the gospel itself; and by *σάρξ* is designated, not the Jewish dispensation, but the sensuous element of our nature, which finds its gratification in the observance of ceremonial or of external rites. See under Phil. iii. 4; Rom. iv. 1. It is too restricted on the part of Chrysostom, Rückert, and Schott to give *σάρξ* any immediate reference to circumcision, though it is not excluded; and too vague on the part of Theodoret to render *πνεῦμα* by *χάρις*, and on the part of Winer to describe it as *indoles eorum qui mente Deum colere didicerunt.* The folly was extreme—to go back from the spiritual to the sensuous, from that which reaches the soul and fills it with its light, life, and cheering influence, or from the gift of Pentecost, to the dark economy, which consisted of "meats, and drinks, and divers washings." Shall he who has been conscious of his manhood, and exulted in it, dwarf himself into a child, and wrap himself in swaddling bands? It was so foolish to turn round so soon after they had so auspiciously begun; though there is no allusion here or in the context, as Wolf and Schott think, to the

image of a race. Lightfoot's allusion to a sacrifice is far-fetched; as is the similar notion of Chrysostom, that the false teacher slew them as victims.

Ver. 4. *Τοσαῦτα ἐπάθετε εἰκῇ; εἴ γε καὶ εἰκῇ*—"Did ye suffer so many things in vain, if it be really in vain?" We hold this to be the right translation of the verb, that it has not a neutral sense, and that it cannot be used *in bonam partem*—"have ye experienced so many blessings in vain?" The verb has such a meaning in extra-biblical writings, but not in itself—never having it when used absolutely, such a sense being determined by the context, or by the addition of such words as *εὖ, χάριν, ἀγάθα*, etc. Rost und Palm, *sub voce;* Joseph. *Ant.* iii. 15, 1; *ἀγαθὸν καὶ κακὸν πάσχουσι*, Artemidorus, iv. 67; *παθὼν ἀγαθὸν μέγα*, Theognis, 342, p. 20, ed. Welcker; *ὧν πέπονθεν οὐκ ἔχει χάριν*, Chares, *ap. Stobæi Florileg.* xvii. 3, vol. i. p. 345, ed. Gaisford; Kypke and Raphel. *in loc.*, and Hombergk's *Parerga*, p. 278; Bos, *Ellips.* p. 131. In Homer and Hesiod it never has such a sense at all; nor in the Hellenistic Greek (Septuagint and Apocrypha); nor in the New Testament, though it occurs in it above forty times, and eleven times in the Pauline writings. But this meaning is given it here by Schomer, the first apparently to propose it, and by Borger, Flatt, Homberg, Winer, Wieseler, Bagge, Holsten, Sardinoux, De Wette, Usteri, Schott, Trana, Ewald, Hilgenfeld, Jowett, and the lexicographers Robinson, Wahl, Bretschneider, and Wilke. The sense then will be, Did ye experience so many things,—or, "Have you had all those experiences in vain?" (Jowett.) But the proper translation is the natural one—"Did ye suffer so many things in vain?" Such a reference to previous suffering is surely not "unlike the noble spirit of the apostle;" for he is rebuking that inconsistency which, as it turns its back on blessing, forgets the lessons of persecution. The Syriac appears to favour this view—"have ye borne;" and the Vulgate has *passi estis*. But if the verb do refer to suffering, what sufferings are spoken of? Not

1. Suffering with the apostle himself, though they had borne with him most patiently. Such is Bengel's view, unsupported alike by the diction and by the context. Nor is it

2. Sufferings of bondage which were brought upon them by their false teachers. For, as Alford remarks, a different tense would have been employed, as the apostle would consider them

as suffering from that source still. But the aorist refers to a specific period in their past history. The appeal would also be in vain; for the Galatians, so long as their delusion lasted, would not admit that they were suffering in this sense. The ceremonial under which they were brought was hailed by them as a means of perfection, and not a source of suffering. The apostle alludes to a previous epoch. And

3. To the sufferings endured by them on their first conversion, when the Crucified One was so vividly set before their very eyes, and they received the Spirit, and began in the Spirit. Thus Theodoret, *ὑπὲρ τοῦ Χριστοῦ τὰ παθήματα*; and Augustine, *multa jam pro fide toleraverant.* It is objected, first, that there is no historical account of persecution endured by the Galatian churches; but the silence of the Acts of the Apostles can furnish no argument. The record is there so very brief and incidental—it is not even a sketch. We cannot suppose that the Jews were less busy in Galatia than in other places, as at Antioch in Pisidia, Lystra, and Thessalonica. 1 Thess. ii. 13, 14.[1] The probability is, that the Galatians suffered like so many of the infant churches, and suffered just because they professed faith in the doctrines of the cross—apart from any Jewish modification, supplement, or admixture: v. 11, vi. 12. It is objected, secondly, by Meyer and Usteri, that the idea of suffering is not in harmony with the course of thought. But surely the appeal is quite in keeping with previous statements. The argument rests on the folly of the Galatians. It was folly to be so bewitched as to revert to the law, which did not and could not give them the Spirit; folly to begin in the Spirit, and apostatize to the flesh which could not perfect them; and folly assuredly all the more unaccountable, after they had suffered so severely for their first and opposite views and opinions. They were so foolish as to renounce blessings which they had once prized, nay, for which they had also undergone persecution. Men naturally cling to that for which they have suffered, but they had in childish caprice flung it away. The apostle thus appeals first to what they had enjoyed,

[1] Justin Martyr boldly says, as if the fact were notorious and undeniable, "Other nations have not inflicted on us such wrongs as you have;" adding, that "chosen men were sent from Jerusalem" to stir up the heathen governors against the Christians.—*Dialog. cum Tryph.* § 17.

and then to what they had endured, as the proof of their folly —their senselessness. See under Phil. i. 29.

Εἴ γε καὶ εἰκῇ—"if indeed they be in vain." The particle εἴγε, different from εἴπερ, does not express doubt,—the usage, according to Hermann, being, *εἴπερ usurpatur, de re quæ esse sumitur sed in incerto relinquitur utrum jure an injuria sumatur; εἴ γε, autem, de re quæ jure sumpta creditur. Καί* signifies truly or really—if it really be in vain. Klotz-Devarius, ii. 308; Hartung, i. 136. If what has been said is true, and it must be true, those sufferings are in vain—though he is loath to believe it. There is therefore no need, first, to weaken the sense, and render the clause, *si modo frustra, si modo dicere ita liceat* (Morus); nor secondly, with the Greek fathers, and many others, as Bengel and Hofmann, to suppose the apostle as hinting, on the one hand, that possibly after all the εἰκῇ might be prevented; nor, thirdly, with Augustine, Meyer, Wieseler, etc., as surmising, on the other hand, that worse than εἰκῇ may be dreaded—*ne ad perniciem valeat.* The Syriac reads, "And I would—ܘܐܝܠܘ—that it were in vain."

Ver. 5. *Ὁ οὖν ἐπιχορηγῶν ὑμῖν τὸ Πνεῦμα, καὶ ἐνεργῶν δυνάμεις ἐν ὑμῖν, ἐξ ἔργων νόμου, ἢ ἐξ ἀκοῆς πίστεως;*—"He then that ministereth to you the Spirit, and worketh miracles in you, doeth He it by the works of the law, or by the hearing of faith?" The οὖν is continuative, or rather resumptive,—is "then," not "therefore," taking up again, after a momentary digression, the question of ver. 2, which has not yet been formally answered. The first participle ἐπιχορηγῶν signifies to furnish, to minister to: Sir. xxv. 22; 2 Cor. ix. 10; Col. ii. 19; Eph. iv. 16. Its original meaning in connection with the furnishing of a chorus on some public occasion is lost sight of, and the generosity of the act, not the purpose of it, remains in the verb. *Χορηγοῦσι οἱ πλούσιοι*, Xen. *Athen.* i. 13. The ἐπί does not signify, as often, "additional," but probably specifies direction. The Spirit came down ἐπί—upon them. Of that Spirit so furnished, the apostle gives a specimen—*ἐνεργῶν δυνάμεις ἐν ὑμῖν.* The ἐν is not "among," as Winer and others take it, but "in," its natural sense. Matt. xiv. 2; 1 Cor. xii. 6; Phil. ii. 13. These δυνάμεις are works of power, which the Spirit alone can effect—the result of His influence and inhabitation. They are not, perhaps, to be confined to miracles, but may comprehend other results of divine energy. The Galatian believers were conscious of the Spirit's presence and working within them, as they had felt the pulsations of the new life, and perhaps could speak with tongues, and they were therefore prepared to answer the interrogation. But there are two questions—What is the tense of the participles? and to whom does the apostle refer? Peter Lombard, Erasmus, Macknight and even Augustine, Doddridge, Riccaltoun, and Brown understand the apostle to apply these participles to himself—"out of modesty declining to name himself" (Locke). In some inferior sense they might be true of him. But the apostle was not likely so to characterize himself as if he stood in God's stead. Could he say that he furnished the Spirit when he was only at best the vehicle of communication, or that he wrought these miracles in them when his hands simply conveyed the energy? The participles portray the source, and not the mere medium. In fact, these two clauses give only the reverse view of ver. 2. There the reception of the Spirit is spoken of, here it is the donation of the Spirit; there it is man who gets, here it is God who gives. See also under i. 6.

Nor do the participles refer to the same point of time with ἐλάβετε, as they are not aorists. The Greek commentators, followed by Semler and Bengel, take them as imperfects, and as referring to the time when the apostle was among the Galatians. But as the reference is to God, it is most natural to take the participles as presents; and the present tense may refer not specially to divine gift as continuous, but may be used in a substantival sense to characterize God as the Giver,—this function of supplying the Spirit specially belonging to Him. Winer, § 45, 7. See under i. 23. God, whose prerogative it is to give the Spirit and work miracles,—does He, is He in the habit of giving the one and doing the other by the works of the law or by the hearing of faith? In the second verse of the chapter the apostle refers to the period when they received the Spirit; and in this verse, while he refers to God, it is to God not simply as giving the Spirit at that precise period, but to the principle on which He usually acts, or the instrumentality which He usually employs, in the bestowment of such gifts. See under ver. 2.

Example is often more pointed and powerful than theoretical illustration, just as for geographical instruction a map excels a verbal description of a country. The Jews boasted of Abraham, their forefather, and of their being Abraham's progeny. "We be Abraham's seed" was their characteristic vaunt, and they believed that because of this relationship all spiritual blessing was chartered to them. Matt. iii. 9; John viii. 33. Some of their sayings were—"All Israel hath part in eternal life;" "Great is the virtue of circumcision—no circumcised person enters hell." "Your Rabbins," said Justin Martyr, "delude themselves and us in supposing that the kingdom of heaven is prepared for all the natural seed of Abraham, even though they be sinners and unbelievers." See Wetstein on Matt. iii. 9. Such being their trust in Abraham and in lineal descent from him, his justification was a ruling precedent for all those who truly hoped to be saved after his example. If he, then, was justified without circumcision, and prior to it, how could Judaizers insist on its necessity? But his justification was prior to his circumcision, nay, his circumcision was but the seal of a righteousness already possessed by him. Abraham was not circumcised in order to be justified; he was circumcised because he was justified. Let the example of Abraham, then, decide the controversy, for Judaizers cannot in loyalty refuse to be bound by it. It is surely enough for you to be as he was, and to accept the doctrine which his life suggests and embodies. Ought it not by common consent to be a divine precedent to all generations? At once, then, without warning, and without any connecting particle, does he add—

Ver. 6. *Καθὼς 'Αβραὰμ ἐπίστευσε τῷ Θεῷ, καὶ ἐλογίσθη αὐτῷ εἰς δικαιοσύνην*—"Even as Abraham believed God, and it was counted to him for righteousness." The apostle does not answer his own question: he takes for granted that every one will reply, "By the hearing of faith,"—faith being the leading term, which is now illustrated in the case of Abraham. He thus passes so far from the point of the interrogation, which was the supply of the Spirit, and takes up another topic—justification by faith. But by *καθὼς* both themes are associated, as indeed they really are in ver. 3. The reception of the Spirit implies justification, and is a blessing either dependent upon it or collateral with it. So related to each other are the two gifts, that the apostle binds them together in the following illustration, which, after dwelling on law, curse, faith, righteousness, life, returns to the leading question as answered in ver. 14.

The connecting compound *καθώς* (a later form of *καθά*, *Phryn.* ed. Lobeck, p. 426) is not to be causally rendered as by Gwynne—"Forasmuch as Abraham believed God, therefore know ye," etc.; for such abruptness mars the consecutive force of the argument, since *καθώς* introduces the illustrative example. The verse is a quotation from Gen. xv. 6, as given in the Sept., and as in Rom. iv. 3, Jas. ii. 23. The Hebrew of the last clause is somewhat different: וַיַּחְשְׁבֶהָ לּוֹ צְדָקָה, "and He counted it to him as righteousness." The nominative to the verb *ἐλογίσθη* in the Greek translation is *τὸ πιστεῦσαι.* The meaning of *εἰς* after *λογίζεται* has been viewed in various ways. Some give it the sense of destination, one of its common uses—his faith was counted unto, or, in order to, righteousness; that is, it was the means of securing righteousness to Abraham. Writers on systematic theology have generally adopted this exegesis, as indicating the connection of an instrumental faith with the righteousness of Christ. Thus Gerhard, *Loci Com.* i. vii. 238: *Fides . . . dicitur nobis imputari ad justitiam quippe cujus est organum apprehendens.* Many also have held that faith must mean here the object of faith,—"that," as Bishop Davenant says, "being ascribed to faith itself which is due in reality to Christ." *Disputatio de Justitia*, cap. xxviii. Others take it as the state of mind which was regarded by God as true faith, and therefore instrumental to the obtaining of righteousness. But the phrase seems to be more idiomatic in meaning, and, according to Fritzsche, *λογίζεταί τι εἴς τι* is equivalent to *λογίζεταί τι εἰς τὸ ὥστε εἶναι τι*—*ita res æstimatur, ut res sit, h.e. ut pro re valeat.* Fritzsche ad Rom. ii. 26. The one thing is regarded as being the other thing, or its equivalent. Thus Acts xix. 27, the temple of the great goddess Diana *εἰς οὐδὲν λογισθῆναι*—"should be counted for nothing," or regarded as nothing; Rom. ii. 26, *οὐχὶ ἡ ἀκροβυστία αὐτοῦ εἰς περιτομὴν λογισθήσεται;*—"shall not his uncircumcision be counted for circumcision?" the one state being regarded as the other state; Rom. ix. 8, *ἀλλὰ τὰ τέκνα τῆς ἐπαγγελίας λογίζεται εἰς σπέρμα*—"but the children of the promise are counted for a seed," or are reckoned as a seed. So too in Septuagint: 1 Sam. i. 13, *καὶ ἐλογίσατο αὐτὴν Ἠλεὶ εἰς μεθύουσαν*—"and Eli regarded her (Hannah) as a drunk woman;" Isa. xl. 17, *καὶ εἰς οὐδὲν ἐλογίσθησαν αὐτῷ*—"and they (all the nations) are counted to Him for nothing"—*quasi non sint, sic sunt coram eo* (Vulg.); Wisd. ix. 6, "for though a man be never so perfect among the children of men, yet if Thy wisdom be not with him," *εἰς οὐδὲν λογισθήσεται*—"he shall be counted for nothing," or, as in the Authorized Version, "he shall be nothing regarded." Such an idiom is plainly tantamount to a simple predication. Compare Wisd. v. 4, xv. 15; Mark x. 8. The preposition is used in the same way after verbs denoting to make or constitute, as Acts xiii. 22, v. 36; with the verb of existence—"they shall be *εἰς σάρκα μίαν*," Matt. xix. 5; or after *γίνεσθαι*—*ἐγένετο εἰς δένδρον μέγα*—in our version, "waxed a great tree." Acts v. 36, vii. 21; Rom. xi. 9; 1 Cor. xv. 45; Bernhardy, pp. 218, 219. See also Rost und Palm, *sub voce*, p. 804. This interpretation gives no support to the theory that the verb *by itself* means to impute or reckon to another what does not belong to him—the notion of Jonathan Edwards, Arminius, and many others, who confound the signification with the sense of the term. Nor will its use in Philem. 18 justify such an assumption, for there the meaning is settled by the circumstances and the context. It is the same with the corresponding Hebrew verb חָשַׁב, which, when it means to reckon to any one, does not by itself determine whether such reckoning be rightly or wrongly made. This inferential or ethical sense is to be gathered from the connection. According to this idiom, the faith of Abraham was accounted to him as his righteousness, or God regarded his faith as his righteousness.

The factitive verb *δικαιόω* is peculiar in its uses, and occurs 37 times in the New Testament. It is used absolutely of God, Luke vii. 29; of man, Luke x. 29, Rom. ii. 13; and also relatively, as in a judicial sense, Ps. lxxxii. 3, Matt. xii. 37. In the general classical use of the word in reference to acts or events, there is a kind of legal element involved, or a judgment formed or a decision come to (Thucyd. v. 26); and in the case of persons, the verb means to act justly toward them, to right them, to put them in a right relative position. And so the verb came to denote to condemn, to punish, to put a criminal in a right position in reference to the law and society.[1] Thucyd. iii. 40; Herod. i. 100; Ælian, *Var. Hist.* v. 18. In the Septuagint it represents the *Pihel* and *Hithpahel* of צָדַק, the former, צִדֵּק, at least five times—Job xxxii. 2, xxxiii. 32; Jer. iii. 11; Ezek. xvi. 51, 52—in all which vindication is the idea, righting one's self or others by a judgment pronounced. The *Hiphil* הִצְדִּיק occurs many times. In Ex. xxiii. 7, Deut. xxv. 1, 1 Kings viii. 32, 2 Chron. vi. 23, Isa. l. 8, it describes God's vindication or judicial approval; in 2 Sam. xv. 4, Job xxvii. 5, Ps. lxxxii. 3, Prov. xvii. 15, Isa. v. 23, it is used of men, and of them under a legal aspect, as of Absalom promising to right every suitor who came to him, or that he would declare in his favour,—of Job vowing that he could not vindicate or pronounce sentence of acquittal on his criminators—"miserable comforters,"—of judges who are summoned to give decisions based on character, and who, if they act in a contrary spirit, have a woe pronounced on them, and are, from their unjust sentences, "an abomination to God." The phrase as occurring in Dan. xii. 3 is of doubtful meaning, and the word in Isa. liii. 11 involves the question under discussion. The Greek term is frequently found, besides, in the Septuagint and Apocrypha with a similar reference, though not always so distinctly as in the previous instances,—the reference in the majority of cases being to an opinion or a judgment uttered or an acquittal pronounced, and not to heart or character made better inherently. The phrase in Ps. lxxiii. 13 is an apparent exception, where, however, ἐδικαίωσα represents a different Hebrew term, זָכָה, and it is the rendering in several places of the Hebrew

[1] In mediæval Latin, *justificare* meant to condemn. *Non tam justitiam exercere quam judicio dato damnare, vel per judicium compellere.* Du Cange, *sub voce.* "Justify" had the same meaning in old Scotch. Thus in Pitscottie's *History* it is said, "Writings were brought to the Duke of Albany, telling him that he should be justified on a certain day"—*i.e.* executed. In the *Complaint of Scotland,* "He gart bryng furth the presoners to be justifiet" = to execute justice on them. The words of Bellendene, "the child was justifiet in presence of mony peple," are rendered by Boethius—*multis conspicientibus furcâ est suspensus.* James IV., in a letter to Charles VII. of France, says, "The chief rebels who were found in the camp"—*pœna suspendii justificavimus*—"we have justified by hanging." See Jamieson's *Scottish Dictionary*, under Arettyt—Justifie. Hesychius gives only this meaning. See *Cicero in Verrem.* v. 57.

שָׁפַט, to judge. In Ps. li. 4 the *Kal* of צָדַק is rendered by ὅπως ἂν δικαιωθῇς ἐν τοῖς λόγοις σου—"in order that Thou may be just in Thy words," or, "that Thy rectitude may be made apparent in Thy utterances." The common meaning is thus forensic in nature—to righten a man, or to give him acceptance with God, Rom. iii. 24, 26, 28, v. 1, vi. 7; or from its nature as acquittal from a charge—παρὰ Θεῷ—"at the bar of God." It is used in ii. 17, in opposition to "found sinners," or being under the curse. It means thus to give one the position of a δίκαιος, or to righten him in relation to God by releasing him from the penalty, so that he is accepted by the gracious Judge, and at the same time to purify and perfect him—a process which, beginning at the moment of his justification, stretches on through many a struggle to its complete development. Thus the blessing of Abraham, or justification by faith, and the reception of the Spirit the Worker of spiritual renewal, are regarded as collateral or as interconnected gifts in the 14th verse. To condemn is the opposite of to justify—κατάκριμα is the opposite of δικαίωμα (Rom. v. 16): but condemnation is not making a man a criminal, it is proving or asserting him to be one; so justification is not making a man righteous, but declaring him to be righteous, not for his own merit, but through his faith in the righteousness of Christ—that faith being the means of vitalizing the soul at the very moment of its being the instrument of release and acceptance. Δικαιοσύνη might be taken in a broad sense as covering the whole of that rightening which a sinner needs and through faith enjoys; that is, righteousness both imputed and inherent. But specially in such passages as this, where the leading thought is release from the curse which violation of the law has induced and perpetuated, its reference is rather to the basis than to the method of justification—to that, on his possession of which a sinner is rightened in relation to the law, relieved from its penalty. Δικαιοσύνη is not to be confounded with δικαίωσις which in Rom. iv. 25 is opposed to the παραπτώματα on account of which Christ was delivered up, and is the realized result of His resurrection; while in Rom. v. 18 it is defined by ζωῆς, as obtained δι' ἑνὸς δικαιώματος. J. A. Turretine, Wesley, Moses Stuart followed by Dr. Brown, take δικαιοσύνη Θεοῦ as meaning generally God's method of justification or of justifying a sinner. The explanation is vague, unless method mean something more than plan or outline, and include also basis and result, and it will not fit in to many passages where the phrase occurs. But δικαιοσύνη is said to refer to moral condition, as "nothing can be more inapplicable than a Greek noun ending in οσυνη to a mere business of *reputation* or *extrinsic change*." Knox's *Remains*, vol. i. 303. But, first, there are passages where the word cannot bear such a meaning as applied to God's dealing with sinners, so that it has not this moral sense uniformly; secondly, in its meaning as the basis of justification, it is moral in the sense of being personal, or in our individual possession; and thirdly, in another aspect, δικαιοσύνη may be regarded as the "moral" state of one who is δίκαιος at God's tribunal, or as that quality which characterizes him before God. The meaning of the term may be thus conserved without making the ground of justification inherent righteousness—without grounding, as Mr. Knox and others do, justification on sanctification. The compound term justification would naturally signify "making righteous"—*justum facere*, and several Romish theologians lay hold of this as an argument; but the word belongs not to the classic Latin, and came into general use as a representative of the Greek δικαιόω. Still the word, from its composition, is unfortunate, especially when ranged by the side of sanctification—"making holy." The analogy taken from the verbs "magnify" and "glorify" as applied to God will not hold, for "justify" belongs to the relation of God to man. Not a few theories about different kinds of justification are wanting in any sound scriptural basis;—some confounding it with election, faith in that case being only its proof, not its instrument; others assuming a first, and a final justification at the last day; and others laying no small stress on the difference between an actual and a declarative justification—a theory apparently necessitated by the attempt to reconcile the statements of the apostles James and Paul, but not indispensable by any means to a true adjustment of their language: thus Cunningham, *Historical Theology*, vol. ii. p. 67; Buchanan, *Doctrine of Justification*, p. 233, etc., Edin. 1867. Owen distinguishes between justification and justifaction!

The passage before us implies that Abraham had no righteousness, or was in want of a righteousness which no law could provide for him, and that Jehovah reckoned faith to him as, or in lieu of, such a personal righteousness which he had not. A new principle was brought in by God Himself; as the Hebrew text so distinctly expresses it—"He counted his faith to him for righteousness;" and the non-righteous Abraham stood before the divine tribunal acquitted and accepted as truly as if he had possessed a personal righteousness through uniform obedience. His faith, not as an act, but as a fact, put him into this position by God's own deed, without legal fiction or abatement. He believed God; that is, God in the promise given by Him in Gen. xv. 5: "And He brought him forth abroad, and said, Look now toward heaven, and tell the stars, if thou be able to number them. And He said unto him, So shall thy seed be." He was lifted into acceptance with God, however, not on account of his faith, but through it laying hold of the promise. That faith had no merit; for what merit can a creature have in believing the Creator's word?—it is only bare duty,—but Abraham's trust in God introduced him into the promised blessing. His faith rested on the promise, and through that faith he became its possessor or participant. That promise, seen in the light of a previous utterance, included the Messiah; and with all which it contained, and with this as its central and pre-eminent object, it was laid hold of by his faith, so that his condition was tantamount to justification by faith in the righteousness of Christ. In Abraham's case the promise was vague—the Redeemer had not become incarnate, and righteousness had not been formally provided; but now the person and work of Christ are distinctly set before us as the immediate object of saving faith—the characteristic doctrine of the New Testament. Tholuck indeed objects that the parallel between Abraham and believers is not complete—*unvolkommene*—Abraham's faith being his righteousness, and Christ's righteousness being reckoned to believers. But the promise included Him whose day Abraham rejoiced to see, and whatever was included in the promise was grasped by his faith Compare Alford and Meyer on Rom. iv. 3, and Philippi on the same verse in reply to Tholuck and Neander. And this righteousness is not innocence, as Bishop O'Brien more than once represents it in his *Treatise on the Nature and the Effects of Faith*, 2d ed. p. 186. That the justified person has sinned, is an element of his history which can never be obliterated; nay, it is confessed in all the songs of the saints, and the atoning work of Christ ever presupposes it. He who believes becomes righteous, not innocent as if he had never broken the law or had uniformly kept it; for he has sinned, and Omnipotence itself is unable to reverse a fact. But from all the penal effects of his sin he is graciously absolved, and is treated as righteous by God.

It was faith, then, and faith alone, which was accounted to Abraham for righteousness. Bishop Bull maintains that faith justifies, not as "one single virtue," but as being the germ of holiness, or as "comprehending all the works of Christian piety." St. Paul, he affirms, is to be interpreted from St. James, not St. James from St. Paul. Be that as it may, the Pauline doctrine is, that justification is by faith alone—*fide sola sed non fide quæ est sola;*[1] that is, this faith, while alone it justifies, does not remain alone—it proves its vitality or justifying nature by clothing itself with good works. The function of faith as justifying differs in result from its function as sanctifying; but it sanctifies as surely as it justifies. "God infuses righteousness in the very act of justifying." Davenant. Its sanctifying power is as certain as its justifying influence, and therefore the view of Bishop Bull is superficial: "Whoso firmly believes the gospel, and considers it with due attention, will *in all probability* become a good man." No such probability is hazarded in the New Testament—absolute certainty is asserted. One may ask, in fine, how far Bishop Bull's theory about the nature of faith—*fides formata*—differs from that of Bellarmine and that of the Tridentine theology which represents no less than six graces as co-operating with faith in a sinner's justification. See also Newman, *Lectures on Justification.*

The discussion of the doctrine of imputation belongs to systematic theology, and it has been ably treated, with varying opinions and conclusions—as in the treatises of Hooker, Owen, Martensen, Dick, Wardlaw, Edwards, Hodge, Cunningham, and Buchanan. See other authors in Buchanan's Notes.

It may be added, in conclusion, that it has been often

[1] Bellarmine puts the difference between the Romish and Reformed creed on the point thus: his own party teaching *Fidem non justificare solam, sed tamen posse esse solam;* but his opponents, *Fidem solam justificare, nunquam tamen posse esse solam.*

asked why faith should have been constituted the one instrument of justification; and various answers have been given. It may be replied that the loss of faith in God brought sin and death into the world. The tempter insinuated doubts of God's disinterestedness, as if He had been jealous, and had selfishly forbidden access to the tree of the knowledge of good and evil, since those who partook of the fruit would become gods and rise to a feared equality with Himself. The insinuation prevailed,—His creatures so poisoned against Him, gave up confidence in Him, and fell into spiritual death. And surely the restoration of this confidence or faith in God is, and must be in the nature of things, the first step toward pardon, acceptance, or reinstatement—toward reunion with the one Source of life. Still, faith is indispensable only as instrument or condition, not for any merit in itself. The phrases *ἐκ πίστεως*, or *διὰ πίστεως*, or *ἐν* or *ἐπὶ τῇ πίστει*, are used, but never *διὰ πίστιν*—on account of faith—which would be allied to the *justitia inhærens* of Thomas Aquinas, and the *meritum ex congruo* of Peter Lombard. See under ii. 16. The earlier fathers were not accustomed to minute doctrinal distinctions, and they often write without precision—their thoughts occupied with the entire process of salvation, without any minute analysis of its separate parts. Such freedom produces apparent inconsistency in careless utterances which may be variously expounded. So that the patristic history of the doctrine of justification has been viewed from opposite points, and been to some extent interpreted in the light of previous opinions. See, for example, on the one hand, Davenant's *De Justitia*, cap. xxix.; Faber's *Primitive Doctrine of Justification*, chap. iv.; and on the other hand, Bellarmine's *De Justificatione*, and Newman. See also Donaldson's *Critical History of Christian Literature and Doctrine.*

Ver. 7. *Γινώσκετε ἄρα ὅτι οἱ ἐκ πίστεως, οὗτοί εἰσιν υἱοὶ Ἀβραάμ*—"Know ye therefore that they who are of faith, those are the sons of Abraham." This verse is an inferential lesson which he charges them to learn. The verb is better construed in the imperative than in the indicative, which is preferred by Jerome, Beza, Rückert, Alford, Lightfoot, etc.; for the apostle is not taking for granted that they know it, but he is enjoining their knowledge of it, and he proceeds to expound and prove it to them. *Cognoscite ergo*—Vulgate. The particle *ἄρα* gives peculiar force to the imperative: "therefore," it being admitted that Abraham's faith was the undoubted means of his justification. Hartung, p. 443; Klotz-Devarius, ii. 167. Compare 2 Tim. iii. 1, Heb. xiii. 23. The phrase *οἱ ἐκ πίστεως* is more than a mere periphrasis for *οἱ πιστεύοντες*. The preposition represents origin—genetic relation. Rom. ii. 8, iii. 26, iv. 14; John xviii. 37; Winer, § 47. The aspect of thought is not simply—those who possess faith but those who are sprung of faith; yet not specially here the faith of Abraham (Windischmann),—faith being at once the formative and the distinctive principle. The pronoun *οὗτοι*, so placed, has a sharp exclusiveness of meaning,—those, and those alone—those and none other. Bernhardy, p. 283. The contrast to *ἐκ πίστεως* is not *ἐκ σαρκός*, as Chrysostom wrongly illustrates, but specially *οἱ ἐξ ἔργων* in ver. 10, though at the same time it is implied that mere natural descent does not entitle a man to be ranked in this spiritual progeny of Abraham. It is not Abraham's blood, but Abraham's faith which forms the filial bond. The phrase *υἱοὶ Ἀβραάμ* is expressive, and is meant to be so. Rom. iv. 12–18; Schoettgen, *in loc.* vol. i. p. 731. To be his children is to have what he had, and that is faith; and to be what he was, and that is to be justified. Faith is the common principle between father and children; justification is the common blessing, or the gift of righteousness is the common inheritance. Only such as have faith—and the point is not raised whether they be Gentiles or of the line of Isaac and Jacob, whether they be of the circumcision or of the uncircumcision—they alone are true Abrahamids—*σπέρμα Ἀβραάμ*. The aspect of thought is different here from that in ver. 29, where to be Abraham's seed is said to result from connection with Christ. The conclusion is levelled directly against proud Judaizing errorists, who insisted more on imitation of Abraham's circumcision than on the possession of Abraham's faith,—thus misunderstanding the place, nature, and meaning of the seal and rite, and deluding their victims away from the Spirit to trust in externalism, and seek for perfection in the flesh.

Ver. 8. *Προϊδοῦσα δὲ ἡ γραφή*—"But the Scripture foreseeing." The particle *δέ* is transitional ("but," not "and," as in our version), to urge an additional but different aspect of the same truth (Klotz-Devarius, vol. ii. 523),—that there is community of blessing with Abraham, and that this was no novelty. It had been described or foretold at a very early period, for it is found in the inspired record of the patriarch's life. In the words προϊδοῦσα ἡ γραφή the Scripture is personified, from the divine power and presence originating and pervading it. The Scripture embodies the mind of God, and that God being omniscient, His Scripture foresees as well as narrates, glances into the future with the same eye as it sweeps round the present or looks back into the past. Prophecy in a book coming from the All-knowing One is as natural as history; but there is no distinction meant here and on this point between divine and human writing (Hofmann). This species of personification is not uncommon in Jewish books. Surenhusius, *Bib. Katall.* 567; Schoettgen, *in loc.* vol. i. 732. Rom. iv. 3; John vii. 38. The Syriac reads ܡܛܠ ܓܝܪ ܕܩܕܡ ܝܕܥ ܐܠܗܐ —"for because God knew beforehand."

What the Scripture foresaw is—

Ὅτι ἐκ πίστεως δικαιοῖ τὰ ἔθνη ὁ Θεός—"that of faith God justifies the nations." The verb is present, not, as Meyer and De Wette argue, because the future time is taken as present, there being no time with the Unchanging One; nor merely, as Alford, because it is God's one way of justification; nor, as Ellicott, because the reference is to eternal and immutable decrees; nor, as Trana and Bengel, a view from the apostle's own position: but rather because it is God's continuous and uniform way of justification, and that by which He may be characterized. The words ἐκ πίστεως have the emphasis—that out of which justification springs—faith as opposed to works; for it is of this means or source of justification that the apostle's quotation and reasoning are a proof. Winer, xl. 2; Schmalfeld, § 54.

The ἔθνη are supposed by Estius, Alford, and Winer to include all nations—Jew and Gentile, the word being accepted in its widest significance. But we are inclined to take it in its more common and current usage, and therefore that in which it would be most likely understood by those whom the apostle addressed—the signification which it has in ver. 14. It there denotes the Gentiles, or other races than the Jews. Not only were his own race to be justified by faith such as his, but races alien to him and his should be justified precisely in the same way. The Scripture notified to Abraham the glad tidings beforehand—*προευηγγελίσατο,*—a word occuring in Philo, but found only here in the New Testament. This early prophetic notification made to Abraham was committed to writing—*ἡ γραφή*, and its substance was—

Ὅτι ἐνευλογηθήσονται ἐν σοὶ πάντα τὰ ἔθνη—"that there shall be blessed in thee all the nations." This second double compound verb rests on high authority, and it is plural, though in concord with a neuter nominative. Kühner, § 424, *a.* *Ὅτι* is recitative, or introduces the quotation. The words, however, are not found as the apostle quotes them. In the Septuagint occur: Gen. xii. 3, *ἐνευλογηθήσονται ἐν σοὶ πᾶσαι αἱ φυλαὶ τῆς γῆς*; xviii. 18, *ἐνευλογηθήσονται ἐν αὐτῷ πάντα τὰ ἔθνη*. The quotation represents both passages, as it so far combines them. The difficulty lies in the determination of the meaning of *ἐν σοί.*

1. It has been common to take it as meaning virtually "in thy seed"—thy seed as embodied in thee, and that seed meaning Christ. This view has been held by many, as by Œcumenius and Jerome, and more recently by Estius, Hunnius, Rambach, Bullinger, a-Lapide, Borger, Bagge, and Schott. In that case *ἐν* would signify *per*, through—through thee, or thy seed springing out of thee. But (1.) the mere words cannot bear this meaning—it is a foreign sense imposed upon them; (2.) it would not sustain the inference of the following verse—"blessed with Abraham;" (3.) nor would it warrant the language of the 14th verse, in which a certain blessing is called the blessing of Abraham; and (4.) it would forestall the new and peculiar argument of the 16th verse.

2. Nor can the phrase mean, as Calvin, Brown, Semler, Rosenmüller, and Baumgarten-Crusius suppose, "along with," or "in the same manner as;" for then the statement of the following verse, so far from being a deduction from this one, would only be a repetition of its sentiment, and the logical link expressed by *ὥστε* would be broken. Calvin is content with a reference to Abraham as *commune exemplar*, and Augustine with an *imitatione fidei;* while Chrysostom explains *ἐν σοί* by *τὴν πίστιν μιμησάμενοι*, and that in contrast to their possessing *τὴν φυσικὴν συγγένειαν.*

3. The meaning, then, seems to be, that Abraham is pic-

tured as the root and representative of all the faithful. They are in him as spiritual children in a spiritual ancestor or federal head, and are therefore included in his blessing—are blessed in him. It is only a quotational illustration of the truth announced in the previous verse. Gwynne, afraid lest the phrase "in thee" as so explained should lead to theological error, presses the meaning so far down that "father of the faithful" is only analogous to "Jabal, father of such as dwell in tents," "Jubal, father of all such as handle the harp." Wieseler understands "in thee" = "having a share in thy blessing," which indeed is the result.

And what is the εὐλογία, blessing, promised or predicted? It does not seem to be merely the reception of the Spirit, that being a result of the blessing, ver. 14 (De Wette, Wieseler); nor is it properly salvation as a whole, or the benefits attached to it (Hofmann); but it is specially that blessing which has immediate and uniform connection with faith and righteousness, *i.e.* justification. The quotation is adduced to prove that God justifies the Gentiles by faith, and it is this phase of blessing which has been since the conclusion of the previous chapter especially before the apostle's mind, and which he now proceeds more fully to illustrate. It was the free nature of this blessing and its dependence on faith alone which the Judaizers so strenuously and malignantly impugned. The "blessing" is in contrast also with the "curse" so soon referred to, and that curse is the penalty of a broken law. The prophecy does not teach that when men wish to bless one another, they shall take Abraham for a proverbial example, and say, God bless thee as He blessed Abraham (Jowett). But God, foreseeing His own gracious and uniform process of justifying the Gentile races through faith, made it known to Abraham, even while disclosing to him the blessing of his own promised and direct posterity. God revealed it, not to some heathen prince or priest, one of the Gentiles himself, but to the father of the Jewish race. He wrapped up blessing for the world in benediction given to the Abrahamids. And the words are surely "good tidings," fully warranting the epithet; for they show that the non-Abrahamic races were not utterly cast off, though they were not comprised in the covenant, and that they do not need to seek admission into that covenant by circumcision in order to obtain righteousness before God. It is Abraham's faith, not Abraham's blood, which brings them into federal or genetic unity with him.

Ver. 9. Ὥστε οἱ ἐκ πίστεως, εὐλογοῦνται σὺν τῷ πιστῷ Ἀβραάμ—"So then they which are of faith are blessed together with the faithful Abraham." Ὥστε expresses a consequence. Schmalfeld, *Synt.* § 155. The deduction is not specially from ἐνευλογηθήσονται (Alford and Ellicott), but it rests also upon ἐν σοί. Believers are ideally Abraham's children, inheriting his righteousness, for it had been fore-announced—"In thee shall all nations be blessed;" therefore those who believe are really blessed along with believing Abraham. Faith brings them into such a filial union with Abraham, that they are as if contained in him—ἐν σοί, and are through the same faith blessed along with him—σὺν τῷ Ἀβραάμ. Οἱ ἐκ πίστεως, as before, has the emphasis. The aspect of relation is now changed: it was ἐν, now it is σύν. In the one the idea is that of unity; in the second, that of company. "In him," as children in an ancestor, are they blessed, according to the promise in the quotation, and therefore "with him;" in fellowship with him are they blessed, he and they together—they being ἐκ πίστεως, and he being πιστός. For τῷ πιστῷ is prefixed to Abraham, to prevent any mistake as to that in which this unity and community consist. The adjective is used in an active sense. See under Eph. i. 1. It is altogether wrong in Grotius to take σύν as equivalent in meaning to καθώς or ὥσπερ, "in the same way." The apostle's representation is by no means so vague. The assertion is directed against that error which insisted on the Gentile races submitting to the seal of Abraham's race and lineage before they could enjoy his blessing. It attacks *l'orgueilleux egöisme des Juifs* (Sardinoux), which mistakes the ground of Abraham's justification, and would frustrate the promise which Jehovah made to him. Judaizing was opposed alike to the example of Abraham and this early statement of Scripture. The apostle had therefore been preaching no novelty when he preached to the Gentiles, and Jews too, a free and complete salvation, simply through faith in the Crucified One. Chrysostom describes the apostle in the conclusion of this verse as συλλογιζόμενος—Those who are of faith are Abraham's children; Abraham's children are blessed; therefore those who are of faith—believers—are blessed with believing Abraham.

Ver. 10. *Ὅσοι γὰρ ἐξ ἔργων νόμου εἰσίν, ὑπὸ κατάραν εἰσίν*—"For as many as are of the works of the law are under curse." The *γάρ* introduces another argument from the opposite point of view. Believers alone are blessed; and that they who are of faith are alone blessed is plain from the fact, that they who stand in antagonism to them, or they who are of the works of the law, are under curse—are not only negatively unblessed, but positively under curse. The *ἐκ* is expressive, denoting origination and that dependence which it characterizes, as in *οἱ ἐκ πίστεως*. It is not simply *οἱ ἐργαζόμενοι*, men in the act of working, but men whose character and hopes have their origin and shape out of works of the law. All such—*ὅσοι*—as are under law are *ὑπὸ κατάραν*. Compare *ὑπὸ χάριν*, Rom. vi. 14. The preposition is used in an ethical sense (Matt. viii. 9; Rom. iii. 9, vii. 14; 1 Cor. ix. 20; Winer, § 49, *k*); the original image of position, "under," fades away in familiar usage, and the idea remains of subjection. *Κατάρα* is plainly opposed to *εὐλογία*, and denotes here the penalty of sin. They are under the penalty, according to the apostle's proof, not merely because they have broken, but because they are breaking, the law. Their obedience is neither complete nor uniform. They are under the curse, and the law cannot deliver them; for the function of law is to arraign, convict, and punish. By it is "the knowledge of sin," it shows their conduct to be out of harmony with its requirements, and thus by its demonstration all the world becomes guilty before God. "For," as the apostle adds in proof, *γέγραπται γὰρ, ὅτι*. *Ὅτι* by authority of A, B, C, D, F, א, and it introduces the quotation: "for it has been written," and still stands written—

Ἐπικατάρατος πᾶς ὃς οὐκ ἐμμένει ἐν πᾶσι τοῖς γεγραμμένοις ἐν τῷ βιβλίῳ τοῦ νόμου, τοῦ ποιῆσαι αὐτά—"Cursed is every one who continueth not in all things which have been written in the book of the law, to do them." The quotation is from Deut. xxvii. 26, but not precisely in harmony with the original Hebrew or the Septuagint. The Hebrew is: אָרוּר אֲשֶׁר לֹא־יָקִים אֶת־דִּבְרֵי הַתּוֹרָה־הַזֹּאת לַעֲשׂוֹת אוֹתָם; and the Septuagint reads: *ἐπικατάρατος πᾶς ἄνθρωπος ὃς οὐκ ἐμμένει ἐν πᾶσι τοῖς λόγοις τοῦ νόμου τούτου ποιῆσαι αὐτούς*. The

Hebrew wants the πᾶς and πᾶσι. Jerome, however, says that he saw CHOL in the Samaritan Text—*Quam ob causam Samaritanorum Hebræa volumina relegens, inveni Chol quod interpretatur* OMNIS *sive* OMNIBUS *scriptum esse, et cum Septuaginta interpretibus concordare.* And he accuses the Jews of making the deletion wilfully, though the motive he ascribes to them is somewhat puerile—lest they too should be under curse; for the omission does not change the sense, and the verse is a summary conclusion of all the Ebal curses recorded in the previous paragraph. Surenhusius well says: ארור האיש, *maledictus vir iste, id est quisque, et in responsione dicitur, "respondit totus populus, dixitque Amen." Biblos Katall.* p. 569. The verb ἐμμένει, "to stand in," "to continue" (Thucydides, iv. 118; Polyb. iii. 704; Acts xiv. 22; Heb. viii. 9), is sometimes followed by the simple dative, but here by ἐν,—not, however, as if the relation were doubly marked. The directive ἐπι in the adjective ἐπικατάρατος is based upon an image the inverse of that implied in the previous ὑπό. He who is ὑπὸ κατάραν is truly ἐπικατάρατος. The term does not belong to classic Greek. The "all things which are written in the law" are the sphere in which any one must abide who purposes to do them; but if he leave this sphere and break any of them, he is cursed—the emphasis being placed on ἐπικατάρατος. The last clause, τοῦ ποιῆσαι αὐτά, is the infinitive of design, such an infinitive being, as Winer remarks, § 44, 4, *b*, almost peculiar to Luke and Paul. It grew out of the ordinary meaning of the genitive as denoting result, for purpose and result are closely associated. This usage, which is also found in the classical writers after the age of Demosthenes, is common in the Septuagint, the translation being partly induced by the Hebrew infinitive with ל prefixed. Thiersch, *De Pent.* p. 173. The apostle's meaning is, that confessedly every one fails to keep all the written enactments of the law; therefore every one seeking salvation by his own obedience is under curse. He is striving to obtain blessing from a code which has condemned and cursed him, to win life from a law which has wrought his death. Ps. xiv. 3; 1 Kings viii. 46. It is useless to refute the notion of Semler and others, that the law here is the ceremonial law, and the curse the civil penalty that followed trespass or neglect.

This is one argument fortified by Scripture; and the apostle adduces another, and a more sweeping one. This tenth verse states the principle—no obedience save what is uniform and universal can be accepted; no one renders this, or can render it; therefore they who yet are legalists are under the curse, and the word of God has emphatically said so. But he now states as a result the broad fact fortified by Scripture too, that justification is impossible by the law, for it is declared to depend not on obedience, but simply and solely on faith.

Ver. 11. *Ὅτι δὲ ἐν νόμῳ οὐδεὶς δικαιοῦται παρὰ τῷ Θεῷ δῆλον*—"But that in the law no one is justified before God is evident." Flatt gives the connection in this way: because no man is justified by the law in God's sight, it is clear that the just shall live by faith. But the second *ὅτι*, introducing a quotation which contains an argument, must be causative in signification. Bengel seems to take *δῆλον ὅτι* as one word—*δηλονότι, id est*—"As concerns the fact that no one is justified in the law before God, it is beyond all doubt true that the just shall live by faith." Homberg suggests that a point is to be placed after *Θεῷ*—*ut τὸ δῆλον sequentia regat*—"since no one is justified in the law before God, it is plain that the just shall live by faith." Hofmann adopts a similar view, taking *δῆλον ὅτι* adverbially, and regarding the following clause as an explanatory parenthesis, and a protasis or premiss to vers. 13, 14. But 1 Cor. xv. 27 and 1 Tim. vi. 7 will not bear out this construction which is never used by the apostle; and so far from being an incidental insertion, this quotation is an essential portion of the argument, which is made up of a series of brief statements fortified by a series of Scripture proofs. *Δέ* is more than continuative. It introduces not an additional argument merely, but one of another kind. Justification is not of works, for legalists are under curse, since they cannot render perfect obedience, is the one argument; but the second is, Justification cannot depend on works, for the Scripture asserts its connection with faith. It seems to many as if some objection had started itself to the apostle's mind. Brown puts it thus: "But are not justification by the law and justification by believing reconcilable? may they not be coincident?" But the verse does not afford a reply to such a question, nor does it seem to be the objection present to the apostle's thought. De Wette, followed by Ellicott, supposes it to be, "but lest any one should imagine that if a man did so continue in all things written in the book of the law, he should be blessed." Granting that this hypothesis might be started, the answer must have been in the affirmative, for perfect obedience must secure acceptance; though on another view it must be in the negative, since no man ever did find acceptance by works, and justification before God has uniformly been by faith. And such is his answer to the supposed challenge. We see no need, however, for accounting for the chain of argument by forging such a link of association. Justification cannot be by law, for legalists are under a penalty; and he says now, Justification as a fact has never been by works, but invariably by faith. The verb δικαιοῦται is therefore in the ethical present—it is God's characteristic and invariable way of justification. The phrase παρὰ τῷ Θεῷ has a judicial aspect. Rom. ii. 13; 2 Thess. i. 6; 1 Pet. ii. 20; Rost und Palm, *sub voce.* The phrase ἐν νόμῳ is not *nach der Norm des Gesetzes* (Wieseler), but may mean, by or through law as instrument, as Meyer maintains, for, as he says, " Χριστός is in contrast to it." But ἐν may have a wider meaning: no one is justified "in the law"—in any aspect of it or in any connection with it, for justification is found wholly beyond its sphere. The proof of the position is again taken from Scripture, but the quotation is so well known that there is no introductory formula—

Ὅτι ὁ δίκαιος ἐκ πίστεως ζήσεται—"because the just shall live by faith." Codices D[1] and F, agreeing with the Syriac and the Itala, have ὅτι γέγραπται γάρ, F omitting δῆλον. The quotation is from Hab. ii. 4—וְצַדִּיק בֶּאֱמוּנָתוֹ יִחְיֶה, "the just man by his faith shall live;" and is rendered by the Septuagint, ὁ δὲ δίκαιος ἐκ πίστεώς μου ζήσεται. The apostle omits μου. The pronoun μου, if not an error—and its position differs in the MSS.—indicates another Hebrew reading, and may be used objectively: "by faith in me," that is, God. The rendering of אֱמוּנָה by πίστις is found also in Aquila, Symmachus, and Theodotion, but with the reading αὐτοῦ or ἑαυτοῦ. Orig. *Hex.* vol. ii. p. 372, ed. Montf. But "his faith" may mean either *ex fide ejus*—faith in Him—God, or *ex fide sua*—his own faith. The idea of stedfastness expressed by the Hebrew noun implies faith, and it is commonly rendered πίστις in the Septuagint; though only in this place it is translated faith in the Authorized Version, its usual renderings being "steady," "faithful," "faithfulness," "truth," "truly," "verily," "stability," and "set," as in the phrase "set office"—margin "trust." The quotation occurs again in Rom. i. 17, and in Heb. x. 38.

It is difficult to determine the connection, whether *ἐκ πίστεως* belongs to *ὁ δίκαιος* before it—the man just by faith shall live, or whether it belongs to *ζήσεται* after it—the just shall live by his faith. Interpreters are greatly divided. The first view is supported by Cajetan, Pareus, Bengel, Michaelis, Semler, Morus, Rückert, Usteri, Hilgenfeld, Meyer, Brown, Alford, Sardinoux, Bisping, Umbreit on Rom. i. 17. In favour of this view it may be said, that the apostle's aim is to show the source of justification, and not the means or foundation of spiritual life; his theme being justification by faith, not life by faith. Besides, as Meyer says, *ὁ δίκαιος ἐκ πίστεως* stands opposed to *ὁ ποιήσας αὐτά* in the following verse. The other view is held by many old interpreters—by Borger, Schott, Matthies, Winer, De Wette, Ellicott, Middleton, Wieseler, Bagge, Ewald, Holsten, Hofmann, Philippi on Rom. i. 17, Delitzsch on Hab. ii. 4.

And 1. The original Hebrew is in favour of this meaning. The first clause reads, "See, the proud, his soul is not upright in him; but the just shall live by his stedfastness." See Fürst, *Lex. sub voce.* The first clause of the verse in the Septuagint is wholly different from the Hebrew, though there is quite a harmony of sense with the second.

2. The order of the Greek words is also in its favour. It is not *ὁ ἐκ πίστεως δίκαιος*. Great stress, however, cannot be laid on this argument, for it has been replied that the apostle quotes the words as they stand in the Septuagint. But it may be answered, the apostle quotes them in the sense which they bear in the Septuagint, which is a true translation of the original, though the first part of the verse would seem to be rendered from a different Hebrew text (Hitzig).

3. There is the contrast *ἐκ πίστεως ζήσεται* and *ζήσεται ἐν αὐτοῖς—ἔργοις*,—phrases directly antagonistic; the one living by faith, the other living in works—life and its source, life and its element.

4. The apostle's theme is justification by faith. Now justification and life are not different, as Alford's objection would imply; he who is justified or rescued from the curse—

that curse being death—lives *παρὰ τῷ Θεῷ*. The apostle has spoken of his own experience as a justified man under the more subjective aspect of life in the end of the second chapter, and the same idea recurs to him as suggested by a quotation from the Old Testament. No man is justified in or by the law before God, for the justified man lives by faith—faith giving him life, or rescuing him from death as the penalty of the law which he has broken. Or the statement, he is justified by faith, is the inference, inasmuch as he lives by faith—life being the result of justification, or rather coincident with it.

The *ἐκ* denotes origin—out of faith comes life. Abiding faith is continuous life. If faith vary, life flickers, it is so susceptible and so dependent on faith; or, to speak differently, the Spirit of life cannot dwell in an unbelieving heart. The apostle adds—

Ver. 12. *Ὁ δὲ νόμος οὐκ ἔστιν ἐκ πίστεως*—"But the law is not of faith." This *δέ* introduces the minor proposition of the syllogism. The law is in no sense connected with faith in its origin, essence, or working—does not spring from it, and in no way belongs to it. Theodoret says truly, *ὁ νόμος οὐ πίστιν ζητεῖ, ἀλλὰ πρᾶξιν ἀπαιτεῖ.* The law is not, as Dr. Brown paraphrases, "the way of justification by the law," but the law itself as an institute, the Mosaic law being the reference, and on this point representing all law. The insertion of *ζήσεται* after *πίστεως*, which Gwynne "confidently presses as the true grammatical construction," would be a clumsy and unsatisfactory interpolation.

Ἀλλ᾽ ὁ ποιήσας αὐτὰ ζήσεται ἐν αὐτοῖς—"but he who hath done these things shall live in them." The *ἀλλά* is strongly adversative. The Received Text has *ἄνθρωπος* after *αὐτά* on such slender authority as D[3], K, L, and it was probably taken from the quotation as it stands in the Septuagint, Lev. xviii. 5. The Hebrew clause is, אֲשֶׁר יַעֲשֶׂה אֹתָם הָאָדָם וָחַי בָּהֶם; and the whole verse in the Septuagint is, *καὶ φυλάξεσθε πάντα τὰ προστάγματά μου καὶ πάντα τὰ κρίματά μου, καὶ ποιήσετε αὐτά· ἃ ποιήσας αὐτὰ ἄνθρωπος ζήσεται ἐν αὐτοῖς.* The *αὐτά* are the *προστάγματα* and *κρίματα* of the previous clauses. Compare Neh. ix. 29; Ezek. xx. 21; Baruch iv. 1. As in the previous quotation, there is no formula as *γέγραπται*, nor does it need to be understood. The apostle uses a well-known quotation, and does not need to name it as such; but there is a formula employed in Rom. x. 5. The emphasis is on the aorist ποιήσας. Doing, not believing, is always connected with the law. It prescribes obedience, and threatens penalty. Works, not faith, belong to it. It does not recognise faith, for it says, Do, and then thou shalt live. He who has kept these laws lives in them as the element of his life. *Præcepta legis non sunt de credendis, sed de faciendis* (Thomas Aquinas). The two quotations are placed almost side by side. Faith and obedience are very opposite in nature, and so are a life of faith and a life of legal obedience. Perfect obedience would secure life; but there is, and there can be, no perfect obedience. All are therefore under the curse who are under the law, and the law has no justifying power; but by a new principle which the law knows nothing of, and which is quite opposed to law in essence and operation, are men justified—to wit, by faith. These two verses are a species of inverted syllogism. The major is, "The just shall live by faith;" the minor is, "but the law is not of faith;" and the conclusion is, therefore "in the law no one is justified before God." See under ii. 16, etc.

Ver. 13. *Χριστὸς ἡμᾶς ἐξηγόρασεν ἐκ τῆς κατάρας τοῦ νόμου*—"Christ redeemed us from the curse of the law." There is no connecting particle, and the abruptness of the asyndeton gives vividness to the expression. Compare Col. iii. 4; Dissen, *ad Pind.* Excur. ii. p. 277. Olshausen needlessly supposes a μέν in ver. 10 and a δέ in this verse to be left out. As many as are of the works of the law are under the curse—"Christ redeemed us from the curse of the law." There is no doubt, whatever general truth may be inferred from the passage, that the ἡμεῖς are specially or primarily, if not solely, Jews. If the law, as seems clear, be the Mosaic law or the published law of God, then its curse lay upon the Jews who were guilty of violating it, and to them the threatening of ver. 10 applies. The ἡμάς also stands in contrast to εἰς τὰ ἔθνη, who are not included in it. Freed from the curse through faith in Him who bore it, why should they be so rigid and undutiful in enjoining that law on the Gentiles? That law did not originally include the Gentiles under its sway,—it in fact severed Israel and non-Israel, Jew and Gentile. The *us* and the *we* are, therefore, properly those who in ver. 23 are said to be *ὑπὸ νόμον*, and also in iv. 5, and not heathen also (Pareus, Winer, Matthies, Baumgarten-Crusius). The law of Moses is wrongly affirmed by Winer to have authority over the heathen. The apostle gives a different view of the heathen world in Rom. ii. 14, 15, and states a contrary doctrine—that they are "without law." So far, indeed, as the Mosaic law is unnational, or so far as it is a proclamation of earlier moral law springing out of those essential and unchanging relations which creatures bear to God and to one another, it must bind all races.

The aorist verb *ἐξηγόρασεν*—"bought us out," redeemed or ransomed—corresponds very much to the other terms employed elsewhere—*λυτρόω, ἀπολύτρωσις*. The preposition in a compound verb in the later Greek is not to be unduly pressed, as Ellicott remarks, and as Thiersch has illustrated, *De Pent. vers. Alex.* p. 82. The simple verb occurs 1 Cor. vi. 20, vii. 23; 2 Pet. ii. 1; Rev. v. 9, xiv. 3, 4. The idea is deliverance by ransom. See under Eph. i. 7, v. 2, v. 25; Col. i. 14. The curse of the law is its penalty of death, under which it holds us in terrible bondage. The mode in which the action asserted by the verb was done is told by the following participial clause—

Γενόμενος ὑπὲρ ἡμῶν κατάρα—"having become a curse for us," *γενόμενος* having the stress upon it. The noun *κατάρα* is the abstract, and without the article points out that the curse which He became was full—not circumscribed or modified—wide as the curse of the law. 2 Cor. v. 21. Cursed is every one who has not kept the law—*ἐπικατάρατος*—Christ became *κατάρα*—not an accursed one, but curse. No element of the *κατάρα* that fell on the sinner is beyond the sphere or influence of the *κατάρα* which He became; *γενόμενος*—not under the curse originally, but filled with blessedness, the law having no claim on Him derived from previous or personal violation of any of its statutes.

He became a curse *ὑπὲρ ἡμῶν*, for us. See what is said under i. 4. While *ὑπέρ* signifies primarily on behalf of, or for the good of, it may here bear in combination the meaning of "in room of," as certainly in John xiii. 37, 38, 2 Cor. v. 20, in Philem. 13, and in Plato, *Ὡμολογήκαμεν· ἐγὼ ὑπὲρ σοῦ ἀποκρινοῦμαι*, *Gorgiás*, 515, D, *Opera*, vol. ii. p. 305, ed. Stallbaum. Compare Usteri, *Paulin. Lehrb.* p. 117. If substitution be not formally expressed, it is certainly implied in this striking declaration. He became the curse that lay upon us, and thus ransomed us out of it.

A quotation is introduced as proof of the last statement by *γέγραπται γάρ*, "it has been" and it stands "written," as in the Textus Receptus; but the *ὅτι γέγραπται* has in its favour A, B, C, D[1], F, with the Vulgate and several of the Latin fathers.

Ἐπικατάρατος πᾶς ὁ κρεμάμενος ἐπὶ ξύλου—"Cursed is every one that hangeth upon a tree." The quotation is taken freely from Deut. xxi. 22, 23. The Hebrew of the clause is כִּי־קִלְלַת אֱלֹהִים תָּלוּי—for he that is hanged is accursed of God; the Greek, *ὅτι κεκατηραμένος ὑπὸ Θεοῦ πᾶς κρεμάμενος ἐπὶ ξύλου*. The whole place is given in our version thus: "And if a man have committed a sin worthy of death, and he be to be put to death, and thou hang him on a tree; his body shall not remain all night upon the tree, but thou shalt in any wise bury him that day; (for he that is hanged is accursed of God;) that thy land be not defiled, which the Lord thy God giveth thee for an inheritance." The clause "and he be to be put to death," is properly "he be put to death," for crucifixion was not a Hebrew punishment. The common version of the clause under consideration is the correct one—"the curse of God;" though another rendering has been sometimes given—"He that is hanged is an insult to God"—*ὕβρις Θεοῦ*,—the rendering of him whom Jerome calls *Ebion ille hæresiarches semichristianus et semijudæus*. The rendering of the Peshito, of the Targum of Jonathan, and of the Greek translators Aquila, Symmachus, and Theodotion, is a modification of this view. Jerome also makes allusion to an *altercatio* between Jason and Papiscus—a controversy referred to also by Celsus and Origen—in which the words in dispute are rendered *λοιδορία Θεοῦ*. See Prof. Lightfoot's note on the subject. The words *ὑπὸ Θεοῦ* are omitted in the quotation, and *ἐπὶ ξύλου* is added from the previous verse. Lightfoot says that the words *ὑπὸ Θεοῦ* are "instinctively" omitted by Paul; but they are really implied in the citation—the criminal having broken God's law bore God's curse; and in their application to Christ, it is still God's law whose curse was borne by Him, though the *ὑπὸ Θεοῦ* fades into the background, as it is not essential to form a result of the present argument. Bähr and Hofmann suppose the words to be omitted on purpose to keep out the idea expressed, as, among other grounds, it might be a stumbling-block to the unsettled Galatians. The citation is thus made as to sense—a citation the force and truth of which his readers must at once admit. Suspension from a stake (though ξύλον in later Greek and in the New Testament signifies also a living tree) was a posthumous degradation awarded to certain classes of criminals put to death probably by stoning. Crucifixion was not a Jewish punishment, but the dead criminal was exposed on a stake by the hands. A man so hanged was a curse, and was not on that account to remain exposed all night, because the land had been consecrated to God. So the very means of Christ's death showed it to be an accursed death. His being hanged on a tree proved that He was made a curse. The manner of the death, besides being in consonance with prophecy, was a visible proof and symbol of its real nature; for "He bore our sins on His own body on the tree." He bore the curse of a broken law, and the mode of His death signally showed that He became a curse, for, by being suspended on a stake, He became in the express terms of the law a curse. Acts v. 30, x. 39; 1 Pet. ii. 24. And this declaration was a continuous stumbling-block, as Jerome testifies, and as may be seen in Tertullian, *Adversus Judæos*, § 10, *Opera*, vol. ii. p. 727, ed. Œhler; in Justin Martyr, *Dial. cum Tryph.* § 96, *Opera*, vol. ii. p. 327, ed. Otto; and in Aristo Pellaeus, some fragments of whom may be found, with annotations, in Routh's *Reliq. Sac.* vol. i. p. 95, etc. Jewish contempt styled the Saviour "the hanged man," as may be seen in the second chapter of the first part of Eisenmenger's *Entdeckt. Judenthum*, "on the slanderous names which the Jews give to Christ." Eisenmenger did with a will this work, which is a curious, erudite, and ponderous indictment against the Jewish nation.

Ver. 14. *Ἵνα εἰς τὰ ἔθνη ἡ εὐλογία τοῦ Ἀβραὰμ γένηται ἐν Χριστῷ Ἰησοῦ*—"in order that to the Gentiles the blessing of Abraham might come in Christ Jesus." The *ἵνα* points to the final purpose expressed by *ἐξηγόρασεν* and the clauses connected with it, and not simply with *γενόμενος ὑπὲρ ἡμῶν κατάρα*, as Alford, after Theophylact, Œcumenius, Winer, Usteri, and Schott; and *ἡ εὐλογία τοῦ Ἀβραάμ* is the blessing possessed or enjoyed by Abraham—not the blessing promised to him, as Wieseler and Schott argue, but the blessing itself, justification by faith, ver. 6. Ellicott and Trana make it the genitive of object, the blessing announced to Abraham; the promise was vouchsafed to him, and he enjoyed the reality. The apostle does not allude by contrast in *εὐλογία* to *κατάρα* in the previous verse, though it may not be altogether excluded, but he re-introduces the idea of vers. 5–9. Winer takes the blessing generally as *felicitas*, but too vaguely; Gwynne as the "Spirit"—a confusion of ideas; and Wieseler, the collective blessing of God's kingdom. These are included as results, but the blessing to which the apostle gives prominence is justification by faith, as in ver. 8. The Scripture foresaw that God would justify the heathen by faith—*τὰ ἔθνη*; and Christ became a curse, that upon the same *τὰ ἔθνη* the blessing of Abraham might come. Besides, it is the object of the apostle to vindicate the doctrine of justification by faith, for it was endangered by the false teaching of the Judaizers. The heathen are foreshown to be justified by faith, and it was contravening this foreannouncement to insist on something more than faith in order to justification. For the phrase *γένηται εἰς*, "should come to" or "should reach," compare Acts xxi. 17, xxv. 15; 2 Cor. viii. 14; Rev. xvi. 2. The preposition retains its local meaning, and does not signify, as in Peile's paraphrase, "in reference to" the nations. Winer, § 49, *a*. The *ἔθνη* are the heathen in contradistinction to the Jews, and not the peoples generally, as Estius, Olshausen, and Baumgarten-Crusius suppose. This blessing of Abraham comes upon the Gentiles *ἐν Χ. Ι.*, in Christ Jesus—the element in which it is found, conveyed, and enjoyed—not in the law, which claims perfect obedience, and inflicts a curse on all transgressors. But why this connection? Christ became a curse that the blessing of Abraham might come, not on his own descendants, but on the Gentiles—the moment lying on the words *εἰς τὰ ἔθνη*, from their position. Through His death comes justification, or deliverance from the curse, and acceptance with God,—the curse of the law being borne by Him,—and that death, the infinite merit of which flows over to the Gentile, at the same time (though the idea is not formally introduced here) put an end to the typical and national economy from which the Gentiles were excluded, and introduced a new dispensation without distinction of race or blood. Besides the expiation of guilt in Christ's death, which is the express and special thought of the apostle, there was in it also the fulfilment of the old symbols, with their consequent abolition, and the inauguration of a system of world-wide adaptation and offer. The blessing so specially characterized as Abraham's, and so founded on Christ's expiation, passes over to those who bear no natural kinship to him—"aliens," "strangers," "afar off"—who, looking up to the Source of all spiritual good, may say, "Doubtless Thou art our Father, though Abraham be ignorant of us, and Israel acknowledge us not."

Ἵνα τὴν ἐπαγγελίαν τοῦ πνεύματος λάβωμεν διὰ τῆς πίστεως—"in order that we might receive the promise of the Spirit through faith." This second *ἵνα* is co-ordinate with the first, and is of climactic force. Rückert after Chrysostom maintains the second clause to be subordinate to the first, and to express the result of it. Schott has a similar view. Flatt renders this second *ἵνα*, "so that." The conjunctions *ἵνα—ἵνα*, co-ordinate or parallel, are found in Rom. vii. 13, 2 Cor. ix. 3, Eph. vi. 19. It is also something more than an explanation, the error of Grotius, Estius, and Koppe. In the first plural *λάβωμεν* the "we" includes probably both Jews and Gentiles. He does not say *λάβωσι*, as Chrysostom reads, in direct reference to the Gentiles just referred to, nor does he formally express *ἡμεῖς* as in contrast to *τὰ ἔθνη*, but he employs the simple verb. Having specified the Gentiles, and recurring to the use of "we," the probability is that he means "we"—both Gentiles just referred to, and Jews, the subject of the previous paragraph. Hofmann, Beza, Bengel, and virtually Brown, confine the subject of the verb to the Jews—*Judæi benedictioni in Christo propinqui.* What they should receive, the apostle styles—

Τὴν ἐπαγγελίαν τοῦ πνεύματος—"the promise of the Spirit." The verb *λάβωμεν* may mean to receive it in full, or into conscious possession. The *ἡ ἐπαγγελία τοῦ πνεύματος* is no Hebraism standing for *τὸ ἐπαγγελθὲν πνεῦμα*—the promised Spirit; and as little can it mean *promissio spiritualis*—Calvin, Pareus, Zegerus. The genitive is that of object—the promise which has the Spirit for its object; or perhaps is the genitive of nearer specification or definition, as Wieseler takes it. The genitives which admit of the resolution referred to are very limited. Winer, § 34. See Fritzsche also on the phrase *ἐν καινότητι ζωῆς*, ad Rom. vi. 4, vol. i. p. 367. Were the genitive that of subject, as Winer takes it, it would mean, as he phrases it, *bona illa quæ a divino spiritu promissa sunt.* But the Spirit Himself stands out as the special subject of promise: Joel ii. 28; Luke xxiv. 49; Acts i. 4, ii.; Eph. i. 13. In the apostle's idea, the Spirit does not give the promise, but seals it in personal realization. The Spirit is a characteristic prediction of the Old Testament, and the Paraclete is Christ's pre-eminent promise in the New Testament. Thus it is plain that the apostle recurs in this clause to the question of the second verse, *τὸ πνεῦμα ἐλάβετε;*—"Did ye receive the Spirit?" and he answers that question by various connected arguments, referring to Abraham—to faith as opposed to law and works—to the curse of the law and Christ's endurance of it, in order that the promise of the Spirit may be enjoyed as an actual blessing. His questions were, "Did ye receive the Spirit *ἐξ ἔργων*?" ver. 2; "Does God furnish the Spirit *ἐξ ἔργων*?" ver. 3. No; and the answer is elaborated in a series of pithy and pointed sentences, "compactly built together," till he ends the demonstration, and sets down as the proved result—*διὰ τῆς πίστεως*. For *νόμος* and *ἔργα* are associated with *κατάρα*, and Christ became *κατάρα* for us, that justification might come to the Gentiles, according to the old promise that all the nations should be blessed in Abraham, their faith and not their blood being their bond of union with him; their faith being at the same time inseparably connected with their possession of the Spirit—God's great promise to believers.

Ver. 15. *Ἀδελφοὶ, κατὰ ἄνθρωπον λέγω*—"Brethren, I speak after the manner of men"—I am going to use a human analogy, or to propose an illustration from a human point of view. "Brethren, yet beloved and cared for," though they are censured as senseless in their relapse; affectionate remembrance naturally springing up at this pause in the argument. The phrase *κατὰ ἄνθρωπον* has various shades of meaning, as may be seen by comparing Rom. iii. 5, 1 Cor. ix. 8 with 1 Cor. iii. 3, xv. 32, Gal. i. 11. See Wetstein on Rom. iii. 5. The point of the statement is, that if it be true beyond doubt of a human covenant, it applies much more to a divine covenant—*a minore ad majus.*

Ὅμως ἀνθρώπου κεκυρωμένην διαθήκην οὐδεὶς ἀθετεῖ ἢ ἐπιδιατάσσεται—"though it be but a man's covenant, yet when it has been confirmed, no one annulleth or addeth to it"—imposeth new conditions. Διαθήκη is rightly rendered covenant, for the context demands such a sense. Such is its constant meaning in the Septuagint, and its uniform use in the New Testament—Heb. ix. 15, 17 being no exception. The classical meaning of the plural form of the word and the *testamentum* of the Vulgate have given currency to the other translation of "testament," which is adopted here by Luther, Erasmus, and Olshausen. The Hebrew בְּרִית, as a name both of the Abrahamic and Mosaic covenants, is always represented by it. Suidas defines it by *συνθήκη*, a covenant in the strictest sense; but it has a wider significance than this allied term. Yet the meaning is not so general as dispensation or arrangement—*dispositio* (Winer, Matthies, Usteri, Schott, Hofmann, Hauck,[1] and virtually Brown); the usual sense fits in to the illustration. The participle *κεκυρωμένη* is applied to the ratification of a bargain, Gen. xxiii. 20; of a public measure, Thucyd. viii. 69; of a treaty of peace, Polyb. i. 6; and of laws, Andocides, *De Myster.* p. 27, ed. Schiller. The confirmation might be effected in various ways, as by an oath, Heb. vi. 13–18, or by the erection of a memorial or witness, Gen. xxxi. 44–53. The adverb *ὅμως* is not to be taken as *ὁμῶς*, "in like manner" (Morus, Jatho), but it signifies "yet," or "though,"—not *doch selbst* (Zachariæ, Matthies) nor *quin imo* (Wolf). Windischmann, Olshausen, and Rückert refer it to *κατ' ἄνθρωπον*, and take it as *tamen* or *certe*—"I speak only as a man"—one certainly cannot abrogate a man's testament; but the point is missed in this exegesis. Some connect it with *ἀνθρώπου*—"yet *even a man's* covenant no one annulleth" (Gwynne, Matthias). Bagge lays the emphasis on the participle *κεκυρωμένην*, and connects *ὅμως* with it—"no one sets aside a covenant, although ratified by man." But the illustration is broader in its basis, for *ὅμως* logically belongs to *οὐδείς*, and is out of its order by an idiomatic displacement. 1 Cor. xiv. 7; Winer, 61, 4. This trajection happens oftenest with participles—*participio suo præmitti solito*. Stallbaum, *Phædo*, 91, C; Plat. *Opera*, vol. i. p. 155; Xen. *Cyrop.* v. 4, 6; Thucyd. vi. 69. The sense then is, though it be a man's covenant, when it is confirmed no one yet or notwithstanding annuls it or adds to it. The last verb sig-

[1] *Studien und Kritiken*, p. 512, 1862.

nifies to add or to supplement (*superordinat*, Vulgate), and by its composition—*ἐπί*—it hints what the supplement is, or insinuates that it is contrary to the contents of the covenant or purpose of its author (Erasmus, Winer). Joseph. *Bell. Jud.* ii. 2, 3, where *ἐπιδιαθήκη* means a second will; *Antiq.* xvii. 9, 4. After a man's covenant has been duly ratified, no one dares to set aside or supplement it with any new matter or any additional stipulations. It stands good beyond strife and cavil against all opposition and argument. *'Ανθρώπου* is emphatic, to mark the contrast; for if it be so with a mere man's covenant, how much more so with God's, which was also a ratified covenant! To add to a covenant is virtually to annul it; the Judaistic dogma, under the guise of a supplement, was really an abrogation of the original promise or covenant.

Ver. 16. *Τῷ δὲ 'Αβραὰμ ἐῤῥέθησαν αἱ ἐπαγγελίαι, καὶ τῷ σπέρματι αὐτοῦ*—"Now to Abraham were the promises made, and to his seed." The non-Attic form *ἐῤῥέθησαν* has the support of the best MSS., as A, B[1], C, D[1], F, א, etc.; Lobeck, *Phrynichus*, p. 441; Buttmann, vol. ii. p. 121. It is needless and irrelevant on the part of Schott, De Wette, and Hilgenfeld, to make vers. 15–17 a syllogism, and this verse the minor premiss. A more definite contrast must in that case have been expressed, and the parenthetical and explanatory clause *οὐ λέγει* would destroy the symmetry. The minor premiss is in ver. 17, and this verse is rather a subsidiary illustration of some points or words in the covenant, the validity of which he is just going to prove. Thus—

1. The plural *αἱ ἐπαγγελίαι* is not one promise, but many, or the promise repeated in varying terms: Gen. xii. 3, xiii. 15, xv. 18, xvii. 8, xxii. 16–18. The arrangement of the words gives the emphasis to *καὶ τῷ σπέρματι αὐτοῦ* by severing it from *τῷ 'Αβραάμ*.

2. The promises were spoken not to Abraham only, but to Abraham and his Seed. This Seed he explains to be Christ, so that until the Seed came, the promise was not fulfilled; it was still a divine promise awaiting its fulfilment when the law was given, and could not therefore be set aside by it, or be clogged with new clauses. The force of the argument lies in this, that the seed is not Abraham's natural progeny, to which

[1] So, too, in the palimpsest recently published by Tischendorf, Leipzig 1865.

Canaan had been given, but Christ, who did not come into the world till the fulness of time. The simple dative, not that of relation, is here employed, and the meaning is not, for Abraham and his seed (Matthias, Vömel), nor "through" or "in reference to Abraham and his seed" (Brown), but the Seed is characterized as the party to whom the promises were uttered or given.

3. The point of the argument then is the quotation *καὶ τῷ σπέρματί σου*, the very words employed by God. For he explains—

Οὐ λέγει· Καὶ τοῖς σπέρμασιν, ὡς ἐπὶ πολλῶν, ἀλλ' ὡς ἐφ' ἑνός· Καὶ τῷ σπέρματί σου, ὅς ἐστι Χριστός—"He saith not, 'And to seeds,' as of many, but as of one, 'And TO THY SEED,' which is Christ." The *καί* is plainly a part of the quotation, which must be taken either from Gen. xiii. 15 or from xvii. 8, and therefore not from Gen. xxii. 18, as Tertullian and many after him have supposed. The apostle now explains the meaning and the unipersonal reference of the singular *σπέρμα*. *Οὐ λέγει*, referring back to *ἐῤῥέθησαν*, probably in this instance not impersonal (Lightfoot), for *Θεός* is emphatically implied in the context and in *ἐῤῥέθησαν*. He who spoke the promises used this phrase, "And to thy seed." In the two clauses *ἐπί* with the genitive has some trace of its local meaning, "on"—the utterance of God in the promise rests not on many, but on one—like *scribere super*. Winer, § 47, 9. There are several instances in classical Greek. Ast, *Lex. Plat. sub voce*. *Λεγόμενον ἐπὶ τῶν θεῶν τούτων*, Ælian, *Var. Hist.* i. 31; Plato, *Charmides*, 155, D; and Stallbaum's modification of Heindorf's note, which, however, is not applicable here, vol. ii. 132-3; Diodor. Sic. i. 12. For the attraction in *ὅς*, which has not *ἑνός* for its antecedent (Beza), see Winer, § 24, 3; Mark xv. 16; 1 Tim. iii. 15.

The apostle's argument is, that the singular *σπέρμα* signifies what the plural *σπέρματα* could not have suggested. This plural is indeed found in 4 Macc. xvii. 1, *τῶν 'Αβραμιαίων σπερμάτων*; but this use is not so natural. Comp. in poetry, Æschylus, *Supp.* 290; Sophocles, *Œdip. Col.* 1275. The Hebrew term זֶרַע is used in the plural, with quite a different meaning, to signify "grains of seed," 1 Sam. viii. 15, and in Dan. i. 12, where it is rendered "pulse" in our version. On this account the plural זְרָעִים could not have been employed in such a promise, and therefore the apostle's argument from it would be void. The plural, however, is used in Chaldee in the sense of posterity; and the apostle's inference only implies, that had a plural been employed in the promise, his reasoning could not have been sustained. It is also true, on the other hand, that *σπέρμα* may have a plural signification, as in Rom. iv. 18, ix. 7, where the apostle's argument depends on it, as also in ver. 29 of this chapter. The singular זֶרַע denotes a man's offspring as a collective unit, not its separate individuals but in their related oneness, the organic unity of the branches with the root. In the promise made to Abraham, however, the singular term is not a collective unity, but has an unipersonal sense which no plural form could have borne, such as בָּנִים, וּבָנֶיךָ. The singular form thus gives a ground for the interpretation which he advances. The Septuagint had already given a similar personal meaning to *σπέρμα—αὐτός σου τηρήσει κεφαλήν*, Gen. iii. 15. That seed is Christ—not Jesus in individual humanity, but the Messiah so promised. The posterity of Abraham was embodied in Him; He was its summation and crown. It would never have existed but for Him, nor could its mission to bless all nations be fulfilled but in Him. For Him was Abraham chosen, and Canaan promised and conferred. In typical fore-union with Him was the old economy organized, and its testimony to Him was the soul of prophecy. The seed of Abraham blessed the world by the circulation of its oracles in a Greek translation, its code being a protest against polytheism, against atheism — the negation of the Infinite, and against pantheism—the absorption of the finite,—a vindication of the dignity of man as made in God's image, and of the majesty of law as based on His authority; while it made a special providence a matter of daily experience, and disclosed the harmony of mercy with the equity and purity of divine legislation. Babylon, Egypt, and Phœnicia had contributed to the education of humanity, which was also mightily advanced by the genius of Greece and the legislation of Rome. But Judaism diffused a higher form of truth: it taught religion—the knowledge and worship of that God who was in Christ, in whom all the spiritual seed are comprehended, in whom they were chosen, and in whom they have died, been raised, and enthroned in the heavenly places. In the Old Testament there are glimpses of the same truth; for the servant of Jehovah is sometimes the Messiah in person, sometimes Israel either national or spiritual, and sometimes Messiah combining in Himself and identified with the theocratic people. Messiah was the Lord's servant, and so was Israel; their service, either individual or collective, had its root and acceptance in Him. Israel was God's son, His first-born—closely related to Him, reflecting His image, and doing His will among the nations; and Messiah's relations and functions are described in similar language. In this way Moses, in his time, bore "the reproach of Christ;" and in the Gospel of Matthew (ii. 15) a prophetic utterance regarding the chosen people is said to be fulfilled in the child Jesus—"Out of Egypt have I called my son." Hos. xi. 1. The same truth is more vividly brought out in the New Testament—the identity of Christ and Christ's. "Why persecutest thou me?" said Jesus to the persecutor. The apostle "fills up that which is behind of the afflictions of Christ in his flesh for His body's sake," and he says, "The sufferings of Christ abound in us;" and again, "For as the body is one, and hath many members, and all the members of that one body, being many, are one body: so also is Christ." Acts ix. 4; 1 Cor. xii. 12; 2 Cor. i. 5; Heb. xi. 26. See under Eph. i. 23 and Col. i. 24.

The meaning is not, Christ and His church (Augustine, Beza, Matthies, Jatho); nor the church under a special aspect, as Bengel and Ernesti; but Christ Himself, embodying at the same time His church—the Head with its members in organic unity.

Ver. 17. *Τοῦτο δὲ λέγω*—"This, however, I say," or, my meaning is. The *δέ* serves to resume or restate the argument, applying the previous principle underlying a man's covenant to the point under discussion in the form of an implied inference.

Διαθήκην προκεκυρωμένην ὑπὸ τοῦ Θεοῦ εἰς Χριστὸν ὁ μετὰ τετρακόσια καὶ τριάκοντα ἔτη γεγονὼς νόμος οὐκ ἀκυροῖ, εἰς τὸ καταργῆσαι τὴν ἐπαγγελίαν—"a covenant which has been before confirmed by God for Christ, the law, which was four hundred and thirty years after, does not invalidate, so as to do away the promise." The words *εἰς Χριστόν* of the Received Text are doubtful. They are found in D, F, K, L, majority of cursives, the Syriac version (ܡܩܕܡ ܒܡܫܝܚܐ), the Claromontane Latin, and the Greek fathers; but are wanting in A, B, C, א, in the Vulgate, Coptic, and in Jerome and Augustine. The words are therefore suspicious, though Ewald, Wieseler, Hauck, and Hofmann vindicate their genuineness; and were they genuine, they cannot mean "in Christ" as in the Authorized Version, nor "with Christ" as Scholefield, nor "until Christ" as Borger, but "for Christ." Jelf, 625; iv. 11, v. 10; Rom. ii. 26; 2 Cor. xii. 6, etc. The phrase, however, is quite in harmony with the statement of the previous verse: the covenant was ratified with Abraham and his Seed, or its primary object was Christ—not in Him, but with a view to Him was it confirmed. The covenant was ratified "before" by God with Abraham, the *προ* in the participle being in contrast with the following *μετά*. The ratification took place when the covenant was made. In one instance there was a sacrifice; in another an oath, when God "sware by Himself." If a man's covenant on being confirmed cannot be set aside or interpolated with new conditions, much more must God's covenant remain unchanged, unvitiated, unabrogated. The law, so unlike it in contents and purpose, can be no portion of it; and the priority of the covenant by four centuries is additional proof of its validity: the law, that was introduced so long after it, can have no retrospective annulling influence over it. *Magnitudo intervalli auget promissionis auctoritatem* (Bengel, Koppe, Meyer). The *γεγονώς* means "that came into existence" with the act of legislation at Mount Sinai. The *εἰς* introducing the last clause gives the purpose of *ἀκυροῦ*: "so as to do away with the promise"—the promise which was so much the core of the covenant, and so identified with it that they are convertible terms. Rom. i. 20; 1 Thess. ii. 16.

The law came in "430 years after the promise"—*μετὰ ἔτη τετρακόσια καὶ τριάκοντα.* The apostle thus puts the interval in specific numbers. If the period from the promise to the Exodus was 430 years,[1] as the apostle asserts, then the sojourn

[1] After the promise twenty-five years elapsed to the birth of Isaac, Abraham being seventy-five when he came into Canaan, and 100 years old when Isaac was born, Gen. xii. 4, xxi. 5; Isaac was sixty years old when Jacob was born, as is related in Gen. xxv. 26; Jacob was 130 years

in Egypt could not have been 400 years; or if it lasted 400 years, then the apostle's chronology is defective by more than 200 years. But in Ex. xii. 40 the abode in Egypt is said to be "430 years;" in Gen. xv. 13 the time of affliction is predicted to be 400 years, the statement being quoted by Stephen in his address, Acts vii. 6. There is thus a very marked difference of computation, and the apostle has followed the chronology of the Septuagint. It reads in Ex. xii. 40, *ἡ δὲ κατοίκησις τῶν υἱῶν Ἰσραὴλ ἣν κατῴκησαν ἐν γῇ Αἰγύπτῳ καὶ ἐν γῇ Χαναάν, [αὐτοὶ καὶ οἱ πατέρες αὐτῶν,] ἔτη τετρακόσια τριάκοντα*—the clause within brackets being found in Codex A, and there being other minor variations. The Samaritan Pentateuch reads similarly. The apostle adopts this chronology of the Alexandrian translators, who might, from their residence in Egypt, have some special means of information on the point. Josephus, *Antiq.* ii. 15, 2, says "that they left Egypt in the month Xanthicus . . . 430 years after our forefather Abraham came into Canaan, but 215 years after Jacob's removal into Egypt." Josephus, however, with strange inconsistency, had announced another chronology in his *Antiquities*, ii. 9, 1, and he

old when he went down to Egypt;—these periods producing 215 years. Similarly as to the length of the abode in Egypt. It is stated, Gen. xli. 46–7, that Joseph was thirty-nine years old when Jacob went down to Egypt; and as Jacob was 130 at the same period, it follows that Joseph was born when his father Jacob was ninety-one. Jacob's marriage with Rachel took place when he was about seventy-eight, and at the same time as his marriage with Leah. Levi, Leah's third son, could not have been born before Jacob's eighty-first year, and he was therefore about forty-nine at the settlement in Egypt. Levi lived 137 years in all, eighty-eight of them in Egypt. Amram married his father's sister Jochebed, "the daughter of Levi, whom his mother bare to Levi in Egypt." Now Jochebed must have been born within eighty-eight years after the arrival in Egypt, and Moses her son was eighty years at the Exodus. Giving her the full age of forty-seven when he was born, you make the sojourn 215 years. But if the sojourn in Egypt was 430 years, then, allowing Jochebed to have been born in the last year of her father's life, she must have been 262 years when Moses was born. In this way the apostle's shorter chronology may be made out and sustained. It is the result of an implicit faith in entangled theories of the succession and duration of Egyptian dynasties for Bunsen to lengthen the sojourn in Egypt to 1500 years, or for Lepsius to shorten it to ninety, or for Engelstoft to make it only a century. See Schöttgen's *Horæ Heb.* p. 736; Augustine, *De Civitate Dei*, xvi. 24, *Opera*, vol. vii., Gaume, Paris 1838; also Rosellini, *Monumenti dell' Egitto*, vol. i. 293.

follows it also in his *Jewish War*, v. 9, 4. Philo adopts it, *Quis rerum divinarum hæres*, § 54, *Opera*, vol. iv. p. 121, ed. Pfeiffer; so also Theophilus, *ad Autolycum*, iii. 10, p. 215, ed. Otto. Hengstenberg, Kurtz, Hävernick, Ewald, Tiele, Reinke, Delitzsch, and Hofmann support this view, and disparage the Alexandrian reading as a clumsy and artificial interpolation. But the apostle adopted the Hellenistic chronology, and it can be satisfactorily vindicated out of many distinct intimations and data even in the Hebrew Text. There seem to have been two traditions on the subject, and Josephus apparently acknowledged both of them. It is ingenious but baseless to attempt a reconciliation by supposing that the promise may be regarded as made to Jacob just before he went down to Egypt, so that 430 years can be allowed for the sojourn (Olshausen), or by maintaining that the "land not theirs" of the Abrahamic promise comprehends Canaan as well as Egypt. See Usher's *Chron. Sac.* cap. viii. As to the possible rate of increase of population during 215 years, see the calculations in Birks, *The Exodus of Israel*, chap. iii.

Ver. 18. *Εἰ γὰρ ἐκ νόμου ἡ κληρονομία, οὐκ ἔτι ἐξ ἐπαγγελίας*—"For if the inheritance be of the law, it is no more of promise." The *γάρ* shows strongly the basis of the previous statement—if the law abrogate the promise, inheritance comes of law; but law and promise are quite antagonistic in nature, so that if it be of law, the promise is completely set aside. The one hypothesis excludes the other—there is no middle ground. *Ἐκ* has its usual significance of origin, and *οὐκ ἔτι* is used in a logical sense—"no more," not in point of time, but by force of inference. Winer, § 65, 10. The "inheritance" was to Abraham the land of Canaan; and as the name is naturally employed in connection with the Abrahamic covenant, of which it was the characteristic term and gift, it became a symbol of spiritual blessing, or of "the better country," as the apostle argues in Heb. xi. It does not mean expressly the Holy Spirit (Gwynne).

Τῷ δὲ Ἀβραὰμ δι' ἐπαγγελίας κεχάρισται ὁ Θεός—"but God has given it to Abraham by promise." "By promise," or "through promise"—through the medium of promise; not exactly in the form of promise (Rückert, Peile), though that is the result. The verb is used in its common transitive signification, the inheritance being understood; and the perfect tense denotes the duration of the gift. Compare Rom. viii. 32; 1 Cor. ii. 12; Phil. i. 29. It alters the connection to make Christ the object of the gift, as Grotius; or to supply no object at all, as Schott, Olshausen, and Matthias (*gratiosum se ei exhibuit*); or to take the verb in a passive sense, God giving Himself as the inheritance, as Caspari. This is not the usage of the New Testament which never identifies God with the inheritance, but describes Him as its Giver, Lord, and Possessor. Rom. viii. 17; 1 Cor. vi. 9, xv. 50; Eph. v. 5; Jas. ii. 5. The object of the apostle is to show the validity of the promise having for its gift the inheritance, which, if it be of law, cannot be of promise; but the fact is, that God gave it to Abraham by promise, and it cannot be of law. What is expressed as the subject of the first or conditional clause is naturally supplied as the object of the second or demonstrative clause, resting on the great historical fact which was universally admitted. The point of the argument is lost in generality if no accusative be supplied. For the verse is a species of dilemmatic syllogism,[1] the first giving the hypothesis—disjunctive major—if the inheritance be of the law, it is no longer of promise; the minor being, but God has given it to Abraham by promise; and the conclusion is so self-evident that it does not need to be expressed—therefore it is not of the law. For similar reasoning, see Rom. iv. 13, etc. If, then, the law cannot upset the promise, and yet if that law be of divine origin and introduction, what is its use and meaning? It must serve some purpose worthy of its Author, though its functions be very different from those assigned it by the Galatian Judaists. Therefore the apostle puts the question—

Ver. 19. *Τί οὖν ὁ νόμος;*—"What then is the law?" "What thanne the lawe?" (Wycliffe.) *Τί* is not for *διὰ τί*—"wherefore" (Schott, Brown, Wieseler, Bagge, and Jatho); nor is *ἐτέθη*, as the latter thinks, the natural supplement, *ἐστι* being quite sufficient. The passages adduced in proof by Wieseler have a verb expressed, and one of a different character. The *τί* is the neuter, employed in reference to the abstract nature of the subject. It often occurs with such a meaning. Bernhardy, p. 336. The law—not "the

[1] Sir Wm. Hamilton's *Logic*, vol. i. pp. 350–1.

ceremonial law" alone (Gwynne)—is not useless, as might be conjectured; it is in no sense περιττός, ἀλλὰ πάνυ χρησίμως ἐδόθη (Chrysostom), for—

Τῶν παραβάσεων χάριν προσετέθη—"on account of the transgressions it was superadded." The compound verb is to be preferred, on preponderant authority, to the simple ἐτέθη of the Received Text, which has little in its favour—D, F, and the Latin versions (*posita est*), Clement, Origen, and Eusebius in some quotations. There may have been a temptation to substitute the simple verb, as the compound might seem opposed to ἐπιδιατάσσεται of ver. 15—"addeth thereto."

The idiomatic χάριν, originally *in gratiam*—"in favour of," "for the sake of"—came at length to signify generally "on account of," a definite purpose being involved. Many examples may be found in Ellendt (*Lex. Soph. sub voce*), who explains it as *in gratiam alicujus, inde alicujus aut hominis aut rei causa significans, quanquam minime semper gratia adsignificatur;* and in Ast (*Lex. Platon.*), who says: *Præpositionis instar ita ponitur, ut verti possit "causa" et "propter."* Various meanings have been assigned to the expression, "on account of the transgressions."

1. Many give it the sense of to restrain transgressions—Clement, *Homil.* xi. 16, παραπτωμάτων χάριν ἡ τιμωρία ἕπεται—the result being that "He may present them pure in the day of universal judgment." Many of the fathers and the older expositors held this opinion, followed by Neander, Olshausen, De Wette, Baur, and others. This is one of the ends of law generally, since it commands obedience to its statutes and threatens a penalty on transgressors. But the term employed is παραβάσεων, not ἁμαρτία, and implies in itself the existence of a law or legal standard, without which sins could scarcely bear such an appellation: "where no law is, there is no transgression."

2. Some attach the meaning to the phrase—"the law was superadded for the sake of transgressions," to multiply them. Alford, Meyer, Wieseler, Lipsius, and Hofmann, who put it in various phases. But such a view is extreme, for it is the application to a passing phrase such as this of the formal argument of the apostle in a theological section of the Epistle to the Romans, v. 20, etc. It is true that the law does this in various ways, for it irritates man's fallen and perverse nature,

and brings about that love of forbidden things which the apostle pictures in Rom. vii.—*ut transgressio sit et abundet.* Luther.

But 3, probably the phrase means that the law multiplies transgressions chiefly by detecting them, and bringing men to a knowledge of them. "I had not known sin but by the law: for I had not known lust except the law had said, Thou shalt not covet;" "sin that it appear sin;" "that sin by the commandment might become exceeding sinful." Rom. vii. 7–13. So Calvin, Winer, Matthies, Windischmann, Ellicott. Meyer's objection to this opinion, resting on his view of the uniform meaning of *χάριν*, falls to the ground. This view is thus the virtual basis of the one enunciated before it, as it is principally by the knowledge of transgressions that they are multiplied. For the law so instructs in the nature of sin, that what before was reckoned innocent is seen to be transgression, and what was regarded as trivial comes to be recognised as "exceeding sinful." Through this detection transgressions are of necessity multiplied in number and intensified in enormity. Gwynne's notion is inadmissible, that the phrase refers to the work of the priesthood in offering sacrifice "on behalf of sins." It must not be forgotten, too, that the law is here regarded as an intermediate dispensation, as is intimated in the following clause—*προσετέθη, ἄχρις οὗ.* The purpose of the superaddition of the law was connected with the coming of Christ—that is, to prepare for it, by so deepening the sense of sinfulness that men, convicted of so often breaking it, could not look to it for righteousness, but must be "shut up unto the faith which should afterwards be revealed." The Mosaic dispensation, provisionally introduced between the Abrahamic promise and the coming of the Seed, was a preparative or an educative instrument, not merely in its typical services as foreshowing the realities of atonement and pardon, but in the ethical power of multiplying transgressions through the light which it cast upon them, and of convincing those who were under it of the necessity of Christ's advent in order to release them from its curse. The function of the law was to produce profounder views of the number and heinousness of sins, as preparatory to the appearance of Him who came to deliver from its awful penalty, so that, under the pressure of such convictions, His redemption might be welcomed as a needed and an adapted blessing. Thus the law did not add to the promise, but was a different institute altogether; as Meyer remarks, "it was not an ἐπιδιαθήκη," or anything connected with the ἐπιδιατάσσεται of the fifteenth verse. And it was also temporary—

Ἄχρις οὗ ἔλθῃ τὸ σπέρμα ᾧ ἐπήγγελται—"until the Seed to whom the promise has been made shall have come." This use of the subjunctive proceeds upon this, that the apostle throws himself back to the time when the law was given, which thereby becomes to him present time, and from it he looks down into the future, though historically that future was now past time. Winer, § 41, 1; Jelf, § 841. The particle ἄν is not used, as the period referred to is a definite one, without any contingency. Stallbaum, *Plato, Phædo* 62 C, *Opera*, vol. i. p. 32; Hermann, *de Part.* ἄν, pp. 110-12, *omittitur* ἄν *in re certa designanda;* Klotz-Devarius, ii. 368, *non adjuncta* ἄν *ubi eventus per se ponitur.* The Seed is Christ—ᾧ, to whom, not εἰς ὅν, but the ordinary dative (Winer, Usteri), as ver. 16 shows. It seems better to take the verb as passive, for then it is in harmony with ἐῤῥέθησαν, ver. 16. The Vulgate has *promiserat*, and Bengel and Flatt prefer it. Compare 2 Macc. iv. 27 and Rom. iv. 21, Heb. xii. 26, in both which places the Authorized Version prefers the active. Bretschneider in his *Lexicon* gives the meaning, *cui demandatum est ut legem mosaicam tollat*—a meaning unauthorized by New Testament usage and unnatural in the context. It serves no purpose, as in many editions of the New Testament, to make this clause a parenthesis. The same sense might have been expressed by two finite verbs and a conjunction. Hermann, *Vigerus*, vol. ii. p. 614, London 1824. The next clauses point out the mode in which the law was superadded, and the first is—

Διαταγεὶς δι᾽ ἀγγέλων—"being ordained by means of angels"—*ordinata*, Vulgate; *disposita*, Clarom.,—the aorist denoting time contemporaneous with the former verb προσετέθη. The phrase διατάσσειν νόμον is to enact a law: νόμον διέταξε Κρονίων, Hesiod, *Opera et Dies* 276, ed. Goettling; τόν γε νόμον διατάττειν, Plato, *Leg.* 746 E. Comp. Judg. v. 9. So in his address Stephen says that they received the law εἰς διαταγὰς ἀγγέλων—"at the enactments of angels," εἰς as in Matt. xii. 41. But the word will not bear the sense of "promulgate," as many have wrongly conjectured. The phrase δι᾽ ἀγγέλων signifies by the instrumentality of angels, whatever that instrumentality may mean, and is not to be diluted into "in the presence of" (Calovius, Loesner), or "under the attestation of" (Peile). Nor can *ἀγγέλων* signify men—messengers (Zegerus), nor priests, *ἱερέας*, as Chrysostom alternatively puts it. The angels are not the source of the law in any sense (Schultess); *διά* implies only instrumentality. But in some way or other as God's instruments they enacted it, so that it was *ὁ δι' ἀγγέλων λαληθεὶς λόγος*—"the word spoken by angels." Heb. ii. 2; Winer, § 47, 1. The divine precepts were by them made audible to the people, or they had mysterious connection with the awful phenomena which enshrined the majesty of the Lawgiver. Josephus holds fast the distinction—*τῶν ἐν τοῖς νόμοις δι' ἀγγέλων παρὰ τοῦ Θεοῦ μαθόντων*. *Antiq.* xv. 5, 3. It is one thing to originate a law, and a different thing to enjoin it. The special point is, that the law was not given immediately by God, but mediately by angels—they came between God and the people; but Jehovah, without any intervening agency, and directly, spoke the promise to Abraham. No allusion is made to angels in the portions of Exodus which relate the giving of the law. The first reference is in the last blessing of Moses, Deut. xxxiii. 2: "The Lord came from Sinai, and rose up from Seir unto them; He shined forth from Mount Paran, and He came with ten thousands of saints: from His right hand went a fiery law for them." The special clause is וְאָתָה מֵרִבְבֹת קֹדֶשׁ—"He came from the midst of thousands of holy ones." But the Seventy had a different reading, or fused together two readings, and translate, *σὺν μυριάσι Κάδης*,—adding, *ἐκ δεξιῶν αὐτοῦ ἄγγελοι μετ' αὐτοῦ*. Not a few expositors follow the Sept. rendering, which requires the pointing קָדֵשׁ, and render, from the heights of Kadesh; but the Hebrew will not bear such a rendering. Aquila has *ἀπὸ μυριάδων ἁγιασμοῦ*; Symmachus, *ἀπὸ μυριάδος ἁγίας*; the Vulgate, *cum eo sanctorum millia*. So also the Targums. The common rendering is the best. The angels appear already in connection with God, Gen. xxviii. 12; and as "God's host," Gen. xxxii. 1, 2. The "holy ones" of the Hebrew text cannot be the Jewish people, as is thought by Luther, Vatablus, and Dathe; for He came not with them, but to them. Again, in Ps. lxviii. 17 there is a similar allusion: "The chariots of God are two myriads, thousands repeated (or thousands on thousands): the Lord is with them, Sinai is in His holy place." Jewish tradition gradually enlarged on these hints, though the word angels occurs in none of the original clauses, and made such a romance out of them as may be found in Eisenmenger's *Entdecktes Judenthum*, vol. i. 308, etc. The mention of angels in connection with the law is not specially meant to shed lustre upon it, as in Acts vii. 38 and Heb. ii. 2; but the object here is to show that the employment of angels—glorious though these beings are—in the enactment of it proves its inferiority to the promise, which was directly given by Jehovah in sole majesty to Abraham, no one coming between them. And for the same end it is added—

'Εν χειρὶ μεσίτου—"in the hand of a mediator." Meyer takes the clause in a historical sense: Moses having received from God the tables of the law, carried them to the people. Ex. xxxii. 11, xxxiv. 29. But idiomatic usage shows that *ἐν χειρί* has much the same meaning as *διά*, the Hebrew phrase בְּיַד, which it often represents in the Septuagint, having this general signification. Ex. xxxv. 29; Lev. x. 11, xxvi. 46; Num. iv. 38, 41–45, xv. 23; Josh. xiv. 2; 2 Chron. xxxiii. 8; in all which places the phrase is by the hand of Moses. Compare 1 Kings xii. 15, Jer. xxxvii. 2, Prov. xxvi. 6. As the giving of the law is described here, there can be no doubt that Moses is the mediator, whatever might be the position of the high priest in subsequent times. Moses thus describes his own mediation: "I stood between you and the Lord at that time" —*ἀναμέσον Κυρίου καὶ ὑμῶν*. Sept. Deut. v. 5, 27. Philo says, that on hearing the sound of the idolatry connected with the worship of the golden calf, and receiving the divine command, he sprang down to be "a mediator and reconciler"—*μεσίτης καὶ διαλλακτής*. *Vita Mosis*, iii. 19. The name mediator, סַרְסוּר, is often given to Moses in the rabbinical writings. See Schoettgen and Wetstein. The allusions in Heb. viii. 6, ix. 15, xii. 24, also plainly recognise the mediatorship of Moses. Origen started the opinion that the mediator was Christ, and was followed by Athanasius, Ambrose, Jerome, Augustine, Chrysostom, Hilary, Victorinus, and others; but Basil, Gregory of Nyssa, and Theodore of Mopsuestia, Theodoret, Epiphanius, and others rightly maintain that the mediator was

Moses, and the most of modern commentators adhere to the same view. Schmieder takes him to be the angel of the covenant (*Nova Interpretatio*, Gal. iii. 19, 20), as does also Schneckenburger. This angel is often referred to in the Old Testament, but there is no ground for the opinion that He is referred to here, and in those simple terms. But Moses did the work of a mediator—went from the people to God, and came from God to the people; the first function more priestly, and the second more prophetic, in character. Through his mediatorial intervention the law was superadded, but the promise was made by Jehovah to Abraham without any one between them. On the other hand, it is held by Calvin, Meyer, Wieseler, Winer, Schott, Baumgarten-Crusius, and Alford, that the apostle refers to angels and a mediator in order to illustrate the glory of the law. But even in Heb. ii. 2, "the word spoken by angels" is put in contrast to the "salvation spoken by the Lord," and is regarded as inferior to it, the argument being from the less to the greater. The contrast formally stated there is implied here—the *majus* did not need to be expressed: the covenant was *confirmed by God; God gave it* to Abraham by promise; *God is one.* Is the law against the *promises of God?* It is no objection to say that the employment of a mediator is no mark of inferiority, since the new dispensation has its Mediator too; for, first, the contrast is not between the law and the gospel, but between the law and the earlier promise; and secondly, the Mediator of the new covenant is the Son of God—no mere man, as Moses; and, as Professor Lightfoot says, "the argument here rests in effect on our Lord's divinity as its foundation." Nor could it be "unwise," as Meyer argues, in the apostle to depreciate the law in writing to those who were zealots about it; for he only states in these two clauses two facts about it which they could not gainsay, and he quietly leaves them to draw the inference. Nor is his object to enhance the solemnity of the giving of the law as a preparation for Christ; for that is not the theme in hand—it is the relation of the law superinduced because of transgressions, to the older promise, and the function of a law as a pædagogue is afterwards introduced. Granting that its enactment by angels glorifies the law, it is yet inferior to a word immediately spoken by the God of angels. The argument of the verse is: 1. The law has no organic relation to the promise, was neither a new form of it nor a codicil to it, did not spring out of it, but was superadded as a foreign and unallied element. 2. The law has functional connection with sin; the promise regards an inheritance. 3. The law was provisional and temporary only; the promise has no limitation of time, and is not to be superseded. 4. The law was given by a species of double intervention—the instrumentality of angels and the mediation of Moses; the promise was given directly and immediately from God's own lips, no one stepping in between its Giver and its recipient—neither angel ordaining it nor man conveying it. 5. The promise, as resting solely on God, was unconditioned, and therefore permanent and unchanging; the law, interposed between two parties, and specially contingent on a human element, was liable to suspension or abolition. 6. This law, so necessitated by sin, so transient, so connected with angelic ordinance and human handling, was an institute later also by far in its inauguration—was 430 years after the promise.

Ver. 20. Ὁ δὲ μεσίτης ἑνὸς οὐκ ἔστιν, ὁ δὲ Θεὸς εἷς ἐστίν—"Now a mediator is not of one, but God is one;" equivalent to saying, No mediator can belong to one party—ἑνός emphatic—but two parties at least are always implied. It is philologically wrong in Hauck to regard μεσίτης as meaning "one taken out of the midst," and equivalent to intercessor or representative, for it is "middleman." The verse defines by the way what a mediator is, δέ being transitional, and ὁ μεσίτης giving the specific idea—virtually every mediator, "denoting in an individual a whole class." Winer, § 18. Matt. xii. 35; John x. 11; 2 Cor. xii. 12. Compare Job ix. 33. Meyer quotes Hermann: *Articulus definit infinita . . . aut designando certo de multis, aut quæ multa sunt cunctis in unum colligendis.* Præf. ad *Iphig. in Aulide*, p. xv. Lipsiæ 1831. In every work of mediation there must be more than one party, and thus at the giving of the law in the hand of a mediator there were two parties—God on the one side, and the Jewish people on the other, there being a covenant or contract between them. This view of the clause is held generally by Theodoret, Luther, Keil, Usteri, Rückert, De Wette, etc. The numeral ἑνός must be masculine, in correspondence with the following εἷς; but Koppe and Bengel supply νόμου, Borger πράγματος, Keil *μέρους*, Sack *τρόπου*, Rosenmüller and Steudel *σπέρματος*, understanding by it believers, also Gurlitt who limits it to heathen believers (*Stud. u. Kritik.* 1843), and Jatho who restricts it to Christ, the one Seed. Some, with a wrong interpretation of the clause ending with *ἀγγέλων*, take the singular *ἑνός* in contrast: Moses was not a mediator of one, *i.e.* God, but of many, *i.e.* angels; as Schultess, Schmieder, Caspari, Huth, Schneckenburger, and Gfrörer in his *das Jahrhundert des Heils*, i. 228, etc.

"But God is one"—*ὁ δὲ Θεὸς εἷς ἐστιν*. *Δέ* adversative; *ἑνός* being numerical, so must *εἷς*. God is one, and is therefore mediatorless. God Himself without any intervention speaks the promise to Abraham; the promise is conveyed through no third party, as was the law. Whatever contingency might be in the law and its conveyance by a mediator who went between God and the people, there can be none with regard to the promise, the direct and unconditioned word of Jehovah Himself alone. The all-inclusive One uttered the words, "In thy seed shall all nations of the earth be blessed," to Abraham immediately, no one placing himself between them. God the Giver is one (not two—Himself and a mediator) in the bestowment of that absolute promise, which the introduction of the law four centuries afterwards cannot modify or set aside. It is not necessary for this interpretation, as some object, that the historical *ἦν* should be employed, as the present is commonly employed in a definitive sentence. The clause, "but God is one," does not announce dogmatically the unity of the Godhead, as do several similar utterances in the Pentateuch. Whatever doctrinal ideas the words might suggest, they are here used on purpose to deny all duality in the bestowment of the promise, the *ὁ μεσίτης* as implying more than one—*ἑνὸς οὐκ*—being in contrast with God, who is one—*εἷς*. The law, in the period of introduction, in its temporary and provisional nature, and in the mediatorial process by which it was given, is so different from the promise and its method of bestowment, that the apostle next puts the question sharply, "Is the law then against the promises of God?" This view, which appears to be the simplest, as well as grammatically correct and in harmony with the context, has been opposed by many, who take *ὁ μεσίτης* to refer to the mediator just mentioned—either Christ or Moses—the verse being then regarded as descriptive of his relations or functions; some supposing it to state an objection, others regarding it as the refutation of one.

The interpretations which have been given of this verse, so difficult from its terse brevity, amount to several hundreds;[1] and it would be a vain attempt to enumerate or classify them. Suffice it to say, first, that it is in vain to attempt to displace the verse, as if it were spurious, for it is found without variation in all MSS.,—or as if it were made up of two glosses, first written on the margin, and then carelessly taken into the text (Michaelis, Lücke, *Stud. u. Kritik.* 1828). Equally vain is it to rewrite it, as if the first words should be τὸ δὲ σπέρμα (Gödör); or to change the accentuation of ἕνος, and give it the unwarranted signification of annual—"the yearly mediator is no more," οὐκ ἔστιν (Weigand). As little to the purpose are such eccentric interpretations as that of Bertholdt, who takes ἑνός to refer to Abraham, because he is called הָאֶחָד in Isa. li. 2; or that of Kaiser, who supplies υἱός—"Moses is not the son of One, that is God, but Christ is;" or that of Holsten, that ὁ μεσίτης is the law standing between two things—the promise and the fulfilment; or that of Matthias, who, overlooking the contrast between ἑνός in the first clause and εἷς in the second, understands the second clause thus—"God (and not fallible man) is one of the two parties,"—his conclusion being, that therefore the law, though given by angels, is of divine origin; and then, giving the κατά of the following verse the sense of "under," he makes the question to be, "Does the law fall under the idea of promise?" or, "Does the law belong to the category of the promises?"—or that of Hermann, who, preserving the numerical meaning of εἷς, and regarding it as part of the minor proposition of a syllogism, brings out this odd sense: *Deus autem unus est; ergo apud Deum cogitari non potest interventor, esset enim is, qui intercederet inter Deum et Deum, quod absurdum est;*—but the *reductio* assumed as an inference is wholly foreign to the verse and context, and his further exposition proceeds on the sense of *testamentum*, as given to διαθήκη;—or that of Ewald, whose interpretation is not dissimilar in some points, but who, instead of saying "between

[1] Weigand in 1821 reported and examined 243 interpretations, and controversy on the passage may be seen still in several recent numbers of the *Stud. u. Kritiken.*

God and God," speaks of two "innerly different Gods, or an earlier and a later God." So Bagge—"There are not two gods, —one giving the promise, the other the law,—but One only;" and similarly Vömel. Bengel's general view is, "The party to whom the mediator belonged is different from God—namely, the law. There is not one God before and another after the giving of the law. Before the law He transacted without a mediator; the mediator belongs to the law, but the promise to God." Quite apart from the meaning and the course of argument is the opinion that makes εἷς mean ὁ αὐτός, *unus idemque* (Semler), or *sibi constans* (Beza), or that regards ἑνός as ἑνότητος—a mediator implying diversity of opinion (Gabler, Schöttgen). The exegesis of Dr. Brown is ingenious but philologically baseless, because ἑνός and εἷς never signify immutable, as Borger and Koppe contend. "The law was given by the hands of Moses as a mediator. But was he not the mediator of Him who is one and the same, unchangeable? Now God, who appointed Moses mediator, is one and the same, unchanged and unchangeable." To give ἑνός a numerical meaning in the first clause, but εἷς an ethical meaning in the second clause, is not consistent (Schleiermacher, Usteri). Koppe, Cameron, Sack, and Barnes who gives his exegesis as original, educe this meaning: "While there may be many mediators, God is one, consistent with Himself, so that the two dispensations cannot be opposed." Hilgenfeld, after Matthies, in the same way gives εἷς the sense of absolute unity—*monarchie*. See also Baumgarten-Crusius, Lipsius, *Rechtfertigung*, p. 77. Somewhat similarly Luther: *Neque Deus eget mediatore, cum sit ipse unus secum optime conveniens;* and again, *Deus neminem offendit ergo non indiget ullo mediatore.* Luther's opinion is so far reproduced in Matthies; in Rink—"God is eternal unity" (*Stud. u. Kritik.* 1834), and in De Wette—"God is essential unity." Windischmann has a more complex and untenable view: "God is one—the Giver as the Father, the Receiver as the Son—united,"—*unmittelbar dem Geber und dem Emptfänger nach.* So too his co-religionist Bisping, "The promise was given immediately to the Seed, that is Christ, who is God and man in one person. The promise made by God to God needed no mediator." And similarly also Wilke. It is loading the verse with an inferential sense to explain, that as God is but one of the parties concerned, and as Moses was mediator between God and the Jews only, his mediation could have no effect on a promise which included Gentiles as well as Jews (Locke, Whitby, Chandler); or to conjecture that the apostle's words suggest an allusion to the unity of man—to whom God is one and alike—and to the unity of man with God (Jowett); or to argue, God is one only, one part only, and the Israelites as being the other part are bound to obey the law—*Deus est unus, una (altera) tantummodo pars est gens Israel* (Winer, with whom agree virtually Kern, Paulus, and Sardinoux); or to affirm, God is one, not the other party, and stands therefore not under the law, so that the freedom of Christ the Son of God from the law is established (Steinfass).

Those interpretations which give ὁ μεσίτης a personal reference, and identify it with either Christ or Moses, labour under insuperable difficulties. The fathers generally held the former view, as Chrysostom, Ambros., and Jerome, and many others. The exegesis of some of this class may be thus reported: "The law was given in the hand of a mediator—Jesus Christ. Now He is not the mediator of the one dispensation only, but of the other also. But God is one—the one God gave the law and the promises, and in both cases He has employed the same mediator." But the mediator of the context is very plainly Moses, and that paraphrase assumes greatly more than the text asserts. Similar objections may be made to another form of the same exegesis: "Now the mediator (Jesus Christ) does not belong to one part of the human race, but to both Jew and Gentile, even as the one God is God of both." Others give it this form: "Christ is the mediator between two parties; but God is one of those parties, the elect being the other." Or, "God is in Himself One; so likewise was He one of the parties, the other party being the children of Israel."[1] But the majority hold the reference to be to Moses, as Theodoret, Bengel, Schultess, Jatho, Brown, Hofmann, Wieseler. Theodoret explains: "But Moses was not the mediator of one, for he mediated between God and the people; but God is one. He gave the promise to Abraham, He appointed the law, and He has shown the fulfilment of the promise. It is not one God who did one of these things, and another God the other." Others, as Noesselt,

[1] *The Epistle to the Galatians*, by Sir Stafford Carey, M.A., 1867.

follow the form already given with Christ as mediator: "Moses was not the mediator of the one seed, containing both Jews and Gentiles; but God is one, standing in a common relation to both Jews and Gentiles." The one seed, however, is Christ; and ἑνός is masculine, as the construction plainly determines. Piscator brings out a different conclusion: "God who gave the law by Moses is one, and therefore, being unchanged, still will punish such as break His law; therefore justification by works is impossible." Another form of the exegesis is that of Pareus (1621)—"a mediator implies two parties, out of which one must be transgressors, in reference to ver. 19. But the transgressing party cannot be God, who is one—*justitia et sanctitate semper sibi constans*." Cameron puts it thus: "A mediator (Moses) does not belong to the Sinaitic covenant only, but also to the Abrahamic or Christian covenant (Christ); but God is one—both covenants originate in Him." Wessel takes the genitive ἑνός in the sense of dependence—"the Mediator Christ is not of one God, *i.e.* is not subject to Him as a creature, though officially He became a mediator, nay, He is Himself the One God;" as if the apostle had wished to vindicate Christ's divinity from some objection based upon His economic subordination. Turner regards the verse as an assertion of the great characteristic of the gospel, that "the illustrious Mediator thereof is not the Mediator of one race or class or body of men, as Moses, but of all, as God is one and the same, equally the Father of all." The objection to this and other similar interpretations need not now be recounted. Wieseler's notion is, that the failure of the mediation of Moses—since it concerned not God, but man also—arose out of his having to do with men who have not obeyed the law; the apostle's purpose being to show how the divinity of the law may be reconciled with its sin-working power. The first part of this exegesis is adopted by Kamphausen in Bunsen's *Bibel-werk*. Hofmann's interpretation of the first clause virtually is: "The mediator Moses did not concern himself with the one united seed, as such a unity, according to ver. 28, exists only in Christ, but with a multitude of individuals;" and his interpretation of the second clause is, that it stands in contrast to the phrase "ordained by angels," and asserts the divine unity as opposed to the multitude of those spirits. See Meyer and Wieseler on this interpretation.

Ver. 21. Ὁ οὖν νόμος κατὰ τῶν ἐπαγγελιῶν τοῦ Θεοῦ; μὴ γένοιτο—"Is then the law against the promises of God? God forbid." The οὖν *aperte collectivam vim præ se fert.* Klotz-Devarius, ii. p. 717. "Promises" in the plural may refer to its repetition at various times and in various forms. The genitive τοῦ Θεοῦ may, as read in the light of the context, characterize the promises as God's in a special sense—His as given by Him singly, and without any intervention. The sense proposed by Gwynne, "God in contrast with any other beings," is feeble. The question anticipates a natural objection, which the previous reasoning would suggest—not the statement merely of the 20th verse (Meyer, Winer), nor merely the clause "because of transgressions" in the 19th verse (Estius, Bengel, De Wette); for neither of these two statements by itself leads to the objection which the apostle starts and refutes. The οὖν takes up the entire description. If the law cannot set aside the promise,—if law and promise are so opposite principles, that if the inheritance be of law, it can no longer be of promise,—if the manner in which the promise was given surpasses in true divineness that in which the law was announced, the query at once rises—a query that seems to cast discredit on the previous reasoning by reducing it to an absurdity—"Is the law then against the promises of God?" No. There is a wide difference, but no antagonism. The promise is not touched or altered by it, and it had its own function to discharge as a preparative institute. For μὴ γένοιτο, see under ii. 17. Nay more—

Εἰ γὰρ ἐδόθη νόμος ὁ δυνάμενος ζωοποιῆσαι, ὄντως ἐκ νόμου ἂν ἦν ἡ δικαιοσύνη—the order in the last clause having the authority of A, B, C; ℵ places ἦν before ἄν, and the Received Text places ἄν before ἐκ νόμου, while D omits it; F, G leave out ἂν ἦν, and B has ἐν νόμῳ—"for if there had been given a law which was able to give life, verily by the law should have been righteousness"—the argument for the μὴ γένοιτο. For the form of the hypothetical proposition, see Jelf, § 851, 3. The νόμος is the Mosaic law, and the article following confines it to the special quality—to that defined by the participle. Compare Acts iv. 12, x. 41, Rom. ii. 14; Winer, § 20, 4. The verb ζωοποιῆσαι is "to quicken," "to impart life," to bestow that ζωή which Christ speaks of as the sum or result of all His blessings, John iii. 16, etc. Life is opposed to that death which sin has wrought within us, and is not specially a new moral life (Rückert, Winer, Matthies, Olshausen, Ewald). To give life is only here another and more subjective form of saying to bestow the inheritance, and in using the term the apostle is mentally referring to vers. 11, 12. If the law could have given life, truly—*ὄντως*, emphatic in position—"in very truth from the law (as its origin) righteousness would have been."

Δικαιοσύνη is the one indispensable condition or means of life or justification, and not the result (Wieseler). To give life, the law must confer righteousness—*ὁ δίκαιος ζήσεται*. The law is not against the promises of God; it comes not into rivalry with them, for it has a different aim and work, being superadded on account of transgressions. If it could have justified, righteousness would have sprung from it, and the promises would have been by it annulled, or rather superseded. But no one can obey the law, and win righteousness by his obedience to it. Righteousness is found in a very different sphere—that of trust in the divine promise, iii. 10–13. Law and promise are so far removed from one another in character and operation, that the one comes not into collision with the other as if to counterwork it. The law, as Chrysostom says, is *οὐκ ἐναντίος τῆς χάριτος ἀλλὰ καὶ συνεργός*. Nay, as the apostle proceeds to illustrate, the law cannot be hostile to the promise, for both are portions of one divine plan carried out in infinite wisdom and harmony. For the law subserves the promise, one of its special functions being to produce such convictions of sin as "shut up" men to faith in the promise as the only means of salvation—the teaching of the following verse. But this verse looks back to ver. 18, and its declaration, as the next verse does to ver. 19, the connection of the law with sin.

Ver. 22. *Ἀλλὰ συνέκλεισεν ἡ γραφὴ τὰ πάντα ὑπὸ ἁμαρτίαν*—"But the Scripture shut up all under sin." *Ἀλλά* is strongly adversative—"but, on the contrary,"—the statement following being in direct contradiction to the preceding one: so far from righteousness being of the law, the Scripture embodying that law shuts up all men under sin, as unrighteous and beneath its curse. Therefore the law, which encloses all under sin and its penalty, cannot by any possibility be the source of life. The phrase ἡ γραφή is so far personified, as doing what God its author does. Rom. xi. 32. It may signify the Old Testament as a whole, or, as being in the singular, some special portion of it, as Ps. cxliii. 2, or Deut. xxvii. 26. Compare for use of singular Luke iv. 21, and chiefly in John, as John xix. 37, xx. 9, etc., in many of which places the quotation is not given, but only referred to. The συν in the verb συνέκλεισεν does not mean that all are shut up *together*—*omnes simul* (Bengel, Usteri), for the verb is sometimes applied to individuals, and means to hem in *on all sides*. Sept. Ps. xxxi. 9; Polybius, xi. 2, 10. Compare Herod. vii. 41; Pol. i. 17, 8. Many of the fathers, followed by Calvin, Beza, and others, suppose that "Scripture" means the law. It indeed contains, expounds, and enforces the law, but it is not to be identified with it. Nor does the verb mean merely, convinced them of sin—ἤλεγξεν (Chrysostom, Hermann), for this subjective experience was not always effected as a reality; but the Scripture so shut them up objectively under sin as to bring out their inability to obtain righteousness by the law. Bishop Bull and others assign a declaratory meaning to the verb—*conclusos declaravit;* and similar reference to the verdict of Scripture is alleged by Schott, Winer, Wieseler, Usteri, Hofmann, in the same way as an analogous dilution—*permisit, demonstravit* —is proposed for the same verb in Rom. xi. 32 by so many expositors. Such a meaning is only inferential as to result. The Scripture was the divine instrument of this spiritual incarceration, in which sin has the lordship over its prisoners. Bondage and helplessness are intended by the phrase—not, however, to produce despair, but to serve a very different purpose. There was little need for Jerome's caution, *nec vero æstimandum scripturam auctorem esse peccati, . . . judex non est auctor sceleris.* The neuter plural τὰ πάντα (not ἔθνη, Grotius) is certainly more comprehensive than the masculine, though it is putting undue pressure on it to extract the signification of *man and man's things* (Bengel),—*humana omnia, non modo omnes sed etiam omnia* (Windischmann, Hofmann),—Brenz including especially the lower animals. The statement is certainly true, but the following verse is rather against such a view as required by the context, and the masculine is used in Rom. xi. 32 to express an analogous thought. The neuter sets out the comprehensive or unindividualized generality of the statement. Winer, § 27, 5. Compare John vi. 37, xvii. 2, 1 Cor. i. 27, Col. i. 20, 2 Thess. ii. 6, and examples in Poppo, *Thucydides,* Prolegom. i. 104; thus, too, *quæcunque* for *quemcunque,* Sallust, vol. ii. p. 68, ed. Kritz. And the purpose is—

Ἵνα ἡ ἐπαγγελία ἐκ πίστεως Ἰησοῦ Χριστοῦ δοθῇ τοῖς πιστεύουσι—"in order that the promise by faith in Christ Jesus might be given to them who believe." The telic *ἵνα* expresses the divine purpose of the previous statement. It cannot mean the mere result, or be taken *logice—quo appareret dari,* as Winer, Burton, Peile, Koppe, Semler. The promise, *ἐπαγγελία,* is the abstract, tantamount in this clause to the blessing promised. It is connected with faith—*ἐκ,*—for the words are to be construed with *ἐπαγγελία,* and qualify it. That faith belongs to, rests on, *I. X.* as its object. Gwynne's notion of its being a subjective genitive has a precarious foundation. The article is not inserted before *I. X.*, as no defining limitation is intended. Winer, § 20, 2. The antithesis looks back to *ἐκ νόμου* in the 21st verse—the promise springs out of faith, and is conditioned by it. It has no connection of origin or stipulation with the law. Originating in faith, and dependent on faith, it is given *τοῖς πιστεύουσιν*—they only being its recipients. It is harsh to connect *ἐκ πίστεως* with *δοθῇ,* and the repetition of idea is not a mere emphatic tautology (Winer); but the apostle first says that the promise is one which from its nature is conditioned by faith, and then he adds, it is given to those in whom this condition is realized, or the defining element of this promise and the requisite qualification for receiving it are ever one and the same—faith. The Galatians accepted the last part of the statement, that the recipients of the inheritance were believers; but they demurred to the first part, that the promise is of faith, for they practically held that it was to some extent connected with works of law, and was partially suspended on the performance of them. Therefore the earnest apostle first defines the promise as "of faith," and then limits the reception of it to those "who believe," that there might be no possible mistake as to his meaning. The shutting up of all under sin shows the impossibility of salvation by works, and brings out clearly the connection of salvation with the promise and faith. The next verses look back to the clause of ver. 19 in which the intermediate duration of the law is stated.

Ver. 23. *Πρὸ τοῦ δὲ ἐλθεῖν τὴν πίστιν, ὑπὸ νόμον ἐφρουρούμεθα συγκεκλεισμένοι εἰς τὴν μέλλουσαν πίστιν ἀποκαλυφθῆναι* —"But before the faith came, we were kept in ward, shut up under the law for the faith to be afterwards revealed." The perfect participle of the Received Text has C, D[3], K, L in its favour, with several of the Greek fathers, and is adopted by Tischendorf; while the present *συγκλειόμενοι* has A, B, D[1], F, א. The last, accepted by Lachmann, is apparently the better supported by MSS., though it may be suspected of being a conformation to the verb *ἐφρουρούμεθα*. *Δέ* leads on to another explanatory thought—to an additional element of contrast, and it stands third in the clause on account of the prepositional phrase. Hartung, i. 190; Klotz-Devarius, ii. 378. The particle is postponed, *ubi quæ præposita particulæ verba sunt aut aptius inter se conjuncta sunt aut ita comparata, ut summum pondus in ea sententia obtineant.* Poppo, *Thucyd.* i. 302. The article specializes the faith as that just mentioned—"the faith of Jesus Christ"—not in an objective or theological sense, the body of truth claiming faith or the gospel, as many of the older commentators supposed, with Schott, Bisping, Gwynne, Brown, etc. It is subjective faith placed under an objective aspect (see under i. 23), or an inner principle personified. It is not "Christ" (Pelagius, Bullinger), nor "Christ and the preaching of the doctrine of faith" (Brenz). The faith with this special aspect and object did not come till Christ came, till the promised Deliverer or Christ appeared in human nature, and under the human name Jesus, ver. 22. Under the law, faith in Him unincarnate did exist, and certainly such faith did justify; for the "non-justification of the Jew antecedent to the coming of Christ," asserted by Gwynne, is tantamount to his non-salvation, and contradicts many utterances and thanksgivings of the Old Testament. The pre-Christian faith resting ideally on One to come, brought them acceptance and pardon, for men are saved not by the doctrine, but by the fact of an atonement; though faith in Him as really existent, or as Jesus, came with Himself into the world. Faith came when prophecy merged into history, and prior to the incarnation the Jews were under the pressure of law—the reference in the verb and participle being to them and their law.

The verb ἐφρουρούμεθα is not *asservabamur*—the notion of ἀσφάλεια is not in the context (Winer, Usteri, Schott),—but *custodiebamur*, kept under guard—ὥσπερ ἐν τειχίῳ τινί (Chrysostom). They were under guard, being or having been shut up—literally, *concluded*,[1] to retain the translation of the previous verse; the συν not referring to those who form the object of the verb, but expressing the fulness of its action—shut round so that escape is impossible. The meaning is not that the pædagogic power of the law—*severa legis disciplina* (Winer)—restrained sin, for such a sense is not found in the context, which refers not to the moral restraint of the law, but the helplessness of the law to bring righteousness or justification. The connection of συγκεκλεισμένοι is disputed. Some, as Œcumenius, Theophylact, Augustine, Raphelius, Wolff, Bengel, and Hofmann, connect it directly with εἰς. If the reading of the perfect tense be admitted, this connection becomes impossible, for it supposes the act to have been done when the law was given; whereas standing by itself, or unconnected with εἰς, it denotes the completeness and permanence of the state. The meaning of the participle directly joined to εἰς has been thus given by Borger: *eo necessitatis redigere ut ad fidem tanquam sacram anchoram confugere cogatur*, or *conclusi adeoque reservati atque adacti ad fidem*. The construction is justifiable, for there are several examples of it. See Fritzsche on Rom. xi. 32; Raphel. *in loc.*; Schweighaüser, *Lex. Polyb. sub voce.* Yet it does not fit in here so well, as "shut up to the faith" would imply the existence of "the faith" during the act or the period of the incarceration. But during the whole of that period it had not yet come, as the apostle expressly argues. The εἰς either of time or destination is more in harmony with the verb in the imperfect, ἐφρουρούμεθα—"we were kept in ward until the faith came," or rather "for the faith about to be revealed." The law was an institute of intermediate and temporary guard and bondage, but it had a blessed purpose. *Εἰς* is not temporal (Borger, Matthies, Brown), a sense it very seldom has, and one unneeded here after the distinct temporal assertion,

[1] Thus Hooker, "The very person of Christ was, only touching bodily substance, *concluded* in the grave."

"before the faith came." The preposition has its ethical meaning of aim or object (not *in adventum ejus fidei*, Augustine). Donaldson, § 477; Jelf, § 625, 3. The temporally qualifying epithet *μέλλουσαν* seems taken out of the usual order that it may have the emphasis, and that the idea expressed by it may be put into the foreground, as in Rom. viii. 18, x. 4. The faith was future when the law was given, and from his assumed standpoint the apostle specializes it; but it was revealed when the apostle wrote—*revealed*—divinely disclosed—the theme and the mode being alike of God. Matthias connects *ἀποκαλυφθῆναι*, not with *μέλλουσαν*, but with *συγκεκλεισμένοι*, giving *εἰς* a temporal signification, as if the purpose were to show them openly as persons who, through the guardianship of that law, must remain under its curse till they were freed from it by faith. The Jews, during the continuance of that law, were in spiritual bondage and seclusion; as obedience could not win righteousness for them, they were helpless; and all this that they might pass into freedom when the Seed came, and faith in Him gave them emancipation and acceptance with God. From a law, the curse of which so terribly enslaved them, they were to pass into faith and deliverance. The very contrast should have rejoiced them, as it did the apostle himself, for his own experience gave proof and power to his theology. And yet they were seeking back to that law, and ignoring that faith, which unmixed and by itself, had been the instrument of righteousness to Abraham, and would be the same to all his spiritual children. The law had its own work to do, but that work did not result in the gift of the Spirit, or in the perfection of those under it, iii. 2–5; its work was done in its own sphere which was one of curse and confinement, and done under an economy which was a parenthesis in the divine government, brought in and moulded with a view to the introduction of a better and nobler dispensation, the characteristic principle of which is faith. The law was not, and was not meant to be, a final economy.

Ver. 24. *Ὥστε ὁ νόμος παιδαγωγὸς ἡμῶν γέγονεν εἰς Χριστόν*—"So that the law has become our tutor (pædagogue) for Christ." Wycliffe has "under-maister;" "schoolmaster" is in Tyndale, Cranmer, and the Genevan; the Rheims has "pedagogue;" and the interpolated words *to bring us* are taken from the Genevan, Tyndale rendering "unto the time of Christ." Ὥστε marks the conclusion from the preceding statements, and especially from ἐφρουρούμεθα. We are the children of God; and the law prior to the coming of faith acted toward us as our pædagogue, with all his vigorous discipline and vigilant superintendence. The pædagogue was not the διδάσκαλος or παιδόνομος,[1]—*non magister et pater* (Jerome). The term, as its composition implies, is one *qui puerum manu prehensum ducit . . . ad magistrum.* The pædagogue was usually a slave selected for his fidelity, to whom was entrusted the complete supervision of the children of a family from their sixth or seventh year till they arrived at puberty.[2] Under his charge they went to and from school—*gymnasia;* he accompanied them in their walks and recreations, as responsible for their personal safety; and he guarded them against evil society and immoral influences. Horace, *Sat.* lib. i. vi. 81, 4. A pædagogue is accused of the opposite, *Athenæus,* vii. 279, *Opera,* vol. iii. p. 16, ed. Schweighaüser. He was therefore obliged to maintain the rigid discipline which was commonly associated with the name. Not only were pædagogues called *assidui* and *custodes,* but their functions came to be associated with moroseness and imperious severity.[3] Their countenance became proverbial for its sourness. It represents in the Jerusalem Targum the Hebrew אֹמֵן, "nursing father," of Num. xi. 12; and the Syriac renders it by ܬܪܘܢܐ, "monitor." The apostle in 1 Cor. iv. 15 puts pædagogue in contrast with "father."

[1] The two are sharply distinguished: τὸν παιδαγωγὸν καὶ τὸν διδάσκαλον, Plato, *De Legibus,* vii. 14; and the corresponding verb is often used in this distinctive sense. Compare Xenophon, *De Lac. Rep.* ii. 1; Quintil. *Inst. Or.* i. 1, 8, 9; and on the character and qualifications of a proper pædagogue, Plutarch, *De Liberis Educandis,* vii., *Opera,* vol. i. p. 12, 13, ed. Wittenbach.

[2] Thus, in Plato, Socrates says to the boy Lysis, "Who then governs you? My pædagogue, he said. Is it so that he is a slave? How could he be otherwise?—our slave however. . . . And by doing what, then, does this pædagogue govern you? Of course, said he, he conducts me to my masters," etc. *Lysis,* 208 E, vol. iv. p. 136, ed. Stallbaum.

[3] *Tristior et pædagogi vultus.* Suetonius, *Nero,* xxxvii. Συβαρίτης ἀνὴρ παιδαγωγὸς, τοῦ παιδὸς ὃν ἦγε διὰ τῆς ὁδοῦ, ἰσχάδι περιτυχόντος καὶ ἀνελομένου, ἐπέπληξεν αὐτῷ ἰσχυρότατα. Ælian, *Hist. Var.* xiv. 20. He is called *Magister* in Terence, *Andria,* i. 1.

In the later days of Rome the young slave pædagogue was delicately trained, his office in the palace degenerated into that of a mere ornamental attendant on his imperial master, and naturally pædagogue was shortened into the modern *page*. The Rabbins took the word into their language, making it פדגוג, and associated with it the additional idea of a closer superintendence, as in food,[1] etc.

Thus the surveillance of a pædagogue carried with it the idea of a strictness bordering on severity, and of an inferior but responsible position. The law was in the place of a pædagogue to the Jews—hard, severe, unbending in its guardianship of them when they were in their minority,—it being implied in the illustration, however, that all the while they were children. The pædagogic function of the law was not in the repression of sins (De Wette, Baur); it was given "for the sake of transgressions," to produce such convictions of guilt and helplessness as prepared for faith in Christ. Its types and ceremonial services conduced to the same result. The phrase *εἰς Χριστόν* is very naturally understood as meaning "to Christ,"—the pædagogue bringing the child to the Teacher. So the Greek fathers, with Erasmus, Elsner, etc. But this idea does not suit the imagery, for Christ is here not regarded at all as a Teacher, but rather as a Redeemer, as the following clause distinctly implies, as well as the commencing imagery of the next chapter. Nor is the *εἰς* temporal, *usque ad* (Morus, Rosenmüller, Rückert, Bagge), but telic; it expresses the spiritual design of the previous pædagogy: it was for Christ, as its ultimate purpose. Winer, § 49, *a.* The statement is therefore a virtual reply to the objection, "Is the law against the promises of God?" No, it is a pædagogue with a view to Christ, and to Christ the Seed were the promises made. The next clause explains the *εἰς Χριστόν*, or shows in what sense we ought to regard it—in order that we might be justified by or out of faith; *ἐκ πίστεως*, as in contrast to *νόμος*, having the emphasis. See under ii. 16, iii. 6. See Suicer on *νόμος*.

Ver. 25. Ἐλθούσης δὲ τῆς πίστεως, οὐκέτι ὑπὸ παιδαγωγόν

[1] *Rex filio pædagogum constituit et singulis diebus ad eum invisit, interrogans eum, Num comedit filius meus? Num bibit filius meus? Num in scholam abiit? Num ex schola rediit?* *Tanchuma*, 35, 1, in Schoettgen's *Horæ*, i. p. 741.

ἐσμεν—"But the faith being come, we are no longer under a pædagogue." The *δέ* is adversative—introduces a contrasted statement. The preposition *ὑπό* ("under," "under the power of," Krüger, § 68, 45, 2) is here followed, as always in the New Testament, by an accusative, as in Rom. iii. 9, 1 Cor. ix. 20, Gal. iv. 2, 21; but in Attic Greek it is sometimes followed by a dative. The pædagogy was from its very nature temporary; it ceased when the faith came. The coming of faith being identical with the coming of the object of that faith—the Seed or Christ for whom the pædagogy was instituted as its purpose—marks at the same time the period when the children pass from the austere constraint and tutelage of the law into maturity and freedom. The noun, though repeated, has not the article after the preposition, the personality of the pædagogue being merged in his work—"no longer under pædagogy" (Meyer). Winer, 19, 2, *b*. And the reason is annexed—we are not children, but are now sons full-grown—*υἱοί*, not *παῖδες*.

Ver. 26. *Πάντες γὰρ υἱοὶ Θεοῦ ἐστε διὰ τῆς πίστεως ἐν Χριστῷ Ἰησοῦ*—"For ye all are sons of God through the faith in Christ Jesus." "You all," Jews and Gentiles also, spoken to in the second person, the previous clause being in the first person—himself and the Jewish believers who were once under the law. 1 Thess. v. 5. Usteri and Hofmann wrongly on this account take the address in *ὑμεῖς* to be, "you believing Gentiles," the former interpolating thus: though "we are no longer under a pædagogue, how much less you who were never under him!" The sons of God are sons in maturity, enjoying the freedom of sons, and beyond the need and care of a rigorous pædagogue. The *υἱοί* has the stress upon it in tacit contrast to *νήπιοι*,—*τεκνίον* being John's favourite term, with a different ethical allusion. See under iv. 6, 7; Rom. viii. 14. Theodore of Mopsuest. connects the sonship with *τελειότης*. It was by the instrumentality of faith that they were sons of God; and that faith—the faith already referred to—was *ἐν X. I.*; and there being no article after *πίστεως* to specialize it, the clause represents one idea. See under Eph. i. 15.

Some would join the words *ἐν X. I.* to *υἱοὶ Θεοῦ*, as Usteri, Schott, Windischmann, Wieseler, Ewald, Jowett, Hofmann, Riccaltoun, and Lightfoot. But this construction is against the natural order of the words, and would be a repetition of *διὰ τῆς πίστεως* as expressing mode. *Πίστις* stands alone in the two previous verses, as in direct contrast to *νόμος*, and now its fulness of power is indicated by the adjunct "in Christ Jesus." The construction with *ἐν* is warranted, though Riccaltoun denies it. Eph. i. 15; Col. i. 4; 1 Tim. iii. 13; 2 Tim. iii. 15; Sept. Ps. lxxviii. 22; Jer. xii. 6. See p. 168. "Sons of God"—not "ye will be" (Grotius), but "ye are sons." Sons as His creatures, for Adam was "the son of God;" and the prodigal son did not cease to be a son, though he was a lost and wandered one, nay, the father recognised the unbroken link. "We are also His offspring," said the apostle on Mars Hill, sustaining a filial relation to Him, and still bearing His image, though many of its brightest features have been effaced. But now we are "sons of God by faith in Christ Jesus"—by that faith forgiven, accepted, regenerated, adopted—born of God, and reflecting the paternal likeness—loved, blessed, and disciplined by Him—trained to do His will and to submit to it—enjoying the free spirit which cries "Abba, Father," and prepared in all ways for His house of many mansions.

Ver. 27. *Ὅσοι γὰρ εἰς Χριστὸν ἐβαπτίσθητε, Χριστὸν ἐνεδύσασθε*—"For as many of you (ye whosoever) as were baptized into Christ, ye put on Christ." This verse confirms, and at the same time explains, the statement of the previous verse.

Those who, like Prof. Lightfoot, separate *ἐν X. I.* from *πίστεως* connect thus: "In Christ Jesus, I say, for all ye who were baptized into Christ put on Christ." Those, on the other hand, who keep the words in their natural connection, give this as the argument: "Ye are sons of God; for in being baptized, ye put on Christ who is the Son of God." *Si autem Christum induistis, Christus autem filius Dei, et vos eodem indumento filii Dei estis.* But the statement is not so minute as to show *τὸν τῆς γεννήσεως τρόπον* (Theodoret). Chrysostom says that already they had been proved to be sons of Abraham, but now sons of God. The phrase *εἰς X.* is "into Christ," into union and communion with Him, and differs from baptism either *ἐν τῷ ὀνόματι*, or even *εἰς τὸ ὄνομα.* When a purpose is specified, as *μετάνοια*, Matt. iii. 11, or *ἄφεσις τῶν ἁμαρτιῶν*, Acts ii. 38, *εἰς* means "with a view to;" but when followed as here by a person, it has the same meaning as in the phrase, "believed into

Christ." See under ii. 16. This is the true baptism, Acts viii. 16. But the thing signified does not always or necessarily accompany the sign. Estius remarks, *Ex quo liquet non omnes omnino baptizatos Christum induisse;* and Peter Lombard, *Alii per baptismum inducunt Christum tantum sacramento tenus.* See Jerome and Calvin *in loc.*[1] Both verbs are aoristic, and the two acts are marked as identical in point of time. The figure of "putting on, being clothed with," is a common one in relation to "power," Luke xxiv. 49; "armour of light," Rom. xiii. 12; "the Lord Jesus Christ" as a command, Rom. xiii. 14; "incorruption, immortality," 1 Cor. xv. 53, 54; an "house from heaven," 2 Cor. v. 3; the "new man," Eph. iv. 24, etc. The figure is also common in the Sept.: "the Spirit," 1 Chron. xii. 18; "salvation," 2 Chron. vi. 41; "the Spirit of the Lord," 2 Chron. xxiv. 20; "shame," Job viii. 22; "righteousness," Job xxix. 14, Ps. cxxxi. 9; "fear" (thunder), Job xxxix. 19; "shame and dishonour," Ps. xxxiv. (xxxv.) 26; "majesty," "strength," Ps. xcii. (xciii.) 1; "honour and majesty," Ps. ciii. (civ.) 1; "cursing," Ps. cviii. (cix.) 17; "salvation," Ps. cxxxi. (cxxxii.) 17; "glory," or beautiful garments, Isa. lii. 2; "garments of salvation," Isa. lxi. 10, etc.: and often, too, in the Apocrypha—1 Macc. i. 29; Wisd. v. 19; Sir. xlv. 10. Distinct examples are found in the classics: *οὐκέτι μετριάζοντες, ἀλλὰ τὸν Ταρκύνιον ἐνδυόμενοι, Dionys. Halicar.* xi. 5, *Opera*, vol. i. p. 657, ed. Hudson; *ἐνέδυ τὸν σοφιστήν*, Libanius, *Ep.* 956; *nisi proditorem palam et hostem induisset*, Tac. *Annal.* xvi. 28. See Wetstein on Rom. xiii. 14, and for some rabbinical examples, Schoettgen on the same place. The classical passages clearly show, that when one man is said to put on another, the full assumption of his nature or character is meant—the personation of him in thought and act. There is therefore no need to resort to any such image as the *toga virilis* (Bengel), or the stoling of the high priest at his consecration (Jatho; Deyling, *Observ.* iii. 406), or to baptismal robes, which were not then in existence (Beza). Bingham, *Antiq.* xi. § 11, 1.

What is it, then, to put on Christ? If to put on a tyrant, as in one of these examples, be to change natures with him, to put on Christ is to exchange our natural character for His—is to become Christ-like in soul and temperament—is to be in the world

[1] See Mozley's *Primitive Doctrine of Regeneration*, London 1855.

as He was in the world, the "same mind being in us which was also in Him,"—every one in all things a representative of Him, —His "life" thus "made manifest in our mortal flesh:" *ἐν αὐτῷ δεικνὺς τὸν Χριστόν* (Chrys.). Wieseler, overlooking the striking peculiarity of the language, identifies the phrase with the putting on of "the new man," Eph. iv. 24, Christ being only a concrete ideal term. But while the result is the same, the modes of conception are different; and in this place the second clause is moulded from the first, and expresses vividly the connection of Christ with spiritual renovation as its source and image. Chrysostom says, "He who is clothed appears to be that with which he is clothed"—*ἐκεῖνο φαίνεται ὅπερ ἐνδέδυται.* On Rom. xiii. 14, *Opera*, vol. ix. p. 767, ed. Gaume. It is also to be borne in mind, that while it is here said that those who were baptized into Christ put on Christ, the apostle elsewhere exhorts those who had been baptized still to put on Christ, Rom. xiii. 4. Believers baptized professedly put on Christ, but the elements of the Christ-like are to be ever developing within them—the new life is ever to be ripening to maturity.

Ver. 28. *Οὐκ ἔνι Ἰουδαῖος, οὐδὲ Ἕλλην· οὐκ ἔνι δοῦλος, οὐδὲ ἐλεύθερος· οὐκ ἔνι ἄρσεν καὶ θῆλυ*—"There is among such neither Jew nor Greek, there is among such neither bond nor free, there is not among such a male and a female." The *ἔνι* is supposed by Buttmann, Kühner, Winer, and Robinson to be another form of the preposition *ἐν* with a stronger accent, after the analogy of *ἔπι* and *πάρα*,—"the notion of the verb being so subordinated that it is dropped" (Kühner, § 379, 2). But what then is to be said of clauses in which *ἔνι* and *ἐν* are used together, as 1 Cor. vi. 5; Xen. *Anab.* v. 3, 11; Plato, *Phædo*, 77 *E?* Others take it as a contracted form of *ἔνεστι*. The sense is not different, whatever view be adopted. In the New Testament it is usually preceded by *οὐκ*, as 1 Cor. vi. 5, Col. iii. 11, Jas. i. 17. *Οὐκ ἔνι* is a strong negative—"there is not among you," almost equivalent in strength to "there cannot be among you." De Wette denies the reference "in you," and understands it, "there is not in this putting on of Christ;" others give it "in Christ" (Koppe, Webster and Wilkinson), or in that state (Hofmann). But this narrows the reference, and does not harmonize with the last personal clause. In the spiritual family of God, the distinctions of race, social position, and even of sex, are lost sight of. National, social, and sexual distinctions cease to exercise their special influence. The Jew is not to the exclusion of the Greek, nor the Greek to the exclusion of the Jew—*οὐδέ*; the bond is not accepted to the refusal of the free, nor the free to the refusal of the bond. Not that in themselves such distinctions cease to exist, but they interfere not with spiritual oneness and privilege. They are so noted in the world as to divide society: Jew and Greek are in reciprocal alienation; bond and free are separated by a great gulf; to the male much was accorded in prerogative which is denied to the female, such as the ordinance on which the Judaists insisted; but these minor characteristics are now merged in a higher unity among the children of God. Such differences were specially prominent and exclusive in ancient times. 1 Cor. xi. 7–9.

The generalized neuters *ἄρσεν καὶ θῆλυ* are not connected, as the previous two pairs, by *οὐδέ*, but by *καί* (Gen. i. 27; Mark x. 6), for the distinction is not of race or rank, but of physical and unchangeable organization. Duality is denied: there is no longer a male and a female—no longer the two, but only one. The distinction in its ethical consequences ceases to exist: as a member of the spiritual family, the woman is equal to the man; there is not a man and a woman, but simple humanity. Having put on Christ, the woman is a child of God, equal to the man in all filial honour and enjoyment. See under Col. iii. 11. Some minor points of difference yet remain, as the apostle insists in 1 Tim. ii. 12, v. 9, etc., but they interfere not with the general statement. The reason is subjoined—

Πάντες γὰρ ὑμεῖς εἷς ἐστε ἐν Χριστῷ Ἰησοῦ—"for all ye are one (person) in Christ Jesus." The *πάντες* of the Received Text is well supported, but *ἅπαντες* is found in A, B[2], ℵ. The masculine is now employed, not the neuter *ἕν*, as it implies conscious oneness. Theodoret says, *τὸ εἷς ἀντὶ τοῦ ἓν σῶμα.* The unity is organic, not unconscious or fortuitous juxtaposition, but like the union of all the branches with the root, and through the root with one another. There may be many disparities in gifts and graces, but there is indissoluble oneness in Christ Jesus, its only sphere, or through union to Him, its only medium. See under Eph. ii. 15.

Ver. 29. *Εἰ δὲ ὑμεῖς Χριστοῦ, ἄρα τοῦ Ἀβραὰμ σπέρμα*

ἐστὲ, κατ' ἐπαγγελίαν κληρονόμοι—"But if ye are Christ's, then are ye Abraham's seed, heirs according to promise." *Χριστοῦ* is the preferable reading in the first clause; the other words, *εἷς ἐστε ἐν Χ. Ι.* in D[1], T, are a comment; and the *καί* of the last clause of the Text. Recept. is omitted on the authority of A, B, C, D, ℵ, 17, Vulgate, etc. The moment rests on *ὑμεῖς*—you the objects of my present appeal. If ye be Christ's, then (the *οὖν* after *ἄρα* being without good authority) Abraham's seed are ye—the stress being on *τοῦ 'Αβραάμ*—the indubitable conclusion, for Christ is Abraham's Seed, and you belonging to Him—one in Him—must be Abraham's seed also. "And if children, then heirs,"—the emphasis is more on *κατ' ἐπαγγελίαν* (Ewald, Wieseler, Hofmann) than on the concluding word *κληρονόμοι* (Meyer) absolute, or without any annexed genitive as *τοῦ 'Αβραάμ*, for they are heirs not of Abraham, but co-heirs of the same inheritance with him. *Κατ' ἐπαγγελίαν* is "agreeably to promise," the very point which the apostle has been labouring to substantiate, as against the claims made for the law by the disturbers of the churches,—the reference being to ver. 16. "Heirs according to promise;" for "to Abraham and his seed were the promises made," and that promise, containing the inheritance, the law did not and could not set aside—all in illustration and proof of the starting premiss in ver. 7, "They which be of faith, the same are the children of Abraham;" and of the earlier declaration, that justification comes not from works of law, but through faith in the divine promise, as Abraham was justified by faith. But the Galatian legalists ignored these reasonings, and fell into the error of expecting justification from works; an error which, as the apostle has argued, involved the awful consequence of making Christ's death superfluous, counterworked the example of Abraham the father of the faithful, and ignored the promise of inheritance made by God immediately to him—a promise still given to all those who believe, as the seed of Abraham. In a word, he has fully vindicated the sharp words with which the chapter opens, "O foolish Galatians, who has bewitched you?" What folly was involved in their sudden and unaccountable apostasy! See a paper by Riggenbach on "Righteousness by faith"—*Rechtfertigung durch den Glauben*—in the *Stud. u. Kritik.* 1868.

CHAPTER IV

THE apostle had said in the end of the last chapter that those who are Christ's are Abraham's seed, heirs according to promise. The idea suggested by a *κληρονόμος* who is so not through right, but by promise, dwells in his mind, and he now illustrates some of its peculiarities. These he notices, and then works round again to the conclusion—*εἰ δὲ υἱὸς καὶ κληρονόμος*—"but if a son, an heir also," through God. The illustration is parallel in some points to that of the previous section.

Ver. 1. *Λέγω δέ, ἐφ' ὅσον χρόνον ὁ κληρονόμος νήπιός ἐστιν, οὐδὲν διαφέρει δούλου, κύριος πάντων ὤν*—"Now I say, That the heir, as long as he is a child, differeth nothing from a servant (bond-servant), though he be lord of all." This formula introduces a continued explanatory statement: ver. 16; Rom. xv. 8. Otherwise the apostle writes as at iii. 17, *τοῦτο δὲ λέγω*; or as in 1 Cor. i. 12, *λέγω δὲ τοῦτο*; or in 1 Cor. vii. 29, *τοῦτο δέ φημι*. These cases are analogous, but somewhat different in emphasis. The train of thought which he has been pursuing suggests the following illustration. "Now I say," carrying out yet another point of illustration, and by a different figure. The sense is not, "my meaning is this;" but a new phase of argument, connected closely, however, with what goes before, is introduced. For the phrase *ἐφ' ὅσον χρόνον*, see Rom. vii. 1, 1 Cor. vii. 39; and this period is parallel to that of the pædagogy. The apostle states the simple proposition, and does not use the accusative with the infinitive as in Rom. xv. 8, or *ὅτι* as in 1 Cor. i. 12. *Νήπιος* is an infant or minor, and this term or *ἄνηβος* stands opposed to *ἔφηβος* (*παῖς—ἀνήρ*), one who had attained to his majority. In Athens *ἐφηβεία* began at the age of eighteen, and two years elapsed before complete emancipation. In Rome infancy ended at the seventh year, puberty began at the fourteenth, but tutelage lasted till the twenty-fifth. In Scottish law pupillarity extends to fourteen in males, and minority to twenty-one. Among the Hebrews the period of nonage was thirteen years and a day for males, and twelve years and a day for females. Selden, *de Successionibus*, ix., *Works*, vol. ii. p. 25. It disturbs and enfeebles the analogy to attach to νήπιος any ethical meaning, as if "it implied imperfection of understanding as well as of age" (Bagge after Chrysostom). Doubtless it is because the heir is a child that tutors are appointed over him, and youth implies inability; but the apostle refers simply to the fact of childhood in its legal aspect—not to infancy in any physical sense, as might be suggested by the composition of the word. We must not put more into the figure than is warranted by the apostle's own deductions from it. The phrase ὁ κληρονόμος is like ὁ μεσίτης in iii. 20—"the heir," any or every heir as the case may be. Winer, § 18, 1; Dionys. Halic. iv. 9, p. 13, vol. ii. ed. Kiessling. "The heir" is not the possessor, but only the expectant possessor. The inheritance is in reserve for him, Matt. xxi. 38; but he differs nothing from a servant. The genitive δούλου is used as in Matt. vi. 26. See on ii. 6. The heir is nothing different from a bond-servant—the idea being that he has no real possession, no power of independent action—even though he be lord of all: κύριος πάντων ὤν—"being all the while, or though he be lord of all." This concessive use of the participle is common. Jelf, § 697, *d;* Donaldson, § 621. The κυριότης is his *de jure*, not *de facto*—the πάντα being his by right even now from his birth and position. It is not *in eventum*, as Meyer gives it, but now, at the present moment, he is lord of all, though not the actual possessor; yet, though lord of all, he is in dependence and discipline nothing different from a servant who has no right in the inheritance at all.

Ver. 2. Ἀλλὰ ὑπὸ ἐπιτρόπους ἐστὶ καὶ οἰκονόμους, ἄχρι τῆς προθεσμίας τοῦ πατρός—"But is under guardians and stewards, until the term appointed of the father." The Vulgate has *sub tutoribus et actoribus;* Augustine, *procuratores et actores;* Wycliffe, "kepers and tutores,"—*actores* = to "doers" in old Scottish statute. The ἐπίτροπος literally is one on whom charge is devolved, or he might be the guardian of orphan children—ὀρφανῶν ἐπίτροπος, Plato, *Leg.* p. 766, C; Plutarch,

Lycurgus, § 3, p. 66, *Vitæ*, vol. i. ed. Bekker. He is not to be identified with the παιδαγωγός (Elsner), but the heir is under his charge—he has the control of his person. On the other hand, the οἰκονόμος is entrusted with his property, as indeed the name implies—who provides for him and manages his possessions. Luke xvi. 1; Gen. xv. 2; Xen. *Mem.* ii. 10, 4. The word has been disguised into a rabbinical one. Schoettgen, *in loc. et in* Luke viii. 3; Selden as above. In ordinary New Testament use it means overseer, as in Matt. xx. 8, Luke viii. 3; Herod. i. 108; Joseph. *Antiq.* xviii. 6, 6. But it is here employed in a more restricted meaning as a guardian or legal representative, called in Attic process κύριος. Xen. *Mem.* i. 2, 40; Ael. *Var. Hist.* iii. 26. Compare what is said of Moses in Heb. iii. 5. Neither the person nor property of the heir are therefore at his own disposal during his minority—the first is under guardians, and the second under stewards.[1] But the period of subjection is limited, yea, defined—

Ἄχρι τῆς προθεσμίας τοῦ πατρός—"until the term appointed of the father." The term προθεσμία, meaning "appointed before"—προ—prearranged, occurs only here in the New Testament. It is used substantively, though ἡμέρας may be supplied. The word is a legal term found often in classical writers, as meaning the time defined for bringing actions or prosecutions ("*Statute of limitations*"), and it also denotes the period allowed to a defendant for paying damages. Sometimes it signifies any time pre-fixed—τῆς προθεσμίας ἐνισταμένης, Joseph. *Antiq.* xii. 4, 7; but here it denotes the period fixed when the tutorship comes to an end. See Wetstein, *in loc.*

The general meaning of the apostle is quite plain; but some points in the analogy, though they are not essential to the argument, are involved in difficulty. The apostle is not to be supposed to treat the subject with forensic accuracy in minutiæ, but only to bring out the general conception, so that his meaning could be easily apprehended. One question is, "Is the father of the heir described supposed to be dead or

[1] In Scottish law the tutor is vested with the management both of the person and the estate of his pupil, while a curator's sole concern is with the estate; and this has given rise to the maxim, *Tutor datur personæ, curator rei.* Lord Mackenzie, *Roman Law*, p. 143.

alive?" Commentators are divided. That the father is supposed to be dead is the opinion of Theodoret, Rückert, De Wette, Baumgarten-Crusius, Hilgenfeld, Windischmann, and Hofmann. The other opinion, that the father is supposed to be alive, is held by Cameron, Neubour, Wolf, Winer, Schott, Wieseler, Matthies, and Meyer. The question is of little importance in itself, and the settlement of it is not essential to the illustration. It may be argued, on the one hand, that the father is supposed to be dead, because the word ἐπίτροπος so often refers to a guardian of orphans, and the present participle ὤν describes a claim or right scarce compatible with the idea of the father's being alive. There is little force in the opposite argument, urged by Dr. Brown and others, that the supposition of a dead father would not be in harmony with the antitype, the living God of Israel; for the supposed death of the father would only symbolize some change of relation on the part of His children to God. On the other hand, it is in favour of the supposition that the father is alive, that the termination of the minority is said to be fore-appointed by him, whereas were he deceased the interval of minority would be regulated by statute. It may, however, be replied, that the father might fix the period which the law itself had ordained, or that there might be exceptional cases of power granted to a father,[1] or that in Galatia the will of the father was more prominent in such arrangements than in other provinces.[2] To decide either way dogmatically is impossible, though the second view has some probability. The ingenuity of Grotius in saying that the father is supposed to be absent, is parallel to that of Jatho in saying that the child-heir is an adopted child. The apostle simply states a common case—states it as it must have

[1] Thus Justinian, *ad certum tempus vel ex certo tempore vel sub condicione vel ante heredis institutionem posse dare tutorem non dubitatur: Institut.* i. 14, 3;—Gaius, *et ideo si cui testamento tutor sub condicione aut ex die certo datus sit, quamdiu condicio aut dies pendet tutor dari potest: Institut.* i. 186;—and Ulpian also, *tutorem autem et a certo tempore dare, et usque ad certum tempus licet: Digest.* xxvi. 2, 8.

[2] Gaius is sometimes quoted to prove this assertion, but he only affirms that the *patria potestas*—a power supposed to be characteristically and exclusively Roman—prevailed in Galatia: *nec me præterit Galatarum gentem credere in potestatem parentum liberos esse. Institut.* i. 55, p. 19, ed. Böcking, 1855. See also Cæsar, *De Bello Gall.* vi. 19.

often occurred, and as it was best suited to illustrate his argument, in which the sovereign will of the father has a prominent place. He does not say—and it was not essential to his illustration to say—why the heir was thus placed under tutors and stewards. He merely records the common custom, that the heir for a definite period limited by the father's will, was usually so placed, and the occurrence was no rare or abnormal arrangement. Nor, in speaking of the spiritual truth so pictured out under a form of domestic administration, need we be curious or careful to distinguish the respective spheres of the tutors and trustees, as if the first referred to the Jews and the second to the Gentiles (Baumgarten-Crusius), or to inquire who they were, as if the *ἐπίτροπος* were the law and the *οἰκονόμος* the Aaronic priesthood (Windischmann). It is needless to track out points of analogy so minutely, for the apostle himself gives his meaning in the following verse—

Ver. 3. *Οὕτω καὶ ἡμεῖς, ὅτε ἦμεν νήπιοι*—"Even so we also, when we were children"—not individually or in our own previous personal lives, but the reference is to the church in its past immature state. *Καί* is used in the comparison—the heir was for a time *νήπιος*, and we too are *νήπιοι*—in pointed parallel. Klotz-Devarius, vol. ii. 635; Winer, § 53, 5.

Who are meant by *ἡμεῖς* has been disputed. The previous illustration as to spiritual relationship to Abraham and the spheres of law and faith leads naturally to the conclusion that the *ἡμεῖς* are Jewish Christians, especially as the Son of God is declared in the next verse to have been born under law—that is, Jewish law—to redeem them who were under it. Such is the view of Chrysostom, Theodoret, Theophylact, Grotius, Estius, Usteri, Schott, De Wette, Baumgarten-Crusius, and Wieseler. Others suppose that, while the special reference is to Jewish Christians, Gentiles are not excluded—as Koppe, Rückert, Matthies, Olshausen, and Ellicott. But it is difficult to see on what principle the subordinate reference to the Gentiles at this point is proved. The language is not in its favour, the spirit of the context does not imply it, and the direct address to Gentiles is postponed till ver. 8. The Jewish believers were children while the law was over them, and the Son of God was born under that law to redeem them who were under it. A third party take *ἡμεῖς* in a general sense—we Christians:

so Winer, Borger, Trana, Meyer, Bagge, Ewald, and Webster and Wilkinson. The heir while a minor is under tutors and stewards, and differs nothing from a servant; and we too, as long as we were in nonage, were in a similar condition—

Ὑπὸ τὰ στοιχεῖα τοῦ κόσμου ἦμεν δεδουλωμένοι—"were under the rudiments of the world kept in bondage." For the "elements" of the Authorized Version, Tyndale and Cranmer have "ordinaunces," and the Genevan "rudiments." The heir was in all respects as a *δοῦλος*; so we have been and are *δεδουλωμένοι*—perfect participle. Winer, § 45, 1. He is under tutors and guardians; *οὕτως*, so we were *ἦμεν* under *ὑπὸ τὰ στοιχεῖα τοῦ κόσμου*. The verb and participle may thus be taken separately—*ἐστίν*—*ἦμεν*; *δοῦλος*—*δεδουλωμένοι*. The term *στοιχεῖα*, *elementa*, is used in reference to physical elements in 2 Pet. iii. 10-12, Wisdom vii. 17; especially the heavenly bodies—*οὐράνια στοιχεῖα* (Justin, *Apolog.* ii. 5, p. 294, *Op.* vol. i. ed. Otto; and the term by itself has probably the same meaning, as it is said they "never rest or keep Sabbath" in *Dial. c. Tryph.* p. 78, vol. ii. do.). They are defined as "sun, moon, stars, earth, sea, and all in them" in *Clement. Hom.* x. 9, p. 218, ed. Dressel. The common numeration, *τέσσαρα στοιχεῖα*, occurs in Hermas, *Vis.* iii. 13, p. 29, *Nov. Test. extra Canonem receptum*, ed. Hilgenfeld, 1866; Plato, *Timæus*, p. 48, B; Theophilus, *ad Autol.* i. 4, p. 14, ed. Otto. In this sense the word was regarded by many of the fathers (Chrysostom, Theodore Mops., and Pelagius) as referring to new moons, Sabbaths, and festivals ruled by the seasons, etc.; Augustine taking it to describe the Gentile worship of the physical elements—a thought excluded by the *ἡμεῖς*; Hilgenfeld, Schneckenburger, and Caspari, regarding the phrase as denoting the adoration of the stars as living powers—a form of nature-worship with which the Mosaic cultus cannot certainly be identified. But the term *στοιχεῖα* means also in the New Testament rudiments or elementary teaching—*primas legis literas* (Tertullian)—as in Heb. v. 12, where it is opposed to *τελειότης*; in Col. ii. 8 it has much the same meaning as in this place, for there it is opposed to "traditions of men," and in ii. 20, where it is viewed as connected with "ordinances." The noun also denotes letters, alphabetical symbols, what is suited to the tuition of infancy. The genitive *τοῦ κόσμου*, subjective in meaning, may not have a gross materialistic sense (Hofmann), nor that of humanity (Wieseler), but a sense similar to that of its adjective in the phrase ἅγιον κοσμικόν—"a worldly sanctuary," Heb. ix. 1. The words may thus mean "elementary lessons of outward things" (Conybeare). The Jewish economy was of the world as it was sensuous, made up of types appealing to the senses, and giving only but the first principles of a spiritual system. See under Col. ii. 8, 17. Cremer, *sub voce*. Bondage and pupillarity appear to be combined in the illustration—the στοιχεῖα are fitted to the νήπιοι, and necessary to them. The child-heir, when he was a child, was taught only faint outlines of spiritual truth suited to his capacity, and taught them to some extent by worldly symbols—the fire, the altar, and the shedding of blood, δικαιώματα σαρκός, Heb. ix. 10—a state of dependence and subjection compared with the freedom and the fulness of enlightenment and privilege under the gospel, or after the fulness of the time. While the "we" seems to refer so distinctly to Jewish believers as under the law, it may be said, that as in the previous paragraphs the Mosaic law in its want of power to justify represents on this point all law, so this state of bondage under the elements of the world represented also the condition of the Gentile races as somewhat similar in servitude and discipline.

Ver. 4. Ὅτε δὲ ἦλθεν τὸ πλήρωμα τοῦ χρόνου—"But when the fulness of the time was come;" δέ introducing the opposite condition. For πλήρωμα, see under Eph. i. 23. It is the time regarded as having filled up the allotted space, or itself filled up with the inflow of all the periods contained in the προθεσμία of the father. The one clause is parallel to the other. The δουλεία of the heir lasts till the προθεσμία of the father arrives; our spiritual bondage expires with the advent of the fulness of the time—God's set time. The nonage of the church was the duration of the Mosaic covenant. But not till the last moment of its existence, when its time was filled like a reservoir with the last drop, was it set aside, and the ripe or full age of the church commenced—πεπλήρωται ὁ καιρός, Mark i. 15. The fulness of the time was also the fittest time in the world's history. See under Eph. i. 10.

Ἐξαπέστειλεν ὁ Θεὸς τὸν υἱὸν αὐτοῦ—"God sent forth His Son," that is, from Himself. Many passages of Scripture assert this truth of the mission of Christ from the Father. The verb is a double compound. He sent forth "His Son," so named here with a reference to the subsequent *υἱοί*: through His Son they pass from servants into sons. Christ came not without a commission: the Father sent Him; and He undertook the mission, came in love, did His Father's will, "became obedient unto death, even the death of the cross." He was with the Father as His Son prior to His mission—His pre-existence at least is clearly implied, but not impersonal, as Baur (*Paulus*, p. 628), or only ideal, according to the representation of Philo (*Leg. Allegor.* p. 139, *Opera*, vol. i. ed. Pfeiffer).

Γενόμενον ἐκ γυναικός—"born of a woman." The reading *γεννώμενον*, defended by Rinck, has only a very slender support, and is found in no uncial MS. (Reiche). The preposition *ἐκ* indicates origin: Matt. i. 18; John iii. 6; Winer, § 47. No specialty is expressed in *ἐκ γυναικός*, for the reference is not to the virgin birth of our Lord. The meaning is not *de virgine sponsa* (Schott). Nor are Theophylact and Œcumenius justified in regarding the phrase as formally directed against Docetism—*ἐκ τῆς οὐσίας αὐτῆς σῶμα λάβοντα.*

The clause, while it contains the profound mystery of the miraculous conception, does not give it prominence. It says nothing of the supernatural, save the fact of the divine mission and the incarnation, for it had no immediate connection with the apostle's argument. It is the phrase employed to describe human birth in Hebrew: Job xiv. 1, Matt. xi. 11; as Augustine says, *Mulieris nomine non virgineum decus negatur, sed femineus sexus ostenditur.* But there is an implied exclusion of human fatherhood, though not a formal expression of it as Calvin maintains; but he adopted the reading *factum ex muliere* of the Vulgate,—*factum* being by many of the Latin fathers, as Tertullian (*De Carne Christi* xv.), regarded as in contrast with *natum*, and *ex* with *per.* So Estius, Calovius, Perkins. But the phrase "born of a woman" (*ἐκ*, not *διά*), though not intended for the purpose, furnished a fair argument against Docetism,—the *ἐκ* implying *τὴν κοινωνίαν τῆς φύσεως*, as Basil says, *De Spiritu Sancto* v. 12, p. 13, *Opera*, tom. iii., Gaume, Paris. While the previous clause assumes His pre-existence, this asserts His genuine humanity. But Hegel's philosophy ventures a transcendental commentary: God sent His Son—

Das heisst nicht Anderes als, das Selbst-bewusstseyn hatte sich zu denjenigen Momenten erhoben, welche zum Begriff des Geistes gehören, und zum Bedürfniss, diese Momente auf eine absolute Weise zu fassen. See Mansel's *Bampton Lectures*, v. Schelling philosophizes away the fulness of the time thus: *Die Menschenwerdung Gottes ist also eine Menschenwerdung von Ewigkeit;* apparently identifying the incarnation with what divines call the eternal generation.

Γενόμενον ὑπὸ νόμον—"born under the law." 1 Macc. x. 38. The phrase is more common with the simple verb of existence—ch. iii. 25, iv. 21, v. 18. In classic usage a dative is often employed. Rost u. Palm, *sub voce.* It would be forced to change the meaning of this second *γενόμενον,* and render it with Scholefield, "made subject to the law;" or with Luther, *unter das Gesetz gethan.* So also Calvin, Winer, Usteri, Wieseler. For to change the meaning would lose the emphasis involved in the repetition. Christ was not only born a man, but He was born a Jew—one of the seed of Abraham. He was a member of the Hebrew commonwealth by birth, and by the fact of that birth was under the law; so that He was circumcised, presented in the temple by Mary, and baptized by John; and He worshipped in the synagogue, kept the Sabbath, regarded ceremonial distinctions, observed the great feasts, and paid the tax of the half-shekel. The apostle does not mean that after becoming man He did, by a distinct and additional voluntary act, place Himself under the law, but that by His very birth He became subject to the law whose claims upon Him He willingly allowed.

According to promise and prophecy, salvation was to be of the Jews. The woman's Seed was to be specially the Seed of Abraham, through the line of Isaac and Jacob, of the tribe of Judah, and the family of David. He was a "minister of the circumcision," being sent only "to the lost sheep of the house of Israel." And the purpose is then described—

Ver. 5. *Ἵνα τοὺς ὑπὸ νόμον ἐξαγοράσῃ*—"In order that He might redeem those under the law." See under iii. 13. Those under the law are certainly the Jews; and He was born of a woman, born under the law, in order that He might redeem them. As their representative in blood, and in position under the law, He obeyed its precepts and He bore its penalty, so that they were freed from its curse and from its yoke, and became disciples of a more spiritual system, which taught truth in its realities and not in obscure symbols, whose sacrifice was not "the blood of bulls and of goats, and the ashes of a heifer," but "the precious blood of Christ;" which gave them the privilege of kneeling, not toward a mercy-seat of gold, but before the "throne of grace," and whose High Priest had gone into a holiest place beyond the skies. We enter not into the question of the active and passive obedience so often discussed under reference to this verse, but only say that obedience and suffering were ever combined, so that in obeying He suffered, while His suffering was His last and highest act of obedience: "He became obedient unto death."

They were no longer under bondage to a law which Christ had obeyed alike in its requirements and penalty. To the bondage of the law, as we may learn from the second verse, the apostle has special allusion. God's own children living under that law differed little from slaves. Spiritual freedom was denied them. Minute prescriptions were given for diet, dress, travel, labour, for home and for field, for farm and orchard, for private piety and public worship, for ceremonial purity and ethical relations, for birth and marriage, for each day and for the Sabbath-day, for trade and for war, for child and for parent, for tax and for tithe. The entire and multifarious code lay a heavy burden upon them,—nothing was left as a matter of choice to them,—almost in nothing were they masters of themselves; so that the national life must have been to a great extent mechanical—a routine of obedience into which they were so solemnly drilled—the service of *δοῦλοι*. Law cannot save; it has no means of deliverance within itself. Nor could they throw the burden off. They durst not dismiss the tutors and guardians, nor proclaim of their own power that their minority had ceased and that they henceforth assumed the position of men. They had to wait the fore-fixed time of the father. But now from the burden of the law they are delivered, as they had been redeemed from its curse, though certainly the curse was also an element of the burden. See under iii. 10–14.

Ἵνα τὴν υἱοθεσίαν ἀπολάβωμεν—"in order that we might receive the adoption of sons." Rom. viii. 15, 23; Eph. i. 5. The apostle again uses the first person plural, and the use of it may resemble iii. 14. The redemption of those who were under the law was necessary to the adoption both of Jews and Gentiles. So that the second *ἵνα* is scarcely co-ordinate with the first, but introduces a higher ulterior purpose common in its realization both to Jew and Gentile. Compare iii. 15, Eph. v. 25. Both clauses are connected with the one finite verb, but the lines of connection are not parallel, the first clause—"that He might redeem those under the law"—specially linked with the one nearest to it—"born under the law," and the second with the more remote one—"born of a woman." Jelf, § 904, 3. The blessing is *υἱοθεσία*, not simply *υἱότης*—not sonship natural, but sonship conferred. Rückert, Usteri, Schott, and Brown deny this, and refer it to the change by which the heir who had been under tutelage passes to his majority, and is recognised as a son. That is straining the analogy. Hesychius rightly defines the term—*ὅταν τὶς θετὸν υἱὸν λαμβάνῃ.* Diodor. Sic. iv. 39; Herod. vi. 57. They had been in bondage; but they were freed from it now, and adopted into the household. By no other process could they enter into the family—they were not of it, but were brought into it. And they are freed from legal burden before they are adopted; nay, their emancipation from servitude is virtually their adoption. Both are gifts—Christ died to redeem them, and they receive the other from God. The idea of receiving "back" or recovering is not in the verb, though Augustine argues, *non dixit, accipiamus sed recipiamus*, and Jowett paraphrases, "receive back our intended blessing." The *ἀπο-* may sometimes signify "again," Luke xv. 27; Liddell and Scott. Adam had a *υἱότης* before his fall—he was *υἱὸς Θεοῦ*; and in this sense our adoption is reinstating us in the family. But the new sonship is so different, that it can scarce be termed a recovery, since it is far more—it is a higher relation than man originally possessed. For it is the image of the second Adam to which we are to be conformed, and the inheritance is in heaven, and no mere paradise restored on earth. Nor, as Meyer remarks, was the *υἱοθεσία* which belonged to the Jews really lost. Ex. iv. 22; Hos. xi. 9. The nation was still in theocratic covenant with God. Chrysostom gives the verb another meaning—to receive as one's due, for the promise was made of old (Theophylact, Bengel). Such a sense may sometimes be inferred from the context, as in Luke vi. 34; in the other passages —Luke xxiii. 41; Rom. i. 27; Col. iii. 24—a distinct term is found which formally conveys this sense. But the idea is here foreign to the train of thought. Nor can the notion of Schott and Rückert be sustained, that ἀπο- means *inde*, or as the fruit of the redemption; the notion is implied in the context, but not directly expressed by the verb. The verb is used simply as elsewhere—Luke xvi. 25; Col. iii. 24—"to receive into possession from," pointing ideally to the source. Through faith, the apostle had said, believers are Abraham's seed, and children according to promise; and how faith confers adoption upon us is told us in these verses. Christ's incarnation and death intervening—the curse and yoke of the law being taken away—by faith in Him he who was a servant is gifted with the position and privileges of a son. See under iii. 26. That sonship is now enjoyed, but its fulness of blessing and fellowship waits the coming of the Lord Jesus. For it is added—

Ver. 6. Ὅτι δέ ἐστε υἱοί. It is difficult to say whether ὅτι be demonstrative or causal—whether it mean "that"—as a proof that, or "because"—*quoniam* in the Vulgate and Claromontane Latin. The question then is, Is the sending forth of the Spirit of His Son regarded by the apostle as the proof or as the result of sonship? The conjunction will bear either meaning; the causal meaning is the simpler syntax, but the demonstrative meaning is more in unison with the argument. To render "because ye are sons" seems to interfere with the formal conclusion of the following verse—ὥστε—"wherefore thou art no more a servant, but a son." He would be taking for granted their sonship before he had proved it as his conclusion—there would be an assumed result, and then a formal conclusion. But with the other rendering, "that," or "in proof that ye are sons," the apostle is only adding another argument—forging a last link in the demonstration. Christ was born a man, and born under the law, to redeem such as were under the law, that we from being servants might be adopted as sons; and that this is your position is proved by your possession of His Spirit.

Critics are divided. The causal meaning is held by Luther, Bengel, Olshausen, De Wette, Hilgenfeld, Alford, Windischmann, Lightfoot, Trana, Bisping, and Meyer in his third edition, having maintained the other view in his first and second editions. The demonstrative meaning is held by the Greek fathers, who found no difficulty in the construction, by Ambrosiaster, Koppe, Flatt, Borger, Rückert, Schott, Jatho, Brown, Ellicott, and Wieseler who renders somewhat differently by *quod attinet ad id, quod*—*εἰς ἐκεῖνο,*—*ὅτι.*

In adopting the demonstrative meaning we admit a breviloquence, which, however, can be well defended. Winer, § 66, 1; Demosthenes, *contra Pantæn.* p. 110, vol. ii. *Opera*, ed. Schaefer. In confirmation of the same view the *ἐστε* speaks, for it has the emphasis and not *υἱοί*, and the verb is that of actual present state. In such a case, too, one would expect *ὑμῶν*, which, however, is a correction, probably for this reason, of the better supported *ἡμῶν*.

"And that ye are sons." The *δέ* introduces the statement, not, however, as opposed to what precedes, but as something yet different—a step in advance. The words *τοῦ Θεοῦ* found in D, F, and in the Latin fathers (Augustine, however, excepted), are an unwarranted exegetical supplement.

Ἐξαπέστειλεν ὁ Θεὸς τὸ πνεῦμα τοῦ υἱοῦ αὐτοῦ εἰς τὰς καρδίας ἡμῶν—"God sent forth the Spirit of His Son into our hearts." The authorities for the *ὑμῶν* of the Received Text are D[3], E, K, L, Chrysostom, Theodoret, Augustine, the Vulgate, Coptic, and Syriac; while *ἡμῶν* has in its favour A, B, C, D[1], F, א, with many of the fathers, such as Basil, Tertullian, Jerome, and Hilary. The reading *ὑμῶν* might have been a conformation to the previous *ἐστε*. But the change of person is as in Rom. vii. 4. The appeal is to them directly in the previous *ἐστε*; but the apostle at once and now includes himself with them, when he adds a clause descriptive of spiritual experience. The *τὸ πνεῦμα τοῦ υἱοῦ αὐτοῦ* is the Holy Spirit, in no sense "spirit" meaning disposition or temper—*sensus christianus*—or a filial nature (Gwynne); *ὁ Θεὸς ἐξαπέστειλεν τὸν υἱὸν αὐτοῦ*, and similarly *ἐξαπέστειλεν ὁ Θεὸς τὸ πνεῦμα τοῦ υἱοῦ αὐτοῦ*. The mission is first of the Son and then of the Spirit on the part of the Father, implying by the parallel language the personality of the Spirit. And He is the Spirit of His Son, who dwelt in Him, as He has secured His gracious influences, and as it is His "things" which the Spirit shows, one of His special functions being to deepen in all the sons their resemblance to the elder brother—the Son of God. Rom. viii. 9. In the fulness of the time God sent forth His Son, and no doubt in the fulness of the time, too, God sent His Spirit into their hearts—the time fore-appointed for their ingathering and conversion—in that crisis of their history which Himself had set apart, iii. 2. The aorist does not represent the fulness of the Spirit's outflow upon them, but the fact that the Spirit was sent into their hearts when they believed and were adopted. The Spirit of His Son is a token of its adoption to every child, for it is the bond of union with Him who is "the first-born among many brethren." That Spirit is sent into the "heart," the central seat or organ of the inner life and power, which the Spirit of God's Son inhabits, and out of which He cries through us, Abba, Father. The *ἐστέ υἱοί* seems to have suggested the correlative appellation *τοῦ υἱοῦ αὐτοῦ*. There is thus triune operation—Father, Son, and Spirit—in providing, securing, and enjoying this adoption. And that Spirit in their hearts is represented as—

Κράζον, 'Αββᾶ ὁ πατήρ—"crying, Abba, Father." Mark xiv. 36. In Rom. viii. 15 the aspect of thought is, *ἐν ᾧ κράζομεν 'Αββᾶ, ὁ πατήρ*; and in ver. 26 of the same chapter it is said of the Spirit, *ὑπερεντυγχάνει ὑπὲρ ἡμῶν*. The Spirit in our hearts cries—no Hebraism meaning "making to cry." But the Divine Agent Himself, as the Spirit of adoption, is represented as crying. For the impulse is His, the realized sonship is of Him, the deepened sense of want is of His creation, in the heart whence rises the tender and earnest address, Abba, Father. The nominative is used as the vocative. Matt. xi. 26; Bernhardy, p. 67; Krüger, § 45, 2, 6, 7. But why the double appellation, first in Aramaic and then in Greek, as in Mark xiv. 36, Rom. viii. 15? The childlike lisp in the word Abba, and its easy labial pronunciation, may account for its origin, but not for its use here (Olshausen); nor can Dr. Gill be listened to in his dream that "the word being the same pronounced backwards or forwards, shows that God is the Father of His people in adversity as well as in prosperity." It is a superficial explanation of the formula to allege, with Beza, Schott, Usteri, and Conybeare, that *ὁ πατήρ* is merely, like the Abaddon-Apollyon of Rev. ix. 11, explanatory of the Aramaic Abba. For why should such a translation be made by Jesus in the garden, where no human ear heard Him, and by Paul when writing to the Romans of the Spirit of adoption? Nor is it more likely that the double appellation is meant to convey what the elder interpreters find in it—to wit, that it was uttered to point out the spiritual brotherhood of all men in all languages. This opinion, so naturally suggested, cannot certainly apply to the individual address of the Saviour in Mark xiv. 36. But one may say, in the first place, that endeared repetition characterizes a true child, as it clings to the idea of fatherhood, and loves to dwell upon it. In the second place, the use of the Aramaic term must have arisen in the Jewish portion of the church, with whom it seems to have been a common form of tender address. And then, as believing Jews used another tongue in foreign countries, they appear to have felt the ὁ πατήρ to be cold and distant, so that, as to the Lord in His agony, the vernacular term impressed on the ear and heart of childhood instinctively recurred. *Ὁ πατήρ* is what the apostle wishes to say; but in a mood of extreme tenderness, speaking of God's children and of their yearning filial prayerfulness and confidence in approaching and naming Him, he prefixes the old familiar term *Ἀββᾶ*. It was no absolute term at first, like some other names, but ever a relative one. So Jesus, realizing His Sonship with unspeakable intenseness, in that awful prayer names His Father *Ἀββᾶ ὁ πατήρ*. The double appellation could only arise among a bilingual people, where certain native words were hallowed, and in moments of strong emotion were used along with their foreign equivalent. And soon the phrase became a species of proper name, so that in heathen countries *Ἀββᾶ ὁ πατήρ* passed into an authorized formula. As this formula commences prayer, so we have a similar concluding one, but in reverse order, *ναὶ Ἀμήν*, Rev. i. 7. Similar expressions are found in the rabbinical books. Schoettgen, vol. i. p. 252. Selden's explanation is, that the use of the name implies the change of a slave to a freeman; but the apostle is proving a different point—that of sonship or adoption. *Works*, vol. ii. p. 14. Lightfoot affirms that the form אָבִי signifies a master as well as a father, but the form אַבָּא denotes only a natural father (*Hebrew and Talmudic Exercitations on Mark*, *Works*, vol. xi. p. 438). In Chaldee with a single ב it is said to mean a natural father, with a double ב a father in a spiritual sense. The Syriac renders simply "Father, our Father."

The apostle now comes to the conclusion or application to which he has been working in the three preceding verses, connected as they are so closely with the illustration which begins the chapter.

Ver. 7. *Ὥστε οὐκέτι εἶ δοῦλος, ἀλλὰ υἱός*—"Wherefore thou art no longer a slave, but a son." The first term introduces the statement as a result from what precedes, and it is followed here by the indicative, as often at the commencement of a sentence. Winer, § 41, 5; Klotz-Devarius, ii. p. 771. See under ii. 13. The comparative term *οὐκέτι* refers back to the *δουλεία* in ver. 3. The address is narrowed down in this pointed appeal from the first person plural in ver. 5, through the second person plural in ver. 6, to the second person singular. Compare Rom. xi. 17, xii. 20, 1 Cor. iv. 7, x. 29, for a similar form of individualizing appeal.

Εἰ δὲ υἱός, καὶ κληρονόμος—"but if a son, also an heir." The two positions are identical—the one is bound up in the other. The slave is no heir, but he who is a son is also an heir by the fact of his being a son. Rom. viii. 17, *εἰ δὲ τέκνα, καὶ κληρονόμοι.* If thou art a son, in addition to such sonship thou art an heir—an heir of the promise made by God to Abraham and his seed. See under Eph. i. 11. That thou art a son is proved from thy possession of the Spirit; no longer a slave—thou canst say, Abba; and if a son, then also an heir.

The Received Text reads, *κληρονόμος Θεοῦ διὰ Χριστοῦ*—"an heir of God through Christ"—a reading quite in harmony with the context. This reading is found in C[3], D, K, L, א[3], the Claromontane which reads *et hæres Dei per Christum,* and the Gothic version. Chrysostom and Theodoret follow the same reading, and there are other smaller variations. The simpler and shorter reading—*διὰ Θεοῦ*—is supported by A, B, C[1], א[1], the Vulgate which has *hæres per Deum,* Ambrosiaster, Augustine, Pelagius, with Clement, Basil, Athanasius, Cyril, Didymus among the Greek fathers. F reads *διὰ Θεόν,* and some MSS. have *διὰ Ἰησοῦ Χριστοῦ.* Some versions seem made from a text which read simply *Θεοῦ,* while others must have read *Θεοῦ διὰ τοῦ πνεύματος.* This variety of reading shows that emendation has been at work, and that the similar phrase in Rom. viii. 17—*κληρονόμοι μὲν Θεοῦ συγκληρονόμοι δὲ Χριστοῦ*—has suggested the different readings. Some indeed—as Rückert and De Wette, and as Griesbach thinks probable—suppose that all the words after *κληρονόμος* are spurious additions, as in iii. 29. But the MSS. all declare, with one exception (C at first hand), for some addition. Rinck and Usteri maintain the reading *διὰ Χριστοῦ*, as if *Θεοῦ* from Rom. viii. 17 were first written above *Χριστοῦ* and then exchanged for it. Lachmann and Tischendorf adopt the shorter reading. It is needless to object with Matthæi that the orthodox wrote *διὰ Θεοῦ* for *διὰ Χριστοῦ*, for the reading *διὰ Θεοῦ* is as old as Clement of Alexandria; nor could the hostility to Arianism suggest such a change. Reiche, Fritzsche, and Hahn defend the Received Text. Fritzsche supposes that the copyists first confounded *Θεοῦ* with *Χριστοῦ per oculorum errorem*, then omitted *διὰ Χριστοῦ*, and then wrote *διὰ Θεοῦ*—a critical hypothesis not very credible. If we accept *διὰ Θεοῦ*, the curter reading, all the others can be, by a series of natural emendations, easily accounted for, and by the desire to express the mediation of Christ. But *διὰ Θεοῦ* is in harmony with the whole passage. The agency of God in the process of adoption has special prominence. The time "appointed of the father" is the express terminus of the *δουλεία* in the figure. Then it is *ἐξαπέστειλεν τὸν υἱὸν αὐτοῦ*, then *ἐξαπέστειλεν ὁ Θεὸς τὸ πνεῦμα*—that Spirit which cries *ὁ πατήρ*; and the clear and undeniable conclusion is, we are brought into the position of sons *διὰ Θεοῦ*—through God's agency. Thus there is no occasion to adopt the view of Windischmann which takes *Θεοῦ* in its widest sense of God—Father, Son, and Spirit,—the Father sending the Son and the Spirit, the Son redeeming us, and the Spirit completing our sonship. The noun is anarthrous, as it often is after prepositions. Winer, § xix. It would seem, too, that God the Father is directly referred to; for He adopts, sends His Son to provide for it, and His Spirit as the proof of it, so that we become sons, also heirs, "through Him." No genitive follows *κληρονόμος* in this clause, but it has *Θεοῦ* in Rom. viii. 17; *τῆς βασιλείας*, Jas. ii. 5. The inheritance is also referred to in iii. 18, 29.

The declaration, "if a son, then an heir," is based on a general law or instinct—"The parents lay up for the children."

Perhaps this common practice is enough for the apostle's argument. But if the statement is regarded as a special declaration based on legal enactment, the reference cannot be to the Hebrew law which gave the first-born a double portion and excluded daughters; for there is in Christ neither male nor female, and each one is an heir. The allusion is rather to Roman law, under which all the children inherited equally. Thus Gaius: *sui autem et necessarii heredes sunt velut filius filiave.—Sui autem heredes existimantur liberi qui in potestate morientis fuerint, veluti filius, filiave, nepos neptisve ex filio . . . nec interest utrum naturales sint an adoptivi, suorum heredum numero sunt.—Institut.* ii. 156, iii. 2, ed. Böcking. *Sui et necessarii heredes* were quite in this position—if children, then heirs. The Athenian law, which, however, made no distinction between real and personal estate, was not so precise: it gave sons an equal right, the son being merely bound to give his sisters a marriage-portion.[1]

The apostle now turns to the Gentile portion of the church, and impresses on them the folly of placing themselves under bondage to the Mosaic law.

Ver. 8. *'Αλλὰ τότε μὲν, οὐκ εἰδότες Θεόν*—"Howbeit at that time indeed, not knowing God." The *ἀλλά* introduces the statement of their condition, and throws it into striking contrast with the conclusion arrived at in the preceding verse. Sons you are now, but the time was when it was different with you. In the adverb *τότε* the allusion is not formally to ver. 3 (Winer), but generally to their previous state—to the *ἔτι* in *οὐκέτι*. It does not signify vaguely *πάλαι*, as Koppe and Flatt take it, and the stress is on the *μέν*—"indeed," "truly." The *οὐκ εἰδότες*, as Meyer remarks, forms one *conceptus—ignorantes*. Winer, § 55, 5; Gayler, p. 287. This ignorance of God was a characterizing fact—no mere opinion of the writer. 1 Thess. iv. 5; 2 Thess. i. 8. See under Eph. ii. 12—*ἄθεοι*.

'Εδουλεύσατε τοῖς φύσει μὴ οὖσι θεοῖς—"ye were in bondage to them which by nature are not gods," or, "to gods which

[1] This division among sons was the same as the custom of gavel-kind in Kent, which, according to Selden, was all but universal in England before the time of the Norman conqueror, and the same as the present law of France, where there is also no preference of males over females, and no distinction of real and personal estate. See also a dissertation by Fritzsche in *Fritzschiorum Opuscula*, p. 143.

by nature are not." The former negative is historic—οὐ; but this is subjective—μή. The order of the words in the Received Text is τοῖς μὴ φύσει οὖσι θεοῖς, which is found in D[3], F, G, K, L, some minuscules, and in Chrysostom, Theodoret, and the Philoxenian Syriac. The other arrangement is found in A, B, C, D[1, 3], E, א, and in the Vulgate, Gothic, Coptic, etc. The last order, which is also best substantiated, is the more emphatic—it denies them in the apostle's estimation to be gods in any sense; whereas the other order would say less strongly that they were gods—not so indeed by nature, but converted against their nature into gods by human superstition. By the use of μή the apostle gives in his own judgment a denial of the divinity of those objects of worship (Winer, § 55, 5), 1 Cor. viii. 4, 5, 6, called by him δαιμόνια in 1 Cor. x. 20. The dative φύσει is that of characterization (Madvig, § 40), and means "by nature," or essentially, in opposition to what is accidental or derived from circumstance. See under Eph. ii. 3. The aorist ἐδουλεύσατε refers simply to the past period of their ignorance. During this period, and confined to that period over and gone, they were servants (Kühner, § 401)—in slavery to gods which in no sense were gods, and had no real right to be so named. Idolatry characterized them. "Gods and lords many" were worshipped and served among them in their state of ignorance, or because of it, as the participle may have a quasi-causal sense. The Galatians probably inherited the "abominable idolatries" of their Gallic ancestors. "*Natio est omnis Gallorum admodum dedita religionibus*."—Cæsar, *de Bello Gall.* vi. 16. Diodorus speaks of the Galatian δεισιδαιμονία, which led them to lavish gold on their gods and temples, though they were fond of money to excess, v. 27. The native Phrygian idolatry may have been partially adopted on the Gallic occupation of the province—the worship of Cybele; and there may have been combined with it some elements of Hellenic superstition. Wernsdorff, *De Republica Galat.* § 32; Pausanias, *Descrips. Græc.* vii. 17, 10, vol. ii. p. 584, ed. Schubart et Walz. The apostle does not enter into particulars, as there may have been variations among the three leading tribes,—the general fact suffices for his purpose. These words cannot be addressed to Jewish believers, as Theodoret seems to imagine. The scholiast quoted in Usteri says that the keeping of times marked by sun and moon is to be in slavery to those heavenly bodies—a species of idolatry.

Ver. 9. *Νῦν δὲ γνόντες Θεόν, μᾶλλον δὲ γνωσθέντες ὑπὸ Θεοῦ*—"But now having known God, or rather being known by God." The *νῦν δέ* stands in contrast to the *τότε μέν*. There seems no true ground for making any distinction here between *εἰδότες* and *γνόντες*, as is done by Olshausen, as if the former meant rather external knowledge—*mehr blos ausserliche Wissen*, and the second inner knowledge. There is more truth in Professor Lightfoot's distinction, that the first refers to absolute and the second to relative knowledge—the difference between "to know" and "to come to the knowledge of." 1 John ii. 29. At least the following verses do not warrant Olshausen's distinction, for John vii. 27—especially John viii. 55—would seem to reverse it, where Jesus says of His Father: *καὶ οὐκ ἐγνώκατε αὐτόν· ἐγὼ δὲ οἶδα αὐτόν*. In 2 Cor. v. 16, the words *εἰ δὲ καὶ ἐγνώκαμεν κατὰ σάρκα Χριστόν* do not certainly imply an inner or active knowledge. The Galatians had come to the knowledge of God—of God in Christ, the one living and true God—the only object of genuine worship and trust. And this knowledge had been carried to them by the gospel, and by the preaching of Christ. "No man knoweth the Father but the Son, and he to whomsoever the Son shall reveal Him." The apostle, however, at once corrects himself, and adds—

Μᾶλλον δὲ γνωσθέντες ὑπὸ Θεοῦ—"but rather were known of God." Compare for a similar change of voice, Phil. iii. 12. In *μᾶλλον δέ* lies the notion of a climactic correction of the previous clause. Raphelius, *in loc.; hic est corrigentis ut sæpissime alibi*, Stallbaum, *Plato*, *Sym.* 173, E; Bornemann, *Xen. Cyrop.* p. 354. Rom. viii. 34; Eph. v. 11. The phrase has been variously understood.

1. The most improbable interpretation is that of Beza, a Lapide, Koppe, and others, who give the participle the sense of the *Hophal* conjugation in Hebrew—*scire facti*, "being made to know." It is forced and unnecessary. Winer, § 39, 3, n. 2.

2. Some, as Grotius, give the simple sense of *approbati*, which the usage does not warrant.

3. Others, as Borger, Winer, Rückert, Usteri, Schott, and virtually Trana and Ewald, attach the meaning *anerkannt seid*

—acknowledged by. But this direct meaning does not seem proved by any distinct instance in the New Testament. Matt. xxv. 12; Phil. iii. 12; 2 Tim. ii. 19. The sense, then, seems to be that of the Greek fathers, that they had not so much known God, as they had been taken into knowledge by God. 1 Cor. viii. 2, xiii. 12—προσληφθέντες ὑπὸ Θεοῦ (Theophylact). It was not that by any intuition or argument they had arrived at the knowledge of God; but the apostle glorifies the divine agency in their enlightenment, and refers to their condition, rather than their actual knowledge. God knew them ere they knew Him, and His knowing them was the cause of their knowing Him. See many examples from the Old Testament in Webster and Wilkinson. *Nostrum cognoscere est cognosci a Deo* (Luther). Matthies understands the clause as referring "to the Spirit of God knowing Himself again in them;" but Kimmel justly calls this exegesis *ein Hegel'scher dem Paulus fremder Sinn.* Jowett's statement is not unlike that of Matthies. Compare for another form of putting the same truth, 1 John iv. 10, Isa. lxv. 1. Recognition, conversion, and other blessings are implied, though not expressed in the clause. That He did not know them before the gospel came among them argues no defect in His omniscience. The language is warranted by usage. But brought into His knowledge, they saw light in His light. The gospel, he who preached it, and the Spirit who accompanied it, were alike of Him, and given to them. Their privilege thus began with His gracious knowledge of them, not their apprehension of Him. The apostle feels that this is the truer way of stating the case—giving the grace of God the glory, and putting their apostasy in a yet more awful light, it being an ungrateful rebellion against God's kindness, as well as a relapse into what was unsatisfying and obsolete.

And the startling question then comes—

Πῶς ἐπιστρέφετε πάλιν ἐπὶ τὰ ἀσθενῆ καὶ πτωχὰ στοιχεῖα; —"how is it that ye are returning again to the weak and beggarly elements?" In the question begun by πῶς that surprising inconsistency is rebuked. Their going back is something amazing—"Who bewitched you?" After your high privilege conferred on you, your emancipation from the servitude of idols, your pure theology, yea, and your being taken into the knowledge of God, how comes it that you, so preciously blessed, are turning, and that without any tempting bribe, or any plausible benefit—turning "to the weak and beggarly elements?" The adverb πάλιν does not mean "back"—*retro*—as in Homer, but as usually in the New Testament, "again"—*iterum*. Damm. *Lex. Homer. sub voce.* Ellicott says that the notion of back is involved in the verb; but ἐπι does not necessarily imply it, for ὀπίσω and εἰς τὰ ὀπίσω are often connected with it. Comp. also Acts xiv. 15, xv. 19, 1 Thess. i. 9. The present tense shows the act to be going on—the apostasy to be proceeding. See under i. 6.

For στοιχεῖα, see under ver. 3.

These elements are stigmatized as ἀσθενῆ—"weak," wholly inadequate to secure justification or provide spiritual deliverance (Rom. viii. 3); and πτωχά—"beggarly,"—an epithet often used in its literal sense as applied to persons, and here signifying that they were endowed with no clusters of spiritual blessing, and were not fraught with "the unsearchable riches of Christ." Heb. vii. 18.

Οἷς πάλιν ἄνωθεν δουλεύειν θέλετε—"to which ye are desiring again afresh to be in bondage." Wisd. xix. 6. The English version, the Syriac, and Vulgate omit the translation of one of the two adverbs, probably regarding them as synonymous—an opinion adopted by Borger. The emphasis lies on πάλιν ἄνωθεν—once in bondage, and again anew placing themselves under it, as if the first slavery had been forgotten. "Ye desire" to be in it again, and are anew beginning to place yourselves beneath it. Strange to say, of their own accord they were wishing to be in this servitude "afresh." As their condition struck him—their divine deliverance, their spiritual freedom, and their willing relapse into servitude—he naturally asks πῶς, is it possible? One difficulty lies in πάλιν, if the στοιχεῖα as in ver. 3 be restricted to the Mosaic ritual. Were the Gentiles under στοιχεῖα previously as well as the Jews? There is no sure historical ground for alleging that the persons so addressed had been proselytes (Olshausen, Credner), though in all probability many of the class existed in the churches of Galatia and in all the early churches, as if the meaning were—ye are going again into bondage to the Mosaic ritual, since in some sense they had been in it, and afresh they were recurring to its στοιχεῖα. This notion cannot be sustained, and therefore it is probable that the heathen *cultus* receives by implication the same name from the apostle as do the Jewish ordinances. While there was not identity, there was such similarity between them that they may be both comprehended under the same epithet, though such a comparison as that of Grotius between *castratio* and *circumcisio* is simply absurd. The system into which they were relapsing was of a like character to that under which they had been originally enslaved. For it was ritualistic in a high degree, with its orgies and mutilations. Such a ceremonial institute, hedging in a man with its rigid *minutiæ*, and binding him to the punctilious observance of them, was an intolerable yoke like Judaism. Besides, even in paganism, with all its follies and falsehoods, there were rudiments of truth. The worship of many gods proved the felt need of some god, the altar with its victims implied convictions of sin, and the lustrations betokened the conscious want of purity. Thus under such systems, and not wholly overlaid by them, were some "elements" of religious verities, in harmony with irrepressible spiritual instincts and yearnings, educated by such discipline into an intensity which must in many instances have prepared for the reception of that gospel which meets all wants and satisfies all awakened longings—verifying what Tertullian calls *testimonium animæ naturaliter christianæ*. Augustine also gives another aspect of the same opinion. He had said in his treatise *De Vera Religione*, written by him when a young man (A.D. 390), that Christianity belonged to later times—*nostris temporibus;* but in his *Retractationes*, composed towards the close of his life, he explains the assertion, and distinguishes between the *res* and the *nomen*, the latter having originated at Antioch; but of the former he uses the following words: *nam res ipsa, quæ nunc christiana religio nuncupatur, erat apud antiquos, nec defuit ab initio generis humani, quousque ipse Christus veniret in carne, unde vera religio quæ jam erat, cœpit appellari christiana.* Compare Acts x. 34, 35. The *Retractationes* and the *De Vera Religione* are in the first volume of Augustine's *Opera*, pp. 20, 1202, Gaume, Paris. Other fathers had similar views. Clement and Origen speak of the dark night of paganism as having had its stars which called to the morning star which stood over Bethlehem; Justin Martyr describes a ray of divine light shining in the soul, and turning toward the divine light as a plant to the sun. "Obey your philosophers," says Theodoret to the heathen, "for they fore-announced our doctrines." *Græcarum affectionum Curatio*, p. 483, vol. iv. *Opera*, ed. Sirmondi, Lutetiæ 1642. Clement also asserts of the Greek philosophy that it led to Christ—*ἐπαιδαγώγει . . . εἰς Χριστόν*. *Strom.* i. 5, 28. The apostle himself on Mars' hill, penetrating to the instinctive feeling which underlies idolatry, and recognising that inner necessity under which man must worship, uttered a kindred statement when he virtually identified the God who had the altar wanting a name with the object of his preaching: "What therefore, not knowing it, ye worship, that proclaim I unto you." Not that the "unknown God" was really Jehovah, but the inscription implied that He was not found in their lists, and was beyond the circuit of their recognition; and taking up this idea of a divinity above and beyond their pantheon, he expanded and applied it. Acts xvii. 23. See also Pressensé's *Religions before Christ:* Clark, Edinburgh; Max Müller's *Chips from a German Workshop*, Preface, and Essays in first volume, London 1867. It may be said, too, the apostle argues that the abrogation of the Mosaic law in the death of Christ was essential to the adoption of the Gentiles—to their becoming the seed of Abraham, or free children; so that the Mosaic institute—this thing of weak and beggarly elements—prior to Christ's death really held Gentiles in bondage, and why should they now relapse into servitude under it? They differed nothing from servants, as truly as the Jews while the Jewish law was in force; how was it, then, that they were desiring to go back to that law, and be in subjection to it over again?

The apostle now adduces a specimen of the bondage into which they were so willing to fall—the ritualistic observance of certain portions of the Jewish sacred kalendar—

Ver. 10. *Ἡμέρας παρατηρεῖσθε, καὶ μῆνας, καὶ καιροὺς, καὶ ἐνιαυτούς*—"Ye are observing days, and months, and seasons, and years." The force of the middle voice cannot be expressed in English, but it deepens the sense = religious assiduity. Many give this verse an interrogative form, as Koppe, De Wette, Hilgenfeld, Meyer, Bisping, and Trana; as also the editors Griesbach, Knapp, Tischendorf, and Lachmann.

But the form of solemn statement is in better harmony with the context. The question had been put already, πῶς—how comes it? It may appear incredible, but alas it is true—"Ye are observing days," etc. And the statement lays foundation for the mournful declaration of the following verse—φοβοῦμαι ὑμᾶς. The compound verb παρατηρεῖν in its original sense is "to watch carefully," as being παρα, near to, Acts ix. 24; next "to watch closely," Ps. cxxix. 3, and with evil purpose, Mark iii. 2, Luke vi. 7; and then, as here, "to observe carefully," to keep in a religious spirit,—not however superstitiously, as Sardinoux, Winer, and Olshausen assert, for the verb is applied to the keeping of the seventh day or Sabbath by Josephus, *Antiq.* iii. 3, 5. The observance may appear superstitious to the onlooker, but the idea is not contained in the verb, nor that of *præter fidem* (Bengel, Wessel, Wordsworth). "Days ye are observing," the moment being on ἡμέρας, as their observance would of course be more characteristic in its frequency. The "days" were the Jewish Sabbath, with other times of religious observance appointed by the law. The "months" were probably the new moons—days indeed, but observed with periodical exactness: Isa. lxvi. 23. The seventh month had a sacredness attached to it like the seventh day. The καιροί were the seasons of festival, as the passover, pentecost, and feast of tabernacles: Lev. xxiii. 4; 2 Chron. viii. 13. The ἐνιαυτοί, years, may be the seventh or sabbatic year and the year of jubilee. Compare Judith viii. 6; Philo, *De Septen.* p. 286. The two last terms do not stand for καιροὺς ἐνιαυτοῦ (Borger, Wahl).

The order of the terms is progressive—days, months, seasons, years. The last, supposing it to refer to the sabbatic year, they could not have observed more than once; and to infer from the present tense of the verb that they were then in the act of observing such a year, is in the highest degree precarious. Wieseler so calculates it, that from autumn 54 to autumn 55 there was a sabbatic year, within which period the epistle was written during the apostle's sojourn at Ephesus. *Chronologie des Apostolischen Zeitalters*, p. 287. But the epistle may have been written from Macedonia two or three years later. Michaelis, from the allusion to a sabbatic year in 1 Macc. vi. 53, which he places 162 years B.C., finds that the 49th year after Christ was the thirtieth sabbatic year from that period, and therefore he dates this epistle in 49. But he admits his ignorance as to the Jewish mode of calculation, whether they uniformly adhered to the seventh year on its recurrence, or began a new reckoning from the year of jubilee; as in the former case the 56th year would be the sacred year, and in the other it would be the 57th. "Introduction" by Marsh, vol. iv. p. 11. The sabbatic year and that of jubilee applied only to Canaan, its soil and the people on it; and it is not easy to see how it could be kept in other countries where Jews might own no land, nor engage in its cultivation. The reconstitution of society every fiftieth or jubilee year belongs also to the promised land, as really as the sacrifices to the central altar in Jerusalem, and its arrangements could not have been to any extent carried out among foreigners. If the statement in 2 Chron. xxxvi. 21, "Until the land enjoyed her sabbaths, for as long as she remained desolate she kept sabbath to fulfil threescore and ten years," mean that those years of desolation are a penalty chronologically parallel to a series of neglected sabbatic years, then the neglect must have extended backward 490 years, dating from the time of Solomon. These sabbatic years might be early neglected; for a nation that could subsist without cultivation of the soil for a year must either store up with cautious forethought, or enjoy a signal blessing from the God of the seasons. Such storing was not enjoined, as direct fulness of blessing was promised; but during so many periods of apostasy the promise of temporal abundance would be suspended, and the observance of the sabbatic year fall into desuetude. Lev. xxv. 18–22. But the year of jubilee, fraught with so many kind provisions to the slave, the debtor, and the poor, and involving so many changes of social relation to rural property, was more likely to be partially observed, for those to be especially benefited by it would naturally clamour for it. The prophets do not upbraid the nation for neglecting it; Josephus asserts that it was kept; and there is no ground for Michaelis and Winer to question its observance, or for Kranold and Hupfeld to deny it. Diodorus also makes allusion to the strict entail of Jewish property, and the testimony of Jewish tradition is unanimous on the point. Saalschütz, *Das Mosaische Recht*, xiii.; Keil, *Handbuch d. Bib. Archäol.* vol. i. p. 374. No such stress can be laid, as Ginsburg does, on Ezek. xlvi. 17 as to the uniform keeping of the jubilee; for the chapter is an ideal sketch of a re-distribution of the territory, and the re-organization of the national worship. Art. Jubilee, Kitto, *Bib. Cyclop.* 3d edition.

It is going too far on the part of Bullinger and Olshausen to affirm, that in this verse by synecdoche a part is put for the whole, *i.e.* the customs mentioned stand for all the customs. Nor can it be, as Rückert says, that only such customs are mentioned as were common to Jews and Gentiles; for, as Olshausen remarks, no relapse to Gentilism is apprehended. The apostle does not certainly speak of two of the Jewish "elements"—distinction of meats and drinks, and circumcision. There is no substantial evidence for saying that, as proselytes, those Galatians had been circumcised already; for it may be, as Meyer observes, that they had not yet relapsed so far as to be circumcised: v. 2, 3, 12, vi. 12, 13. The accumulation of terms of time, not meant to be exhaustive, may denote generally sacred periods, or it may be "a rhetorical description of those who observed times and seasons" (Alford). Dean Alford adds, "Notice how utterly such a verse is at variance with any and every theory of a Christian Sabbath, cutting at the root, as it does, of ALL *obligatory observance of times as such.*" This generalization is far too sweeping; for,

1. It makes assertion on a subject which is not before the mind of the apostle at all. Nothing is further from his thoughts, or his course of rebuke and expostulation, than the Christian Sabbath and its theme—the resurrection of Christ.

2. The apostle is not condemning the obligatory observances "of times as such," but he is condemning the observance only of the times which the Galatians, in their relapse into Judaism, kept as sacred; for their keeping of such Jewish festivals was the proof and result of their partial apostasy.

3. Nor is it even Jewish festivals as such which he condemns, for both before and after this period he observed some of them himself.

But, first, he condemns the Galatian Gentiles for observing sacred Jewish seasons, which, not being intended for them, had therefore no authority over them. The Gentile keeping of Jewish sabbaths, or of passovers, pentecosts, new moons, and jubilees, was in itself a wrong thing—a perilous blunder then as it would be a wretched anachronism now. And secondly, he condemns the observance of these "times," because the Galatians regarded such observance as essential to salvation, and as supplementing faith in the atoning work of Christ. These limitations are plainly supplied by the context, and the true theory of a Christian Sabbath, or rather Lord's day, is not in the least involved in the discussion.

The apostle having described their perilous and unsatisfactory condition, adds in sorrowful tone—

Ver. 11. *Φοβοῦμαι ὑμᾶς, μή πως εἰκῇ κεκοπίακα εἰς ὑμᾶς*—"I am afraid of you, lest perhaps I have in vain bestowed labour on you." Winer, in his Commentary and in his Gram. § 66, 5, *a*, regards this construction as a species of attraction—that in which the principal clause attracts something from the dependent one; and he is followed by Usteri, Wieseler, Hilgenfeld, and Jatho. But the supposition is not necessary. In such cases the object of the one clause is the subject of the other; but the pronoun is object here in both clauses, and the repetition of it intensifies the meaning, or gives distinct emphasis to the declaration. I am afraid of you is a definite idea, and the reason of the *φόβος* is then stated. The *κατά* suggested by Turner is not needed, as in such a sense the verb governs the simple accusative—the accusative of equivalent notion. Jelf, § 550, *b;* Kühner, § 857. Compare Plato, *De Leg.* x. p. 886, *A ;* Diodor. Sic. iv. 10 ; Soph. *Œd. Tyr.* 767.

In the perfect *κεκοπίακα*, and after *μή πως*, is the idea of enduring labour, and the indicative means that the apprehension expressed by *φοβοῦμαι* (Winer, § 56) is realized—the fear has become a matter of fact. Gayler, p. 317 ; Klotz-Devarius, vol. i. 129. See under ii. 2. So Theodoret, but not Chrysostom, who gives it a different turn—"the wreck has not happened, but I see the storm travailing with it." Comp. under Phil. i. 16, Col. iv. 17.

In the phrase *εἰς ὑμᾶς* the preposition implies direction, Rom. xvi. 6, not *in vobis* as the Vulgate, nor *propter vos* even, but *in vos*, upon you, as having been directed to them. Bernhardy, p. 217. His labours had them for their special aim and object.

It must have been a sad thought to the large-hearted apostle that his toils, anxieties, and prayers were proving themselves so far in vain. Surprised was he at the speedy revolution of sentiment, and indignant also toward the false teachers who had been seducing them. It cannot, however, be inferred from *ὑμᾶς* after *φοβοῦμαι* that the apostle is blaming them as if the Judaizers could not have done it without their assistance. However true the sentiment may be, that they were a willing prey to the false teachers, these simple words will not bear it; and the passage in Acts v. 26 adduced by Storr in defence is quite different in structure.

Ver. 12. *Γίνεσθε ὡς ἐγώ, ὅτι κᾀγὼ ὡς ὑμεῖς*—"Become ye as I am, for I also am become as you are." For somewhat similar phraseology, כָּמוֹנִי כָמוֹךָ, compare 1 Kings xxii. 4, 2 Kings iii. 7. These brief and terse words can only be explained from the context. He has been speaking of their returning to Judaism—to the weak and beggarly elements, and of the anxiety which their dangerous state caused him. As a personal argument and illustration he refers now to himself and the position he sustained toward the same weak and beggarly elements. "Become ye as I am, for I too am become as you,"—become free from Judaism as I, for I also am free from it like you—as if I too were a Gentile. Or, become ye as I—*εἰμί* or *γέγονα* being supplied—free from the law, in no sense recognising its obligation upon you,—for I have become as you; a Jew though I be, I am as regards the law quite like you Gentiles; or, Reciprocate my feeling and relation to Judaism: ii. 14; 1 Cor. ix. 20, 21; —*me imitamini gentiliter viventem, quia et ego gentiliter vivo*, as Pelagius gives it. Such generally is the view of Usteri, Winer, Hilgenfeld, Fritzsche, De Wette, Meyer, and Wieseler. The appeal is direct: I am afraid of you, lest my labour upon you be in vain. It will not be in vain if ye will become as I am in reference to the law; for toward that law I have become as you Gentiles to whom that law was not given, and over whom therefore it has, and was meant to have, no jurisdiction.

Another view has been given by the Greek fathers. "Become as I am, for I was once a very zealot for Judaism, as you are." Thus Chrysostom: *τοῦτον εἶχον πάλαι τὸν ζῆλον· σφοδρὰ τὸν νόμον ἐπόθουν.* Vatablus, Semler, and Matthies hold this view: "I once thought as you do, but I have changed my opinion; so do ye:" ye will not be the first who renounced the Mosaic law; or, ye can do what I wish you to do, since I have done it. But the words will not bear this interpretation. For, first, the appeal is not to Jews, but to those who had been Gentiles; and secondly, ἤμην, the word to be supplied, in that case must have been written, as the emphasis would be on it: so, as has been remarked, Justin, *Orat. ad Græcos*, writes, γίνεσθε ὡς ἐγὼ ὅτι κἀγὼ ἤμην ὡς ὑμεῖς, p. 12, vol. i. *Opera*, ed. Otto.[1] The context would only warrant the supplement of ἐγενόμην, which would not bear the sense assumed. Others, as Jerome, a Lapide, Rückert, and Olshausen, take another view. Thus Olshausen: "I always sought to look at matters from the same point of view as you did; so do ye act now also in the same spirit toward me." But this is too vague, and puts the two clauses out of unison.

Different is the interpretation of a fourth party, who suppose the words to refer to a reciprocation of love: Love me as I love you. This view is held by Luther, Beza, Calvin, Grotius, Cramer, Gwynne, Bagge, and Brown. 1 Kings xxii. 4. But the Greek phrase γίνεσθε ὡς certainly will not bear such fulness of meaning. It is true, at the same time, that the apostle's under-current of appeal is to his love to them and their former attachment to him. Afraid of them he was, yet he would have them act in love to him, so as to imitate him; and he goes on to refer to that affection which once subsisted between them. This interpretation has been thought by some to derive some countenance from the following clause, as they understand it: "I love you still, I do not feel toward you as an injured man." But the next clause begins apparently a new declaration, and is indeed a motive for them to become as he was. The apostle adds, however—

'Αδελφοί, δέομαι ὑμῶν—"Brethren, I beseech you." These words have been taken to refer to the following statement by Chrysostom and his followers, with Rückert, Koppe, and others. But there is no request contained in the following clauses at all, so that the phrase cannot be a preface to them. The request lies in the previous part of the verse.

The paragraph now commencing extends to the sixteenth

[1] Cureton found this treatise in a Syriac recension ascribed to some one called Ambrose, "a chief man of Greece," *Spicilegium Syriacum*, xi. 61. Otto after Tillemont and Maran defends its genuineness, but Grabe, Semisch, Neander, and others have doubted or denied it on good grounds.

verse. It is an appeal to their previous conduct and attachment, and it is adduced as a motive why they should follow the earnest counsel, *γίνεσθε ὡς ἐγώ*. The succession of aorists shows that the apostle writes of a previous point of time, probably his first visit to them. So that he says generally—

Οὐδέν με ἠδικήσατε—"in nothing did ye wrong me;" on the contrary, they did treat him with extreme kindness. But, 1. Beza, Bengel, and Rückert give by a meiosis this turn to the words, that "he forgave the anxiety and sorrow which they had occasioned him;" that "he would forgive and forget all" (Ewald). 2. The clause is not a mitigation of the previous rebuke, or something said in contrast to soothe them (Chrysostom, Estius, Winer). 3. Some, as Ambrosiaster, a Lapide, and Schott, put the emphasis wrongly on *μέ*, and bring out this contrast: "ye did not wrong me, but ye wronged yourselves." 4. Grotius and Rettig give it another point: "you have done nothing against me, but against God and Christ." These four forms of evolved contrast are alike to be rejected. They do not give the aorist its proper past signification which it must have, as is indicated by the following series of verbs in the same tense.

Ver. 13. *Οἴδατε δέ*—"But ye know." So far from doing me any injury, your treatment of me was the very opposite—ye wronged me in nothing; on the other hand, *δέ*, ye know that. *Δέ* is wanting in D[1], F, but found in A, B, C, and it is supported by the Vulgate. The demonstrative *ὅτι* introduces the series of clauses describing the facts of his first reception, which were matter of knowledge to them. He does not say, Ye remember, as if an act of reminiscence were needed, but, Ye know. And first he says—

Ὅτι δι' ἀσθένειαν τῆς σαρκὸς εὐαγγελισάμην ὑμῖν τὸ πρότερον—"that on account of weakness of my flesh I preached the gospel unto you the first time." The phrase *τὸ πρότερον*—Vulgate, *jam prius*—might point to an early time, or formerly: John vi. 62, vii. 51, ix. 8; Sept. Deut. ii. 12, Josh. x. 9 (Usteri). But it here refers to the apostle's first visit. Heb. iv. 6, vii. 27. Had he been once only in Galatia, the phrase would have been superfluous. The article gives emphasis to the expression. Some indeed affirm that Paul paid only one visit to the Galatian province. Thus Grotius interprets against the true construction—*nempe cum præsens essem, nam et absens eos docet;* but a simple *docet* falls short of that oral teaching which is expressed by the verb εὐαγγελισάμην. The phrase δι' ἀσθένειαν τῆς σαρκός, literally rendered, can have only one meaning—"on account of infirmity of the flesh," that is, on account of bodily weakness. Winer, § 49, *c.* This meaning of σάρξ is found in Acts ii. 26, 31, Col. i. 22, and such is the regular sense of διά with the accusative. On account of bodily infirmity the apostle preached during his first visit to Galatia. We cannot explain it. Either, travelling through the country, he was seized with sickness, and being unable to prosecute his journey, he employed his leisure in preaching; or, some malady detaining him longer in the province than he had intended or expected, he devoted what strength he had, or what strength was returning to him, to a hearty and successful proclamation of the good tidings. This strictly grammatical sense given to the clause is in complete harmony with the context, as the exegesis of the following verse will show; and to suppose a change of case is contrary to any real example in the New Testament. It is wrong, therefore, to evade this literal and only admissible meaning by giving the preposition the meaning of "under," as is done by not a few commentators. Thus Chrysostom: "While I preached to you, I was scourged, I suffered a thousand deaths; yet ye thought no scorn of me." Œcumenius and Theophylact explain it as μετ' ἀσθενείας, and the Vulgate, *per infirmitatem.* Luther, too, Olshausen, Matthies, follow this exegesis; and Brown says it is equivalent to ἐν ἀσθενείᾳ. Jowett's explanation is similar, and also that of Turner. In such a case διά would require the genitive, for such a phrase as διὰ νύκτα belongs to poetry. Bernhardy, p. 236. Some dilute the meaning, as Calvin: *abjectus et in hominum conspectu nullius pretii;* and similarly Rosenmüller, Koppe, and Borger. Others understand the phrase of persecutions. Thus Grotius: *per varios casus, per mille pericula rerum perrexi, ut vos instituerem.* Jatho, going still beyond this, and taking σάρξ as denoting sinful humanity, gives the weakness of humanity to save itself as the ground of all Paul's preaching. Bengel gets clear of the supposed difficulty by the allegation that sickness was not the cause of the preaching, *sed adjumentum cur Paulus efficacius prædicaret.*

Similarly Schott—that the apostle continuing to preach *assidue et alacriter*, notwithstanding his sickness, had a great effect on the minds of tho Galatians. Semler thinks that the phrase refers to timidity, which kept the apostle from openly withstanding the supporters of Judaism! Baumgarten-Crusius takes the allusion to be to some *Befangenheit und Verlegenheit*—perplexity and dilemma—occasioned by the antipathy to him of the Jewish element in those communities. Lastly, Jerome propounds this strange explanation: *Per infirmitatem autem non suæ sed audientium, qui non poterant carnem subjicere verbo Dei.* Estius, Hug, and Rettig follow him. But there wants some qualifying particle to bring out such a meaning, and the μοῦ of the following verse seems to decide that the reference is to himself. Gwynne denies that the grammatical sense suits the context, and suggests that it would have fitted the apostle, instead of saying "on account of," to say "in spite of, my weakness in the flesh." Peile also calls the proper translation "utterly irreconcilable" with the context, adding, "we would gladly read δι' ἀσθενείας." Jowett thus defends his view: "In the interpretation of διά we have to choose between ordinary Greek usage and the sense of the passage;" but how, except through the Greek usage, can the sense of this or any Greek passage be ascertained? Nor have the prepositions such "uncertainty of usage" as he ascribes to Paul. Classical precision may not be uniformly predicated of them, but their generic sense is always preserved even in rhetorical accumulations. The plain meaning then, without resort to grammatical torture, undue dilution, or remote reference, is, that in some way or other unknown to us, but quite known to the Galatians, bodily weakness led the apostle to preach, or to continue to preach, in Galatia at his first visit; and he goes on to say, that in spite of this, he met with a most cordial welcome, and with great success. It is needless to allege that if he had been sick or ill, he could not have preached. For what know we of the real nature of the malady? It might be so severe or of such a character as to prevent him from travelling, but not from preaching. What know we of his bodily infirmities, caught by infection or brought on by persecution? —for "he was in stripes above measure, in prisons more frequent,"—or created by numerous causes, for he was "in weariness and painfulness, in hunger and thirst, in fastings often, in cold and nakedness." What know we of the maladies and sudden attacks incident to a constitution which had been so tried and enfeebled, and into which had been sent also a thorn in the flesh? (Suicer, *sub voce ἀσθένεια.*)

Ver. 14. *Καὶ τὸν πειρασμὸν ὑμῶν ἐν τῇ σαρκί μου οὐκ ἐξουθενήσατε οὐδὲ ἐξεπτύσατε*—"And your temptation in my flesh ye despised not nor loathed"—"abhorred," Tyndale and the Genevan. The reading of the first part of this clause is involved in difficulty, whether it should be *τὸν πειρασμὸν ὑμῶν*, or *τὸν πειρασμόν μου τόν* of the Received Text. The first reading, *ὑμῶν*, is found in A, B, C[2], D, F, ℵ[1], 17, 39, 67[2] (C[2] having *ὑμῶν τόν*, ℵ[3] *τόν*). It is also found in the Coptic and Latin versions, and among the fathers in Jerome, Augustine, Ambrosiaster, Sedulius. Mill in his appendix adopts it, and so does Lachmann. On the other hand, the received reading *μου τόν* is found in D[2, 3], E, K, L, the great majority of MSS., in the Syriac and Gothic versions, and in Chrysostom, Theodoret, Œcumenius, Basil, etc. It is adopted by Tischendorf, Griesback, Hahn, and Reiche. Diplomatic or uncial authority and that of versions is in favour of *ὑμῶν*. This pronoun *ὑμῶν*, in the interpretation of the Greek fathers, would appear to them unintelligible; for they understand the trial of dangers and persecutions, and there was thus a temptation to omit it or change it. Lachmann wrongly places a colon after *ἐν τῇ σαρκί μου*. The reading with *ὑμῶν* is the more difficult, and was therefore more liable to be altered. There is no occasion to render *καί*, *et tamen*, as Winer does; it simply connects the clauses. The two compound verbs rise in emphasis. The first verb *ἐξουθενέω* (*οὐθέν* being a later form of *οὐδέν*, *Phrynichus*, ed. Lobeck, p. 181) is "to set at nought," "to despise." The second verb *ἐκπτύω* means "to spit out," as in Homer—*στόματος δ' ἐξέπτυσεν ἅλμην πικρήν*, *Od.* v. 322; and this, as well as the compound with *ἐν*, is used only in the natural sense. Then it means to spit as if in disgust—to loathe. Some of the other compounds are treated in *Phrynichus*, ed. Lobeck, p. 17. The simple verb is used in the earlier Greek, *Soph. Antig.* 649, and *ἀποπτύειν* would have been the more correct form here; but apparently the preposition of the first verb is repeated in the alliteration. The absolute *οὐ* is followed by the relative *οὐδέ*, the second clause not being intended when the first was formed in the mind of the writer. Jelf, § 776, 1, *b.* The verb describes a feeling excited by what is revolting. See Kypke *in loc.* The Vulgate has *non reprobastis aut respuistis.* By *πειρασμός* the apostle characterizes something which had a distinct tendency to produce those feelings — something in the physical malady or in his appearance under it which subjected the Galatians to the temptation of contemning and loathing him. Either the disease of itself had a tendency to produce this disgust and revulsion, or it may be that there was a temptation to set at nought and nauseate a professed teacher of a new religion so afflicted and disabled, reject his claims, and turn a deaf ear to his teaching. The words *ἐν τῇ σαρκί μου* define the seat of the *πειρασμός*, and being without the article, form with it one conception. Winer, § 20, 2. It has also been shown that *πειράζειν ἐν* occurs, as in Plato, *Phil.* p. 21, A. The expression is elliptical. "Your trial you did not reject" = that which originated or caused the trial. For nouns in *μος*, see Lobeck, *Phrynichus*, p. 511. So far from his weakness in the flesh tempting them to cherish any such feeling toward him, he adds in very graphic phrase—

'Αλλ' ὡς ἄγγελον Θεοῦ ἐδέξασθέ με, ὡς Χριστὸν 'Ιησοῦν— "but ye received me as an angel of God, as Christ Jesus." The vivid contrast in *ἀλλά* is, that so far from in any sense contemning him, they honoured him with an eager and intense welcome—they received him as an angel of God. Of course, in both clauses the apostle speaks in accordance with their present knowledge of divine revelation, not according to any knowledge they had possessed before he preached to them, for that would imply that he found them in possession of the gospel on his first visit to them. He therefore speaks of angels and Christ, as they understood them now, since their conversion. They received him as an angel. 1 Sam. xxix. 9; 2 Sam. xiv. 17, xix. 27. The angel is the highest and most glorious among creatures, and many appearances and visits of angels are recorded in the Old Testament. They received him not only as a "legate of the skies," but as Christ Jesus, the Lord of the angels. As you would receive an angel, nay, as you would receive Christ Jesus, did you receive me. Compare Luke x. 16, 2 Cor. ii. 10, v. 10, 11. The apostle, in spite of

bodily malady, was most enthusiastically welcomed and revered. He says this to their credit, and he affectionately recalls it. How lovingly they greeted him, and how studiously they consulted his welfare, untempted by what might have produced a very opposite result!

Ver. 15. Mournfully but sharply does he now turn round and ask—

Τίς οὖν ὁ μακαρισμὸς ὑμῶν; This reading has D, K, L in its favour, with the majority of MSS. and fathers. Another reading—*ποῦ οὖν ὁ μακαρισμός*—is found in A, B, C, F, G, ℵ, and in the Vulgate and Syriac versions. The Greek fathers refer to the various reading. Theodoret says, *ὁ γὰρ τίς ἀντὶ τοῦ ποῦ τέθηκε,* and he and Theodore Mops. and Severianus explain *τίς* by *ποῦ.* The particle *ποῦ,* though well supported, has the aspect of an emendation in that it appears to simplify the question—Where has it all gone to? "Where is the blessedness ye spake of?" With *τίς, ἦν* must be supplied, as it is written in D, E, K; F (G having *η*): "Of what sort or nature was your boasted blessedness?" The adjective refers to quality, as it usually does, not to quantity, though this last sense is given to it by Luther, Beza, Borger, Hilgenfeld, Reiche, Wieseler, and Brown. The question has more point if *τίς* bear its common significance. The *οὖν* is simply retrospective, implying here no logical inference. Donaldson, § 548, 31. The noun *μακαρισμός*—not *μακαριότης,* blessedness—means pronouncing blessed, as does the allied verb *μακαρίζω.* Rom. iv. 6, 9; Luke i. 48; James v. 11; Sept. Gen. xxx. 13; Ast, *Lexicon Platon. sub voce.* Bengel gives another meaning to *τίς*: *quæ causa*—what was the ground of this gratulation?—and he is followed by Jatho, Matthies, Schott, and to some extent Alford—"worth what?" "of what weight or value?" That the *μακαρισμός* was by Paul on the Galatians, is on the one hand the opinion of Jerome, who says, *vos eo tempore quo evangelium juxta carnem susceperatis—beatos dicerem,*—of Theodoret and the Greek fathers. On the other hand, Estius, Locke, and Wordsworth understand that the apostle himself is the object of the congratulation on the part of the Galatians. Locke's paraphrase is, "What benedictions did you then pour out upon me!" and his note is, "The context makes this sense of the words so necessary and visible, that it is to be wondered how any one could overlook it." If the apostle had meant felicitation upon himself, he would have stated it in some distinct way, but *ὑμῶν* stands without any addition. They had felicitated themselves on the apostle's ministry among them, even though they knew that it was what might be called an accident of illness which kept him so long in their province, apparently in opposition to his original plan of travel. Amidst their earnest self-congratulations, they forgot not the instrument of the blessedness which they boasted of. They pronounced themselves happy in enjoying such a ministry, and they vied with one another in kindness to the minister; for in proof he says—

Μαρτυρῶ γὰρ ὑμῖν ὅτι εἰ δυνατὸν τοὺς ὀφθαλμοὺς ὑμῶν ἐξορύξαντες ἐδώκατέ μοι—"for I bear you record, that if it had been possible, ye would have plucked out your eyes and have given them to me." The verb *μαρτυρῶ* is here followed by the dative of person in favour of whom the *μαρτυρία* is given, and also, as frequently, by the demonstrative *ὅτι*, equivalent to an accusative with the infinitive.

The participle *ἐξορύξαντες* is often employed in this idiom—perhaps more frequently than other terms. The imperative *ἔξελε* is used in Matt. v. 29, and *ἔκβαλε* in Mark ix. 47. Compare Judg. xvi. 21; 1 Sam. xi. 2; Joseph. *Antiq.* vi. 5, 1; Herod. viii. 116. The phrase *τοὺς ὀφθαλμοὺς ὑμῶν* is not "your own eyes," as Ellicott remarks, but simply "your eyes." No emphasis is intended. Compare John iv. 35. "Ye would have given them to me." The *ἄν* before *ἐδώκατε* in the Received Text is rejected on the authority of A, B, C, D[1], F, G, ℵ. The use of *ἄν* would have indicated hypothetical reality, but without *ἄν* it is more rhetorically emphatic, and means that the act would have been done if the restriction in *εἰ δυνατόν* had not intervened. John ix. 33, xv. 22. Hermann, *de Particula ἄν, Opuscula*, vol. iv. cap. xi. p. 57; Jelf, § 858, 1. The phrase *εἰ δυνατόν* is not to be pressed as meaning an absolute impossibility, but in a popular sense that such a token of love was impracticable—*pro evangelico lumine sua lumina tradidissent.* What higher expression of self-denied and ardent attachment to himself could the apostle describe? As Alford remarks, "The position of the words *τοὺς ὀφθαλμοὺς ὑμῶν* strongly supports the idea that the apostle uses the clause proverbially." And the expression is a common one based on nature, and found in a great variety of authors. Compare Deut. xxxii. 10, Ps. xvii. 8, Prov. vii. 2, Zech. ii. 8; Callim. in *Dian.* p. 21, ed. Blomfield; in Latin, Horace, *Sat.* ii. 5, 33; Terence, *Adelph.* v. 7–5; Catullus, iii. xiv. See Wetstein *in loc.* The meaning then is, that they would have parted with anything, even the most precious—have endured no common self-torment—in the depth of their professed attachment to him.

But some give the phrase a more literal significance, or rather suppose a more literal reason for the use of the figure. They suppose that the ἀσθένεια was some kind of ophthalmic disorder. The meaning in that case is, the Galatians would have parted with their eyes to him, could the gift have relieved the apostle. Lomler, Rückert, Schott, and others advocate this view, which is favoured also by Conybeare. We would not, however, call it with Schmoller *abgeschmackt*, nor say with Bisping *fast lächerlich ist es;* for some form of it may have been mixed up with his malady. But, as has been remarked, the emphasis is neither on ὑμῶν nor μοί. Nor is there any distinct proof in the apostle's language at any time, or in the record of his life, that he was vexed with any eye-illness. See Essay at end of this section.

Ver. 16. Ὥστε ἐχθρὸς ὑμῶν γέγονα ἀληθεύων ὑμῖν;—"So then, have I become your enemy because I tell you the truth?" By ὥστε an interrogative inference is made—"so then," or "as matters now are." *Ergo* is so used in the Latin versions. Plato, *Phædrus*, 231, B; Klotz-Devarius, vol. ii. 776. Meyer connects ὥστε directly with τίς οὖν ὁ μακαρισμὸς ὑμῶν, but the connection is better taken with the entire verse or paragraph—not a direct conclusion, as the result of the previous statement. The term ἐχθρός is taken in a passive sense by Estius, Koppe, Rosenmüller, Trana, and Meyer in his second edition. The context agrees with such a sense. Their feeling toward him had been that of extreme kindness and indulgence, and he might ask, Have I, who once was the object of your intense affection, become the object of your hatred? the two states being brought into distinct contrast. The genitive is probably used because ἐχθρός is a virtual substantive—Am I become the hated of you? But we prefer the active sense, with many of the ancient versions, and with Bengel, Beza, Grotius, Rückert,

Schott, Hilgenfeld, Meyer, and Ellicott. Such is the prevailing meaning of the word, adjective and substantive, in the New Testament; and it is followed here, as usually, by the genitive of person (Sophocles, *Ajax*, 500; Demosthenes, *de Legat.* 439, 19, p. 279, vol. i. *Opera*, ed. Schaefer), whereas in the passive sense it takes the dative. The perfect γέγονα expresses the change as over, and as resulting in a permanent state—Am I become your enemy? Nor is this meaning out of harmony with the context. There had been mutual ascriptions of blessedness because they enjoyed the labours of such a benefactor. Have I then, from being esteemed and welcomed as your best benefactor, come to be regarded as your enemy? There is no ground for Olshausen's supplement, "and can those be your friends?" as there is no ἐγώ expressed. At a later period, as we have seen, the Judaizers called him ὁ ἐχθρὸς ἄνθρωπος. *Clement. Hom.* p. 4, ed. Dressel. The participle ἀληθεύων has a causal force—"because I tell the truth to you;" the use of the present not confining it to the moment of writing; nor is it "because I have told you the truth," though the idea of the past is not excluded. The state is expressed in its whole duration. Winer, § 40, 2, *c*, § 45, 1; Schmalfeld, pp. 91, 92, 405; Acts xix. 24; 1 Pet. iii. 5. The participle probably means simply "speaking the truth"—referring to oral address, and not to upright conduct. Matthias, as his wont is, would alter the punctuation, and connect ἀληθεύων with the next verse.

To what period, then, does the apostle refer? Not (1) to the letter he is writing, as he could not know of its result, though this is the view of Jerome, Luther, Koppe, and others;—nor (2) to his first visit, for they received him then as an angel, nay, as Christ Jesus Himself; nor then could the Judaizing teachers have had any scope for labour. Some time had elapsed before they made their appearance, as is implied in iii. 2–5, and expressly stated in v. 7: "Ye did run well." So that (3) the probability is that he refers to what took place on his second visit, when the evil was fermenting which speedily developed into such pernicious results. That the speaking of unwelcome truth creates enmity has passed into a proverb. Terent. *Andr.* i. 1, 40. While the apostle could go far in the way of accommodation to prejudice, and in matters indifferent, he would on no account sacrifice any element of truth. Whatever on any pretence or to any degree endangered truth met at once from him with vehement and persistent opposition, no matter what hostility, misapprehension, or prejudice his fidelity might create against himself. The truth was Christ's, and he dares not compromise it; himself was Christ's, and in Christ's spirit he "endures all things for the elect's sake." And as the truth endangered in Galatia was truth alike precious and prominent in the gospel—truth resting on the perfection of Christ's work, and involving the freeness of His salvation—it must be upheld at all hazards. Still the apostle must have keenly felt this revulsion of sentiment toward himself; for his was not an impassible nature, with nerves that never tingled and a surface that no weapon could pierce. On the contrary, with a woman's tenderness, his sympathies were acute, profound, and ever active: "Who is weak, and I am not weak? who is offended, and I burn not?" Had the change of feeling toward him been only characteristic caprice, he would have cared less; but it involved a departure from the gospel which he had proclaimed, and which was divine alike in origin, substance, and results.

NOTE ON PAUL'S "INFIRMITY IN THE FLESH"—"THE THORN IN THE FLESH"

GAL. IV. 13, 14, 15. *Οἴδατε δὲ ὅτι δι' ἀσθένειαν τῆς σαρκὸς εὐηγγελισάμην ὑμῖν τὸ πρότερον, Καὶ τὸν πειρασμὸν ὑμῶν ἐν τῇ σαρκί μου οὐκ ἐξουθενήσατε οὐδὲ ἐξεπτύσατε· ἀλλ' ὡς ἄγγελον Θεοῦ ἐδέξασθέ με, ὡς Χριστὸν Ἰησοῦν. Τίς οὖν ἦν ὁ μακαρισμὸς ὑμῶν; μαρτυρῶ γὰρ ὑμῖν ὅτι εἰ δυνατὸν τοὺς ὀφθαλμοὺς ὑμῶν ἐξορύξαντες ἐδώκατέ μοι*—"Ye know how, on account of infirmity of the flesh, I preached the gospel unto you at the first. And your temptation which was in my flesh ye despised not, nor loathed; but received me as an angel of God, even as Christ Jesus. What then was the blessedness ye spake of? for I bear you record, that, if it had been possible, ye would have plucked out your eyes, and have given them to me."

2 COR. XII. 7. *Καὶ τῇ ὑπερβολῇ τῶν ἀποκαλύψεων ἵνα μὴ ὑπεραίρωμαι, ἐδόθη μοι σκόλοψ τῇ σαρκί, ἄγγελος Σατᾶν ἵνα με κολαφίζῃ, ἵνα μὴ ὑπεραίρωμαι*—"And lest I should be exalted above measure through the

abundance of the revelations, there was given to me a thorn in the flesh, the messenger of Satan to buffet me, lest I should be exalted above measure."

According to one probable hypothesis, the Epistle to the Galatians and the second Epistle to the Corinthians were written about the same period, and it is a natural conclusion that the reference in the two preceding paragraphs is to the same sharp distressing visitation. But surmises as to the nature of the malady so referred to in both epistles in these strong and significant terms, have been numerous and conflicting. Plainly it was no merely inner disease, the effects or concomitants of which were either not visible, or, if perceptible, affected no one with disgust—*ἐξεπτύσατε*. But it was an infirmity which could not be concealed, which obtruded itself on all with whom the apostle came into contact, and was so revolting in its nature as to excite nausea in spectators, and tempt them to reject his preaching. The apostle does not disguise its tendency, though he does not unfold its nature or give it any specific name. The Galatians knew it so well that the merest allusion was sufficient for them. Their perfect knowledge of it is thus the cause of our ignorance of it. But there are allusions to some sickness or other peculiar malady in other portions of the second Epistle to the Corinthians so striking and peculiar, that there is every probability of their identity with this *ἀσθένεια*. Thus 2 Cor. i. 8–10—"For we would not, brethren, have you ignorant of our trouble which came to us in Asia, that we were pressed out of measure, above strength, insomuch that we despaired even of life: but we had the sentence of death in ourselves, that we should not trust in ourselves, but in God which raiseth the dead; who delivered us from so great a death, and doth deliver; in whom we trust that He will yet deliver us." These remarkable words have been referred by many, as Neander and Wieseler, to the tumult at Ephesus, as told in Acts xix. The objection, that Paul would have written "in Ephesus," and not vaguely "in Asia," if he had alluded to that city, is without real force, though he generally so names it, as in the first epistle, 1 Cor. xv. 32, xvi. 8. But the life of the apostle does not seem to have been in peril at Ephesus; the tumult was stupid and aimless, and did not last long; and if he had been martyred, it would have been in the sudden confusion and excitement. Hours of dreadful anticipation would in that case have been spared him. Nay, so far as the record tells, it could not be said of him, that during the riot he was in anguish or felt himself in danger. But in the verses quoted he speaks of being "weighed down beyond strength, so that we despaired even of life." These terms certainly are inapplicable to such a sudden or momentary terror as the swift gathering of a mob might produce; they rather describe the result of sore personal sickness, so long, heavy, oppressive, and continuous, that "we utterly despaired even of life." That sickness was *καθ' ὑπερβολήν* in itself grievous, and on this account *ὑπὲρ δύναμιν*, beyond our power of endurance. The visitation so characterized must have a load of unwonted pressure, for the apostle is of all men least prone to exaggerate in personal matters. To "despair even of life," implies a period of suffering so tedious and heavy that it gradually extinguished all hope of recovery. The expression, to "have the sentence of death in ourselves," inclines us again to the same view: the malady was felt to be a deadly one; the prospect of restoration to health was so wholly gone, that his trust was not in God for it, but for a blessed resurrection — "in God which raiseth the dead;" and his unexpected recovery was signally due to Him "who rescued us from so great a death." Such is a probable meaning of the paragraph. In ver. 4 the apostle speaks generally of tribulations, and, viewed in a special aspect, they are called "the sufferings of Christ," as He still endures them in His members. But in ver. 8 he passes from the general reference to a specific instance, which indeed might be aggravated by surrounding persecution, and by his deepening anxiety for the welfare of the churches—"affliction, anguish of heart, and many tears," 2 Cor. ii. 4. In 2 Cor. x. 10 the apostle quotes a bitter criticism of his opponents on himself and his writings, in which occurs the phrase, *ἡ δὲ παρουσία τοῦ σώματος ἀσθενής*—a sentence referring not to stature or physical constitution, but to the impressions of frailty and sickness which his appearance indicated. Nay, he had said to the same church, 1 Cor. ii. 3, "I was with you in weakness, and in fear, and in much trembling:" the weakness was probably physical weakness, nervous susceptibility increased by his intense anxiety as to the results of his preaching. He could not indeed be what Jowett calls him, "a poor decrepid being afflicted with palsy;" for surely in such a case he could not have done the work which so few could have done, or borne the trials which so few could have faced. One may remark, too, the specialty of emphasis in the phrase, "Luke the beloved physician," as if he had endeared himself to the apostle, who stood in need so often of his medical sympathy and skill. He might not be unlike what Luther calls him, *ein armes dürres Mannlein wie Magister Philippus* (Melancthon); for there is throughout his epistles a deep current of allusion to weakness, to mental depression, to nervous apprehension, to hindrances in his labours which distressed him, and a consequent sense of humiliation which always chastened him. These were mortifying drawbacks to his eagerness and success.

Still farther, there is a very strong probability that in the apostle's malady there was some prominent characteristic, to which passing allusions are thus made, and of which a more formal account is given by himself in 2 Cor. xii. 1. Even there the result is dwelt upon, but the nature of the infliction is not clearly described. He had been describing many of his outer sufferings, and the last of them, referred to so solemnly and under an adjuration, must have made an indelible impression on him—the kind of ignominy and humiliation attaching to his undignified mode of escape from Damascus—"through a window, in a basket was I let down by the wall." He almost shrinks from telling the adventure: such is its nature that he is afraid that his sober statement may not be credited, and therefore it is prefaced, "The God and Father of our Lord Jesus Christ, which is blessed for evermore, knoweth that I lie not." Perhaps, however, these words belong to the previous catalogue of sufferings, or they form a preface to some other statements, which after all have been withheld. He then comes at length to his inner experiences, connected with his highest glory and with his deepest and most trying weaknesses. In these infirmities would he glory, as they were either coincident with or resulted from the noblest privilege which he had enjoyed. He proposes to give them—for he was forced to it—a specimen of his glories and his infirmities, his enjoyments of visions and revelations—those states of spiritual ecstasy in which, with a partial or total cessation of self-consciousness, he was brought into immediate communing with the Master, beheld His glory, and listened to His voice; in which truth in its beauty and power was flashed upon him, and glimpses into the glories and mysteries of the spiritual world were suddenly vouchsafed to him. Both forms of ecstasy combined (for the vision included the revelation) had already been enjoyed by him. The person of Christ was usually the object of the vision, and the disclosure of His will the theme of the revelation. And the amazing incident is told by him as of a third person while he unfolds the exalted and perilous honour, but he resumes the first person when he comes to speak of the resulting infirmity. "I know a man in Christ, fourteen years before, whether in the body I know not, or out of the body I know not, God knoweth,—(I know) such an one snatched up as far as the third heaven. And I know such a man, whether in the body or without the body I cannot tell, God knoweth, that was caught up to paradise, and heard unutterable utterances, which it is not lawful for a man to speak." This repetition with a difference refers apparently to two raptures; and we may almost infer from the construction, broken and resumed, asserted and repeated, that the remembrance of the indescribable glory, and his untraceable translation into it, produced a momentary maze or mental bewilderment like that which preceded or followed the mysterious ascensions. The "third heaven" is evidently the highest heaven—it was no common honour; and paradise may not be a distinct, loftier, or remoter region, but perhaps a portion of the same glorious abode. Probably, as this name was given to the garden of Eden, the scene of original innocence, it was transferred to that peculiar sphere of the third heaven where human spirits are gathered together in restored purity and felicity, in the immediate presence of God on His throne—that paradise where the Saviour unveils His glory, and admission into which He promised to the penitent thief on the cross. That the apostle saw the divine essence is maintained by Augustine, Anselm, Aquinas; but what he saw he tells not, what he heard could not be disclosed. If we were even allowed to repeat the songs and voices, still language would be wholly inadequate as a vehicle, for words want power to bear on them a description of the "far more exceeding and eternal weight of glory." But how he reached the third heaven he knew not, only it was under a swift and sudden spell—he was snatched away, and by no self-analysis could he unravel the psychological mystery. So contrary was it to all experience, so little was he under the guidance of ordinary consciousness, and of the common influences of space and time, that he could not tell whether he was in the body or out of the body. Yet he speaks of himself as a man caught up, of passing from one region to another, and of hearing words. His whole inner nature was under the influence of the divine charm, in whatever way it was effected, though hearing in the ordinary sense implies organs of sensation. "Of such a one will I glory"—one so strangely honoured as to be for a season among the blessed in their exalted sphere,—of such an one so singled out would he glory, but he would not glory of himself; not denying the identity of "such an one" with himself, but drawing probably this distinction, that in enjoying the translation he was not himself, but in some way beyond himself. Still he would boast of his infirmities, for these were himself, elements of continuous consciousness, struggle, and depression. Nay more, if he did glory, he should not be "a fool;" for in referring to visions and revelations he was only speaking the truth without exaggeration; but he forbears, for this reason, that he does not wish to be judged by such an abnormal standard—this enjoyment of ecstasies which they could not comprehend. He would not be the object of any idolatrous veneration because access had been given to the light inaccessible; but he would be judged by the common criterion—what they saw him to be, what they heard of him, that is, by their own experience of him, in his daily life, and by his work which was ever patent and palpable to them. He would glory in his infirmities; and he adds, "And for this purpose, that through the excessive abundance of the revelations I might not be unduly exalted, there was given unto me a thorn in the flesh, a messenger of Satan, that he may buffet me, that I might not be unduly exalted." The language implies that the *σκόλοψ τῇ σαρκί* was produced by the excess of the revelations, or it was so connected with them in time and circumstance that it was felt to have resulted from their excess—*τῇ ὑπερβολῇ*,—they were so many and so grand, that while the spirit might enjoy them, the flesh was so weak that it was worn out by them. This conscious link between the thorn and the revelation was the appointed means of keeping the apostle humble: what he had enjoyed might have elated him, but it had a sting left behind it which ever abased and tortured him. That the visitation had wrought out its purpose is apparent from many allusions, and from this late record of his unprecedented honours, for he does not seem to have told them before. The words imply that there might have been undue elation, but that it was most surely prevented. It may be added that Lucian sneers at the apostle's rapture, calling him *ἀναφαλαντίας, ἐπίρρινος, ἀεροβατήσας*, *Philopat.* 12, p. 249, *Opera*, vol. ix. Bipont. The visions are also mocked in the *Clementines*, xvii. 19.

The term *σκόλοψ* occurs only here in the New Testament, and originally signifies a pointed stake, defined by Hesychius *ξύλον ὀξύ*, for fixing heads on; as in Homer, *Il.* xviii. 177, *κεφαλὴν . . . πῆξαι ἀνὰ σκολόππεσσι*,—or for impaling a person, Eurip. *Bacchae*, 983; *ἢ σκόλοψι πήξωμεν δέμας*, *Iph. in Taur.* 1431. Lucian calls Jesus *τὸν ἐν τῇ Παλαιστίνῃ ἀνασκολοπισθέντα*, *De Morte Peregrini*, 12, p. 279, vol. viii. Bipont. In the Septuagint it seems to be employed to denote a sharp-pointed stake, but one not so large as that a head could be set on it or a body impaled on it—a stake in miniature, virtually a thorn: *σκόλοπες ἐν τοῖς ὀφθαλμοῖς ὑμῶν*, "thorns in your eyes," Num. xxxiii. 55; similarly Ezek. xxviii. 24, and in Hos. ii. 6, where it represents the Hebrew סִיר, *spina.* *Ἄκανθαι καὶ σκόλοπες ὀδύνας σημαίνουσι διὰ τὸ ὀξύ*, Artemidorus, *Oneirocritica*, iii. 33, p. 280, vol. i. *Opera*, ed. Reiff. The Syriac renders by ܫܘܟܐ ܠܒܣܪܝ, "a thorn in my flesh." It is therefore extreme in Dean Stanley to take the image as that of impaling or crucifying, or at all analogous to the phrase, "I am crucified with Christ." Impalement would scarcely be a congruous image for physical suffering in one who travelled and laboured like the apostle. The references to crucifixion and its agonies are of a different nature. But he might bear about a sharp-pointed stake in his flesh which no power could extract, and which was producing a rankling festering wound and torture. Now the *τῇ σαρκί* here appears to be parallel to the *ἐν τῇ σαρκί μου* of Gal. iv. 13—something which had its origin in those superabundant revelations, which vexed and humiliated the apostle, and was of a nature so visibly painful, and withal so offensive, that it became a trial to spectators and listeners. The thorn was "given him" by God, and was also "an angel of Satan that he may buffet me"—the last clause describing the action not of the thorn, but of the angel of Satan. It is a superficial and unbiblical supposition of Turner, that this clause may have no more real meaning in it than the popular expressions, "St. Vitus' dance" or "St. Anthony's fire," in which there is not the least idea of supernatural agency. Scripture does not so sport with the awful names and agencies of the fallen spirit-world. "The devil and his angels" is a phrase found in Matt. xxv. 41. The thorn was employed by this evil spirit as a means of buffeting him. That he might be humble was God's purpose; that he might be humiliated was the purpose of Satan's angel,—that is, brought into contempt, and restrained in his work, his influence lessened, and himself harassed and agonized. May not this help to explain the allusion in 1 Thess. ii. 18, "We would have come unto you, but Satan hindered us?" This buffeting might produce nervous tremors, apprehensions, and a chronic lowness of spirits. Amid all his enthusiasm and chivalry, he needed frequent comfort and assurance; so that we find the voice saying to him at Corinth, "Be not afraid;" in his confinement in Jerusalem, "Be of good cheer;" and during the voyage to Rome, "Fear not." Acts xviii. 9, xxiii. 11, xxvii. 24. Another result in such circumstances might be, that strong craving for human sympathy which is often manifested by him. See Howson, *Lectures on St. Paul*, p. 72, 2d edition.

It is difficult to say at what period these revelations were given. It was fourteen years before he wrote his second epistle to the Corinthians. The period could not therefore be that of his conversion, as is thought by Damasus, Thomas Aquinas, Œder, Keil, and Reiche, for considerably more than fourteen years must have elapsed since that turning-point in his life. Others identify the rapture with the trance in the temple, and the vision and commission connected with it, which himself describes in Acts xxii. 17–20, as Spanheim, Lightfoot, Rinck, Schrader, Osiander, Wieseler. If this vision took place at his first visit to Jerusalem three years after his conversion, the dates are more in harmony, though the chronology of the apostle's life is very uncertain. The year of his conversion cannot be definitely fixed, opinions varying from the years 33 to 42 A.D. But if it happened, as there is strong probability for believing, in the end of 37 or in 38, and the 2d Epistle to the Corinthians was written in 57 or 58, then the "three years after" of Gal. i. 18, the date of his first visit to Jerusalem, would be in 40 or 41—more than fourteen years before this allusion in 2 Cor. xii. 2. There are other ways, however, of manipulating these dates: Wieseler, for example, places the conversion in the year 40. Still, though on such a computation the dates might thus be brought to correspond, the two accounts are by no means in unison; for the apostle "utters" what he saw in the temple, and recounts also what he "heard." Wieseler argues, indeed, that as the description of the rapture follows close on the reference to the escape from Damascus, its date must naturally be assigned to the first visit to Jerusalem: Gal. i. 18. But, as Meyer remarks, the apostle in the beginning of 2 Cor. xii. goes on to tell something distinctly new, and quite different from the incidents of previous rehearsal. Wieseler also labours hard to prove against Ebrard and Meyer, that the *ἄῤῥητα ῥήματα* are not things impossible, but only unlawful for a man to utter: *die nicht gesagt werden dürfen,—quæ non licet homini loqui.* But *ἄῤῥητα ῥήματα* is a phrase not to be identified with *ἀλάλητοι στεναγμοί*, Rom. viii. 26, for those groanings are often inarticulate *suspiria de profundis.* Nor does this interpretation much help him; for certainly the apostle felt at liberty to record what was said to him in the temple ecstasy, though it is possible that some other portion of that revelation may come under the category of "unutterable utterances." At all events, the two accounts do not present any palpable data for their identification; so that the period and place of the "visions and revelations" are unmarked as an epoch in the history of the Acts of the Apostles. He did not so glory in the honour as to be often alluding to it; it had left him a broken and shattered man.

We can only form an inferential judgment as to the nature of this stake in the flesh, and can more easily assert what it was not than define what it really was. But—

I. The reference in Galatians cannot be to the carnal style of his preaching, the first of four interpretations given by

Jerome—*Quasi parvulis vobis atque lactentibus per infirmitatem carnis vestræ jam pridem evangelizavi . . . apud vos pene balbutiens.* This notion is wholly unwarranted by the pointed words.

II. Nor can the thorn be anything external to him, such as persecution, or any form of fierce and malignant opposition on the part of enemies, or of one singled out as ἄγγελος Σατᾶν, like Alexander the coppersmith, or Hymenæus, or Philetus, who are instanced by Chrysostom. Thus Chrysostom explains "my temptation in the flesh:" "While I preached unto you, I was driven about, I was scourged, I suffered a thousand deaths, yet ye thought no scorn of me." Similarly Eusebius of Emesa, Theodore of Mopsuestia, Theodoret, Œcumenius, Theophylact, Ambrosiast.; and also Calvin, Beza, Fritzsche, Schrader, Hammond, Reiche. Augustine, on the verse in Galatians, says, Neque respuistis, *ut non susciperetis communionem periculi mei.* It was very natural in those days, when the gospel everywhere encountered fanatical opposition and numbered its martyrs by hundreds, to suppose that the eager apostle, so often thwarted and maligned, so often suffering and maltreated, summed up all elements of antagonism into the figure of a thorn in the flesh, and personified them as a messenger of Satan buffeting him. The Canaanites, the ancient and irritating enemies of the chosen, are called "thorns." But this opinion is baseless. For, 1. His weakness is identified with himself: it clung to him, and he could not part with it; it was a stake in his flesh. But he might occasionally avoid persecution, as when he escaped from Damascus and when he left Ephesus. 2. Such persecution could not load him with a sense of humiliation in presence of others, or produce that loathing to which he refers. 3. These persecutions, whether from Judaizers or other foes, were so bound up with his work, that he could scarcely seek in this special and conclusive form to be delivered from them, vers. 8–10.

III. A third theory refers the thorn to some inner temptation which fretted and distracted him. And,

1. Some describe those trials as temptations to unbelief, the stirring up of remaining sin, or as pangs of sorrow on account of his own past persecuting life. So generally Gerson, Luther, Calvin, Osiander, Calovius. Gerson describes it as consisting

de horrendis cogitationibus per solam suggestionem inimici phantasiam turbantis obtingentibus. Luther supposed them to be blasphemous suggestions of the devil, as if they had been a parallel to his past experience and conflicts. Calvin says, more distinctly, *Ego sub hoc vocabulo comprehendi arbitror omne genus tentationis quo Paulus exercebatur. Nam caro hic, meo judicio, non corpus, sed partem animæ nondum regeneratam significat.* Now no statement of such a nature occurs in any other part of the apostle's letters; and though the second descriptive clause, "a messenger of Satan," may correspond so far with the hypothesis, the first phrase, "thorn in the flesh," indicates something not in his mind, but acting from without or from his physical organism upon it. And it is called ἀσθένεια—ἀσθένεια σαρκός.

2. Not a few, perhaps led by the *stimulus carnis* of the Vulgate, take the phrase to mean temptation to incontinence. It is not to be wondered at that such should be the opinion of celibates and of monks who fled from the world and from duty, but felt to their vexation that they could not flee from themselves. There seems to have been an early impulse to this view. Augustine's words tend in that direction—*accepit stimulum carnis. Quis nostrum hoc dicere auderet, nisi ille confiteri non erubesceret?—Enarrat.* in Ps. lviii. p. 816, vol. v. *Opera*, Gaume. Jerome, too, says: *Si apostolus . . . ob carnis aculeos et incentiva vitiorum reprimit corpus suum.—Epist. ad Eustoch.* p. 91, vol. i. *Opera*, ed. Vallars. Primasius gives it as an alternative, *alii dicunt titillatione carnis stimulatum.* Gregory the Great describes the apostle after his rapture thus: *Ad semetipsum rediens contra carnis bellum laborat.—Moral.* lib. viii. c. 29, p. 832, vol. i. *Opera*, ed. Migne. In mediæval times this was the current opinion, as of Salvian, Thomas Aquinas, Bede, Lyra, Bellarmine, and the Catholic Estius, a Lapide, and Bisping. Cardinal Hugo condescended to the time of the temptation, viz. after the apostle's intercourse with the charming Thecla, as related in the legendary *Acts.* Zeschius *de stimulo carnis*, in the *Sylloge Dissertationum* of Hasæus and Ikenius, vol. ii. 895. See *Acta Apost. Apocrypha*, Tischendorf's edition, p. 40. Thecla's heathen mother complains of her as wholly absorbed in Paul's preaching, and waiting on it "like a cobweb fastened to the window" in which she sat; and it is in this legend, so old that Tertullian refers to it, that the apostle's

appearance is described—*ἄνδρα μικρὸν τῇ μεγέθει, ψιλὸν τῇ κεφαλῇ, ἀγκύλον ταῖς κνήμαις, εὐεκτικόν, σύνοφρυν, μικρῶς ἐπίρινον, χάριτος πλήρη.*—*Acta Apostolorum Apocrypha*, p. 41, ed. Tischendorf. The words of Estius are: *Apostolum per carnis stimulum indicare voluisse incentivum libidinis quod in carne patiebatur*, adducing in proof 1 Cor. ix. 27 and Rom. vii. 23, neither of which places refers to sensuality. And a Lapide claims something like infallibility for this opinion, insisting on it as an instance of the *vox populi, vox Dei*.

The objections to this view are many and convincing. For,

(1.) Such a *stimulus* could not be said to be given him by God as a special means of humbling him, and in coincidence with superabundant visions and revelations.

(2.) Nor could the apostle have gloried in this temptation, ver. 9.

(3.) Nor would it have exposed him to scorn or aversion; the struggle would have been within, and could not have been described as in this passage of Galatians.

(4.) And lastly, the apostle declares his perfect freedom from all such temptations. "I would," he affirms, referring to incontinency and to marriage,—"I would that all men were even as I." 1 Cor. vii. 7. "Ah! no, dear Paul," Luther says, "it was no such trial that afflicted thee."

IV. The trial and the thorn in the flesh seem to be rightly referred to some painful and acute corporeal malady which could not be concealed, but had a tendency to induce loathing in those with whom he had intercourse, which he felt to be humbling and mortifying to him as a minister of Christ, and which seems to have been connected with the many visions and revelations having a tendency to elate him. Generally, that is the view of Flatt, Billroth, Emmerling, Rückert, Meyer, De Wette, Professor Lightfoot, Alford, Howson, Chandler. Böttger, who regards Galatia as comprising Lystra and Derbe, thinks that the illness was caused by the stoning in the former of those places. But from that stoning there was an immediate recovery, and it could scarcely be the "thorn in the flesh." See Introduction.

One hypothesis on this point, viz. that feeble or defective utterance is meant, has been suggested by the statement of the apostle, when he says that, in the judgment of his opponents, his "speech was contemptible." This adverse criticism, however, does not refer to articulation, but to argument; for he "came not with the enticing words of man's wisdom." Still the words may imply that his oratory had some drawbacks, which made it inferior in power to his epistolary compositions.

Others, again, take the malady to be defective vision,[1] and the opinion is based to a large extent on what he says in the verses prefixed to this Essay: "I bear you record, that if it had been possible, ye would have plucked out your eyes and have given them to me." The theory is plausible, but it wholly wants proof, unless some unauthorized additions be made to the inspired statements. For—

1. The translation of the verse on which such stress is laid is wrong: it is not "your own eyes," but simply your eyes, unemphatic. See on the verse.

2. The mere defect of vision could not of itself induce that contempt and loathing which his trial implies, as in ver. 14.

3. The thorn in the flesh was given him fourteen years before he wrote his second Epistle to the Corinthians; but his conversion, accompanied by the blinding glory of Christ's appearance, to which his ophthalmic weakness has been traced, happened at a considerably earlier period.

4. The arguments adduced to prove that the apostle's eyesight was permanently injured by the light "which shone from heaven above the brightness of the sun" at mid-day are not trustworthy. That he was blinded at the moment is true, but he recovered his sight when there "fell from his eyes as it were scales." All miracles appear to be perfect healings, and restorations of vision are surely no exceptions. The verb *ἀτενίζω*, which is referred to in proof, will not bear out this conjecture. For in Acts xxiii. 1 *ἀτενίσας* characterizes the apostle's act before he began his address, and describes naturally a sweeping and attentive scrutiny, but with no implied defect of vision. In Luke iv. 20 the same verb describes the eager gaze of the synagogue of Nazareth upon Jesus about to address them—*οἱ ὀφθαλμοὶ ἦσαν ἀτενίζοντες αὐτῷ.* In Luke xxii. 56 it depicts the searching survey of the damsel in the act of detecting Peter as one of the twelve—*καὶ ἀτενίσασα αὐτῷ.* In Acts

[1] See an ingenious paper in Dr. John Brown's *Horæ Subsecivæ*, written by one of his relatives.

i. 10 it paints the long and wondering look of the eleven after their ascending Lord—ὡς ἀτενίζοντες ἦσαν. In Acts iii. 4 it marks the fixed vision of Peter on the man whom he was about to heal; in vi. 15 it represents the rapt stare of the audience on Stephen, "when his face shone as the face of an angel;" in vii. 55, the intense vision of Stephen himself, when he "looked up and saw the glory of God, and Jesus standing at the right hand of God;" and in x. 4, the awestruck look of Cornelius at the angel. See also Acts xiv. 9. In these examples from Luke—and twice the reference is to Paul, xiii. 9, xxiii. 1—the look is one of earnest and strong vision, and therefore the occurrence of the same verb in xxiii. 1 cannot form any ground for the opinion which we are controverting; for in making a virtual apology the apostle does not say, "Pardon me, I did not see," but "I wist not"—perhaps = I forgot at the moment—"that he was the high priest." The allusion also to the "large letters" in which he wrote the Galatian Epistle, and to the marks of the Lord Jesus which he bore, admit of a different and satisfactory interpretation.

5. Nor can the interpretation of δι' ἀσθένειαν in the paper referred to be sustained. The writer gives it this sense: "By the infirmity of my flesh I proclaimed to you the good news;" that is, his defective vision was a lasting proof of his conversion and of the truth of Christ's resurrection and glory, and such evidence so adduced they did not despise nor reject. But "reject" is not the rendering of the last verb, and δι' ἀσθένειαν can only mean "on account of"—certainly not "by means of." See on the verse.

6. Lastly, if the thorn in the flesh be identified with defective vision produced by the light which blinded him at his conversion, then, as we have said, the proposed identification is contradicted by the apostle's own chronology in 2 Cor. xii. 2.

The hypothesis of some severe physical malady was among the earliest started on the subject. The language of Irenæus is vague indeed, yet it seems to refer to corporeal ailment; for in illustrating the infirmities of the apostle, he adds, as given in the Latin version, *homo, quoniam ipse infirmus et natura mortalis*, v. 3, 1.

But of the precise form of the malady there are very various opinions. Hypochondriacal melancholy is supposed by some (Bartholinus, Wedel). Hæmorrhoids is the conjecture of Bertholdt. Thomas Aquinas gives as one opinion, not his own, *morbus Iliacus, seu viscerum dolor.*[1] Basil held the opinion that the thorn was some disease; for, treating of the use of medicine, he speaks of it in connection with, or under the same category as, the healing of the impotent man at Bethesda, Job's affliction, and the ulcered beggar Lazarus. *Regulæ Fusius Tractatæ, Opera,* vol. ii. 564, Gaume, Paris 1839. Gregory of Nazianzus, at the end of his twentieth Oration, solemnly appeals to his departed brother—*ὦ θεῖα καὶ ἱερὰ κεφαλή*—to arrest some malady in him which he calls by Paul's words, *σκόλοπα τῆς σαρκός*. His annotator Nicetas describes it as a disease of the kidneys or of the joints—*ποδάγρα*, adding that some explained Paul's thorn in the same way. Greg. Naz. *Opera,* ii. p. 785, ed. Paris 1630. Baxter thought the disease may have been stone—his own torment; his tormentor is preserved in the British Museum. An old and prevailing opinion refers it to some affection of the head. This opinion is alluded to by Chrysostom—*τινὲς μὲν οὖν κεφαλαλγίαν τινὰ ἔφασαν*. Primasius gives as an alternative: *Quidam enim dicunt eum frequenti dolore capitis laborasse: ad* 2 Cor. xii. *Patrolog.* vol. lxxviii. p. 581, Migne. Tertullian says: *Sed et ipse datum sibi ait sudem . . . per dolorem, ut aiunt, auriculæ vel capitis* (*De Pud.* cap. v.), and his editor Rigalt wonders at the opinion. In another allusion, in a passage where he is discussing the power of Satan, he simply says: *In sanctos humiliandos per carnis vexationem. De Fuga in Persecutione,* cap. ii. Pelagius, while recording the opinion that persecutions are meant—*persecutiones aut dolores*—adds: *Quidam enim dicunt eum frequenter dolore capitis laborasse: ad* 2 Cor. xii. Jerome, too, in giving other conjectures, speaks in general terms: *Aut certe suspicari possumus, apostolum eo tempore quo primum venit ad Galatas ægrotasse . . . nam tradunt eum gravissimum capitis dolorem sæpe perpessum.* This ancient and traditionary notion of some physical ailment is the correct one, though of its special character we are necessarily ignorant. But mere headache, grievous and overpowering, could scarcely have produced such an effect as

[1] The *σκόλοψ* in this case was supposed probably to refer to impalement: *adactum per medium hominem qui per os emergat stipitem.*

is implied in the verbs "despised not nor loathed." Its accompaniments or results might, however, have this tendency. Ewald makes it *fallende Sucht*, or something similar, and also Ziegler, Holsten, and Professor Lightfoot. This opinion has several points in its favour. If mental excitement, intense or prolonged, produces instant and overpowering effect on the body, how much more the ecstasy which accompanies visions and revelations! An "horror of great darkness" fell upon Abraham when a vision was disclosed to him (Gen. xv. 13). The prophet Daniel "fainted, and was sick many days," after a revelation from the angel Gabriel; and after a "great vision," he says, "There remained no strength in me: for my comeliness was turned in me into corruption, and I retained no strength"—"straightway there remained no strength in me, neither is there breath left in me." Dan. viii. 27, x. 8, 17. The beloved disciple who had lain in His bosom says, "When I saw Him, I fell at His feet as dead." Rev. i. 17. If communications of the more common kind, like those vouchsafed to Daniel, produced such debility and reaction, what would be the result of such a bewildering rapture into paradise, and the visions which followed it? If his nervous system had been weakened by previous manifestations, might not this last and grandest honour bring on cerebral exhaustion, paralysis, or epileptic seizure, with all those results on eye, feature, tongue, and limb which are so often and so shockingly associated with it? And the infliction was a chronic one, as may be inferred; it was a stake in his flesh, hindering his work as directly as Satan might wish, exposing him to the contemptuous taunts of Jews and Judaists, and to loathing on the part of his friends. This theory appears to suit all the conditions of this mysterious malady. Its paroxysms seem to have recurred at intervals, the first attack being fourteen years before the writing of the second Epistle to the Corinthians—that is, perhaps, about the year 44; another at his first visit to Galatia, probably in 52; and then when he was writing the second Epistle to the Corinthians and this to the Galatians, perhaps about 58, according to the view we have given in the commencement of this paper.

One is amazed at the work which men with a strong will can brace themselves up to do in the midst of extreme suffering and weakness. Chrysostom, King Alfred,[1] William the Third, Pascal, Richard Baxter, Robert Hall, and Robertson of Brighton are examples of "strength made perfect in weakness."

[1] Asser's *Life of Alfred*, p. 66, etc. A mysterious disease—a "sudden and overwhelming pain," which from childhood had seized him, and recurred in another form with frightful severity at his marriage-feast—"tormented him day and night from the twentieth to the forty-fourth year of his life. If even by God's mercy he was relieved from this infirmity for a single day or night, yet the fear and dread of that dreadful malady never left him, but rendered him almost useless, as he thought, for every duty, whether human or divine."—Bohn's *Antiquarian Series: Six old English Chronicles.* In describing the battle of Landen, Macaulay characterizes the two great leaders, William and Luxemburg, as "two sickly beings, who in a rude state of society would have been regarded as too puny to bear any part in combats. In some heathen countries they would have been exposed while infants. . . . It is probable that among the hundred and twenty thousand soldiers who were marshalled round Neerwinden under all the standards of Western Europe, the two feeblest in body were the hunchbacked dwarf who urged forward the fiery onset of France, and the asthmatic skeleton who covered the slow retreat of England."—*History of England*, vol. iv. pp. 409, 410.

CHAPTER IV. 17–31

AWARE by what means this alienation of feeling had been produced, he now reverts to those by whose seductive arts and errors it had been occasioned—

Ver. 17. *Ζηλοῦσιν ὑμᾶς οὐ καλῶς*—"They are paying court to you, not honestly." I may be reckoned your enemy because I have told you the truth; but these men, who so zealously court you, and profess such intense regard for you, are not actuated by honourable motives,—their purpose is selfish and sinister. Hofmann connects this verse with the preceding one, as if it were the result—*ζηλοῦσιν ὑμᾶς*. But the connection is unnatural, and *ὥστε* in such a case would probably be followed by an accusative with the infinite. A. Buttmann, p. 210. The verb, like others in *οω*, seems to have a factitive sense—to show or display *ζῆλος*; but it may be shown in various ways, and from a variety of motives—for one or against one. Matthias translates it *eifern machen sie euch*—they create zeal in you—a meaning unproved. Followed by an accusative of person or thing, it may mean to desire him or it ardently, to be eager for: 1 Cor. xii. 31, Soph. *Ajax*, 552; and sometimes in a bad sense it denotes to be jealous or envious of: Acts vii. 9, James iv. 2, Sept. 2 Sam. xxi. 2. Calvin, Beza, and others give the meaning, "they are jealous of you;" but the same verb in the next clause cannot bear this signification. Some of the fathers assume the sense of envy or emulation; Chrysostom explaining it thus: "They wish that they may occupy the rank of teachers, and degrade you who now stand higher than they to the position of disciples." See Plutarch, *Mor.* p. 831, vol. iv. *Opera*, ed. Wittenbach. Their obsequious attentions were *οὐ καλῶς*—in no honourable way, but insincerely, and for their own unworthy ends: Jas. ii. 3; and *ἔφθιθ' οὐ καλῶς* describes the manner of Agamemnon's death, Æschylus, *Eumenides*, 461. The apostle gives no formal nominative to the verb: who the persons so stigmatized were, all parties knew in the Galatian churches, and he does not condescend even to name them. This wooing of their converts is one of the elements of that witchery referred to in iii. 1. The word "affect" in the Authorized Version, from the Latin *affectare*, is used in its older sense, as in Shakspeare—

> "In brief, sir, study what you most affect;"

And in Blair's *Grave*—

> "While some affect the sun, and some the shade."

The apostle explains οὐ καλῶς in the next clause, or rather gives one illustration of it—

'Αλλὰ ἐκκλεῖσαι ὑμᾶς θέλουσιν—"nay, they desire to exclude you." 'Αλλά here has a limiting or corrective power. Kühner, § 322, 6. It introduces a different idea, yet not one directly opposite. Klotz-Devarius, ii. 23. Instead of ὑμᾶς, Beza conjectured ἡμᾶς; but the reading has no support. De Wette, however, advocates it on account of the easy sense which it suggests—"they wish to exclude us from all fellowship with you and influence over you." For the same reason Macknight says, "I suppose it to be the true reading." Beza suggested it *ex ingenio*. The Syriac translator seems to have read ἐγκλεῖσαι, as the rendering is ܠܡܚܒܫܟܘܢ ܗܘ ܨܒܝܢ—"they wish to include" or "shut you up."

The reference in ἐκκλεῖσαι has been understood in various ways—they desire to exclude you, from what or whom?

1. Erasmus, followed by a Lapide, supposes the exclusion to be from Christian liberty,—the former giving it as *a libertate Christi*, and the latter *a Christo et christiana libertate.* So Estius, and Bagge who explains "from gospel truth and liberty." Prof. Lightfoot has "from Christ." This does not tally, however, with the design alleged in the next clause.

2. Wieseler and Ewald suppose the exclusion to be from salvation—*aus dem Himmelreiche*, from the kingdom of heaven, according to the former,—*vom ächten Christenthume* according to the latter; and the notion of Borger, Flatt, and Jatho is not dissimilar—"from the Christian community." But though such

might be the feared result, it is not alleged. The Judaists made it their distinctive dogma that salvation was to be had through faith in Christ, but only on compliance with the Mosaic law, so that a church of circumcised believers would be to them a true object of desire. The next clause suggests also a separation of persons.

3. Chrysostom, Theophylact, and Œcumenius suppose the exclusion to be "from perfect knowledge, having had imparted to them what is mutilated and spurious." Thus Theophylact: ἐκβαλλεῖν τῆς τελειοτάτης ἐν Χριστῷ καταστάσεως καὶ γνώσεως.

4. Some take it to mean exclusion from the apostle himself, as Luther, Calvin, Bengel, Olshausen, Winer, Gwynne, and Trana. Reiche has *ab apostolo ejusque communione.* But with a meaning so definite, pointed, and personal, one would have expected the genitive pronoun to be expressed.

5. Some suppose the exclusion to be from the sounder portion of the church. Hilgenfeld writes: *aus dem Paulinischen Gemeindeverbande.* Meyer includes the apostle also. This generally seems to be the idea. Their desire was to remove these Galatian converts from the sounder portion of the church, adhering of course to the apostle in person and doctrine, and form them into a separate clique. The emphasis from position lies on the verb, and the αὐτούς of the next clause suggests a personal contrast. The allusion is thus left general; the antithesis to the αὐτούς is only understood—"they" as a party naturally stand opposed to the party who hold the Pauline doctrine, and bear no altered relation to the apostle. The idea of compulsion found in the verb by Raphelius, Wolf, and Zachariæ, does not belong to it; the examples quoted for the purpose fail to prove it (Meyer). And their design was—

Ἵνα αὐτοὺς ζηλοῦτε—"in order that ye may zealously affect them." They attach themselves to you, that by drawing you off from those who are of sound opinion, ye may attach yourselves to them. The verb must have the same sense in the last clause as in the first. The syntax is somewhat solecistic. The verb ζηλοῦτε, though preceded by ἵνα, is in the present indicative—not the Attic future, as Jatho says; for the instances adduced by him from Thucydides are presents, and not futures. There is no difference worthy of the name among the MSS., though Fritzsche lays stress on MS. 219², which reads ζηλῶτε. So also in 1 Cor. iv. 6 ἵνα is followed by the present indicative. The connection is illogical in thought—design implying something future, possible, etc. Some therefore are disposed to take ἵνα as an adverb; Meyer, followed by Matthias, rendering it *ubi*, *quo in statu*, and he rests his interpretation on grammatical necessity. There is no instance, however, of such an adverbial usage in the New Testament, for the passages sometimes adduced will not support the conjecture. Mullach, *Grammatik der Griechischen Vulgar-sprache*, p. 373. The idiom is English, however: "now is the hour come that"—ἵνα—or "when," "the Son of man should be glorified;" but ἵνα has its usual telic significance in the original text. Far rather may it be admitted that the construction is one of the negligences of the later Greek, or it may be traced to some peculiarity in the conception of the apostle. Winer, § 41, 5, 1. In both instances found in the New Testament the verbs end in οω. A. Buttmann, p. 202. The usage of ἵνα with the indicative present is found in later Greek, of which Winer has given instances—as from the apocryphal books: *Acta Petri et Pauli* 15, but Tischendorf's text reads ἀπόληται; *Acta Pauli et Theclæ* 11, and there too various readings are noted by Tischendorf, *Acta Apocrypha*, Lipsiæ 1851. An additional clause, ζηλοῦτε δὲ τὰ κρείττω χαρίσματα, taken from 1 Cor. xii. 3, is here inserted by D¹, F, and is found in Victorinus, the Ambrosian Hilary, and in Sedulius.

Ver. 18. Καλὸν δὲ ζηλοῦσθαι ἐν καλῷ πάντοτε—"But it is good to be courted fairly at all times." The reading τὸ ζηλοῦσθαι is found in D, F, G, K, L, and almost all MSS. A, B, C omit τό; B and ℵ read ζηλοῦσθε (with the Vulgate—*æmulamini*—and Jerome), which from the Itacism was the same in sound with ζηλοῦσθαι; ζηλοῦσθαι without τό is the reading of A, C, D, F, K, L, and is preferable. The δέ is, as usual, adversative. The interpretation given of the previous verse rules that of the present one. They display zealous attentions toward you, and desire to form you into a clique that you may display zealous attentions toward them. It is not the mere zealousness I object to. To have zealous attentions shown toward one in a good cause always is a good thing. Such seems the natural order of thought: the words are repeated from the previous verse. Such paronomasia, or rather annominations, are not unfrequent, and are very common in tho Old Testament. Winer, § 68, 2; Lobeck, *Paralip.* p. 501. The previous καλῶς suggests καλόν and ἐν καλῷ; ζηλοῦσιν and ζηλοῦτε suggest ζηλοῦσθαι. This last word is to be taken in a passive sense, for no instance of a middle voice sense has been adduced. The infinitive has more force with the article. Winer, § 44, 2, *a.* The use of ἐν καλῷ for καλῶς is suggestive: the exchange implies a difference of meaning; and we agree with Meyer, that it refers not to manner, like the adverb, but to sphere—"in a good thing." Nor does this, as Ellicott objects, alter the meaning of the verb from "*ambiri*" to *admirari;* for surely one may say it is good to be courted in a good way, or to be courted in a good cause, though we do not hold to the sense of the Greek fathers, as if the phrase pointed out that which excited the ζηλοῦν. The reference is not to that which draws forth the ζηλοῦν, but to that in which it operates, implying also the motives of those who feel it. Such seems the most natural construction of the words. The goodness of the ζῆλος depends upon its sphere, the emphasis being on καλόν—good it is to be courted in a good thing, as when the gospel in its simple truth is earnestly urged upon you. The apostle does not object to the mere fact of zealous attention being shown to the Galatians, but first to its way—οὐ καλῶς, that it was dishonourable; and then to the sphere of it, that it was not in a good thing—ἐν καλῷ, for it was pressing on them a subverted gospel, and endangering their soul's salvation. The statement is a general one—a species of maxim; but to the Galatians, as the objects of the verb, the apostle plainly refers. The phrase ἐν καλῷ does not refer to purpose (Reiche), nor is the meaning so vague as *bona est ambitio in re bona* (Wahl, Schott). Πάντοτε, "always,"—a word refused by purists. Phrynichus, p. 105, says, that instead of it ἑκάστοτε and διαπαντός are to be used; similarly Zonaras, *Lex.* p. 1526. It is added—

Καὶ μὴ μόνον ἐν τῷ παρεῖναί με πρὸς ὑμᾶς—"and not only when I am present along with you." In πρὸς ὑμᾶς, as in later usage, the idea of direction is almost wholly dropped. John i. 1. The infinitive again has the article, giving it force and vividness. The language plainly implies that the ὑμεῖς are supposed to be the objects of the previous ζηλοῦσθαι, and the meaning is: The being paid court to in a good cause is praiseworthy, not only at all times, but by every one; in my absence from you, in my presence with you: I claim no monopoly of it. I do not wish to have you all to myself. Whoever in my absence shows you zealous attentions, if his zeal be in a good thing, does what I cannot but commend.

But there are other interpretations which cannot be entertained. Locke gives ἐν καλῷ a personal reference—"it is good to be well and warmly attached to a good man," that is, himself the apostle—"I am the good man you took me to be." Estius writes, *Ut æmulemini magistros vestros, qualis ego imprimis sum, id enim intelligi vult.* He is followed by Chandler, whose words are, "I am still worthy of the same share of your affection, though I am absent from you; therefore it is neither honourable nor decent for you to renounce my friendship," etc. Macknight's paraphrase is, "Ye should consider that it is comely and commendable for you to be ardently in love with me, a good man, at all times." But this surely is not the apostle's usual mode of self-reference.

Some again regard the apostle himself as the object of ζηλοῦσθαι (Reiche, Hofmann); and Usteri gives this sense: "How much was I the object of your ζῆλος when I was with you! As it has so soon ceased in my absence, it must have lost much of its worth." But this takes off the edge of the statement, and its consecutive harmony with the preceding verse; and in such a case, as Meyer says, you would expect με to have been expressed.

Others, as Bengel, take ζηλοῦσθαι in the middle—*zelare inter se*—to be zealous for one another; but we have no example of such a meaning. Others, taking the word in a passive sense, bring out nearly the same meaning, referring to what is said in vers. 13–15—their warm reception of the apostle and his doctrine when he was present, and their revolution of feeling as soon as he was absent.

Some adopt the meaning of the middle or active voice. Thus Olshausen generally, but away from the context, "Zeal is good when it arises in a good cause, ζηλοῦσθαι being equivalent to ζηλοῦν;" Luther, *Bonum quidem est imitari et æmulari alios, sed hoc præstate in re bona semper.* While Beza makes the apostle the subject of the verb—*absens absentes vehementissime conplector*,—Morus makes him the object: *Laudabile autem est sectari præceptorem in re bona semper.* Koppe thus writes: *Optem vero ut hanc istorum hominum erga vos invidiam concitetis semper constanter sequendo doctrinam meam.* He is virtually followed by Paulus, Rückert, and Brown who thus renders Koppe's thought: "Ye were once the subject of their envy, and I would God ye were the subject of their envy still. I wish your place in their estimation had been the same in my absence that it was when I was present with you." But this sense, allowing the verb to have the meaning "to envy," does not tally with the same interpretation of the previous verse; for, as Meyer hints, they had not been the objects of such envy in the apostle's presence, as the last clause of this verse with such an interpretation would plainly intimate. Lastly, Bagge strangely gives this translation: "It is good to call one's self blessed in the truth at all times."

The apostle suddenly changes his tone; his mood softens into tenderness, like the mother beginning with rebuke and ending in tears and embraces.

Ver. 19. *Τεκνία μου*—"My little children." B, D[1], F[1], ℵ, read *τέκνα*, a reading which Lachmann adopts, though it is an evident emendation. *Τεκνία* has in its favour A, C, D, K, L, ℵ[3], with Chrysostom and Theodoret among the Greek fathers, and also the Vulgate. The apostle is not in the habit of using the diminutive; its use here is therefore on purpose: 1 Cor. iv. 14, 17; 2 Cor. vi. 13, xii. 14; Phil. ii. 22. But the Apostle John employs it frequently: John xiii. 33; 1 John ii. 1, 12, 28, iii. 7, 18, iv. 4, v. 21; though with the genitive *Θεοῦ* he uses *τέκνα.* This clause is joined, or, as one might say, is tacked on, to the previous one by Bengel, Rückert, Usteri, and Schott; and such is the punctuation in the text of Knapp, Scholz, and Lachmann. See Hofmann. But such a connection is exceedingly unsatisfactory, as there is no direct address. The *δέ* of the following verse (20) has led some to this mode of division, as if it began a new thought.

Οὓς πάλιν ὠδίνω—"whom I travail in birth with again." This change of gender according to the sense is frequent. Matt. xxviii. 19; Rom. ix. 22, 24; Winer, § 24, 3. The verb *ὠδίνω* is spoken of the mother, not of the father—*parturio*,

Vulgate. It does not mean *in utero gestare*, as is the opinion of Heinsius, Grotius, Koppe, Rückert; but is "to travail," to be in the throes of parturition. Rev. xii. 2. Compare Num. xi. 2; Ps. vii. 14; Cant. viii. 15; Isa. xxxiii. 4, xxvi. 17, 18, liii. 11, lxvi. 7, 8; Rom. viii. 22, 23. The image of paternity is the usual one with the apostle: 1 Cor. iv. 15; Philem. 10. There does not seem to be any foundation for Wieseler's idea, that in πάλιν the allusion is to παλιγγενεσία; it is simply to the previous agonies of spiritual birth when he was present with them. At the first he had travailed in birth with them; and now the process, with all its pain and sorrow, was being repeated. The sense of the verb in such a context is not mere sorrow, but also enduring anxiety and toil. No wonder that those who had cost him so much were so dear to him—τεκνία μου—whom he had begotten in the gospel. See Suicer, *Thesaur. sub voce.*

Ἄχρις οὗ μορφωθῇ Χριστὸς ἐν ὑμῖν—"until Christ be formed in you." The words ἄχρι and μέχρι are distinguished by Tittmann, as if the first had in prominence the idea of *ante*, the entire previous time, and the second that of *usque ad*, the end of the time specially regarded—a hypothesis which Fritzsche on Rom. v. 14 has overthrown. Klotz-Devarius, ii. p. 224. The passive μορφωθῇ with the stress upon it, not used elsewhere, expresses the complete development of the μορφή—the form of Christ. Sept. Isa. xliv. 13. The metaphor is slightly changed, and the phrase does not probably refer to regeneration (it is not till Christ be born in you), but to its fully formed and visible results. The Galatian churches might be regenerate, for they had enjoyed the Spirit: the apostle's anguish and effort were, that perfect spiritual manhood might be developed in them. The figure is therefore so far changed; for they were not as an embryo waiting for birth,—the child is formed ere the pangs of maternal child-bearing are felt. The apostle's maternal pain was not because a full-formed child was to be born, but because his little children were dwarfing and not rising up to manhood—were still τεκνία. See under Eph. iv. 13. These earlier pangs he had felt already when they became his little children; but, now that they were born, he was in labour a second time, πάλιν, that they might come to manhood, and be Christians so fully matured that indwelling truth should be their complete safeguard against seduction and error. It is no argument against giving πάλιν a reference to his first visit that he describes it as joyful; for his spiritual anxiety was none the less deep, and his agony of earnestness none the less intense, till the truth of the gospel should take hold on them and Christ be formed in them—their life. Besides, the mere pain of parturition is not the only point of comparison. The formation of Christ within them is the purpose of his travail of soul. For "Christ" is the one principle of life and holiness,—not Christ contemplated as without, but Christ dwelling within by His Spirit; not speculation about His person or His doctrine, nor the vehement defence of orthodox belief, not the knowledge of His character and work, nor profession of faith in Him with an external submission to the ordinances of His church. Very different—Christ in them, and abiding in them: His light in their minds, His love in their hearts, His law in their conscience, His Spirit their formative impulse and power, His presence filling and assimilating their entire inner nature, and His image in visible shape and symmetry reproducing itself in their lives. Rom. viii. 29. What Christian pastor would not toil, and pray, and yearn for such a result, to "present every man perfect in Christ Jesus?" Col. i. 28; Eph. iv. 13. Calvin says well: "If ministers wish to do any good, let them labour to form Christ, not to form themselves in their hearers." The figure is virtually reproduced in describing the fruits of martyrdom, as Prof. Lightfoot remarks, in the Epistle of the Churches of Vienne and Lyons; but there is this difference, that in that epistle it is the church, the "virgin mother," who brings forth. Euseb. *Hist. Eccles.* v. 1, § 53, etc. The notion of a second conversion urged by Boardman cannot be based on this verse: *Higher Christian Life*, pt. iii. See Waterland, vol. iv. p. 445. Yet Calvin writes, and Gwynne calls him "drowsy and oblivious" for so writing: *Semel prius et concepti et editi fuerant, jam secundo procreandi erant post defectionem;* but he adds, *Non enim abolet priorem partum, sed dicit iterum fovendos utero esse, tanquam immaturos fœtus et informes.* Augustine says: *Formatur Christus in eo, qui formam accipit Christi.*

Ver. 20. Ἤθελον δὲ παρεῖναι πρὸς ὑμᾶς ἄρτι—"I could wish indeed to be present with you now." The δέ is not redundant (Scholefield), but is used after an address, as often after questions, and after a vocative with a personal pronoun. Bernhardy; A. Buttmann, p. 331. There is a subadversative idea in the transition. He had spoken of his being present with them; in his memory a chord is struck; it vibrates for a moment while he calls them little children, for whom he is suffering birth-pangs; and then he gives expression to his feeling, "I could wish, yea, to be present with you." Hilgenfeld's separation of this verse from the one before it, as if it began a new sentence, is unnatural. His absence stands out in contrast to his ideal presence. The imperfect ἤθελον is rightly rendered "I could wish,"—a wish imperfectly realized, but still felt; for there underlies the idea, "if it were possible," *si possim*, or *wenn die Sache thunlich wäre.* Acts xxv. 22; Rom. ix. 3. It is the true sense of the imperfect, the act being unfinished, some obstacle having interposed. Bernhardy, p. 373; Kühner, § 438, 3; Hermann, *Sophocles*, *Ajax*, p. 140, Lipsiæ 1851. The particle ἄν is not understood (Jowett); for the use of ἄν, as Hermann remarks, would have brought in a different thought altogether—"but I will not." *Opuscula*, iv. p. 56. See Fritzsche on Rom. ix. 3. For πρὸς ὑμᾶς, see under ver. 18, and for ἄρτι, see under i. 9.

Καὶ ἀλλάξαι τὴν φωνήν μου—"and to change my voice." The tense of the verb is altered, and such an alteration is not infrequent. Winer, § 40, 2. Could we lay any stress upon the alteration here, it might point out that the change of voice was the effect of the realized wish to be present with them. *Φωνή* may refer more to the tone than the contents of speech, for it would still be *ἀληθεύων.* But of what nature is the change expressed by the verb?

1. The change seems to be in oral address—φωνή, and not in allusion to anything which he was writing, for he could easily change the tone of the epistle. He supposes himself present, and may allude to strong and indignant declarations and warnings made during his second visit. 2. The change is not from milder to sterner words, as is wrongly held by Wetstein, Michaelis, Rosenmüller, Rückert, Baumgarten-Crusius, Webster and Wilkinson, for hard words are not written by him now, but his soul is filled with love and longing —*τεκνία μου.* 3. According to Hahn, the change is from argument to accommodation and the allegory of the following

paragraph. *Biblical Repository*, vol. i. p. 133. But such an explanation is artificial and unnatural. 4. The change, as Meyer and others think, is to a milder tone than that which he had just been employing. Such appears to be the dictate of his present mood of mind as he pens this sentence. His soul is softened toward them—*molliter scribit, sed mollius loqui vellet* (Bengel). 5. A variety of changes are supposed to lurk in the word by many expositors, for they imagine the change to be suited to changing circumstances. Such is the view of Theodoret, Luther, Winer, De Wette, Schott, Brown, Estius, and Bisping. Thus Luther: "That he might temper and change his voice, as he saw it needful." Thus, too, a Lapide: *Ut quasi mater nunc blandirer nunc gemerem nunc obsecrarem nunc objurgarem vos.* But the simple verb ἀλλάξαι will not bear such a variety of implied meanings, and, as Meyer suggests, such a clause would have been added as πρὸς τὴν χρείαν, Acts xxviii. 10. Fritzsche's notion is untenable in its extravagant emphasis: *Vel severius, vel lenius cum iis agere, prout eorum indoles poposcerit.* In the two examples of the phrase cited by Wetstein, the first, referring to the croak of the raven, has πολλάκις qualifying the verb, and the second is precise and simple in meaning. Artemidorus, *Oneiro.* ii. 20, p. 173, vol. i. ed. Reiff; Dio Chrysostom, *Orat.* 59, p. 662, vol. ii., *Opera*, ed. Emperius, 1854. Lastly, the meaning assigned by Wieseler to the verb cannot be sustained; for, according to him, ἀλλάσσειν means *austauschen*, to exchange, not simply to change, as if the apostle longed to exchange words or to converse freely with them. It is true that ἀλλάσσειν and μεταλλάσσειν, both followed by ἐν, are used in Rom. i. 23 and 25 in senses not very different, save that the compound is the more emphatic, and the latter in ver. 26 is followed more distinctly by εἰς, though ἀντί is a common classical usage, or a genitive—τί, τινος. In order to bear out the sense given by Wieseler, some supplementary clause with a preposition is therefore indispensable. The passages quoted from the Septuagint will not bear him out, as there is only the accusative here; in Lev. xxvii. 3, 33 there is also a dative, καλὸν πονηρῷ; in Ps. cv. 20 the preposition ἐν follows the verb as in Romans; and in Ex. xiii. 13 there occurs the simple dative. Comp. Jer. ii. 11, xiii. 23; Gen. xxxi. 7; Esdras vi. 11, etc.

The apostle adds the reason—

Ὅτι ἀποροῦμαι ἐν ὑμῖν—"for I am perplexed in you." Hofmann unnaturally connects *ἐν ὑμῖν* with the previous clause, and Matthias, with as little reason, joins the whole clause to the following verse, as the ground of the question which it contains. The verb *ἀπορέω* (*ἄπορος*, impassable, as applied to hills or rivers) signifies "to be without means," to be in difficulty or in perplexity. In the New Testament it is construed with *εἰς*, referring to a thing, Acts xxv. 20, and also with *περί*, Luke xxiv. 4, as well as *ἐν*. The verb is here passive with a deponent sense. Grammatically, in the purely passive sense it might mean, "I am the object of perplexity," as the passive of an intransitive verb. Bernhardy, p. 341; Jelf, § 367. The meaning would then be that assigned by Fritzsche, *Nam hæretis quo me loco habeatis, nam sum vobis suspectus;* and this meaning coalesces with his interpretation of the previous clause. But the usage of the New Testament is different, as may be seen in John xiii. 22, Acts xxv. 20, 2 Cor. iv. 8. Gen. xxxii. 7; Sirach xviii. 7; also, Thucydides, ii. 20; Xen. *Anab.* vii. 3, 29; Schoemann, *Isæus*, p. 192. The phrase *ἐν ὑμῖν* points to the sphere of his perplexity. Winer, § 48, *a*; 2 Cor. vii. 16. The doubts of the apostle were not merely what to think of them or of their condition, but how to reclaim them. How to win them back he was at a loss; and therefore he desired if possible to be present with them, and if possible to adopt a milder tone, if so be they could be recovered from incipient apostasy. The *ἐν* is not *propter* (Bagge), but has its usual meaning, denoting the sphere in which the emotion of the verb takes place. Such is apparently the spirit of the verse.

Ver. 21. *Λέγετέ μοι, οἱ ὑπὸ νόμον θέλοντες εἶναι, τὸν νόμον οὐκ ἀκούετε;*—"Tell me, ye who desire to be under the law, do ye not hear the law?" The appeal is abrupt—*urget quasi præsens* (Bengel). The parties addressed are not persons of heathen birth (Flatt, Rückert), nor specially of Jewish birth (Schott, De Wette), but those who had a strong desire to place themselves under the law, in whom the Judaistic teaching had stirred up this untoward impulse, which Chrysostom says came from their *ἀκαίρου φιλονεικίας*. The phrase, "Do ye not hear the law?" is supposed by Meyer and others to mean, "Do ye not hear the law read?" But the plain meaning of the terms is the best. The verb ἀκούετε is not to be taken as signifying "do ye understand?" (Jerome, Borger, Olshausen, Küttner, and others), nor as denoting, "Do ye not submit to the law?" (Gwynne), which is utterly wrong, or as having any modification of that sense; but it is, "Ye who would submit to the law, give ear to its statements." The reading ἀναγινώσκετε is an old gloss found in D, F, found also in the Latin version (*legistis*) and in several of the fathers, and may have been suggested by the reading of the law in the synagogues, or by a wish to give a more palpable form to the question. The repetition of νόμος is emphatic: in the first clause it is the legal institute; in the second with the article it is the book of the law. Luke xxiv. 44; Rom. iii. 21. Hofmann needlessly takes the whole verse as one thought—"Tell me (οἵ relative), ye who desiring to be under the law do not hear the law;" but this view does not harmonize with the beginning of the next verse. The apostle now sets before them a striking lesson of the law, so presented and interpreted as to be specially intelligible to them, as being also quite in harmony with their modes of interpretation—

Ver. 22. *Γέγραπται γάρ, ὅτι Ἀβραὰμ δύο υἱοὺς ἔσχεν· ἕνα ἐκ τῆς παιδίσκης, καὶ ἕνα ἐκ τῆς ἐλευθέρας*—"For it is written that Abraham had two sons; one by the bond-woman, and one by the free woman." The γάρ introduces illustrative proof. It tacitly takes for granted a negative reply to the previous question, and thus vindicates the propriety of putting it: Klotz-Devarius, ii. 234; or it may mean *profecto—doch wohl:* Ellendt, *Lex. Soph.* i. 332. The two mothers Hagar and Sarah are particularized by the article as well known: Gen. xvi. and xxi. *Παιδίσκη* sometimes, however, means a free-born maiden, as in Ruth iv. 12, Xen. *Anab.* iv. 3, 11. But in Gen. xxi. 10 it represents in the Sept. the Hebrew אָמָה, and in Gen. xvi. 1 the Hebrew שִׁפְחָה, and in the New Testament it is used only in the sense of slave. *Νεᾶνις* was the earlier Greek term. *Phrynichus*, ed. Lobeck, 239; Cremer's *Lex. sub voce ἐλεύθερος*.

The apostle refers to some very remarkable points in Abraham's domestic history with which they must all have been well acquainted—

Ver. 23. Ἀλλ' ὁ μὲν ἐκ τῆς παιδίσκης, κατὰ σάρκα γεγέννηται· ὁ δὲ ἐκ τῆς ἐλευθέρας, διὰ τῆς ἐπαγγελίας—"Howbeit he of the bond-maid was born after the flesh, but he of the free woman by the promise." Ἀλλά—"howbeit" (though both were sons of the same father)—introduces the difference between the two sons in their birth, probably with the underlying idea of difference, too, in their character and destiny. *Κατὰ σάρκα* (Rom. ix. 7-10) means that Ishmael was born in the usual course of nature, and implies that Isaac was not; for he was born "by virtue of the promise," as is recorded in Gen. xviii. 10. There was a promise also connected with Ishmael's birth, though that birth in itself implied nothing out of the ordinary course of nature; whereas in Isaac's case there was miracle, when Sarah, "past age," gave birth to a son in fulfilment of the promise. Gen. xvii. 15, 16, xviii. 10, 11, 14; Rom. ix. 9. But for the promise, there would have been no such birth.

Ver. 24. *Ἅτινά ἐστιν ἀλληγορούμενα*—"which things," "which class of things," or "all those things are allegorized"—*quæ sunt per allegoriam dicta*, Vulgate. The meaning of the clause is not, "which things have been allegorized" already—namely, by the prophet Isaiah in the quotation made afterwards from Isa. liv. 1 (Brown after Vitringa, Peirce, and Macknight). For the quotation comes in as part of the illustration, not as an instance or example. A formal reference to an allegory framed by Isaiah, or to one found in his prophecies, would have necessitated a past participle; but the use of the present participle describes the allegory as at the moment under his hand. *Ἅτινα* brings together not the persons simply, but in their peculiar relations; not the births merely, but their attendant circumstances. The verb *ἄλλο—ἀγορεύειν* is to express another sense than the words in themselves convey. Wycliffe renders: "the whiche thingis ben seide bi anothir understondinge." Suidas thus defines *ἀλληγορία* : *ἡ μεταφορά, ἄλλο λέγον τὸ γράμμα καὶ ἄλλο τὸ νόημα.* The verb signifies either to speak in an allegory (Joseph. *Ant. Introd.* iv.), or to interpret an allegory. Plutarch, *Op. Mor.* p. 489, D, vol. iv. ed. Wittenbach; Clem. Alex. *Strom.* v. 11, p. 563. An allegory is not, as it has been sometimes defined, a continued metaphor; for a metaphor asserts one thing to be another, whereas an allegory only implies it. To be allegorized, then, is to be interpreted in another than the literal sense. The simple historical facts are not explained away as if they had been portions of a mere allegory, like the persons and events in Bunyan's *Pilgrim;* but these facts are invested with a new meaning as portraying great spiritual truths, and such truths they were intended and moulded to symbolize. But to say that a portion of early history is allegorized is very different from affirming that it is an allegory, or without any true historical basis. Luther says that Paul was "a marvellous cunning workman in the handling of allegories," and he admits that "to use allegories is often a very dangerous thing,"—adding: "Allegories do not strongly persuade in divinity; but, like pictures, they beautify and set out the matter. ... It is a seemly thing to add an allegory when the foundation is well laid and the matter thoroughly proved." The allegory used by the apostle here is quite distinct from the τύπος in 1 Cor. x. 11, where certain historical events are adduced as fraught with example and warning to other men and ages which might fall into parallel temptations. Yet Chrysostom says, "Contrary to usage, he calls a type an allegory;" but adds correctly: καταχρηστικῶς τὸν τύπον ἀλληγορίαν ἐκάλεσεν; "This history not only declares what appears on the face of it, but announces somewhat further, whence it is called an allegory."

The allegory is here adduced not as a formal or a prominent proof, but as an illustrative argument in favour of what had been already proved, and one fitted to tell upon those whose modes of interpreting Scripture were in harmony with it. "Ye that desire to be under the law, do ye not hear the law?" Prefaced by this personal appeal, it starts up as a vindication on their own principles, the justness of which would be recognised by the apostle's Judaistic opponents. His early rabbinical education, and some familiarity, too, with the peculiarities of the Alexandrian school of thought and theosophy, may have suggested to him this form of discussion as an *argumentum ad hominem;* but it would be rash to say that the apostle invented this allegory to suit his purpose. It is not as if he had said, Those things may be turned to good account in a discussion of this nature; but his inspiration being admitted, his meaning is, they were intended to convey those spiritual lessons. Such an allegorical interpretation is therefore warranted, apart from his employment of it in the present instance. It is not wholly the fruit of subjective ingenuity—*ein blosses Spiel seiner Phantasie* (Baur)—or an accommodation to rabbinical prepossession. The history by itself, indeed, affords no glimpse into such hidden meanings. But Abraham and his household bore a close historical and typical connection with the church of all lands and ages, and God's dealings with them in their various relations foreshadowed His dealings with their successors, as well the children by natural descent and under bondage to the law—Hagar, Ishmael—as those after the Spirit and in the possession of spiritual freedom—believers—blessed in Abraham, along with believing Abraham, and heirs through promise. Faith and not blood is the bond of genetic union; but the natural progeny still hates and persecutes the spiritual seed, as at that time in Galatia. God repeats among the posterity what He did among their ancestors; the earlier divine procedure becomes a picture of the later, and may therefore on this true basis be allegorized. To take out the lasting lessons from the history of Abraham's family, and the divine actings in it and toward it, is to say in the apostle's words, "which things are an allegory." The migration from Ur is somewhat similarly treated, though not in the same form, in Heb. xi. 14, 15, 16. If the outlines of such allegorical treatment were current in the apostle's days,—if it was an acknowledged method of exposition,—then one may conjecture that the favourite allegory among Jewish teachers would be to picture Isaac as the Jewish church, and Ishmael as the Gentiles; but the apostle affirms the reverse, and makes Hagar's child the Jewish representative.

Philo allegorizes those points in Abraham's history which are selected here for the same purpose by the apostle. But a comparison will show that the process and aim of the two writers are widely different. According to various assertions met with in Philo's *Treatises*, Abram is the soul in its advance toward divine knowledge; the very name, which means "high father," being suggestive, for the soul reaches higher and higher, through various spheres of study, to the investigation of God Himself. Salvation implies change of abode; therefore Abraham left his native country, kindred, and father's house,—that country being the symbol of the body, his kindred of the outward senses, and his father's house denoting speech. A somewhat different explanation is given in his *De Mut. Nom.* Abram signifies high father, but Abraham elect-father of sound,—sound being equivalent to speech, father the same as mind, and elect a special quality of the wise man's soul. Sarai, signifying "my princess," stands for "the virtue which rules over my soul;" but she does not as yet bring forth for Abraham—divine virtue is barren to him for a time. He must first cohabit with Hagar; there must be a preparatory connection with the handmaiden; and she represents the encyclical knowledge of wisdom and logic, grammar and geography, rhetoric and astronomy, all of which are mastered by an initiatory course of mental discipline.[1] Philo describes at length the various elements of this intermediate instruction. Hagar, in her race, name, and social position, is profoundly symbolic; for she is of Egypt, the land of science, her name means emigration, and she is slave to the princess. The same relation that a mistress has to her handmaidens, or a wife to a concubine, Sarah or wisdom has to Hagar or worldly education. Hagar at once bears a son; that son is Ishmael, who represents sophistry. Abraham then returns to Sarah, and she too at length bears a son: her son is Isaac, who typifies wisdom; and this is happiness, for the name Isaac signifies laughter. That is to say, the mind, after previous initiation and discipline, enters profitably on higher prolific study; or when Sarai, "my authority," is changed into Sarah, "my princess" = generic and imperishable virtue, then will arise happiness or Isaac. Then, too, the rudimentary branches of instruction, which bear the name of Hagar and her sophistical child called Ishmael, will be cast out. "And they shall suffer eternal exile; God Himself confirming their expulsion, when He orders the wise man to obey the word spoken by Sarah." "It is good to be guided by virtue when it teaches such lessons as this."—*De Cherub.* p. 2, vol. ii. *Op.* ed. Pfeiffer. Thus Philo and Paul have in their allegory little in common, save the selection of the same historical points. In the hands of Philo the incidents become fantastic, unreal, and shadowy—fragments of a dim and blurred

[1] Not unlike the studies of the Trivium and Quadrivium, thus expressed in a mediæval line:

"Lingua, tropus, ratio, numerus, tonus, angula, astra."

outline of spiritual and intellectual elevation and progress. The allegory of Clement is similar to that of Philo. *Strom.* p. 284, ed. Sylburg. But the apostle's treatment, on the other hand, is distinct and historical, without any tinge of metaphysical mysticism. In a word, the difference between Paul's allegorizing and that of Philo and of the Christian fathers, such as Clement and Origen, is greatly more than Jowett asserts it to be—is greatly more than a difference "of degree." For there is on the part of the apostle a difference of style and principle in the structure of it, and there is a cautious and exceptional use of it. It never resembles the מדרש of the Jewish doctors, or the dreamy theosophy of the Cabbala. See Maimonides, *Moreh Nevochim*, iii. 43. See Professor Lightfoot's note.

The Old Testament has many historical facts which surely involve spiritual lessons, and pre-intimate them as distinctly, though not so uniformly, as the Aaronic ritual typifies the great facts of redemption, it being *ἀντίτυπα, ὑπόδειγμα, σκιά*. The prospective connection of the old economy with the new is its great characteristic—the connection of what is outer and material with what is inner and spiritual in nature. But this connection must be of divine arrangement and forecast, otherwise it could not furnish such illustrations as are presented in this paragraph. While this is the case, every one knows that allegorization has been a prevailing vice in biblical exposition—that the discovery of occult meanings, and of typical persons and things, has done vast damage to sound commentary. There is scarcely an event, person, or act, that has not been charged with some hidden sense, often obscure and often ludicrous, the analogy being frequently so faint that one wonders how it could ever have been suggested. Amidst such confusion and absurdity which defy hermeneutical canons and apostolical example, it is surely extreme in Dean Alford to characterize as "a shallow and indolent dictum, that no ancient history is to be considered allegorical but that which inspired persons have treated allegorically." We may at least be content with the unfoldings of the New Testament; and he who "reads, marks, learns, and inwardly digests" the Scriptures will be under little impulse to handle the word of God so fancifully as to be accused of handling it deceitfully.

The apostle now unfolds the allegory—

Αὗται γάρ εἰσιν δύο διαθῆκαι—"for these women are two covenants." The article *αἱ* before the last noun is omitted on the preponderant authority of all the uncials, though it occurs in א[1], but not in א[3]. The *αὗται* are the two mothers Hagar and Sarah, not Ishmael and Isaac (Jowett), nor is *αὗται* for *ταῦτα* (Balduin, Schmoller); and in the allegory they represent two covenants, not revelations (Usteri). The construction is as in Matt. xiii. 39, xxvi. 26–28, 1 Cor. x. 4, Rev. i. 20.

Μία μὲν ἀπὸ ὄρους Σινᾶ, εἰς δουλείαν γεννῶσα, ἥτις ἐστὶν Ἄγαρ—"one indeed from Mount Sinai, bearing children into bondage, which," or, "and this is Hagar." The local *ἀπό* indicates place or origin—this covenant originated or took its rise from Mount Sinai. The particle *μέν*, *solitarium*, is followed by no corresponding *δέ*, as the other point of the comparison is not brought into immediate prominence, but passes away into the general statement. Winer, § 63, 2. For *γεννῶσα*, see Luke i. 13, 57; Xen. *De Rep. Lac.* i. 3. The last words are "for bondage," or "into a state of bondage;" the children of the bond-mother according to law inherit her condition. Hofmann connects the words "from Mount Sinai" closely with the participle "bearing children." The pronoun *ἥτις*, *quippe quædam*, is a contextual reference. The Sinaitic covenant is thus represented by Hagar.

What the apostle says in the following verse has given rise to numerous differences of opinion, and there is also conflict about its various readings. The Received Text has—

Ver. 25. *Τὸ γὰρ Ἄγαρ Σινᾶ ὄρος ἐστὶν ἐν τῇ Ἀραβίᾳ*—"For Hagar (not the person, but the name) is Mount Sinai in Arabia"—the neuter *τό* with the feminine *Ἄγαρ* in its abstract form specifying the thing itself in thought or speech. Kühner, vol. ii. § 492; Winer, § 18; Eph. iv. 9. In the *Clementine Homilies*, xvi. 18, occurs *τὸ Θεός*; *τὸ δ' ὑμεῖς ὅταν εἴπω τὴν πόλιν λέγω*, Dem. *De Corona*, p. 162, vol. i. *Op.* ed. Schaefer.

But the reading has been disputed. *Τὸ δὲ Ἄγαρ* has the authority of A, B, D, E, and of one version, the Memphitic; but *γάρ* has in its favour C, F, K, L, א, the Vulgate, Syriac, and many of the fathers. The first reading given is found in K, L, the great majority of cursives, both Syriac versions, and in the Greek fathers. On the other hand, the reading τὸ γὰρ Σινᾶ ὄρος ἐστὶν, omitting Ἄγαρ, is found in C, F, G, ℵ, the old Latin, the Vulgate, the Greek fathers Origen (according to the Latin version), Epiphanius, Cyril, Damascenus, in Ambrosiaster or the Ambrosian Hilary, in Augustine, Jerome, Pelagius, and, as Prof. Lightfoot says, probably "all the Latin fathers,"—*apud omnes Latinos interpretes*, says Estius. Beza omitted Ἄγαρ in his first and second editions, but afterwards inserted it—*nolui tamen receptam Græcam lectionem immutare.* Now, to account for these variations, it may be said on the one side, that the juxtaposition of γὰρ Ἄγαρ may have led to them, so that the one or other of the like words was omitted, and δέ inserted, either for the connection, or as suggested by the μέν in the previous verse. So Tischendorf, Meyer, Reiche, Winer, Ewald, Ellicott, and Alford. It may be replied, however, on the other side, that the words τὸ γάρ might be easily turned into τὸ Ἄγαρ, Ἄγαρ being found in the immediate context, while δέ or γάρ was inserted for the contextual sequence. With this hypothesis the other variations may also be more easily accounted for. Our reading is adopted by Lachmann, Fritzsche, De Wette, Hofmann, Wieseler, Prof. Lightfoot, and by Bisping and Windischmann who may be supposed to be partial to Latin authority. Bentley adopted the same view, as may be seen in his text, as given in Ellis's *Bentleii Critica Sacra*, p. 108, London 1862; and in his letter to Mill (p. 45) he supposes that the verse was originally a gloss: *ea verba de libri margine in orationem ipsam irrepsisse.* Mill was not averse to the same conjecture, as his note indicates, and Kuster adopted the same view. This reading is moreover natural and plausible: "for Sinai is a mountain in Arabia," not according to the order of the words, "for Mount Sinai is in Arabia." The moment is on the last words, "in Arabia;" that is, among the descendants of Hagar, or beyond the limits of Canaan in a land of bondmen. The site and origin of the one covenant, which is Hagar bearing children into bondage, is Sinai, and that Sinai is a mountain in the country of Hagar's offspring. The Arabs are named from Hagar Ἀγαρηνοί in Ps. lxxxiii. 7, in parallelism with Ishmaelites; Ἀγαραῖοι, 1 Chron. v. 10, 19; Baruch iii. 23. The Targumist renders Shur (wilderness of Shur) by Hagar—הגרא—Hagra, as in Gen. xvi. 7. Compare Ewald,

Geschichte des Volkes Israel, vol. i. 452, 3d ed., and his *Nachtrag über den Namen Hagar-Sinai*, in his *Die Sendschr. d. Apost. Paulus*, p. 493. Strabo, on the authority of Eratosthenes, joins with the Ἀγραῖοι the Nabatæans and Chauloteans, xvi. 4, 2; Pliny, *Hist. Nat.* vi. 32. The clause then is a parenthetical remark suddenly thrown in, to sustain and illustrate the allegory of Hagar the bond-woman representing the covenant made at Sinai,—for indeed that Sinai is a mountain in Arabia, the country of Hagar's descendants.

If the common reading be adopted, there are several difficulties in the way of interpretation: "For this Hagar (the object of allegory, not the person) is Mount Sinai in Arabia." The meaning of the clause is not, the woman Hagar is a type of Mount Sinai (Calvin, Estius); the neuter article forbids it. Others suppose the meaning to be: Hagar is the name of Mount Sinai in Arabia; or, that mountain is so named by the Arabians—*apud Arabes* (Meyer); is so named in the Arabian tongue: Matthias, offering to supply διαλέκτῳ. But ἐν τῇ Ἀραβίᾳ is taken most simply and naturally as a topographical notation. The apostle is thus supposed to refer to the meaning of the word Hagar, and to say that in the tongue of the natives it is the name of Mount Sinai, or, as Tyndale renders, "for Mount Sinai is called Hagar in Arabia." There is, however, no distinct proof of this assertion. It may be true, but there is no proper evidence of its truth. The tribes sprung of Hagar might give the great mountain their own name and that of their famous ancestress; but no instance of this has been adduced by any one. A Bohemian traveller named Harant visited the country in 1598, and he says "that the Arabian and Mauritanian heathens call Mount Sinai Agar or Tur." His work, named *Der Christliche Ulysses*, published at Nürnberg in 1678, was translated out of Bohemian into German (see Prof. Lightfoot), and the quotation from it is generally taken from Büsching's *Erdebeschreibung*. Granting that he reports what he heard with his own ears, it is strange that his statement has been confirmed by no succeeding traveller. His authority is rendered suspicious also by some of Prof. Lightfoot's remarks.

It has been alleged, too, that the words Hagar and Sinai are the same in sense, and that the apostle meant to assert by the way this identity of meaning. But granting that Sinai, סִינַי, means "rock" or "rock-fissures," the Hebrew name הָגָר—هاجر, *hajar*, in Arabic—cannot bear such a signification, for it denotes "fugitive" or "wanderer," or, as Jerome gives it, *advena vel conversa.* It is true that there is an Arabic word of similar sound, حجر, which means "stone," but it would be represented in Hebrew by חָגָר, *hhagar*—the words differing distinctly in the initial consonants. Freytag, *sub voce.* These consonants are indeed sometimes interchanged, but הגר and חגר belong to different families of words. It will not do to allege with Meyer that allegory interpretation is easily contented with the mere resemblance of names, as in the case of Nazarene, Matt. ii. 23; Siloam, John ix. 7; or to allege that yet, with all these objections to the common reading, it may be held that Paul, when he went into Arabia, as he says in i. 17, may have heard Sinai get the provincial name of Hagar. There was apparently a place of this name not far from Petra, but Petra itself never seems to get the designation of El-hhigr. Hilgenfeld refers for a similar clause to a reference to Ramah in Justin Martyr, *Dial. c. Tryph.* c. 78.

Συστοιχεῖ δὲ τῇ νῦν Ἱερουσαλήμ—"and indeed she ranketh with the present Jerusalem." Tyndale and Cranmer render "bordereth upon;" the Vulgate, *conjunctus est;* and the Arabic translator gives it as "contiguous to,"—rendering Arabia by El-Belka, which was on the east of the Jordan. Jerome, Chrysostom (*ἅπτεται*), and Theophylact hold this view, which is also adopted by Baumgarten-Crusius; but it is geographically wrong, unless you maintain with some that Sinai belongs to the same mountain range with Sion—a very strange conjecture (Genebrardus, *ad Psal.* cxxxiii.). The erroneous *mons qui conjunctus est* of the Vulgate is explained away by Thomas Aquinas, as referring not to *spatii continuitas* but to *similitudo.* Wycliffe, however, translates it, "whiche hil is ioyned to it," that is, to Jerusalem. The nominative is either *Ἄγαρ* or *διαθήκη*, as in the Claromontane Latin *quæ*, but not *τὸ ὄρος*, as in the Vulgate *mons qui* (Jerome, Chrysostom, Hofmann). The verb in military phrase signifies "to be of the same file with," Polybius, x. 23, *Op.* Tit. 111, p. 39, ed. Schweighaeuser. The corresponding noun is used of alphabetic letters pronounced by the same organ, or metaphysically of things in the same category. The meaning is not "stands parallel to" (Winer, Rückert), but "corresponds to." The δέ marks something additional or new in the progress of the statement. The Jerusalem "that now is" is not opposed by this epithet to the earlier Salem (Erasmus, Michaelis), but to the Jerusalem of that day, the Jewish metropolis under the law in contrast with the Jerusalem which is from above; though the first is characterized temporally, and the other from its ideal position. The "Jerusalem that now is" is the symbol of the nation, under the bondage of the law—

Δουλεύει γὰρ μετὰ τῶν τέκνων αὐτῆς—"for she is in bondage with her children." Matt. xxiii. 37. The reading γάρ has preponderant authority over δέ. The nominative is not Hagar nor διαθήκη (Gwynne), but the "Jerusalem that now is," as the clause assigns the reason for the correspondence of the ἡ νῦν Ἱερουσαλήμ with Ἄγαρ or διαθήκη. Jerusalem is in bondage with her children, as Hagar the bond-mother with her son Ishmael. It cannot refer to civil bondage to Rome (Bagge). Augustine, on Ps. cxix. (cxx.), expounds this allegory at some length: the word Kedar in the last clause of ver. 5, *inhabitavi cum tabernaculis Cedar*, naturally suggested Ishmael and the allegory, p. 1954, *Opera*, vol. iv. Gaume. The apostle has been describing this very bondage—"under the law," "under pædagogy," "under tutors and governors," "in bondage unto the elements of the world."

Ver. 26. *Ἡ δὲ ἄνω Ἱερουσαλὴμ ἐλευθέρα ἐστίν, ἥτις ἐστὶ μήτηρ [πάντων] ἡμῶν*—"But the Jerusalem above is free, and she is our mother." The πάντων is doubtful, though received by Lachmann on the authority of A, C[3], K, L, א[3]; but is rejected by Tischendorf on the authority of B, C[1], D, F, א[1], with the Syriac, Latin, and Coptic versions, and the majority of the fathers. The insertion may have come from the parallel clause, Rom. iv. 16, πατὴρ πάντων ἡμῶν. The phrase with the addition is found, as Prof. Lightfoot quotes, in Polycarp, § 3, and in Irenæus, v. 35, 2, at least in the Latin translation—*mater omnium nostrum*, p. 815, *Op.* vol. i. ed. Stieren. The δέ is opposed to the last clause: "on the contrary." The epithet ἄνω cannot refer in a temporal sense to the Salem of Melchisedec (Michaelis, Paulus), nor in a local sense to the upper city — the city of David, the Acropolis (Vitringa, Elsner, Zachariæ),—for it is the new covenant that Sarah symbolizes, and the *νῦν* of the previous verse is opposed to it. Nor does it mean the New Testament (Grotius, Rollock), based on the meaning of Jerusalem as signifying "vision of peace." Nor is it directly the church of the New Testament (Sasbout, a Lapide, Bullinger). It is the heavenly—*ἄνω*—as opposed to the earthly Jerusalem, the ideal metropolis of Christ's kingdom —the church before the second advent and the kingdom of glory after it—the "heavenly Jerusalem," Heb. xii. 22; but different in conception and symbol from the new Jerusalem, Rev. xxi. 2. The phrase is also a rabbinical one, for the Rabbins speak of the Jerusalem שֶׁל מַעְלָה. But their heavenly Jerusalem was merely the counterpart of the earthly one in everything; as the book Sohar says, "Whatever is on earth is also in heaven,"—one argument being that the pattern of the tabernacle in heaven was shown to Moses, so that the one constructed might be a fac-simile; and the tabernacle is called by the apostle "the pattern of things in heaven." Schoettgen's *Horæ Heb.* vol. i. p. 1205; Wetstein *in loc.*; Witsius, *Miscellanea Sacra*, vol. ii. p. 199. Not that the apostle thought of it as the Rabbins did; it was to him the metropolis in which believers are now enfranchised as citizens, Phil. iii. 20, not the triumphant church in heaven (Rosenmüller, Winer), nor what Hofmann calls *die in der Person Christi schon himmlisch vollendete Gemeine.* And she—*ἥτις*—"is our mother,"—no one of us is excluded; for the Jerusalem is not the visible church with many in it who are not believers, but the invisible or spiritual church, all whose members, whether Jews or Gentiles, are true disciples. The apostle does not develop the contrast with technical fulness. It might have been, *δευτέρα δὲ ἀπὸ ὄρους Σιὼν εἰς ἐλευθερίαν γεννῶσα, ἥτις ἐστὶ Σάῤῥα . . . συστοιχεῖ δὲ τῇ ἄνω Ἱερουσαλήμ.* The parallel is broken in the apostle's haste; he seizes only on the salient points; the doctrine imaged out was of more importance than the formal or rhetorical symmetry of the figure. The apostle, as has been remarked, uses *Ἱερουσαλήμ*, the more sacred name, as in the Apocalypse, but in referring to the earthly capital in i. 18, ii. 1, he uses *Ἱεροσόλυμα*, the name found also in the fourth Gospel.

Ver. 27. *Γέγραπται γάρ, Εὐφράνθητι στεῖρα ἡ οὐ τίκτουσα·*

ῥῆξον καὶ βόησον ἡ οὐκ ὠδίνουσα· ὅτι πολλὰ τὰ τέκνα τῆς ἐρήμου μᾶλλον ἢ τῆς ἐχούσης τὸν ἄνδρα—"For it is written, Rejoice, thou barren that bearest not; break forth and cry, thou that travailest not: because many are the children of the desolate one more than of her who has an husband," or "the man." The quotation is according to the Septuagint from Isa. liv. 1, and the idiomatic variations between it and the Hebrew are of no real importance—the Greek using the article and present participle for the Hebrew præterite. After *ῥῆξον*, *φωνήν* may be understood, or *βοήν*, or *εὐφροσύνην*, but such an ellipse is common. The term רִנָּה, "joyous shouting," is omitted by the Seventy. The Hebrew idiom רַבִּים מִן is correctly imitated in the Greek *πολλὰ τὰ τέκνα . . . μᾶλλον ἤ*, and is different from *πλείονα ἤ*, for both are to have many children, but the children of the desolate are far to outnumber the other; and the past participle בְּעוּלָה is paraphrased by *τῆς ἐχούσης τὸν ἄνδρα*—"the man" whom the desolate woman has not. The two women contrasted, in the apostle's use of the quotation, are Sarah, and Hagar who had Abraham—*τὸν ἄνδρα*—when Sarah gave him up to her, and was the first of the two to have children.

The address of the prophet is to the ancient Israel, not to Jerusalem simply, or because in it no children were born during the Babylonish exile. Her desolate condition is to be succeeded by a blessed prosperity, and by the possession of Gentile countries. Zion in her youth had been espoused by Jehòvah to Himself, but the nuptial covenant had been broken and she had been repudiated, and had suffered the reproach of such widowhood, "forsaken and grieved in spirit." But re-union is promised on the part of the divine Husband under the claim of a *Goel* or Redeemer, and by a new and significant title, "God of the whole earth." In a gush of wrath He had hidden His face a moment, but in everlasting kindness would He have mercy on her (compare li. 2). The result is a numerous progeny. What the precise historic reference of the prophecy is, it is needless to inquire. Under its peculiar figure, so common in the prophets, it portrays, after a dark and sterile period, augmented spiritual blessings, and suddenly enlarged numbers to enjoy them, as the next chapter so vividly describes. In the apostle's use of the quotation, and in accordance with the context,

Hagar—she that hath τὸν ἄνδρα—is the symbol of the theocratic church with its children in bondage to the law; and Sarah—she that was desolate—is the symbol of the New Testament church, composed both of Jews and Gentiles, or the Jerusalem above which is our mother. Compare Schöttgen *in loc.* The prophecy is adduced to prove and illustrate this maternal relation. Some of the fathers took a different view of this prophecy. The Roman Clement, Origen, Chrysostom, and many others, suppose her "that bears not, the barren one," to be the Gentile church as opposed to the Jewish church or synagogue; but this is against the scope and language of the allegory. The Jerusalem that now is is the Jewish dispensation, the children of the bond-maid Hagar; the Jerusalem above, which prior to the advent was sterile and childless—Sarah—is now a fruitful mother, her children greatly more numerous than those of her rival, for all believers like her son Isaac are the seed of Abraham, children of promise.

Ver. 28. *Ὑμεῖς δέ, ἀδελφοί, κατὰ Ἰσαάκ, ἐπαγγελίας τέκνα ἐστέ*—"But ye, brethren, as Isaac was, are children of promise." The Received Text has ἡμεῖς ἐσμέν, and the reading is well supported, having in its favour A, C, D[3], K, L, א, four MSS., the Syriac, Vulgate, Coptic, and Gothic versions, with several of the Greek fathers and Augustine. The other reading has in its favour B, D, F, four MSS., the Claromontane Latin, Origen, Irenæus, Ambrose. This difference of reading would seem to show that ἐσμέν, supposed to look back to ἡμῶν in ver. 26, has been probably conformed to ver. 31, whereas the other reading is free from any such suspicion. The δέ is more than transitional; it implies a contrast to the children of her who had the husband. The idiomatic phrase κατὰ Ἰσαάκ is, after the example of Isaac, he being the norm or pattern. Winer, § 49; Eph. iv. 24; Col. iii. 10; 1 Pet. i. 15; Kypke *in loc.* And being not children κατὰ σάρκα, "ye are children of promise," as Isaac was, as has been stated in ver. 23. The genitive ἐπαγγελίας denotes the source, and is equivalent in sense to διά, as the context shows. It does not mean *liberi promissi* (Bloomfield, Brown), nor children possessed of the promise, but distinctly children by means of the promise.

Ver. 29. *Ἀλλ' ὥσπερ τότε ὁ κατὰ σάρκα γεννηθεὶς ἐδίωκε*

τὸν κατὰ πνεῦμα, οὕτω καὶ νῦν—"But as then he who was born after the flesh persecuted him who was born after the Spirit, so it is also now." The *ἀλλά* is adversative, warning those who like Isaac are children of promise to anticipate and prepare for persecution. For *κατὰ σάρκα*, see under ver. 25; *κατὰ πνεῦμα* is the opposite—the one was born naturally, the other supernaturally, or by promise, realized by the agency of the Holy Spirit. The verb *ἐδίωκεν* is imperfect—the action in some shape yet ideally continues. Winer, § 40, 3. What the persecution was, it is difficult to decide. The Old Testament implies it, and Jewish legend amplifies it; so that as a fact it was well known at least to one section of the Galatian church. The words in Gen. xxi. 9 are וַתֵּרֶא שָׂרָה אֶת־בֶּן־הָגָר . . . מְצַחֵק, rendered in the Septuagint—*ἰδοῦσα δὲ Σάῤῥα τὸν υἱὸν Ἄγαρ . . . παίζοντα μετὰ Ἰσαὰκ τοῦ υἱοῦ αὐτῆς*. Lightfoot conjectures that the Hebrew verse may have originally ended בִּבְנָהּ בְּיִצְחָק, and that the words implied in the Greek may have dropped out on account of the homœoteleuton. The Hebrew then is, "And when Sarah saw the son of Hagar laughing." Sarah's consequent anger implies that he was laughing at, mocking or jeering, her son Isaac. Isaac's own name was laughter, and Ishmael may have turned it into boyish ridicule. He was laughter to his mother in one sense, but to his brother in a very different sense—the one laughed for him, the other at him. For *παίζω*, Prov. xxvi. 19, Jer. xv. 7, xxxi. 4. That the Hebrew word has such a meaning is plain from Gen. xix. 14: "Lot seemed as one that mocked;" Gen. xxxix. 14: "He hath brought in an Hebrew unto us to mock us;" and in ver. 17. In 2 Sam. ii. 14 a word from the kindred root שָׂחַק denotes the "combat" which Joab proposes, and which he grimly calls a "play" or sport. These instances dispose of Jowett's statement, that "the word neither in the Hebrew nor the Seventy admits the sense of mocking." It was natural that Ishmael, now sixteen years of age, and for many years regarded and no doubt courted as the heir of Abraham's wealth, should regard with peculiar jealousy the younger child who had ousted him; and it was natural for him to make mockery of him, or to laugh at or make himself merry over the idea of one so much younger and feebler becoming the ultimate possessor. Some such sense belongs to the Hebrew term, for it must account for Sarah's displeasure, since it was not without cause; so that, as Kalisch says, "the Septuagint and Vulgate translations are inappropriate." See Keil and Delitzsch, and Tuch *in loc.* The traditions took two different shapes—one, that of insolence and blows, as Beresch. R. 53: *Tulit Ishmael arcum et sagittas, et jaculatus est Isaacum, et præ se tulit ac se luderet.* Beer, *Leben Abraham*, p. 49, and his authorities, p. 169. *Lusio illa illusio erat* (Augustine). The other shape was that of merriment, as at the weaning feast. The Book of Jubilees (Ewald, *Jahrb.* iii. 13) represents Ishmael as dancing, pleasing Abraham, and creating jealousy in Sarah. The narrative in Genesis thus sustains of itself the use which the apostle makes of it, especially when set in the light of those national legends with which many of his readers must have been well acquainted. The enmity began early as between the representative Ishmael and Isaac; it was continued between their descendants, Hagarites and Israelites (Ps. lxxxiii. 7; 1 Chron. v. 10, 19); and it was still manifested in the enemies of a free spiritual faith—those after the flesh, Jews and Judaists, Abraham's natural progeny—trusting in carnal ordinances, and persecuting those after the Spirit, who are his spiritual children through faith in Christ. As it was then, οὕτω καὶ νῦν, "so is it now." 1 Thess. ii. 15. What the nature of the opposition carried on in Galatia was, we know not. But it is alluded to in iii. 4, v. 11. The Judaizers were keen and unscrupulous opponents, and must have had at command many weapons of insult, raillery, and persecution. Heidegger, *Hist. Patriarcharum*, ii. p. 205.

Ver. 30. Ἀλλὰ τί λέγει ἡ γραφή; Ἔκβαλε τὴν παιδίσκην καὶ τὸν υἱὸν αὐτῆς, οὐ γὰρ μὴ κληρονομήσῃ ὁ υἱὸς τῆς παιδίσκης μετὰ τοῦ υἱοῦ τῆς ἐλευθέρας—"Nevertheless what saith the Scripture? Cast out the bond-maid and her son, for the son of the bond-maid shall in nowise inherit with the son of the free woman." This quotation is from the Septuagint, with a necessary alteration. The words in Gen. xxi. 10 are those of Sarah: τῆς παιδίσκης ταύτης μετὰ τοῦ υἱοῦ μου Ἰσαάκ, as D^1, F, and some of the fathers read; but her wish became the divine command, and the apostle naturally adapts it as τῆς παιδίσκης μετὰ τοῦ υἱοῦ τῆς ἐλευθέρας. Nothing is said of Sarah as to her jealousy or heartlessness, for it was her premature plot to expedite the promise that led to the birth of

Ishmael; and nothing is said of Abraham's natural displeasure at Sarah's request, for those domestic incidents belong not to the allegory, with which alone the apostle is concerned. See Turner, *Genesis*, p. 283. What saith the Scripture? The ἀλλά introduces a thought in cheering contrast to the previous statement. The significant question leads to a conclusive and definite reply: "Cast out the bond-maid and her son;" their doom was immediate and complete expulsion from the Abrahamic household. There could be no division of the inheritance, no joint heirship. For the son of the bond-maid shall in nowise inherit —*οὐ μὴ κληρονομήσῃ*, the verb having the emphasis, the future *κληρονομήσει* being read in B, D, א, as in the Septuagint. As Winer remarks, on account of the various readings, and the use of the subjunctive more than of the future in the New Testament, the rule of Hermann is not to be pressed. Hermann says, Note on Soph. *Œdip. Col.* 848, that the aorist subjunctive is used *aut in re incerti temporis, sed semel vel brevi temporis momento agenda;* while the future, *ad ea pertinet quæ aut diuturniora aliquando eventura indicare volumus, aut non aliquo quocunque, sed remotiore aliquo tempore dicimus futura esse.* The application of this canon to the New Testament or the Septuagint has no sure ground. Thiersch, *Pent.* p. 109. The remark applies to the later Greek also. Gayler, *De Part. neg.* pp. 433, 440; Baumlein, *Griech. Part.* p. 308; Winer, § 56, 3. The double negative is intensive, at least in this place, though it had become a familiar unemphatic formula, and it is of frequent occurrence in the Septuagint. An explanation will be found in Donaldson, *Cratylus*, § 394, and *Gram.* § 544.

The command is precise and unambiguous. Ishmael must be sent away, that Isaac alone may inherit. Ishmael had no title. The case of Jephthah's disinheritance is not wholly analogous, for he was the son of "an harlot," "a strange woman," not of a secondary wife. Selden, *De Success.* cap. iii., *Works*, vol. ii. p. 11. The two children, so different in temper and social position, could not have lived together; coheritage was divinely prohibited; the purpose of God necessitated separation. The bond-mother and her son must go out into the wilderness. Isaac, the free woman's child, remains at home, and succeeds to the inheritance. The lesson from this portion of the allegory is, that Judaism is in no sense to be combined with Christianity; that they were intended to be kept asunder, and to no extent to be amalgamated; that they are so opposed in genius and working—flesh and spirit, bondage and freedom—that any compromise between them is impossible. The inheritance belongs alone to Abraham's spiritual seed, and cannot be obtained by mere natural descent from the patriarch. And all this on highest authority, that of Scripture, to whose teachings they professed to yield implicit obedience. Not many at this period could acquiesce in this teaching; for Judaism was still tenaciously clung to by myriads who believed, and who could not so fully emancipate themselves from early bias and national prepossession as did the apostle of the Gentiles. See under ii. 1–10.

Ver. 31. *Διό, ἀδελφοί, οὐκ ἐσμὲν παιδίσκης τέκνα, ἀλλὰ τῆς ἐλευθέρας*—"Wherefore, brethren, we are children not of a bond-woman, but of the free woman." The *ἄρα* of the Received Text is not very strongly supported, and there are other minor variations, apparently emendations suggested by some difficulty felt about *διό*. According to Meyer, followed by Ellicott, this verse begins a short semi-paragraph, which passes on in the next verse to an exhortation. The common interpretation, on the other hand, is to regard the verse as the conclusion from the previous argument. This appears to be the most natural form of connection. Prof. Lightfoot remarks that the particle is chosen "rather with a view to the obligation involved in the statement, than to the statement itself: Wherefore, let us remember that we are, etc." The apostle's use of *διό* is so various that no argument can be based on its occurrence here. Donaldson, *Cratylus*, § 192. He may refer back to *κληρονομήσῃ* (Alford), but he rather sums up the whole argument. We are children of promise, he had said, persecuted it is true, but the persecution does not prevent or interrupt our heirship; the bond-woman's child is expelled, the free woman's son inherits alone: we inherit by the same title; "wherefore" our inheritance by such a title is a proof that we are the children not of a bond-woman, but of the free woman. While *διό*—*δι' ὅ*—may begin a new paragraph, but not without connection with what has preceded, it often connects clauses: Rom. iv. 22, 2 Cor. iv. 13, v. 9, xii. 10, Phil. ii. 9; and it precedes an inference in

Matt. xxvii. 8, Luke i. 35, Rom. i. 24, xv. 7. The article is omitted before παιδίσκης, not perhaps because it is emphatically prefixed to its governing noun (Middleton, *Greek Art.* p. 50; Winer, § 19, 2, *b*), but as generalizing the assertion—not of a, or any, bond-woman (compare iv. 11), for this noun has the article throughout the paragraph. The next verse is the practical appeal which, based on the allegory, is suddenly and somewhat sternly addressed to them, and followed up by a series of severe and solemn warnings.

CHAPTER V

VER. 1. This verse is closely connected with the immediately preceding one, and is, as we have just said, the prime inferential and practical lesson. But it is difficult, if not impossible, to fix on the correct reading, there being so many variations affecting both the sense and the connection.

The Stephanic text reads: *τῇ ἐλευθερίᾳ οὖν ᾗ Χριστὸς ἡμᾶς ἠλευθέρωσε, στήκετε.* The *οὖν*, the *ᾗ*, and the *ἡμᾶς* are matter of doubt and of various reading. *Οὖν* is omitted in D, in the Latin and Syriac, and in Theodore Mops. Theodoret, Jerome, Ambros., Pelagius, C³, K, L, many cursives, Damascenus, Theophylact, Œcumenius, place *οὖν* after *ἐλευθερίᾳ*; while it is put after *στήκετε* in A, B, C¹, F, ℵ, the Coptic version, and in Origen, Cyril, and Augustine. The best authority places the particle after *στήκετε*. Then *ᾗ* is omitted in A, B, C, D¹, ℵ; but it (*τῇ ἐλευθερίᾳ ᾗ*) is found in D³, E, K, L, in the majority of cursives, and in the most of the Greek fathers, and is adopted by Tischendorf, Scholz, Rinck, Reiche, Ellicott; while the reading *ᾗ ἐλευθερίᾳ* is found in F, G,—the Claromontane Latin and Vulgate reading also *quâ libertate*, followed by the Gothic, Victorinus, Augustine, and Jerome. The authority for this peculiar reading is chiefly Latin, and it may have been a re-translation of the Latin idiom *qua libertate*. But the omission of *ᾗ* makes the clause and the connection difficult, though the omission is really well supported. The omission is adopted by Alford—"with liberty did Christ make you free," beginning thus the new statement. It may be said that *ᾗ* was omitted from its closeness to the same letter beginning *ἡμᾶς* (Wieseler), and it may be replied that it got in from an unwitting repetition of the same first letter (Meyer). The *ἡμᾶς* stands before *Χριστός* in A, B, D, F, ℵ; but after it in C, K, L, ℵ³, and in several of the versions, in some of the Greek fathers, and many of the Latin ones, the Vulgate having *Christus nos*, and Ulphilas *uns Christus*. The first order is therefore the better sustained, and Χριστὸς ἡμᾶς may have been written to avoid ᾗ ἡμᾶς, found in the codices referred to. According, then, to diplomatic evidence, the best supported reading is—

Τῇ ἐλευθερίᾳ ἡμᾶς Χριστὸς ἠλευθέρωσε· στήκετε οὖν—"For freedom did Christ free us: stand therefore." This is adopted by Lachmann, Meyer, Usteri, Hofmann, and Alford. Prof. Lightfoot does not set it aside altogether, but retains it as an alternative reading. See Mill, Griesbach, Winer.

1. Retaining the ᾗ, some join the first clause to the previous verse—"We are children not of the bond-woman, but of the free woman, in that freedom with which Christ made us free." So Schott, and Prof. Lightfoot who puts the alternative: "Ye are sons by virtue of the freedom which Christ has given, or children of her who is free with that freedom which Christ has given us." So Wycliffe, the Genevan and the Rheims versions. But the connection is loose and pointless, and στήκετε becomes in that case abrupt and unsupported.

2. Some connect it with στήκετε, and give the dative the sense of *quod attinet ad*—stand fast in respect to, or rather in, the liberty for which Christ did make us free (Ellicott, Winer). The ᾗ may be by attraction, or it may be ablatival—"with which." Piscator, Rückert, Hilgenfeld, Wieseler, and the Vulgate—*quâ libertate.*

3. Adopting the reading which we prefer, the sense will be: "with liberty did Christ make us free (the dative instrumental): stand therefore;" or, "for liberty Christ freed us; make a stand,"—it being the *dativus commodi*, and the stress being on ἐλευθερίᾳ. A. Buttmann, p. 155. We are children of the free woman—beyond doubt it is; for liberty Christ did free us: v. 13; John viii. 36. The verb στήκετε, unknown in classical Greek, derives its specialty of sense from the context. 2 Thess. ii. 15. See under Phil. i. 27. Chrysostom says by the word "stand fast" he indicates their vacillation—τὸν σάλον.

The verb ἐνέχομαι is "to be held in" or "by," either physically, as τῇ πάγῃ, Herod. ii. 121, or ethically, as δόγμασιν, Plutarch, *Symp.* ii. 3. See Kypke *in loc.* It means to be held fast in, or so held that there is difficulty or impossibility of escape. Mark vi. 19; Luke xi. 53; Sept. Gen. xlix. 23; Ezek. xiv. 4. The phrase ζυγῷ δουλείας is the "yoke of bondage," though both nouns want the article. Winer, § 19, 1; Soph. *Ajax*, 944; Sept. Cant. v. 1. The genitive δουλείας, which deprives its governing noun of its article, denotes the characterizing quality or element of the yoke. The πάλιν is explained by a reference to iv. 9, if the allusion be definite—once under a yoke of heathenism, they would be involved again in a yoke of heathenism; or if the genitive be indefinite, the meaning would be—once in bondage, and again to be held fast in it, without formally specifying its nature.

Ver. 2. Ἴδε ἐγὼ Παῦλος λέγω ὑμῖν—"Behold I Paul say to you." The proper accentuation of ἴδε has been disputed. In later Greek it is a paroxyton, but in Attic Greek an oxyton. Winer, § 6, 1; Moeris, p. 193. This accentuation is followed by Lachmann and Tischendorf. The particle occurs frequently in the Gospels, ἰδού being commoner in the Epistles; and here it sharply summons attention to what follows, as a warning of highest moment. In the ἐγὼ Παῦλος is the direct interposition of the apostle's own authority, as in 2 Cor. x. 1, Eph. iii. 1. The name would suggest what he has said so solemnly of himself in the beginning of the epistle—"Paul an apostle, neither of men nor by man," etc. The words are therefore decidedly more than what Jowett calls "an expression of his intimate and personal conviction." Other allusions given to the phrase by commentators seem to be inferential and distant. Thus Grotius—*apostolus . . . quod illi vestri doctores de se dicere non possunt;* Koppe—*cujus animi candorem et integritatem nostis;* Wetstein, followed by Prof. Lightfoot—*ego quem dicunt circumcisionem predicare;* Wieseler—*in Gegensatze zu dem Irrlehrer;* Borger—*ego vero, idem ille Paulus quem tam impudenter calumniantur;* Brown—"*who ardently loves you, and whom you once ardently loved;*" Sardinoux—*il pose son nom . . . par sentiment paternel de la confiance que les Galates avaient pour lui.* Of course, when the apostle asserts his authority, he virtually puts himself into opposition to the false teachers, and the name might suggest many associations in connection with his previous residence among them. But the phrase especially places his personal or official authority in abrupt and warning emphasis. It is in no sense a pledge—*pignori quasi nomen suum obligat* (Trana), nor an oath (S. Schmid), nor is it based on any suspicion that the Judaizing teachers gave out that they were at one with him in doctrine (Jatho).

Ὅτι, ἐὰν περιτέμνησθε, Χριστὸς ὑμᾶς οὐδὲν ὠφελήσει—"that if ye be circumcised"—"if ye be getting yourselves circumcised"—"Christ shall profit you nothing." (See under i. 8.) The present subjunctive indicates the continuance of the habit. He says not, that they had been circumcised, but "if ye be getting yourselves circumcised." Klotz-Devarius, vol. ii. 455. The future form of the second clause is referred by Meyer, as is his wont, to the second coming—the *parousia*. But the future here simply indicates certainty of result. Winer, § 40, 6; Matt. vii. 16. The warning is strongly worded. Circumcision and salvation by Christ are asserted to be incompatible. The false teachers said, "Except ye be circumcised, ye cannot be saved;" and the apostle affirms, in the teeth of this declaration, "Of what advantage shall Christ be to you, if ye are trusting in something else than Christ—in the blood of your foreskin, and not in His atoning blood?" It is of course to the Gentile portion of the church that the apostle directly addresses himself. The circumcision of one who was a Jew wholly or on one side might be pardoned as a conformity to national custom, and as a sacred token of descent from Abraham, if it was meant to involve no higher principle. But when heathens were circumcised, they wore a lie in their flesh, for they had no connection with Abraham; and to declare circumcision to be essential to their salvation was not only enforcing a national rite on those for whom it was never intended, but was giving it a co-ordinate value with the death of Christ—as if that death had failed to work out a complete salvation. Conformity to Judaism so taught and enjoined, interfered with the full and free offer of pardon by the Son of God: it raised up a new condition—interposed a barrier fatal to salvation; for it affirmed that the Gentile must become a proselyte by initiation, and do homage to the law, ere he could be profited by faith in Christ. It brought two contradictory principles into operation, the one of which neutralized the other: if they trusted in Christ, there was no need of circumcision; if they observed circumcision, they would get no benefit from Christ, for they were seeking justification in another way. "What a threat!" exclaims Chrysostom; "good reason for his anathematizing angels."

Ver. 3. *Μαρτύρομαι δὲ πάλιν παντὶ ἀνθρώπῳ περιτεμνομένῳ*—"Yea, I testify again to every man getting himself circumcised"—*circumcidenti se*, Vulgate, the chief stress being on *παντί*. Acts xx. 26; Eph. iv. 17. But Chrysostom's explanation dilutes the sense, "Lest you suspect that I say it of enmity, I testify not to you only, but to every one." The particle *δέ* is more than transitional (Wieseler), but is neither *enim* nor *potius;* according to Hermann, *ad Vigerum*, No. 343, it is in this connection represented by *autem*, as in the Vulgate. Hilgenfeld supposes that *Θεόν* is understood after *μαρτύρομαι*, as if he called God to witness. But such an accusative is not necessary. "I obtest"—I solemnly do testify. Josephus, iii. 8, 3. In *πάλιν* reference is not made, as Meyer and Wieseler suppose, to previous oral warnings when he was with them, but plainly to the *λέγω* of the previous verse—"I say"—"once more I testify." It is out of the question to give it the meaning of *porro* with Borger, or *contra* with Koppe and Wahl. The verse does not indeed repeat the statement of the preceding one; but the apostle makes an extended affirmation, which is also an additional one—*πάλιν*, the second verb being a solemn repetition of the preceding one. He has said, if ye be circumcised; and now he obtests to every one not as having been circumcised, but as now submitting to circumcision; not simply assuming the possibility of the occurrence, or regarding it as actually accomplished, but vividly representing every one who gets himself circumcised as putting himself under covenant to obey the whole law. The obtestation is not to the Jews who may have been circumcised in infancy, nor to the heathen who may at any earlier period, and prior to the introduction of the gospel, have become proselytes; but to the Gentile converts who might persist in undergoing the rite on the principles and with the motives of the Judaizing teachers. And his solemn averment is—

Ὅτι ὀφειλέτης ἐστὶν ὅλον τὸν νόμον ποιῆσαι—"that he is a debtor to do the whole law." Circumcision, as the initiatory rite—*inaugurale sacramentum* (Dickson)—is to be regarded not merely in itself, but in the connected obligations under which it brought one. It was a pledge to obey the whole law. The person who on purpose submitted to circumcision did by that act place himself under the law, as he who is baptized is brought into a similar relation to the law of Christ, or as a foreigner whose naturalization pledges him to observe the law of the land. And such circumcision bound a man not to obey this or that department of ordinances, but to do the "whole law"—the emphasis being on ὅλον. The law is a code one and indivisible in origin and authority, however ramified its statutes; therefore an elective obedience to preferred precepts is not to be permitted. Chrysostom thus illustrates the obligation in reference to the ceremonial law: A man circumcised is bound to offer sacrifices, and such oblations necessitate the observance of sacred seasons and the visitation of sacred places. The precise allusion or inference which the apostle has in his mind has been disputed. Some, as Usteri and Rückert, suppose it thus: A debtor to obey the whole law, which you can never do, so that you are under the curse. But in order to such an application, the apostle did not need to emphasize ὅλον, for law in no sense can justify: iii. 1. Winer brings out this conclusion, *Debetis totam legem recipere, h. e. religionem Christianam omnem abjicere.* But the object of the apostle seems to be, not to prove that by being circumcised a man places himself under stipulation to obey the whole law—an impossibility, and therefore subjects himself to the curse,—but rather to show the utter incompatibility between the law and the gospel, or that any one so acting places himself under the very yoke from which Christ came to redeem him. He has spoken of this bondage in the previous section, which is wound up with "stand fast, and be not entangled again in the yoke of bondage." It is the bondage rather than the curse of the law which at the moment is uppermost in his mind; and this voluntary circumcision is a first step toward self-subjugation, for it binds a man to do the whole law. Perhaps, as Estius has remarked, the Judaists disguised or evaded this inference of the apostle, that circumcision puts a man under covenant to do the whole law, as indeed their own conduct seems to have illustrated. See vi. 13. Compare Rom. ii. 25.

Ver. 4. *Κατηργήθητε ἀπὸ τοῦ Χριστοῦ, οἵτινες ἐν νόμῳ δικαιοῦσθε*—"Ye were done away from Christ, whoever of you are being justified by law." The article τοῦ is doubtful. It is omitted in B, C, D[1], F, ℵ, and by Lachmann; but it is found in A, D[3], K, L, and almost all MSS., and it is inserted by Tischendorf. The first verb denotes the dissolution of all connection between them and Christ. It is not common in classic Greek, or even in the Septuagint where it occurs only four times; but it is one of the compound verbs often used by the apostle, and is here followed by *ἀπό*. Rom. vii. 2, 6. Fritzsche suggests that it is a *structura prægnans—καταργεῖσθαι καὶ χωρίζεσθαι ἀπό*, *Ad Rom.* vii. 2, vol. ii. pp. 8, 9; Winer, § 66, 2; Poppo's *Thucydides*, i. 1, 292. The tense of the verb points to a previous time, the time when they began their course of defection—then they were done away from Christ. The sentence is an asyndeton, or without any connecting particle, and the syntax is changed to the second person—a sudden and striking application of the previous verse—as if reverting to the ὑμῖν and ὑμᾶς of the second verse. He had said, Christ shall profit you nothing; and he explains the reason: Ye were done away from Christ, for He profits only those who are in union with Him. The branch cut off from the living trunk soon withers and dies. The emphasis is on the verb beginning the sentence (Œcumenius), on the perilous state described by it; and, that there may be no mistake, he adds with special point—

Οἵτινες ἐν νόμῳ δικαιοῦσθε—"whoever of you are justified by the law," or "as being persons who." The compound οἵτινες points them out as a class—*quippe qui*. The ἐν is not distinctly instrumental, but as usual indicates the sphere, though it may be what Donaldson calls instrumental adjunct, § 476. The law is regarded as that within which the supposed justification takes place, or, in another aspect, it is supposed to be the means of it. The present δικαιοῦσθε is what is called the subjective present—justified in their own feeling or opinion, ὡς ὑπολαμβάνετε (Theophylact). Schmalfeld, p. 91. De Wette and Windischmann give it the sense of justified in your idea and intention; "who seek to be justified," Rückert and Baumgarten; and Bagge puts it still more remotely, "who think that ye are to be, and so seek to be justified." But it is not the seeking of justification, but the dream of having it, that the apostle describes. When in their heart they thought themselves justified in the sphere of law, they became nullified from Christ; yea, he adds, τῆς χάριτος ἐξεπέσατε—"from grace ye fell away." Ἐξεπέσατε is the Alexandrian mode of spelling for ἐξεπέσετε. Lobeck, *Phryn.* p. 724; Winer, 13, 1. With the genitive it signifies tropically "to fall off" or "away from." 2 Pet. iii. 17; Sirach xxxiv. 7; Ast, *Lexicon Platon. sub voce.* Χάρις is not here the subjective influence of grace, but is in opposition to ἐν νόμῳ. The contrast is implied in Rom. v. 2. Compare 2 Pet. iii. 17. Law and grace are in direct antagonism. Justification by the one is of debt, by the other is of favour. The justified person works out his acceptance in the one case; he simply receives it in the other. If a man then imagines that he is justified by law, he has renounced grace as the principle of justification. He who is circumcised comes under pledge to obey the whole law; but obedience to law is wholly different in nature and operation from faith in Christ, so that he who looks to law renounces connection with Christ. Christ's method of justification is wholly of grace, and those who rely on law and merit are in opposition to grace—are fallen out of it. The clause has really no bearing on the doctrine of the perseverance of the saints, or on their possible apostasy. See, however, Wesselius *in loc.*

Ver. 5. Ἡμεῖς γὰρ Πνεύματι ἐκ πίστεως ἐλπίδα δικαιοσύνης ἀπεκδεχόμεθα—"For we by the Spirit are waiting for the hope of righteousness from faith." Tyndale's translation is an exegetical paraphrase: "We look for and hope in the Sprite to be justified thorow fayth." The γάρ introduces the proof, based on a contrary experience. The Judaists and their party thought themselves justified by works of law; we, on the other hand, by the Spirit, who cometh not through works but faith, are waiting for the hope of righteousness, which has also faith as its source. The ἡμεῖς are the apostle and those who, like him, so thought and felt that Christ did profit them, who also still clung to Christ, and had a living interest in His gracious process of justification.

Πνεύματι is the dative of instrument—by the assistance of the Spirit—not as if it were ἐν πνεύματι. It plainly in such a context refers to the Holy Ghost, though, like a proper name, it wants the article. The older interpretation of Wolff, Rambach, that the word means *doctrina evangelii,* is baseless. 2 Cor. iii. 6, adduced in proof, presents a sentiment of a different nature and contrast. Nor is it *spiritus pro fide* (Beza), nor *evangelium* (Seb. Schmid), nor *promissio gratiosa* (E. Schmid). Middleton, Peile, Brown, and Windischmann take it adverbially—"spiritually," or in a spiritual manner, *nach geistiger Weise*. Middleton, *Greek Art.* p. 126. Grotius, Borger, and Fritzsche are disposed to regard it as referring to the human spirit; the first explaining it by *intra animam*, the second by *interioribus animi sensibus*, and the third by *mente: Opuscula*, p. 156. This interpretation takes a very low and incorrect view of the apostle's statement. Akin to it is another opinion which takes πνεύματι as the human spirit enlightened and spiritualized by the Holy Spirit (Rosenmüller, Morus, Paulus, Winer). Winer explains it, *in Christi communione;* Baumgarten-Crusius, *der höhere, heilige Lebensgeist*. But the apostle often refers to the Spirit of God as the gift of Christ, as dwelling and working in the heart of believers, and creating and sustaining such graces as that of hope here referred to. Many expositors suppose an ideal contrast in πνεύματι to σαρκί, as characterizing the genius and form of Jewish observance. But the apostle refers not so much to legal observance by contrast in this verse as to the result of it,—not to the pursuit of righteousness on the part either of legalists or believers, but to the condition into which those who trust in Christ are brought by the Spirit, who cometh from the hearing of faith. Rather, perhaps, the contrast is: Ye are fallen away from Christ; we, on the other hand, are enjoying the Spirit of Christ given to those redeemed by Him, trusting in Him, in union with Him, and therefore no longer under the law, but heirs, and full of the hope of future blessing: iii. 5, 6, 7; Rom. viii. 15; Eph. i. 13.

Luther and some others wrongly join πνεύματι to ἐκ πίστεως—*spiritu qui ex fide est*—since, as Meyer remarks, no contrast is made with any other spirit; it is the contrast to ἐν νόμῳ of the previous verse. The double compound verb ἀπεκδέχομαι signifies "to wait for," and so to be in earnest and constant expectation of (Rom. viii. 19, 23, 25; 1 Cor. i. 7; Phil. iii. 20; Heb. ix. 28; 1 Pet. iii. 20), the sub-local reference being to the place whence the object is expected to come. Fritzschiorum *Opusc.* p. 156; Eurip. *Alcest.* 130. It is needless to suppose that there is a pleonasm (Jowett), or to imagine that the apostle originally intended to write ἔχομεν (Winer, Usteri, Schott); or, with Matthies, to give the verb the unjustifiable sense of *accipimus*, *wir fassen*. Ἐλπίς is used with another compound, προσδέχομαι, in Acts xxiv. 15 and Tit. ii. 13. It is not formally, but in thought, a cognate accusative, like ζῆν βίον, though Winer in his commentary styles it a pleonasm, and likewise Usteri. Lobeck, *Paralip.* p. 501. Wieseler objects that the noun and verb are not synonymous in meaning; but in these passages quoted, the accusative connected with the verb contains the object of hope,—future good or blessing being the object of expectation, for hope is the expectation combined with the desire of blessing to come.

In the phrase ἐλπίδα δικαιοσύνης the difficulty is to define the relation of the genitive. First, it may be the genitive of object, righteousness itself being the object of hope. So Theophylact, Winer, Usteri, Rückert, Schott, Olshausen, and Meyer. In that case the meaning is, we wait for the hoped righteousness—*justitia sperata*—righteousness itself being the object of hope. But the genitive, even with such a meaning, can scarcely be that of apposition (Wieseler, Gwynne). Or, secondly, it may be the genitive of subjective possession—the hope which belongs to righteousness, or that blessing connected with righteousness which is the object of hope. So Pelagius, Hunnius, Bengel, Borger, Windischmann, Bisping, Bagge, and Jowett. Thus Beza makes it *coronam gloriæ—spem quam justitia præbet.* Rosenmüller and Koppe err when they give δικαιοσύνη the meaning of *omnis felicitas.* In this view of the relation indicated by the genitive we are inclined to concur. For,

1. To expect hoped-for righteousness is an idea that enfeebles the argument, and places believers in no strong position as against legalists. They think themselves justified—we hope to be justified. To describe a condition opposed to their delusions about justification, something stronger than mere hope might be expected.

2. Righteousness to believers is a present possession, and as such the apostle usually represents it. Faith brings righteousness now, and such is the illustration in the third chapter. Ellicott's objection to this, that the Jew regarded δικαιοσύνη as something outward, present, realizable, is of little weight;

for what is inner may be regarded equally as present and realizable. It is true, as Neander says, that δικαιοσύνη is one of those divine results which "stretch into eternity;" but it is perfectly possessed in time, though not in its fullest development. Thus σωτηρία is enjoyed as soon as faith is possessed; but that salvation has a fulness still to be revealed, as is indicated in Rom. xiii. 11, Heb. ix. 28. Adoption may be described in similar terms.

3. Alford remarks that ἐλπίδα has the emphasis: this, however, does not favour his view, but ours. We believers have not only righteousness really now, but we are waiting also for the realization of the great hope wrapt up in it; we believers have now and in reality what you legalists imagine you have—justification; nay, we are cherishing the hope which it excites and sustains. Rom. viii. 30. The hope belonging to this righteousness is final acceptance—future blessedness and glorification, though we do not, as Ellicott, affix this idea to δικαιοσύνη itself, but take it as one of the assured and hoped-for results to which it leads.

The phrase ἐκ πίστεως is opposed to ἐν νόμῳ, and probably belongs to δικαιοσύνη, though some would connect it otherwise, as if the meaning were—We by the Spirit and out of faith do expect. It is noticeable that all the nouns in this and the following verse want the article. Gersdorf, *Beiträge zur Sprachcharact.* p. 273, etc.

Ver. 6. Ἐν γὰρ Χριστῷ Ἰησοῦ οὔτε περιτομή τι ἰσχύει οὔτε ἀκροβυστία—"For in Christ Jesus neither circumcision availeth anything nor uncircumcision." The clause ἐκ πίστεως is prominent and regulative in the previous verse, and the reason is given in the verse before us. Πίστις stands opposed to everything legal—to law, to ritual, to works of any sort. And why? The reason is introduced by γάρ.

The phrase ἐν Χριστῷ Ἰησοῦ is sadly diluted if made to mean *in lege Christi* (Grotius), *in Christi regno* (Pareus), or *Christi judicio* (Koppe and Flatt), or as if it were παρὰ Χριστῷ, or *Christi religio* (Morus). The union is that of personal union; and, as Ellicott remarks, the addition of Ἰησοῦ is not to be overlooked. Circumcision availeth nothing—does not create a deeper union into Christ Jesus, or excite a livelier hope, or confer a firmer hold on righteousness. This is an idea immediately present to the apostle's mind, and the one which pervades the previous verse, nay, is the very text of the epistle. But he adds—

Οὔτε ἀκροβυστία. See under ii. 7. It is a very wrong and perilous thing to be circumcised in order to righteousness, as he has so strenuously insisted; but he is not to be misunderstood, for the mere fact of uncircumcision has in itself no merit, and helps not to a deeper interest or fellowship in Christ. The uncircumcised has nothing to boast of over the circumcised; if both be in Christ, their condition is equal—is influenced neither by the presence of the mere external rite, nor by the want of it.

Ἀλλὰ πίστις δι' ἀγάπης ἐνεργουμένη—"but faith working through love" is of avail—*τι ἰσχύει.* The emphasis is on *πίστις*, as might be expected. The theological dispute is concerning *ἐνεργουμένη*—whether it has an active or a passive signification. That it may have the latter is undoubted, as Polybius, i. 13, 5; Joseph. *Antiq.* xv. 5, 3. See Rost und Palm *sub voce.* But *ἐνεργεῖσθαι*, not used of persons in the New Testament, has uniformly an active meaning—*operatur*, Vulgate. Winer, § 38, 6; Rom. vii. 5; 2 Cor. i. 6, iv. 12; Eph. iii. 20; Col. i. 29; 1 Thess. ii. 13; 2 Thess. ii. 7; Jas. v. 16. The faith shows from itself its efficacy through love—the real signification of the dynamic middle voice. Through love it operates, manifests its vitality and power—*ζῶσα δείκνυται* (Theophylact). He on whom faith is reposed, becomes naturally an object of love. If I believe that the Son of God in my nature died for me, and, yet wearing that nature, in it reigns over me, pleads for me, and fills me with His Spirit that I may finally and fully bear His image—such a faith must induce love within me toward Him and towards all that bears His image. And thus the three grand graces are referred to here—faith, hope, and love. 1 Thess. i. 3; Col. i. 4. While faith is child-like and hope is saint-like, love is God-like.

Tertullian, however, renders—*fides quæ per dilectionem perficitur;* Bellarmine and Estius take the same view; and the Council of Trent cites the clause so translated in proof of their favourite doctrine of *fides formata*, Sess. vi. c. 7. Bisping and Windischmann, though they do not hold the participle to be passive, will not part with the doctrine which the passive is adduced to support; the one saying, that in any case the essential meaning of the clause is unchanged, and the other, that either way it remains a strong proof of the Catholic doctrine. But the theory sets aside the Pauline theology of justification.

The apostle then recurs to the Galatians in direct personal appeal, referring to their previous state of spiritual prosperity, and how they had so quickly declined from it; warning them at the same time of the rapidity of spiritual declension when it once begins, and throwing blame on their seducers whose arts had prevailed.

Ver. 7. *'Ετρέχετε καλῶς*—"Ye were running well." The meaning of the figure is apparent: ii. 2; Phil. iii. 14; 2 Tim. iv. 7. They had been making rapid progress in the right course, but they had suddenly and unaccountably deflected. Legalism and internal dissensions (ver. 15) had got in among them. Ye were running well, and the hope was that ye should reach the goal and win the garland. The second member of the verse drops the transparent figure, which it identifies with obedience to the truth. Truth was the course, and obedience was the progress. Such is the eulogy; and now, without any connecting particle, the sudden question is put—a question of sorrow and surprise—

Τίς ὑμᾶς ἐνέκοψεν τῇ ἀληθείᾳ μὴ πείθεσθαι;—"Who did hinder you that ye should not obey the truth?" The Received Text has *ἀνέκοψεν* on the authority of a few minuscules, while the other reading has vastly preponderant authority. Erasmus edited *ἀνέκοψε*, and from him it passed into the Elzevir copies. Usteri is inclined still, but on feeble grounds, to receive it; and he reckons the next words a gloss. The verb *ἐγκόπτειν* is "to strike in," to hinder as by breaking up a road, and is used classically with the dative of a person, as in Polybius, xxiv. 1, 12; but it is also construed with the accusative: Acts xxiv. 4; 1 Thess. ii. 18. Compare Lucian, *Nigrinus*, § 35, vol. i. p. 24, ed. Dindorf.

Τῇ ἀληθείᾳ μὴ πείθεσθαι—"that ye should not obey the truth." The article *τῇ* is wanting in A, B, and ℵ. Chrysostom omits this clause; and after *πείθεσθαι* F and G add *μηδενὶ πείθεσθε*—*nemini consenseritis* in Lucifer and Ambrosiaster—evidently an interpolation, though it is defended by Koppe and Semler. Jerome remarks in reference to those words, that they are found *nec in Græcis libris, nec in his qui in apostolum commentati sunt.* Windischmann, however, is not wholly adverse to it, if thus connected with the former clause—"be persuaded by no one not to obey the truth." The μὴ before πείθεσθαι is not properly pleonastic, though the two translations correspond in sense—"who hath hindered that ye should not obey the truth?" or, "who hath hindered you from obeying the truth?" Meyer indeed says, it is *das gewöhnliche pleonastische nach verbis des Hinderns.* See Hermann, *Vigerus,* No. 271. The opinion is common, but the particle μή expresses the intended negative result contained in the infinitive. Jelf, § 749; Klotz-Devarius, vol. ii. p. 668; Madvig, § 210.

The truth is the truth of the gospel. See under ii. 5, 14. That truth is opposed in the apostle's mind not simply to what is false, but to every modification or perversion of it, under any guise which would rob it of its efficacy, mar its symmetry, or in any way injure its adaptation to man. And the truth is to be obeyed; not simply understood or admired, but obeyed. This clause omitted by Chrysostom has been wrongly placed at the end of iii. 1 in the Received Text.

Ver. 8. Ἡ πεισμονὴ οὐκ ἐκ τοῦ καλοῦντος ὑμᾶς—"The persuasion is not from Him who calleth you." The change of ἡ into ᾗ by Vömel is needless, though Tyndale's version is not unlike—"even that counsel that is not of Him," etc.—an answer to the previous question, "who was a let unto you, that ye should not obey the truth?" The verse is also regarded by Erasmus and Beza as the answer to the previous question, Who hindered you?—the persuasion not of Him that calleth you. But, as De Wette remarks, the article would in that case be repeated after πεισμονή. The word πεισμονή, suggested by the paronomasia, presents a difficulty; it occurs very rarely, being found neither in classic Greek nor in the Septuagint. It is found in the commentary of Eustathius on Homer several times, and in Justin Martyr, *Apol.* i. 53, Chrysostom on 1 Thess. i. 4, and Epiphanius, *Hæres.* xxx. 21. The citation from Ignatius is more than doubtful, as the Codex Colb., instead of οὐ πεισμονῆς τὸ ἔργον, reads οὐ σιωπῆς μόνον τὸ ἔργον, and the reading is adopted by Dressel. The question is, whether the word should be taken in an active or a passive sense—whether it signify *Ueberredung* or *Folgsamkeit, assen-*

tiendi facilitas aut persuadendi sollertia, persuading or persuadedness. The signification of *credulitas* given by Estius, of obstinacy by Bengel, of *Eigensinn* by De Wette, may not be admitted. The noun, as far as its form is concerned, may have either meaning. 1. The Greek fathers give it the passive sense. Theophylact explains it by τὸ πείθεσθαι, and Œcumenius by τὸ πεισθῆναι. This interpretation is adopted by many—as Winer, Rückert, Matthies, Olshausen, Reiche, and Prof. Lightfoot. The meaning then would be—this conviction or state of mind you are in, cometh not of Him that calls you. But this would be a truism, and the active sense of καλοῦντος is in that way overlooked. 2. But secondly, the πεισμονή and καλοῦντος are in contrast: it comes from a source opposed to the divine call. It is not the state of being persuaded, but the art or process of persuading, which comes into direct conflict with divine call. The Judaistic arts and arguments were not in harmony with the effectual calling of God. The one is πεισμονή—persuasion—ἐν πειθοῖς σοφίας λόγοις—art and arguments—on merely human and specious principles; the other is κλῆσις, the summons of God to life and truth in Christ. The apostle goes back in idea to τίς ὑμᾶς ἐνέκοψεν; the Judaizers are present to his mind from this question on through several verses and to the end of the twelfth verse. It is their work which he thus pictures; their πεισμονή was the preaching of another gospel, the bewitching of the Galatians. Were the apostle repeating the idea in μὴ πείθεσθαι, he would probably have expressed it in its negative form, and with the addition of a pronoun, as indeed is supplied by Jerome who gives both views, and by Augustine and Ambrosiaster. The active meaning is abundantly warranted. Justin Martyr, *Apolog.* i. 53; Epiphanius, *Hæres.* xxx. 21. This is the meaning given by Beza, Piscator, Borger, a Lapide, Usteri, Schott, Hilgenfeld, Meyer, Wieseler, and Trana. Reiche, adopting the passive sense, proposes to read the verse interrogatively, and wonders that nobody has thought of it: Is not persuasion—obedience—from God who calls you? This is not very different from omitting οὐκ altogether: Persuasion is of Him that calleth you; and so οὐκ is omitted in D[1] and some Latin codices referred to by Jerome who, however, after saying that in some Latin codices the reading *ex Deo* was a corruption from *ex eo*, assigns a theological reason for the omission of the negative οὐ: *verum simpliciores quique putantes se deferre Deo ut persuasio quoque nostra in ejus sit potestate, abstulerunt partem orationis* non. In the phrase ἐκ τοῦ καλοῦντος ὑμᾶς, the present participle, as Meyer suggests, may be taken substantively (Madvig, § 180), or it may bear its usual meaning —who is calling you still. Winer, § 45, 7. The reference is to God, as in i. 6, 15, not to the apostle (Locke, Paulus, Doddridge, and Macknight), nor to Christ (Theophylact). Because of the use of the uncommon word πεισμονή, and the various readings of this and the previous verse, Schott says that he conjectures, *haud temere*, the whole verse to be a gloss; it is wanting, he adds also in proof, in the Æthiopic version.

Ver. 9. *Μικρὰ ζύμη ὅλον τὸ φύραμα ζυμοῖ*—"A little leaven the whole lump leaveneth." This is a proverbial saying, delivered here as a warning. Matt. xiii. 33, xvi. 11; Mark viii. 15; Luke xiii. 21; 1 Cor. v. 6. The figure—applied in a bad sense, save in Matt. xiii. 33, Luke xiii. 21—may refer either to the false teachers or to their doctrine. Luther, Chrysostom, Calvin, a Lapide, Matthies, and Meyer refer it to the latter. The meaning in that case is, that the introduction of minute error has a tendency to corrupt the whole mass of truth. Alford differently—"corrupts the whole mass of Christians," taking ζύμη in the abstract and φύραμα in the concrete. It refers to persons, Rom. xi. 16, and here the Judaists are in the apostle's mind. True indeed, as Meyer says, the apostle nowhere lays stress on their number; yet the following ὁ ταράσσων might seem to indicate that the Judaists were not many. The question is, Who hindered you? and the assertion that the hindrance was occasioned by the πεισμονή refers to the teachers; so that the proverb may mean, that though like leaven they may appear small in comparison with the lump, yet by assiduity and influence they may and will infect and debase the *entire* society—ὅλον being emphatic. Such is the better view, as being more in harmony with the context. Theophylact refers the little leaven to circumcision—*μία οὖσα ἐντολή*; but that can scarcely be the apostle's reference: it is the doctrine connected with it which he has chiefly in view.

Ver. 10. The apostle so far modifies his statement, or

rather expresses a confidence that the whole lump will not be so leavened. Still there is no connecting particle; each statement stands out vividly by itself—

'Εγὼ πέποιθα εἰς ὑμᾶς ἐν Κυρίῳ—"I have confidence in" or "toward you in the Lord." The emphatic use of the pronoun *ἐγώ* is, "I for my part." There is a tacit contrast to what goes before, which some copyists filled in by *δέ*, as in C^1, F, and which Lachmann so far acknowledges as to put it within brackets in his text. The verb is used with *ἐπί* and an accusative—*ἐφ' ὑμᾶς*—2 Thess. iii. 4, 2 Cor. ii. 3; it has also, as here, the momentous adjunct *ἐν Κυρίῳ*, in Phil. ii. 24, 2 Thess. iii. 4; with a different aspect of relation it is also followed by *ἐπί* with a dative, 2 Cor. i. 9, Heb. ii. 13, and by the simple dative, Phil. i. 14, 2 Cor. x. 7, which designates the region or ground of confidence. *Εἰς ὑμᾶς* is "in reference to you." Wisdom xvi. 24; Winer, § 49, *a*, *c*; Bernhardy, p. 220. He based his confidence not on his own pointed reproof, solemn expostulation, or tender reminiscences; not on their affection toward him, or their probable recognition of the truth and reappreciation of it when they should bethink themselves. He might not overlook those elements indeed, but he says boldly, *ἐν Κυρίῳ*. Compare Rom. xiv. 14. We have in these three verses in succession, *πείθεσθαι—πεισμονή—πέποιθα*. His confidence was—

"Οτι οὐδὲν ἄλλο φρονήσετε—"that ye will think nothing different"—that is, that ye will be of the same mind with me. Acts xxviii. 22; Phil. i. 7, iii. 15. The reference seems directly to be to what he has been enjoining and illustrating in the previous sections; but as that includes the germ of his preaching, the inference is fair, that the entire circle of the apostle's public instruction is comprehended. We do not, like Ellicott, make the last the immediate reference; nor does the use of the future justify the supposition, for it naturally refers to the period when the epistle should be read, not excluding, of course, the anticipated and lasting result.

The apostle's confidence was, that the persuasive arts of the Judaizers should fail; that their success should be only temporary; and that the mass, after the novelty had worn off and they had come to themselves, should be of his mind—should settle down into harmony with him in reference to all the distinctive or characteristic truths of the gospel which he had proclaimed. See under Phil. iii. 15.

The apostle has been verging for some time toward the next declaration—the stern censure of the false teachers—

Ὁ δὲ ταράσσων ὑμᾶς βαστάσει τὸ κρίμα—"but he that troubleth you shall bear his judgment." The *δέ* marks a contrast between the apostle's confidence in returning harmony of opinion with himself, as just expressed, and the perversions and disturbances created by the Judaists. The singular *ὁ ταράσσων* is not collective for *οἱ ταράσσοντες* (i. 7), nor is it used as representing a class. Winer, § 27; 2 Cor. xi. 4. Nor, probably, does it specify any particular individual or any well-known person directly, as Erasmus, Bengel, Usteri, and others suppose; for the *ὅστις ἂν ᾖ* generalizes the expression. The phrase simply takes an individual of a class, and holds him up for the moment to notice, so that what is true of him is true of the entire party of which he is the representative. Madvig, § 14. It matters not—

Ὅστις ἂν ᾖ—"whoever he may be." Acts iii. 23. There is in this clause no direct reference to personal character, relation, or state, though they may be all included. The common reference has been to station—high station; as by Theophylact and Theodoret—*μεγάλοι, ἀξιόπιστοι*, and they are followed by Luther, Rückert, and De Wette. The sentiment may be true, but it is not directly expressed. Whoever he may chance to be—no matter what his position, influence, or pretensions—he shall bear his judgment. Lightfoot's filling up, "however he may vaunt his personal intercourse with the Lord," is a very unlikely supposition. Some, according to Jerome, found in this clause a quiet reference to Peter.

Βαστάσει τὸ κρίμα. Κρίμα is the judgment or sentence—whatever its nature—pronounced by the *κριτής*, and by contextual reference it is here a condemnatory judgment. Rom. iii. 8. We have *λαμβάνειν κρίμα* in Luke xx. 47, Rom. xiii. 2, Jas. iii. 1. In the Septuagint it represents the Hebrew נָשָׂא in its various senses. Compare 1 Cor. xi. 29, 1 Tim. v. 12. The image of a load in *βαστάσει* is found in Hebrew usage. Locke, Borger, and Macknight regard the *κρίμα* as excommunication; Jatho refers it to other church penalties, and placing a comma after *φρονήσετε*, he supposes the apostle to express his confidence that the church would agree in judgment with him against the offenders; but the apostle refers the judgment to God—ἀνταπόδοσις Θεοῦ (Hesychius). Tischendorf writes ἐὰν, after A, B, ℵ. See on this spelling, Winer, § 42, 6; Hermann, *ad Viger*. 835. *Κρίμα* is accented *κρῖμα* in classical writers. See under ii. 9. Lipsius, *Grammatische Untersuchungen*, p. 40.

The apostle immediately adds—

Ver. 11. Ἐγὼ δέ, ἀδελφοί, εἰ περιτομὴν ἔτι κηρύσσω, τί ἔτι διώκομαι;—"But I, brethren, if I still preach circumcision, why am I still persecuted?" The first ἔτι is omitted in some MSS. The difficulty of the temporal allusion may have suggested the omission. He never or at any time preached circumcision since he became an apostle. The ἐγώ is again emphatic in position and expression—"as for me;" and the δέ is not transitional simply, but indicates a contrast. There were troublers among them, and they shall bear their judgment. Such a crimination did not apply to him, though he had been unjustly charged. It would seem that some of these troublers alleged his patronage, and were sheltering themselves under his example. He had circumcised Timothy; nay, to Jews he became as a Jew; and his practice, misunderstood, might be quoted in favour of Judaizing inconsistency. But, in direct opposition to all arguments and apologies, he says, "As for me, if I still preach circumcision, why am I still persecuted?" *Εἰ κηρύσσω*—if I preach—if it be a fact that I preach. See under i. 9. The ἔτι refers to a period prior to his conversion, when, of course, circumcision was a prominent article of his creed and advocacy. He may have taken the word *κηρύσσω* from his present form of labour, and applied it, though not with perfect accuracy, to his previous maintenance of Judaism in its integrity (i. 14). The present tense is used, as if borrowed from the allegation of his opponents—he preaches yet circumcision,—*περιτομήν* having the stress. To preach circumcision is to maintain the observance of it to be necessary to salvation, and that all Gentile converts should submit to it as essential to their admission to the church, and their hope of final acceptance.

The apostle's reply to the charge of preaching circumcision is decisive—τί ἔτι διώκομαι—"why am I still persecuted?"

This second ἔτι may be regarded, but not necessarily, not as temporal, but as logical—Rom. iii. 7, ix. 19—"If I preach circumcision, what reason is there that I should be persecuted?" The fact of his being persecuted by the Jews and Judaists was surely a proof that he was neither preaching circumcision, nor was regarded by them as preaching it. Had he been preaching circumcision, would not they have joyfully clung to him? The conclusion is inevitable—

Ἄρα κατήργηται τὸ σκάνδαλον τοῦ σταυροῦ—"then the offence of the cross is done away with." 1 Cor. i. 23. A and C, 39, 40, add τοῦ Χριστοῦ, and so Jerome with the Coptic and Æthiopic versions. The addition is an exegetical emendation. The Syriac version takes the clause interrogatively, and Knapp and Vater so point it. Bengel is not disinclined to it, and Usteri and Ewald adopt it. But there is no necessity for it, and the statement by such a turn becomes feebler in character. The particle ἄρα leads to a somewhat unexpected conclusion (Klotz-Devarius, ii. p. 160. See under ii. 17, 21)—"those things being so"—"then after all," *ergo* in the Latin versions. The noun σκάνδαλον occurs often in the New Testament and the Septuagint, and properly is not offence, but that at which one stumbles or takes offence—found with its literal meaning, Lev. xix. 14—ἀπέναντι τυφλοῦ οὐ προσθήσεις σκάνδαλον, but only tropically in the New Testament. Morus and others understand σταυρός figuratively, as denoting suffering on account of Christ. But this sense weakens the declaration, for the apostle speaks directly of Christ's cross as involved in the controversy, and in the phrase adduced from Matt. xvi. 24 it is his own cross that a man is asked to take up. The offence of the cross is the offence which the Jews took at the idea of salvation through the Crucified One, and Him alone: vi. 12; 1 Cor. i. 17; Phil. ii. 8. Salvation by the blood of the cross was a sore stumblingblock to their national pride—an open affront to their cherished theology; for He that died on Calvary had been rejected by their people, and doomed for blasphemy and treason to a public execution. To speak of that instrument of shame and agony as the means of salvation inflamed their bitterest prejudices, and chafed them into an unscrupulous and malignant hostility, which plumed itself on doing God service when it put down and thwarted in every way, even unto death, the preachers and disciples of a crucified Messiah. 1 Thess. ii. 15.

Ver. 12. Ὄφελον καὶ ἀποκόψονται οἱ ἀναστατοῦντες ὑμᾶς —"I would that they would even cut themselves off who are unsettling you." The verb ἀναστατοῦν is defined by Hesychius as ἀνατρέπειν. Acts xvii. 6, xxi. 38. The term is of deeper meaning than ταράσσοντες in i. 7—not only troubling, but unhinging you. The ordinary classic phrase is ἀνάστατον ποιεῖν. Sturz, *De Dialect. Alexandrinâ,* p. 146. Symmachus, however, employs the verb, Ps. lix. (lviii.) 11; and Aquila, Ps. xi. (x.) 12. Bengel takes quite a peculiar view of the connection. Ὄφελον, according to him, should stand by itself, as being a curt answer to the previous clause taken interrogatively —"Is then the offence of the cross ceased?" "I wish it were; he shall bear his judgment, . . . and they who are unsettling you shall be cut off." (Similarly Bagge.) Besides the disjointed construction, the insulation of ὄφελον and the wrong translation of the middle verb forbid this exegesis. Ὄφελον is very rarely joined with the future, so that D, F have ἀποκόψωνται—an evident emendation. Lucian gives such a connection as an example of a solecism, *Pseudosophista,* p. 216, vol. iv. Bipont. The word is allied to ὤφειλε—ὤφελον. Matthiæ, § 513; 1 Cor. iv. 8; 2 Cor. xi. 1; Klotz-Devarius, 516. D^3, K, L have ὤφελον. The future is here used virtually for the optative, and the word is treated as a mere particle, Winer, § 41; A. Buttmann, § 185. In the use of the term in 1 Cor. iv. 8, 2 Cor. xi. 1, there is a tinge of irony.

What then is the meaning of ἀποκόψονται? 1. It cannot bear the passive sense—the *abscindantur* of the Vulgate, or "were cut off" of the English version. Winer, § 38, 4. The usage, though it occurs in classical writings, does not seem to be found in the New Testament. The Gothic, too, has *vainei jah usmaitaindau;* and the Syriac has the common idiom, "cutting were cut off." Calvin interprets it in the same way —*exitium imprecatur impostoribus illis,* and he vindicates the exegesis: "And yet I should not wish that a single individual perish thus; but my love of the church, and my anxiety for her interests, carry me into a kind of ecstasy—*quasi in ecstasin* —so that I can think of nothing else." Bagge explains it— "cut off from a position of hope that they may ever accept the salvation of Christ." The interpretation of Wieseler and Schmoller is similar to Calvin's; so Hammond, and Chandler who renders—"excluded from the church, disowned by you as brethren;"—"were themselves cut off from the society of the church with the circumcising knife of excommunication" (Boston).[1] But the passive translation is grammatically untenable; and if excommunication were the penalty, the apostle in his plenary authority would have pronounced the sentence himself.

2. Retaining the proper middle signification, the verb has been supposed to mean "cut themselves off, or get themselves cut off, from fellowship with you." Generally this view is held by Erasmus, Beza, Piscator, a Lapide, Bengel, Windischmann, Webster and Wilkinson, Ellicott; and Gwynne who renders—"that they would even beat themselves away!" But this meaning is unusual; the *καί* in this case also loses its emphasis; and why in such a crisis did the apostle only wish for the severance and not at once command it, as in 1 Cor. v. 11? There may be an allusion to the ἐνεκόψε of ver. 7, both being compounds of the same verb; but the paronomasia will not bear out Gwynne's idea—"Instead of intercepting the progress of others, make away with yourselves," for the *καί* again becomes meaningless, and the wish amounts to little. But the words of the apostle are sharp and precise.

3. The meaning is keener than this, that they may be deprived of all opportunity of seducing you (Wolf, Baumgarten), and greatly stronger than that of doing penance—*Busse thun.*

4. Nor is the meaning merely in a tropical sense, *utinam spadones fient propter regnum cœlorum, et carnalia seminare cessabunt;* the view of Thomas Aquinas, and of Augustine who calls it *sub specie maledictionis, benedictio.* Some admit in the phrase a reference to circumcision—"would execute upon themselves not only circumcision, but excision also" (Conybeare). Bengel too: *Quemadmodum præputium per circumcisionem abscinditur, ut quiddam, quo carere decet Israelitam; ita isti tanquam præputium rejiculum de communione sanctorum abscindentur et anathema erunt.*

5. Another and literal sense has been given, which some

[1] *Paraphrase on Galatians. Whole Works of Thomas Boston of Ettrick,* vol. vi. p. 273, Aberdeen 1849.

brand as indelicate, which Bagge calls "a positive insult to St. Paul," which Gwynne stigmatizes as "a filthy witticism," and of which even Le Clerc writes, *Imprecatio scurræ est non Pauli*, viz. I would that they would not only circumcise, but even castrate themselves;—Chrysostom saying, *μὴ περιτεμνέσθωσαν μόνον, ἀλλὰ καὶ ἀποκοπτέσθωσαν*; and Jerome as decidedly, *non solum circumcidantur sed etiam abscindantur*—would not only circumcise, but eunuchize themselves. Now, 1. this is the proper meaning of the term, to hew off limbs—*κάρη, αὐχένα, τένοντας*: *Iliad*, ix. 241; *Odyss.* x. 127; Rost u. Palm *sub voce*. 2. This verb and its noun are the technical terms employed for this act: Arrian, *Epictetus*, ii. 20. *Γάλλος ὁ ἀπόκοπος ἤτοι ὁ εὐνοῦχος*, Hesychius; Lucian, *Eunuchus*, p. 210, vol. v. *Opera*, Bipont. 3. The word bears the same meaning in the Septuagint: *οὐδὲ ἀποκεκομμένος*, Deut. xxiii. 1; also Philo, *De Leg. Spec.* § 7; *De Victis Offer.* § 13. See Wetstein *in loc.* A portion of the passage quoted by Bentley (*Critica Sacra*, p. 48) from Dio Cassius is a various reading. Dio Cassius, lib. lxxix. 11, p. 448, vol. ii. *Op.* ed. Dindorf. 4. Both the name and the thing were familiarly known in Galatia, especially in the town of Pessinus, where, on Mount Dindymus, Cybele had her shrine, which was served by emasculated priests. Lucian, *Cronosolon*, § 12, p. 16, vol. ix. *Op.* Bipont. Justin Martyr also uses the verb of the priests of the mother of the gods: I. *Apolog.* p. 70, E, p. 196, vol. i. *Opera*, ed. Otto. See also Bardesanes, Cureton's *Spicileg. Syr.* p. 32. Strabo also mentions the *ἀπόκοποι Γάλλοι*, xiii. 4, 14, p. 87, vol. iii. *Geograph.* ed. Kramer. Reference may also be made to the wild wail of the *Carmen*, lxiii. of Catullus. Diodorus Siculus, iii. 31, p. 247, vol. i. *Opera*, ed. Dindorf. Such a mutilation must have been so well known in the province of Galatia, that the apostle's words in connection with the *περιτομή* of the previous verse could scarcely have conveyed any other allusion to a Galatian reader; and this reconciles us to this third interpretation. The verb could not have the same hard sound to them as it has to us. 5. The *καί* in this way preserves its ascensive force—not only circumcise, but even eunuchize themselves. In a similar spirit and play of terms, the apostle says, Phil. iii. 2, 3: *βλέπετε τὴν κατατομήν· ἡμεῖς γὰρ ἡ περιτομή*. Circumcision to a Gentile was a mere bodily mutilation of the same kind as that of the priests of Cybele. See under Phil. iii. 2. Such an ἀποκοπή was quite on a level with their περιτομή: let them show their extravagant attachment to the rite by imitating the degraded ministers of Cybele. Luther writes, *Allusit ad circumcisionem, q. d. cogunt vos circumcidi utinam ipsi funditus et radicitus excindantur.* Such is the view of all the Greek fathers, of Jerome, Ambrosiaster, Augustine, and of Winer, Matthies, Schott, Olshausen, Usteri, De Wette, Hilgenfeld, Alford, Ewald, Jowett, and Prof. Lightfoot. It is needless to apologize for the apostle's words, as springing either from *Judaicus furor*, as Jerome says, or, as he further hints, from human frailty, since the apostle was a man *adhuc vasculo clausus infirmo.* Nor does it serve any purpose to call the imprecation simply prophetic (Pareus) or ecstatic (Calvin). It is a bitter sarcasm on the fanatical fondness for circumcision, and the extravagant estimate of its value, which these Judaistic zealots cherished, and which they were putting into prominence with persistent vehemence—a scornful and contemptuous estimate of the men, and of the mere mutilation for which they had such a passion.

Ver. 13. Ὑμεῖς γὰρ ἐπ' ἐλευθερίᾳ ἐκλήθητε, ἀδελφοί—"For ye for your part were called to liberty, brethren"—ὑμεῖς being emphatic from its position. Γάρ is "not merely a particle of transition" (Brown); nor is it to be referred to a more remote sentiment—"Let them not revolutionize you, for ye were called to freedom" (Webster and Wilkinson); nor is it connected with ὄφελον—"Would that the offence of the cross were done away; would that the Jews no longer rejected the doctrine that the law cannot justify, for ye were called" (Bagge). Gwynne needlessly throws the connection back to the last verse of the previous chapter. But γάρ refers back to the immediately preceding statement, and is a justification of the strong and indignant feeling expressed against the Judaizers, since they were fighting against the very freedom into which they had been called. Some difficulty about the meaning and reference of γάρ seems to have suggested the alteration into δέ, as in F, G, and in Chrysostom. The ἐπί expresses the object or design of the verb—called that you might be free. 1 Thess. iv. 7; Eph. ii. 10; Xenophon, *Anab.* vii. 6, 3; Winer, § 48, *c*; Jelf, 634, 3. It is the state for which, or for the permanent enjoyment of which, they had been called. To a state of liberty, permanent and unvarying, had they been summoned—freedom from that legal yoke under which the reactionists would bind them, and from which they had been delivered so wholly that they were under no obligation to conform either occasionally or partially, for such conformity impaired the breadth and fulness of their liberty. Law and its bondage were in direct antagonism to faith and its freedom. For κλῆσις, see under i. 6, Eph. iv. 1. And he names them "brethren," in affectionate counsel. Possibly ἐκλήθητε here was suggested by the previous phrase, ἐκ τοῦ καλοῦντος: the persuasion to bow to the servitude of the law did not come from Him who called them to freedom. But he adds the salutary caution—

Μόνον μὴ τὴν ἐλευθερίαν εἰς ἀφορμὴν τῇ σαρκί—"only turn not your liberty into an occasion for the flesh." The ellipse is emphatic in its conciseness. F, G supply δῶτε after σαρκί; and so Jerome and the Vulgate, *detis*. Meyer proposes τρέπετε, De Wette τρέψητε, and Hofmann ἔχετε. The want of a verb in similar cases with μή is not uncommon. Winer, § 64, 6; Matt. xxvi. 5; Sophocles, *Antig.* 577; Klotz-Devarius, ii. 669; Hartung, ii. 153. Some versions get out of the difficulty by recurring to the nominative. Thus the Syriac—"Only let not your liberty be for an occasion to the flesh;" and similarly Tyndale and the Genevan. The noun ἀφορμή signifies in martial phrase, a base of operations, as in Thucydides, i. 90; then a starting-point, an occasion or opportunity—with λαμβάνειν to take it, or with διδόναι to afford it. The dative σαρκί is that of *dativus commodi*—the flesh taking advantage of the occasion. Rom. vii. 8, 11; 2 Cor. v. 12, xi. 12; 1 Tim. v. 14. The σάρξ is man's unrenewed nature,—not simply his corporeal organism with its passions and appetites, but his whole nature ethically viewed as under the dominion of sin—sense and selfishness. See under ver. 19, and under Eph. ii. 3. See also Wieseler's long note. They had been exhorted to stand fast in the liberty, but they are specially cautioned not to abuse it. They were to be on their guard against antinomian licentiousness; for, though they were not under the law as a means of justification, they were still under it as their rule of life. The probable reference, as the succeeding context hints, is to whatever is opposed to the mutual service of love enjoined in the next clause,—perhaps that selfishness and self-importance which some among them seem to have cherished,—and to their contemptuous disregard for such as had not arrived at their cherished independence. The making freedom an occasion for the flesh is an extravagance which has been often witnessed; as with the German Anabaptists in the peasant wars of the days of Luther, and among the Fifth Monarchy men of the English Puritans. In the quaint words of a recent Irish theologian, "If the devil cannot stop the coach, he mounts the box and drives." Compare Rom. vi., Jude 4.

Ἀλλὰ διὰ τῆς ἀγάπης δουλεύετε ἀλλήλοις—"but by love be in bondage to," or "be serving, one another." A different reading, *τῇ ἀγάπῃ τοῦ Πνεύματος*, is found in D, F, 31, in the Claromontane, Vulgate, Gothic, and Coptic versions; but it is evidently an emendation, or an attempt to express a contrast to *σαρκί*. The article *τῆς* emphasizes the love as possessed and manifested by them, and *διά* points it out as the instrument of this mutual service. While there was *ἐλευθερία*, there was also to be *δουλεία*; not that of fear, as under the law, but that which springs from a faith working by love. Mutual service in their spiritual freedom was to be the result of mutual love, each serving and being served in turn,—a result which could not be obtained if they remained apart in cold and haughty isolation. Comp. Rom. xvi. 8, 22; 1 Cor. ix. 19; 1 Pet. ii. 16; 2 Pet. ii. 19. The law had occasioned no little disputation among them, was the source out of which had sprung those factious alienations; and yet what is the spirit of that very law? Is it not as follows?

Ver. 14. *Ὁ γὰρ πᾶς νόμος ἐν ἑνὶ λόγῳ πεπλήρωται*—"For the whole law has been fulfilled in one word." Codices K and L have *λόγος* instead of *νόμος*—an evident blunder. D[1] and F prefix *'ν ὑμῖν* to *ἐν ἑνὶ λόγῳ*—a plain interpolation; Tertullian has *in vobis*. Marcion, as quoted by Epiphanius, substituted *ὑμῖν* for *ἐν ἑνὶ λόγῳ*, and he seems to have read the verse thus: *ὁ γὰρ πᾶς νόμος ἐν ὑμῖν πεπλήρωται*; thus out of enmity against the Mosaic law, as some alleged, altering the apostle's meaning, and omitting *ἐν τῷ* that the following clause might not seem to be a quotation.

The reading *πεπλήρωται* is found in A, B, C, א, 17, 21, 23, 37, 39–71, in Marcion as quoted by Epiphanius, in Tertullian against Marcion, in Damascenus, and Augustine, who, however, often reads *impletur*. The reading is adopted by Lachmann and Tischendorf. *Πληροῦται* of the Received Text has in its favour D, F, K, L, Chrysostom, Theodoret, and many of the versions, as the Claromontane and Vulgate, the Gothic, Coptic, and Syriac. It is also advocated by Reiche at some length. The external testimony for *πληροῦται* is not however preponderant, and it is impaired by the suspicion which Meyer alleges, that the mechanical copyist did not understand the full force of the perfect. The present, besides, would mean that the process of fulfilment was still going on; whereas the perfect signifies, has been and is still fulfilled, is in a fulfilled state, or has received its full complement of obedience in this: "Thou shalt love thy neighbour as thyself." A. Buttmann, p. 172.

The position of the words *ὁ γὰρ πᾶς νόμος* is peculiar, but not without example: Acts xx. 18; 1 Tim. i. 16. In *γάρ* the connection is manifest: by their love they were to be serving one another, and for this reason, that love by divine appointment was the fulfilment of the law. The phrase *ἐν ἑνὶ λόγῳ* means, in this one utterance or precept—*πᾶς* and *ἑνί* being in contrast. But,

1. The notion attached by Grotius to *πληροῦται* is peculiar: The law is filled up, or is fulfilled—*sicut rudimenta implentur per doctrinam perfectiorem*. That is, the law itself gets an addition which perfects it. But the apostle is not speaking of the law as a code which may receive any enlargement, but of the obedience which it exacts. How could the Mosaic law be made perfect by the addition of one of its own precepts, and how could *πᾶς* stand in such a statement as Grotius supposes?

2. Not a few give *πεπλήρωται* the meaning of—is summed up, *comprehenditur*, like *ἀνακεφαλαιοῦται* in Rom. xiii. 9. This is the view of Luther, Calvin, Borger, Jaspis, Winer, Usteri, Reiche, and Olshausen. But though the meaning of the two phrases be not dissimilar, still the verb before us will not bear the signification thus assigned to it. Its proper meaning is distinctly to be given it, as other clauses of the New Testament show. So that we prefer—

3. The interpretation which gives the verb its common signification; and such is the view of Chrysostom and his followers, of Rückert, Matthies, Schott, De Wette, Meyer, Baum-

garten-Crusius, and Wieseler. Thus Matt. iii. 15, Rom. viii. 4, Col. iv. 17, Gal. vi. 2, Acts xiii. 25, Rom. xiii. 8. See under next clause.

The apostle adds—

'Εν τῷ, 'Αγαπήσεις τὸν πλησίον σου ὡς σεαυτόν—"is fulfilled in this, Thou shalt love thy neighbour as thyself." The repetitive words *ἐν τῷ* are omitted by D[1], F, the Itala and Vulgate, by Marcion, and many of the Latin fathers, as Jerome and Pelagius, but without any ground. *Σεαυτόν* has the authority of A, B, C, D, E, K, א, etc.; *ἑαυτόν* is read only in F, G, L, and many cursives. It is, however, defended by Meyer, but now abandoned by Tischendorf. It is true that *ἑαυτόν* does not change the sense, for it may be used in the second person: Winer, § 22, 5; Matt. iii. 9; John xii. 8; Acts xiii. 46; Phil. ii. 12; A. Buttmann, p. 99. But the external authority for *σεαυτόν* preponderates, and the accidental dropping of a *σ* after *ὡς*, ending with the same letter, may have given rise to the variation.

The quotation is from Lev. xix. 18, וְאָהַבְתָּ לְרֵעֲךָ כָּמוֹךָ, translated in Septuagint as it is found here: "And thou shalt love thy neighbour as thyself." The future for the imperative is common in Hebrew. Thiersch, *De Pent.* p. 156, etc. The meaning of *πλησίον* in the quotation is somewhat different from the original, where it denotes brother Jews. Here its reference seems specially to fellow-Christians, and generally to fellow-men. See Augustine, *De Doct. Christ.* i. 31. The question, "Who is my neighbour?" was in its wide sense answered by Christ in the parable of the good Samaritan; and that answer is, Every one needing thy help, be his blood or creed what it may, is thy neighbour.

1. But what is meant by loving one's neighbour as one's self? It does not mean with the same amount, but with the same kind of love,—which realizes or acts out the spirit of brotherhood,—which seeks for a neighbour what you seek for yourself, and feels his welfare involved in your own. According to Gwynne, it comprises both "manner and degree."

2. But how does this love of a neighbour fulfil the law? And the first question then is, What is the law referred to? Some, as Koppe, Brown, and Gwynne, suppose it the law of Christ; others, as Beza and Locke, the second table of the law;

others, as Schöttgen and Rückert, the divine law generally; others only the moral law, as Estius and Baumgarten-Crusius; others, as Macknight, hold that "the whole law" signifies those parts of the Mosaic law which enjoined men's duty to their neighbour; and similarly Turner. It seems a certain and necessary conclusion, that the whole law is that very law to which the apostle has referred so often in a variety of aspects. In what other sense could those who had heard the epistle read understand it? What is said is true of the Mosaic law in itself, and as a representative portion of God's great legislation. Secondly, the difficulty yet remains, how loving one's neighbour fulfils the whole law? Did the whole law mean only the whole law in reference to our neighbour, it would be easily understood. Love of neighbour would fulfil it in its various precepts; for what but the want of love, what but selfishness, leads any one to kill, or commit adultery, or steal, or perjure himself, or covet? If he loved his neighbour as himself, no such breaches of the divine code would be possible for him—murder would be to him as suicide, and false witness like self-crimination. The great Teacher has said, "Thou shalt love the Lord thy God with all thy heart, and with all thy soul, and with all thy mind, and with all thy strength. This is the first commandment." Mark xii. 30. But if one obeys the second commandment, which is "like unto" the first, he also obeys the first. For right love of neighbour implies the love of God, and is one of its tests or visible fruits. "If he love not his brother whom he hath seen, how can he love God whom he hath not seen?" No one can love his neighbour with the prescribed measure and character of love, unless he love God; for that neighbour is loved because he is God's child and bears His image. The love of the child presupposes as its root the love of the All-Father; obedience to the second commandment depends upon and comprises obedience to the first; and therefore love, in its inner spring, essence, and motive, fulfils the law. Disputes about that law were apparently running high among the Galatians, and were creating alienation, schism, and hatred; and yet the spirit of that law is love, showing itself in mutual service. Thus the apostle says, He who loves his neighbour *νόμον πεπλήρωκε*; and again, *πλήρωμα οὖν νόμου ἡ ἀγάπη*—"love is the fulfilment of the law." Rom.

xiii. 8, 10. And this is the royal law. Jas. ii. 8. Calvin says "that the doctors of the Sorbonne argued, that as the rule is superior to what it directs, so the love of ourselves must always hold the first rank." This, he affirms, is not to interpret but to subvert our Lord's words, adding—*asini sunt qui ne micam quidem habent caritatis.*

Ver. 15. The apostle enforces these thoughts by the emphatic warning—

Εἰ δὲ ἀλλήλους δάκνετε καὶ κατεσθίετε—"But if one another ye bite and devour." The image is taken from the preying of wild beasts. The first verb *δάκνω*—used literally, Xen. *Anab.* iii. 2—is employed in this tropical sense in Arrian's *Epict.* ii. 22. It means more than to vex or thwart (Robinson); it is to inflict deep piercing spiritual wounds—to lacerate character and feeling. A similar figure occurs in Ps. xxvii. 2; and Horace has *dente mordeor invido: Carmina,* iv. 3. The second verb denotes an action consequent upon the first. The animal bites, and then devours. The idiom is different in Greek and English: the first is, "to eat down," "to eat up." The verb—used literally of animals, Matt. xiii. 4, etc.; and of the action of fire, Rev. xi. 5—signifies here the utter spiritual waste which animosity creates and hurries on. Not content with wounding others, it would trample them and spoil them in its voracity and rage. 2 Cor. xi. 20. Both Cyprian and Marian. Victor have for the second verb, *accusatis.* Chrysostom says: "To bite is to satisfy a feeling of anger, but to devour is a proof of extreme savagism—*θηριωδίας ἐσχάτης.*" And the caution is added—

Βλέπετε μὴ ὑπὸ ἀλλήλων ἀναλωθῆτε—"see that by one another ye be not consumed;" the emphasis lying on *ἀλλήλων*—a reciprocal pronoun, realizing vividly the scene or object of the action, and in contrast to the previous clause—"serving one another in love." *Βλέπετε* is followed as often by *μή* and the subjunctive aorist. Winer, § 56; Gayler, 323. *'Αναλίσκω,* which appears to be climactic after *δάκνετε* and *κατεσθίετε,* is often used of killing or destroying. 2 Macc. ii. 10; Æschylus, *Agam.* 570, *τί τοὺς ἀναλωθέντας ἐν ψήφῳ λέγειν;* Thucydides, viii. 65. It is also employed in the sense of spending or squandering money, and thereby exhausting it. Here it pictures spiritual devastation and wreck, when, in consequence of brawling and contention, the spiritual life should go out, and the community itself be broken up and ended. Mutual destruction is the natural result of fierce mutual quarrel. Neither gains the victory—both perish. Koppe refers the result cautioned against to the interference of the Roman magistrates, who might interdict their religion; and Grotius points to it as a divine judgment. Both opinions are contrary to the verse and context.

Ver. 16. *Λέγω δέ, πνεύματι περιπατεῖτε*—"Now I say, According to the Spirit walk." The first words are a formula introducing a further explanation, and refer back to the first part of ver. 13—*εἰς ἀφορμὴν τῇ σαρκί*; the intervening verses being suggested by the last clause of the same verse—*διὰ τῆς ἀγάπης*. . . *Δέ* is not merely continuative, but points to the difference of theme. Had the apostle referred, as Gwynne supposes, to the immediately preceding verse, and merely proceeded with a specific and opposed injunction, λέγω would have been superfluous. It always introduces continued explanation: iii. 17, iv. 1. For *περιπατεῖτε*, see under Eph. ii. 2. The dative *πνεύματι* is that of norm—*κατὰ πνεῦμα*, Rom. viii. 4 (Meyer, Usteri)—indicating the rule or manner. Winer, § 31, 6; Gal. iii. 17; Rom. iv. 12; Phil. iii. 16. Fritzsche regards it as the *dativus commodi* (on Rom. xiii. 13), because in such a verb as the one occurring in this clause, *nulla notionis eundi ratio habetur;* and Hofmann similarly refers it to the power of the Spirit, like *πνεύματι ζῆν*. Wieseler takes it as instrument, the Spirit being the path in which they walk. Similarly Gywnne —"the Spirit, the agent, being regarded as the instrument." *Πνεῦμα* is the Holy Spirit; for it is the same Spirit that is spoken of in vers. 18 and 22, and therefore is not the spiritual part of our nature, nor the human spirit in unity with the Divine Spirit (Beza, Rückert, De Wette, Schott, Olshausen, and Brown); some epithet or addition would need to be added to the simple *πνεῦμα* to give it such a meaning. Nor can the phrase be diluted into "after a spiritual manner" (Peile, and Theodoret who calls it *ἐνοικοῦσαν χάριν*). The want of the article does not forbid the reference to the Holy Spirit; for *πνεῦμα* came at length to be treated as a proper name. See under Eph. i. 17.

Their whole course of life in thought and act, in all its

manifestations, was to be in the Spirit who is the source of all good and gracious impulse. He is within believers the living, ennobling, and sanctifying power; and susceptibility of influence—of check and guidance—from Him, in all points of daily life, was to characterize them—

Καὶ ἐπιθυμίαν σαρκὸς οὐ μὴ τελέσητε—"and (so) ye shall not fulfil the lust of the flesh." This translation is accepted by perhaps the majority of expositors. The clause is a conclusion following an imperative—do the one, and the other shall follow; the *καί* being consecutive. Winer, § 53, 3; Matt. xxii. 32; Luke vi. 37; 2 Cor. xiii. 11. See under Phil. iv. 7. The double negative *οὐ μή* is intensive, as if it were *μηδαμῶς*. Lobeck, *Phrynichus*, p. 724; Winer, § 56, 3. See under iv. 30. The aorist subjunctive is often employed in such negative utterances, especially in later Greek. Donaldson, *Cratyl.* 394; Krüger, § 53, 7, An. 6.

But another rendering has been adopted, and the verb is taken as an imperative—"and fulfil not the lust of the flesh;" the verse consisting in this case of an affirmative and a negative imperative connected by the simple copula. This is the view of Castalio, Beza, Koppe, Usteri, Baumgarten-Crusius, Ewald, and Meyer. The verb may indeed be taken in an imperative sense, there being apparently similar instances of such an imperative use of the second person subjunctive, and the aorist subjunctive being abundantly used in later Greek for the future. Gayler has given many examples from the classics, and a table of them from the Sept., p. 440, 1, etc. But there is no clear example of this construction in the New Testament, and there is often difference of reading in such cases as here. D[3], E have *οὐ μὴ τελέσετε*, as if from the Latin versions, which give *non perficietis*. The context following plainly presupposes an assertion made, not a prohibitive command given, and assigns the reason for making it: If ye walk by the Spirit, ye shall not fulfil the lusts of the flesh; for the two courses are incompatible —the one excludes the other. It is questionable if the use of *τελεῖν* will bear out the inference of Calvin—"The spiritual man may be often assaulted by the lusts of the flesh, but he does not fulfil them." See the use of *ποιεῖν* in John viii. 44, Eph. ii. 3, compared with Rom. ii. 27, Jas. ii. 8. For *σάρξ*, see under Eph. ii. 3; Delitzsch, *Bib. Psychol.* v. 6, *die unauf-*

gehobene Antinomie; Müller, *die Christ. Lehre von der Sünde,* vol. i. p. 442, etc.

Ver. 17. Ἡ γὰρ σὰρξ ἐπιθυμεῖ κατὰ τοῦ πνεύματος, τὸ δὲ πνεῦμα κατὰ τῆς σαρκός—"For the flesh lusteth against the spirit, and the spirit against the flesh." The reason or ground of the previous statement is assigned—γάρ. The flesh and spirit are powers in one and the same person. The same verb ἐπιθυμεῖ, as a *vox media,* is used of both, to mark the reflex antagonism. There is no zeugma (Bengel), and no similar verb needs to be supplied, as is done by Prof. Lightfoot. The verb is often followed by the genitive, accusative, or infinitive; but here by κατά, as marking the direction of the ἐπιθυμία,—a hostile direction being implied—Matt. x. 35, xxvii. 1; Acts vi. 13; 1 Cor. iv. 6, etc.—though not overtly stated, as by ἀντί. The flesh longs and wrestles for its former predominance; it is ever in the position of lusting against the spirit, and the spirit is always and unweariedly beating back and resisting the impulses and yearnings of the flesh. According to Meyer, Wieseler, and others, it is wholly or partially wrong to compare this mutual struggle with that depicted in Rom. vii. which in their opinion characterizes the unrenewed, as in such the struggle is between σάρξ and νοῦς. See Hodge *in loc.* Flesh and the spirit are ever so opposed, that to walk by the spirit is to preclude the fulfilment of the lust of the flesh. This inner warfare is not unknown to classical writers; it is in some aspects a matter of daily experience with all men. Euripides, *Medea,* 1077; Arrian, *Epictetus,* ii. 26; Xenophon, *Cyro.* vi. 1, 41; Cicero, *Tusc.* ii. 21; Ovid, *Metam.* vii. 19; Seneca, *Ep.* 25. See Wetstein *in loc.* and Schoettgen, vol. i. p. 1178.

Ταῦτα γὰρ ἀλλήλοις ἀντίκειται—"for these are opposed the one to the other." The order of the Received Text is found only in K, L, ℵ, some versions and fathers. But its δέ is supported by A, C, D[3], K, L, ℵ[3], etc., and is accepted by Tischendorf, 7th ed.; while γάρ is found in B, D[1], F, ℵ[1], the Latin versions and fathers, and is preferred by Lachmann. The evidence is pretty fairly balanced. But it may be said on one side, δέ may have been inserted by copyists to avoid the repetition of γάρ; on the other, that γάρ was inserted to prevent the repetition of δέ. The recurrence of δέ, however, would not be so strongly felt as that of γάρ, and would less likely lead to change; moreover, γάρ repeated is a characteristic of the apostle's style. Were the sentence a repetition of the preceding, δέ, as De Wette argues, would be the more appropriate; but it explains, or rather assigns a reason for the reciprocal hostility —"for they are contrary the one to the other." The pronoun ταῦτα is not the τὸ ἐπιθυμεῖν τὴν σάρκα τὸ πνεῦμα (Baumgarten-Crusius, Gwynne), a mere truism, but πνεῦμα and σάρξ themselves. They maintain this reflex warfare, and they cannot coalesce, for they are contrary the one to the other. There is no use in making the clause an explanatory paraphrase (Rückert and Schott), and giving it this sense—"for they are in their nature opposed to one another." But there is at the same time no tautology, and the apostle is describing an actual contest.

Ἵνα μὴ ἃ ἂν θέλητε ταῦτα ποιῆτε—"that ye may not do those things whatsoever ye may wish." For the use of ἄν, see Winer, § 42, 3, *b*; Kühner, § 428, *a*. *Ἵνα* is not to be explained ecbatically, or as denoting simply event—ὥστε μή, as in our version, "so that," and by Luther, Usteri, Baumgarten-Crusius, De Wette, Bisping, Brown, Gwynne, Prof. Lightfoot, and several others. The conjunction is therefore to be taken in its full telic force—the constant mutual contest has this in view—ἵνα. The emphatic ἀλλήλοις of the previous clause governs the interpretation. On either side is the will influenced and counteracted. It is therefore one-sided, on the one part, to give this meaning only in reference to the second clause of the verse; that is, by the struggle of the spirit ye may not do what things your fleshly will would prompt you to do. Such is the view of Chrysostom—"that you may not permit the soul to proceed in its evil desires." He is followed by Theodoret, Œcumenius in one of his explanations, Grotius, Beza, Bull, Neander. Though θέλω may refer to the carnal will in John viii. 44 and in 1 Tim. v. 11, there is no reason to impose such a sense upon it in this place. Dr. Brown, in vindication of the same view, argues that the clause is an illustration of the statement, "If they walked by the spirit, they would not fulfil the lusts of the flesh." But this is to forget the vital connection of the two clauses. Bagge holds the same view, adding, "How any other sense than this is to be extracted from the words of the apostle, I do not comprehend." And it is as one-sided, on the other part, to give the opposite meaning in sole reference to the first clause of the verse; that is, that by the struggle of the flesh ye may not do what the spirit prompts you to do. Such is the opinion of Luther, Calvin, Estius, Usteri, Schott, De Wette, Baumgarten-Crusius, Bisping, and virtually Prof. Lightfoot. Θέλω points indeed, in Rom. vii. 15, etc., which Lightfoot calls "the parallel passage," to the will in its direction toward good, as the context very plainly shows; but there is no such contextual guidance found in this place. Both these interpretations are therefore wrong; for the words are used of actual contest, not of decided mastery on either side. The phrase ἀλλήλοις ἀντίκειται describes not only actual antagonism, but undecided result. It is true in the case of all who are born again, that the conflict ends in the victory of the spirit; but the apostle here does not include the issue, he speaks only of the contest. So that the exegesis is preferable which includes both sides of the statement: "The spirit wrestles against your doing the things which ye would on the impulse of the flesh, and the flesh struggles against your doing the things which ye would on the impulse of the spirit." In this case no inferred ethical notion is attached to θέλητε, and the clause describes the nature of the contest between the flesh and the spirit. Thus Œcumenius in one of his interpretations, Bengel, Meyer, and Winer, who has, *scil.* τὸ πν. *impedit vos quo minus perficiatis* τὰ τῆς σαρκός, *contra* ἡ σάρξ *adversatur vobis ubi* τὰ τοῦ πνεύματος, *peragere studetis*. The idea of Wieseler is somewhat different, and amounts to this, that the man does not do the thing, τοῦτο, which in each particular case he would do. If he wills to do good, he cannot do it; if he wills to do evil, he cannot do it: whatever he does is in opposition to his will. But this view is too precise and definite for the more general picture which the apostle presents. Hofmann's notion is, that the object of the willing is not to be thought of, whether good, or bad, or both; but that, while the contest lasts, your deed is not one of your self-willing, and that when the contest ends, you come to peace when you walk by the Spirit of God. This is true; but it is rather an inference from the statement than a reproduction of the statement itself. The apostle depicts the inner warfare of renewed men, especially in the earlier stages of faith, when the old nature has not been beaten back and conquered, and the new nature has not risen up to the fulness of mastery—when the feebleness of a partial sanctification is unable to work out its purposes, through the many temptations and hindrances yet lurking in the heart. He states a general principle which every one acknowledges as verified in his own experience. The soul in which dwells the Spirit of God is unable to realize its own ideal on the one hand, though it is still approaching it; and on the other hand, it is kept not from sinning, but from falling into many sins to which the power of former habit most especially exposes it. The Galatians were in such a distressing condition at that moment, recurring at the same time to carnal ordinances instead of giving His own place and pre-eminence to the Spirit; going back from their higher experiences to lower and legal institutions. See under iii. 3. Gwynne says somewhat inconsistently, that the experience of ver. 17 is not "of the regenerate character;" but in whom else than a regenerate man does the Spirit of God so dwell? He admits that the experience of the persons spoken of, though it do not belong to the regenerate character, may apply to such as are "babes in Christ;" but the "babe" is surely the child of the new birth.

Ver. 18. *Εἰ δὲ πνεύματι ἄγεσθε, οὐκ ἐστὲ ὑπὸ νόμον*—"But if ye be led by the Spirit, ye are not under the law." *Δέ* introducing a new and contrasted thought: in opposition to this fluctuation of purpose and impotence of will—"but." The dative *πνεύματι* is that of instrument. Winer, § 31, 7; Krüger, § 48, 6, p. 286; Rom. viii. 14; in another aspect, 2 Tim. iii. 6. To be led by the Spirit, in the full sense of it, is to be under His benign and powerful influence in all thoughts, aspirations, and acts,—to be yielded up to His government without reserve, —to have no will without His prompting it, no purpose without His shaping it,—is to be everywhere and in all things in willing submission to His control, and always guarding against any insubordination which may "grieve the Holy Spirit of God." When men are in this condition, it is true of them—"Ye are not under the law;" not, ye will not be as a result, but "ye are"—a parallel condition. To be led by the Spirit is much the same as to walk by the Spirit, ver. 16. In what sense are those led by the Spirit not under the law?

Not, 1. Because you have no need of it—the opinion of

Rückert, Matthies, Schott;—*οὐ δεῖται τῆς ἀπὸ τοῦ νόμου βοηθείας, τίς χρεία νόμου;* (Chrysostom). This idea is not in the full extent of it warranted by anything in the context.

Nor, 2. Because the law is something foreign—an alien principle; for the law of the Spirit is engraven in his heart (Usteri). This is not fully found in the context. Nor is it,

3. Because the law finds in you nothing to forbid or condemn (Meyer, Wieseler, Ellicott). This is a strong statement, and one that actual experience does not verify. If the apostle be supposed to describe an ideal state, in which no element of the flesh had any power, and in which the whole man was under the willing, unresisted government of the Spirit, the statement would be true; for in a perfect saint the law would "have nothing to forbid, because nothing forbidden is desired, and nothing to be condemned, because nothing condemnable is done" (Windischmann). So far, indeed, as a man is guided by the Spirit, so far the law has nothing to condemn in him,—the law cannot be against the fruits of the Spirit. But the apostle is not describing what might be, or what ought to be, but what is. But,

4. As to be under law is to be under its authority, to be in bondage to it, so not to be under it is to be freed from its yoke—*terrente, premente, vindicante* (Estius, Lightfoot, Hofmann). The Galatians were putting themselves again in subjection to law, and ignoring the free government of the Spirit. To be led by the Spirit is incompatible with being under the law. See the beginning of chap. iii. To be under the law is thus to acknowledge its claim, and to seek to obey it in hope of meriting eternal life; but the believer dies to the law, and rises into "newness of life,"—is influenced by the Spirit of God as a guiding power within him; and "where the Spirit of the Lord is, there is liberty." According to Rückert and Schott, one might expect the apostle to say, If ye are led by the Spirit, *perficietis quod tanquam πνευματικοί volueritis.* It serves no purpose to make the verse a parenthesis (Koppe, Flatt). The *σάρξ* and *νόμος* are placed under the same category. In the former verse it was flesh and spirit, here it is spirit and law. For the flesh is in subjection to the law, and the law condemns it. All about it is under the law, which at the same time, so far from checking or subduing, only irritates it, and helps it to develop its

worst manifestations. See under iii. 19. The law is helpless for its deliverance. In this special case believers in Christ entered into a new dispensation, the special characteristic of which was the Spirit, according to Christ's promise; and all who possessed His gracious influences were no longer under the law—a ministration of death, but had come into the possession of spiritual power and freedom,—their will, moved by a higher will, was growing able to realize its own purposes. Or, more generally, believers pass out of the dominion of law—mere law, having died to it; their hearts filled by the Spirit of God are under the government of a new principle. In this sense the law does not condemn them, as they are forgiven, and obedience to it is not the condition of their forgiveness; for there is "no condemnation to them which are in Christ Jesus." Nor are they under the law in regard to their sanctification: as long as they were under it, they were disobeying it, and were slavishly struggling to escape its penalty. Not that they allow themselves to act contrary to it, but a higher power legislates within them, able at the same time to ensure obedience to its edicts,—that obedience being not a servile submission to law, but a willing conformity to the example of Him who loved us and gave Himself for us. They are not under the law to command them sternly; they are guided and influenced by the Spirit of God—a divine law, an enshrined authority within them. There is in these statements no antinomianism, or "going on in sin that grace may abound." The Spirit by whom we are led is the Spirit of holiness, and the flesh is crucified. The difference is as between formal law in outer statute, cold and dead as the tables of stone on which it was engraved, and a law within, a living power, fulfilling itself in love, and gradually working out a universal compliance; for "sin shall not have dominion over you, for ye are not under law, but under grace," and Christ is Sanctification as well as Righteousness. *Οὐ νόμῳ ἀπειλοῦντι δούλοις, πνεύματι δὲ τῷ ἄγοντι τέκνα Θεοῦ.* Cramer's *Catena in loc.* Luther writes, "When I was a monk, I thought by and by that I was utterly cast away, if at any time I felt the lust of the flesh, if I felt any evil emotion. If at that time I had rightly understood those sentences of Paul, I should not have so miserably tormented myself, but should have thought and said to myself, as I commonly now do—Martin, thou shalt not utterly be without sin, for thou hast flesh; thou shalt therefore feel the battle thereof. Despair not, therefore, but resist it strongly."

Ver. 19. *Φανερὰ δέ ἐστιν τὰ ἔργα τῆς σαρκός*—"Now manifest are the works of the flesh;"—*φανερά* having the stress upon it, yet not so as to mean that the works of the flesh are so open that one led by the Spirit does not first need the teaching of the law about them—what to do, what to refrain from, in reference to them (Hofmann). Meyer connects this clause with the one before it, and as a closer explanation of "ye are not under the law"—to show what the sinful principle produces when the Holy Spirit does not lead men; and Ellicott more distinctly calls it "the open difference between the works of the flesh against which the law is ordained, and the fruits of the Spirit." Probably this is too narrow a connection. The flesh is spoken of in the entire short paragraph in its lusting and warrings, in contrast with the Spirit in its wrestlings and leadings. Those who are guided by the Spirit are not as such under the law; but the flesh is under law, under its sentence and dominion: manifest are its works, and the law cannot but condemn them as *ἔργα*—works—done by the evil and unrenewed nature. It is needless to press a contrast in *φανερά* with the fruit of the Spirit as being more hidden, and as needing to be educed and specified. The works of the flesh are notorious, and notoriously of a corrupt origin. *Σάρξ* is, very plainly, greatly more than the sensual part of fallen nature, for many of these *ἔργα* are intellectual or spiritual in nature. See under Eph. ii. 3, and under ver. 16. The apostle proceeds to give a specimen catalogue—

Ἅτινά ἐστι—"of which class are"—*qualia sunt* (Jelf, 816, 5), or less likely, *quippe quæ* (De Wette). They are sins no doubt very common in the Gentile world, and characterized the Galatian people. Thomas Aquinas well says—*cum apostolus in diversis locis diversa vitia et diversimode enumerat, non intendit enumerare omnia vitia ordinate et secundum artem, sed illa tantum in quibus abundant et in quibus excedunt illi, ad quos scribit.*

The Received Text begins with *μοιχεία*, on the authority of D, F, K, L, ℵ[3], the Claromontane Latin, the Gothic, the Phil., Syriac, and many of the Greek and Latin fathers; while F,

G make it plural, with several of the following words, as does Origen. But the preferable reading omits the word, as in A, B, C, ℵ[1], 17, Vul., Cop., etc. Probably the insertion was a reminiscence of Matt. xv. 19, Mark vii. 21.

Πορνεία—"fornication." 2 Cor. xii. 21. Scarcely reckoned a sin in heathen opinion.

Ἀκαθαρσία—"uncleanness," "impurity," including unnatural lusts, so common in Greece and the East. See Döllinger's *The Gentile and the Jew*, vol. i. 377–431; vol. ii. 197, 238, 273, etc., Eng. trans.

Ἀσέλγεια—"lasciviousness"—probably from *ἀ—θέλγω*. Mark vii. 22; 2 Cor. xii. 21; Eph. iv. 19. Donaldson derives it from *a* and *σαλαγ*., foulness. Benfey (*Wurzellexicon, sub voce*) proposes another derivation: from *ἀσ*., satiety, and *ἀλγ*. *ἄλγος*, *die Sucht*. Suidas takes it from *a*, and *Σέλγη*, a Pisidian town of notorious debauchery. It is defined in the *Etymologicum Magnum* as *ἑτοιμότης πρὸς πᾶσαν ἡδονήν*. That it did not signify lasciviousness always, is plain from its use by Demosthenes, where it means insolence. The blow which Meidias gave was in character with *ἡ ἀσέλγεια*—the outrageousness—of the man. *Orat. cont. Meid.* 514, p. 327, vol. i. *Opera*, ed. Schaefer. In a similar way, the term wantonness, which had at first a more general signification, has passed in English into the meaning of open sensuality. It is the self-asserting propensity indulged without check or regard to ordinary propriety, especially in libidinous gratification. Tittmann, *De Synon.* p. 81; Trench, *Synon.* p. 64; Wetstein *in loc.*

Ver. 20. *Εἰδωλολατρεία*—"idolatry"—worship of images or false gods, not a species of the former sensualities (Olshausen), though perhaps not without reference to the idol feasts, which were often scenes of revelry and lust. 1 Cor. v. 11. The worship of God might be mingled with that of the national divinities. Acts xv. 20; compare 2 Kings v. 18. The word was also applied to various sins, as undue devotion to anything to the exclusion of the Highest. See under Eph. v. 5; Col. iii. 5.

Φαρμακεία—not poisoning, or the use of *φίλτρα* (Plat. *Leg.* xi. 12), but, from its connection with the previous sin, "sorcery," or, as defined by Suidas, *γοητεία*. It is often used in this sense in the Sept.: Ex. vii. 11, 22, viii. 18, Isa. xlvii. 9, 12; and in the Apocrypha: Wisdom xii. 4, xviii. 13. *Φάρμακον* is found also in 2 Kings ix. 22, and along with *πορνεῖαι* is ascribed to Jezebel. The words again occur twice over, Nah. iii. 4, in a description of the sin and doom of Nineveh. Comp. Rev. ix. 21, xviii. 23, xxi. 8, xxii. 15. The term, from its association with idolatry, denotes incantation—superstitious dealings with the spirit-world. These practices were common in Asia Minor. Acts xix. 18.

Ἔχθραι—"hatreds"—breaches of the law of love, apt to deepen into malignity. Sept. 1 Macc. xiii. 6, 2 Macc. iv. 3.

Ἔρις—"strife." Codices C, D[2, 3], E, F, K, L have the plural; the singular being found A, B, D[1], א, and it is preferred by Lachmann and Tischendorf. Rom. xiii. 13. In 2 Cor. xii. 20 the three next words occur in the same order. In such strife, love by which the law is fulfilled becomes wholly lost, for it springs out of these "hatreds," and is nursed by them.

Ζῆλος. Codices C, D[2,3], K, L, א, and very many versions and fathers, have the plural; but B, D[1], E (*ζήλους*, a misprint, being read in F) have the singular, and it is found in several of the fathers. Amidst such variations, it is hard to say whether the singular or plural ought to be adopted. Only there was some temptation from the following plurals to change these singular forms into plural ones for the sake of uniformity. *Ζῆλος* is used in a good sense, John ii. 17, Rom. x. 2, 2 Cor. ix. 2; and also among the classics: *ζῆλος τῶν ἀρίστων*, Lucian, *Adv. Indoct.* 17; *ζῆλος καὶ μίμησις*, Herodian, ii. 4. But here it signifies rivalry, jealousy in the dark sense, mingled with envy (Rom. xiii. 13; 1 Cor. iii. 3; 2 Cor. xii. 20), and burning like fire: *πυρὸς ζῆλος*, Heb. x. 27; Sept. *ἐν πυρὶ ζήλου*, Zeph. i. 18, iii. 8, as applied to God; also *ζῆλον πικρόν*, Jas. iii. 14. Trench, *Syn.* p. 99. See under iv. 17.

Θυμοί—"outbursts of anger." The word comes from *θύω*, and it, according to Donaldson (*Cratyl.* § 471), from *θε*, to place, as in *τίθημι*, which, on the principle that "the same root may suggest contrasted ideas," signifies also to run, as in *θέειν*, like "fast" in English, which means both "fixed" and "rapid." The noun therefore means—impulse toward a thing; and in Plato, *De Republica* 440, it signifies the "will"—"disposition" in general, *Legg.* v. 731, B, though he explains it as signifying anger in the *Cratylus*, 419, E: *θυμὸς δὲ ἀπὸ τῆς θύσεως καὶ ζέσεως τῆς ψυχῆς ἔχοι ἂν τοῦτο τὸ ὄνομα.* See Stallbaum's note. It is therefore more demonstrative than *inimicitia hominis acerbi et iracundi*, for it is *excandescentia* (*quum bitumen et sulphur additum est, excandescet*). Cato, *R. R.* 95. The plural *θυμοί* denotes here, concrete manifestations of the abstract sin. Lobeck, *Soph. Ajax*, p. 274, 3d ed. Similarly *σοφίαι*, Aristoph. *Ran.* 688; *φιλοσοφίαι*, Plato, *Theaet.* 172, C; *θάνατοι, αἵματα*, etc., Bernhardy, pp. 62, 63. *Θυμοί* are those explosions of rage that proceed from a vindictive heart and an ungovernable temper. See under Eph. iv. 31.

Ἐριθεῖαι—"caballings." The word is not derived from *ἔρις*, though both may come from the root *ἔρω, ἔρδω.* It is allied to *ἐριθεύω* as *δουλεία* to *δουλεύω.* The Homeric *ἔριθος* is a day-labourer, one who works for hire—used of reapers and slaves, and is connected by some with *ἔριον*, wool. It means first of all, labour for hire, then intriguing or canvassing for office—*καὶ γὰρ ἡ ἐριθεία εἴρηται ἀπὸ τῆς μισθοῦ δόσεως*, Aristot. *Pol.* v. 2, 3; Suidas, *sub voce δεκάζεσθαι.* It then comes naturally to signify party-spirit,—thus Hesychius, *Ἠριθεύετο . . . ἐφιλονείκει*,—and is opposed to *χρηστομαθεία* in Ignat. *Ep. ad Philad.* § 8. In the New Testament it is opposed to *ἀγάπη*, Phil. i. 16, 17; in Jas. iii. 14, 16 it is coupled with *ζῆλος* as here, and as something more active and mischievous, leading to *ἀκαταστασία*; in Phil. ii. 3, with *κενοδοξία*, vainglory, which often prompts to it, and as opposed to *σύμψυχοι, τὸ ἓν φρονοῦντες*, and to *τῇ ταπεινοφροσύνῃ ἀλλήλους ἡγούμενοι ὑπερέχοντας ἑαυτῶν.* It stands between *θυμοὶ* and *καταλαλιαί* in 2 Cor. xii. 20. See Rom. ii. 8. It is thus dark, selfish, unscrupulous intriguing, that alike sacrifices peace and truth to gain its end. See under Phil. i. 17.

Διχοστασίαι—"divisions," the decided and violent taking of a side on selfish and unyielding grounds.

Αἱρέσεις—"factions," the result of the former—divisions organized into factions, but without the ecclesiastical meaning which a Lapide, Crocius, and others assign to the term. The word is applied to the party of the Sadducees, Acts v. 17; to that of the Pharisees, Acts xv. 5; to that of the Christians—*τῶν Ναζωραίων αἱρέσεως*, Acts xxiv. 5; and in 1 Cor. xi. 19 it is applied to parties within the church. The Judaizers were producing such results in the Galatian churches by their self-willed and bitter reactionary agitations.

Ver. 21. *Φθόνοι, φόνοι*—"Envyings, murders." The second term *φόνοι* is omitted in B, ℵ, several cursives and fathers, Jerome; but it is found in A, C, D, F, G, K, L, majority of MSS., and in the Latin and Syriac versions. It is admitted by Lachmann, but rejected as doubtful by Tischendorf. The omission was probably owing to the similarity of sound (Gleichklang); but the paronomasia is in the apostle's style. Rom. i. 29, *φθόνου, φόνου*; Winer, § 68; *φθόνου, φόνου τε*, Eurip. *Troades*, 770–1; Bötticher, *de Paronom.* Lipsiæ 1828.

Φθόνος—envy—is the desire to appropriate what another possesses. It has no redeeming feature about it: *ἐπιεικές ἐστιν ὁ ζῆλος καὶ ἐπιεικῶν, τὸ δὲ φθονεῖν φαῦλον καὶ φαύλων*, Arist. *Rhet.* ii. 9, 10; or *πρῶτον μὲν ζῆλος ἀπὸ ζήλου δὲ φθόνος*, Plato, *Men.* 242; Trench, *Synon.* 1st ser. p. 99.

Φόνοι—"murders"—the sudden or the deliberate sacrifice of any human life that stands in the way of self-advancement, or it may be a deed of vengeance.

Μέθαι, κῶμοι—"drunkenness, carousals." "Drunkenessis, immesurable etyngis" (Wycliffe); "ebrieties, commessations" (Rheims); "dronkenes, glottony" (Genevan). The last Greek term is the more comprehensive one. Judith xiii. 15, *ἐν ταῖς μέθαις αὐτοῦ.* In Rom. xiii. 13 the words are joined; also in Dio Cassius, *οὐδὲν ἄλλο ἢ μέθαι τε καὶ κῶμοι*, p. 272, *Opera*, vol. ii. ed. Bekker. The second term—in Latin *comissationes*—is described by Hesychius as being *ἀσελγῆ ᾄσματα, πορνικά, συμπόσια, ᾠδαί.* So Plato, *Theaet.* 173, D; Herod. i. 121. See Becker's *Charicles*, vi., and *Gallus*, x. Compare Isa. v. 11, 12, Amos vi. 4–6, 1 Thess. v. 7, 1 Pet. iv. 3.

And not only these sins, but—

Καὶ τὰ ὅμοια τούτοις—"and such like." Luther says—*addit et iis similia quia quis omnem lernam carnalis vitæ recenseat?* Ed. 1519.

These works of the flesh have been often divided into four classes. Any classification or system, however, is scarcely to be expected; but each term of the catalogue may have been suggested by some law of association, especially as some of the terms are similarly arranged in other places. In the first class are sensual sins—fornication, impurity, wantonness; in the second class are sins of superstition—idolatry and sorcery; in the third class, sins of malice and social disorder—hatred, strife, jealousy, wraths, caballing, divisions, heresies, envying, murders; and in the fourth class are sins of personal excess—drunkenness and revellings. In the first class, the first term, which has a distinct meaning, may have suggested the other and allied vices—miscellaneous and grosser aspects of forbidden indulgence. The two terms of the second class are somewhat similar,—the first more precise in meaning, and the second more comprehensive—all occult dealings with the powers of evil. In the third class there is a climactic enumeration—hatreds ripening into strife; jealousy venting itself in passionate outbursts; cabals yet darker and more selfish; divisions, the result of deepening hostility; envyings quite fiendish in nature; and murders—the extreme result, and no uncommon thing in such countries, to obtain an end and consummate an intrigue by the removal of a rival. In the fourth class are first the simple term drunkenness, and the more inclusive term after it, referring either to scenes of dissipation so gay and wanton, or to orgies so gross and sensual, that they may not be described; and the terms stand each in its own prominence, unconnected by any particle,—an asyndeton common before such phrases as *τὰ τοιαῦτα, οἱ ἄλλοι*. Jelf, § 792, 2.

Ἃ προλέγω ὑμῖν, καθὼς καὶ προεῖπον—"concerning which I tell you before, as also I did foretell you." Engl. Ver.: "as I have also told you in time past." The *καί* is not in B, F, א[1], nor in the Vulgate, and is bracketed by Lachmann; but it is retained on the authority of A, C, D, K, L, א[4], almost all MSS., and the majority of versions. The *ἅ* is not governed by *πράσσοντες* (Olshausen, Schott), but by *προλέγω*, as an accusative of contents (*Inhalt*), and may be resolved by "*was anbetrifft*"—*quod attinet ad ea quæ*. Scheuerlein, p. 55; Thucyd. ii. 62, and Poppo's note. The anacoluthon and the position of the relative, used in a sense absolutely, emphasize it. John viii. 54. The *προ* in both verbs is "beforehand"—not before they come to light (Matthies); nor does the *προ* in *προεῖπον* mean "already" (Baumgarten-Crusius), but before the event, 1 Thess. iii. 4, or the day of retribution. He gives them a present fore-warning, ere it is too late; and this was by no means the first warning he had given them—"as also I did foretell you;" that is, when he had been with them; both during his first and second sojourn, he had forewarned them as he now is writing to them. The theme of forewarning then and now was—

Ὅτι οἱ τὰ τοιαῦτα πράσσοντες βασιλείαν Θεοῦ οὐ κληρονομήσουσι—"that they who are doing such things shall not inherit the kingdom of God." The contents of the *προλέγω* are prefaced by *ὅτι*, and described by *τὰ τοιαῦτα*—such things as these—the sins referred to and all similar sins, the article *τά* specifying the things as a class; "*de toto genere eorum qui tales sunt, usurpatur.*" Kühner, *Xen. Mem.* i. 5, 2. The verb *ποιεῖν* and *πράσσειν* may sometimes be distinguished, as John iii. 20, 21; Xen. *Mem.* ii. 9, 4; but as, with these exceptions and John v. 29, the verb occurs only in Luke and Paul, and characterizes their style, it would be wrong to lay any stress on its use. The persons described are they who are doing and continuing to do such things, and are not *λυπηθέντες εἰς μετάνοιαν*—they shall not inherit the kingdom of God. 2 Cor. v. 10; Rom. xiv. 10. They prove by their perseverance in such practices that they are not led by the Spirit; that they are not justified through faith; that they are not children, and therefore not heirs of the promise: 1 Cor. vi. 9, 10. See under Eph. v. 4. Heaven, according to the popular adage, is a prepared place for a prepared people. The kingdom of Christ exists on earth, with Him as its Head and Defence, and only those who are qualified, through a change inwrought and sustained by His Spirit, are admitted into it in its ultimate and glorious form in heaven. The inheritor of the kingdom must be brought into congenial harmony with its occupations and enjoyments. They "which do such things" prove their want of meetness "for the inheritance of the saints in light," and therefore cannot enter it; it has no attraction for them, and they could find no enjoyment in it. See under Col. i. 12.

Ver. 22. *Ὁ δὲ καρπὸς τοῦ πνεύματος*—"But the fruit of the Spirit,"—passing by *δέ* to this contrasted catalogue. Both *ἔργα* and *καρπός* are, as Meyer says, in themselves *voces mediæ*, no ethical quality being essentially attached to them. Nay, we find them reversed in Sept. Prov. x. 16, *ἔργα δικαίων—καρποὶ δὲ ἀσεβῶν.* Still one may suppose that the terms are here changed for good reason, inasmuch as Paul uses *καρπός* on the good side; and, as Ellicott remarks, even in Rom. vi. 21 it means, "what good result had ye in those things whereof ye are ashamed?" If, then, there be an intended distinction, what is it? Not because those graces are regarded more as feelings or dispositions than as acts (Rückert, and virtually Hofmann); nor because they are beneficent and delightful (Winer, Usteri, Schott, Alford); but because they spring out of one living root, as the singular seems also to indicate. The *καρπός* may show itself in *ἔργα* which in their collective form make up the *καρπός*; but here it is regarded in its unity of source and development. Its origin is "the Spirit;" not man's spirit, or the new and better mode of thinking and feeling to which men are formed by the Holy Spirit (Brown), but the Holy Spirit Himself, the Author of all spiritual good. Those who are led by the Spirit not only do not do the works of the flesh, but they bring forth the fruit of the Spirit. It is wrong and forced to seek a detailed antagonism in the two lists. The apostle's eagerness did not give him leisure to arrange such parallels or work out symmetrical antitheses.

The first of the graces is *ἀγάπη*—"love"—the root of all the other graces,—greater than faith and hope, for "God is Love;" love to God and all that bears his image, being the essence of the first and second tables of the law,—all the other graces being at length absorbed by it as the flower is lost in the fruit. 1 Cor. xiii.; Rom. xii. 9.

Χαρά—"joy." Joy is based on the possession of present good, and here means that spiritual gladness which acceptance with God and change of heart produce. For it is conscious elevation of character, the cessation of the conflict in its earlier stage (v. 16, 17), the opening up of a new world, and the hope of final perfection and victory. It is opposed to dulness, despondency, indifference, and all the distractions and remorses which are wrought by the works of the flesh. This joy is the spring of energy, and praise wells out of the joyful heart. Where the heart is gladness, the instinctive dialect is song. May not the joy of restoration at least equal the joy of continuous innocence? It is therefore here not merely nor prominently *Mitfreude*, joy in the happiness of others (Grotius, Zachariæ, Stolz, Koppe, Borger, Winer, Usteri, Hofmann), nor joy as opposed to moroseness (Calvin, Michaelis), though these aspects or manifestations are not excluded. This joy is "joy in the Holy Ghost" (Rom. xiv. 17), the "joy of faith" (Phil. i. 25), "joy of the Spirit" (1 Thess. i. 6), "joy in the Lord" (Phil. iii. 1); and the welcome addressed to the faithful servant is, "Enter thou into the joy of thy Lord."

Εἰρήνη—"peace" with God primarily, and peace within them; and not simply so, but concord—peace with those around them. See under Phil. iv. 7.

Μακροθυμία—"long-suffering" (longanimitie, Rheims)—is opposed to *shortness* of temper—*ὀξυθυμία*, Eurip. *Andr.* 728. It enables us to bear injury without at once avenging ourselves: *βραδὺς εἰς ὀργήν*, Jas. i. 19; 1 Cor. xiii. 4. See under Eph. iv. 2.

Χρηστότης—"kindness"—occurs in Paul's writings only, as in 2 Cor. vi. 6, where also it is joined to the previous term; in Tit. iii. 4, where, along with *φιλανθρωπία*, it is ascribed to God our Saviour; and in Rom. xi. 22, where, along with *ἀποτομία*, it is also ascribed to Him. Compare Rom. iii. 12; Eph. ii. 7; Col. iii. 12; Sept. Ps. cxliv. 7, lxvii. 11. Plato defines it as *ἤθους ἀπλαστία μετ' εὐλογιστίας*, *Defin.* p. 412, E. Phavorinus also defines it as *εὐσπλαγχνία, ἡ πρὸς τοὺς πέλας συνδιάθεσις, τὰ αὐτοῦ ὡς οἰκεῖα ἰδιοποιουμένη*. The meaning is kindness—gentleness, affability, the benign heart and the soft answer, "the gentleness of Christ;" or a serene, loving, and sympathizing temper, the fruit of that Spirit who descended in the form of a dove upon our great Exemplar, and abode upon Him.

Ἀγαθωσύνη—"goodness." The word is Hellenistic (Thom. Mag. p. 921), and occurs in Rom. xv. 14, Eph. v. 9, 2 Thess. i. 11. It is difficult to distinguish it from the previous term. Jerome calls the first *benignitas sive suavitas*, and the second *bonitas*, differing from the former *quia potest bonitas esse tristior et fronte severis moribus irrugata, bene quidem facere et præstare quod poscitur*. It may signify beneficence, specially *Gutigkeit*, (Ewald, Wieseler)—kindness in actual manifestation. 2 Chron. xxiv. 16; Eccl. vii. 15.

Πίστις—"faith" ("faythfulnes," Tyndale, Cranmer)—not simply faith in God in the theological sense (Jerome, Theophylact),—that being implied, as the Spirit dwells only in those who have faith,—nor merely fidelity or good faith (Meyer), nor veracity (Winer); but trust generally, trustfulness toward God and towards man. Confidence in God, in all His promises, and under all His dispensations; and a spirit of unsuspicious and generous confidence towards men,—not moved by doubts and jealousies, nor conjuring up possible causes of distrust, and treasuring up sad lessons from previous instances of broken plight. 1 Cor. xiii. 7.

Πραΰτης—"meekness." The word—so written in A, B, C, ℵ—is sometimes spelled *πραότης*, as in D, E, F, G, K, L. The last is the more Attic form (Photii *Lex.* 447, ed. Porson), though the other may be the earlier. Lobeck, *Phryn.* 403; Lipsius, *Gramm. Untersuch.* pp. 7, 8. See also A. Buttmann, p. 23. It is also sometimes spelled with *iota* subscribed in both forms, but not by Lachmann and Tischendorf. This Christian grace is universal in its operation—submission Godward, meekness manward, which seems to be its special reference. Compare 2 Cor. xi. 1, Matt. v. 5, xi. 29. The meek man bears himself mildly—submissively—in all things, "like a weaned child;" neither arraigns God, nor avenges himself on man. See under Eph. iv. 2; Ecclus. xlv. 4; and the definition in Stobæus, *Flor.* i. 18, p. 8, vol. i. ed. Gassford.

'Εγκράτεια—"temperance"—self-control—the holding in of passions and appetites, distinguished by Diogenes Laertius from *σωφροσύνη* in that it bridles *ἐπιθυμίας σφοδράς*, the stronger desires. Suidas defines it as *ἡ ἕξις ἀήττητος ἡδονῶν.* Acts xxiv. 25; 2 Pet. i. 6; Sept. Sir. xviii. 30. The word is to be taken in its widest significance, and not principally in reference to sexual sin—as Origen: *τὸ δεδομένον ἀπὸ Θεοῦ σῶμα ἄῤῥεν τηρητέον*, *Comm. in Matt.* vol. i. p. 369, ed. Huet. This virtue guards against all sins of personal excess, and is specially opposed to drunkenness and revellings as works of the flesh.

The Cod. D[1], F, the Vulgate, and Claromontane Latin, with some of the Latin fathers, but not Jerome or Augustine, add to the catalogue *ἁγνεία*, *castitas.* Indeed there are twelve terms in the Vulgate for the nine of the Greek text—*patientia, modestia, castitas*—as if it had read *ὑπομονή* and *ἐπιείκεια.* These fruits of the Spirit may be divided into three clusters, with three terms under each. The first three are more distinctive in character, yet of true individual experience—love, joy, peace—graces peculiar to Christianity; the next three are social in their nature, and are climactic illustrations of the command, "Thou shalt love thy neighbour as thyself"—long-suffering, kindness, beneficence; and the three occurring last—trustfulness, meekness, temperance—are perhaps selected and put into contrast with opposite vices prevailing in the Galatian community.

The apostle adds—

Ver. 23. *Κατὰ τῶν τοιούτων οὐκ ἔστιν νόμος*—"Against such there is no law." For *τὰ τοιαῦτα*, see under ver. 21. A similar catalogue from Aristotle occurs in Stobæus, containing *χρηστότης, ἐπιείκεια, εὐγνωμοσύνη, ἐλπὶς ἀγαθή*, and ending with *καὶ τὰ τοιαῦτα. Florileg.* i. 18, p. 16, vol. i. ed. Gassford. The gender of *τοιούτων* is matter of dispute. Is the meaning, "against such" persons as possess the fruit of the Spirit there is no law? or is it, "against such" graces there is no law? The masculine is preferred by the Greek fathers, by Erasmus, Grotius, Bengel, Koppe, Rückert, Hofmann, and Gwynne. But there is no immediate personal reference in the context. *Τὰ τοιαῦτα* are naturally the virtues or elements of Spirit-fruit which have now been enumerated, and all such—all like them; and they apparently correspond to the *τὰ τοιαῦτα* of the 21st verse: so that the neuter is rightly preferred. Those who adopt the masculine reference explain the phrase thus: either such do not need the law, or such the law does not condemn (Rückert, Hofmann). A similar phrase is used by Aristotle: *κατὰ δὲ τῶν τοιούτων οὐκ ἔστι νόμος, αὐτοὶ γάρ εἰσι νόμος, Pol.* iii. 13, 14, p. 83, vol. x. *Opera*, ed. Bekker. Similar explanations have been given with the neuter reference.

1. Some introduce a meiosis, as Beza, Estius, Flatt, and De Wette—*non adversatur, sed commendat*—so far is the law from forbidding such graces, that it much more bids or enjoins them.

2. Winer and Schott thus interpret: "The law is not against those virtues—it has only a negative power to restrain the outbreaks of a sinful will; but in the fruits of the Spirit there is nothing to restrain, and therefore no law exists against them."

3. Usteri and Matthies understand it thus: "Where such

virtues exist, the law is superfluous"—an inference rather than an explanation.

4. But the simplest and easiest reference and meaning are preferable—"against such there is no law," *i.e.* to condemn them. Meyer takes the clause as explanatory of the latter part of ver. 18: "ye are not under the law, the law has no power over you." Probably this may be included, but the direct meaning is, that these graces are condemned by no law; and you may say that this happens, first, from their very nature, and secondly, because, as the fruit of the Spirit, they belong to those who are led by that Spirit, and therefore are not under the law. 1 Tim. i. 9, 10.

Ver. 24. *Οἱ δὲ τοῦ Χριστοῦ* ['*Ιησοῦ*] *τὴν σάρκα ἐσταύρωσαν*—"Now they who are Christ's crucified the flesh." The Received Text is found in D, F, G, L, in the Latin versions, and in many of the versions and fathers. On the other hand, *τοῦ Χριστοῦ 'Ιησοῦ* is found in A, B, C, א (the last adding also *τοῦ κυρίου*, which has been erased), and in some of the versions, as the Ethiopic and Coptic, and in Cyril and Augustine. The order is indeed unusual. The testimony of these old codices is, however, of great weight. Where a similar phrase occurs, as in Acts xvii. 3, Eph. iii. 1, there are also various readings, as might be expected. The δέ is not resumptive of ver. 18 (Bengel), nor yet of ver. 16 (De Wette), nor is it for *γάρ* (Beza). It introduces a new or contrasted view of the subject. The works of the flesh, when the flesh is unchecked, exclude from heaven, but the fruit of the Spirit has no law against it. The Spirit indeed is lusted against by the flesh; and he adds, "now," or "but they who belong to Christ [Jesus] crucified the flesh," and the Spirit has therefore unresisted predominance. Hofmann also connects it closely with the previous verse, and with *τοιούτων* as masculine. Chrysostom inserts a question: they might object, "And who is such a man as this?" this verse being the answer to the objecting interrogation.

The genitive *τοῦ Χριστοῦ* ['*Ιησοῦ*] is that of possession: they belong to Him as bought by Him, delivered by Him, and possessed by Him, through His Spirit producing such fruit. "Christ liveth in me." They who are Christ's cannot but be characterized by the fruit of the Spirit, for they crucified the flesh,—not "have crucified" (Luther, Matthies, Schott), the aorist referring to an indefinite past time, when the action was done. The action is described and then dismissed (Ellicott). That the effects of the crucifixion still remained, is indeed very plain, but the aorist does not say so; it puts it only as a single and separate fact. Donaldson, p. 411. Nor does it mean *quæ fieri soleant*—such a meaning assigned to the aorist is wrong—*vulgo putatur*. Wex, *Soph. Antig.* vol. i. p. 326. The flesh is not the flesh of Christ, as Origen and some of the fathers supposed, meaning, either because our bodies are members of Christ, and therefore one with Him, or *corporea scripturæ intelligentia quæ nunc caro Christi appellatur;* or, as Jerome gives it, *Crucifixit Christi carnem, qui non juxta carnem historiæ militat, sed spiritum allegoriæ sequitur præviantem.* The flesh was crucified once for all when they believed, and it remains dead; it has lost its living mastery through a violent and painful death. They were crucified with Christ in a somewhat different sense, when with Him and in His death they died to the law. The apostle says, "I have been crucified with Christ;" but that *I* includes more than the σάρξ, which was also nailed to the cross. See under ii. 20. But here it is said that they crucified the flesh, their old unrenewed nature: when they believed and were converted, they inflicted death upon it. Col. iii. 5; Rom. vi. 6. In and through union with Christ, believers themselves die to the law and escape its penalty; but at the same time the flesh is also crucified, its supremacy is overthrown. Thus justification and sanctification are alike secured to believers through their union with Christ in His sufferings and death.

Σὺν τοῖς παθήμασι καὶ ταῖς ἐπιθυμίαις—"along with the passions and lusts." See under Col. iii. 5; 1 Thess. iv. 5; Rom. vi. 5, vii. 5. *Παθήματα*, allied to πάθος, are mental states more passive in character, and ἐπιθυμίαι are desires more active in pursuit, in reference to all those spheres of forbidden gratification to which the θυμός is ever prompting. It has attached to it such epithets as κακή, Col. iii. 5, σαρκικαί, 1 Pet. ii. 11; and such genitives as τῆς ἀπάτης, Eph. iv. 22, φθορᾶς, 2 Pet. i. 4. Trench, *Synon.* p. 161, 2d ser.

Ver. 25. *Εἰ ζῶμεν πνεύματι, πνεύματι καὶ στοιχῶμεν*—"If we live by the Spirit, by the Spirit also let us walk." The ζῶμεν has the stress in the first clause, and the repeated πνεύματι has it in the second. There is no connective particle, the asyndeton making the inferential counsel based on the previous condition assumed to be true, all the more vivid.

The dative πνεύματι is not that of manner—"if we be spiritually affected." Middleton (*Greek Art.* 349), who adds, "I understand it as a caution against the mischievous consequences of trusting to the all-sufficiency of faith." But such a dilution robs both verse and context of the contrast between σάρξ and πνεύμα; the Spirit being represented, too, as the source of life, of guidance, and of all superiority to the works of the flesh.

Nor is the dative to be rendered "to the Spirit" (Prof. Lightfoot), as in the clauses τῇ ἁμαρτίᾳ ἀποθανεῖν, Rom. vi. 2, 11, or κυρίῳ ζῶμεν, Rom. xiv. 6, 8 (Fritzsche on Romans, vol. iii. p. 142); for in that case it would not differ materially in meaning from the clause which follows it as the inference,—to live to Him and to walk in Him, being only differing phases of the same relation. They are all but identical, and the one could not therefore form a ground for the other. The Spirit is plainly viewed here as having so close a connection with our life, that it forms the basis of a solemn injunction, which no one recognising such a connection would think of gainsaying.

The dative is probably instrumental (Rückert, Schott, and Hofmann), or as Meyer calls it, ablatival. Winer, § 31, 7. Thus, the first dative may be used somewhat loosely, from correspondence with the second, in an injunction so brief and distinct, and in which the very order of the words imparts point and emphasis. The second dative, as the usage of the verb indicates, is that of norm, as in ver. 16. Fritzsche gives it in paraphrase: *Si vitam spiritui divino debemus, ad spiritum etiam dirigamus vitam*—*Ad Rom.* vol. iii. p. 142; A. Buttmann, p. 160, 22, *b*. The verb signifies to advance in order or in a row—in battle order, and hence, ethically, to walk according to rule; perhaps, from its literal meaning, having the sense of a more definite walk than the vaguer περιπατεῖν. Polyb. xxviii. 5, 6; Sext. Empir. p. 640, ed. Bekker; Phil. iii. 16; Rom. iv. 12; and Acts xxi. 24, where an explanatory participle is used instead of a dative.

The apostle announces a general maxim, and puts himself among those whom he addressed. He takes for granted that his first principle will not be disputed, that the one source of life is the Spirit; and his argument then is: If we live by the Spirit, if the flesh being crucified there springs up a new life, and if that inner life be originated and fostered by the Spirit, let our whole conduct be in harmony with the character and workings of this holy Life-giver. Should not the outer life be in unison with its inner source? Should not the fruit of the Spirit adorn him who lives by the Spirit? It would be grievous inconsistency for us to admit as an undoubted fact that we live by the Spirit, and yet to be producing the works of the flesh. Though we had the law, we could not live up to the law, the *σάρξ* was only irritated and condemned by it. But with this higher principle of life within us, let us walk according to His guidance and strength. He gives ability to follow His impulses, for He enjoins no duty for the performance of which He does not implant sufficient grace. Nay, if we walk by the Spirit, it then becomes an impossibility for us to fulfil the lusts of the flesh: ver. 16.

Ver. 26. *Μὴ γίνωμεθα κενόδοξοι*—"Let us not become vainglorious." The verb is to be taken with its proper significance; not vaguely, let us not be, but "let us not become"—Vulgate, *efficiamur*—not *simus*, as Beza and Calvin. Beza's dogmatic objection to *efficiamur* is, that men are born such by nature; but, as Meyer remarks, believers have been born again. They were in circumstances and under temptations by which they might easily become vainglorious. In the verb itself and its person, by which the apostle classes himself among them, is a spirit of mildness in rebuke and warning. *Κενοδοξία* is glory without basis, conceit, and is defined by Suidas *ματαία τις περὶ ἑαυτοῦ οἴησις*. See under Phil. ii. 3, where it is opposed to *ταπεινοφροσύνη*; Wisd. xiv. 14; Polyb. xxvii. 6–12, xxxix. 1, 1; 2 Macc. v. 9. This vainglory is unworthy of us. 1 Cor. i. 31, "He that glorieth, let him glory in the Lord." 2 Cor. x. 17. The exhortation of the apostle is general, and is not to be confined to Judaizing sympathizers on the one side (Theophylact), nor, on the other side, to those remaining true to the apostle (Olshausen)—their vainglory resting on their continued faithfulness. *Quisque gloriæ cupidus est . . . a vera gloria discedit* (Calvin).

Ἀλλήλους προκαλούμενοι—"provoking one another"—as Chrysostom adds: *εἰς φιλονεικίας καὶ ἔρεις*. The verb means to invite or challenge to combat. Xen. *Cyr.* i. 4, 4; Diodor. Sic. iv. 58; often in Homer, *Il.* iii. 432, vi. 50, 218, 285; Polyb. i. 46, 11; Wetstein *in loc.* Such provocation was the natural result of that vainglory against which he is warning.

'*Αλλήλοις φθονοῦντες*—"envying one another." B, G, several MSS. and Greek fathers, read *ἀλλήλους*, which is adopted by Lachmann and Lightfoot; but the text is supported by A, C, D, F, K, L, א, etc. The other reading may have arisen from a careless repetition of the previous *ἀλλήλους*. The verb *φθονεῖν*, which does not occur elsewhere, governs here the dative of person. There are, however, other constructions in classic writers. Kühner, § 578. The provocations referred to excited responsive envyings; the strong challenged the weak, and the weak envied them in turn. Perhaps, however, it is too precise to make such a distinction, for those even of the same party might occasionally provoke and envy one another.

The apostle in this verse "works around," as Lightfoot observes, to the subject of ver. 15. The divisions in the church were naturally destructive of brother-love, and showed themselves in those works of the flesh—hatred, strife, jealousy, angers, intrigues, divisions, separations, envyings. But against these are ranged the fruit of the Spirit—love, joy, peace, long-suffering, gentleness, goodness, trustfulness—graces specially needed by the Galatian churches in this crisis, as they were tempted to vainglory, to challenge and envy one another; the *φθονοῦντες* of this verse recalling the *φθόνοι* of ver. 21.

CHAPTER VI

SOME begin this chapter with the previous verse; such as Meyer, Olshausen, Brown, and Hofmann. But there is really no ground for such a division. Nay, while there is a succession of hortatory statements down to ver. 10, there is a change of person in this first verse; while *ἀδελφοί* often marks a transition to a new subject, though, from the nature of the case, it is here closely connected with the preceding paragraph. So much statement about the Spirit as our life, and about its fruit, may have suggested the appeal to the *πνευματικοί*, and the use of that term. At the same time, the restoration of a fallen brother in a spirit of meekness, is a duty quite opposed to that vainglory which the apostle has been condemning.

Ver. 1. The apostle, in drawing to a close, becomes the more affectionate and direct in his practical counsels and warnings; and he calls them again, in pointed and prominent love, *ἀδελφοί*, the emphasis being on this term, as if the clouds were lifting and the sun were shedding a parting ray.

Ἐὰν καὶ προλημφθῇ ἄνθρωπος ἐν τινὶ παραπτώματι—"if a man be even surprised in any trespass." The phrase *ἐὰν καί* does not put a case for mere illustration, like *καὶ εἰ*. Klotz-Devarius, vol. ii. p. 519. For the Alexandrian spelling of the verb, as supported by the best MSS., see Tischendorf's *Prolegomena*, p. xlvii. The meaning of the verb has been variously given, the difficulty lying in the reference indicated by *προ*.

1. Some deny, indeed, that the meaning of the verb is at all modified by the *προ*; at all events, the Greek fathers make no account of it: *οὐκ εἶπεν ἐὰν πράξῃ, ἀλλ' ἐὰν προληφθῇ, τουτέστιν ἐὰν συναρπαγῇ* (Chrysostom). But the influence of *προ* is felt in the signification of the verb, which is, to take before a certain time, or before another; to get the start, or in some

way to anticipate, etc. The Vulgate renders, *etsi præoccupatus*.

2. What may be called the incidental temporal reference may be discarded, either that προ means *before* the arrival of the epistle—*anteaquam hæc epistola ad vos veniat* (Grotius), or to a repetition of an offence committed *before—iterum peccantem* (Winer, Matthies), or that the λαμβάνεσθαι takes place *before* the καταρτίζειν (Olshausen). In the first two cases the emphasis of καὶ προλημφθῇ is not brought out; and the last opinion is a truism, for it is implied in the very terms of the injunction. The idea of Bengel, that the meaning is, *ante captus fuisse dicatur, qui nos, non laesus, laesit*—who injures us *before* we injured him—is quite foreign to the context.

3. The most common mode of interpretation has been to give the προ the notion of "*before* one is aware," as in the English Version, "if a man be overtaken," be surprised, by a fault, before he has time to think of it. This idea is implied in the interpretation of the Greek fathers, and is followed by most: *Si quis improviso (citius quam expectaverit s. quam sibi cavere potuerit) peccato quodam fuerit abreptus;* or as Thomas Aquinas, *imprudenter et ex surreptione lapsus*. That the verb may bear such a meaning is not denied, but ἐν must then be regarded as instrumental or local (Rückert)—taken as if in a snare. Such a meaning evidently extenuates the sin referred to, and such an extenuation is contended for by this class of commentators. But such an extenuation diminishes also the necessity for so solemn an injunction as to restoration. A man surprised or betrayed suddenly into sin has an apology which in itself contains a claim for restoration, and it scarcely needed an admonition to remind the spiritual members of this duty. Besides, the καί has its intensive force, and προλημφθῇ is emphatic in position, indicating that the offence or sin is something which in its nature might repel sympathy and preclude restoration.

4. So that we prefer to take the verb as meaning, "if a man be surprised in a fault," not into a fault—caught in it, not by it—*overtaken* in a fault, by detection, and *before* he can escape. So Ellicott, Alford, Prof. Lightfoot, and Meyer in his first and second editions. Thus Wisdom xvii. 16: εἴ τι γὰρ γεωργὸς ἦν τις ἢ ποιμὴν . . . προληφθεὶς τὴν δυσάλυκτον ἔμενεν ἀνάγκην. Kypke, *Observ.* ii. 298. See John viii. 4.

This exegesis preserves the unity of the sentence. For the *καί* is intensive,—not a case put for argument, as by *καὶ εἰ*, but a strong case which might occur. Klotz-Devar. ii. 519. The noun *παράπτωμα* has not the idea of inadvertence in it, but is an act of sin, a falling away from a divine precept,—any particular trespass. See under Eph. ii. 1; Rom. v. 15, 16, 20. It is the translation of various Hebrew words in the Sept.: Ps. xix. 13; Ezek. xiv. 13; Job xxxvi. 9; Ezek. iii. 20;—2 Cor. v. 19; Eph. i. 7; Col. ii. 13.

Luther lays stress on the *ἄνθρωπος*. "This term, a name of man, helpeth somewhat also to diminish or qualify the matter, as if he should say, What is so proper to man as to fall, to be deceived and to err? (Lev. vi. 3.)" But though the idea of weakness may be found in the word in certain positions, as when it is in contrast with God, the term is here only a general expression.

The appeal is direct and immediate—

Ὑμεῖς οἱ πνευματικοὶ καταρτίζετε τὸν τοιοῦτον—"do ye the spiritual ones restore such a person." The verb often means to refit or repair what is injured. Matt. iv. 21; Mark i. 19. It is applied in Galen to the setting of a bone; but Beza's application of such an image here is not at all necessary: *Nitimini eum, quasi luxatum membrum.* So Hammond, Bengel, Brown. The ethical sense is a common one. Herodotus, v. 106, *κεῖνα πάντα καταρτίσω . . . ἐς τὠυτό*. Chrysostom renders it *διορθοῦτε*, Theodoret *στηρίζετε*.

The *πνευματικοί* are not the presbyters (Hammond), nor those who thought themselves spiritual (Windischmann), but those in possession of that *πνεῦμα* on which such stress has been laid in the previous paragraph, those truly endowed with this divine gift; and because they were so endowed, they were to restore the fallen brother. Those ruled by the *σάρξ* could not do this duty; the spirit of provocation and envy already referred to quite unfitted them for such delicate work; they might only taunt, rebuke, and glory over an offending brother taken *flagrante delicto.* The *πνευματικοί* were therefore the best class in the church—the ripe, the experienced, the advanced in Christian excellence; and such a class is opposed to the *ὡς σαρκικοί, ὡς νήπιοι ἐν Χριστῷ*, in as far as *ζῆλος καὶ ἔρις* had place among them. 1 Cor. iii. 1–3. The *οἱ πνευματικοί* are thus different from *οἱ δυνατοί*, Rom. xv. 1; at least it is a very different relation of parties in the church which is there referred to, for it is the strong and the weak in reference chiefly to dietetic ceremonialism.

The restoration of the sinning member to his normal state is to be carried out—

'Εν πνεύματι πραΰτητος—"in the spirit of meekness." The genitive is that of the characterizing moral quality—*die dominirenden Eigenschaften*, Scheuerlein, p. 115. Winer, § 34, 3, *b*. It is not to be diluted into *πνεῦμα πρᾳΰ* (Borger, Koppe, Brown); nor is *πνεῦμα* directly or immediately the Holy Ghost, as the Greek fathers and many after them suppose; nor is it a mere abstract characterization (Moeller), but rather their own spirit. The "spiritual," led and endowed by the Spirit, had as one of His gifts—as one of His inwrought elements of character—a spirit of meekness. In 1 Cor. iv. 21 we have the phrase *ἐν ἀγάπῃ πνεύματί τε πρᾳότητος*, where the two nouns refer alike to inner disposition. See under v. 22, 23. The restoration of a fallen brother is not to be undertaken in a distant or haughty spirit, or in a hard, dictatorial, or censorious style, which dwells bitterly on the sin, or brings its aggravations into undue relief, or condemns in self-complacent severity the weakness which led to the fall. The spirit of meekness compassionates while it must blame, soothes while it may expostulate; its fidelity is full of sympathy—itself the image of that gentleness which in the benign Exemplar did not "break the bruised reed, nor quench the smoking flax." In the exegesis of Rückert and Usteri the term *πνεῦμα* is all but superfluous.

And the duty of restoring an erring brother is to be done all the while under this self-applied caution—

Σκοπῶν σεαυτὸν μὴ καὶ σὺ πειρασθῇς—"considering thyself, lest thou also shouldest be tempted." The apostle suddenly appeals to each and every one of the spiritual. This individualizing use of the singular is no such solecism as Jerome apologizes for—*profundos sensus aliena lingua exprimere non valebat*. This change of number is not uncommon: ch. iv. 7. Jelf, § 390; Winer, § 63, 2. D^1 and F change the second person into the third—an evident and clumsy emendation.

The participle may have its temporal meaning, this self-consideration being an accompaniment of the duty enjoined.

Calvin regards it as a warning against sin in the form of harshness exceeding the due limits; and again he says, "Whatever be our acuteness in detecting the faults of others, we are backward to acknowledge our own." But these interpretations do not tally with the caution given in the next clause. The participle rather gives a subsidiary reason why the restoration is a duty, and especially why it should be gone about in a spirit of gentleness. Schmalfeld, § 207, 2, 3. For it is added, "lest thou also (as well as he) shouldest be tempted." The subjunctive aorist is used—the thing apprehended, being still future, may not happen. Winer, § 56, *β*; Gayler, p. 325. See 1 Cor. vii. 5, 1 Thess. iii. 5, Jas. i. 14. That which has happened to him who has been caught in a fault may happen to any of you. Each of you is liable to temptation, and under a sense of that liability should act toward the lapsed one in a spirit of gentleness: his case may be thine; for thou art what thou art only by the grace of Him "who is able to keep thee from falling." The statement is in contrast to that vainglory which leads to provocation and envy; and these beget self-conceit and censoriousness. Lachmann connects this clause with the following verse. But the connection is unnatural. The liability of one's self to fall through temptation has a natural relation to the duty of restoring a fallen brother—not so much with bearing one another's burdens; the *καὶ σύ* refers to *τοιοῦτον*, but the reference would be virtually lost in Lachmann's construction with *ἀλλήλων*.

Ver. 2. *'Αλλήλων τὰ βάρη βαστάζετε*—"One another's burdens do ye bear." This verse broadens the sphere of duty enjoined in the previous verse; or it presents that duty in a form not specialized as in the first verse: the spirit that restores a fallen brother should pervade ordinary Christian relations. The *βάρη* have been unduly narrowed in the definition of them. They are not weaknesses simply, as in Rom. xv. 1, but also errors, trials, sorrows, sins, without any distinct specification. And they are not merely to be tolerated, they are to be taken up as "burdens;" for the verb implies this. Matt. xx. 12; Acts xv. 10. Whatever forms a burden to our brethren we are to take upon ourselves, and carry it for them or with them, in the spirit of Him "who bore our sins and carried our sorrows." The burden to be borne is not to be limited to *ψυχὴ ὑπὸ τῆς τοῦ ἁμαρτή-*

ματος συνειδήσεως βεβαρημένη. Theodore Mops. There does not therefore seem to be any covert allusion to the self-imposed burdens of the law (Alford). The emphasis is on *ἀλλήλων*, giving distinctness to the duty as a mutual duty: "Weep with them that weep." Mutual interposition in sympathy and for succour in any emergency—fellow-feeling and fellow-helping—is the duty inculcated, as opposed to that selfish isolation which stands aloof, or contents itself with a cheap expression of commiseration, or an offer of assistance so framed as to be worthless in the time or the shape of it. The apostle exemplifies his own maxim, 2 Cor. xi. 29.

The reading of the next clause is doubtful. The Received Text has *καὶ οὕτως ἀναπληρώσατε τὸν νόμον τοῦ Χριστοῦ*—"and so fulfil the law of Christ." This reading is supported by A, C, D, K, L, א, nearly all MSS., and is found in the Syriac (Philox.), and in many of the Greek fathers. It is also adopted by Griesbach, Scholz, Reiche, Alford, and Tischendorf in his 7th ed. The other reading is the future *ἀναπληρώσετε*—"and so ye shall fulfil the law of Christ." It is supported by B, F, G, two MSS., the Vulgate and Claromontane Latin, the Syriac (Peschito), the Armenian, Coptic, Sahidic, and Ethiopic versions, Theodoret (MS.), and some of the Latin fathers; and it is admitted by Lachmann, Meyer, and Ellicott. Diplomatic authority is in favour of the common text; but the versions give decided countenance to the other reading in the future, which Alford regards "as a probable correction, the imperative aorist being unusual" (Winer, § 43). The difference is but that of a single letter, and one may suppose that a copyist might change the future to make both clauses imperative. The present would have been "natural" (Ellicott), but the *καὶ οὕτως* seems to point to the future. It is impossible to come to a definite conclusion, and the meaning is not really affected whatever reading be adopted.

Borger, Rückert, Brown, and others are wrong in assigning the compound *ἀναπληροῦν* the mere sense of the simple *πληροῦν*. The preposition gives the idea of a complete filling, of a filling up. Col. i. 24; Phil. ii. 30; 1 Thess. ii. 16; Sept. Ex. xxiii. 26; Strabo, vi. p. 223; Joseph. *Antiq.* v. 6, 2; Tittmann, *De Syn.* p. 228; Winer, *De verborum cum præp. composit. in N. T. usu*, iii. pars 11.

The "law of Christ" is not simply the law of love, or His new commandment which is only one precept of His law (Theodoret, De Wette, Usteri), but His entire code, which indeed is summed up in love. Whoso, from right motive and in true form, bears the burdens of others, has so drunk into the spirit of Christ who carried our burdens, has so realized the gentleness and sympathy of His example who "came not to be ministered unto, but to minister," that he fully obeys His law, —a law which reprobates all hard, sullen, and self-absorbed individualism, and is fulfilled in love to God and to all that bears His image. The explanation of Chrysostom, *κοινῇ πάντες*—"fulfil it in common by the things in which ye bear with one another, each completing what is wanting in his neighbour,"—is not to the point. The injunction is meant for Christians, and there is a contrast recorded (Rev. ii. 2) in praise of the church of Ephesus: *ὅτι οὐ δύνῃ βαστάσαι κακούς*. There may be a tacit reference to the *νόμος* which the Galatians, under the teaching of the Judaizers, were taught to obey, but which was not in authority or contents the law of Christ. See under v. 14.

Ver. 3. *Εἰ γὰρ δοκεῖ τις εἶναί τι, μηδὲν ὤν*—"For if any one think himself to be something, while he is nothing." This verse is closely connected by *γάρ* with the one before it, either as an *argumentum e contrario* for the immediately preceding clause (Meyer), or as a confirmation, by showing the evils of the opposite course (Ellicott). Hofmann refers it more to the mutuality of the duty than to the duty itself. The apostle had already said, "Considering thyself, lest thou also be tempted;" consciousness of frailty leads to mutual attachment, and shows the need of mutual support. But self-importance based on self-ignorance is the grand hindrance to the duty of mutual burden-bearing. If a man thinks himself so perfect that he can have no burden which others may carry with him, or for him; if he regards himself so far above frailty, sin, or sorrow, that he neither needs nor expects sympathy nor help,—he will not readily stoop to bear the burdens of others. On the meaning of *εἶναί τι*, etc., compare Acts v. 36, 1 Cor. iii. 7, xiii. 2, 2 Cor. xii. 11. The phrase *μηδὲν ὤν* is expressive—"being nothing," all the while he is thinking himself something,—the condition affirmed in *ὤν* underlying the mental action in *δοκεῖ*.

The participle has its common temporal signification. The use of the subjective μηδέν is not, as Ellicott warns, to be overpressed, since it is the prevailing usage with participles in the New Testament. Here, however, and in such a verse, it may have its proper signification—not simply objective οὐδέν, but μηδέν: "nothing," not ironically, nor merely in the writer's opinion (Gwynne); nor "if he would come to himself, and look on the real fact, nothing" (Alford); but in sober judgment, according to true estimate, nothing. On δοκεῖ, see Trench, *Synon.* ii. § 30. The phrase is a common one. Plato, *Apolog.* 41, E, ἐὰν δοκῶσί τι εἶναι μηδὲν ὄντες; Arrian, *Epictet.* ii. 24, δοκῶν μέν τι εἶναι ὢν δ' οὐδείς; Euripides, *Electra*, 370, ἄνδρα . . . τὸ μηδὲν ὄντα; *Supplices*, 424, πονηρὸς ἀξίωμ' ἀνήρ . . . οὐδὲν ὤν. See examples in Wetstein; in Kypke, ii. 291; and in Raphel. ii. 457. See also under ii. 6, 9. Some, as Baumgarten, Hensler, Jatho, and Hofmann, connect the words with the concluding sentence—he deceiveth himself, as being one who is nothing; but the connection weakens the force of the declaration, and takes away the point and antithesis of the previous clause. Such a one—

Φρεναπατᾷ ἑαυτόν—"deceiveth his own mind"—an example of "vainglory." The Received Text, which reverses this order, has good but not decisive authority; A, B, C, א giving the order we have preferred. The verb is only found here in the New Testament, but in no earlier Greek writers, though it occurs afterwards in the ecclesiastical authors. The noun φρεναπάτης, however, is found in Tit. i. 10. The word, probably coined by the apostle, denotes a self-deception of a nature solely subjective; corresponding, therefore, to the previous δοκεῖ in the premises. Comp. Jas. i. 26. This self-conceited and in result self-duped man is incapable of bearing others' burdens, and is insensible to the obligation. The true estimate of ourselves, which we ought to cherish, is given us in Luke xvii. 10.

Ver. 4. Τὸ δὲ ἔργον ἑαυτοῦ δοκιμαζέτω ἕκαστος—"But let each one prove his own work." While a momentary introspection may lead to morbid self-exaltation, the actual judgment passed on deeds may conduce to a proper estimate; δέ being in contrast with what is said in the previous verse of self-inflation and self-deception: let there be account taken of "work." The stress is from its position on ἔργον, which is deepened by ἑαυτοῦ, and which, as Meyer remarks, is collective in meaning, as in Rom. ii. 15, 1 Pet. i. 17, Rev. xxii. 12. See Winer, § 27, 1, and the limits which he gives to the collective singular. His work—his own work—himself embodied in act,—*τὸν ἑαυτοῦ βίον* (Theodoret),—the outer shape and expression of the inner realities,—let him test this, put it to the proof; the *δοκιμάζειν* responding to the *δοκεῖ*, and being its grand corrective. Such is the meaning of the verb—to prove, to put to the test, Luke xiv. 19; 1 Cor. iii. 13, xi. 28; 1 Thess. ii. 4. It does not mean *probatum reddat, sc. deo*, as is thought by Beza, Piscator, Wesselius, Justinianus, Rückert, Matthies. Theophylact thus explains: *ἐξεταζέτω μετὰ ἀκριβείας τὰς ἑαυτοῦ πράξεις, τοῦτο γὰρ τὸ, δοκιμαζέτω.* Œcumenius, more pointedly: *καὶ ἑαυτὸν ἐρευνᾷ ἀκριβῶς.*

Καὶ τότε εἰς ἑαυτὸν μόνον τὸ καύχημα ἕξει, καὶ οὐκ εἰς τὸν ἕτερον—"and then he shall have ground of boasting only in relation to himself, and not in relation to the other." Let him put his work to the test,—not this act or that act, but his whole work in its complex unity,—"and then," *καὶ τότε*, that is, when he shall have done this; it being implied that his work has stood the test, though there is no formal ellipse, as Estius, Borger, Turner, and others suppose. *Καύχημα*, not *καύχησις*, is not glorying (Bagge), but the ground of glorying, Rom. iv. 2, compared with Rom. iii. 27; 1 Cor. v. 6, ix. 15, 16; Phil. i. 26, ii. 16. Ellicott takes the article *τό* in its pronominal meaning—*his* ground of boasting. Middleton, *Gr. Art.* v. 3. But it may be quite as well taken in its ordinary signification—that ground of boasting which he may find after putting his work to the proof. The future *ἕξει* refers to the having as subsequent to the previous testing, and carries in it no allusion to the last judgment, though many expositors hold such an opinion. The phrase *εἰς ἑαυτὸν μόνον ἕξει* is taken by some to mean, "and then he shall hold his glorying to himself." So Hilgenfeld: *seinem Ruhm für sich selbst zu behalten, mit gegen Andere geltend zu machen.* So Koppe, Storr, Flatt, and Usteri. But while the verb may have such a meaning, it is better to take the words in their ordinary signification, especially as *εἰς* is employed, which does not stand exactly for *κατά*, as in Theodoret—*κατὰ σεαυτὸν σεμνύνου*; nor for *παρά*, as in Winer's opinion, quoting

Rom. iv. 2; the next clause showing the inapplicability of such a meaning here. Nor does it mean *contra* (Schott), as apparently in Luke xii. 10; for "against himself" would not in this clause be a natural idea, though it would apply in the last clause, as "against the other." De Wette, giving εἰς the same translation, *für*, in both clauses, alters the indicated relation in the second, making the first *zu seiner eigenen Freude*, and the second *um sie damit zu reizen und herauszufordern*. Jatho also gives the preposition the sense of *für* in the first clause, and of *gegen* in the second. But εἰς must bear the same meaning in both clauses, and it signifies "in reference to," *quod attinet ad*. Acts ii. 25; Rom. iv. 20; 2 Cor. xi. 10; Eph. iii. 16; Xen. *Anab.* i. 9, 16; Kühner, ii. § 603; Bernhardy, p. 221. In reference to himself—ἑαυτόν emphatic—he shall have ground of glorying, καὶ οὐκ εἰς τὸν ἕτερον—"and not in reference to the other,"—that is, the other with whom he brings himself into ideal comparison or contrast. Οὐκ is objective—not as matter of opinion, but as matter of fact; and the article is not to be overlooked. Rom. ii. 1, xiii. 8; 1 Cor. vi. 1, x. 24. But in this καύχημα, real or imaginary, is there a slight irony? Theophylact, after Chrysostom, says that the apostle speaks συγκαταβατικῶς οὐ νομοθετικῶς; and that there is irony in the clause is the opinion of Justinianus, Bengel, Olshausen, Baumgarten-Crusius, and Alford. This, however, does not appear likely; for the apostle is not bitter or scornful in tone: he does not deny that there may be matter of glorying; he only shows how it often and wrongly bases itself on vain and fallacious comparison with others. A man may test his own work; but he cannot know "the other," and test his work. The Pharisee did not, could not, know the downcast suppliant when he thanked God that he was so much better than "this publican." But if a man examine himself, and find not only faults and frailties, but also germs of grace and goodness, then has he ground of glorying, in reference to himself, not certainly in himself, but in the mercy and power of the Saviour in him. This is really glorying in the Lord. 1 Cor. i. 31; 2 Cor. x. 17. Compare xii. 5, 9, where to glory in infirmities is really to glory in that grace which such infirmities attract to themselves, but for which His grace could not have proved its sufficiency, and without which His strength could not have demonstrated its perfection. Thus Castalio says: *probitas in re, non in collatione;* and Calvin writes: *ea demum est vera laus, non quam aliis detrahendo nobis conciliamus, sed quam habemus sine comparatione.* "The other" does not in any way enter as an element into that experience which concerns himself alone; for his own numerous imperfections, which pressing upon his notice and filling him with profound regrets, prevent him from judging his neighbour or exulting over him. Humility and thankfulness ever characterize this glorying in reference to himself, one reason being—

Ver. 5. *Ἕκαστος γὰρ τὸ ἴδιον φορτίον βαστάσει*—"For each one shall bear his own burden." The *γάρ* does not indicate an ellipse—"such comparative rejoicing is worthless, for;" but rather it refers to the last clause—"and not in reference to the other." No one can glory in reference to his neighbour; for he will find on that self-inspection recommended that he has many frailties in himself—something which clings to him, and ever rebukes conscious or self-exultant comparison. This is more natural than the connection with the clause, "Let every one prove his own work—for every one must bear his own burden,"—the connection of Beza, Matthies, Hofmann; but the intervening clauses declare against it. *Φορτίον*—a diminutive in form only—is something which one carries, a pack. Ecclus. xxi. 16, *ὡς ἐν ὁδῷ φορτίον*; Xen. *Mem.* iii. 13, 6, *εἰ καὶ φορτίον ἔφερε.* But the *βάρη* of ver. 2 means loads—heavy loads, which they are asked to carry in sympathy, which some refused to carry; while *φορτίον* is a burden which each one has—something individual, and of which one cannot rid himself. The *βάρη* are always heavy; but you may have on the one hand *φορτία βαρέα*, Matt. xxiii. 4, and on the other a *φορτίον ἐλαφρόν*, Matt. xi. 30. The Vulgate and Claromontane wrongly render both Greek words by *onus;* but the Syriac rightly renders the first by ܝܘܩܪܐ, *onus*, and the second by ܡܘܒܠܬܐ, *sarcina.* This "burden" is not "punishment," as is supposed by Theodoret, Jerome, Luther, Erasmus, Calvin, Grotius, a-Lapide, Estius, Bengel, and Rückert. For the *φορτίον* is borne now; and because each one now bears it, and feels its weight, he is not to form hard opinions or pronounce unjust decisions about others. Nor is it simply responsibility (Gwynne), but his own peculiar (*ἴδιον*) present sin and weakness, which ought to lead him to be charitable. The idea of either future punishment or responsibility is foreign to the course of thought. And the future has its ethical signification—shall bear = must bear, from the very nature of things. Winer, § 40, 6; Bernhardy, pp. 377–8; Kühner, 446, 3. The verse expresses a general truth which is or shall be ever realizing itself as a thing of moral necessity. Bisping and Windischmann take the future as the previous ἕξει—he will find at the end of his self-examination that he is to bear his own burden. This is unnecessary. In fine, there is no discrepancy between this and the second verse. The two verses are like two stars revolving round each other. The second verse enjoins sympathy and mutual burden-bearing; while this verse describes that individual load which each one carries, and which no one can bear for him.

Ver. 6. *Κοινωνείτω δὲ ὁ κατηχούμενος τὸν λόγον τῷ κατηχοῦντι ἐν πᾶσιν ἀγαθοῖς*—"But let him who is taught in the word communicate with him who teacheth in all good things." The verb *κατηχέω*, besides its literal signification, denotes to communicate information orally—to sound it in one's ears, Acts xxi. 21, 24; or to teach by means of oral instruction, Acts xviii. 25, 1 Cor. xiv. 19; sometimes with *περί* and a genitive, referring to the contents, Luke i. 4; or with *ἐκ*, Rom. ii. 18, referring to the source. Sometimes it has both a genitive of thing and person, Acts xxi. 24. The word, however, seems here to signify to teach or instruct generally. Such instruction was in the early church usually oral, and could at that time be nothing else; but the oralness of it ceases to be recognised as a primary and distinctive feature. Thus the Greek fathers explain the word simply by *διδασκόμενος* or *μαθητευόμενος*; Hesychius explaining *παιδευόμενος*. It came to denote familiar tuition; and the *κατηχούμενοι*, as opposed to the *πιστοί*, were persons under preliminary instruction in the elements of Christianity. The passive participle *κατηχούμενος* is here followed by the accusative of reference or second government, Winer, § 32, 5; or, as Schmalfeld calls it, "of qualitative object," § 25. Jelf, § 579; Suicer, *sub voce*. *Ὁ λόγος* is the gospel. Acts xiii. 26, xv. 7, xx. 32; Luke i. 2, v. 1; Eph. i. 13.

The duty of him who is instructed in the word is expressed

by κοινωνείτω . . . τῷ κατηχοῦντι—"let him share with him that teacheth." The verb is sometimes used with the genitive, "to partake *of*," Heb. ii. 14; and sometimes with the dative, "to share *in*," Rom. xii. 13, xv. 27, 1 Tim. v. 22, 1 Pet. iv. 13; Wisdom vi. 25, οὐ κοινωνήσει σοφίᾳ. It is also found with the dative of person, the thing being governed as here by ἐν, or by εἰς, as in Phil. iv. 15. Plato, *De Repub.* v. 453. In the New Testament the prevailing if not uniform sense is intransitive, though not in classical usage. Xen. *Mem.* ii. 6, 22; Polyb. ii. 42, 5; Plato, *De Leg.* viii. 844. It may stand, according to Thomas Magister, either ἀντὶ τοῦ συμμετέχω σοι, or ἀντὶ τοῦ μεταδίδωμι . . . ὧν ἔχω. The sense is then strictly, not—let him communicate, but, let him be in communication with; and it may be either as giver or receiver—the last in Rom. xv. 27, and the first in Rom. xii. 13. The transitive sense would seem to require τῶν ἀγαθῶν, but ἐν agrees with the intransitive—the sphere of communication. Franke (in Wolf) joins the phrase ἐν πᾶσιν ἀγαθοῖς with the immediately preceding words, τῷ κατηχοῦντι—with him that teacheth in all good things. But in that case the accusative would be employed.

The meaning of the phrase itself has been disputed. Marcion (in Jerome), Hennike, Matthies, Meyer, Schott, Trana, Jatho, Sardinoux, and Keerl understand it of spiritual things; Vömel supplying this contrast—*in allem Guten, nicht in Irrlehren.* See Mynster's *kleine theol. Schriften*, p. 70. The words may bear such a meaning. The article is wanting here; so that τὰ ἀγαθά, John v. 29, and τὸ ἀγαθόν in the following ver. 10, are not adducible in proof. Were this the sole view, the communication would be tantamount to imitation, or the connection between teacher and taught was to refer to all kinds of spiritual good—getting it, or rather giving it, as the injunction is upon "the taught." But the singular is more in Paul's style when he refers to ethical good. Col. i. 10; Heb. xiii. 21, ἐν παντὶ ἔργῳ ἀγαθῷ; Rom. ii. 10, xii. 2, 9, xiii. 3, xvi. 19; Eph. vi. 8; 1 Thess. v. 15; Philem. 6, etc.; Sept. Isa. vii. 15. The reference to temporal things is the almost unanimous opinion of ancient and modern interpreters. Ἀγαθά has this sense, Luke xii. 18, 19, xvi. 25, and often in the Septuagint, 2 Sam. vii. 28, 1 Chron. xvii. 26, 2 Chron. xviii. 12, 17. Comp. Luke i. 53. At all events, it is virtually the same doctrine which he teaches in 1 Cor. ix. 11. Compare 1 Thess. ii. 6, 9, 1 Tim. v. 17, 18. The occurrence of πᾶσιν is somewhat difficult, and the expression is vague. Wieseler therefore includes both ideas in the reciprocal sense—the taught being in communication with the teacher in temporal things, as the teacher is in communication with the taught in spiritual things. See also Bagge, Gwynne, Schmoller.

It is somewhat difficult to trace the connection; but it seems to be suggested by the last verse. The δέ may continue the thought under another aspect; thus, he had said, "Bear one another's burdens"—now—δέ, this is one form in which the precept may be obeyed;—or he had said, Every man must bear his own load; but—δέ, this does not exempt you from bearing the burden of your teachers. It is an obligation not to be slighted, or left to mere caprice. So-called voluntaryism is not optionalism. The duty consists (Theophylact) in the giving to the pastor of "food, raiment, honour," etc.—τροφῆς, ἐνδύματος, τιμῆς; "for thou receivest more than thou givest—spiritual things for carnal things." Keerl takes the connection from ver. 1, understanding by "him who is taught in the word" the fallen brother who has been restored, while the intervening verses guard the "spiritual" restorers against pride. But this connection is artificial and narrow.

Ver. 7. The connection again is rather obscure. Chrysostom, Theophylact, Œcumenius, Luther, Hunnius, Grotius, Bagge, Gwynne connect the verse with the immediately preceding one. Thus also Prof. Lightfoot, who thus paraphrases: "What, you hold back! Nay, do not deceive yourselves." But such a connection is too limited to warrant the broader statement of the following verses. Some would refer the first clause, "Be not deceived," to what follows. But probably the warning has been suggested by the preceding context, and not simply or solely by the previous verse, as there is no formal connecting particle. The paragraph treats of duties which spring out of love, the fruit of the Spirit, and are themselves forms of spiritual beneficence or well-doing,—duties, however, which one may be tempted to neglect, or regard only in a negative aspect, so far as not to be acting in direct opposition to them. One may let a fallen brother alone, but without insulting him when he is down. One may refuse to bear another's burden, but without adding to its weight. One may decline communication in temporal things with a spiritual teacher, but without inflicting on him a positive and harmful expenditure. Men may in this way deceive themselves; or in some other form selfishness and the world may so hold them in bondage, that they may be sowing to the flesh. In passing from the more ideal to the more palpable forms of Christian beneficence, the apostle throws in the awful warning of the verse before us—

Μὴ πλανᾶσθε, Θεὸς οὐ μυκτηρίζεται—"Be not deceived, God is not mocked." The same abrupt warning is found in 1 Cor. vi. 9 as a sudden and earnest dissuasive from sinful practices which exclude from heaven; in the same epistle, xv. 33, as a guard against Epicurean indulgence; and in Jas. i. 16, where it is rendered, "Do not err." The warning implies a liability to deception or error: in this case the deception appears to be, that a man may be sowing to the flesh, and yet be hoping to reap of the Spirit, or that for him might be changed the unchangeable order which God has ordained—"like seed, like harvest." The verb *μυκτηρίζω*, from *μυκτήρ*, is to turn up the nose at, to sneer at, to mock. Sept. Job xxii. 19; Ps. lxxx. 7; Isa. xxxvii. 22; Jer. xx. 7,—there representing the Heb. לָעַג; Prov. i. 30, xii. 8; 1 Macc. vii. 34, 39. Quintilian defines *μυκτηρισμόν*, *simulatum quidem, sed non latentem derisum*, ix. 8. In the life of Claudius, part of a letter of Augustus has *σκώπτειν καὶ μυκτηρίζειν*: Suetonius, p. 636, Valpy 1826. So Horace has *naso suspendis adunco*, *Satir.* i. 6, 5; *naribus uti*, *Ep.* i. 19, 45. God is not mocked, either in reality or with impunity (Ellicott); there is no such thing as mocking God. Wieseler takes the verb in the middle, "God will not suffer Himself to be mocked"—*non sinit sibi irrideri.* The expression is a strong one, taken from that organ of the face by which we express careless contempt. Men may be imposed on by a show of virtue on the part of one who all the while scorns their weakness, but God cannot be so mocked.

Ὃ γὰρ ἐὰν σπείρῃ ἄνθρωπος, τοῦτο καὶ θερισει—"for whatsoever a man may sow, that also shall he reap." The *γάρ* is confirmative; *σπείρῃ* is subjunctive present, though the subjunctive aorist is the more common after *ἐάν*; and the consequent clause is usually a future—*θερίσει.* Winer, 41,

2, *b*; Klotz-Devarius, iii. 453, 4. Let him sow what he likes, *τοῦτο* with emphasis—that and that only, that and nothing else, shall he also reap; *καί* with its ascensive power—the sower is also the reaper. The future refers to the judgmont, when the results of present action shall be felt in their indissoluble relations. The reaping is not only the effect of the sowing, but is necessarily of the same nature with it. He that sows cockles, cockles shall he also reap; he that soweth wheat, wheat also shall he reap. It is the law of God in the natural world—the harvest is but the growth of the sowing; and it illustrates the uniform sequences of the spiritual world. The nature of conduct is not changed by its development and final ripening for divine sentence; nay, its nature is by the process only opened out into full and self-displayed reality. The blade and the ear may be hardly recognised and distinguished as to species, but the full corn in the ear is the certain result and unmistakeable proof of what was sown. And the sowing leads certainly, and not as if by accident, to the reaping; the connection cannot be severed—it lies deep in man's personal identity and responsibility. Cicero gives the quotation, *ut sementem feceris, ita metes*, *De Orat*. ii. 65. *Ὁ σπείρων φαῦλα θηρίσει κακά*, *Gorgias*, in Aristot. *Rhet*. iii. 3. Æschylus, *Prom*. 322, *σὺ δὲ ταῦτα αἰσχρῶς μὲν ἔσπειρας, κακῶς δὲ ἐθέρισας*. Plato, *Phædr*. 260, D, *καρπὸν ὧν ἔσπειρε θερίζειν*. Comp. Ps. cxxvi. 5, 6, Hos. viii. 7, x. 12, Job iv. 8, Prov. xxii. 8, 2 Cor. ix. 6.

Ver. 8. The previous verse presented the mere figure of sowing and of reaping, with certainty of reaping what may happen to have been sown. But the seed may be of two kinds, or the seed may be sown with two different purposes, and each purpose naturally and necessarily leads to its own result—

Ὅτι ὁ σπείρων εἰς τὴν σάρκα ἑαυτοῦ, ἐκ τῆς σαρκὸς θερίσει φθοράν—"For he who is sowing unto his flesh, from the flesh shall reap corruption." The various readings are of little value: only by an evident correction, F, G read *τῇ σαρκί*; and so the Vulgate and Claromontane, *in carne sua*. Matthias divides *ὅτι* into *ὅ τι*, and joins it to the previous clause: *was es auch sein möge*,—a useless suggestion. The statement is confirmatory—*ὅτι*, and the phrase *εἰς τὴν σάρκα* does not

present the flesh as the field in or on which the seed is sown—
—*tanquam in agrum* (Bengel, Borger, Brown); for ἐν and ἐπί are employed for this purpose: the former in Matt. xiii. 24, 27, Mark iv. 15, Ex. xxiii. 16, Hos. ii. 23; the latter as in Matt. xiii. 20, 23, Mark iv. 16, 20, 31. *Εἰς*, however, is found Matt. xiii. 22, Mark iv. 18, and is regarded by Ellicott as signifying "among." But εἰς in that place may bear its own meaning of "on"—the seed was sown on the thorns, which were invisible at the moment, and under the ground; and thus εἰς πέτρας τε καὶ λίθους σπείροντας, Plato, *De Leg.* viii. 838, E. The verb is sometimes followed with the accusative of the seed, Matt. xiii. 24, Herod. iv. 17, and sometimes with the accusative of the field sown, Sept. Ex. xxiii. 10, Xen. *Cyr.* viii. 3, 28. *Εἰς* is to be taken here in an ethical sense, "with a view to;" and σάρξ is the unregenerate nature—the leading sense of the word throughout the epistle—the nature which specially belongs to him—ἑαυτοῦ, but not emphatic. The "flesh" is thus neither the field nor the seed; but that for the gratification of which the seed is sown, or that which forms the ruling end to the man's desires and actions, which governs and moulds the aspirations and workings of his present life. The seed sown is much the same as the ἔργα τῆς σαρκός. It is too narrow an interpretation to refer it to undue care for the wants of the present life (Calvin), or to a "sumptuous table and viands" (Chrysostom and his followers), or to withholding support from the ministers of God's word, and feeding and caring for themselves only (Luther, Olshausen). The reference to circumcision (σάρξ), allowed by Pelagius, Schoettgen, Rückert, and Usteri, may be at once discarded; and any allusion to such asceticism as that which characterized the Encratites is also out of the question. Jerome condemns Cassian or Tatian as finding in the clause a prohibition of marriage. See also in Luther.

The harvest is φθορά—"corruption." The noun means something more than that "the flesh is a prey to corruption, and with it all fleshly desires and practices come to nothing" (Alford, after Chrysostom and De Wette). 1 Cor. vi. 13, xv. 42, 50. It is here opposed to ζωὴν αἰώνιον, and must have its strongest and most awful signification, as in 1 Cor. iii. 17, 2 Pet. ii. 12. It may have been suggested by the use of σάρξ; but in meaning it is tantamount to ἀπωλεία,

Phil. iii. 20. Compare Matt. vii. 13, Rom. ix. 22. Hesychius defines *φθορά* by *ὄλεθρος*. Herod. vii. 18; Thucyd. ii. 47; Plato, *Leg.* 677; Sept. Ps. ciii. 4, Jonah ii. 7. The meaning, then, is different only in form from Rom. viii. 6, *τὸ φρόνημα τῆς σαρκὸς θάνατος*. Rom. viii. 13, vii. 23.

But the converse is also true—

Ὁ δὲ σπείρων εἰς τὸ πνεῦμα, ἐκ τοῦ πνεύματος θερίσει ζωὴν αἰώνιον—"but he who is sowing to the Spirit, from the Spirit shall reap life eternal." As in v. 16, etc., the Spirit is not the higher or renewed part of man's own nature (Rückert, Schott, Olshausen, Borger, Baumgarten-Crusius, Brown, and others), but the Spirit of God; and there is no *ἑαυτοῦ* with it as with *σάρκα*. Sowing to the Spirit produces "eternal life" as its harvest. Matt. xix. 16, 17, xxv. 46; Mark x. 17, 30; Luke x. 25, xviii. 18; John iii. 15, 16, v. 24, etc. etc. *Αἰώνιος* is an epithet of quantity, not of quality. Compare its use with *δόξα*, 2 Cor. iv. 17, 2 Tim. ii. 10, 1 Pet. v. 10; with *σωτηρία*, Heb. v. 9; with *παράκλησις*, 2 Thess. ii. 16; with *κληρονομία*, Heb. ix. 15. The future verb refers to the harvest at the end of the world, though indeed it is enjoyed even now. John iii. 36, v. 24, vi. 47. The clause is virtually the same in meaning with *τὸ δὲ φρόνημα τοῦ πνεύματος ζωή*, Rom. viii. 6, 13. The *ζωὴ αἰώνιος* has reference specially to blessedness in the future world, as the fruit of present grace and holiness, and as the object of hope. Rom. ii. 7, v. 21, vi. 22; 1 Tim. i. 16; Tit. i. 2, iii. 7. The life created by the Spirit, and sustained through believing oneness with Christ, can have neither pause nor end. It is immortal from its living union with Him who "only hath immortality."

The continued and wilful indulgence of our unrenewed nature becomes its own penalty, as it does not realize the end of its being, and unfitting itself for blessedness, sinks and darkens into ruin; but the work of the Spirit of God, fostered within us and consciously elevated into predominant and regulative influence, ripens surely into blessedness. The process in both cases is a certain one—*θερίσει*—as certain as that between sowing and reaping; and the identity of the harvest with the seed sown is emphatically marked—*ἐκ τῆς σαρκός . . . ἐκ τοῦ πνεύματος*.

The apostle now encourages to the second kind of sowing—

Ver. 9. *Τὸ δὲ καλὸν ποιοῦντες μὴ ἐγκακῶμεν*—"But in well-doing let us not be faint-hearted." The *ἐκκακῶμεν* of the common text, after C, D[3], K, L, does not seem to be a Greek word at all. See under Eph. iii. 13. Similar variation occurs also in Luke xviii. 1, 2 Cor. iv. 1, 16, 2 Thess. iii. 13. Meyer, however, prefers *ἐκκακῶμεν*, regarding the other as an emendation—*als Besserung*, and this as an oral form introduced into his epistles by Paul. The form *ἐγκακῶμεν* is supported by A, B, D[1], ℵ. The pronunciation and spelling of the two words are so like, that one needs not wonder at the variations. Both forms, however, occur in Hesychius; but neither the one nor the other is found in the Sept. The form *ἐνκ.* occurs in Polybius, iv. 19, 10; Symmachus, Gen. xxvii. 46, Num. xxi. 5, Isa. vii. 16; and in Theodotion, Prov. iii. 11, where the Sept. has *ἐκλύου*. The meaning is not essentially different; the verb compounded with *ἐκ* meaning to faint so as to back *out* of, and the verb with *ἐν* to lose courage *in* course of action. The *δέ* introduces a new address in contrast with the sowing to the flesh already described: "but for our part." Hartung, i. p. 166, states the case, and adds, that in such places it appears to take the place of *οὖν*. The phrase *τὸ καλόν*, here emphatic, signifies that which is beneficent, or what is absolutely good, beautifully good. See under next verse. 2 Thess. iii. 13. It is beneficence in its highest aspect, such as was embodied in a gracious miracle of healing—*καλῶς ποιεῖν*, Matt. xii. 12. It may here cover the ground of the previous context, as the duties there set forth are distinctive elements of the *τὸ καλόν*—acts of generosity, robed in that love which is itself perfection. Compare Luke viii. 15; Xen. *Cyr.* v. 3, 2. There is a *levis paronomasia* between *καλόν* and *-κακῶμεν*—in well-doing let us not be ill-hearted. And the duty is enforced by the cheering prospect—

Καιρῷ γὰρ ἰδίῳ θερίσομεν, μὴ ἐκλυόμενοι—"for in due time we shall reap, if we faint not." The unwearied well-doing is now understood as a sowing, and the figure of reaping is again introduced.

The phrase *καιρῷ ἰδίῳ* means "in due time," or at the proper season—the appointed time of the harvest. Compare the plural form, 1 Tim. ii. 6, vi. 15. It is a species of temporal dative, specifying the time within which the action takes place, Winer, § 31, 9; and usually it is expressed by *ἐν*. Krüger,

§ 48. "The harvest is the end of the world." Matt. xiii. 30. It is no objection to say, as is done by De Wette, that well-doing brings its own reward even now. 2 Cor. ix. 8, 9. For the figure is here preserved in harmony, and the sowing lasts all our lives. The time is with God, and His time for the harvest must be the right time and the best time. We are not to lose heart because the interval of labour may appear long, and the crop may not seem to be of speedy growth; for He is Judge, the seasons are in His hand, and at the divinely meted out period the invitation will be issued, "Thrust in thy sickle and reap." The concluding words bear upon the same thought—

Μὴ ἐκλυόμενοι—"if now we," or "provided that we faint not"—that is, in our well-doing. The sentence is thus conditional, or, as Krüger calls it, *hypothetische, im Falle—wenn*, § 56, 11: we shall reap only if we do not faint,—the tense of the participle connecting it with our present state. The participle *ἐκλυόμενοι* is stronger than the verb *ἐνκακῶμεν*. Bengel says of them, *ἐκκακ. est in velle, ἐκλυ. est in posse.* The first is weakness of heart; and the second, as the result of the first, describes relaxed effort, prostration of power,—spoken of corporeal fainting in Matt. xv. 32, and of mental exhaustion, Heb. xii. 3, 1 Macc. iii. 17; Joseph. *Antiq.* v. 2, 7. The view of the connection here given is the general view, enforcing the need of patience. Matt. xxiv. 13; Jas. v. 7; Rev. ii. 10. Some, however, take *μὴ ἐκλυόμενοι* in a merely temporal or predicative sense: we shall reap, and in reaping be unwearied. Thus Theodoret: *πόνου δίχα θερίσομεν τὰ σπειρόμενα.* This is tantamount to saying, *Nulla erit satietas vitæ æternæ*, and is pointed at in Luther's translation, *ohne aufhören;* the Vulgate having *non deficientes*, and the Claromontane *non fatigati.* See also Anselm, Homberg, and Usteri. Rückert and Schott are wrong, as Meyer shows, in objecting to this interpretation the occurrence of *μή* with the participle,—the prevailing usage in the New Testament (Winer, § 55, 5; Krüger, § 67, 7, etc.; Gayler, p. 274). But the exegesis, though grammatically tenable, is defective and unnatural. The last words are an emphatic warning, and describe the one condition on which the reward can be enjoyed; and while there is much about the working or sowing, there is nothing about the reward which may induce that fainting or down-heartedness against which the apostle guards. Similar repetitions occur in the apostle's writings, Rom. v. 15, 16, 17, 2 Cor. xii. 7, Gal. iii. 22, Eph. vi. 19, 20; John iii. 22. Hofmann begins a new sentence with the words, but the connection is awkward. Distinct encouragement is given us—the encouragement of the husbandman in sowing his fields, the bow in the cloud assuring him that seed-time and harvest shall not fail. The Christian doctrine of reward is in perfect harmony with the doctrine of grace.

Ver. 10. *Ἄρα οὖν ὡς καιρὸν ἔχομεν*—"So then as we have opportunity." The particles *ἄρα οὖν* indicate an inferential exhortation; the first, *ἄρα*, meaning "such being the case;" *οὖν*, therefore, *igitur*, being an argumentative conclusion. Klotz-Devarius, ii. 717. Compare Rom. v. 18, vii. 3, 25, viii. 12; Eph. ii. 19; 1 Thess. v. 6; 2 Thess. ii. 15. The particle *ὡς* has had different meanings assigned to it.

1. Beza, Bengel, Matthies, Schott, Olshausen, and Keerl regard it as meaning "so long as," or while,—*dum*, Vulgate,—a sense not warranted by Pauline usage, but which is expressed rather by *ἕως*.

2. Koppe, Paulus, Usteri, and De Wette render it "because,"—a signification not found in the Pauline writings, not even in 2 Tim. i. 3.

3. Knatchbull, Homberg, Wolf, Zachariæ, and Hilgenfeld give it the meaning of "as often as," or "when," *i.e.* as often as we have opportunity. This meaning, which overlooks the reference to the *καιρός* of the previous verse, is involved in the simple and grammatical interpretation, next given.

4. Meyer, Wieseler, Hofmann translate it "as," "in proportion as," or, in proportion to the circumstances. The *καιρός* here refers to the *καιρός* of the preceding verse: as there is one *καιρός* for reaping, there should be also one for sowing; and in proportion as we have it, so ought we to improve it; the season for reaping is coming, the season for sowing is fast passing away.

Καιρός is not *χρόνος*, *tempus*, but here *tempus opportunum;* though it has not that sense always, for it may be *importunum.* The Latin has no term for it, as Augustine complains, *Ep.* 197, 2. Ammonius says: *ὁ μὲν καιρὸς δηλοῖ ποιότητα χρόνου, χρόνος δὲ ποσότητα.* Trench, *Syn.* ii. p. 27. The phrase is a common one. See Wetstein *in loc.*, and see under Eph. v. 16.

Ἐργαζώμεθα τὸ ἀγαθὸν πρὸς πάντας—"let us do that which is good toward all." A, B[2], L, some MSS. read *ἐργαζόμεθα*, but the text has preponderant authority. Lachmann, in his smaller edition, adopted *ἐργαζόμεθα*, and read the clause interrogatively—an abrupt and unnatural exegesis. The indicative would not be a stronger hortative form, as Meyer remarks, and Winer in his *Grammar*, though not in his *Commentary*. The usage is foreign to the New Testament, at least in non-interrogative clauses. See John xi. 47, where, however, there is a question. But *ο* and *ω* are liable to be interchanged by copyists, as in Rom. v. 1,—the *ο* induced here by the previous *ἔχομεν*, *θερίσομεν*, and no version is in favour of the change. *Τὸ ἀγαθόν* is commonly taken to mean, either what is good in itself, Rom. ii. 10, vii. 19, xiii. 3—thus, too, *ἀγαθοποιεῖν*, 1 Pet. ii. 15, 20, iii. 6, 17, and *ἀγαθοεργεῖν*, 1 Tim. vi. 18; or what is good in result—an act of kindness or beneficence, Rom. xii. 21, 2 Cor. ix. 8, Philem. 14: so *ἀγαθοποιεῖν*, Luke vi. 33, 35; Sept. Num. x. 32, Judg. xvii. 13, Zeph. i. 13. The latter meaning is generally preferred. Meyer and Hilgenfeld, however, take it in the first sense. But there is no occasion to limit the meaning of the epithet; it is the thing which is good in each case, as the case may occur. The good thing may vary according to various wants, for it is to be done *πρὸς πάντας*—"towards all." Winer, § 49, *h*. The entire paragraph has the idea of doing good underlying it: the restoration of a fallen brother, ver. 1; the bearing of one another's burdens, ver. 2; communication on the part of the taught to the teacher, ver. 3; unwearied well-doing, ver. 10; and this verse seems to sum up all these thoughts into one vivid injunction, which not only comprises them all, but enjoins similar social duty in all its complex variety. Whatever its immediate form, whether kindness, or beneficence, or mercy, whether temporal or spiritual in character, it is still good in its nature, and is "the good thing," adapting itself to each case as it may turn up, in reference to all, generally or more specially.

Μάλιστα δὲ πρὸς τοὺς οἰκείους τῆς πίστεως—"but specially to them who are of the household of faith." The *δέ* is omitted in the Authorized Version. *Μάλιστα δέ* (*μάλιστα* superlative of *μάλα*) does not put the two classes in opposition, though the sub-adversative meaning of *δέ* is not lost. First a wider class is spoken of, and then a narrower class within it is pointed out, and by certain qualities distinguished from it. 1 Tim. v. 8, 17. The *οἱ οἰκεῖοι* are those belonging to the *οἰκία*—relatives, domestics. Thus Ammonius, *οἱ κατ' ἐπιγαμίαν ἐπιμιχθέντες τῷ οἴκῳ*; and Hesychius, *οἱ κατ' ἐπιγαμίαν προσήκοντες*; and it represents שְׁאֵר, *consanguineus*, Lev. xviii. 6, 12, 13. It means also one's own, or in a personal sense, what is not acquired,—*οἰκεῖα ξυνέσις*, mother-wit, Thucyd. i. 138; and in a national sense, *οἰκ. σῖτος*, home-grown corn, Thucyd. ii. 60. In a more general sense it signifies relatives, familiars, friends, associates—the idea of the *οἰκία* receding into the background, especially when the word is followed by the genitive of an abstract noun. See *sub voce*, Ast, *Lexicon Platon.*; Ellendt, *Lex. Sophocl.* Instances of the last signification are such as *οἰκεῖοι φιλοσοφίας*, Strabo, i. 13, p. 11, vol. i. ed. Cramer; *γεωγραφίας οἰκεῖος*, Strabo, i. 25, p. 20, ed. Cramer; *οἰκείους ὀλιγαρχίας*, Diod. Sic. xiii. 91, vol. i. p. 779, ed. Dindorf; *οἰκεῖοι τυραννίδος*, Diod. Sic. xix. 70, vol. ii. p. 1409; *πολιτικῆς ἀρετῆς οἰκεῖος*, Plutarch, *Philop.* p. 397; Sept. Isa. lviii. 7 (see Wetstein *in loc.*). Meyer, Ellicott, Alford, Borger, Baumgarten-Crusius, Trana, and Hofmann take the word, thus explained, as simply meaning, "those who belong to the faith." On the other hand, Beza, Schott, Rückert, Olshausen, Wieseler, Bisping, Schmoller, Bagge, Lightfoot, keep the original idea, which is also given in the English version—*domestici fidei*, Vulgate. Eph. ii. 19; 1 Tim. iii. 15; Heb. iii. 6; 1 Pet. ii. 5, iv. 17. Meyer's objection, that the clause, to get this meaning, must be *τοὺς ἡμῶν οἰκείους*, is naught, as the idea of "our" is implied; for, when a believer characterizes fellow-believers as a household, he does not need to say *ἡμῶν*, inasmuch as the *οἰκία τῆς πίστεως* is a common heritage. Perhaps, after all, the truth in this passage lies between these two extremes. The reference to the spiritual *οἰκία* may not be in formal prominence, and yet the image may have suggested the phrase to the apostle, as denotive of a close and mutually recognised relationship. The duty inculcated in the verse is not indeed to be graduated, but fellow-believers have a primary claim. For one form of the duty in this nearer relation, as enjoined on the Galatian churches, see 1 Cor. xvi.

1, 2—"the collection for the saints." There is no ground for the supposition of Jerome, that "teachers" are meant by the phrase: *domesticos fidei magistros nominat.*

The verse enjoins generally φιλανθρωπία, man-love, and especially φιλαδελφία, brother-love—the love of the ὁμόπιστοι, the family feeling of Christianity. Julian (*Ep.* 49) admits that Christians did obey this injunction: τρέφουσιν οἱ δυσσεβεῖς Γαλιλαῖοι πρὸς τοῖς ἑαυτῶν καὶ τοὺς ἡμετέρους. Tertullian, *Adver. Marc.* iv. 16.

Ver. 11. Now follows what is virtually a postscript, which glances at some points already advanced, characterizes in a new light the Judaizing teachers, gives fervent utterance in contrast to his own great and unchanging resolves, touches on the absorbing spirituality of the gospel and his relation to the Master and His cross, and ends with earnest benediction. Thus it begins somewhat abruptly—

Ἴδετε πηλίκοις ὑμῖν γράμμασιν ἔγραψα τῇ ἐμῇ χειρί—"Ye see," or "look ye with how large letters I have written to you with mine own hand." There are two marked divisions of opinion as to the meaning of πηλίκοις γράμμασιν, and two also as to the reference in ἔγραψα. The idea of the English version, that the first words assert the length or size of the epistle, is maintained by many, as Erasmus, Luther, Calvin, Beza, a-Lapide, Bengel, Borger, Schott, Olshausen, Neander, Baumgarten-Crusius, Hofmann, and Turner; and they, of course, hold in general that the entire epistle was written by his own hand. The Authorized Version, "how large a letter," follows some of its predecessors, as Tyndale, Cranmer, and the Genevan. Wycliffe has "with what manner of letters." To sustain the Authorized Version, it may be said that γράμματα, something written, may be rendered epistle, as the Latin *literæ.* 1 Macc. v. 10; Acts xxviii. 21; Ignat. *ad Rom.* viii. It may denote not only writings, letters or despatches, but a single letter or epistle—Thucydides, i. 30, where γράμματα is identified with ἐπιστολή in the preceding paragraph, and vii. 8, where a similar identification occurs. So, too, in Hebrew, הַסְּפָרִים, writings, 2 Kings xix. 14, rendered in our version "a letter," is followed first by a plural suffix, agreeing with it in form, and then by a singular suffix, agreeing with it in sense. In the parallel passage, Isa. xxxvii. 14, both the suffixes are singular, and the Septuagint renders in the singular, *βιβλίου . . . αὐτό.* The rabbinical expositors needlessly explain the use of the plural in different ways, Kimchi giving it a distributive meaning, and Luzzato supposing that it was customary to send duplicates of the same epistle. See Keil on the passage in Kings, and Alexander on that in Isaiah. But there are objections to taking the noun in this sense here. For, 1. The apostle never once employs *γράμματα* with this meaning, but uses *ἐπιστολή* no less than seventeen times. This place, therefore, can scarcely be regarded as an exception; at least there is nothing to induce us to suppose that in his choice of the term there is a solitary deviation from his usual style. 2. The accusative, were such the meaning, would naturally be expected. The cognate dative *γράμμασιν γράψαι*, like *εἶπε λόγῳ*, is not found in Paul's writings. 3. The meaning assigned to this unusual idiom—*eine höhere Innigkeit und Starke*—is not to be recognised, especially in a clause which has two other datives of person and instrument. The uncommon construction with a dative, and the selection of the term *γράμμασιν*, lead us therefore to conclude that the apostle means to say something more than that he has written a letter. 4. With the admission that *γράμματα* may not mean epistle, but a thing written, an alphabetic letter, the same signification may be ascribed to the clause: "with how many letters," is virtually, how long or large a letter. Hesychius defines *πηλίκον* by *οἷον, ὁποῖον.* Laurent adopts this definition, *qualibus literis*, as in the Vulgate: "mark you with what kind of letters I have written;" simply calling attention to the handwriting of his first letter to them (*Neutest. Studien*, p. 5, Gotha 1866). But *πηλίκοις* is not *πόσοις*, and means, not "how many," but "of what size;" for it applies not to number or character, or, as Ellicott expresses it, "it denotes geometrical, not numerical magnitude." Sept. Zech. ii. 2, *τοῦ ἰδεῖν πηλίκον τὸ πλάτος αὐτῆς ἐστιν καὶ πηλίκον τὸ μῆκος*; Heb. vii. 4, *θεωρεῖτε δὲ, πηλίκος οὗτος*—used in the same sense, though with an ethical application. Compare Plato, *Men.* p. 82, D, where *πόσοι* often occurs in the question, as *πόσοι ποδές*? whereas *πηλίκος* refers to the whole length of a line so measured: similarly *do.* p. 83, E, 85, A. 5. Nor can the epistle be really or absolutely called a long one, unless in connection with the emphatic clause, "with mine own hand." The Syriac omits the epithet altogether. The phrase *πηλίκοις γράμμασιν* in the dative seems then to mean, "with how large letters or characters,"—*γράμμασιν* being used as in Luke xxiii. 38,[1] 2 Cor. iii. 7. Why the apostle should have employed so large characters, whether it were from the necessity of age, or from infirmity, or from want of habit in writing Greek, it is impossible to say.

Inferential meanings have been superimposed upon the words. Thus Chrysostom and his followers suppose the allusion to be to the misshapen aspect of the letters, and so Estius, Winer, Rückert, Usteri, Hilgenfeld, and Alford. Chrysostom says: *τὸ δὲ, πηλίκοις, ἐμοὶ δοκεῖ οὐ τὸ μέγεθος, ἀλλὰ τὴν ἀμορφίαν τῶν γραμμάτων ἐμφαίνων λέγειν.* But *πηλίκοις* does not mean *ποίοις*, and size and awkwardness are different things, though perhaps to those who wrote a smaller hand elegance might appear to be incompatible with largeness. Nor can it be averred, with Chrysostom and Jerome, that the apostle did not know how to write Greek well; his early education at Tarsus forbids the supposition. At all events, the words do not of themselves convey such an idea; and though the great size of the letters would differ from ordinary handwriting, it might not present sprawling and unsightly characters. Why, then, did he call their attention to the size of the characters which he employed? Theodore of Mopsuestia says: *μέλλων καθάπτεσθαι τῶν ἐναντίων, ἄγαν μείζοσιν ἐχρήσατο γράμμασιν ἐμφαίνων ὅτι οὔτε αὐτὸς ἐρυθριᾷ οὔτε ἀρνεῖται τὰ λεγόμενα*—an opinion virtually acquiesced in by Lightfoot. But it does not follow that boldness of handwriting is any natural or undeniable proof of distinct and unabashed statement. Pelagius puts it thus: *Intelligite quod non timeam qui literas manu mea nuper scripsi.* Jerome gives another view: *Ne aliqua suppositæ epistolæ suspicio nasceretur.* Such a guard against forgery not only implies that his handwriting was already known to them, but the same purpose might have been served by a brief salutation.—Meyer, who restricts the reference to ver. 12, or to 12–16 or 18, puts down the large letters to the apostle's desire to impress his readers with the importance of the statements so written. But the sentiments in the conclusion of the epistle

[1] This refers to the reading of the Received Text. See Tischendorf's note *in loc.*

are not more momentous than those which occur in the body of it. Any amanuensis also, as Wieseler remarks, could easily have used such large characters, if so instructed.

But what is the reference of ἔγραψα? The verb is what is called the epistolary aorist—"I have written," and it is used in reference to the point of time when the epistle should be received and read: ἴδετε—as if the letter were in their hands, and before their eyes—"Look you with what large characters I have written." The phrase may either characterize the postscript only, or it may comprehend the whole epistle. The verb itself will scarcely decide the question. Generally it is used of what precedes in a document, and it naturally occurs at its virtual conclusion, as in Rom. xv. 15, 1 Pet. v. 12. It is employed also in reference to the previous portion of a letter, as in 1 Cor. ix. 15, Philem. 19, 21, 1 John ii. 14, 21, 26, v. 13. The instances of its reference, with its proper sense, to some former communication, are of course not in point. 1 Cor. v. 9; 2 Cor. ii. 3, 4, 9; Winer, § 40, 5, *b*. 2. That ἔγραψα might refer to what follows, is not to be denied—the mind of the writer not looking, indeed, to what he is to write, but specially to the period of the reception of his letter by those for whom he is writing; as in the instance cited from the *Martyrdom of Polycarp*, x. § 1, in which the church of Smyrna say, ἐγράψαμεν ὑμῖν, which, occurring just after the opening salutation, refers to the subsequent sections of the epistle. *Patres Apostol.* p. 392, ed. Dressel. Compare Thucydides, i. 1; Poppo *in loc.* Similarly, too, we have ἔπεμψα, Acts xxiii. 30. Compare ἔπεμψε, Xen. *Anab.* i. 9, 25, ii. 4, 16, on the first of which places Kühner remarks, *Aoristus positus est respectu habito temporis quo alter donum accipiebat.* 2 Cor. ix. 3; Eph. vi. 22; Col. iv. 8. The phrase τῇ ἐμῇ χειρί, occurring also in other epistles, shows that the apostle usually employed an amanuensis; and especially after letters had been forged and circulated in his name, he attached some autographic sentence at the close, frequently a benediction or salutation—Ὅ ἐστι σημεῖον ἐν πάσῃ ἐπιστολῇ, 2 Thess. iii. 17. Compare Rom. xvi. 21, 22, 25; 1 Cor. xvi. 21; Col. iv. 18. The Ambrosian Hilary notes *in loc.*: *Ubi enim holographa manus est falsum dici non potest, ne forte circumventi excusarent de epistola, quasi aut falsa esset, aut non esset apostoli, nolentes se reprehendi.*

Augustine gives the meaning as *cave ne quisquam sub nomine Epistolæ ejus fallat incautos.* While the body of the epistle was written by a secretary, the apostle subjoined with his own hand some concluding sentence; and it has been argued that such is the case in the epistle before us—an opinion held by Jerome, Grotius, Meyer, Bisping, Jowett, Lightfoot, and Bagge. Admitting the possibility of the exegesis, we are inclined to deny its probability. For, 1. What may be called the natural reference of ἔγραψα is to the previous portion of the epistle. The present γράφω appears to be used in such a case, and in reference to what is immediately under hand, as in 1 Cor. iv. 14, xiv. 37, 2 Cor. xiii. 10, 2 Thess. iii. 17, 1 John ii. 12, 13; Winer, 40, 5, *b*. 2. 2. Nor is there any indication of any breach, or pause, or change, as in Rom. xvi. 24, 25, and in 2 Thess. iii. 17. Instead then of saying, with Lightfoot, that "at this point the apostle took the pen from his amanuensis," we are inclined rather to say, that at this point the apostle pauses, and reading what he has written, the form of the handwriting struck him, and he adds abruptly the words of the verse before us. 3. The ὑμῖν comes in naturally, too, on the same supposition: *mei pectoris apud vòs index* (Erasmus). He had not dictated the epistle to another, but he had written it himself; no one came between him and them, not even a secretary. 4. It would also be odd if a sentence calling attention to the handwriting should be the first specimen of it, and the asyndetic nature of the construction is in favour of the same view. 5. The τῇ ἐμῇ χειρί has in this way a special significance, from the fact that he had written all the epistle with his own hand, and not merely a few concluding clauses. Thus the entire letter seems to have been written by the apostle himself; such a deviation from his wont being adduced apparently as a proof of his earnest regard for them, and of his profound anxiety about them in the present perilous crisis. The "large characters" would convey to their minds, who knew him so well with his habits and infirmities, something perhaps which we may not be able to recognise. He puts himself to the trouble of framing those great characters from personal interest in them, and the document was meant as a circular for all the Galatian churches. See under ἀσθένεια, iv. 13. *Utinam*, adds Pareus, αὐτόγραφον *apostoli nobis habere et videre liceret.* Compare what is said in Eusebius vi. 24 of the ὁλόγραφοι ἐπισημειώσεις of Origen, and the note in Heinichen, vol. ii. 221; and also another note to v. 20, *do.* p. 98. It is needless to inquire into the kind of letter, uncial or cursive, which the apostle employed on this occasion, or whether the material was papyrus (2 John 12) or vellum (2 Tim. iv. 13)—the former being the more difficult to write upon, and that perhaps generally used (3 John 13).

Ver. 12. The apostle now shows up the hollowness of the Judaists, and utters his last warning against them. They were not conscientious in insisting on circumcision as indispensable to salvation. Their motive was to screen themselves from persecution, and to gain a good report among the Jews. The enmity of these Jews toward those of their brethren who made a Christian profession was greatly modified by the thought, that they had not only not ceased to observe the Mosaic ordinance themselves, but were actually forcing it on Gentile converts. This manifestation of zeal for the law was regarded as a compensation for their abandonment of the synagogue; any Gentiles who might submit to circumcision being apparently counted as so many Jewish proselytes—the successful proselytizers propitiating in this way their angry and vindictive kinsmen. But this their real motive they speciously veiled.

Ὅσοι θέλουσιν εὐπροσωπῆσαι ἐν σαρκί—"As many as desire to make a fair show in the flesh." The connection proposed by Alford is, "As my epistle, so my practice. My *γράμματα* are not *εὐπρόσωπα*, and I have no sympathy with those who desire to make a fair show in the flesh." But such a connection is not very obvious, and it assumes a meaning of *πηλίκοις* which the epithet does not warrant. The verb occurs only here, but the form *εὐπροσωπίσθησαν* occurs in Symmachus as his rendering of נָעֵמוּ, Ps. cxl. 6; Orig. *Hex.* vol. i. p. 684, ed. Montfaucon, Paris 1713. But we have the adjective, Sophocles, *Ajax*, 1009, *δέξαιτ' ἂν εὐπρόσωπος*; *φίλον . . . εὐπρόσωπον καὶ καλόν*, Aristoph. *Plut.* 976, in an ideal sense; and in Demosthenes, *λόγους εὐπροσώπους καὶ μύθους*, *De Corona*, vol. i. p. 176, ed. Schaefer. See other examples in Wetstein and Kypke *in loc.* There are also other compounds, as Aristoph. *Nubes*, 363; and Cicero has the clause, *nec enim conquisitores φαινοπροσωπεῖν audent*, *Epist. ad Attic.* vii. 21, and he uses the verbal adjective, *do.* xiv. 22. See Rost und

Palm, *sub voce.* The verb in the verse means to assume a specious appearance. It is not *placere*, as in the Vulgate, but rather that by which the pleasing is carried out. Chrysostom explains it by *εὐδοκιμεῖν*. The meaning is not in result very different from that given by the scholiast—*ὅσοι θέλουσιν ἀρέσκειν Ἰουδαίοις*.

As for *ἐν τῇ σαρκί*, 1. some refer it to fleshly things, specially to circumcision, as Beza, Winer, Olshausen, Schott. But this sense is too restricted and technical in itself, though it was also so far in the apostle's mind, as is plain from what is stated in the following clause. Michaelis takes it as the flesh of the Galatians; but this meaning would require *ὑμῶν*, and the *σάρξ* is the errorists' own sphere of pretentious display.

2. Others give the weak sense, *apud homines*—among or before men. The Greek fathers and others hold this view. It is indeed implied in the verb, but not expressed by this phrase.

3. Others again, as Meyer and Bagge, make it all but equivalent to *σαρκικοὶ ὄντες*, a sense which is only inferential.

4. The *ἐν* denotes the sphere in which the specious appearance shows itself, and *σάρξ* is still the unrenewed nature cropping out under its more special aspect of sensuousness and externalism. It was a sphere opposed to the Spirit in principle and result,—the sphere of the flesh, on which they had fallen back after having begun in the Spirit, and which still lusted against the Spirit, which negatived the freeness of justification, and which developing self into selfishness, and originating dark and pernicious "works," severs its victim from the "fruits" of love, joy and beneficence. So far from "crucifying the flesh," they cherished it, nay, wished to make a fair show in it,—to appear so well in what was specially opposed to the grace and genius of the gospel as to disarm the enmity of their Jewish brethren.

Of the party, larger or smaller in number, who made this fair show in the flesh, the apostle says—

Οὗτοι ἀναγκάζουσιν ὑμᾶς περιτέμνεσθαι—"these are compelling you to be circumcised,"—*οὗτοι* emphatic: it is those who, or these and none other,—these are the very class who are forcing circumcision upon you; that is, their teaching, example, and influence amount to a species of moral compulsion. Comp. ii. 3, 14. The present denotes an action going on, not completed. Bernhardy, p. 375; Schmalfeld, § 54, 4. And all this for this end—

Μόνον ἵνα τῷ σταυρῷ τοῦ Χριστοῦ μὴ διώκωνται—"only lest they should suffer persecution for the cross of Christ." The indicative *διώκονται*, adopted by Tischendorf, has in its favour A, C, F, K, L, and many MSS. But it appears to be a blunder in writing *ο* for *ω*—no uncommon occurrence, as Rom. v. 1 and in ver. 9 of this chapter. The unsolecistic reading is supported by B, D, E, א, and many MSS.; and the order *ἵνα μὴ* of the Received Text is found in F, K, L, and some of the fathers, but the other order is found in A, B, C, D, א, in the Vulgate, Gothic, Syriac, and Jerome, etc. See A. Buttmann, *Gr.* § 139, 39.

For *μόνον*, see ii. 10. They make a fair show in the flesh, only their purpose in doing so is a very selfish and unworthy one; it is to escape persecution. The dative is that of ground, or of proximate cause. "From signifying the *αἴτιον* or *ὑφ' οὗ*, the dative naturally passed on to the expression of the *αἰτία* or *δι' ὅ*—'on account of which.'" Donaldson, § 451. Plato, *Menex.* p. 238, D, where three similar datives occur in succession. Winer, § 31, 6; Bernhardy, p. 102. Compare Rom. xi. 20, 30, 2 Cor. ii. 13. On the other hand, Jerome, Luther, Tyndale, Grotius, Winer, De Wette, Conybeare, and Ewald take the dative as that of instrument—lest they should be persecuted with the cross of Christ: *Ne participes fiant crucis suppliciorum Christi*, h.e. *qualia Christus nuper subiit.* Winer, comparing 2 Cor. i. 5 and Col. i. 24. But the cross of Christ always with the apostle means more than mere suffering; it signifies the atoning death of the Son of God, as in ver. 14 and in v. 11. The cross of Christ offered salvation without works of law of any kind; dispensed with the observance of Mosaic rites and ordinances as a condition of acceptance with God; gave welcome to the heathen without obliging them to become Jewish proselytes as a requisite preliminary step; and therefore the profession or preaching of it stirred up the malignant hostility of the Jews, as it destroyed their national distinction and pre-eminence, and placing the Gentile world on a level with them, desecrated in their imagination all which they and their fathers had revered and cherished for ages. To escape the enmity of the Jews so fiercely fighting for their institutions, the Judaists insisted on circumcising the Gentile converts, and thus attempted to propitiate their opponents by showing that, in attaching themselves to the gospel, they had not deserted the law,—nay, that they enjoined its observance on all who proposed to become members of the church, and were on this account enabled to carry Jewish influence into spheres of society which the synagogue had not in itself the means of reaching. But this syncretistic mixture of law and gospel veiled the cross and its salvation, so free and fitting to mankind without distinction of race or blood; so that their profession was deceptive, perilous in its consequences, and prompted and shaped by an ignoble and cowardly selfishness; it was a "fair show," but only in the sphere of fleshly things, and assumed on purpose to avoid persecution. They wanted that earnest perception and belief of the one saving truth of which the cross is the centre, and that courage in holding it in its simplicity and purity against all hazards, which the cross inspires. In proof of his statement, that their motive is selfish and cowardly—the avoidance of persecution—the apostle adds—

Ver. 13. *Οὐδὲ γὰρ οἱ περιτεμνόμενοι αὐτοὶ νόμον φυλάσσουσιν*—"For not even do they who are getting themselves circumcised keep the law." The reading *περιτετμημένοι* appears to be an evident correction—the reading of B, L, and the Claromontane Latin, and is adopted by Reiche, Meyer, Ewald, and Usteri. The other reading of the present participle has in its favour A, B, C, D[1], F, א, several versions and fathers. The present participle middle describes the party as in continuous activity. To regard it as denoting those merely who had been circumcised, changes the prevailing nominative from the false teachers to their pupils. Is it then of the persons seduced into circumcision that the apostle says that they do not keep the law, though by the act of circumcision they took on them an obligation to obey it? Neander and Windischmann so understand it—that is, of persons born heathens induced by the Judaists to submit to circumcision, and becoming the organs and agitators of the Judaizing party. But may not born Jews, so loudly insisting on circumcision, also receive the appellation? Or does he not refer rather to the whole faction, circumcised itself and forcing circumcision on others, which, professing such respect for the initiatory rite, is by no means sincere, for it neglects the law, and does not carry out its obedience to the requisite extent? The *οἱ περιτεμνόμενοι* includes both aspects of these questions, but does not decide whether the clique was Jewish or heathen in origin, and it depicts the whole party as being busily engaged in carrying out their Judaizing tendencies, to whom circumcision was everything, to whom it was a distinctive watchword; they prided themselves on possession of it, and persistently pressed it on others. This is the meaning in effect contended for by Hilgenfeld, Holsten, Lightfoot, and Gwynne, who take the phrase in a substantive sense—"the circumcisers for themselves," or "the circumcision party." The participle thus loses its temporal reference. Winer, § 45, 7. Hilgenfeld quotes the Acts of Peter and Paul—*οὗτοι οἱ περιτεμνόμενοι*, § 63, ed. Tischendorf. While this is grammatically warranted, it is not strictly necessary. The participle characterizes the Judaists by their factional distinction. Hofmann makes it characterize Jews in general, the errorists being depicted in their Jewish quality, like *ἀποθνήσκοντες* characterizing men in general, or rather the Levites, in Heb. vii. 8, and different from *θνητοί*. But such a generalization is beyond the scope of the apostle's argument.

The wretched inconsistency of the Judaistic party is made apparent—*οὐδὲ γὰρ*, "not even they," keep the law. The emphatic *νόμος*, though without the article, does not mean law as a principle (Lightfoot, Peile), nor moral obedience (Middleton, *Greek Art.* p. 306), nor the obligations arising out of the law (Gwynne); but the law of Moses given to the nation of the Jews—the code to which Gentile converts became debtors by their circumcision. The noun is often anarthrous, as being so definite and distinctive in itself. Winer, § 19, 1. See under ii. 16, pp. 163–4. *Φυλάσσειν τὸν νόμον* is to keep or obey the law; under a different aspect the *νομοφύλαξ* was one who guarded the law from infraction. Plato, *Leg.* 755, A. They do not observe the whole law, but make selections among its precepts, though the entire code is based on the one divine authority. It is true, as Theodoret remarks, that their distance from Jerusalem—*πόῤῥω τῶν Ἱεροσολύμων*—made it impossible for them to keep the feasts, offer sacrifice, and abstain from ceremonial impurities; but the apostle speaks not of geographical inability, but of moral inconsistency. Nor is there such a latent thought in the phrase as that of Jerome, that the law cannot be fully obeyed, *propter infirmitatem carnis.* Nor is it the ceremonial law simply that the apostle refers to, for one peculiar Jewish inconsistency was the attention paid to ceremonial in preference to moral duties. Matt. xxiii. 3, 4. The apostle makes no sort of apology for them, he simply exposes the hollowness of their zeal for the law; and might he not have had in his eye such inconsistencies as he so sternly reprimands in Rom. ii. 17–24? Had they been actuated by honest zeal, they would strive to obey the whole law. They were actuated by another and a sinister motive—

Ἀλλὰ θέλουσιν ὑμᾶς περιτέμνεσθαι ἵνα ἐν τῇ ὑμετέρᾳ σαρκὶ καυχήσωνται—"but they desire to have you circumcised in order that they may glory in your flesh"—*αὐτοί* and *ὑμετέρᾳ* being in contrast. Wieseler, Ewald, and some others take *σάρξ* as in ver. 12—man's fleshly nature, of which suffering themselves to be circumcised was an outflow. Thus Bagge —"that they may glory in your carnality," that you have yielded to their influence, and followed their example. But the supposed parallel in ver. 12 is not to be insisted on; for the pronoun *ὑμετέρα* emphatic gives to *σάρξ* a distinctive reference, especially in so close a connection with *περιτέμνεσθαι.* Therefore it is to be taken in its literal significance—either *corpus mutilatum* (Borger, Winer, Meyer), or *præputium ipsum abscissum* (Beza, Rückert). So too Theophylact, *ἵνα ἐν τῷ κατακόπτειν τὴν ὑμετέραν σάρκα καυχήσωνται ὡς διδάσκαλοι ὑμῶν.*

This clause is not opposed to the last clause of the twelfth verse. In the twelfth verse one motive is assigned to the false teachers—they spread their Judaistic notions that they might not be persecuted; here another motive is imputed to them—that they might glory over the circumcision of their converts. This last motive expounds the process by which the former works itself out. Their power to get their followers circumcised, or the circumcision of Gentile converts manœuvred so effectively by them, was paraded before their fanatical countrymen, who could not persecute a party that in bringing men over to Christianity made them, and insisted on making them, at the same time Jewish proselytes; inconsistent and capricious relation to the law on the part of the agitators being overlooked and forgiven, in consideration of the primary honour they were doing to Moses under a profession of serving Christ. They might say, We are doing more for the spread of Judaism than its most rigid adherents, affirming of this and that one circumcised as the condition of his joining the church, *hic quoque per me factus est Judæus* (Morus). The apostle gives the clique no credit for sincerity, as if they were acting like men under prejudice or partial enlightenment; he imputes to them cowardice, hypocrisy, and self-interestedness. Theirs was not a mistaken zeal, like that which characterized himself in the earlier part of his life: they were mean and mercenary in their opposition to the apostle, and utterly craven in soul in their relation to their Jewish brethren.

Ver. 14. *'Εμοὶ δὲ μὴ γένοιτο καυχᾶσθαι εἰ μὴ ἐν τῷ σταυρῷ τοῦ Κυρίου ἡμῶν 'Ιησοῦ Χριστοῦ*—"But as for me, far be it to glory save in the cross of our Lord Jesus Christ." *'Εμοί*, emphatic in position, is the dative of ethical relation (Winer, § 31, 4; Thucydides, ii. 7, and Arnold's note): *ἐμοὶ δέ*—but as far as regards me, in contrast with them and their *καύχησις* in the circumcision of their misguided converts. The *σάρξ* in which the Judaists wished to make a fair show is the representative element of a system directly and wholly opposed to that, of which *σταυρός* is the central principle and in which the apostle gloried. For *μὴ γένοιτο*, see ii. 17. The formula is here followed by the infinitive, as in Sept. Gen. xliv. 7, 17, Josh. xxii. 29, xxiv. 16, 1 Macc. ix. 10, xiii. 5, 9, 10. It occurs also in a positive form, *λαβεῖν μοι γένοιτο*, Xen. *Cyr.* vi. 3, 11; and *ὧν ἔφη μηδενὶ γένοιτο πεῖραν ὑμῶν λαβεῖν*, Polyb. xv. 10, 4. The phrase "God forbid" really expresses the strong emotion or revulsion of feeling which interjects these decided words.

The Saviour is named "our Lord Jesus Christ"—the full name adding solemnity to the abjuration, and *ἡμῶν* giving believers like himself a community of interest in Him.

By *σταυρός* some understand sufferings endured for Christ, as in the phrase, taking up one's cross (Luther, Grotius, Koppe, Rosenmüller),—a view alike superficial and out of harmony with the context. The "cross," as it is understood by the majority of interpreters, means the atoning death of the Son of God, in that "suffering, humiliation, and here more specially self-abnegation which is essentially involved in the idea of it" (Ellicott). It carries us back to *σταυρῷ*, with the same meaning, in ver. 12. The Judaizers boasted of their influence, of their converts' conformity to the Mosaic ritual, of the unhappy compromise between law and gospel which they had so far effected, but which secured them from persecution on account of the cross. That cross was to them a *σκάνδαλον* in a variety of ways, especially as the symbol of a full and free salvation through faith, and without any ritualistic observance. But the cross in its expiatory sufferings was everything to the apostle; and in it, and only in it, would he glory.

Δι' οὗ ἐμοὶ κόσμος ἐσταύρωται, κἀγὼ κόσμῳ—"by which the world has been crucified to me, and I to the world." The reading *τῷ* before *κόσμῳ* is doubtful—A, B, C[1], D[1], F, א omit it, while it is found in C[3], D[3], K, L, and many of the fathers. The *ὁ* before *κόσμος* has no authority, though *τῷ* might be omitted for the sake of uniformity, or overlooked on account of the previous *γω*. The antecedent to *οὗ* is matter of dispute and difficulty. Is it "by whom," that is Christ, or "by which," that is the cross? The Vulgate has *per quem*, and it is followed by Luther, Beza, De Wette, Meyer, Baumgarten-Crusius, Bisping, Wieseler, Trana. The reference to *σταυρῷ* is given by Theodoret, and is adopted by Calvin, Bengel, Winer, Usteri, Bagge, Brown, Hofmann, Lightfoot, Jowett, Schmoller, Matthias. The English version has "by whom," with "whereby" in the margin—"whereby" occurring also in Tyndale, Cranmer, and the Genevan. Ellicott's argument, that "as the emphasized *Κυρίου ἡμῶν 'Ιησοῦ Χριστοῦ* just precedes, the relative will more naturally refer to these words," is certainly not conclusive, for the relative does not always refer to the nearest antecedent; and the statement of Alford, that "the greater antecedent *K. ἡ. I. X.*, coming after *σταυρῷ*, has thrown it into the shade," may be met with a simple denial, for it may be replied that *σταυρῷ* has the primary place in the verse, and keeps that place as a prominent object in the apostle's mind till it is reproduced by its verb, the instrument followed by a reference to the act done upon it. Wieseler's argument for *I. X.* as antecedent is weak. "It is not indeed the cross itself," he says, but it is "the personal Christ through the cross that is the source of all our salvation." Nobody denies it, and the apostle uses the term in its connection with the personal Christ, for without Him and His death it is nothing. Windischmann thinks that if *Χριστοῦ* were the antecedent, *ἐν ᾧ* would most naturally have followed it, according to the analogy of many other places, or *συν ᾧ*, as Lightfoot suggests after ii. 20, Col. ii. 20. Nor is it the analogy of the New Testament to represent Christ as the agent of our crucifixion, or as our actual crucifier; for *δι' οὗ* followed by *ἐσταύρωται* most naturally points out the effective cause, and cannot of itself mean, as Ellicott after Meyer gives it, "by whose crucifixion." Besides, the object of the apostle, as the context shows, is to exalt the cross, which among these errorists was depreciated and shrunk from. After all, the sense is not materially different whichever view may be adopted. It was by the cross only in its connection with Christ that the world was crucified to the apostle, or it was only by his union with Christ in being crucified with Him that he was crucified to the world.

Κόσμος wants the article, like a proper name, and rather anomalously, as it usually wants it after a preposition, or in regimen with a previous noun. Winer, § 19. There is inter-crucifixion—the world has died to him, and he has died to the world. The "world" is not *res et religio Judaica;* it is the sphere of things in which the *σάρξ* lives and moves—that in which self and sense delight themselves: opposed to that sphere of things in which the *πνεῦμα* finds its fitting nutriment and exercise, and also to "the new creature" in the following verse. Nor is "the world" the same as the "elements of the world" in iv. 3 (Bagge), but it is wider in significance—*τὰ βιωτικὰ πράγματα* (Theodoret). The term represents wealth, power, pleasure, indulgence, "lust of the flesh, lust of the eyes, pride of life,"—all that draws humanity after it, which so many seem to crave as their only portion, and in which they seem to find their supreme delight. The world in this sense is opposed to God: "the friendship of this world is enmity with God," Jas. iv. 4; 1 John ii. 15. The apostle had long seen all this hostility and hollowness on the part of the world, and so he had done with it. It was crucified to him; it was a thing done to death for him, and he was done to death so far as regarded it. As Schott pithily puts it, *alter pro mortuo habet alterum.* Each had been nailed to the cross; each to other was dead. Christ's cross effected this separation. It was the result of neither morbid disappointment, nor of the bitter wail of "vanity of vanities," nor of a sense of failure in worldly pursuits, nor of the persecutions he had undergone—scourging, imprisonment, hunger, thirst, fastings, and nakedness. By none of these things did he die to the world. But it was by his union with the Crucified One: death in Him and with Him was his death to the world, and the death of that world to him. See under ii. 19, 20, and v. 24.

Ver. 15. The reading varies: the common text begins, *ἐν γὰρ Χριστῷ Ἰησοῦ οὔτε περιτομή τι ἰσχύει.* The better reading is probably *οὔτε γὰρ περιτομή τι ἔστιν οὔτε ἀκροβυστία*—"For neither doth circumcision avail anything nor uncircumcision." *Ἰσχύει* may be borrowed from v. 6, and it is not read in A, B, C, D[1], F, א. The words *ἐν γὰρ Χριστῷ Ἰησοῦ* are found in A, C, D, F, K, L, א. B reads *οὔτε γάρ* with several versions, and with Chrysostom, Jerome, Augustine. The MSS. authority for the longer reading is probably overborne by the fact that it is taken from v. 6, and thus the shorter reading may be preferable. *Γάρ* introduces a confirmatory explanation. For the first clause, see under v. 6.

Ἀλλὰ καινὴ κτίσις—"but a new creature." *Κτίσις* is sometimes active—the act of creation, Rom. i. 20; or passive—what is created, either collectively, Rom. viii. 19, or individually as here and in 2 Cor. v. 17. The phrase is borrowed probably from the בריה חדשה of the Rabbins, and bases itself on such language as Isa. xliii. 18, lxv. 17; Schoettgen, i. 308. Thus you have in Eph. ii. 15, "to make in himself of twain one new man;" iv. 24, "put on the new man;" and in Rom. vi. 6, "our old man is crucified," etc. This spiritual renewal springs out of living union to Christ, and it is everything. For it re-enstamps the image of God on the soul, and restores it to its pristine felicity and fellowship. It is not external—neither a change of opinion, party, or outer life. Nor is it a change in the essence or organization of the soul, but in its inner being—in its springs of thought and feeling, in its powers and motives—by the Spirit of God and the influence of the truth. "All old things pass away; behold, all things are become new." 2 Cor. v. 17. This creation is "new,"—new in its themes of thought, in its susceptibilities of enjoyment, and in its spheres of energy; it finds itself in a new world, into which it is ushered by a new birth.

Ver. 16. *Καὶ ὅσοι τῷ κανόνι τούτῳ στοιχοῦσιν* or *στοιχήσουσιν*—"And as many as are walking, or shall walk, by this rule." For the present we have A, C[1], D, F, Clarom., Syriac, Gothic, Cyril, Jerome, and Augustine. The future has in its favour B, C[2], K, L, א, the Vulgate (*secuti fuerint*), Chrysostom, and Theodoret. As there was a temptation to change to the future, Ellicott holds by the present with Tischendorf. Alford says, on the other hand, "the correction has been to the present," and adds, "no reason can be given why the future should be substituted." So also Lightfoot and Meyer. The future is certainly the more difficult, and looks forward to the time when the epistle should be received, and they should read and understand what is meant by *τῷ κανόνι τούτῳ*. Besides, they were scarcely walking by it just now, but he hoped better things of them. The two *σσ* in the verb might also originate a various reading. The nominative *ὅσοι*, standing absolute for the sake of prominence, necessitates a broken construction. Winer, § 63, 1, *d*. The *ὅσοι* are in contrast to *ὅσοι* in ver. 12, "as many as desire to make a fair show." The *κανών* is in harmony with the verb, it is a line drawn; and the dative is that of norm, as in v. 16, "Walk by the Spirit." The figure of walk falls so far into the background, and the idea remains of "course of life." This rule is plainly that laid down in v. 15: as many as live under the guidance of this great leading principle—that what is outer is nothing, and what is inner is everything; that to be a Jew or Gentile, circumcised or uncircumcised, matters not, is neither privilege nor barrier, while a spiritual change is inclusive of all blessing for eternity,—peace be on all those who adopt this *norma vivendi*.

Εἰρήνη ἐπ' αὐτοὺς καὶ ἔλεος—"peace be on them and mercy"—a benediction—*εἴη*, not *ἐστίν* or *ἔσται*, being understood. The position and order make the whole clause emphatic. The common words are *χάρις καὶ εἰρήνη*, as in i. 3—all blessing. See under Eph. i. 2. Here the result is put first, not as if he did not intend to add any other blessing, but he emphasizes peace as being the distinctive and prominent theocratic gift suggested by the term Israel and in close connection with it. Peace and compassion, or mercy, now, and "mercy of the Lord in that day." 2 Tim. i. 18. The blessing comes—*ἐπί*—on them from above. The prayer is probably a reminiscence of Ps. cxxv.

5, "Peace shall be upon Israel," and of Ps. cxxviii. 6, "Yea, thou shalt see thy children's children, and peace upon Israel."

Καὶ ἐπὶ τὸν Ἰσραὴλ τοῦ Θεοῦ—"and on the Israel of God." The meaning turns on the sense assigned to *καί*. If it be only copulative "and," then the Israel of God is an additional body to the *ὅσοι*, and would mean Jewish believers. But if *καί* be explicative, signifying "to wit," then the Israel of God is the same body with the *ὅσοι*, and is the whole believing community, comprising alike Jews and Gentiles. The one view, that the phrase means Jewish believers, is held by Ambrosiaster, Beza, Grotius, Estius, Schoettgen, Bengel, Schott, Matthies, De Wette, Brown, Ellicott, Trana, and apparently Jowett. The other opinion is held by names as great: Chrysostom, Theodoret, Luther, Calvin, Calovius, Borger, Winer, Olshausen, Meyer, Sardinoux, Lightfoot, Alford. Justin Martyr twice calls believers generally *Ἰσραηλιτικὸν γένος*; and affirming that Christ is the true Israel or wrestler, he calls all who flee for refuge through Him "the blessed Israel." *Dial. c. Tryph.* §§ 11, 125, 135, *Opera*, ii. pp. 42, 418, 446, 446, ed. Otto.

Can *καί* be really explicative? Ellicott says that Meyer's examples do not seem conclusive (1 Cor. iii. 5, viii. 12, xv. 38), nor do they. Still it is to be found in this sense, which Winer (§ 53, 3) calls epexegetical, introducing the same thing under another aspect. But there is no case so peculiarly distinctive in sense as this would be. And,

1. In the quotations commonly adduced to prove this position, that Israel means believers, Gentiles as well as Jews, as Rom. ii. 28, 29, ix. 6–8, Gal. iv. 28, 31, it is Jews by blood who are spoken of or referred to in connection with the appellation.

2. The simple copulative meaning is not to be departed from, save on very strong grounds; and there is no ground for such a departure here, so that the Israel of God are a party included in, and yet distinct from, the *ὅσοι*.

3. The apostle is not in the habit of calling the church made up of Jews and Gentiles—Israel. Israel is used eleven times in Romans, but in all the instances it refers to Israel proper; and so do it and *Ἰσραηλίτης* in every other portion of the New Testament. In the Apocalypse, the 144,000 sealed of Israel stand in contrast to "the great multitude which no man can number,"

taken out of the Gentile or non-Israelitish races. Rev. vii. 9. The "Israelite indeed" is also one by blood. John i. 47; comp. 1 Cor. x. 18. The ὅσοι may not be Gentile believers as such, and opposed to Jewish believers, but the entire number who walk according to this rule; while Paul finds among them a certain class to whom his heart turns with instinctive fondness —"the Israel of God." Jatho's distinction is baseless—the one party being those who, warned by this epistle, should renounce their error and walk according to this rule; and the other, those who had uniformly held the sacred and evangelical doctrine. It may be said indeed, on the one hand, that the apostle has been proving that the Jew, as a Jew, has no privilege above the Gentiles, that both Jew and Gentile are on a level, so that both believing Jews and Gentiles may therefore be called Israel. It may be replied, however, that the apostle never in any place so uses the name, never gives the grand old theocratic name to any but the chosen people.

4. To the apostle there were two Israels—"they are not all Israel which are of Israel,"—and he says here, not Israel *κατὰ σάρκα*, but "the Israel of God," or the true believing Israel; his own brethren by a double tie—by blood, and especially by grace. Was it unnatural for the apostle to do this, especially after rebuking false Israel—the wretched Judaizers—who certainly were not the Israel of God?

Ver. 17. *Τοῦ λοιποῦ, κόπους μοι μηδεὶς παρεχέτω*—"Henceforth let no one cause troubles to me." The phrase *τοῦ λοιποῦ* occurs only here, and is simply the genitive of time, and not the same as *λοιπόν* or *τὸ λοιπόν*, which also occurs. It means at any time in the future—*τὸ λοιπόν* signifying simply "during the future." Hermann, *ad Viger.* p. 706. Let no one cause me troubles or annoyance, doubting his apostolical authority, neutralizing his preaching or misrepresenting its import, and obliging him to write again in so large characters with his own hand. His apostolical authority he had asserted in full, striking, and unqualified terms in the first chapter; and he has it at this point also especially in view, as he adds—

Ἐγὼ γὰρ τὰ στίγματα τοῦ Ἰησοῦ ἐν τῷ σώματί μου βαστάζω—"for I bear in my body the marks of Jesus." The Received Text inserts *Κυρίου* before *Ἰησοῦ* on authority which, though good, is not, owing to other variations, free from suspicion. Ἐγώ emphatic, "it is I who," not ἔχω, but βαστάζω, "not I have, but I carry them" (Chrysostom). The στίγματα are the brands printed upon slaves—and sometimes on captives and soldiers—burnt into them, to indicate their owners. Herod. vii. 233; Rev. vii. 3, xiii. 16, xiv. 1, 9, 11; Vegetius, *De Re Militari*, ii. 5; Spencer, *De Leg. Heb.* xx. 1; Deyling, *Observat. Sacr.* vol. iii. p. 423; Wetstein *in loc.* Slaves attached to temples were tattooed, bore brands upon them. Herod. ii. 113; Lucian, *De Dea Syr.* § 59. This practice in the worship of Cybele might be common in Galatia, though there is little probability that the apostle is referring to it. The genitive Ἰησοῦ is that of possession, not that of author (Gomar, Rückert). He bore on his body the brands of Christ his Master. Indelible marks on his person showed that he belonged to Jesus as His servant. The meaning is not, such marks as Jesus Himself bore (Morus, Borger). Webster and Wilkinson admit the possibility of an allusion to John xx. 25. But such an idea is foreign to the simple statement. The marks of the crucifixion are said to have been borne by St. Francis; and his biographer Bonaventura addresses him in words similar to those of this verse. The wounds are said to have been reproduced in other persons. Windischmann renders the words correctly, and says that the *stigmatization* of St. Francis has no connection with the real meaning of this clause, though he proceeds to defend the possibility and value of such a phenomenon. Bisping rejects also the idea that the apostle's stigmata were in any way connected with the "five wounds," especially as tradition is silent about it. The reader may see a long Catholic note on St. Francis in the commentary of a-Lapide, and as long a Protestant note in that of Crocius. Nor is the meaning, marks borne on account of Christ (Grotius, Flatt, Rosenmüller). The marks are ἐν τῷ σώματι. His body bore such marks of suffering that no one could mistake his owner. 2 Cor. xi. 23. Any allusion to circumcision as one kind of στίγμα is not to be thought of. The warning, then, is not, "Let no man henceforward trouble me, for I have enough to bear already"—the view of Bengel and Winer; but, let no man impugn or doubt my authority,—the στίγματα of Jesus which I carry are the seal of my apostleship, the visible vouchers of my connection with Jesus. The Judaists insisted on circumcision that they might avoid persecution, but he had suffered many things: the stoning must have disfigured him, the scourge must have left its weals on his back—*cicatrices plagarum* (Ambros.),—and the fetter its scars on his limbs. The idea of Chrysostom, that he prided himself in those marks as a "trophy and regal ensign," is not suggested by the solemn mandate of the previous clause. Nor can the notion of Chandler be at all accepted, that the words conveyed a threatening of spiritual punishment to his enemies, as though he had said, "Be it at their peril to give me any further trouble or disturbance on this account."

Then comes the parting benediction—

Ver. 18. *Ἡ χάρις τοῦ Κυρίου ἡμῶν Ἰησοῦ Χριστοῦ μετὰ τοῦ πνεύματος ὑμῶν, ἀδελφοί. Ἀμήν*—"The grace of our Lord Jesus Christ be with your spirit, brethren. Amen." *Χάρις* is invoked to be, not *μεθ' ὑμῶν* or *μετὰ πάντων ὑμῶν*, but *μετὰ τοῦ πνεύματος*. Philem. 25; 2 Tim. iv. 22. These two passages show that no special stress is to be laid on the phrase here. *Πνεῦμα* is not opposed here in any way to *σάρξ*, as in some previous clauses of the epistle (Chrysostom, Beza, Rückert, Usteri, Schott). There are no salutations appended, perhaps because the epistle is an encyclical one, meant for believers throughout the province. The *πνεῦμα* is the higher nature, the region of divine operation in renewal and sanctification—distinct from the *ψυχή* by which it is united to the *σῶμα*. See Heard's *Tripartite Nature of Man*, Clark, Edin. 1868; Delitzsch, *Psychologie*. And the last word *ἀδελφοί* is unusually placed—placed last on purpose. After all his sorrow, amazement, censure, and despondency, he parts with them in kindness; after all the pain they had cost him, yet were they dear to him; and ere he lifts his hand from the parchment, it writes, as a parting love-token—*ἀδελφοί*.

TRANSLATION OF THE EPISTLE

THE following translation professes only to give a tolerably correct version of the epistle, without aiming at elegance or classic purity of style :—

Address and Salutation

PAUL, an apostle, not from men, nor by man, but by Jesus Christ, and God the Father who raised Him from the dead, and all the brethren who are with me, to the churches of Galatia. Grace be to you and peace, from God the Father, and our Lord Jesus Christ who gave Himself for our sins, that He might deliver us out of the present world—an evil one: according to the will of God and our Father; to whom be the glory for ever and ever. Amen.

Challenge

I marvel that you are so soon turning away (are removing yourselves) from Him who called you in the grace of Christ, unto a different gospel, which is not another; save that there are some who are troubling you, and are desiring to subvert the gospel of Christ. But if we, or an angel from heaven, should preach to you any other gospel different from that which we preached to you, let him be accursed. As we have said before, and now again I say, If any man is preaching to you a gospel different from that which ye received, let him be accursed. For do I now conciliate men or God? or am I seeking to please men? If still I were pleasing men, Christ's servant I should not be.

Vindication of his Apostleship

Now I declare unto you, brethren, as to the gospel preached by me, that it is not after man. For neither did I receive it from man, nor was I taught it, but through revelation of Jesus Christ. For ye heard of my manner of life in Judaism, how that beyond measure I was persecuting the church of God, and was destroying it, and was making progress in Judaism beyond many my equals in my own nation, being more exceedingly a zealot for the traditions of my fathers. But when

God was pleased, who set me apart from my mother's womb, and called me by His grace, to reveal His Son in me, in order that I should preach Him among the Gentiles, immediately I conferred not with flesh and blood; neither did I go away to Jerusalem to them who were apostles before me, but I went away into Arabia, and again returned to Damascus. Then after three years I went up to Jerusalem to make the acquaintance of Cephas, and I abode with him fifteen days. And another of the apostles I did not see, except James the Lord's brother. But as to the things which I am writing to you, behold, before God that I lie not. Afterwards I came into the regions of Syria and Cilicia; and I was unknown by face to the churches of Judæa which are in Christ; only they were hearing, that he who once persecuted us is now preaching the faith which he once was destroying. And they glorified God in me.

Equality of Rank with the other Apostles

Then, after fourteen years, I went up again to Jerusalem with Barnabas, taking along with me also Titus; but I went up by revelation. And I communicated to them the gospel which I preach among the Gentiles, but privately to them of reputation, lest I might be running, or have run, in vain. Howbeit not even Titus, who was with me, though he was a Greek, was forced to be circumcised. Now it was because of the false brethren stealthily introduced to spy out our liberty which we have in Christ Jesus, in order that they might bring us into utter bondage; to whom not even for an hour did we yield in subjection, that the truth of the gospel might continue with you. But from those high in reputation (from them who were esteemed something), whatsoever they were, nothing to me it matters; God accepteth no man's person; to me, in fact, those in repute communicated nothing. But, on the contrary, seeing that I have been entrusted with the gospel of the uncircumcision, even as Peter was with that of the circumcision (for He who wrought for Peter toward the apostleship of the circumcision, the same wrought for me also towards the Gentiles), and coming to the knowledge of the grace which was given to me, James and Cephas and John, who are reputed pillars, gave to me and Barnabas right hands of fellowship, that we should go (or preach) to the Gentiles, but they to the circumcision: only they asked us that we should remember the poor, which very thing I also was forward to do.

Conflict with Peter, the Apostle of the Circumcision

But when Cephas came to Antioch, I withstood him to the face, because he had been condemned: for before that certain from James came, he was eating with the Gentiles; but when they came, he withdrew and separated himself, fearing them of the circumcision.

And the other Jews also dissembled with him, so that even Barnabas was carried along with them by their dissimulation. But when I saw that they were not walking uprightly according to the truth of the gospel, I said to Cephas before all, If thou, being a Jew, livest after the manner of Gentiles and not after the manner of Jews, how art thou compelling the Gentiles to live after the manner of the Jews? We by nature Jews, and not of the Gentiles sinners, but knowing as we do that a man is not justified, by the works of the law, except by faith in Jesus Christ, we also believed into Jesus Christ, in order that we might be justified by the faith of Christ, and not by the works of the law, because by the works of the law no flesh shall be justified. But if, while seeking to be justified in Christ, we ourselves were found sinners, is Christ therefore a minister of sin? God forbid. For if the things which I destroyed, these again I build up, I constitute myself a transgressor. For I through the law died to the law, that I might live to God. I have been crucified with Christ: it is, however, no longer I that live, but it is Christ that liveth in me (or, I live however no longer myself, Christ however liveth in me); but the life which I am now living in the flesh, I live in the faith of the Son of God who loved me, and gave Himself for me. I do not frustrate the grace of God; for if righteousness comes through the law, then Christ died without cause.

Warning

O foolish Galatians! who bewitched you, before whose eyes Jesus Christ was evidently set forth in you—crucified? This only I would learn of you, Did ye from the works of the law receive the Spirit, or by the hearing of faith? Are ye so very foolish? Having begun in the Spirit, are ye now being completed in the flesh? Did ye suffer so many things in vain, if it be really in vain? He, then, that ministereth to you the Spirit, and worketh miracles in you, doeth He it by the works of the law, or by the hearing of faith?

Justification by Faith argued and exemplified in Abraham

Even as Abraham believed God, and it was counted to him for righteousness. Know ye, therefore, that they who are of faith, these are the sons of Abraham. But the Scripture foreseeing that of faith God justifies the nations, proclaimed beforehand the glad tidings unto Abraham, "that there shall be blessed in thee all the nations." So then they which are of faith are blessed together with the faithful Abraham. For as many as are of the works of the law are under curse; for it is written, "Cursed is every one who continueth not in all things which have been written in the book of the law to do them." But that in the law no one is justified before God is evident, "because the just shall live by faith." Now the law is not of faith, but "he who hath done these things shall live in them." Christ redeemed us from the curse of the law, having become a curse for us; for it is written, "Cursed is every one that hangeth upon a tree:" in order that to the Gentiles the blessing of Abraham might come in Christ Jesus, in order that we might receive the promise of the Spirit through faith. Brethren, I speak after the manner of men: though it be but a man's covenant, yet, when it has been confirmed, no one annulleth or addeth to it. Now to Abraham were the promises made, and to his Seed. He saith not, "And to seeds," as of many; but as of one, "And to thy Seed," which is Christ. This, however, I say, A covenant which has been before confirmed by God [for Christ], the law, which was four hundred and thirty years after, does not invalidate, so as to do away the promise. For if the inheritance be of the law, it is no more of promise; but to Abraham God has given it through promise. What then is the law? On account of the transgressions it was superadded, until the Seed, to whom the promise has been made, shall have come, being ordained by means of angels in the hand of a mediator. Now a mediator is not of one, but God is One. Is then the law against the promises of God? God forbid; for if there had been given a law which was able to give life, verily by the law should have been righteousness. But the Scripture shut up all under sin, in order that the promise by faith in Christ Jesus might be given to them who believe. Now before the faith came, we were kept in ward, shut up under the law for the faith to be afterwards revealed; so that the law has become our tutor (pædagogue) for Christ, that we might be justified by faith. But the faith being come, we are no longer under a pædagogue. For ye all are sons of God through the faith in Christ Jesus. For as many of you (ye whosoever) as were baptized into Christ, ye put on Christ. There is among such neither Jew nor Greek, there is among such neither bond nor free, there is not among such a male and a female, for all ye are one (person) in Christ Jesus. But if ye are Christ's, then are ye Abraham's seed, heirs according to promise.

Further Illustration from Domestic Law

Now I say, That the heir, as long as he is a child, differeth nothing from a servant (bond-servant), though he be lord of all, but is under guardians and stewards until the term appointed of the father. Even so we also, when we were children, were under the rudiments of the world, kept in bondage. But when the fulness of the time was come, God sent forth His Son, born of a woman, born under the law, in order that He might redeem those under the law, in order that we might receive the adoption of sons: because (or to show) that ye are sons, God sent forth the Spirit of His Son into our hearts, crying, Abba, Father. Wherefore thou art no longer a servant, but a son; but if a son, also an heir through God.

Appeal to the Gentile Portion of the Church

Howbeit, at that time indeed, not knowing God, ye were in bondage to them which by nature are not gods. But now having known God, or rather being known by God, how is it that ye are returning again to the weak and beggarly elements, to which ye are desiring again afresh to be in bondage? Ye are observing days, and months, and seasons, and years. I am afraid of you, lest perhaps I have in vain bestowed labour on you. Brethren, I beseech you, become ye as I am; for I also am become as you are. In nothing did ye wrong me.

Change of Feeling toward him

But ye know that, on account of weakness of my flesh, I preached the gospel unto you the first time. And your temptation in my flesh ye despised not nor loathed, but ye received me as an angel of God, as Christ Jesus. Of what nature, then, was your boasted blessedness? for I bear you record, that if it had been possible, ye would have plucked out your eyes and have given them to me. So then, have I become your enemy because I tell you the truth? They are paying court to you, not honestly; nay, they desire to exclude you, in order that ye may zealously pay court to them. But it is good to be courted fairly at all times, and not only when I am present along with you. My little children, with whom I travail in birth again until Christ be formed in you, I could wish indeed to be present with you now, and to change my voice, for I am perplexed in you.

Appeal to the Jewish Portion of the Church

Tell me, ye who desire to be under the law, do ye not hear the law? For it is written that Abraham had two sons; one by the bond-maid, and one by the free woman. Howbeit he of the bond-maid was born after the flesh, but he of the free woman by the promise. Which things are allegorized, for these women are two covenants; one indeed from Mount Sinai, bearing children into bondage, and this is Hagar (for Sinai is a mountain in Arabia); and indeed she ranketh with the present Jerusalem, for she is in bondage with her children. But the Jerusalem above is free, and she is our mother. For it is written, Rejoice, thou barren that bearest not; break forth and cry, thou that travailest not; because many are the children of the desolate more than of her who has an husband. But ye, brethren, as Isaac was, are children of promise. But as then he who was born after the flesh persecuted him who was born after the Spirit, so it is also now. Nevertheless what saith the Scripture? Cast out the bond-maid and her son, for the son of the bond-maid shall in nowise inherit with the son of the free woman. Wherefore, brethren, we are children not of a bond-maid, but of the free woman.

Warning against Legalism and Judaistic Teachers

With liberty did Christ make us free: stand therefore (or, make a stand), and be not held fast again in a yoke of bondage. Behold, I Paul say to you, that if ye be circumcised, Christ shall profit you nothing. Yea, I testify again to every man getting himself circumcised, that he is a debtor to do the whole law. Ye were done away from Christ, whoever of you are being justified in the law; from grace ye fell away. For we by the Spirit are waiting for the hope of righteousness from faith. For in Christ Jesus neither circumcision availeth anything, nor uncircumcision, but faith working through love. Ye were running well; who did hinder you, that ye should not obey the truth? The persuasion is not from Him who calleth you. A little leaven leaveneth the whole lump. I for my part have confidence in you in the Lord, that ye will think nothing different; but he that troubleth you shall bear his judgment, whoever he may be. But I, brethren, if I still preach circumcision, why am I still persecuted? then the offence of the cross is done away with. I would that they would even cut themselves off who are unsettling you.

Charge against Abuse of Liberty

For ye for your part were called unto liberty, brethren; only turn not your liberty into an occasion for the flesh, but by love be serving one another. For the whole law has been fulfilled in one word: Thou shalt love thy neighbour as thyself. But if one another ye bite and devour, see that by one another ye be not consumed. Now I say, Walk according to the Spirit, and (so) ye shall not fulfil the lust of the flesh. For the flesh lusteth against the Spirit, and the Spirit against the flesh, for these are opposed the one to the other, that ye may not do those things whatsoever ye may wish. But if ye be led by the Spirit, ye are not under the law. Now manifest are the works of the flesh; of which class are fornication, uncleanness, lasciviousness, idolatry, sorcery, hatreds, strife, outbursts of anger, caballings, divisions, factions, envyings, murders, drunkenness, carousals, and such like; concerning which I tell you beforehand, as also I did foretell you, that they who are doing such things shall not inherit the kingdom of God. But the fruit of the Spirit is love, joy, peace, long-suffering, kindness, goodness, faith, meekness, temperance; against such there is no law. Now they who are Christ's crucified the flesh along with the passions and lusts. If we live by the Spirit, by the Spirit also let us walk. Let us not become vainglorious, provoking one another, envying one another.

Christian Charity and Beneficence

Brethren, if a man should be even surprised in any trespass, do ye the spiritual ones restore such an one in the spirit of meekness; considering thyself, lest thou also shouldest be tempted. One another's burdens do ye bear, and so fulfil the law of Christ. For if any one think himself to be something, while he is nothing, he deceiveth his own mind. But let each one prove his own work, and then he shall have ground of boasting only in relation to himself, and not in relation to the other; for each one shall bear his own load. But let him who is taught in the word share with him that teacheth in all good things. Be not deceived, God is not mocked; for whatsoever a man may sow, that also shall he reap. For he who is sowing unto his own flesh, shall from the flesh reap corruption; but he who is sowing unto the Spirit, shall from the Spirit reap life eternal. But in well-doing let us not be faint-hearted, for in due time we shall reap, if now we faint not. So then, as we have opportunity, let us do that which is good toward all, but specially toward them who are of the household of faith.

Visible Proof of Attachment

See in what large letters I have written to you with mine own hand.

Judaistic Inconsistency

As many as desire to make a fair show in the flesh, these are compelling you to be circumcised; only lest they should suffer persecution for the cross of Christ. For not even do they who are getting themselves circumcised keep the law, but they desire to have you circumcised in order that they may glory in your flesh. But as for me, far be it from me to glory, save in the cross of our Lord Jesus Christ, by which the world has been crucified to me, and I to the world. For neither doth circumcision avail anything, nor uncircumcision, but a new creature.

Parting Benediction

And as many as are walking (or shall walk) by this rule, peace be on them, and on the Israel of God. Henceforth let no one cause troubles to me, for I bear in my body the marks of Jesus. The grace of our Lord Jesus Christ be with your spirit, brethren. Amen.

Other Solid Ground Titles

In addition to the book in your hand, Solid Ground is honored to offer other uncovered treasure, many for the first time in more than a century:

PAUL THE PREACHER: S*ermons from Acts* by John Eadie
THE COMMUNICANT'S COMPANION by Matthew Henry
THE CHILD AT HOME by John S.C. Abbott
THE LIFE OF JESUS CHRIST FOR THE YOUNG by Richard Newton
THE KING'S HIGHWAY: *10 Commandments for the Young* by Richard Newton
HEROES OF THE REFORMATION by Richard Newton
FEED MY LAMBS: *Lectures to Children on Vital Subjects* by John Todd
LET THE CANNON BLAZE AWAY by Joseph P. Thompson
THE STILL HOUR: *Communion with God in Prayer* by Austin Phelps
COLLECTED WORKS of James Henley Thornwell (4 vols.)
CALVINISM IN HISTORY *by Nathaniel S. McFetridge*
OPENING SCRIPTURE: *Hermeneutical Manual* *by Patrick Fairbairn*
THE ASSURANCE OF FAITH *by Louis Berkhof*
THE PASTOR IN THE SICK ROOM *by John D. Wells*
THE BUNYAN OF BROOKLYN: *Life & Sermons of I.S. Spencer*
THE NATIONAL PREACHER: S*ermons from 2nd Great Awakening*
FIRST THINGS: F*irst Lessons God Taught Mankind* *Gardiner Spring*
BIBLICAL & THEOLOGICAL STUDIES *by 1912 Faculty of Princeton*
THE POWER OF GOD UNTO SALVATION *by B.B. Warfield*
THE LORD OF GLORY *by B.B. Warfield*
A GENTLEMAN & A SCHOLAR: *Memoir of J.P. Boyce* *by J. Broadus*
SERMONS TO THE NATURAL MAN *by W.G.T. Shedd*
SERMONS TO THE SPIRITUAL MAN *by W.G.T. Shedd*
HOMILETICS AND PASTORAL THEOLOGY *by W.G.T. Shedd*
A PASTOR'S SKETCHES 1 & 2 *by Ichabod S. Spencer*
THE PREACHER AND HIS MODELS *by James Stalker*
IMAGO CHRISTI: *The Example of Jesus Christ* *by James Stalker*
LECTURES ON THE HISTORY OF PREACHING *by J. A. Broadus*
THE SHORTER CATECHISM ILLUSTRATED *by John Whitecross*
THE CHURCH MEMBER'S GUIDE *by John Angell James*
THE SUNDAY SCHOOL TEACHER'S GUIDE *by John A. James*
CHRIST IN SONG: *Hymns of Immanuel from All Ages* *by Philip Schaff*
DEVOTIONAL LIFE OF THE S.S. TEACHER *by J.R. Miller*

Call us Toll Free at 1-877-666-9469

Send us an e-mail at sgcb@charter.net
Visit us on line at solid-ground-books.com
Uncovering Buried Treasure to the Glory of God

Printed in the United States
42571LVS00004B/30

9 781599 250038